PĀLI-ENGLISH
DICTIONARY

BY

A. P. BUDDHADATTA MAHĀTHERA

BKP

Bharatiya Kala Prakashan

Delhi (India)

Published by :
Bharatiya Kala Prakashan
3421-A, IInd Floor,
Narang Colony, Tri Nagar,
Delhi-110035
Phone : 7153083

First Indian Edition : 1999
2011

ISBN: 81-86050-33-7

Printed at :
G. S. OFFSET
N. SHAHADRA, DELHI - 32

FOREWORD

A concise Pali-English Dictionary for use by students in schools and colleges has been a long-felt need. The only available Pali-English lexicon—the work of Childers being long out of print—is the famous publication of the Pali Text Society, but this too is fast becoming rare and difficult to procure. In any case the cost is too heavy for the average student. Hence it is gratifying to note that at long last a reputed scholar has come forward to satisfy this need and after several years of hard work has compiled what may prove to be the standard practical dictionary of the Pali language.

The author is not only an eminent Elder of the Buddhist Order but one of the leading Pali scholars recognized both in the East and in the West as an authority on the subject. His experience as a teacher at Ananda College, Colombo, and the considerable experience he has gained as a writer of text-books for school use, such as the now famous New Pali Course, make him admirably suited for the undertaking. There are but a few Buddhist Elders in direct contact with western scholarship through the English medium and the Rev. Buddhadatta is the most senior among that class of monks.

It is to be observed that the author has kept more or less to the traditional sense of words while not altogether ignoring the meanings given by western scholars in their translations and lexicons. Many errors in the latter sources have also been rectified. But the basic sense adopted is in nearly every instance the traditionally accepted meaning in accord with the commentaries and the glossaries. This, perhaps, is of special value to beginners as thereby they get introduced to the indigenous tradition, thus providing a useful basis on which to build up a more scientific knowledge as the study advances.

I am certain that this dictionary will be found indispensable by all students of the Pali language in acquiring a practical and working knowledge of the subject even at the University level, and also serve as a reliable guide to the more abstruse language of the Tipiṭaka.

O. H. de A. WIJESEKARA
Professor of Sanskrit

University of Ceylon

PREFACE

Some twenty-five years ago when the teaching of Pali was commenced at Ananda College, the text-books used by Buddhist monks, which were centuries old, were found unsuitable for use by its pupils. Mr. P. de S. Kularatna, then principal of Ananda College, who appointed me as tutor in Pali, urged me to produce some suitable text books, and I wrote in three parts the *Pālibhāshāvatarana* in Sinhalese and compiled a Pali Reader named *Pāḷipāṭhāvalī*.

Later I wrote the New Pali Course in two parts for the benefit of those who wished to learn Pali through the medium of English. This book is used even in some foreign countries, and is now in its third edition. A *Higher Pali Course* too is now ready for the press.

There yet lacked for the study of Pali a concise Pali-English Dictionary and an English-Pali Dictionary. The Pali-English Dictionary of the Pali Text Society is too large and too expensive for those studying in schools and colleges. Therefore I prepared two such works during the war, but owing to paper control, which was lifted only recently, the Pali-English Dictionary alone is now appearing in print. The English-Pali Dictionary will be printed as early as possible.

In compiling this work I have constantly referred to the Pali-English Dictionary, published by the Pali Text Society (of England), but I have not followed its method. In some places I have not accepted the meanings and constructions it has given; for instance, the construction of *anabhāva* is given by me as anu + abhāva, in agreement with the commentaries, while the P. T. S. Dictionary gives it as *ana* + *abhāva*. There is no prefix *ana* in Pali, and *na* before a vowel is changed to *an* and not to *ana*. Moreover *na* + *abhāva* would mean "non-cessation", and not "utter cessation" as the P. T. S. Dictionary gives it. Similar is the construction given there for *anugghāṭeti* as *an* + *ugghāṭeti*. The meaning given there for *terovassika* is "lasting over or beyond a year (or season"); here *te* stands, according to the commentary, for three, and *ro* represents "four"; then *terovassika* means: "three or four years old".

I have included some important words missing in that dictionary although my work is of smaller compass. In giving the roots of verbs I have preserved their traditional Pali forms as far as possible though the P. T. S. Dictionary has always followed the Sanskrit Dictionaries.

My thanks are due to Prof. O. H. de A. Wijesekara, M.A., Ph.D., and Dr. G. C. Mendis, B.A., Ph.D., both of the University of Ceylon, who encouraged me to begin this work. Prof. Wijesekara has always readily helped me whenever I met with any difficulty. He has now kindly consented to revise my English-Pali Dictionary.

A. P. BUDDHADATTA

Aggārāma

Ambalangoda

INTRODUCTION

Pali verbs are given here in the third person singular of the Present Tense. As there are different ways of forming the Aorist and Past (Passive) Participle I have given both these forms too under each verb. The P.P. is sometimes separately given when it has some meaning not expressed by the verb, or when it is difficult to understand from which verb it is derived. Ordinary Absolutives ending in *tvā* and *tvāna* are not generally given after the verbs, but the peculiar forms, such as *nikkhamma, pahāya, ucchijja* are given. It is not to be understood, however, that these stems do not have their general forms ending in *tvā* or *tvāna*.

The Pali-English Dictionary of the Pali Text Society has given stems of some Pali nouns with consonantal endings, *viz : satthar, pitar, brahman ;* but I have not followed this method as none of the Pali Grammarians have adopted it. They have always given these stems with vowel endings.

The Secondary Derivatives ending in *tā* are included in the feminine ; they have their neuter forms ending in *tta* and *ttana ;* but for the sake of brevity only one form, either ending in *tā* or *tta* is given in one place.

The masculine nouns ending in *ī* have their feminine stems ending in *inī*, e.g. *hatthī<hatthinī*. Many nouns ending in *a*, such as *kāka, miga, nāga*, have their feminine stems ending in *ī*, and seldom in *inī :*

Masculine	*Feminine*
Kāka	kākī
Miga	migī
Nāga	nāgī ; nāginī.

Some others of the same ending have their feminine forms ending in *ā* or *ānī* :

Khattiya	khattiyā ; khattiyānī
Mātula	mātulānī.

The adjectives ending in *vantu* and *mantu* form their feminine stems by substituting an *ī*, in place of *a*, and sometimes dropping the *n* of the suffix :

Guṇavantu<guṇavantī, guṇavatī.

Satimantu<satimantī, satimatī.

There are two forms of the Present Participle : one ending in *nta* and the other in *māna*. Those ending in *nta* form their feminine stems by substituting an *ī*, in place of *a*, and those ending in *māna* by substituting an *ā* :

Gacchanta<gacchantī
Pacamāna<pacamānā.

The neuter stems of these are similar to those of the masculine.

Some Primary Derivatives such as *dāyaka* form their feminine stems by substituting *ikā*. for *aka* :

Dāyaka<dāyikā
Ārocaka<ārocikā
Pācaka<pācikā.

A. P. BUDDHADATTA

ABBREVIATIONS

a. or *adj.*	..	Adjective
abs.	..	Absolutive
ad.	..	Adverb
aor.	..	Aorist
cpds.	..	Compounds
conj.	..	Conjunction
caus.	..	Causative
Deno.	..	Denominative verb
Des.	..	Desiderative verb
f.	..	Feminine
ger.	..	Gerund
intj.	..	Interjection
in.	..	Indeclinable
inf.	..	Infinitive
m.	..	Masculine
nt.	..	Neuter
Onom.	..	Onometopoetic verb
pass.	..	Passive
pp.	..	Past Participle
pr. p.	..	Present Participle
prep.	..	Preposition
pret.	..	Preterit verb
pt. p.	..	Potential Participle
3.	..	Of the three genders.

ADDITIONS AND CORRECTIONS

Ajjhokirati (adhi + ava + kir + a), to scatter over.

Aṭavimukha, *nt.* outskirts of a forest.

Atiluddha, *a.* very miserly; stringent.

Adissamāna, *a.* not visible.

Adūbhaka, *a.* not treacherous.

Anapekkha, *a.* without expectance.

Anantaraŋ, *ad.* after that.

Antamaso, *in.* at least.

Aparabhāge (*loc.*), afterwards.

Ayutta, *a.* inappropriate. *nt.* injustice.

Avalakkhaṇa, *a.* ugly; having unlucky signs.

Asamekkhakārī, *m.* a hasty person.

Asidhārā, *f.* the edge of a sword.

Āṇatta, *pp.* (of **āṇāpeti**), being ordered.

Āṇāpiya, *abs.* having commanded.

Āḷāhana, *nt.* ground for cremation. **—kicca,** *nt.* cremation. **—ṭṭhāna,** *nt.* the place of cremation.

Uttarāsaṅga, *m.* upper robe.

Uttaritara, *a.* more superior.

Oḍḍeti (uḍ + e), to lay snares; to hang down. *aor.* **—esi.** *pp.* **oḍḍita.**

Ovajjamāna, *pr. p.* being admonished.

Kammaja-vāta, *m.* pangs of child-birth; travail pains.

Kiñci, *in.* something.

Kulūpaga, *a.* one who frequents a family.

Kūṭāgāra, *nt.* a pinnacled building, or such a temporary construction; a catafalque.

Khaṇḍākhaṇḍaŋ, khaṇḍākhaṇḍikaŋ, *ad.* (breaking) into fragments.

Gihībhoga, *m.* enjoyment of a layman.

Guṇahīna, *a.* devoid of virtue

Guḷakīḷā, *f.* playing with balls or marbles.

Ghaŋseti (ghaŋs + e), to rub or knock against. *aor.* **—esi.** *pp.* **—sita.**

Jīvikaŋ kappeti, gets one's living.

Jīvitasaŋsaya, *m.* danger of life.

Jeṭṭhatara, *a.* more old or superior.

Tiṇahāraka, *m.* one who carries grass for sale.

Tena, *in.* on account of it; because of it. **—hi,** *in.* if it is so.

Dātabba, *pt. p.* fit to be given.

Deti (dā + e), to give. *aor.* **adāsi.** *pr. p.* **denta.** *pp.* **dinna.** *abs.* **datvā.** See **Dadāti.**

Nakha-pañjara, *m.* the claw.

Niddhamana, *nt.* a drain or culvert.

Paccupakāra, *m.* help in return.

Pañcāvudha, *nt.* a set of five weapons, *viz.*, sword, bow, dagger, spear and a mace.

Paṭiggaha, *m.* a spitoon.

Padavītihāra, *m.* exchange of steps.

Pākatika, *a.* having the original state ; natural.

Bahūpakāra, *a.* very helpful.

Bhikkhusaṅgha, *m.* congregation of monks.

Mittasanthava, *m.* association with a friend.

Moḷi, *m. f.* top knot of hair ; the crown of the head.

Yāvadatthaŋ, *ad.* as much as one likes ; as far as need be.

Vayovuddha, *a.* advanced in age.

Vayohara, *a.* snatching one's life.

Vihata (*pp.* of **vihanati**), killed; destroyed ; combed or carded (cotton etc.).

Sakkā, *in.* it is possible.

Saṅkhalikā, *f.* a fetter.

Saṅgati, *f.* association.

Sattaratana, *nt.* seven kinds of precious things, *viz.*, gold, silver, pearls, rubies, lapis lazali, coral and diamond.

Samaṇadhamma, *m.* duties of a monk.

Samaṇasāruppa, *a.* lawful for a monk.

Samākula, *a.* crowded or strewn with.

CORRECTIONS

PAGE

41. "Charnel grow" read as "Charnel grove".
44. "To reflect; upon" read as "To reflect upon".
62. **Uḷūka** must stand after **Uḷumpa**.
116. **Dhakkhati** read as **Dakkhati**.
137. **Nijojeti** read as **Niyojeti**.
205. Add "species" to the meanings of **Yoni**.

CONCISE PALI-ENGLISH DICTIONARY

A

A-, prefix *ā* shortened before a double consonant, e.g. **ā + kosati = akkosati**; a negative prefixed to nouns, adjectives, and participles; e.g. **na + kusala = akusala**; the augment prefixed to some roots in the Past and Conditional Tenses; e.g. **akāsi**.

Akaṭa, Akata, *a.* not done; not made; not artificial.

Akataññū, *a.* ungrateful.

Akampiya, *a.* immovable; stable, firm.

Akaraṇa, *nt.* non-action.

Akaraṇīya, *pt. p.* 1. that should not be done; not befitting; 2. *nt.* improper action.

Akaronta, *pr. p.* not doing or performing.

Akāca, *a.* flowless.

Akāmaka, *a.* unwilling.

Akāla, *m.* inappropriate time. *a.* out of season.

Akāsi (aor. of **karoti**), (he) did, made, or performed.

Akiriya, *nt.* non-action;—**vāda**, *m.* the theory that there is no after-effect of action.

Akilāsu, *a.* untiring; active.

Akutobhaya, *a.* safe from every quarter.

Akuṭila, *a.* straight, honest; not crooked.

Akuppa, *a.* steadfast; unshakable.

Akusala, *nt.* demerit; bad action; sin. *a.* unskilful.

Akka, *m.* the sun; swallow-wort plant.

Akkanta, *pp.* stepped upon; trodden; subdued.

Akkandati (ā + kand + a), to wail, to cry. *aor.* —ndi. —**dana**, *nt.* wailing.

Akkamati (ā + kam + a), to step or tread upon; to subjugate. *aor.* **akkami**. —**mana**, *nt.* stepping or treading upon; subjugation.

Akkuṭṭha, *pp.* of **akkosati**.

Akkocchi, aor. of **akkosati**.

Akkosa, *m.* insult; abuse; reproach.—**saka**, *m.* one who insults.

Akkosati (ā + kus + a), to abuse; to revile; to scold. *aor.* **akkosi**. *abs.* **akkositvā**.

Akkha, *nt.* sense organ. *m.* axle; dice; beleric myrobalan; a measurement equal to 20 grains. (**Akkha** in the cpds. such as **visālakkha, sahassakkha** is from the stem **akkhi** = eye).

Akkhaka, *nt.* collar-bone.

Akkhaṇa, *m.* inappropriate time; —**ṇā**, *f.* a lightning.—**vedhī**, *m.* an archer who shoots as quickly as lightning or shoots only to graze the object.

Akkhata, *a.* unhurt; not wounded; faultless.

Akkhadassa, *m.* a judge; an umpire.

Akkhadhutta, *a.* addicted to gambling. *m.* gambler.

Akkhaya, *a.* changeless; eternal; decayless. *nt.* the eternal peace.

Akkhara, *nt.* a letter; a syllable; —**phalaka,** *m.* a board or slate to write on.—**samaya,** *m.* the science of writing and reading.

Akkhāta, *pp.* of **akkhāti.**

Akkhāti (ā + khā + a), to announce; to tell; to declare. *aor.* **akkhāsi.**

Akkhātu, Akkhāyī, *m.* one who relates *or* preaches.

Akkhi, *nt.* eye.—**kūpa,** *m.* socket of the eye.—**tārā,** *f.* pupil of the eye.—**dala,** *nt.* eyelid.

Akkhitta, *a.* not despised or thrown away.

Akkhobha, *a.* imperturbable.

Akkhobhinī, — khohinī, *f.* a number consisting of 42 ciphers; an army of 109,350 soldiers, 65,610 horses, 21870 elephants and 21,870 war chariots.

Akhetta, *nt.* unsuitable place.

Aga, m. mountain; tree.

Agati, *f.* wrong course; prejudice.

Agada, *nt.* medicine, drug.

Agaru, *a.* not heavy; not troublesome. *m.* aloe wood.

Agalu, *m.* aloe wood.

Agādha, *a.* very deep; supportless.

Agāra, *nt.* house; *a* dwelling place.

Agārika, Agāriya, *a.* & *n.* lay man; householder, *m.*

Agga, *a.* the highest; the topmost; *m.* the end; the top.—**tā,** *f.*—**tta,** *nt.* pre-eminence.—**phala,** *nt.* the first harvest of a cultivation; supreme fruit of Arahantship.—**magga,** *m* the highest path of salvation.—**mahesī,** *f.* the queen-consort.

Aggañña, *a.* known as the highest or foremost.

Aggala, *nt.* bolt; latch.

Aggi, *m.* fire.—**kkhandha,** *m.* a great mass of fire—**paricaraṇa** *nt.* fire-worship.—**sālā,** *f.* a heated room.—**sikhā** *f.* flame.—**hutta,** *nt.* fire-sacrifice.

Aggha, *m.* price: value. *nt.* obligation made to a guest.—**kāraka,** *m.* valuator; appraiser.

Agghaka, agghanaka, *a.* (in cpds:) having the value of.

Agghati (aggh + a), to be worth; to deserve. *aor.* **agghi.**

Agghāpana, *nt.* setting a price; valuation.—**naka,** *m.* valuator. —**paniya,** *nt.* that which is to be valued.

Agghika, Agghiya, *nt.* a post decorated with festoons.

Agghiya, nt. an obligation made to a guest.

Agha, *nt.* the sky; grief; pain; sin; misfortune.

Aṅka, *m.* the lap; a mark; sign; numerical figure.

Aṅkita, *pp.* of **aṅketi.**

Aṅkura, *m.* a shoot; sprout; bud.

Aṅkusa, *m.* a pole with a hook used for plucking fruits or to guide an elephant.

Aṅketi aki + e), to mark out; to brand; to put a number on. *aor.* — **esi.** *abs.* **aṅketvā.**

Aṅga, *nt.* a constituent part; a limb; quality.—**paccaṅga,** *nt.* major and minor limbs.—**rāga,** *m.* a cosmatic to anoint the body with.—**vijjā,** *f.* palmistry and other prognostications from the marks on the body.

Aṅgajāta, *nt.* the male or female organ.

Aṅgaṇa, *nt.* an open space; a court yard; impurity of mind.

Aṅgada, *nt.* bracelet.

Aṅganā, *f.* woman.

Aṅgāra, *m. nt.* charcoal; embers.—**kaṭāha**,—**kapalla**, m. pan for holding cinders.—**kāsu**, *f.* a pit full of cinders.—**maŋsa**, *nt.* meat roasted on cinders.

Aṅgika, *a.* (in cpds:) consisting of so many parts; e.g. **duvaṅgika** = consisting of two parts.

Aṅgīrasa,. *m.* the resplendent one; the Buddha.

Aṅguṭṭha, *m.* thumb, the great toe.

Aṅgula, *nt.* an inch; a finger-breadth; *a.* (in cpds:) measuring so many inches.

Aṅguli, *f.* finger; toe.—**pabba**, *nt.* finger-joint.—**muddā**, *f.* signet ring; finger-ring.

Aṅgulīyaka, — **leyyaka**, *nt.* finger-ring.

Acala, *a.* not moving; unshakable.

Acira, *a.* recent; new.—**raŋ**, *ad.* recently; not long ago; before long.—**ppabhā**, *f.* lightning.

Acetana, *a.* senseless; inorganic.

Acela, *a.* void of cloth; naked.—**laka**, *m.* naked ascetic.

Accagā (pret. of ati + gam), he surpassed, overcame.

Accanā, *f.* oblation; respect; honour.

Accanta, *a* perpetual; absolute.—**taŋ**, *ad.* perpetually; extremely; exceedingly.

Accaya, *m.* fault; lapse; passing away. (**accayena** = after the lapse of).

Accādhāya, *abs.* having placed one (leg) upon the other in a slightly changed position.

Accāyika, *a.* urgent.

Accāsanna, *a.* very near.

Acci, *f.* flame.—**mantu**, *a.* having flames; brilliant. *m.* fire.

Accita, (pp. of Acceti). honoured, esteemed.

Accuggata, *a.* very high.

Accuṇha, *a.* very hot. *m.* great heat.

Accuta, *a.* everlasting; not passing away; *nt.* eternal peace.

Accussanna, *a.* much abundant.

Acceti, 1. (ati + i + a), to pass time; to get over. 2. (acc + e), to honour; to respect. *aor.* **accesi**

Accogāḷha, *a.* plunged into a great depth.

Accodaka, *nt.* too much water.

Accha, *a.* clear; pure. *m.* a bear.

Acchati (ās + a; *ā* is shortened and **sa** changed to **ccha**), to sit; to remain. *aor.* **acchi**.

Acchambhī, *a.* fearless; not frightened.

Accharā, *f.* a nymph; snapping of fingers; a short moment.—**saṇghāta**, *m.* snapping of fingers;—**sadda**, *m.* sound of clapping hands.

Acchariya, *nt.* a marvel; wonder; *a.* wonderful; marvellous.

Acchādana, *nt.* clothing.—**danā**, *f.* concealment.

Acchādeti (ā + chad + e), to clothe; to cover with. *aor.*—**esi**. *pp.* **acchādita**,

Acchijja, abs. of the following.

Acchindati (ā + chid + ŋ-a), to rob; to plunder; to take by force; to break off. *aor.* **acchindi**. *pp.* **acchinna**.

Acchecchi (aor. of **chindati**), broke away; cut out; destroyed.

Acchejja, *a.* unbreakable ; indestructible.

Acchera, see **acchariya.**

Aja, *m.* goat.—**pāla,** *m.* goatherd. —**laṇḍikā,** *f.* goats' dung.

Ajagara, *m.* boa constrictor.

Ajañña, *a.* impure; unclean.

Ajā, ajī, *f.* she-goat.

Ajānana, *nt.* ignorance.

Ajānanta, ajānamāna, *pr. p.* not knowing ; ignorant of.

Ajānitvā, ajāniya, *abs.* not knowing ; being unaware of.

Ajina, *m.* a cheetah, i.e. a long limbed beast of cat family with tawny fur and black spots. * *nt.* its hide.—**kkhipa,** *m.* a cloak made of cheetah's hide.—**ppaveṇī,** *f.* a bed-sheet made of cheetah's hide.—**yoni,** *f.* a kind of antelope.—**sāṭi,** *f.* a garment made of skin.

Ajinapattā, *f.* a bat.

Ajini, aor. of **jināti,** to conquer.

Ajimha, *a.* straight ; not crooked.

Ajira, *nt.* court-yard.

Ajīraka, *nt.* indigestion.

Ajeyya, *a.* invincible.

Ajja, *in.* today.—**tana,** *a.* modern ; referring to today.

Ajjava, *m. nt.* uprightness ; straightness.

Ajjita, *a.* earned ; hoarded ; collected.

Ajjuna, *m.* the tree Pentapatera Arjuna ; name of a prince.

Ajjhagā, (pret. of **adhigacchati**) (he) came to ; obtained ; experienced .

Ajjhatta, *a.* personal ; connected with the self.—**taŋ,** *ad.* inwardly.—**tika,** *a.* personal ; inward.

Ajjhappatta, *a.* having fallen upon or approached unexpectedly.

Ajjhabhāsati, (adhi + ā + bhās + a), to address ; to speak. *aor.* —**bhāsi.**

Ajjhayana, *nt.* study ; learning.

Ajjhācarati, (adhi + ā + car + a), to transgress ; to conduct against the rules. *aor.* —**cari.**

Ajjācāra, *m.* transgression ; wrong behaviour ; sexual intercourse.

Ajjhāciṇṇa ,(pp. of **ajjhācarati**). much practised ; habitually done.

Ajjhāpana, *nt.* teaching ; instruction.

Ajjhāpanna, (pp. of **ajjhāpajjati**). become guilty of an offence.

Ajjhāya, *m.* chapter.

Ajjhāyaka, *m.* an instructor ; teacher.

Ajjhāruhati, (adhi + ā + ruh + a), to rise up ; to climb over. *aor.* — **ruhi.** *pp.* **ajjhārūḷha.**

Ajjhāvasati (adhi + ā — vas + a), to inhabit ; to settle down. *aor.* —**vasi,** *abs.* —**vasitvā.**

Ajjhāvuttha, (pp. of the above). inhabited ; occupied.

Ajjhāsaya, *m.* intention ; disposition.—**yatā,** *f.* (in cpds :) the fact of having the intention of.

Ajjhiṭṭha, pp. of **ajjhesati.**

Ajjhupagacchati (adhi + upa + gam + a), to arrive; to reach ; to consent.

Ajjhupagata, pp. of the above.

Ajjhupagamana, *nt.* arrival ; agreement ; consent.

---

* P.T.S.D. gives the meaning "black antilope;" but the Sinhalese term " andun diviyā " shows that it is a kind of leopard.

Ajjhupekkhati (adhi + upa + ikkh + a), to be indifferent; to neglect. *aor.* —**khi.**

Ajjhupekkhana, *nt.*. — **nā,** *f.* indifference; negligence.

Ajjhupeti (adhi + upa + i + a), to come near; to approach. *aor.* —**esi.** *pp.* **ajjhupeta.**

Ajjhesati (adhi + isu + a), to request; to invite. *aor.* —**sayi.**

Ajjhesanā, *f.* request; invitation.

Ajjhesita, *pp.* of **ajjhesati.**

Ajjhokāsa, *m.* the open air.

Ajjhogāhati (adhi + ava + gāh + a), to plunge into; to enter. to immerse. *aor.* — **gahi.**

Ajjhogāḷha, pp. of the above.

Ajjhottharati (adhi + ava + thar + a), to submerge; to overpower. *aor.* — **thari.**

Ajjhotthaṭa, (pp. of the above). spread over; submerged with.

Ajjhohaṭa, pp. of **ajjhoharati.**

Ajjhoharaṇa, *nt.* swallowing; eating.—**raṇīya,** *a.* fit to be swallowed or eaten.

Ajjhoharati (adhi + ava + har + a), to swallow. *aor.* —**hari.**

Ajjhohāra, *m.* swallowing.

Ajjhohita, *pp.* crammed in (the mouth).

Añjati (añju + a), to anoint; to apply collyrium. *aor.*— **añji.**

Añjana, *nt.* collyrium (for the eyes).—**nāḷi,** *f.* a tube for collyrium; toilet box.—**vaṇṇa,** *a.* of the colour of collyrium, i.e. black.

Añjali, *f.* lifting of the folded hands as a token of reverence.—**kamma,** *nt.* the act of salutation.—**karaṇiya,** *a.* worthy of being honoured.—**puṭa,** *m.* folded fingers, in order to retain something in.

Añjasa, *nt.* path; road.

Añjita, pp. of **añjati** or **añjeti.**

Añjeti (añju + e), to anoint with; to apply collyrium. *aor.* —**esi.**

Añña, *a.* other; another; else.

Aññatama, *a.* one out of many; unknown.

Aññatara, *a.* certain; not well-known.

Aññatitthiya, *m.* an adherent of another faith.

Aññattha, aññatra, *ad.* elsewhere; somewhere else.

Aññathatta, *nt.* alteration; change of mind.

Aññathā, *ad.* otherwise; in a different way.

Aññadatthu, *in.* surely; at any rate; on the other hand.

Aññadā, *ad.* on another day; at another time.

Aññamañña, aññoñña, *a.* mutual.—**ñaŋ,** *ad.* one another; each other: mutually.

Aññavihita, *a.* being occupied with something else; distracted.

Aññā, *f.* perfect knowledge; arahantship.

Aññāṇa, *nt.* ignorance.

Aññāta, *a.* 1. (ā + ñāta:), known; understood; 2. (na + ñāta:) unknown; not recognised.

Aññātaka, *a.* not related by blood; unknown; not recognisable.—**vesa,** *m.* disguise.

Aññātāvī, aññātu, *m.* one who knows or has insight. **aññātu-kāma,** *a.* desirous to know.

Aññāya, *abs.* having understood.

Aṭaṭa, *m.* name of a minor hell; a high numeral.

Aṭana, *nt.* roaming about.

Atani, *f.* frame of a bed.

Aṭavi, *f.* forest.—**saṅkhobha,** m. an agitation among wild tribes.

Aṭṭa, *nt.* lawsuit ; watch tower ; a scaffold for workers. *adj.* (from **aṭṭita**:) grieved; afflicted. —**kāra,** *m.* a litigant.

Aṭṭaka, *m.* a high platform or scaffold for watchers or workers.

Aṭṭāna, *nt.* a post incised with squares and used as a rubber by bathing people.

Aṭṭita, *pp.* distressed ; grieved ; afflicted with.

Aṭṭīyati (aṭṭ + ī + ya), to be in trouble ; to be worried. *aor.* **aṭṭīyi.**

Aṭṭīyana, *nt.* —**nā,** f. dislike ; disgust : loathing.

Aṭṭha, *a.* eight.—**ma,**—**maka,** *a.* the eighth.—**mī,** *f.* the eighth day of the lunar month.

Aṭṭhaka, *nt.* a group of eight.

Aṭṭhakathā, *f.* explanation ; exposition ; a commentary.

Aṭṭhaṅgika, *a.* having eight constituents.

Aṭṭhapada, *nt.* a chessboard.

Aṭṭhaŋsa, *a.* octagonal.

Aṭṭhāna, *nt.* a wrong place or position ; an impossibility.

Aṭṭhārasa, *a.* eighteen.

Aṭṭhi, *nt.* bone ; a hard seed.—**kaṅkala,** *m.* the skeleton.—**kalyāna,** *nt.* beauty of teeth. —**maya,** *a.* made of bone.—**miñjā,** *f.* marrow of the bone.—**saṅkhalikā,** *f.*—**saṅghāta,** *m.* the skeleton.

Aṭṭhita, *a.* not steadfast.

Aṭṭhīkatvā, *abs.* having much attention ; being interested.

Aḍḍha, *a.* opulent ; wealthy ; *m.* a half.—**tā.** *f.* opulence.

Aḍḍhatiya, aḍḍhateyya, *a.* consisting of two and a half.

Aḍḍhadaṇḍaka, one half of a stick which is split into two; a short stick.

Aḍḍhamāsa, *m.* a fortnight.

Aḍḍhayoga, *m.* a kind of house which has a roof in the shape of an eagle's wing.

Aḍḍharatta, *nt.* midnight.

Aḍḍhuḍḍha, *m.* three and a half.

Aṇu, *m.* a very small particle ; an atom. *a :* minute ; subtle ; atomic.—**matta,** *a.* of very small size ; tiny.

Aṇḍa, aṇḍaka, *nt.* an egg ; the testicles.

Aṇḍaja, *a.* oviparous ; born of an egg. *m :* a bird ; a serpent.

Aṇḍūpaka, *nt.* a coil ; a pad for keeping something on.

Aṇṇa, *m.* water.

Aṇṇava, *m.* ocean.

Aṇha, *m.* day ; only in cpds. such as **pubbaṇha.**

Ataccha, *a.* false. *nt.* falsehood.

Ati, a prefix giving the meanings : *up to, over, gone beyond, excess* etc.

Atikaḍḍhati (ati + kaḍḍh + a), to pull too hard ; to trouble. *aor.* —**ḍḍhi.**

Atikara, *a.* over-acting.

Atikkanta, pp. of **atikkamati.**

Atikkama, *m.* going over ; passing beyond ; transgression.

Atikkamati (ati + kam + a), to go beyond ; to pass over ; to overcome ; to surpass. *aor.* —**kami.**

Atikhippaŋ, *ad.* too soon.

Atikhiṇa, *a.* blunt.

Atikhīṇa, *a.* much exhausted ; much wasted; shot from (a bow).

Atiga, *a.* (= **atigata,** pp. of **atigacchati**). gone over ; surmounted.

Atigacchati, (ati + gam + a), to overcome ; to surpass ; to surmount. *aor.* — **chi.**

Atigāḷha, *a.* intensive; very tight.

Atighora, *a.* terrible; very fierce

Aticarati (ati + car + a), to transgress; to commit adultery. *aor.* — **cari.**

Aticariyā, *f.* transgression; adultery.

Aticārī, *m.* transgressor; adulteror.—**cārinī,** *f.* an adulteress.

Aticca, *abs.* having passed beyond; having overcome.

Atichatta, *nt.* an extraordinary sunshade.

Atitta, *a.* unsatisfied.

Atittha, *nt.* an unsuitable place, way or manner.

Atithi, *m.* a guest; stranger.

Atidāruṇa, *a.* horrible; very cruel.

Atidivā, *in.* late in the day.

Atidisati (ati + dis + a), to point out; to explain. *aor.* — **disi.**

Atidūra, *nt.* a great distance; *a.* too far; very distant.

Atideva, *m.* a super god.

Atidhamati (ati + dham + a), to beat a drum too often or too loud. — **dhami.**

Atidhāvati (ati + dhāv + a), to run fast; to pass over the limits. *aor.* — **dhāvi.**

Atidhonacārī, 3. one who indulges too much in food, clothes, etc.

Atināmeti (ati + nam + e), to pass time. *aor.* — **esi.**

Atipaṇḍita, *a.* too clever.

Atipapañca, *m.* much delay.

Atipassati (ati + dis + a), to see clearly. *aor.* **atipassi.**

Atipāta, *m.* slaying; killing.

Atipātī, *m.* slayer; destroyer.

Atipāteti (ati + pat + e), to destroy; to kill. *aor.* — **esi.**

Atippago, *in.* too early.

Atibahala, *a.* very thick.

Atibāḷhan, *ad.* too much.

Atibāheti (ati + vah + e), to drive away; to pull out. *aor.* — **esi.**

Atibhaginī, *f.* much beloved sister.

Atibhāra, *m.* too heavy a load.—**bhāriya,** *a.* too heavy; very serious.

Atibhoti (ati + bhū + a), to excel; to overcome. *aor.* **atibhavi.**

Atimaññati (ati + man + ya), to despise. *aor.* — **maññi.**

Atimaññanā, *f.* arrogance; contempt.

Atimanāpa, *a.* very lovely; much beloved.

Atimatta, *a.* too much.

Atimahanta, *a.* immense; enormous.

Atimāna, *m.* pride; arrogance.—**mānī,** *m.* one who is proud.

Atimukhara, *a.* very talkative.

Atimuttaka, *m.* name of a monk; the plant *Guertnera Racemosa.*

Atiyācanā, *f.* begging too much.

Atiyāti (ati + yā + a), to overcome; to excel. *aor.* — **yāyi.**

Atiriccati (ati + ric + ya), to be left over; to remain. *aor.* — **ricci.**

Atiritta, (pp. of the above), left over; remaining.

Atiriva, *in.* excessively; very much.

Atireka, *a.* surplus; extra; exceeding.—**kaŋ,—taraŋ,** *ad.* excessively; very much.—**katā,** *f.* excessiveness.

Atirocati (ati + ruc + a), to outshine; to surpass in splendour *aor.* — **roci.**

Ativatta, *a.* surpassed; overcome.

Ativattati, (ati + vat + a), to pass over; to go beyond.

Ativatteti (ati + vat + e), to overcome. *aor.* — **esi.**

Ativassati (ati + vass + a), to rain down on *or* into. *aor.* — **vassi.** *pp.* **ativuṭṭha.**

Ativākya, *nt.* abuse; rep oach.

Ativāhaka, a. one who carries a burden; a guide.

Ativijjhati (ati + vidh + ya), to see through. *aor.* — **vijjhi.**

Ativiya, *in.* very much.

Ativelaŋ, *ad.* a protracted time.

Atisaya, *m.* abundance. —**yena,** *ad.* exceedingly.

Atisarati (ati + sar + a), to go beyond the limits; to transgress. *aor.* — **sar .**

Atisāyaŋ, *ad.* late in the evening.

Atisāra, *m.* overstepping; dyser tery.

Atisuṇa, *m.* rabid dog.

Atiharati (ati + har + a), to carry over; to bring. *aor.* **atihari.**

Atīta, *a.* past; gone by; *m.* the past.

Atīva, *in.* very much.

Ato, *in.* hence; therefore.

Atta, *m.* soul; oneself.—**kāma,** m. love of self.—**kilamatha,** *m.* self-mortification.—**gutta,** *a.* self-guarded.—**gutti,** *f.* self-care.—**ghañña,** *nt.* self-destruction.—**danta,** *a.* self-restrained.—**diṭṭhi,** *f.* speculation about the soul.—**bhāva,** *m.* personality; individuality.—**vāda,** *m.* the theory of soul.—**vadha,** *m.* self-destruction; suicide.—**hita,** *nt.* personal welfare.

Attaja, *a.* proceeding from oneself; *m.* a son.

Attadīpa, *a.* relying on oneself.

Attaniya, *a.* belonging to the self.

Attantapa, *a.* self-mortifying.

Attapaccakkha, *a.* self-witnessed.

Attapaṭilābha, *m.* acquisition of a personality.

Attamana, *a.* delighted.—**natā,** *f.* joy; pleasure.

Attasambhava, *a.* originating from one's self.

Attahetu, *in.* for one's own sake.

Attāṇa, *a.* without protection.

Attha, *m.* welfare,; gain; wealth; need; want; use; meaning; destruction.—**kkhāyī,** *a.* showing what is profitable.—**kara,** *a.* beneficial.—**kāma,** *a.* well-wishing.—**kusala,** *a.* clever in finding what is beneficial; clever in exposition.—**cara,** *a.* doing good; busy in the interest of others.—**cariyā,** f. doing good. — **dassī,** a. intent upon the good.—**bhañjaka,** *a.* destroying the welfare. —**vādī,** *m.* one who speaks good.

Attha, pres. 2nd pl. of **atthi.**

Atthakathā, *f.* a commentary; explanation of meaning.

Atthagama, *m.* setting down; extinction.

Atthaññū, *a.* one who knows the meaning or what is good.

Atthata (pp. of **attharati**), spread over with.

Atthara, *m.* a rug; a carpet.

Attharaṇa, *nt.* a covering; a bed-sheet.

Attharaka, *m.* one who spreads over.

Attharati (ā + thar + a), to spread; to lay out. *aor.* **atthari.** *caus :* **attharāpeti.**

Atthavasa, *m.* reason ; use.

Atthāya (dat. of **attha**), for the sake of. **Kimatthāya** = what for ?

Atthāra, *m.* spreading out.

Atthi (as + a + ti), to be ; to exist.

Atthika, Atthiya, Atthī, *a.* desirous of ; seeking for.

Atthitā, *f.* **atthibhāva,** *m.* existence ; the fact of being present.

Atthu, (imper. of **atthi**), be it so.

Atra, *ad.* here.

Atraja, a. born from oneself ; *m.* a son.—**jā,** f. a daughter.

At iccha, *a.* very greedy.—**chā,** —**cha ā,** *f.* excessive greed.

Atha, Atho, *in.* then ; and also.

Adaka, *a.* eater.

Adati (ad + a), to eat. *aor.* **adi.**

Adana, *nt.* eating.

Adadi (aor. of **dadāti**), **Adā,** (pret. of **dadāti**), he gave.

Adiṭṭha, *a.* not seen.

Adinna, *a.* not given.

Adu, nt. (of **amu**), such and such a thing.

Adda, *a.* moist ; green.

Addaka, *nt.* fresh ginger.

Addakkhi, aor. of **dakkhati.**

Addasa, Addasā, (pret. of **dakkhati**), he saw.

Addi, *m.* mountain.

Addita, *pp.* afflicted ; oppressed.

Addha, *m.* a half.—**māsa,** *m.* a fortnight.

Addhagata, *a.* one who has traversed the span of life.

Addhagū, *m.* traveller.

Addhaniya, *a.* fit for travelling ; lasting a long period.

Addhā, *in.* indeed ; certainly.

Addhā, *m.* path ; time.

Addhāna, *nt.* a long path, time, or journey.

Addhika, *m.* traveller ; wayfarer.

Addhuva, *a.* unstable ; impermanent.

Advejjha, *a.* doubtless ; uncontradictory.

Adhamma, *m.* misconduct ; false doctrine.

Adhama, *a.* mean ; low ; ignoble.

Adhara, *m.* the lip ; *a.* lower.

Adhi, *prep.* up to ; over ; on ; above.

Adhika, *a.* exceeding ; superior. —**tara,** *a.* much exceeding.

Adhikata, *a.* commissioned with; caused by.

Adhikaraṇa, *nt.* law-suit. *ad.* in consequence of ; because of ; for the sake of.—**samatha,** *m.* settling of a dispute or a lawsuit —**ṇika,** *m.* a judge.

Adhikaraṇī, *f.* a smith's anvil.

Adhikāra, *m.* management ; office ; aspiration.

Adhikoṭṭana, *nt.* executioner's or butcher's block.

Adhigacchati (adhi + gam + a), to attain ; to obtain ; to understand. *aor.* — **gacchi.**

Adhigaṇhāti (adhi + gah + ṇhā), to surpass ; to possess ; to overpower. *aor* — **gaṇhi.**

Adhigata, pp. of **adhigacchati.**

Adhigama, *m.* attainment ; knowledge.

Adhigameti (adhi + gam + e), see **adhigacchati.**

Adhiggahita, pp. of **adhigaṇhāti.**

Adhicitta, *nt.* higher thought ; concentration of mind.

Adhicca (abs. of **adhīyati**), having learnt or recited.—**samuppanna,** *a.* arisen without a cause ; spontaneous.

Adhiṭṭhāti, Adhiṭṭhahati, (adhi + ṭhā + a), to stand firmly ; to determine ; to fix one's attention on. *aor.* —**ṭhāsi,**—**ṭhahi.**

Adhiṭṭhātabba, *pt. p.* fit to be determined.

Adhiṭṭhāna, *nt.* decision ; resolution ; determination.

Adhiṭṭhāya, abs. of **adhiṭṭhāti.**

Adhiṭṭhāyaka, *a.* superintending; looking after. *m.* a superintendant.

Adhiṭṭhita, (pp. of **adhiṭṭhāti**), determined ; undertaken.

Adhipa, Adhipati, *m.* lord ; master ; ruler.

Adhipaññā, *f.* higher wisdom.

Adhipatana, *nt.* attack ; falling upon ; hopping.

Adhipātaka, *m.* a moth ; grasshopper.—**pātikā,** *f.* a flea.

Adhippāya, *m.* intention.

Adhippeta, *pp.* meant,; intended; desired.

Adhibhavati (adhi + bhū + a), to overpower. *aor.* — **bhavi.** *pp.* **adhibhūta.**

Adhimatta, *a.* exceeding ; too much. **-tatā,** *f.* excess ; superabundance.

Adhimāna, *m.* undue estimate of oneself.

Adhimānika, *a.* one who thinks that he has attained some supernatural knowledge not actually being so.

Adhimuccati (adhi + muc + ya), to attach or incline towards ; to possess by a spirit. *aor.* — **mucci.**

Adhimuccana, *nt.* making up one's mind ; possession by a spirit.

Adhimucchita, (pp. of **adhimucchati**), infatuated.

Adhimutta (pp. of **adhimuccati**), intent upon ; inclined to. —**muttika,** *a.* bent on ; attached to.

Adhimutti, *f.* resolve ; disposition.

Adhimokkha, *m.* firm resolve ; determination.

Adhirohanī, *f.* a ladder.

Adhivacana, *nt.* a term ; designation.

Adhivattati (adhi + vat + a), to overpower. *aor.* — **vatti.**

Adhivattha, *a.* inhabiting ; living in.

Adhivasati (adhi + vas + a), to inhabit ; to live in. *aor.* — **vasi.**

Adhivāsaka, *a.* enduring ; patient.

Adhivāsanā, *f.* endurance ; forbearance.

Adhivāseti (adhi + vas + e), to endure ; to wait for. *aor.* —**esi.**

Adhivuttha, pp. of **adhivasati.**

Adhisīla, *nt.* higher morality.

Adhiseti (adhi + si + e), to lie on. *aor.* — **esi.** *pp.* **adhisayita.**

Adhīna, *a.* dependent ; belonging to.

Adhīyati (adhi + ī + ya), to study; to learn by heart. *aor.* **adhīyi.** *pp.* **adhīta.**

Adhunā, *ad.* now ; recently ; newly.

Adho, *in.* under ; below.—**kata,** *a.* lowered ; turned down —**gama,** *a.* going downward.—**bhāga,** *m.* the lower part—**mukha,** *a.* bent over ; with face cast down ; turned upside down.

Anaṅgaṇa, *a.* passionless ; blameless.

Anaṇa, *a.* free of debt.

Anatta, *a.* soul-less. *m.* non-ego.

Anattamana, a. displeased.

Anattha, *m.* harm ; misfortune.

Anadhivara, *m.* the Blessed One.

Ananucchavika, *a.* improper ; not befitting.

Ananta, *a.* endless ; limitless ; infinite.

Anantara, *a.* next ; adjoining ; immediately following.

Anappaka, *a.* much ; many ; not trifling.

Anabhāva (anu + abhāva), *m.* utter cessation.*

Anabhirata, *a.* not taking delight in.

Anabhirati, *f.* discontent ; dissatisfaction ; melancholy.

Anamatagga, *a.* one whose beginning is unknown.

Anaya, *m.* misfortune.

Anariya, *a.* ignoble ; vulgar.

Analaṅkata, *a.* 1. dissatisfied ; 2. not decorated.

Anavaṭṭhita, *a.* unsettled ; unsteady.

Anavaya, *a.* not lacking ; complete.

Anavarata, a. constant.—**rataŋ**, *ad.* constantly ; continually.

Anavasesa, *a.* without any remainder ; complete.—**sesaŋ**, *ad.* fully ; completely.

Anasana, *nt.* fasting.

Anākula, *a.* not confused or entangled.

Anāgata, *a.* not come yet. *m.* the future.

Anāgamana, *nt.* not coming.

Anāgāmī, *m.* one who does not return, i.e. the person who has attained the 3rd Path.

Anācāra, *m.* misconduct ; immorality.

Anātha, *a.* miserable ; helpless.

Anādara, *m.* disrespect ; *a.* disrespectful.—**dariya**, *nt.* disregard.

Anādā, Anādāya, *abs.* (of na + ādāti), without taking.

Anādiyitvā, *abs.* not heeding ; not taking up.

Anāpucchā, *abs.* without asking or permission.

Anāmaya, *a.* free from illness.

Anāmasita, *a.* not touched.

Anāyatana, *nt.* improper place.

Anāyāsa, *a.* free from trouble.—**yāsena**, *ad.* easily.

Anāyūhana, *nt.* non-exertion.

Anāyūhanta, *pt. p.* not exerting.

Anārambha, *a.*free from turmoil.

Anālaya, *a.* free from attachment ; *m.* aversion.

Anāvaṭa, *a.* open ; not shut.

Anāvattī, *m.* one who does not return.

Anāvila, *a.* undisturbed ; clean.

Anāvuttha, *a.* not dwelt in.

Anāsakatta, *nt.* fasting.

Anāsava, *a.* free from intoxicants ; passionless.

Anāḷhika, *a.* poor ; one who does not possess even a measure of rice.

Anikkasāva, *a.* not free from impurity of mind.

Anigha, *a.* free from trouble.

Anicca, *a.* not stable : impermanent.

Anicchanta,—**chamāna**, *pr. p.* unwilling.

Anicchā, *f.* disliking ; despassion.

Aniñjana, *nt.* immobility.

---

* **Ana + bhāva given in P. T. S. D. is not correct.**

Aniñjita, *a.* unshaken; undisturbed.

Aniṭṭha, *a.* unpleasant; not agreeable.

Aniṭṭhita, *a.* unfinished; not completed.

Anindita, *a.* blameless; not reviled.

Anibbisanta, *pr. p.* not finding out.

Animisa, *a.* unwinking.

Aniyata, *a.* uncertain; not settled.

Anila, *m.* wind.—**patha**, *m.* the sky.—**loddhuta**, *a.* shaken by the wind.

Anisammakārī, *a.* not acting considerately; hasty.

Anissara, *a.* having no power or influence.

Anīka, *nt.* an army.—**kagga**, *nt.* array of an army.—**kaṭṭha**, *m.* a royal body-guard.

Anīgha, see. **Anigha**.

Anītika, *a.* free from injury or harm.

Anukaṅkhī, *a.* longing for.

Anukantati (anu + kant + a), to cut into; to shear. *aor.* — **anukanti**.

Anukampaka, **Anukampī**, *a.* compassionate; one who has pity.

Anukampati (anu + kamp + a), to have pity on. *aor.*—**kampi**.

Anukampana, *nt.* **Anukampā**, *f.* compassion; pity.

Anukampita, (pp. of **anukampati**), pitied by.

Anukaroti (anu + kar + o), to imitate; to repeat some action *aor.* **anukari**. *pp.* **anukata**.

Anukāra, *m.* imitation.

Anukārī, 3. imitator.

Anukiṇṇa, (pp. of **anukirati**), strewn with.

Anukubbati, same as **anukaroti**.—**banta**, *pr. p.* imitating.

Anukūla, *a.* favourable; agreeable.—**bhāva**,*m.* complaisance.

Anukkama, *m.* order; succession.—**mena**, *ad.* gradually; in due course.

Anukhuddaka, *a.* minor; less important.

Anuga, *a.* following; followed by.

Anugacchati (anu + gam + a), to follow; to go after. *aor.*—**cchi**.

Anugata, (pp. of the above), accompanied by; gone into.

Anugati, *f.* following; adherence to.

Anugama, *m.*—**gamana**, *nt.* following after.

Anugāmika,—**gāmī**, *a.* going along with; a follower.

Anugāhati (anu + gāh + a), to plunge into; to enter. *aor.*—**gāhi**.

Anugijjhati (anu + gidh + a), to covet. *aor.*— **gijjhi**.

Anugiddha, (pp. of the above), covetous; greedy.

Anugganhāti (anu gah + ṇhā), to help; to have pity on. *aor.* —**ganhi**.

Anugganhana, *nt.* **Anuggaha**, *m.* favour; help; assistance.

Anuggahita, (pp. of **anuggaṇhāti**), commiserated; helped.

Anuggāhaka, 3. helper; a patron.

Anuggiranta, *pr. p.* not uttering; not speaking.

Anugghāṭeti (anu + u + ghaṭ + e), to open; to unfasten. *aor.* — **esi**. *

* P. T. S. D. gives an opposite meaning after showing its construction as: "an + ugghāṭeti."

Anucaṅkamati (anu + kam + a), to follow one who is walking up and down. *aor.* —**kami.**

Anucara, *m.* a follower ; attendant.

Anucarati (anu + car + a), to follow ; to practise. *aor.* —**cari.**

Anucarita, (pp. of the above), accompanied by ; pervaded with ; practised.

Anuciṇṇa, (pp. of **anucarati**), practised; attained ; acquainted with.

Anucināti (anu + ci + nā), to collect or practise. *aor.* —**cini.**

Anucita (na + ucita), *a.* improper ; not befitting.

Anucinteti (anu + cit + e), to think upon ; to consider. *aor.* —**esi.**

Anuccārita, *a.* not uttered or raised up.

Anucciṭṭha, *a.* untouched; (food) that is not left over.

Anucchavika, *a.* suitable ; proper ; befitting.

Anuja, *m.* brother.

Anujā, *f.* sister.

Anujāta, *a.* born after or resembling (his father).

Anujānāti (anu + ñā + nā), to allow ; to give permission. *aor.* —**jāni.**

Anujīvati (anu + jīv + a), to subsist by. *aor.* —**jīvi.**

Anujīvī, 3. a dependent person.

Anuju, *a.* not straight ; crooked.

Anuññā, *f.* sanction ; permission

Anuññāta (pp. of **anujānāti**). allowed; permitted ; sanctioned.

Anuṭṭhahanta,—hāna, anuṭṭhātu, *a.* one who does not rouse himself; inactive (person.)

Anuṭṭhāna, *nt.* inactivity. *a.* not getting up.

Anuḍahati (anu + dah + a), to burn over ; to consume. *aor.* —**ḍahi.**

Anuḍahana, *nt.* burning.

Anutappati (anu + tap + ya), to repent; to regret. *aor.*—**tappi.**

Anutāpa, *m.* remorse ; anguish.

Anutiṭṭhati (anu + ṭhā + a), to stand near by.

Anutīra, *nt.* neighbourhood of a bank or shore.—**tīraŋ,** *ad.* along the bank or shore.

Anuttara, *a.* incomparable ; unsurpassed.—**riya,** *nt.* superiority ; excellency.

Anuttāna, *a.* not shallow ; deep ; obscure.

Anutthunana, *nt.* murmur; wailing; lamentation.

Anutthunanta, *pr. p.* of **anutthunāti.**

Anutthunāti (anu + thu + nā), to moan ; to lament ; to bewail.

Anutrāsī, 3. one who does not fear.

Anudadāti (anu + dā + a), to grant ; to concede.

Anudahati, see **Anuḍahati.**

Anudisā, *f.* an intermediate direction.

Anuddayā, *f.* see **Anukampā.**

Anuddiṭṭha, *a.* not pointed out ; not uttered.

Anuddhaṭa, *a.* not pulled out ; not destroyed.

Anuddhata, *a.* not proud ; not puffed up.

Anudhamma, *m.* conformity with the Law.

Anudhāvati (anu + dhāv + a), to run after. *aor.* —**dhāvi.**

Anunaya, *m.* friendliness.

Anunāsika, *a.* nasal.

Anuneti (anu + nī + e), to conciliate ; to appease. *aor.* —**esi.**

Anunetu, *m.* one who reconciles.

Anupa, *m.* watery land.

Anupakkuṭṭha, *a.* blameless; irreproachable.

Anupakhajja, *abs.* having encroached or intruded.

Anupaghāta, *m.* non-injury; humanity; non-violence.

Anupacita, *a.* not accumulated.

Anupaññatti, *f.* a supplementary regulation.

Anupaṭipāṭi, *f.* succession.—**pāṭiyā,** *ad.* successively; in order.

Anupaṭṭhita, *a.* not present; not arrived.

Anupatati (anu + pat + a), to fall upon; to befall. *aor.* **anupati.**

Anupatita, (pp. of the above), affected with; oppressed by.

Anupatti, f. attainment.

Anupadaŋ, *ad.* word-by-word; close behind.

Anupaddava, *a.* free from danger.

Anupadhāretvā, *abs.* having disregarded; without consideration.

Anupabbajati (anu + pa + vaj + a), to give up worldly life in imitation of another.

Amupameya, *a.* incomparable.

Anuparigacchati (anu + pari + gam + a), to go round about *aor.* —**gacchi.**

Anuparidhāvati (anu + pari + dhāv + a), to run up and down or around. *aor.* —**dhāvi.**

Anupariyāti (anu + pari + yā + a), to go round about. *aor.* —**yāyi.**

Anuparivattati (anu + pari + vat + a), to move round and round; to keep on rolling. *aor.* —**vatti.**

Anuparivattana, *nt.* rolling after; evolving.

Anupalitta, *a.* free from taint; not smeared with.

Anupavajja, *a.* blameless.

Anupavatteti (anu + pa + vat + e), to continue rolling; to wield power in succession. *aor.* —**esi.**

Anupaviṭṭha, pp. of the following.

Anupavisati (anu + pa + vis + a), to go into; to enter. *aor.* —**visi.**

Anupasampanna, *a.* one who has not yet received the full ordination or **upasampadā.**

Anupassaka, 3. observer; one who contemplates.

Anupassati (anu + dis + a), to observe; to contemplate. *aor.* —**passi.**

Anupassanā, *f.* consideration; realization.

Anupassī, see **Anupassaka.**

Anupahata, *a.* not spoilt; not destroyed.

Anupāta, *m.* attack in speech.

Anupātī, 3. one who attacks or follows.

Anupādā,—**pādāya,** *abs.* without grasping.

Anupādāna, *a.* unattached; fuelless.

Anupādisesa, *a.* without any substratum.

Anupāpuṇāti, (anu + pa + ap + unā), to reach; to attain. *aor.* —**puṇi.**

Anupāpeti, caus. (anu + pa + ap + e), to conduct or lead. *aor.* —**esi.**

Anupāya, *m.* wrong means.

Anupālaka, *a.* guarding; protecting. *m.* a protector.

Anupālana, *nt.* maintenance; protection.

Anupāleti (anu + pāl + e), to maintain; to safeguard. *aor.* —**esi.**

Anupucchati (anu + pucch + a), to inquire after. *aor.* —**pucchi.**

Anupuṭṭha, (pp. of the above), being asked or questioned.

Anupubba, *a.* successive; gradual.—**bbaŋ,**—**bbena,** *ad.* gradually; by and by.—**pubbatā,** *f.* graduation; succession.

Anupekkhati (anu + upa + ikkh + a), to consider carefully. *aor.* —**kkhi.**

Anupeseti (anu + pes + e), to send forth after. *aor.* —**esi.**

Anuposiya, *a.* to be nourished or fostered.

Anuppatta, pp. of **anupāpuṇāti.**

Anuppatti, *f.* arrival; attainment. (na + uppatti :) cessation of rebirth.

Anuppadātu, *m.* a giver; one who bestows.

Anuppadāna, *nt.* giving; handing over.

Anuppadinna, pp. of the following.

Anuppadāti (anu + pa + dā + a). **anuppadeti** (anu + pa + dā + e), to give out; to hand over.

Anuppabandha, *m.*—**dhanā,** *f.* continuance.

Anuppharaṇa, *nt.* pervasion; flashing through.

Anubaddha, (pp. of the following), connected with; followed by.

Anubandhati (anu + badh + ŋ -a), to pursue; to follow; to connect. *aor.* — **bandhi.**

Anubandhana, *nt.* connection; chasing; following.

Anubala, *nt.* help : stimulation; a rear-guard.

Anubujjhati (anu + budh + ya), to conceive; to understand. *aor.* — **bujjhi.**

Anubujjhana, *nt.* understanding; awakening.

Anubuddha, (pp. of **anubujjhati**), conceived; known; understood.

Anubodha, *m.* knowledge; understanding.

Anubyañjana, *nt.* a secondary attribute.

Anubrūhita (pp. of the following) improved; strengthened with.

Anubrūheti (anu + brūh + e), to improve; to practise. *aor.* — **esi.**

Anubhavati (anu + bhū + a), to undergo; to partake in; to eat; to experience. *aor.* — **bhavi.**

Anubhavana, *nt.* experiencing of; undergoing; eating.

Anubhavanta, *pr. p.* of **anubhavati.**

Anubhutta, anubhūta, pp. of **anubhavati,** enjoyed; undergone.

Anubhūyamāna, *pr. p.p.* being experienced.

Anubhoti, see **Anubhavati.**

Anumajjati (anu + majj + a), to stroke. *aor.* — **majji.**

Anumajjana, *nt.* stroking.

Anumaññati (anu + man + ya) to assent; to approve. *aor.* — **maññi.**

Anumata (pp. of the above), approved of; given leave.

Anumati, *f.* consent; permission.

Anumāna, *m.* inference.

Anumīyati (anu + mā + ī + ya), to infer; to conclude. *aor.* — **mīyi.**

Anumodaka, 3. one who appreciates; thanksgiver.

Anumodati (anu + mud + a), to rejoice in; to appreciate. *aor.* — **modi.**

Anumodanā, *f.* thanksgiving; appreciation; transference of merit.

Anumodita, pp. of **Anumodati.**

Anuyanta, *pr. p.* following dependent on.

Anuyāta (pp. of **anuyāti**), followed by.

Anuyāti (anu + yā + a), to follow. *aor.* **anuyāyi.**

Anuyāyī, 3. a follower.

Anuyuñjati (anu + yuj + ŋ-a), to engage in; to question; to give oneself up. *aor.* — **ñji.**

Anuyutta (pp. of the above), engaged in; an attendant; a vassal.

Anuyoga, *m.* practice of; devotion to; an inquiry or inquest.

Anuyogī, 3. one who is practising or engaged in.

Anurakkhaka, *a.* protecting; protector.

Anurakkhana, *nt.* preservation; protection.

Anurakkhati (anu + rakkh + a), to guard; to protect. *aor.* — **khi.**

Anurakkhā, *f.* guarding; protection.

Anurakkhī, see **Anurakkhaka.**

Anurakkhiya, *a.* to be guarded.

Anurañjati (anu + rañj + *a*), to attach to; to rejoice. *aor.* — **rañji.**

Anurañjita, pp. of the following.

Anurañjeti (anu + rañj + e), to brighten; to beautify. *aor.* — **esi.**

Anuratta (pp. of **anurañjati**), attached to; fond of.

Anurava, *m.* resounding; echo.

Anurūpa, *a.* suitable; conform with.

Anurodati (anu + rud + a), to cry for. *aor.* — **rodi.**

Anurodha, *m.* compliance.

Anulitta, pp. of the following.

Anulimpati, (anu + lip + ŋ-a); **Anulimpeti** (anu + lip + ŋ-e), to anoint; to besmear. *aor.* —**limpi,** — **esi.**

Anuloma, *a.* regular; not antagonistic; *m.* conformity.—**mika,** *a.* suitable; in proper order.

Anulometi (Deno. from **anuloma**), to be in accordance with. *aor.* — **esi.**

Anuvattaka,—vattī, 3. siding in with; one who follows or acts according to.

Anuvattana, *nt.* compliance; obedience.

Anuvatteti (anu + vat + e), to continue rolling; to wield power in succession. *aor.* — **esi.**

Anuvadati (anu + vad + a), to blame. *aor.* — **vadi.**

Anuvassaŋ, *ad.* annually; in every rainy season.—**vassika,** *a.* annual.

Anuvāta, *m.* a forward or favourable wind.——**vātaŋ,** *ad.* in the direction of the wind.

Anuvāda, *m.* blaming; censure; a translation.

Anuvāsana, *nt.* perfuming.

Anuvāsita, (pp. of the following), perfumed.

Anuvāseti (anu + vas + e), to scent; to impregnate with a good smell. *aor.* — **esi.**

Anuvicarati (anu + vi + car + a), to wander about; to roam. *aor.* — **cari.**

Anuvicarita, (pp. of the above), pondered over; reflected.

Anuvicarana, *nt.* roaming about; strolling.

Anuvicināti (anu + vi + ci + nā), to ponder over; to examine. *aor.* — **cini.**

Anuvicca, (abs. of the above), having known or found out.—**kāra,** *m.* investigation; considerate action.

Anuvijjaka, *m.* examiner; investigator.

Anuvijjati (anu + vid + ya), to investigate; to know thoroughly. *aor.* — **vijji.**

Anuvijjhati (anu + vidh + ya), to pierce; to understand thoroughly. *aor.* — **jjhi.**

Anuvitakketi (anu + vi + takk + e), to reflect; to ponder over. *aor.* — **esi.**

Anuvidita, *pp.* recognised.

Anuviddha, pp. of **anuvijjhati.**

Anuvidhīyati (anu + vi + dhā + ī + ya), to act in conformity with. *aor.* — **īyi.**

Anuviloketi (anu + vi + lok + e), to look over; to survey. *aor.* — **esi.**

Anuvuttha, *pp.* dwelt; lived.

Anuvyañjana, *nt.* a secondary attribute.

Anusakkati (anu + sakk + a), to move back or aside. *aor.* — **sakki.**

Anusaŋvaccharaŋ, *ad.* annually.

Anusañcarati (anu + saŋ + car + a), to walk along; to go round about. *aor.* — **cari.**

Anusañcarita, (pp. of the above) frequented.

Anusaṭa (pp. of **anusarati**), sprinkled with; scattered.

Anusandati (anu + sand + a), to stream along; to be connected with. *aor.* — **sandi.**

Anusandhi, *f.* connection; conclusion.

Anusaya, *m.* proclivity; a dormant disposition.

Anusayati (anu + si + a), to lie dormant. *aor.* — **sayi.**

Anusayita, pp. of the above.

Anusarati (anu + sar + a), to go after; to follow. *aor.* —**sari.** *pp.* — **saṭa.**

Anusavati (anu + su + a), to flow or ooze continually. *aor.* — **savi.**

An (ṇ) usahagata, *a.* having a residium.

Anusāyika, *a.* inherent; chronic.

Anusāra, *m.* following;—**rena,** *ad.* in accordance with.

Anusārī, *a.* striving after; acting in accordance with.

Anusāvaka, *m.* one who announces or proclaims.

Anusāvana, *nt.*—**vanā,** *f.* proclamation.

Anusāvita, *pp.* of the following.

Anusāveti (anu + su + e), to announce; to proclaim. *aor.* —**esi.**

Anusāsaka, *m.* adviser.

Anusāsati (anu + sās + a), to advise; to admonish. *aor.* — **sāsi.**

Anusāsana, *nt.*—**sanī,** *f.*—**sanā,** *f.* advice: instruction.

Anusikkhati (anu + sikkh + a). to learn; to follow one's example.

Anusiṭṭha, pp. of **anusāsati.**

Anusiṭṭhi, *f.* admonition; advice.

Anusūyaka, *a.* not envious.

Anuseti, see **Anusayati.**

Anusocati (anu + suc + a), to bewail. *aor.* — **soci.**

Anusocana, *nt.* bewailing; mourning.

Anusota, *m.* down-stream.—**sotaŋ,** *ad.* along the current.—**tagāmī,** *a.* one who follows the stream.

Anussati, *f.* recollection; memory: mindfulness.

Anussaraṇa, *nt.* remembrance; memory.

Anussarati (anu + sar + a), to remember. *aor.* — **sari.**

Anussaritu, *m.* one who remembers.

Anussava, *m.* hear-say; tradition.

Anussuka, *a.* courageless.

Anussuta, *pp.* heard of.

Anuhīramāna, *pr. p.p.* being held up.

Anūna,—**naka**, *a.* not lacking or deficient; complete.—**natā**, *f.* completeness.

Anūpama, *a.* that which has no comparision.

Anūhata, *a.* not rooted out.

Aneka, *a.* many; various.—**ppakāra**, *a.*—**vidha**, *a.* multifarious; manifold; divers.

Aneja, *a.* free from lust.

Anedha, *a.* fuel-less.

Anesanā, *f.* wrong way of earning.

Aneḷa, **Aneḷaka**, *a.* faultless; pure.

Aneḷagala, *a.* free from dripping saliva.

Anoka, *a.* houseless; free from attachment.

Anokāsa, *a.* having no opportunity, space or time.

Anojā, *f.* a plant with orange-coloured flowers.

Anotatta, *m.* name of a lake in the Himalayas (from which several Indian rivers flow).

Anottappa, *nt.* recklessness.—**tāpī**, *a.* not afraid of sin; reckless.

Anodaka, *a.* waterless.

Anodissaka, *a.* unrestricted; general.

Anonamanta, *a.* not bending down.

Anoma, *a.* superior.—**dassī**, *m.* one who has supreme knowledge.

Anovassaka, *a.* sheltered from the rain.

Anta, *m.* the end; goal; top. *nt.* intestine.—**kara**, *a.* putting an end to.—**kiriyā**, *f.* ending; relief. — **gamana**, *nt.* going to an end; eradication.—**guṇa**, *nt.* mesentery. —**vaṭṭi**, *f.* coils of the intestines.

Antaka, *m.* the Death.

Antara, *nt.* difference. *a.* inner; inter. **antare**, in between.—**kappa**, *m.* intermediatory *kappa*.—**ghara**, *nt.* inner village or house.

Antaraṭṭhaka, *nt.* the coldest eight days of the winter, when snow falls (in India).

Antarantā, *ad.* now and then; occasionally.

Antaradhāna,—**dhāyana**, *nt.* disappearance.

Antaradhāyati (antara + dhe + a), to disappear. *aor.* — **dhāyi.**

Antaradhāpeti (caus. of the above), to cause to disappear

Antaravāsaka, *m.* inner garment.

Antarahita, pp. of **antaradhāyati.**

Antaraṃsa, *m.* space between two shoulders.

Antarā, *ad.* in between; meanwhile.—**magge**, on the way; on the road.

Antarāya, *m.* obstacle; danger.

Antarāyika, *a.* forming an impediment.

Antarāḷa, *nt.* interval.

Antarika, *a.* intermediate; next. —**rikā**, *f.* interval; interstice.

Antavantu, *a.* having an end.

Antika, *a.* (in cpds.) being at the end of; near. *nt.* neighbourhood.

Antima, *a.* last; final.

Antaḷikkha, *nt.* the sky.

Antepura, *nt.* inner town; a harem.—**purika,** *a.* belonging to a harem.

Antevāsika,—vāsī, *m.* one who lives with his master; an attendant; a pupil.

Anto, *in.* inside; within; inner. —**kucchi,** *m. f.* womb.—**gata,** —**gạdha,** *a.* included; contained.—**gabbha,** *m.* innerroom.—**gāma,** *m.* inner village. —**ghara,** *nt.* inner house.—**jana,** *m.* people belonging to the family.—**jāta,** *a.* born in the house; a slave.—**vassa,** *m. nt.* rainy season.

Andu, anduka, *m.* a fetter; a chain.—**ghara.** *nt.* prison.

Andha, *a.* blind; foolish.—**karana,** *a.* blinding; confusing.—**bāla,** *a.* silly; very foolish —**bhūta,** *a.* mentally blind; ignorant.

Andhakāra, *m.* darkness; bewilderment.

Andhantama, *m. nt.* deep darkness.

Andhaka, *m.* gad-fly. *a.* belonging to the Āndhra country.

Anna, *nt.* food; boiled rice —**da,** *a.* one who gives food.—**pāna,** *nt.* food and drink.

Anvagā (3rd. sing. pret.) he followed.

Anvagū (3rd. pl. pret.) they followed.

Anvaddhamāsaŋ, *ad.* twice a month; fortnightly.

Anvattha, *a.* according to the sense.

Anvadeva (anu + eva), *in.* following behind.

Anvaya, *m.* course; conformity; tradition.

Anvahaŋ, *ad.* daily.

Anvāgata, *a.* endowed with; following.

Anvāya, *abs.* having undergone, experienced, or attained.

Anvāyika, *a.* following.

Anvāvisati (anu + ā + vis + a), to take possession of. *aor.* —**visi.** *pp.* **anvāviṭṭha.**

Anvāhata, *a.* beaten; struck.

Anvāhiṇḍati (anu + ā + hid + ŋ-a), to wander. *aor.*—**hiṇḍi.**

Anveti (anu + i + a), to follow; to approach.

Anvesaka, *a.* seeker.

Anvesati (anu + es + a), to seek; to search. *aor.* —**esi.**

Anvesanā, *f.* seeking; search; investigation.

Anvesī, *a.* striving or seeking after. *m.* a seeker.

Apakaḍḍhati (apa + kaḍḍh + a), to draw away; to take off. *aor.* —**kaḍḍhi.**

Apakata, (*pp.* of the following), put off; done away. *nt.* mischief.

Apakaroti (apa + kar + o), to hurt; to offend; to put off. *aor.* —**kari.**

Apakassa, *abs.* (of the following), having drawn aside or removed.

Apakassati (apa + kass + a), to draw aside; to remove. *aor.* —**kassi.**

Apakāra, *m.* injury; mischief.

Apakkama, *m.* removal; departure.

Apakkamati (apa + kam + a), to depart; to go away. *aor.* —**kami.** *pp.* **apakkanta.**

Apakkamma, *abs.* of the above.

Apagacchati (apa + gam + a), to go away; to turn aside. *aor.* —**cchi.**

Apagata (*pp.* of the above), removed; departed; gone away.

Apagabbha, *a.* (apa + gabbha :) not destined to another rebirth; (a + pagabbha :) not haughty.

Apagama, *m.* moving aside; disappearance.

Apacaya, *m.* falling off; diminution; unmaking.—**gāmī,** making for the undoing of rebirth.

Apacāyati (apa + cāy + a), to honour; to respect. *aor.* —**cāyi.**

Apacāyana, *nt.*—**nā,** *f.* worship; reverence.

Apacāyaka, Apacāyī, *a.* paying homage.

Apacāyita, *pp.* of **apacāyati.**

Apacināti (apa + ci + nā), to do away with; to diminish. *aor.* —**cini.**

Apaciti, *f.* respect; expiation.

Apacinana, *nt.* destruction; expiation.

Apacca, *nt.* offspring.

Apaccakkha, *a.* unseen; not realised; not tested.

Apajita, *nt.* defeat. *pp.* defeated.

Apaṇṇaka, *a.* true; faultless.

Apatthaṭa, *a.* not spread out.

Apatthaddha, *a.* not haughty.

Apatthiya, *a.* what ought not to be wished.

Apatha, *m.* a wrong path or way.

Apada, *a.* footless.—**tā,** *f.* footlessness.

Apadāna, *nt.* life history; legend.

Apadisa, *m.* witness; testimony.

Apadisati (apa + dis + a), to call to witness; to quote. *aor.* —**disi.**

Apadesa, *m.* reason; statement.

Apadhāraṇa, *nt.* a lid.

Apanāmana, *nt.* removal; driving away.

Apanāmeti (apa + nam + e), to banish; to remove. *aor.* —**esi.**

Apanidahati (apa + ni + dah + a), to hide; to conceal. *aor.* —**dahi.**

Apanihita, *pp.* of the above.

Apanīta, *pp.* of **apaneti.**

Apanudati (apa + nud + a), to drive away; to dispel. *aor.* —**nudi.**

Apanudana, *nt.* removal; dispelling.

Apanuditu, *m.* dispeller of.

Apaneti (apa + ni + a), to take away; to remove. *aor.* —**esi.**

Apamāra, *m.* epilepsy.

Apara, *a.* another; other; western.

Aparajju, *ad.* on the following day.

Aparajjhati (apa + radh + ya), to offend against; to do some crime. *aor.* —**jjhi.**

Aparaddha, (*pp.* of the above), guilty; failed.

Aparanta, the last end; the future; name of a country in Western India.

Aparanna, *nt.* leguminous seeds (such as peas) other than cereals.

Aparappaccaya, *a.* not relying on others.

Aparājita, *a.* unconquered.

Aparādha, *m.* offence; guilt.

Aparādhika,—rādhī, *a.* guilty; criminal.

Aparāpariya, *a.* ever-following; successive.

Apariggahita, *a.* unoccupied; not possessed.

Aparicchinna, *a.* unlimited; not separated.

Aparimāṇa, *a.* limitless ; immeasurable.

Aparimita, *a* unlimited ; measureless.

Apalāyī, *a.* not running away ; fearless.

Apalāleti (apa + lāl + e), to caress ; to fondle. *aor.* —**esi.**

Apalibuddha, *a.* unhindered ; free.

Apalikhati (apa + likh + a), to scrape ; to lick off. *aor.* —**likhi.**

Apalikhana, *nt.* licking off ; scraping.

Apalokana, *nt.* leave ; consent.

Apalokita, *pp.* of the following.

Apaloketi (apa + lok + e), to look up to; to obtain permission from ; to give notice. *aor.* —**esi.**

Apavagga, *m.* final delivery ; the end.

Apavadati (apa + vad + a), to reproach ; to blame. *aor.* —**vadi.**

Apavāda, *m.* reproach ; blaming finding fault.

Apaviddha, (*pp.* of **apavijjhati**), thrown away ; rejected.

Apasakkati (apa + sakk + a), to go aside ; to move. *aor.* —**sakki.** *pp.* —**sakkita.**

Apasakkana, *nt.* moving aside.

Apasavya, *nt.* right side.

Apasādana, *nt.* disparagement.

Apasādita, *pp.* of the following.

Apasādeti (apa + sad + e), to deprecate ; to decline ; to disparage. *aor.* —**esi.**

Apasmāra, see **apamāra**,

Apassaya, *m.* support ; a bolster ; a head-rest. —**yika**, *a.* reclining on.

Apassita, (*pp.* of the following), leaning against ; depending on.

Apasseti, apassayati, (apa + si + e *or* aya), to lean against ; to depend on. *aor.* —**sayi.**

Apassena-phalaka, *nt.* a bolster slab.

Apahattu, *m.* one who removes.

Apaharati (apa + har + a), to remove ; to take away; to rob. *aor.* —**hari.** *pp.* **apahaṭa.**

Apaharaṇa, *nt.* removal ; stealing.

Apahāra, *m.* taking away ; robbing.

Apākaṭa, *a.* unknown.

Apācīna, *a.* westerly.

Apācī, *f.* southern direction.

Apāda, apādaka, *a.* footless ; creeping.

Apāna, *nt.* breathing out.

Apādāna, *nt.* separation ; the ablative.

Apāpuraṇa, avāp—, *nt.* a key.

Apāpurati, Avā— (apa + ā + pur + a), to open.

Apāya, *m.* the hell ; state of loss and woe ; lapse ; loss.—**gāmī**, *a.* going or conveying to the state of misery.—**mukha**, *nt.* cause of ruin.—**sahāya**, *m.* a spendthrift companion.

Apāra, *a.* limitless ; without a further shore. *nt.* the near bank.—**neyya**, not leading to the other shore; unattainable.

Apāruta, *a.* open.

Apālamba, *m.* leaning board (of a carriage).

Api, *in.* and ; even ; and then.—**ca**, but ; further.—**ca kho**, and yet ; still.—**nu**, used in an interrogative sense.—**nāma**, if (we) may.—**ssu**, so much so.

Apidhāna, *nt.* a cover ; lid.

Apilāpana, *nt.* non-floating.

Apiha, Apihālu, *a.* not greedy.

Apekkha, — khaka, — khī, *a.* waiting for; looking for; a candidate; expectant.

Apekkhati (apa + ikkh + a), to long for; to expect. *aor.* **—khi.**

Apekkhana, *nt.* **Apekkhā,** *f.* hope; desire; expectance.

Apekkhita, *pp.* of **apekkhati.**

Apeta, (*pp.* of Apeti), gone away, rid of; without.—**tatta,** *nt.* absence.

Apeti (apa + i + a), to go away; to disappear. *aor.* **apesi.**

Apetteyyatā, *f.* irreverence against father.

Apeyya, *a.* not drinkable; that should not be drunk.

Appa, appaka, *a.* small; little; insignificant. *nt.* a little. —**kasirena,** *ad.* with little difficulty. — **kicca,** *a.* having few duties.

Appakiṇṇa, *a.* not crowded; quiet.

Appagabbha, *a.* not proud or impudent.

Appaggha, *a.* of a little value.

Appaccaya, *m.* sulkiness. *a.* without a cause.

Appaṭigha, *a.* unobstructive; without anger.

Appaṭipuggala, *m.* matchless person.

Appaṭibaddha, *a.* not connected with.

Appaṭibhāṇa, *a.* bewildered.

Appaṭima, *a.* incomparable.

Appaṭivattiya, *a.* not to be rolled back.

Appaṭivāna, *a.* not shrinking back.

Appaṭividdha, *a.* not attained or understood.

Appaṭisandhika, *a.* incapable of rebirth; unmendable.

Appaṇā, *f.* fixing of thought on an object; attainment of a trance.

Appatikuṭṭha, *a.* not despised.

Appatiṭṭha, *a.* without a footing or help.

Appatissa, — ssava, *a.* not docile; rebellious.

Appati (ṭi) hata, *a.* not smitten; unobstructed.

Appatīta, *a.* displeased.

Appaduṭṭha, *a.* not angry; not corrupt.

Appadhaṃsiya, *a.* not to be violated.

Appamaññā, *f.* infinitude; a technical term including four qualities of mind, *viz.* love, pity, sympathy, and disinterestedness.

Appamatta, *a.* (a + pamatta :) vigilant; careful; alert. (appa + matta :) slight; insignificant. – **ttaka,** *nt.* a trifle.

Appamāṇa. *a.* boundless; unlimited.

Appamāda, *m.* vigilance; earnestness.

Appameyya, *a.* immeasurable.

Appavatti, *f.* noncontinuance; nonexistence.

Appasāda, *m.* displeasure; dislike.

Appassaka, *a.* possessing little; poor.

Appassāda, *a.* having little enjoyment.

Appasattha, *a.* (appa + sattha = caravan :) having few companions. (a + pasattha :), not being praised.

Appasanna, *a* displeased; not believing.

Appasamārambha, *a.* of little trouble.

Appahīna, *a.* not removed or destroyed.

Appāṇaka, *a.* breathless; not containing insects.

Appātaṅka, *a.* free from illness.

Appiccha, *a.* easily satisfied; desiring little.—**tā,** *f.* contentment.

Appita, (*pp.* of **appeti**), applied.

Appiya, *a.* unpleasant; disagreeable.

Appekadā, *ad.* (api + ekadā), sometimes.

Appeti (ap + e), to apply; to fix on. *aor.* **appesi.**

Appeva, appeva nāma, *in.* it is well, if.

Appesakka, *a.* of little influence.

Appossukka, *a.* inactive.

Apphuṭa, *a.* unpervaded.

Apphoṭita, (*pp.* of the following), clapped. *nt.* clapping of hands.

Apphoṭeti (ā + phuṭ + e), to snap the fingers; to clap the hands.

Aphala, *a.* fruitless; vain; useless.

Aphassita, *a.* not touched.

Aphāsu, *a.* uneasy; difficult; troublesome.—**ka,** *ni.* illness.

Abaddha, abandhana, *a.* unfettered; free; not bound.

Ababa, *nt.* name of a purgatory; a numeral with 76 ciphers.

Abala, *a.* weak; feeble.

Abbaṇa, *a.* woundless.

Abbata, *a.* without moral obligations.

Abbuda, *nt.* a tumour; the foetus in the 2nd week after conception; cause of disunion; name of a purgatory.

Abbūhati (ā + vi + ūh + a), to draw off; to pull out. *aor.* **abbūhi.**

Abbūḷha, *pp.* of the above.

Abbokiṇṇa, *a.* uninterrupted; constant; not crowded.

Abbocchinna, *a.* uninterrupted.

Abbohārika, *a.* negligible.

Abbha, *nt.* sky; cloud.—**kūṭa,** *nt.* the summit of a storm-cloud. —**paṭala,** *nt.* a mass of clouds.

Abbhaka, *nt.* graphite; plumbago.

Abbhakkhāti (abhi + ā + khā + a), to slander; to speak against. *aor.* —**khāsi.**

Abbhakkhāna, *nt.* false accusation; slander.

Abbhañjati (abhi + añj + a), to anoint; to lubricate. *aor.*—**ñji.**

Abbhañjana, *nt.* anointing; oiling; unguent.

Abbhatīta, *a.* gone by; past.

Abbhanumodanā, *f.* great appreciation; rejoicing after merit.

Abbhantara, *nt.* the inside; interior. *a.* inner; internal.—**tarika,** *a.* intimate; confident.

Abbhāgata, 3. a guest; a stranger. *pp.* arrived.

Abbhāgamana, *nt.* arrival; coming forward.

Abbhācikkhati (abhi + ā + cikkh + a), to accuse; to culminate. *aor.* —**khi.**

Abbhācikkhana, *nt.* accusation; slander.

Abbhāhata (*pp.* of **abbhāhanati**), attacked; afflicted.

Abbhukkiraṇa, *nt.* drawing out; sprinkling.

Abbhukkirati (abhi + u + kir + a), to sprinkle over. *aor.* —**kiri.**

Abbhuggacchati (abhi + u + gam + a), to rise up; to be diffused. *aor.* —**gacchi.**

Abbhuggata, *pp.* of the above.

Abbhuggamana, *nt.* rising over.

Abbhuggirati (abhi + u + gir + a), to raise up or brandish something in a threatening manner. *aor.* —**giri.**

Abbhuggiraṇa, *nt.* brandishing.

Abbhuṭṭhāna, *nt.* rising ; getting up ; progress.

Abbhuta, *a.* wonderful ; marvellous. *nt.* a wonder ; a marvel; a bet.

Abbhudeti (abhi + udi + e), to rise ; to come into existence. *aor.* **—esi.**

Abbhunnata, *a.* risen high ; high.

Abbhumme, *intj.* alas !

Abbhuyyāti (abhi + u + yā + *a*), to march against. *pp.* **—yāta.**

Abbhokāsa, *m.* unsheltered place ; open air.—**kāsika**, *m.* one who lives in the open air.

Abbhokiṇṇa, *a.* crowded.

Abbhokiraṇa, *nt.* sprinkling ; movements of a dancer.

Abbhokirati (abhi + ava + kir + a), to sprinkle over. *aor.* **—kiri.**

Abhabba, *a.* unable ; not proficient.—**tā**, inability ; impossibility.

Abhaya, *a.* safe ; fearless. *nt.* safety.

Abhayā, *f.* yellow myrobalan.

Abhāva, *m.* disappearance ; absence ; non-becoming.

Abhāvita, *a.* not developed ; not practised.

Abhikaṅkhati (abhi + kakh + ŋ - a), to long or wish for. *aor.* **—khi.** *pp.* **—khita.**

Abhikaṅkhana, abhikaṅkhit , *nt.* hope ; longing ; wish.

Abhikaṅkhī, *a.* wishing for ; desirous.

Abhikiṇṇa, (*pp.* of the following), strewn over with.

Abhikirati (abhi + kir + a), to scatter over ; to sprinkle.

Abhikūjati (abhi + k j + a) to warble ; to sing (of birds). *aor.* **—kūji.**

Abhikūjana, *nt.* singing of birds.

Abhikūjita, *pp.* resounding with (the song of birds).

Abhikkanta, (*pp.* of **abhikkamati**), gone forward ; past ; most pleasant. *nt.* going forward.

Abhikkama, *m.* going forward.

Abhikkamati (abhi + kam + a), to proceed. *aor.* **—kami.**

Abhikkhaṇa, *a.* constant.—**ṇaŋ**, *ad.* constantly ; often.

Abhikkhaṇati (abhi + kha + a), to dig up. *aor.* **—khaṇi.**

Abhikkhaṇana, *nt.* digging.

Abhigajjati (abhi + gad + ya), to roar ; to thunder. *aor.* **—gajji.**

Abhigijjhati (abhi + gidh + ya), to crave for. *aor.* **—jhi.**

Abhigijjhana, *nt.* craving ; greed.

Abhigīta, (*pp.* of **abhigāyati**), sung for.

Abhighāta, *m.* impact ; contact ; killing.

Abhighātana, *nt.* slaying ; destroying.

Abhighātī, *m.* enemy ; destroyer.

Abhijappati (abhi + jap + a), to pray for ; to mumble. *aor.* **—jappi.**

Abhijappana,—jappita, *nt.* mumbling ; wish ; talk.

Abhijāta, *a.* well-born ; of noble birth.

Abhijāti, *f.* rebirth ; descent ; species.

Abhijānana, *nt.* recognition ; recollection.

Abhijānāti (abhi + ñā + nā), to know fully or by experience ; to be aware. *aor.* **—jāni.**

Abhijigiŋsati (abhi + har + sa)*, to wish to overcome. *aor.* —**giŋsi.**

Abhijjanaka, abhijjamāna, *a.* not breaking or separating.

Abhijjhā, *f.* covetousness.—**lu,** *a.* covetous.

Abhijjhāyati (abhi + jhe + a), to wish for; to covet. *aor.* —**jhāyi.**

Abhijjhita, *pp.* of the above.

Abhiñña, *a.* knowing; possessed of knowledge.

Abhiññā, *f.* special knowledge; supernomal power.

Abhiññā,—ñāya, *abs.* having understood well.

Abhiññāta, (*pp.* of abhijānāti), well-known; recognised.

Abhiññeyya, *a.* that which should be well understood.

Abhiṇha, *a.* continuous; habitual.—**haŋ,** *ad.* often; repeatedly.

Abhiṇhaso, *ad.* always: repeatedly.

Abhitatta, (*pp.* of **abhitapati**), scorched by heat; heated.

Abhitapati (abhi + tap + a), to shine. *aor.* —**tapi.**

Abhitāpa, *m.* extreme heat.

Abhitāḷita, *pp.* of the following.

Abhitāḷeti (abhi + tāḷ + e), to beat; to hammer; to hit a drum, etc. *aor.* —**esi.**

Abhituṇṇa, (*pp.* of the following), overwhelmed.

Abhitudati (abhi + tud + a), to pierce; to prick; to incite. *aor.* —**tudi.**

Abhito, *in.* round about.

Abhitoseti (abhi + tus + e), to please thoroughly. *aor.* —**esi.**

Abhittharati (abhi + thar + a), to make haste. *aor.* —**thari.**

Abhitthavati (abhi + thu + a), to praise. *aor.* —**thavi.**

Abhitthavana, *nt.* praise.

Abhitthuta, *pp.* of **abhitthavati.**

Abhittunāti (abhi + thu + nā), to praise. —*aor.* —**thuni.**

Abhidosa, *m.* last evening.—**dosika,** *a.* belonging to the last evening. (See also **Ābhi—**)

Abhidhamati (abhi + dham + a), to blow on. *aor.* —**dhami.**

Abhidhamma, *m.* the analytic doctrine of the Buddhist Canon. —**mika,** *a.* one who teaches Abhidhamma.

Abhidhā, *f.* **Abhidhāna,** *nt.* name; appellation.

Abhidhāvati (abhi + dhāv + a), to run towards; to hasten. *aor.* —**dhāvi.**

Abhinata (*pp.* of **abhinamati**), bent; bowed down to.

Abhinadati (abhi + nad + a), to resound. *aor.* —**nadi.**

Abhinadita, *pp.* of the above. *nt.* the noise.

Abhinandati (abhi + nand + a) to rejoice at. *aor.* —**nandi.**

Abhinandana, *nt.* rejoicing; delight.

Abhinandita, (*pp.* of **abhinandati**), *nt.* an object of pleasure.

Abhinandī, *a.* one who rejoices; enjoying.

Abhinamati (abhi + nam + a), to bend; to bow down. *aor.* —**nami.**

Abhinava, *a.* new; fresh.

Abhinādita, *pp.* resounded with.

Abhinikūjita, a resounded with (the song of birds).

---

* *Har* is changed to *giŋ; gi* is doubled and the former *gi* is changed to *ji.*

Abhinikkhamati (abhi + ni + kam + a), to go forth from : to retire from the world. *aor.* —**khami**. *pp.* —**khanta**. *abs.* —**khamma**.

Abhinikkhamana, *nt.* renunciation ; retirement from the household life.

Abhinikkhipati (abhi + ni + khip + a), to lay down. *aor.* —**khipi**. *pp.* —**khitta**.

Abhinikkhipana, *nt.* putting down.

Abhinipajjati, (abhi + ni + pad + ya), to lie down on. *aor.* —**pajji**. *pp.* —**panna**.

Abhinipatati (abhi + ni + pat + a), to fall down ; to rush on. *aor.* —**pati**.

Abhinipāta, *m.*—**pātana**, *nt.* falling against ; rushing on ; attacking.—**pātī**, *a.* falling on.

Abhinipphajjati (abhi + ni + pad + ya), to become accomplished. *aor.*—**jji**. *pp.* —**nipphanna**.

Abhinipphatti, *f.* production ; accomplishment.

Abhinipphādita, (*pp.* of the following), produced ; accomplished.

Abhinipphādeti (abhi + ni + pad + e), to produce ; to bring into existence. *aor.* —**esi**.

Abhinibbatta (*pp.* of —**nibbattati**), reproduced ; reborn.

Abhinibbatti, *f.* birth ; becoming.

Abhinibbatteti (abhi + ni + vat + e), to reproduce ; to bring into existence. *aor.* —**esi**.

Abhinimmita, *pp.* of the following.

Abhinimmiṇāti (abhi + ni + mā + ṇā), to create, to produce ; to make. *aor.* —**miṇi**.

Abhiniropana, *nt.* fixing upon ; application.

Abhiniropeti (abhi + ni + rup + e), to implant. *aor.* —**esi**. *pp.* —**pita**.

Abhiniviṭṭha, (*pp.* of the following), attached to ; clinging on.

Abhinivisati (abhi + ni + vis + a), to cling to ; to adhere. *aor.* —**nivisi**.

Abhinivesa, *m.* inclination ; tendency.

Abhinisīdati (abhi + ni + sad + a), to sit near. *aor.* —**nisīdi**. *pp.* —**nisinna**.

Abhinissaṭa (*pp.* of **abhinissarati**), escaped or removed from.

Abhinīta (*pp.* of **abhineti**), brought to.

Abhinīhaṭa (*pp.* of the following), taken out.

Abhinīharati (abhi + ni + har + a), to take out ; to direct to ; to aspire. *aor.* —**hari**.

Abhinīhāra, *m.* taking out ; aspiration ; resolution.

Abhipatthita, *pp.* of the following.

Abhipattheti (abhi + path + e), to long or hope for. *aor.* —**esi**.

Abhipāleti (abhi + pāl + e), to protect ; to preserve. *aor.* —**esi**. *pp.* —**pālita**.

Abhipīḷeti (abhi + pīḷ + e), to oppress ; to squeeze. *aor* —**esi**. *pp.* —**pīḷita**.

Abhippakiṇṇa (*pp.* of **abhippakirati**), completely strewn with.

Abhippamodati (abhi + pa + mud + a), to rejoice ; to satisfy. *aor.* —**modi**. *pp.* —**dita**.

Abhippasanna (*pp.* of —**pasīdati**), having faith in ; devoted to.

Abhippasāda, *m.* faith ; devotion.

Abhippasāreti (abhi + pa + sar + e), to stretch out. *aor.*—**esi.**

Abhippasīdati (abhi + pa + sad + a), to have faith in ; to devote. *aor.* —**sīdi.**

Abhibhavati (abhi + bhū + a), to overcome ; to conquer. *aor.* —**bhavi.**

Abhibhavana, *nt.* overcoming ; vanquishing.

Abhibhavanīya, *a.* what should be overcome.

Abhibū, *m.* conqueror ; overlord.

Abhibhūta (*pp.* of **abhibhavati**), overpowered ; vanquished.

Abhimaṅgala, *a.* lucky ; auspicious.

Abhimata (*pp.* of **abhimaññati**), intended ; wished for.

Abhimaddati (abhi + madd + a), to crush ; to subdue. *aor.* —**maddi.** *pp.* —**maddita.**

Abhimaddana, *nt.* crushing ; subjugation.

Abhimanthati (abhi + manth + a), —**mantheti** (abhi + manth + e), to crush ; to churn ; to agitate. *aor.* —**manthi,** —**esi.** *pp.* —**manthita,** —**mathita.**

Abhimāna, *m.* self-respect.

Abhimukha, *a.* facing ; present ; face to face with. *m.* the front. —**khaŋ,** *ad.* towards.

Abhiyācati (abhi + yāc + a), to beg ; to entreat. *aor.* —**yāci.**

Abhiyācana, *nt.* —**nā,** *f.* request ; entreaty.

Abhiyācita (*pp.* of **abhiyācati**), being requested.

Abhiyāti (abhi + yā + a), to go against. *aor.* —**yāyi,** *pp.* —**yāta.**

Abhiyuñjati (abhi + yuj + ŋ – a), to practise ; to charge (in a law-suit) ; to question. *aor.* —**yuñji.** *pp.* —**yutta.**

Abhiyuñjana, *nt.* trial ; practice ; observance.

Abhiyoga, *m.* observance.

Abhirakkhati (abhi + rakkh + a), to protect. *aor.* —**rakkhi.**

Abhirakkhana, *nt.* —**rakkhā,** *f.* protection.

Abhirata (*pp.* of **abhiramati**) fond of ; indulging in.

Abhirati, *f.* delight ; contentment.

Abhiraddha, *pp.* satisfied ; propitiated.

Abhiraddhi, *f.* satisfaction.

Abhiramati (abhi + ram + a), to enjoy ; to find pleasure in. *aor.* —**rami.**

Abhiramana, *nt.* enjoyment; sport.

Abhiramāpeti (abhi + ram + āpe), to cause one to take pleasure. *aor.* —**esi.**

Abhirāma, *a.* pleasant ; agreeable.

Abhiruci, *f.* wish ; longing.

Abhirucita, *pp.* wished for ; liked ; agreeable.

Abhirucira, *a.* much pleasing ; very beautiful.

Abhiruyha, abs. (of **abhiruhati**), having ascended.

Abhirūpa, *a.* lovely ; handsome.

Abhiruhati, —**rūhati,** (abhi + ruh + a), to ascend ; to go up. *aor.* —**ruhi.**

Abhirūhana, *nt.* ascension ; climbing.

Abhirūḷha (*pp.* of **abhiruhati**), ascended ; risen up.

Abhiroceti (abhi + ruc + e), to like ; to find delight in.

Abhilakkhita, (*pp.* of the following), marked by.

Abhilakkheti (abhi + lakkh + e), to mark ; to design. *aor.* —**esi.**

Abhilāpa, *m.* talk ; speech.

Abhivaṭṭa, —vaṭṭha, (*pp.* of **abhivassati**) rained upon.

Abhivaḍḍhati (abhi + vaḍḍh + a), to grow ; to increase ; to outgrow. *aor.* **—vaḍḍhi.**

Abhivaḍḍhana, *nt.*— **vaḍḍhi,** *f.* growth ; increase.

Abhivaṇṇita, *pp.* of the following.

Abhivaṇṇeti (abhi + vaṇṇ + e), to praise; to expound or explain. *aor.* **—esi.**

Abhivandati (abhi + vand + a), to bow down ; to honour. *aor.* **—vandi.** *pp.* **—vandita.**

Abhivandiya, *abs.* (of the above), having bowed down to.

Abhivassati (abhi + vass + a), to rain over. *aor.* **—vassi.**

Abhivādana, *nt.* **—nā,** *f.* salutation ; bowing down.

Abhivādeti (abhi + vad + e), to bow down ; to salute. *aor.* **—esi.** *pp.* **—vādita.**

Abhivādetabba, *pt. p.* fit to be worshipped or honoured.

Abhivijināti (abhi + vi + ji + nā), to conquer. *aor.* **—jini.** *pp.* **—vijita.**

Abhivisiṭṭha, *a.* most excellent.

Abhivuṭṭha, see **abhivaṭṭha.**

Abhivuddhi, see **abhivaḍḍhi.**

Abhisaṅkhata, (*pp.* of **—saṅkharoti**), prepared ; arranged ; restored.

Abhisaṅkharaṇa, *nt.* restoration ; arrangement.

Abhisaṅkharoti (abhi + saŋ + kar + o), to restore ; to arrange ; to prepare. *aor.* **—khari.**

Abhisaṅkhāra, *m.* accumulation ; preparation.

Abhisaṅga, *m.* sticking ; cleaving.

Abhisajjati (abhi + sad + ya), to be angry ; to be attached. *aor.* **—sajji.**

Abhisajjana, *nt.* cleaving ; anger.

Abhisañcetayita, *nt.* thought out ; intended.

Abhisañceteti (abhi + saŋ + cit + e), to think out. *aor.* **—esi.**

Abhisaṭa (*pp.* of **abhisarati**), visited ; approached by.

Abhisatta (*pp.* of **abhisapati**), accursed.

Abhisaddahati (abhi + saŋ + dah + a), to believe in. *aor.* **—dahi.**

Abhisanda, *m.* outflow ; result.

Abhisandana, *nt.* flowing ; outcome ; result.

Abhisandati (abhi + sand + a), to flow out ; to ooze. *aor.* **—sandi.**

Abhisandahati (abhi + saŋ + dah + a), to joint ; to put together. *aor.* **—sandahi.**

Abhisapati (abhi + sap + a), to curse ; to accurse ; to take an oath.

Abhisapana, *nt.* an oath ; cursing.

Abhisamaya, *m.* realization ; penetration.

Abhisamecca, *abs.* (of **abhisameti**), having understood thoroughly.

Abhisameta, —samita, (*pp.* of **abhisameti**), completely realized.

Abhisametāvī, *a.* one who possesses complete insight.

Abhisameti (abhi + saŋ + i + a), to attain ; to realize. *aor.* **—esi.**

Abhisamparāya, *m.* future rebirth ; next world.

Abhisambujjhati (abhi + saŋ + budh + ya), to gain the highest wisdom. *aor.* **—jjhi.**

Abbhisambuddha, *pp.* of the above.

Abhisambodhi, *f.* the highest enlightenment.

Abhisambhunāti (abhi + sambh + uṇā), to be able; to attain. *aor.* —**bhuni.**

Abhisammati (abhi + sam + a), to cease; to pacify. *aor.* —**sammi.**

Abhisāpa, *m.* a curse.

Abhisārikā, *f.* a courtesan.

Abhisiñcati (abhi + sic + ŋ – a), to sprinkle over; to consecrate. *aor.* —**siñci.**

Abhisitta, *pp.* of the above.

Abhiseka, *m.* —**secana,** *nt.* consecration, ablution; sprinkling.

Abhiseceti, *caus.* of **abhisiñcati.**

Abhihaṭa, *pp.* of **abhiharati.**

Abhihaṭṭhuŋ (= abhiharituŋ) *inf.* to bring near.

Abhihata, *pp.* of the following.

Abhihanati (abhi + han + a), to strike; to hit. *aor.* —**hani.**

Abhiharati (abhi + har + a), to bring to; to offer. *aor.* —**hari.**

Abhihāra, *m.* bringing near; offering.

Abhihita (*pp.* of **abhidhāti**), spoken; *nt.* a word; saying.

Abhīta, Abhīru, Abhīruka, *a.* fearless; brave.

Abhūta, *a.* not real; false. *nt.* falsehood.—**akkhāna,** *nt.* a lie. —**vādī,** *m.* a liar.

Abhejja, *a.* not to be split or divided.

Abhojja, *a.* unfit to be eaten.

Amacca, *m.* a privy councillor; a fellow-worker.

Amajja, *nt.* that which is not intoxicating.—**jjapa,** *a.* one who does not take strong drinks; abstaining from intoxicants.

Amata, *nt.* ambrosia; the deathless state.—**tandada,** *a.* bringing the deathless state.—**pada,** *nt.* conveying to deathlessness. —**magga,** *m.* path to deathlessness.

Amattaññū, *a.* immoderate.—**ñutā,** *f.* immoderation.

Amatteyya, *a.* not respecting one's mother.—**yatā,** *f.* disrespect towards one's mother.

Amanussa, *m.* a demon; a ghost; a deity.

Amama, *a.* unselfish; free from longing.

Amara, *a.* immortal; deathless.

Amarā, *f.* an eel.

Amala, *a.* pure; stainless; faultless.

Amātāpitika, *a* parentless; an orphan.

Amānusa, *a.* non-human.

Amāmaka, see **Amama.**

Amāvasī, *f.* new-moon day.

Amita, *a.* boundless; immeasurable.

Amitta, *m.* enemy.

Amilāta, *a.* not withered.

Amilātā, *f.* a medicinal plant, *aloe vulgaris.*

Amissa, *a.* unmixed.

Amu, *pron.* such and such.

Amucchita, *a.* not infatuated; not greedy.

Amutta, *a.* not released or free from.

Amutra, *ad.* in such and such a place.

Amogha, *a.* not empty; not futile.

Amoha, *m.* wisdom.

Amba, *m.* mango tree. *nt.* mango fruit.—**pakka,** *nt.* ripe mango.—**pāna,** a syrup made from mangoes.—**piṇḍī,** *f.* a bunch of mangoes.—**vana,** *nt.* —**saṇḍa,** *m.* a mango grove. —**laṭṭhikā,** *f.* a mango plant.

Ambara, *nt.* a cloth ; the sky.

Ambā, *f.* mother.

Ambila, *a.* sour. *m.* sour taste ; acid.

Ambu, *nt.* water.—**cārī,** *m.* a fish.—**ja,** *a.* aquatic ; *nt.* a lotus. *m.* a fish.—**da,**—**dhara,** *m.* a cloud.

Ambujinī, *f.* lotus pond.

Ambho, *in.* hollo ! hey! (a particle employed to draw attention).

Ammaṇa, *nt.* a standard measure of grain, which is about five bushels.

Ammā, *f.* mother. (Vocative **amma** is often used to address a girl or a daughter).

Amha, (personal pron). I, we.

Amhi (1st. sing. of *as,* to be) I am.

Amha, amhā, (*pl.* of the above), we are.

Aya, *m.* income ; *m. nt.* iron.

Ayaŋ, (Nom. sing. of **ima**) *m. f.* this person.

Ayana, *nt.* path.

Ayasa, *m. nt.* ill repute ; disgrace.

Ayathā, *in.* false. (Found in cpds. such as **ayathābhāva** = unreality).

Ayira, ayiraka, see **ayya, ayyaka.**

Ayo (*aya* becomes ayo in cpds :) —**kūṭa,** *m.* iron hammer.—**khīla,** *nt.* iron stake.—**guḷa,** *m.* iron ball.—**ghana,** *nt.* iron club.—**maya,** *a.* made of iron. —**saṅku,** *m.* iron spike.

Ayogga, *a.* unfit ; not suitable.

Ayojjha, *a.* unconquerable.

Ayoniso, *ad.* improperly ; unjudiciously.

Ayya, *m.* gentleman; lord; master. *a.* noble.

Ayyaka, *m.* grandfather.

Ayyakā, ayyikā, *f.* grandmother.

Ayyā, *f.* mistress ; lady.

Ara, *nt.* spoke of a wheel.

Arakkhiya, *a.* not to be guarded.

Araja, *a.* free from dust or impurity.

Arañjara, *m.* a big jar ; gallipot.

Arañña, *nt.* forest.—**ka,** *a.* belonging to or living in a forest. —**vāsa,** *m.* dwelling in a forest. —**vihāra,** *m.* forest hermitage. —**āyatana,** *nt.* forest haunt.

Araññānī, *f.* a big forest.

Araṇa, *a.* peaceful ; passionless.

Araṇi, *f.* a piece of wood for kindling fire by friction.—**mathana,** *nt.* rubbing of two sticks in order to kindle fire.

Arati, *f.* nonattachment ; aversion.

Aravinda, *nt.* a lotus.

Araha, *a.* worthy of ; deserving. —**ddhaja,** *m.* monks' yellow robe.

Arahati (arah + a), to be worthy of ; to deserve.

Arahatta, *nt.* state of an arahant ; final emancipation.—**phala,** *nt.* final emancipation. —**magga,** *m.* the path to emancipation.

Arahanta, *m.* one who has attained the Summum Bonum.

Ari, *m.* enemy.—**ndama,** 3. tamer of enemies ; a conqueror.

Ariñcamāna, *a.* not giving up ; pursuing earnestly.

Ariṭṭha, *a.* cruel ; unlucky. *m.* a crow ; nimb tree ; soapberry tree. *nt.* medicinal spirit.

Aritta, *nt.* a rudder. *adj.* not empty or futile.

Ariya, *a.* noble, distinguished. *m.* a noble man; one who has attained higher knowledge.—**kanta,** *a.* agreeable to the Ariyas.—**dhana,** *nt.* sublime treasure of the Ariyas.—**dhamma,** *m.* noble practice.—**puggala,** *m.* one who has attained higher wisdom.—**magga,** *m.* the path to attain higher wisdom.—**sacca,** *nt.* an established fact; noble truth.—**sāvaka,** *m.* disciple of the noble ones.—**yūpavāda,** *m.* insulting a saint.

Arisa, *nt.* hemorrhoids; piles.

Aru, *nt.* **Arukā,** *f.* an old wound; a sore.—**kāya,** *m.* heap of sores.—**pakka,** *a.* decaying with sores.

Aruṇa, *m.* the dawn; ruddy colour; *a.* reddish.—**vaṇṇa,** *a.* of the reddish colour.—**ṇuggamana,** *nt.* appearance of the reddish colour before sunrise.

Arūpa, *a.* formless; incorporial; nonsubstantial.—**kāyika,** *a.* belonging to the formless beings.—**bhava,** *m.* formless existence.—**loka,** *m.* the world of the formless.—**pāvacara,** *a.* belonging to the realm of arūpins.

Arūpī, *m.* the formless being.

Are, *in.* he! hollo! I say!

Ala, *m.* *nt.* claw of a crab, etc.

Alakka, *m.* a rabid dog.

Alakkhika, *a.* unlucky; unfortunate.

Alakkhī, *f.* misfortune; bad luck.

Alagadda, *m.* snake.

Alagga, *a.* not stuck or attached.

Alaggana, *nt.* non-attachment.

Alaṅkata (*pp.* of **alaṅkaroti**:) decorated. *adj.* done up.

Alaṅkaraṇa, *nt.* decoration; doing up.

Alaṅkaroti (alaŋ + kar + o), to adorn; to decorate.

Alaṅkāra, *m.* decoration; an ornament.

Alajjī, *a.* shameless; not afraid of sin.

Alattaka, *nt.* lac.—**kata,** *a.* lacquered; varnished with lac.

Alasa, *a.* idle; lazy.—**tā,** *f.* sloth; laziness.

Alasaka, *nt.* indigestion.

Alaŋ, *in.* enough! have done with! stop! *adj.* able; suitable.—**kammaniya,** *a.* fit for the purpose.—**pateyyā,** *f.* a woman of marriageable age.

Alāta, *nt.* firebrand.

Alāpu, Alābu, *nt.* long white gourd.

Alābha, *m.* loss; missing of gain.

Ali, *m.* a bee; a scorpion.

Alika, *nt.* lie; falsehood.

Alīna, *a.* not sluggish; active.

Alobha, *m.* disinterestedness.

Alola, Alolupa, *a.* not covetous or distracted by desires.

Alla, *a.* moist; wet; green; fresh.—**dāru,** *nt.* green wood.

Allāpa, *m.* conversation.

Allīna (*pp.* of the following), stuck; clung.

Allīyati (ā + li + ya), to cling to; to stick to.

Allīyana, *nt.* sticking; clinging.

Avakaḍḍhati (ava + kaḍḍh + a), to draw back. *aor.* —**kaḍḍhi.**

Avakaḍḍhana, *nt.* drawing away or back.

Avakaḍḍhita, *pp.* pulled down; dragged away.

Avakassati (ava + kass + a), see **Avakaḍḍhati.**

Avakārakaŋ, *ad.* scattering about.

Avakāsa, *m.* chance ; room ; opportunity.

Avakirati (ava + kir + a), to pour down ; to throw out ; to scatter. *aor.*—**kiri.**

Avakiriya, *abs.* (of the above), having scattered or thrown away.

Avakujja, *a.* face downward ; bent over.

Avakkanta, (*pp.* of **avakkamati**), beset with; overwhelmed by.

Avakkanti, *f.* entry.

Avakkamati (ava + kam + a), to enter ; to overwhelm. *aor.* —**kami.**

Avakkamma, *abs.* (of the above), having entered or moved aside.

Avakkāra, *m.* throwing away ; refuse.—**pāti,** *f.* a slop basin.

Avakkhitta, *pp.* of the following.

Avakkhipati (ava + khip + a), to throw down ; to drop ; to cast down. *aor.* —**khipi.**

Avakkhipana, *nt.* putting or throwing down.

Avagacchati (ava + gam + a), to attain ; to obtain ; to understand. *aor.* —**cchi.**

Avagata, *pp.* of the above.

Avagāhati (ava + gāh + a), to plunge into ; to enter. *aor.* —**gāhi.** *pp.* —**gāḷha.**

Avagāha, *m.* —**hana,** *nt.* plunging into ; entering.

Avaca, *a.* low. (Only in the combination **uccāvaca**).

Avacanīya, *a.* not to be admonished.

Avacara, *a.* moving in ; frequenting.

Avacaraka, 3. a spy ; of bad character.

Avacaraṇa, *nt.* behaviour ; occupation ; dealing.

Avajāta, *a.* illegitimate ; low-born.

Avajānana, *nt.* contempt ; despising.

Avajānāti (ava + ñā + nā), to despise. *aor.* —**jāni.**

Avajita, *pp.* of the following.

Avajināti (ava + ji + nā), to defeat ; to reconquer. *aor.* —**jini.**

Avajīyati (ava + ji + ya), to be diminished or undone.

Avajja, *a.* unblamable ; faultless.

Avajjha, *a.* not to be killed or punished.

Avaññā, *f.* contempt ; disrespect.

Avaññāta, *pp.* of **avajānāti.**

Avaṭṭhāna, *nt.* **Avaṭṭhiti,** *f.* position ; posture.

Avaḍḍhi, *f.* decay ; loss.

Avaṇṇa, blame ; disrepute.

Avataraṇa, *nt.* **Avatāra,** *m.* descending ; entering ; plunging into.

Avatarati (ava + tar + a), to descend ; to enter ; to plunge into. *aor.* —**tari.**

Avatiṇṇa, (*pp.* of the above), fallen into ; affected with.

Avatthaṭa, *pp.* of **avattharati.**

Avattharaṇa, *nt.* an array ; covering over ; overpowering.

Avattharati (ava + thar + a), to cover over ; to overpower. *aor.* —**thari.**

Avadāta, *a.* white ; clean.

Avadhāraṇa, *nt.* emphasis; selection.

Avadhārita, *pp.* of the following.

Avadhāreti (ava + dhar + e), to select ; to affirm. *aor.* —**esi**

Avadhi, *m.* boundary ; limit.

Avanati, *f.* stooping ; bending.

Avani, *f.* the earth.

Avabujjhati (ava + budh + ya), to understand. *aor.* **—bujjhi.**

Avabodha, *m.* knowledge; understanding.

Avabhāsa, *m.* light; appearance.

Avabhāsati (ava + bhās + a), to shine. *aor.* **—bhāsi.** *pp.* **—sita,** resplendent; lit with.

Avamaṅgala, *nt.* bad luck; ill omen. *adj.* unlucky.

Avamaññati (ava + man + ya), to slight; to despise. *aor.* **—maññi.**

Avamaññanā, *f.* **Avamāna,** *m.* **Avamānana,** *nt.* contempt; disregard; disrespect.

Avamāneti (ava + man + e), to despise; to disrespect. *aor.* **—esi.**

Avayava, *m.* limb; a part; a constituent.

Avaruddha, *pp.* of the following.

Avarundhati (ava + rudh + ŋ – a), to put under restraint; to besiege; to imprison. *aor.* **—rundhi.**

Avalambati (ava + lab + ŋ –a), to hang down. *aor.* **—lambi.** *pp.* **—lambita.**

Avalambana, *nt.* hanging down; help.

Avalikhati (ava + likh + a), to scrape off; to cut into slices. *aor.* **—likhi.**

Avalitta, *pp.* of the following.

Avalimpati (ava + lip + ŋ — a), to smear; to plaster. *aor.* **—limpi.**

Avalekhana, *nt.* scraping off.— **kaṭṭha,** *nt.* bamboo stripes used for scraping.

Avalepana, *nt.* smearing; plastering.

Avalehana, *nt.* licking.

Avasara, *m.* chance.

Avasaṭa, *pp.* of the following.

Avasarati (ava + sar + a), to go down; to arrive. *aor.* **avasari.**

Avasāna, *nt.* the end; conclusion; cessation.

Avasiñcati (ava + sic + ŋ — a), to pour over; to sprinkle. *aor.* **—ñci.**

Avasiṭṭha, (*pp.* of **avasissati**), remaining; left over.

Avasitta, *pp.* of **avasiñcati.**

Avasissati (ava + sis + ya), to be left over; to remain over. *aor.* **—sissi.**

Avasussati (ava + sus + ya), to dry up; to wither. *aor.* **—sussi.**

Avasussana, *nt.* drying up; withering.

Avasesa, *nt.* remainder; *adj.* remaining.

Avasesaka, *nt.* what is left over

Avassaŋ, *ad.* inevitably.

Avassaya, *m.* support; help.

Avassika, *a.* newly ordained; having no years to count after one's ordination.

Avassita, *pp.* of **avasseti.**

Avassuta, *a.* filled with desire; lustful.

Avasseti (ava + si + e), to lean against; to depend on. *aor.* **avassayi.**

Avahaṭa, *pp.* of **avaharati.**

Avaharaṇa, *nt.* **avahāra,** *m.* theft; removal.

Avaharati (ava + har + a), to steal; to take away. *aor.* **—hari.**

Avahasati (ava + has + a), to deride; to laugh at. *aor.* **—hasi.**

Avāpuraṇa, *nt.* a key.

Avāpurati (ava + ā + pur + a), to open. *aor.* **—puri.**

Avikkhepa, *m.* calmness; balance of the mind.

Aviggaha, *m.* the body-less, i.e. the god of love.

Avijjamāna, *a.* not existing.

Avijjā, *f.* ignorance.—**jogha,** *m.* the stream of ignorance.

Aviññāṇaka, *a.* senseless.

Avidita, *a.* unknown.

Avidūra, *a.* near; not far. *nt.* neighbourhood.

Aviddasu, *m.* a fool.

Avinibbhoga, *a.* indistinct; that cannot be separated.

Avinīta, *a.* untrained; uneducated.

Avippavāsa, *m.* presence; attention.

Avibhūta, *a.* not clear or distinct.

Aviruddha, *a.* not contrary; friendly.

Avirūḷha, *a.* not grown or spread. —**rūḷhi,** *f.* nongrowth; cessation of rebirth.

Avirodha, *m.* absence of opposition.

Avivayha, *a.* difficult to bear; unfit to be married.

Avisaŋvāda, *m.* truth.—**vādaka,** —**vādī,** *a.* one who speaks truth.

Avihiŋsā, *f.* humanity; absence of cruelty.

Aviheṭhaka, *a.* not hurting or harassing.

Aviheṭhana, *nt.* non-hurting.

Avīci, *a.* waveless. *f.* one of the great hells.

Avīta, *a.* not free from.

Avītikkama, *m.* non-transgression.

Avuṭṭhika, *a.* rainless.

Avekkhati (ava + ikkh + a), to look at; to consider. *aor.* **avekkhi.** *pp.* **avekkhita.**

Avekkhana, *nt.* looking at; consideration.

Avecca, *abs.* having known.—**ppasāda,** *m.* perfect faith.

Avebhaṅgiya, *a.* not to be distributed.

Avera, *a.* friendly. *nt.* kindness.

Averī, *a.* free from enmity.

Avelā, *f.* improper time.

Avyatta, *a.* not manifest; not learned.

Avyaya, *nt.* indeclinable particle; absence of loss.—**yena,** *ad.* without any expenditure.—**yībhāva,** *m.* the compound which has an indeclinable as its member.

Avyākata, *a.* not designated.

Avyāpajjha, *a.* free from oppression or suffering.

Avyāpāda, *m.* freedom from malice.

Avyāvaṭa, *a.* not occupied; not worrying.

Avhaya, *m.* name; calling. *adj.* (in cpds.) having the name of.

Avhayati (ā + vhe + a).

Avhāti (ā + vhā + a), to call; to address; to summon. *aor.* **avhayi.**

Avhāta (*pp.* of **avhāti**), called; named.

Avhāna, *nt.* name; calling.

Avheti, see **avhāti.**

Asakiŋ, *ad.* more than once.

Asakka, Asakkuṇeyya, Asakkonta, *a.* unable; impossible.

Asaṅkiṇṇa, *a.* unmixed; not crowded.

Asaṅkhata, *a.* unconditioned; unprepared.—**dhātu,** *f.* the unconditioned state.

Asaṅkheyya, *a.* incalculable; *nt.* the highest numerical written with 141 ciphers.

Asaṅga, *m.* non-attachment.

Asacca, *nt.* falsehood. *adj.* false; not true.

Asajjamāna, *pr. p.* not touching with; not clinging.

Asañña, Asaññī, *a.* unconscious. —**bhava,** unconscious sphere.

Asaññata (= na + saŋyata), unrestrained; intemperate.

Asaṭha, *a.* honest; not fraudulent.

Asati (as + a), to eat. *aor.* **esi.** *pp.* **asita.**

Asatiyā, *ad.* unintentionally.

Asatta, *a.* non-attached.

Asadisa, *a.* incomparable; matchless.

Asaddhamma, *m.* misconduct; sin; sexual intercourse.

Asana, *nt.* eating; food; an arrow. *m.* the tree *Pentaptera Tomentosa.*

Asani, *f.* thunderbolt.—**pāta,** *m.* falling of a thunderbolt.

Asanta, *a.* non-existing; the wicked.

Asantasanta, Asantāsī, *a.* not trembling; fearless.

Asantuṭṭha, *a.* unhappy; not pleased with.

Asantuṭṭhi, *f.* displeasure; dissatisfaction.

Asapatta, without enmity; peaceful.

Asappāya, *a.* not beneficial or agreeable.

Asappurisa, *m.* a wicked person.

Asabbha, *a.* impolite; vile. *nt.* vulgar language.

Asabbhī, *m.* the wicked; the vulgar.

Asama, *a.* unequal; matchless.—**sama,** *a.* equal to the matchless.

Asamāna, *a.* unequal.

Asamāhita, *a.* not composed.

Asampakampiya, *a.* not to be shaken.

Asampatta, *a.* not arrived or approached.

Asammūḷha, *a.* not confused (in mind).

Asammosa,—moha, *m.* absence of confusion.

Asayaŋvasī, *a.* not under one's own control.

Asayha, *a.* unbearable.

Asaraṇa, *a.* helpless.

Asahana, *nt.* non-endurance.

Asahamāna, *pr. p.* not enduring.

Asahāya, *a.* lonely; friendless.

Asāta, *a.* disagreeable. *nt.* pain; suffering.

Asādisa, see **Asadisa.**

Asādu, *a.* of bad taste; disagreeable. *nt.* wrong action.

Asādhāraṇa, *a.* uncommon.

Asāra, *a.* worthless; sapless; vain.

Asāraddha, *a.* not excited; cool.

Asāhasa, *a.* not violent; meek.

Asi, *m.* sword.—**ggāhaka,** *m.* sword-bearer (of a king).—**camma,** *nt.* sword and shield. —**patta,** *nt.* blade of a sword.

Asita, *nt.* food; a sickle. (*pp.* of **asati** or **asnāti** :) eaten.

Asita, (na + sita), *a.* black.

Asithila, *a.* stiff; not loose.

Asīti, *f.* eighty.—**ma.** *a.* eightieth.

Asu, Asuka, *a.* such and such.

Asuci, *m.* dirt; excrement; dung; semen. *adj.* impure; unclean.

Asuddha, *a.* unclean.

Asubha, *a.* unpleasant; ugly. *nt.* a corpse.

Asura, *m.* a Titan; an Assirian. —**kāya,** *m.* the nation or an assembly of Asuras.—**rinda,** *m.* the king of Asuras.

Asūra, *a.* cowardly or sluggish person.

Asekha, Asekkha, *a.* one who does not require any further training. *m.* an Arahant.

Asecanaka, *a.* full and delicious in itself.

Asesa, *a.* entire; all.—**saŋ**, *ad.* fully; entirely.

Asoka, *a.* free from sorrow. *m.* the tree *Jonesia Asoka.*

Asobhana, *a.* ugly; improper.

Asnāti (as + nā), to eat.

Asmā, *m.* a stone.

Asmi (1st sing. of **as**), I am.—**māna**, *m.* the pride of self; egotism.

Assa, *m.* a horse; a corner.—**khaluṅka**, *m.* an inferior horse. —**gopaka**, *m.* a groom.—**tara**, *m.* a mule.—**tthara**, *m.* covering for a horse.—**damma**, *m.* a horse to be trained.—**damaka**, *m.* horse-trainer.—**potaka**, *m.* a colt or foal.—**bandha**, *m.* a groom.—**bhaṇḍaka**, *nt.* horse-trappings.—**maṇḍala**, *nt.* racing ground for horses.—**medha**, *m.* horse-sacrifice.—**ratha**, *m.* horse-carriage.—**vāṇija**, *m.* horse-dealer.—**ājānīya**, *m.* a horse of good breed.

Assa (3rd sing. Potential) may be. (Dat. and Gen. sing. of **ima** :) to this; of this.

Assaka, *a.* penniless.

Assakaṇṇa, *m.* Sal tree; name of a mountain.

Assattha, *m.* the holy fig tree. *Ficus Religiosa.*

Assattha (*pp.* of **assādeti**), comforted; consoled.

Assaddha, *a.* faithless; unbelieving.—**dhiya**, *nt.* disbelief.

Assama, *m.* hermitage.

Assamaṇa, *m.* a bogus monk; one who has fallen from the monkhood.

Assayuja, *m.* name of a month, October-November.

Assava, *a.* loyal; attentive. *m.* flow; pus.

Assavaṇatā, *f.* inattention.

Assavanīya, *a.* not pleasant to hear.

Assasati (ā + sas + a), to breathe; to inhale.

Assā, *f.* a mare. (Dat. and Gen. sing. of **ima** :) to her; of her.

Assāda, *m.* **Assādanā**, *f.* taste; enjoyment; satisfaction.

Assādeti (ā + sad + e), to taste; to enjoy. *aor.* —**esi.**

Assāsa, *m.* inhalation; comfort; consolation.

Assāsaka, *a.* that which brings comfort or consolation.

Assāseti (ā + sas + e), to console; to comfort *aor.* —**esi.**

Assu, *nt.* tears.—**dhārā**, *f.* shower of tears.—**mukha**, *a.* with a tearful face.—**mocana**, *nt.* shedding of tears.

Assu, *in.* a particle used in emphatic sense. (3rd. pl. Potential :) may be.

Assuta, *a.* unheard.—**vantu**, *a.* ignorant; one who has no learning.

Aha, *nt.* day. Followed by another word in cpds. it takes the form **aho**, as in **ahoratta.**

Ahata, *a.* new; not spoiled.

Ahaha, *intj.* exclamation of woe. *nt.* an immense number; *m.* name of a purgatory.

Ahaŋ (Nom. sing. of **amha**), I. —**kāra**, *m.* egotism; arrogance.

Ahāriya, *a.* immovable.

Ahi, *m.* snake; serpent.—**guṇṭhika**, *m.* snake-catcher.—**cchattaka**, *m.* a mushroom.—**tuṇḍika**, *m.* snake-catcher.—**pheṇa**, *nt.* opium.

Ahita, *nt.* harm; unkindliness. *adj.* harmful.

Ahirika, *a.* shameless. *nt.* shamelessness.

Ahivātakaroga, *m.* buboenic plague.

Ahiŋsā, *f.* non-hurting.

Ahīnindriya, *a.* not defective of any sense-organ.

Aho, *in.* exclamation of surprise or consternation.

Ahoratta, *nt.* day and night.

Ahosi (*aor.* of **hoti**), he was.—**kamma**, *nt.* an act of thought which has no longer any potential force.

Aŋsa, *m.* *nt.* a part; a side; shoulder.—**kūṭa**, *nt.* shoulder. —**bandhana**, *nt.* shoulder strap.

Aŋsu, *m.* ray of light; a fibre. —**ka**, *nt.* cloth.—**mālī**, *m.* the sun.

Ā.

Ā, *in.* up to. *prep.* from; towards.

Ākaṅkhati (ā + kakh + ŋ—a), to wish for; to desire. *aor.* —**khi**.

Ākaṅkhana, *nt.* **Ākaṅkhā**, *f.* longing; wish; desire.

Ākaṅkhamāna, *pr. p.* wishing; desiring.

Ākaḍḍhati (ā + kaḍḍh + a), to pull; to drag. *aor.*—**ḍḍhi**. *pp.* **ākaḍḍhita**.

Ākaḍḍhana, *nt.* pulling out; dragging.

Ākappa, *m.* deportment.

Ākampita, *pp.* shaken; trembling.

Ākara, *m.* a mine; place of production.

Ākassati (ā + kass + a), to drag; to pull. *aor.* —**ssi**.

Ākāra, *m.* manner; condition; state; appearance.

Ākāsa, *m.* the sky; space.—**gaṅgā**, *f.* the celestial river.—**cārī**, *a.* going through the air.—**ṭṭha**, *a.* situated or living in the sky.—**tala**, *nt.* flat roof of a building.—**dhātu**, *f.* the element of space, i.e. ether.

Ākiñcañña, *nt.* nothingness; absence of any possession.

Ākiṇṇa, *pp.* of the following.

Ākirati (ā + kir + a), to strew over; to scatter. *aor.* **ākiri**.

Ākula, **ākulībhūta**, *a.* entangled; confused.

Ākoṭana, *nt.* knocking; urging.

Ākoṭita (*pp.* of the following), compressed; screened.

Ākoṭeti (ā + kuṭ + e), to knock; to beat down; to compress. *aor.* —**esi**.

Ākhu, *m.* a rat; mouse.

Ākhyā, *f.* name.—**yikā**, *f.* a story.

Ākhyāta, *nt.* predicate; a verb.

Āgacchati (ā + gam + a), to come to; to approach. *aor.* —**chi**, **āgami**.

Āgacchanta, *pr. p.* of the above. coming; approaching.

Āgata, *pp.* of **āgacchati**.

Āgantu, *m.* one who is coming.

Āgantuka, 3. guest; new-comer; stranger.

Āgama, *m.* coming ; approach ; religion ; scripture ; an inserted consonant.

Āgamana, *nt.* oncoming ; arrival.

Āgamayamāna, *a.* waiting for; expecting.

Āgameti (ā + gam + e), to wait for ; to expect. *aor.* **—esi.**

Āgamma, *abs.* (of **āgacchati**), having come ; owing to.

Āgāmī, *a.* coming ; one who comes.—**kāla**, *m.* the future.

Āgilāyati (ā + gilā + ya), to be wearied ; to ache. *aor.* **—lāyi.**

Āgu, *nt.* guilt ; offence.—**cārī**, *m.* a criminal ; a villain.

Āghāta, *m.* anger ; hatred ; collision.

Āghātana, *nt.* slaughter house ; place of execution.

Ācamana, *nt.* rinsing.—**kumbhī**, *f.* water-pitcher used for rinsing.

Ācameti (ā + cam + e), to rinse ; to wash. *aor.* **—esi.**

Acaya, *m.* accumulation.

Ācarati (ā + car + a), to act ; to practise or perform.

Ācariya, *m.* teacher.—**kula**, *nt.* the family or the abode of a teacher.—**dhana**, *nt.* teacher's fee.—**muṭṭhi**, *f.* special knowledge of a teacher.—**vāda**, *m.* traditional teaching.

Ācariyānī, *f.* a woman teacher ; wife of a teacher.

Ācāma, *m.* the scum of boiling rice.

Ācāra, *m.* conduct ; behaviour ; practice.—**kusala**, *a.* versed in good manners.

Ācikkhaka, **Ācikkhitu**, 3. one who tells or informs.

Ācikkhati (ā + cikkh + a), to tell ; to relate ; to inform. *aor.* **ācikkhi**, *pp.* **—khita.**

Ācinanta, *pr. p.* accumulating.

Āciṇṇa, (*pp.* of **ācināti**), practised.—**kappa**, *m.* customary practice.

Ācita, *pp.* of the following.

Ācināti, (ā + ci + nā), to accumulate. *aor.* **ācini.**

Ācīyati (pass. of the above), to be heaped up or accumulated. *aor.*—**yi.**

Ācera, *m.* teacher.

Ājañña, *a.* of good breed.

Ājānana, *nt.* knowledge.

Ājānāti, (ā + ñā + nā), to know ; to understand. *aor.* **ājāni.**

Ājānīya, see **ājañña.**

Ājīva, *m.* livelihood ; living ; subsistence.

Ājīvaka, **ājīvika**, *m.* a kind of non-Buddhist ascetics.

Āṇatti, *f.* command; order.—**tika**, *a.* connected with a command.

Āṇā, *f.* command.—**sampanna**, *a.* authoritative ; influential.

Āṇāpaka, *m.* one who commands or issues orders.

Āṇāpana, *nt.* the act of commanding.

Āṇāpeti (ā + ñā + āpe), to command. *aor.*—**esi.**

Āṇi, *f.* a nail ; linch pin.

Ātaṅka, *m.* illness ; disease.

Ātata, *nt.* a drum with one face. —**vitata**, *nt.* a drum covered with leather on all sides.

Ātatta (*pp.* of **ātapati**), heated ; scorched.

Ātapa, *m.* sunshine.

Ātapati (ā + tap + a) to shine. *aor.* **ātapi.**

Ātapatta, *nt.* sunshade; umbrella.

Ātappa, *m.* ardour; exertion.

Ātāpa, *m.* glow; heat; ardour.

Ātāpana, *nt.* mortification; torture.

Ātāpī, *a.* ardent; strenuous.

Ātāpeti (ā + tap + e), to scorch; to torment. *aor.*—**esi.**

Ātura, *a.* affected with; sick; diseased.

Ādara, *m.* esteem; regard; affection.

Ādā, Ādāya, *abs.* (of **ādāti**), having taken.

Ādātabba, *pt. p.* fit to be taken.

Ādāti (ā + dā + a), to take; to grasp. *aor.* **ādiyi.**

Ādāna, *nt.* taking up; grasping.

Ādāyī, 3. one who takes.

Ādāsa, *m.* mirror.—**tala,** *nt.* surface of a mirror.

Ādi, *m.* starting point; beginning. *adj.* first; beginning with. *nt.* and so on; so forth.—**kammika,** *m.* beginner.—**kalyāṇa,** *a.* beautiful in the beginning.—**ma,** *a.* foremost.

Ādika, *a.* and so on.

Ādicca, *m.* the sun.—**patha,** *m.* the sky.—**bandhu,** *m.* kinsman of the sun; of the Solar race.

Ādito, *ad.* at first; from the beginning.

Āditta (*pp.* of **ādippati**), blazing; burning.

Ādinna (*pp.* of **ādāti**), taken; grasped.

Ādiya, ādiyitvā, *abs.* (of the following) having taken.

Ādiyati (ā + dā + i + ya), to take up; to grasp. (This is a passive base, but has active meaning). *aor.* **ādiyi.**

Ādisati (ā + dis + a), to point out; to tell; to announce. *aor.* **ādisi.**

Ādissa, *abs.* (of the above), having pointed out. *adj.* blamable; fit to be pointed out.

Ādīnava, *m.* disadvantage.

Ādīpita (*pp.* of **ādīpeti**), in flames; ablaze.

Ādu, *in.* or; but.

Ādeyya, *a.* to be taken up; acceptable.

Ādeva, *m.* **Ādevanā,** *f.* lamenting; crying; deploring.

Ādesa, *m.* pointing out.

Ādesanā, Ādisanā, *f.* prophesy; guessing; pointing out.

Ādhāna, *nt.* laying; receptacle; a hedge.—**gāhī,** 3. obstinate person.

Ādhāra, *m.* a container; receptacle; holder; basis; support; stand.—**ka,** *nt.* a stool; a stand.

Ādhāvati (ā + dhāv + a) to run towards.

Ādhāvana, *nt.* onrush.

Ādhipacca, Ādhipateyya, *nt.* lordship; power.

Ādhunāti (ā + dhu + nā), to shake off; to remove. *aor.* **ādhuni.** *pp.* **ādhūta.**

Ādheyya, *a.* belonging to; fit to be borne.

Āna, āṇa, *nt.* breathing; inhalation.

Āṇaka, *m.* a kettledrum.

Ānaṇya, *nt.* freedom from debt.

Ānana, face; mouth.

Ānantarika, *a.* immediately following.

Ānanda, *m.* joy ; pleasure.

Ānandī, *a.* joyful.

Ānayati, see **Āneti.**

Ānāpāna or **āṇāpāṇa** *nt.* inhaled and exhaled breath.

Ānisaŋsa, *m.* profit ; merit ; good result.

Ānisada, *nt.* the buttocks.

Ānīta, (*pp.* of **āneti**), brought.

Ānupubbī, *f.* order ; succession. —**kathā,** *f.* graduated sermon.

Ānubhāva, *m.* power ; splendour ; majesty.

Āneñja, *a.* static ; imperturbable.

Āneti (ā + ni + a) to bring ; to fetch.

Āpa, *m. nt.* water ; liquid. (In some cpds. it becomes **āpo.**)

Āpagā, *f.* river.

Āpajjati (ā + pad + ya), to get into ; to undergo ; to meet with.

Āpaṇa, *m.* bazaar ; market.

Āpaṇika, tradesman ; shopkeeper.

Āpatati (ā + pat + a), to fall or rush on to. *aor.* **āpati.** *pp.* **āpatita.**

Āpatti, *f.* getting into ; an ecclesiastical offence.

Āpadā, *f.* misfortune ; distress.

Āpanna, (*pp.* of **āpajjati**), entered upon ; fallen into.—**sattā,** *f.* a pregnant woman.

Āpāṇa, *nt.* breathing ; exhalation ;—**koṭika,** *a.* limited with the end of life.

Āpādaka, *m.* one who takes care of a child ; a guardian.

Āpādikā, *f.* a nurse ; a foster-mother.

Āpādi, *aor.* of **āpajjati.**

Āpādeti (ā + pad + e =), to nurse; to produce. *aor.* — **esi.**

Āpātha, *m.* sphere or range (of a sense organ).—**gata,** *a.* come into the sphere.

Āpāna, *nt.* drinking hall.—**bhūmi,** *f.*—**maṇḍala,** *nt.* banqueting hall.

Āpānīyakaŋsa, *m.* goblet ; drinking bowl.

Āpāyika, *a.* born in or belonging to a state of misery.

Āpucchati (ā + pucch + a), to enquire after ; to ask permission. *aor.* **āpucchi.** *pp.* **āpucchita.**

Āpuccha,—chiya, *abs.* (of the above), having asked permission or leave.

Āpucchitabba, *pt. p.* to be asked or enquired after.

Āpūrati (ā + pūr + a) to become full ; to increase. *aor.* **āpūri.**

Āpodhātu, *f.* the element of cohesion.

Āphusati (ā + phus + a) to feel ; to attain to.

Ābaddha, *pp.* of **ābandhati.**

Ābandhaka, *a.* tying ; connecting ; fixing.

Ābandhati (ā + bandh + a) to bind to ; to fasten on to. *aor.* **ābandhi.**

Ābādha, *m.* disease ; affliction.

Ābādhika, *a.* sick ; affected with illness.

Ābādhita (*pp.* of **ābādheti**), afflicted ; oppressed.

Ābādheti (ā + badh + e), to oppress ; to harass. *aor.*—**esi.**

Ābhata, *pp.* brought; conveyed.

Ābharaṇa, *nt.* ornament; decoration.

Ābhassara, *a.* radiant.

Ābhā, *f.* **Ābhāsa**, *m.* light; lustre; radiance.

Ābhāti (ā + bhā + a), to shine; to radiate, *aor.* **ābhāsi.**

Ābhidosika, *a.* belonging to the last evening.

Ābhidhammika, *a.* versed in or studying Abhidhamma.

Ābhisekika, *a.* belonging to the consecration.

Ābujati (ā + bhuj + a) to bend; to coil; to contract. *aor.* **ābhuji.**

Ābhujana, *nt.* crouching; bending; soiling.

Ābhoga, *m.* ideation; thought.

Āma, *in.* yes.

Āma, Āmaka, *a.* raw; fresh; uncooked; not ripe.—**gandha**, *m.* verminous odour; flesh.—**kasusāna**, *nt.* charnel grow, where corpses are thrown to be eaten by wild animals.

Āmaṭṭha (*pp.* of **āmasati**), touched; handled.

Āmattika, *nt.* earthernware; crockery.

Āmaddana, *nt.* crushing.

Āmantana, *nt.* calling; invitation; addressing.

Āmantita, *pp.* of the following.

Āmanteti (ā + mant + e), to call; to address; to invite. *aor.* —**esi.**

Āmaya, *m.* illness.

Āmalaka, *nt.*—**lakī**, *f.* emblic myrobalan.

Āmasati (ā + mas + a), to touch; to pat; to rub. *aor.* **āmasi.** *pp.* **āmasita** and **āmaṭṭha.**

Āmā, *f.* a slave woman.

Āmāsaya, *m.* stomach.

Āmisa, *nt.* food; flesh; bait; gain; *adj.* material.—**dāna**, *nt.* donation of requisities (i.e. food, lodging etc).

Āmuñcati (ā + muc + ŋ-a), to put on (some attire); to wear. *aor.* — **ñci.**

Āmutta (*pp.* of the above), dressed or adorned with.

Āmeṇḍita, *nt.* exclamation.

Āmo, see **Āma.**

Āmoda, *m.* pleasure; strong fragrance.

Āmodati (ā + mud + a) to rejoice. *aor.* **āmodi.** *pp.* **āmodita.**

Āmodanā, *f.* rejoicing.

Āmodamāna, *pr. p.* glad; joyful.

Āmodeti (caus. ā + mud + e), to gladden. *aor.*—**esi.**

Āya, *m.* income; profit.—**kammika**, *m.* collector of income.—**mukha**, *nt.* inflow; that which brings income.

Āyata, *a.* long; extended.

Āyatana, *nt.* sphere; region; sense-organ; position.

Āyati, *f.* the future.—**ka**, *a.* belonging to the future.

Āyatikā, *f.* a tube; water-pipe.

Āyatta, *a.* possessed; dependent on; *nt.* possession.

Āyasa, *a.* made of iron.

Āyasmantu, *a.* venerable.

Āyācaka, *a.* petitioner; applicant.

Āyācati (ā + yāc + a) to request; to implore. *aor.* **āyāci.** *pp.* **āyācita.**

Āyācanā, *f.* request; application.

Āyāta, *pp.* of the following.

Āyāti (ā + yā + a), to come; to approach.

Āyāma, *m.* length. *adj.* (in cpds.) having the length of.

Āyāsa, *m.* trouble; sorrow.

Āyu, *nt.* age.—**ka,** *a.* having the age of.—**kappa,** *m.* duration of life.—**kkhaya,** *m.* consummation of life.—**saṅkhaya,** *m.* exhaustion of life.

Āyutta (*pp.* of **āyuñjati**), yoked; connected with; devoted to.

Āyuttaka, *m.* an agent; trustee.

Āyudha, *nt.* weapon.

Āyūhaka, *a.* active; one who strives or collects.

Āyūhana, *nt.* striving; accumulation.

Āyūhati (ā + yūh + a), to strive, to accumulate. *aor.* **āyūhi.** *pp.* **āyūhita.**

Āyoga, *m.* devotion to; exertion; bandage.

Āra, *m.* a needle.—**gga,** *nt.* the point of a needle or an awl.—**patha,** *m.* path of a needle.

Ārakatta, *nt.* the state of being far from.

Ārakā, *in.* away from; far off.

Ārakūṭa, *m.* brass.

Ārakkhaka, 3. a guard; protector; watchman.

Ārakkhā, *f.* protection; care; watch.

Āraññaka,—ñika, *a.* belonging to or living in a forest.

Ārañjita, *pp.* furrowed; slashed; scratched. *nt.* a scar.

Ārata, *pp.* (of **āramati**), keeping away from; abstaining.

Ārati, *f.* abstinence; leaving off.

Āraddha (*pp.* of **ārabhati**), begun; started; firm.—**citta,** *a.* having won the favour.—**viriya,** *a.* strenuous.

Āraddhā, *abs.* (of **ārabhati**), having begun or started.

Ārabbha, *in.* beginning with; referring to; about.

Ārabhati (ā + rabh + a), to begin; to start; to kill; to torture. *aor.* **ārabhi.**

Ārambha, *m.* the beginning; attempt.

Ārammaṇa, *nt.* a sense-object.

Ārā, *in.* away or far from; remote.—**cārī,** 3. living far from.

Ārā, *f.* an awl.

Ārādhaka, 3. one who invites or propitiates.

Ārādhanā, *f.* invitation; accomplishment; winning of favour.

Ārādheti (ā + rādh + e), to invite; to please; to win favour; to attain. *aor.*—**esi.**

Ārāma, *m.* pleasure; delight; a park; a monastery.— **pāla,** *m.* keeper of a park.—**ropa,** *m.* a planter.—**vatthu,** *nt.* site for a garden.—**mika,** *m.* an attendent in a monastery. *adj.* belonging to a monastery.

Ārāmatā, *f.* attachment.

Ārāva, *m.* cry; noise.

Āruppa, *nt. m.* an incorporeal being; formless state.

Āruyha, *abs.* of the following.

Āruhati (ā + ruh + a) to ascend; to mount; climb. *aor.* **āruhi.**

Āruhanta, (*pr. p.* of the above), ascending; climbing.

Ārūḷha (*pp.* of **āruhati**), mounted; embarked.

Ārogya, *nt.* health.—**sālā,** *f.* hospital; sanatorium.

Ārocāpana, *nt.* announcement; information.

Ārocāpeti, *caus.* of **ārocetı.**

Ārocita (*pp.* of the following), told; informed.

Āroceti (ā + ruc + e), to tell; to inform; to announce. *aor.*—**esi.**

Ārodanā, *f.* cry; lamentation.

Āropana, *nt.* putting on; raising up to; committing.

Āropita, *pp.* of the following.

Āropeti (ā + rup + e), to put on; to impeach; to get ready. *aor.*—**esi.**

Āroha, *m.* climbing up; growth; height; a rider.

Ārohaka, *m.* a rider.

Ārohati, see **āruhati.**

Ārohana, *nt.* climbing; ascending.

Ālaggita, *pp.* of the following.

Ālaggeti (ā + lag + e), to hang on; to fasten to. *aor.*—**esi.**

Ālapati (ā + lap + a), to converse; to address. *aor.* **ālapi.**

Ālapana, *nt.* addressing; conversation; the Vocative. — **panā,** *f.* entreaty.

Ālamba, *m.* support; help; anything to hang on.

Ālambati (ā + lab + ŋ-a), to hang on to; to take hold of. *aor.* **ālambi.** *pp.* **ālambita.**

Ālambana, *nt.* a sense-object; hanging down from; support.

Ālambara, *m.* a kind of drum.

Ālaya, *m.* abode; roosting place; desire; attachment; pretence.

Ālasiya, Ālasya, *nt.* sloth; laziness.

Āl(ḷ)āna, *nt.* stake; a post (to which an elephant is tied).

Ālāpa, *m.* talk; conversation; a word.

Āli, *f.* a dike; embankment.

Ālikhati (ā + likh + a) to delineate; to draw some figure. *aor.* **ālikhi.**

Āliṅgati (ā + liṅg + a), to embrace. *aor.* **āliṅgi.**

Āliṅgana, *nt.* embracing.

Ālitta, (*pp.* of **ālimpati** or **ālimpeti**), besmeared or stained with; set with fire.

Ālinda, *m.* a verandah before the house door.

Ālimpana, *nt.* besmearing; burning.

Ālimpita, *pp.* of the following.

Ālimpeti (ā + lip + e), to smear; to anoint; to set fire to. *aor.* —**esi.**

Ālu, *nt.* edible root or bulb; yam.

Āluḷita, *pp.* of the following.

Āluḷeti (ā + luḷ + e), to agitate; to confound. *aor.*—**esi.**

Ālepa, *m.* ointment; plaster.

Ālepana, *nt.* anointing; plastering.

Āloka, *m.* light.

Ālokana, *nt.* a window; looking at.

Ālokasandhi, *m.* a window; an opening to let the light in.

Ālokita (*pp.* of the following), *nt.* looking at or forward.

Āloketi (ā + lok + e), to look at or before. *aor.*—**esi**.

Ālopa, *m.* a morsel; a bit.—**pika** (in cpds). *a.* consisting of morsels.

Āloḷa, *m.* agitation; confusion; uproar.

Āloḷeti (ā + luḷ + e), to confuse; to jumble; to mix. *aor.*—**esi**.

Āvajjati (ā + vajj + a), to reflect upon; to upset (a vessel). *aor.* **āvajji**.

Āvajjita (*pp.* of the following) considered; turned over.

Āvajjeti (ā + vajj + e), to muse; to observe; to turn over. *aor.*—**esi**.

Āvaṭa (*pp.* of **āvarati**), covered; veiled; prohibited.

Āvaṭṭa, *m.* circumference; a whirlpool; twisting.

Āvaṭṭati (ā + vaṭṭ + a), to turn forward and backward; to rotate. *aor.* **āvaṭṭi**.

Āvaṭṭana, *nt.* revolving; temptation; possession by some spirit.—**ṭanī**, *a.* enticing.

Āvaṭṭeti (ā + vaṭṭ + e), to turn round; entice; to convert.

Āvatta (*pp.* of **āvattati**), fallen back to. *nt.* winding; turn; bent.

Āvattaka, **Āvattī**, *a.* coming back; one who returns.

Āvattati (ā + vat + a), to go back; to turn round. *aor.* **āvatti**. *pp.* **āvattita**.

Āvattana, *nt.* turning; return.

Āvattiya, *a.* turnable; returnable.

Āvatteti, see **Āvaṭṭeti**.

Āvatthika, *a.* befitting; original.

Āvaraṇa, *nt.* shutting off; hindrance; a bar; a screen.

Āvaraṇīya, *adj.* apt to obstruct.

Āvarati (ā + var + a), to shut out from; to obstruct. *aor.* **āvari**.

Āvarita, *pp.* of the above.

Āvalī, *f.* a row; a string.

Āvasati (ā + vas + a) to live; to reside; to inhabit. *aor.* **āvasi**.

Āvasatha, *m.* abode; dwelling; rest-house.

Āvaha, **Āvahanaka**, *a.* (in cpds). bringing; bearing; conducive.

Āvahati (ā + vah + a), to bring; to cause; to conduce. *aor.* **āvahi**.

Āvahana, *nt.* bringing; conveyance.

Āvāṭa, *m.* a pit.

Āvāpa, *m.* potters' furnace; an oven.

Āvāsa, *m.* home; dwelling place.—**sika**, *a.* resident.

Āvāha, *m.* **Āvāhana**, *nt.* taking in marriage; wedding.

Āvi, *in.* openly; before one's eyes.

Āvijjhati (ā + vidh + ya), to encircle; to go round; to whirl round; to pierce through. *aor.* —**jhi**.

Āvijjhana, *nt.* going or whirling round.

Āviñjati (ā + vij + ŋ-a), to pull as in milking; to churn; to agitate. *aor.*—**ñji**.

Āviñjanaka, *a.* swinging round; hanging loose; used for pulling. —**rajju**, *f.* the rope to raise a latch; whirling rope used in churning milk.—**naṭṭhāna**, *nt.* place outside the door where the rope is hanging with which the latch inside is to be raised.

Āviṭṭha, *pp.* of **āvisati.**

Āviddha, *pp.* of **āvijjhati.**

Āvila, *a.* stirred up; agitated dirty.

Āvisati (ā + vis + a) to enter; to approach; to be possessed by a spirit. *aor.* **āvisi.**

Āvuṇāti (ā + vu + nā), to string upon; to fix on to. *aor.* **āvuṇi.**

Āvuta (*pp.* of the above and of **āvarati**), strung upon; covered; hindered.

Āvuttha (*pp.* of **āvasati**), inhabited.

Āvudha, *nt.* weapon.

Āvuso, *in.* (vocative), friend; brother. (A form of polite address among monks).

Āveṭhana, *nt.* winding round; ravelling.

Āveṭheti (ā + veṭh + e), to twist or wrap over. *aor.*—**esi.** *pp.* **āveṭhita.**

Āveṇika, *a.* special; exceptional.

Āvelā, *f.* a garland for the head.

Āvellita, *pp.* curved; crooked; curled.

Āvesana, *nt.* entrance; workshop.

Āsaṅkati (ā + sak + ŋ-a), to suspect; to distrust. *aor.* **āsaṅki.**

Āsaṅkā, *f.* doubt; suspicion; fear.

Āsaṅkita, (*pp.* of **āsaṅkati**), apprehensive; doubtful; suspicious.

Āsaṅkī, *a.* see **āsaṅkita.**

Āsajja, *abs.* (of **āsādeti**), having approached, insulted or knocked against.

Āsajjati (ā + sad + ya), to knock against; to become angry; to be attached to. *aor.* **āsajji.**

Āsajjana, *nt.* 1. knocking against; insult; 2. attachment.

Āsati (ās + a), to sit. *aor.* **āsi.**

Āsatta, (*pp.* of **āsajjati**), attached to; clinging; accursed.

Āsana, *nt.* a seat; sitting down. —**sālā,** *f.* a hall with sitting accommodation.

Āsandi, *f.* a long chair; deck-chair.

Āsanna, *a.* near. *nt.* neighbourhood.

Āsabha, *a.* bull-like, i.e. of strong and eminent qualities. —**bhaṭṭhāna,** *nt.* a distinguished position.—**bhī,** *f.* (of **āsabha**), imposing; bold.

Āsaya, *m.* abode; haunt; deposit; inclination.

Āsava, *m.* that which flows; spirit; discharge from a sore; ideas which intoxicate the mind.—**vakkhaya,** *m.* destruction of intoxicants of the mind.

Āsavati (ā + su + a) to flow. *aor.* **āsavi.**

Āsasāna, *a.* wishing; desiring.

Āsā, *f.* wish; desire; hope; longing.—**bhaṅga,** *m.* disappointment.

Āsāṭikā, *f.* fly's egg.

Āsādeti (ā + sad + e), to offend; to assail; to insult. *aor.*—**esi.**

Āsāḷha, *m.* name of a month.—**ḷhī,** *a.* connected with the **āsāḷha** constellation.

Āsāsamāna, *pr. p.* lingering; remaining long.

Āsi, (3rd sing. *aor.* of **as**), he was.

Āsiñcati (ā + sic + ŋ-a), to sprinkle; to pour over. *aor.* **āsiñci.**

Āsiṭṭha (*pp.* of **āsiŋsati**), wished or longed for ; blessed.

Āsitta, *pp.* of **āsiñcati.**

Āsittaka, *nt.* a condiment.—**kupadhāna,** *nt.* receptacle for condiments.

Āsiŋ (1st sing. *aor.* of **as**), I was.

Āsiŋsaka, *a.* wishing ; aspiring after ; a candidate.

Āsiŋsati (ā + siŋs + a), to hope for ; to desire. *aor.* **āsiŋsi.**

Āsiŋsanā, *f.* wish ; hope ; desire.

Āsī, *f.* blessing ; fang of a snake.

Āsītika, *a.* eighty years old.

Āsīna (*pp.* of **āsati**), sat; sitting.

Āsīvisa, *m.* a snake ; whose poison is in the fangs.

Āsu, *in.* quickly.

Āsuŋ (3rd *pl. aor.* of **as**), they were.

Āsumbhati (ā + subh + ŋ-a), to throw down some liquid.

Āsevati (ā + sev + a), to associate ; to practise ; to frequent. *aor.* **āsevi.** *pp.* **āsevita.**

Āsevanā, *f.* practice ; pursuit ; association.

Āha (3rd sing. of Pret). he has said.

Āhacca, *a.* 1. removable ; 2. *abs.* (of **āhanati**) : having knocked or touched.

Āhaṭa (*pp.* of **āharati**), brought.

Āhata (*pp.* of **āhanati**), struck ; affected with ; afflicted.

Āhanati (ā + han + a), to beat ; to strike ; to touch. *aor.* **āhani.**

Āhanana, *nt.* knocking against.

Āharaṇa, *nt.* bringing.

Āharati (ā + har + a), to bring ; to fetch ; to produce. *aor.* **āhari.** *pr. p.* **āharamāna.** *abs.* **āharitvā.**

Āhāra, *m.* food ; nutriment.—**ṭṭhitika,** *a.* subsisting on food.

Āhāreti (ā + har + e), to eat ; to take food. *aor.*—**esi.**

Āhiṇḍati (ā + hiḍ + ŋ-a), to wander about ; to roam. *aor.* **āhiṇḍi.***abs.*—**ḍitvā.**

Āhita, *pp.* put in ; kindled.

Āhu, *pl.* of **āha.**

Āhuti, *f.* oblation ; offering.

Āhuṇa, *nt.* adoration ; oblation. —**ṇeyya,** *a.* worthy of adoration or offerings.

Āhundarika, *a.* crowded ; blocked up.

I.

Ikkhana, *nt.* seeing ; looking at.

Ikkhaṇika, *m.* fortune-teller.—**ṇikā,** *f.* female fortune-teller.

Ikkhati, (ikkh + a), to look at. *aor.* **ikkhi.**

Iṅgita, *nt.* gesture ; sign.

Iṅgha, *in.* come on ; look here.

Iccha, *a.* (in *cpds*). wishing ; longing ; desirous of.

Icchaka, *a.* one who desires.

Icchati (is + a), to whsh ; to desire ; to long for. *aor.* **icchi.** *pr. p.* **icchanta.**

Icchana, *nt.* **Icchā,** *f.* desire ; wish ; longing.—**āvacara,** *a.* moving in desires ; behaving as one likes.

Icchita, *pp.* of **icchati.**

Ijjhati (idh + ya), to thrive ; to succeed ; to prosper. *aor.* **ijjhi.** *pr. p.* **ijjhamāna.**

Ijjhana, *nt.*—**nā,** *f.* success ; thriving.

Iñjati (iñj + a) to move ; to stir. *aor.* **iñji.**

Iñjana, *nt.*—**nā,** *f.* motion ; movement.

Iñjita (*pp.* of **iñjati**), moved ; shaken. *nt.* movement ; vacillation.

Iṭṭha, *a.* pleasing ; agreeable. *nt.* happiness ; pleasure.

Iṭṭhakā, Iṭṭhikā, *f.* tile ; brick. (**Cayaniṭṭhakā**=brick ; **Chadaniṭṭhakā**=tile).

Iṇa, *nt.* debt.—**ṭṭha,** *a.* one who is in debt ; debtor.—**paṇṇa,** *nt.* promissory note.—**mokkha,** *m.* release from debt.—**sāmika,** *m.* creditor.—**sodhana,** *nt.* discharge of debt.

Iṇāyika, *m.* debtor.

Itara, *a.* the other.

Itarītara, *a.* whatsoever ; any.

Iti, *in.* thus. (Used to point out something just mentioned or about to be mentioned, and to show that a sentence is finished). Very often its former **i** is ellided and **ti** only is remaining.—**kira,** *in.* thus I have heard.

Itihāsa, *m.* history ; tradition.

Ito, *in.* from here ; from now ; hence.—**paṭṭhāya,** *in.* henceforth.

Ittara, *a.* short-lived ; brief ; very small or few.—**kāla,** *m.* a short period.

Itthatta (itthaŋ + tta :) the present state ; this life. (itthi + tta :) womanhood ; femininity.

Itthaŋ, *ad.* thus ; in this way.—**nāma,** *a.* called thus ; so-called. —**bhūta,** *a.* being thus ; of this kind.

Itthāgāra, *m.* harem ; seraglio ; harem-ladies.

Itthi (ī), **itthikā,** *f.* woman ; female.—**dhutta,** *m.* one who indulges in woman.—**liṅga,** *nt.* female organ ; feminine quality or gender.—**nimitta,** *nt.* female organ.

Idaŋ (*nt.* Nom. and Acc. sing. of **ima**), this thing.

Idappaccayatā, *f.* having its foundation on this, i.e., causally connected.

Idāni, *ad.* now.

Iddha (*pp.* of **ijjhati**), prosperous; opulent; successful.

Iddhi, *f.* prosperity ; potency ; psychic power.—**pāda,** *m.* basis of psychic power.—**bala,** *nt.* supernatural power.—**mantu,** *a.* possessing psychic powers.—**visaya,** *m.* extent of phychic power.

Idha, *ad.* here ; in this world or existence.

Idhuma, *nt.* firewood.

Inda, *m.* lord ; king ; the Vedic god Indra ; the king of devas.—**gajjita,** *nt.* the thunder.—**gopaka,** *m.* a kind of red insects which come out from the ground after a rain fall.—**ggi,** *m.* lightning.—**jāla,** *nt.* magic.—**jālika,** *m.* magician ; juggler.—**dhanu,** *nt.* rainbow.

Indakhīla, *m.* a door-step ; thres hold ; a strong post before a city gate.

Indanīla, *m.* sapphire.

Indavāruṇi, *f.* cucumber.

Indasāla, *m.* the tree *Vetaria Acuminata.*

Indīvara, *nt.* blue water-lily.

Indriya, *nt.* controlling principal ; faculty ; senses.—**gutti,** *f.* keeping watch over the senses.—**damana,** *nt.* —**saŋvara,** *m.* subjugation of senses.

Indhana, *nt.* fuel ; firewood.

Ibha, *m.* elephant.—**pipphalī,** *f.* a big kind of long pepper.

Irina, *nt.* great forest; desert; barren soil.

Iriyati (iriy+a), to move; to stir; to behave. *aor.* **iriyi.**

Iriyā, iriyanā, *f.* movement of the body; posture.—**patha,** *m.* deportment; four postures, *viz*: walking; standing, sitting, and lying down.

Illī, *f.* a short sword.

Iva, *in.* like; as.

Isi, *m.* a sage; seer.—**pabbajjā,** *f.* leaving the house to become an anchoret.—**patana,** *nt.* name of a place; present Sārnath near Benares.

Issa, *m.* a bear.

Issati (iss+a), to envy.

Issattha, *nt.* archery. *m.* an archer.

Issara, *m.* lord; master; the Creator.—**jana,** *m.* rich or influential people.—**nimmāṇa,** *nt.* the creation.—**nimmāṇa-vadī,** 3. one who believes in a Creator.

Issariya, *nt.* supremacy; domination; wealth.—**mada,** *m.* pride of supremacy.

Issariyatā, *f.* lordship.

Issā, *f.* jealousy; ill-will; envy. —**manaka,** *a.* jealous.

Issāsa, *m.* a bow; an archer.

Issukī, *a.* envious; jealous.

Iha, *in.* here.—**loka,** *n.* this world; present existence.

Ī.

Īgha, *m.* distress; danger.

Īti, *f.* calamity.

Īdisa, *a.* such; such-like.

Īrati (īr+a), to move; to shake; to stir. *aor.* **īri.** *pp.* **īrita.**

Īreti (ir+e), to utter; to speak. *aor.* **īresi.** *pp.* **īrita.**

Īsa, *m.* a lord; ruler.—**dhara,** *m.* name of a mountain.

Īsaka, *a.* little; few.—**kaŋ,** *ad.* a little; slightly.

Īsā, *f.* pole of a plough or a carriage.—**danta,** *a.* having tusks as long as a plough-pole, i.e., an elephant.

Īhati (īh+a), to attempt; to strive after. *aor.* **īhi.**

Īhā, *f.* endeavour; exertion.

U.

Ukkaŋsa, *m.* excellence; superiority.—**ka,** *a.* exalting; praising.

Ukkaŋsanā, *f.* extolling; eulogizing.

Ukkaŋseti (u+kas+e), to exalt; to praise. *aor.* — **esi.**

Ukkaṭṭha, *a.* high; prominent; excellent; specialized.—**tā,** *f.* eminence; superiority.

Ukkaṭṭhita, *pp.* boiled up; seething.

Ukkaṇṭhati (u+kaṭh+-ŋ-a), to be dissatisfied. *aor.* — **ṇṭhi.**

Ukkaṇṭhanā, *f.* dissatisfaction; commotion.

Ukkaṇṭhita (*pp.* of — **ṭhati**), dissatisfied; fretting.

Ukkaṇṇa, *a.* having the ears erect.

Ukkantati (u+kat+ŋ-a), to cut or tear out. *aor.* **ukkanti.** *pp.* —**tita.**

Ukkā, *f.* a torch; a meteor; forge of a smith.

Ukkāra, *m.* dung; excrement.—**bhūmi,** *f.* dung-hill; unclean place.

Ukkāsati (u+kas+a), to cough; to clear one's throat. *aor.* **ukkāsi.**

Ukkāsita (*pp.* of the above), coughed out; *nt.* coughing; clearing of one's throat.

Ukkujja, *a.* set up; upturned.

Ukkujjati (u + kujj + a), to turn up; to bend up. *aor.* — **jji.** *pp.* **ukkujjita.**

Ukkujjana, *nt.* turning up.

Ukkuṭika, *a.* squatting.—**kaŋ,** *ad.* in the posture of squatting.

Ukkuṭṭhi, *f.* shouting out; acclamation.

Ukkusa, *m.* osprey.

Ukkūla, *a.* steep; sloping up.

Ukkoṭana, *nt.* perverting justice by taking bribe etc.

Ukkoṭeti (u + kuṭ + e), to open up again a legal question that has been settled. *aor.* —**esi.** *pp.* —**ṭita.**

Ukkhali, *f.* a pot.—**kā,** *f.* a small pot.

Ukkhitta, (*pp.* of **ukkhipati**) lifted or thrown up; suspended.—**ka,** *a.* suspended person.

Ukkhipati (u + khip + a), to raise, hold, or throw up; to suspend.

Ukkipana, Ukkhepana, *nt.* **Ukkhepa,** *m.* lifting up; raising; suspension.

Uklāpa, *m.* dirt; rubbish. *adj.* dirty; unclean.

Ugga, *a.* huge; fierce; mighty; rising.

Uggacchati (u + gam + a) to rise; to go up. *aor.* — **chi.**

Uggajjati (u + gajj + a) to shout out. *aor.* — **jji.**

Uggaṇhana, *nt.* learning; studying.

Uggaṇhāti (u + gah + ṇhā), to learn; to take up. *aor.* **uggaṇhi.** *pp.* **uggahita.**

Uggaṇhāpeti (*caus.* of the above), to teach; to instruct. *aor.* — **esi.**

Uggaṇhiya,—hitvā, *abs.* having learnt or taken up.

Uggata (*pp.* of **uggacchati**), risen; high; lofty.

Uggama, *m.* **Uggamana,** *nt.* rise; going up; increase.

Uggayha, *abs.* having learnt or taken up.

Uggaha, *m.* **Uggahaṇa,** *nt.* learning; study; taking up.

Uggahita (*pp.* of **uggaṇhāti**), learnt; raised; taken wrongly.

Uggahetu, *m.* one who learns or takes up.

Uggahetvā, *abs.* having learnt or taken up.

Uggāra, *m.* a belch; ejection of wind from the stomach.

Uggāhaka, *a.* one who is learning.

Uggirati (u + gir + a) to lift up; to brandish; to utter; to belch. *aor.* **uggiri.**

Uggilati (u + gil + a) to vomit. *aor.* **uggili.**

Ugghaṭita, *a.* keen; striving.

Uggharati (u + ghar + a), to ooze. *aor.* — **ghari.**

Ugghaŋseti (u + ghaŋs + e), to rub. *aor.* — **esi.**

Ugghāṭana, *nt.* unfastening; opening; that which can be removed; a machine for raising water.

Ugghāṭita, *pp.* of the following.

Ugghāṭeti (u + ghāt + e), to open; to unfasten; to remove; to abolish. *aor.* — **esi.**

Ugghāta, *m.* a jolt or jerk.

Ugghātita, *pp.* of the following.

Ugghāteti (u + ghāt + e), to make a sudden jerk. *aor.* — **esi.**

Ugghosa, *m.*—**sanā,** *f.* a shout; proclamation.

Ugghosita, *pp.* of the following.

Ugghoseti (u + ghus + e), to shout out; to proclaim. *aor.* — **esi.** *pp.* — **sita.**

Ucca, *a.* high; noble.

Uccaya, *m.* accumulation.

Uccākulīna, *a.* of a noble birth.

Uccāra, *m.* dung; faeces; excrement.

Uccāraṇa, *nt.*—**ṇā,** *f.* lifting up; utterance; pronunciation.

Uccārita, *pp.* of the following.

Uccāreti (u + car + e), to utter; to pronounce; to lift up. *aor.* — **esi.**

Uccāliṅga, *m.* a maw-worm; caterpillar.

Uccāvaca, *a.* high and low; various.

Uccāsadda, *m.* loud noise; *adj.* making a loud noise.

Uccāsayana, *nt.* a high bed.

Uccināti (u + ci + nā), to select; to choose; to pick out. *aor.* **uccini.** *abs.* **uccinitvā.**

Ucchaṅga, *m.* the lap; the hip.

Ucchādana, *nt.* rubbing of the body.

Ucchādeti (u + chad + e), to rub the body (in bathing or with perfumes). *aor.* — **esi.**

Ucciṭṭha, *a.* left over (food or drink); impure; used.

Ucchijjati (u + chid + ya, pass. of the following), to cease; to become annihilated. *aor.* — **jji.**

Ucchindati (u + chid + ŋ-a), to break; to destroy. *aor.* — **ndi.**

Ucchinna, *pp.* of the above.

Ucchu, *m.* sugar-cane.—**yanta,** *nt.* sugar-mill;—**rasa,** *m.* treacle; juice of sugar-cane.

Uccheda, *m.* cutting off; perishing; annihilation.—**diṭṭhi,** *f.* belief in the annihilation of the soul.—**vādī,** *m.* one who professes the doctrine of annihilation.

Uju, ujuka, *a.* straight; up-right. — **gata,** — **bhūta,** *a.* straight; upright of life.—**tā,** *f.* rectitude; straightness.

Ujuŋ. *ad.* straightly.

Ujjagghati (u + jaggh + a) to laugh aloud. *aor.* — **ghi.**

Ujjagghikā, *f.* loud laughter.

Ujjaṅgala, *a.* barren; sandy.

Ujjala, *a.* bright; blazing.

Ujjalati (u + jal + a), to shine; to blaze up. *aor.* **ujjali.** *pp.* **ujjalita.**

Ujjavati (u + ju + a), to go up-stream. *aor.* **ujjavi.**

Ujjavanikā, *f.* a vessel going up-stream.

Ujjahati (u + hā + a), to give up. *aor.* **ujjahi.**

Ujjota, *m.* light; lustre.

Ujjotita, *pp.* of the following.

Ujjoteti (u + jut + e), to illuminate. *aor.* — **esi.**

Ujjhati (ujjh + a) to leave; to forsake. *aor.* **ujjhi.** *abs.* **ujjhiya, ujjhitvā.**

Ujjhāna, *nt.* taking offence; complaining.

Ujjhāpana, *nt.* provoking.

Ujjhāpeti (u + jhe + āpe), to irritate; to make one complain. *aor.* — **esi.**

Ujjhāyati (u + jhe + a) to grumble. *aor.* **ujjhāyi.**

Ujjhita, (*pp.* of **ujjhati**), forsaken; cast away; thrown out.

Uñchati, (uch + ŋ-a), to seek alms; to glean. *aor.* **uñchi.** *pp.* **uñchita.**

Uñchā, *f.* anything gathered for sustenance.—**cariyā,** *f.* wandering for gleaning.

Uññātabba, *pt. p.* contemptible; despicable.

Uṭṭhahati Uṭṭhāti (u + ṭhā + a), to stand up; to arise; to be active. *aor.* **uṭṭhāsi, uṭṭhahi.** *pp.* **uṭṭhita.**

Uṭṭhahitvā, uṭṭhāya, *abs.* (of the above), having got up or arisen.

Uṭṭhātu, *m.* one who gets up or rouses himself.

Uṭṭhāna, *nt.* getting up; rising; origin; energy; industry; product.—**ka,** *a.* producing; yielding.— **vantu,** *a.* strenuous.

Uṭṭhāpeti (*caus.* of **uṭṭhāti**), to make rise; to raise; to turn a person out. *aor.* — **esi.**

Uṭṭhāyaka, *a.* (*f.*—**yikā**), active; industrious.

Uṭṭhita (*pp.* of **uṭṭhāti**), got up; arisen; produced.

Uḍḍayhati, *pass.* of the following.

Uḍḍahati (u + dah + a), to burn up. *aor.* **uḍḍahi.**

Uḍḍita, *pp.* of the following.

Uḍḍeti (u + ḍī + e), to fly; to suspend. *aor.* — **esi.**

Uṇṇa, *nt.* **uṇṇā,** *f.* wool; fibre. (With reference to the Buddha:) a hair between the eyebrows.—**nābhi,** *m.* a spider.

Uṇha, *a.* hot. *nt.* heat.

Uṇhatta, *nt.* heat.

Unhīsa, *nt.* a turban.

Utu, *f. nt.* season; climate; the menses.—**kāla,** *m.* the timo of the menses.—**parissaya,** *m.* risk of the seasons. —**sappāya,** *m.* agreeable season or climate.

Utta (=vutta), *pp.* of **vadati.** spoken; uttered. *nt.* utterance.

Uttaṇḍula, *a.* badly cooked (rice), having some unboiled grains.

Uttatta (*pp.* of **uttapati**), heated; molten; shining.

Uttama, *a.* highest; best; noble; excellent.—**ṅga,** *nt.* the most important part, i.e. the head.—**attha,** *m.* the highest gain.—**porisa,** *m.* the greatest man.

Uttara, *a.* higher; further; northern; over. *nt.* an answer; reply.—**attharaṇa,** *nt.* upper cover.—**cchada,** *m.* awning; canopy.—**sve,** *ad.* day after to-morrow.

Uttaraṇa, *nt.* crossing over; overcoming; delivery; passing (of an exam.).

Uttarati (u + tar + a), to come out of water; to go over; to overcome. *aor.* **uttari.**

Uttarā, *f.* the northern direction.

Uttari, Uttariṃ, *ad.* over; beyond; further; moreover; additional.—**karaṇīya,** *nt.* additional duty.—**bhaṅga,** *m.* additional bits; dainty bits.—**manussadhamma,** *m.* extraordinary condition; transcendental norm.— **sāṭaka,** *m.* upper garment.

Uttarīya, *nt.* a cloak.

Uttasati (u + tas + a), to be alarmed or terrified. *aor.* **uttasi.**

Uttasana, *nt.* alarm; terror.

Uttasta, uttrasta (*pp.* of **uttasati**), frightened; terrified.

Uttāna, uttānaka, *a.* lying on one's back; supine; manifest; shallow.—**seyyaka,** *a.* an infant.—**nīkamma,**—**nīkaraṇa,** *nt.* exposition; manifestation.

Uttānīkaroti (uttāna + i + kar + o), to make clear. *aor.* — **kari.**

Uttāpeti (u + tap + e), to heat; to torment. *aor.* — **esi.**

Uttārita, *pp.* of the following.

Uttāreti (u + tar + e), to let cross; to save; to assist. *aor.* —**esi.**

Uttāsa, *m.* terror; fear.

Uttāsana, *nt.* impalement.

Uttāsita, *pp.* of the following.

Uttāseti (u+tas+e), to impale. (*caus.* of **uttasati**) to frighten or terrify. *aor.* — **esi.**

Uttiṭṭhati, (u+ṭhā+a) to rise; to stand up; to strive.

Uttiṇṇa (*pp.* of **uttarati**), crossed over; gone to the other shore; come out of; passed.

Utrāsa, *m.* terror.—**sī,** *a.* fearful; timid.

Uda, *in.* or.

Uda, udaka, *nt.* water.—**kāka,** *m.* a small kind of cormorant. —**dhārā,** *f.* a torrent of water. —**phusita,—bindu,** *nt.* a drop of water.—**maṇika,** *m.* a big jar to keep water.—**sāṭikā,** *f.* bathing mantle.

Udakāyatikā, *f.* water-pipe.

Udakumbha, *m.* water-pot.

Udakogha, *m.* a flood of water.

Udagga, *a.* elated; exultant; joyful.

Udañcana, *nt.* a small vessel with a handle used to take out water from a jar; a bucket.

Udadhi, *m.* ocean.

Udapādi, (*aor.* of **udapajjati**), it arose; originated.

Udapāna, *m.* a well.

Udaya, *m.* rise; growth; increase; income; interest (from money).—**atthagama,** *m.* rise and fall.—**bbaya,** *m.* rise and fall; increase and decrease; birth and death.

Udayanta, *pr. p.* of **udayati.** rising; growing.

Udayati see **udeti.**

Udayana, *nt.* rise; going up.

Udara, *nt.* belly; stomach; interior.—**aggi,** *m.* the digestive faculty.—**paṭala,** *nt.* the mucous membrane of the stomach.—**āvadehakaŋ,** *ad.* filling the stomach to the utmost.

Udariya, *nt.* undigested food in the stomach.

Udahāraka, *m.* carrier of water. (*f.*—**hārikā**).

Udahāriya, *nt.* the act of carrying water.

Udāna, *nt.* an emotional utterance.

Udāneti (u + ā + nī + e), to utter something with intense emotion.

Udāra, *a.* noble; excellent; great; lofty.

Udāsīna, *a.* indifferent; passive.

Udāhaṭa, *pp.* of **udāharati.**

Udāharaṇa, *nt.* example; instance.

Udāharati (u + ā + har + a), to utter; to recite. *aor.*—**hari.**

Udāhāra, *m.* utterance; speech.

Udāhu, *in.* or.

Udikkhati (u + ikkh + a), to look at; to survey. *aor.*—**kkhi.** *pp.* **udikkhita.**

Udikkhitu, *m.* one who looks at.

Udikkhiya, *abs.* (of. **udikkhati**), having seen or looked at.

Udicca, *a.* noble; of the northern origin.

Udita (*pp.* of **udeti**), risen; high; elevated.

Udīraṇa, *nt.* utterance; saying.

Udīrita, *pp.* of the following.

Udīreti (u + īr + e), to utter; to speak. *aor.*—**esi.**

Udukkhala, *m. nt.* a mortar.

Udumbara, *m.* the glomarous fig tree.

Udeti (u + i + a), to rise; to come out; to increase. *aor.* **udesi.**

Udda, *m.* an otter.

Uddasseti (u + dis + e), to show ; to reveal. *aor.*—**esi.**

Uddāna, *nt.* a list ; a table of contents ; a cluster.

Uddāpa, *m.* a bastian.

Uddāma, *a.* out of bounds ; restless

Uddālaka, *m.* the tree *Cassia Fistula.*

Uddālana, *nt.* tearing out.

Uddāleti (u + dāl + e), to tear off. *aor.*—**esi.**

Uddiṭṭha, *pp.* of the following.

Uddisati (u + dis + a), to point out ; to appoint ; to allot ; to recite. *aor.* **uddisi.**

Uddisāpeti (*caus.* of the above), to make recite or allot.

Uddissa (= **uddisiya**), *abs.* of **uddisati,** with reference to ; on account of ; for.—**kata,** *a.* allotted to ; meant for.

Uddīpanā, *f.* explanation ; sharpening.

Uddeka, udreka, *m.* a belch ; spouting out.

Uddesa, *m.* indication ; propounding ; recitation.—**ka,** *a.* one who points out or recites.—**sika,** *a.* indicating ; referring to ; memorial. (In cpds. with **vassa**), of the age of.

Uddha, *a.* upper ; upward.—**agga,** *a.* with the tips turned upwards ; prominent; beneficial —**aggika,** *a.* promoting spiritual welfare.

Uddhacca, *nt.* distraction; flurry; haughtiness.

Uddhaṭa, *pp.* of **uddharati.**

Uddhata, *pp.* agitated; haughty.

Uddhana, *nt.* fire-place ; an oven.

Uddhapāda, *a.* having heels upwards.

Uddhamma, *m.* false doctrine.

Uddharaṇa, *nt.* lifting ; pulling out ; uprooting.

Uddharati (u + har + a), to raise ; to lift ; to pull out ; to remove ; to uproot. *aor.* **uddhari.**

Uddhaŋ, *ad.* high up ; above ; ahead ; hence.—**gama,** *a.* going upwards.—**bhāgiya,** *a.* belonging to the upper part.—**virecana,** *nt.* vomiting ; action of an emetic.—**sota,** *a.* going upwards in the stream of life.

Uddhaŋseti (u + dhaŋs + e), to destroy ; to bring ruin on. *aor.*—**esi.**

Uddhāra, *m.* withdrawal ; pulling out.

Uddhumāta,—taka, *a.* swollen; bloated.

Uddhumāyati (u + dhum + ya), to swell up ; to puff. *aor.*—**māyi,** *pp.*—**māyita.**

Udraya, uddaya, *a.* yielding; causing. (Only in cpds.)

Udrīyati, uddīyati (u + dar + ī + ya), to burst ; to fall into pieces. *aor.*—**yi.**

Udrīyana, *nt.* bursting ; falling down.

Undu(ū)ra, *m.* a rat.

Unnata (*pp.* of **unnamati**), raised ; high ; lofty.

Unnati, *f.* rising ; elevation ; increase.

Unnadati (u + nad + a), to shout ; to roar ; to resound. *aor.* —**nadi.** *pp.* **unnadita.**

Unnama, *m.* elevation.

Unnamati (u + nam + a), to rise up ; to prosper ; to bend upwards. *aor.*—**nami.**

Unnala,—ḷa, *a.* insolent ; arrogant ; proud.

Unnāda, *m.* a shout ; big noise.—**dī,** *a.* noisy ; tumultuous. (*f.*—**dinī**).

Unnādeti (*caus.* of **unnadati**), to make resound.

Upaka (= **upaga**), *a.* approaching; frequenting.

Upakaccha,—ka, *nt.* armpit.

Upakaṭṭha, *a.* near; approaching.

Upakaḍḍhati (upa + kaḍḍh + a), to drag or pull near. *aor.*—**ḍḍhi.** *pp.* —**ḍḍhita.**

Upakaṇṇaka, *nt.* a place where one is able to hear others' whisper.—**ke,** *a.* secretly.

Upakappati (upa + kapp + a), to approach; to be beneficial or suitable.

Upakappana, *nt.*—**nā,** *f.* approach; benefit.

Upakaraṇa, *nt.* instrument; outfit; utensils; requisites; help; support; provisions.

Upakaroti (upa + kar + o), to help; to support; to serve. *aor.*—**kari.**

Upakāra, *m.* help; support; favour.—**ka,** *a.* helping; effective; one who helps.

Upakārikā,—kāriṇī, *f.* benefactress.

Upakārī, *m.* helper; benefactor.

Upakūjati (upa + kūj + a), to sing or chirp. *aor.*—**kūji.**

Upakūjita (*pp.* of the above), resounding or filled with song of birds.

Upakūlita, *pp.* shrivelled; singed; roasted.

Upakkama, *m.* ways; means; expedient; approach; attack.

Upakkamati (upa + kam + a), to strive; to undertake; to begin; to attack. *aor.*—**kami.**

Upakkamana, *nt.* attacking; approach.

Upakkītaka, *m.* a bought slave.

Upakkiliṭṭha, *a.* soiled; impure; stained.

Upakkilesa, *m.* impurity; defilement; anything that spoils or obstructs.

Upakkuṭṭha, *pp.* of **upakkosati.**

Upakkosa, *m.* reproach; censure.

Upakkosati (upa + kus + a), to reproach; to blame; to scold. *aor.*—**kosi.**

Upakkhaṭa, *a.* prepared; administered; brought near.

Upakkhalana, *nt.* stumbling; tripping.

Upaga, *a.* (in cpds.) going to; reaching; coming into; being at; producing.

Upagacchati (upa + gam + a), to approach; to undergo; to undertake. *aor.*—**chi.**

Upagata, *pp.* of the above.

Upagamana, *nt.* approaching; undergoing; undertaking.

Upagūhati (upa + gūh + a), to embrace. *aor.*—**gūhi.** *pp.* **upagūhita.**

Upagghāta, *m.* jolting; sudden jerk.

Upaghāta, *m.*—**tana,** *nt.* knocking against; hurt; injury; killing.

Upaghātaka,—ghātī, *a.* injuring; cutting short; destroying; one who hurts or destroys.

Upacaya, *m.* accumulation.

Upacarati (upa + car + a), to deal with; to be ready. *aor.* **upacari.**

Upacarita (*pp.* of the above), practised; served.

Upacāra, *m.* neighbourhood; preparative or preliminary action.

Upacikā, *f.* termite; white ant.

Upaciṇṇa (*pp.* of **upacināti**), practised; frequented; accumulated.

Upacita, *pp.* of the following.

Upacināti (upa + ci + nā), to collect; to accumulate; to build. *aor.* **upacini.**

Upaccagā (upa + ati + gam + a; 3rd *sing. pret.*) he escaped, passed or overcame.

Upacchindati (upa + chid + ŋ -a), to break off; to interrupt; to destroy. *aor.*—**chindi.**

Upacchinna, *pp.* of the above.

Upaccheda, *m.* stoppage; destruction; breaking off.—**daka,** *a.* destroying; stopping.

Upajīvati (upa + jīv + a), to live on; to depend on. *aor.* —**jīvi.**

Upajīvī, *a.* living on; subsisting by; one who is dependant.

Upajjha, upajjhāya, *m.* spiritual teacher or preceptor.

Upaññāta (*pp.* of **upajānāti**), found out; learnt; known.

Upaṭṭhapeti (upa + ṭhā + e), to provide; to procure; to put forth; to cause to be present or to wait on. *aor.*—**esi.**

Upaṭṭhahati, Upaṭṭhāti (upa + ṭhā + a), to wait or attend on; to care for; to nurse; to serve; to understand. *aor.*—**ṭhahi.**—**ṭhāsi.**

Upaṭṭhahitvā, upaṭṭhitvā, upaṭṭhiya, *abs.* (of the above), having attended on.

Upaṭṭhāka, *m.* a servitor; a nurse; a follower.

Upaṭṭhāna, *nt.* waiting on; looking after; service; understanding.—**sālā,** *f.* a hall for attendance; assembly hall.

Upaṭṭhita (*pp.* of **upaṭṭhāti**), got ready; arrived; present; served by.

Upaḍayhati (upa + dah + ya), to be burnt up. *aor.*—**yhi.**

Upaḍḍha, *a.* half. *nt.* a half.

Upatappati (upa + tap + a), to be vexed or tormented. *aor.*—**ppi.**

Upatāpa, *m.* —**pana,** *nt.* vexation; trouble; remorse.

Upatāpaka, *a.* causing pain or remorse.

Upatāpeti (upa + tap + e), to cause pain; to torment; to harass. *aor.*—**esi.** *pp.*—**tāpita.**

Upatiṭṭhati (upa + ṭhā + a), to stand by; to look after. *aor.* **upaṭṭhāsi.**

Upatthaddha, *a.* stiff; supported by.

Upatthambha, *m.*—**bhana,** *nt.* support; encouragement; a prop.—**bhaka,** *a.* supporting; sustaining.

Upatthambheti (upa + thamb + e), to make firm; to support; to prop up; to sustain. *aor.*—**esi.** *pp.*—**bhita.**

Upatthara, *m.* a carpet; rug; covering.

Upadasseti (upa + dis + e), to make manifest; to show. *aor.* —**esi.** *pp.*—**dassita.**

Upadahati (upa + dah + a), to furnish; to give; to cause. *aor.* —**dahi.**

Upadiṭṭha (*pp.* of the following.) pointed out; put forth; specified.

Upadisati (upa + dis + a), to point out; to advise; to show. *aor.* **upadisi.**

Upadissati (*pass.* of the above), to appear; to be shown up.

Uapdesa, *m.* advice; indication; instruction.

Upaddava, *m.* misfortune; distress; danger.

Upaddaveti (upa + dav + e), to annoy; to trouble. *aor.*—**esi.**

Upadduta, *pp.* of the above.

Upadhāna, *nt.* a pillow. *adj.* causing; imposing.

Upadhāraṇa, *nt.* a receptacle; milk-pail.—**ṇā,** *f.* calculation; consideration.

Upadhārita, *pp.* of the following.

Upadhāreti (upa + dhar + e), to surmise; to look out for; to consider or conclude. *aor.*—**esi.**

Upadhāvati (upa + dhāv + a), to run up to or after. *aor.*—**dhāvi.**

Upadhi, *m.* substratum of rebirth; attachment.—**ka,** *a.* showing attachment to rebirth.

Upanata, *pp.* of **upanamati.**

Upanaddha, *pp.* of the following.

Upanandhati (upa + nah + ya) to bear enmity towards; to grumble at. *aor.*—**ndhi.**

Upanamati (upa + nam + a), to be bent on; to come near; to be present. *aor.*—**nami.**

Upanayana, *nt.* bringing near; the ceremony of subsumption.

Upanayhati (upa + nah + ya), to bear enmity towards; to wrap with. *aor.*—**yhi.**

Upanayahanā, *f.* ill-will; enmity; wrapping over.

Upanāmita, *pp.* of the following.

Upanāmeti (upa + nam + e), to bring near; to offer. *aor.*—**esi.**

Upanāyika, *a.* approaching; conveying.

Upanāha, *m.* ill-will; enmity.—**nāhī,** *a.* one who bears ill-will; finding fault.

Upanikkhitta, (*pp.* of the following), placed by; laid down.

Upanikkhipati (upa + ni + khip + a), to deposit near; to lay up. *aor.*—**khipi.**

Upanikkhipana, *nt.*—**khepa,** *m.* putting down; depositing near.

Upanighaŋsati (upa + ni + ghaŋs + a), to rub up against; to crush. *aor.*—**aŋsi.**

Upanijjhāna, *nt.* consideration; reflection.

Upanijjhāyati (upa + ni + jhā + ya), to meditate upon; to reflect on. *aor.*—**jhāyi.**

Upanidhā, *f.* **upanidhi,** *m.* comparison; pledge.

Upanidhāya, *in.* compared with.

Upanipajjati (upa + ni + pad + ya), to lie down close to. *aor.*—**pajji.** *pp.*—**panna.**

Upanibandha, *m.* close connection; *adj.* dependent on; connected with.

Upanibaddha, *pp.* of the following.

Upanibandhati (upa + ni + badh + ŋ - a), to tie close to; to entreat. *aor.*—**ndhi.**

Upanibandhana, *nt.* close connection; importunity.

Upanisā, *f.* cause; means; likeness.

Upanisīdati (upa + ni + sad + a), to sit close to. *aor.*—**sīdi.** *pp.*—**nisinna.**

Upanissaya, *m.* basis; support; sufficing condition.

Upanissāya, *abs.* depending on; by means of. *ad.* near; close by.

Upanissita (*pp.* of the following), dependent; connected with.

Upanissayati (upa + ni + si + a), to associate closely; to depend on. *aor.*—**sayi.**

Upanīta (*pp.* of **upaneti**), brought for trial; brought up to or into; offered.

Upanīya, *abs.* (of **upaneti**), having brought near; accusing.

Upanīyati (*pass.* of the following), to be brought up to; to be carried away.

Upaneti (upa + nī + e), to bring up to; conduce; to present; to give. *aor.*—**esi.**

Upantika, *a.* near. *nt.* neighbourhood.

Upapajjati (upa + pad + ya), to be reborn in ; to rise. *aor.*—**jji.**

Upapatti, *f.* birth ; rebirth ; approach.

Upapanna (*pp.* of **upapajjati**), possessed of ; come to existence in ; reborn.

Upaparikkhana, *nt.*—**kkhā,** *f.* investigation ; examination.

Upaparikkhati (upa + pari + ikkh + a), to investigate ; to examine. *aor.*—**kkhi.**

Upapāramī, *f.* minor perfection.

Upapīḷaka, *a.* oppressing ; obstructing.

Upapīḷā, *f.* oppression ; obstruction.

Upapīḷeti, see **Pīḷeti.**

Upabbūḷha, *a.* crowded ; in full swing.

Upabrūhana, *nt.* increase ; augmentation.

Upabrūheti (upa + brūh + e), to increase ; to expand. *aor.*—**esi.** *pp.*—**hita.**

Upabhuñjaka, *a.* one who eats, enjoys or undergoes.

Upabhoga, *m.* enjoyment ; profit ; use. *adj.* enjoyable.

Upabhogī, *a.* see **upabhuñjaka.**

Upama, *a.* (in cpds.) like ; similar; having the qualities of.

Upamā, *f.* **upamāna,** *nt.* simile ; parable ; comparison.

Upamita, *pp.* of the following.

Upameti (upa + mā + e), to compare. *aor.*—**esi.**

Upameyya, *a.* that which is to be compared or likened.

Upaya, *m.* attachment.

Upayācati (upa + yāc + a), to beg ; to entreat. *aor.*—**yāci.**

Upayāti (upa + yā + a), to approach.

Upayuñjati (upa + yuj + ŋ - a) to connect with ; to practise. *aor.*—**ñji.** *pp.* **upayutta.**

Upayoga, *m.* connection ; employment ; application.

Uparajja, *nt.* viceroyalty.

Uparata (*pp.* of **uparamati**), desisting or abstaining from ; ceased.

Uparati, *f.* ceasing ; restraint.

Uparamati (upa + ram + a), to desist ; to cease ; to restrain from. *aor.*—**rami.**

Uparāja, *m.* viceroy.

Upari, *in.* above ; on ; upon ; upper.—**ṭṭha,** *a.* topmost ; situated above.—**pāsāda,** *m.* the upper storey of a palace.—**bhāga,** *m.* upper portion.—**mukha,** *a.* face upwards.

Uparima, *a.* upper-most.

Uparujjhati (upa + rudh + ya), to be stopped or ceased. *aor.*—**rujjhi.** *pp.*—**ruddha.**

Uparundhati (upa + rudh + ŋ - a), to keep in check ; to stop or hinder. *aor.*—**dhi.**

Upala, *m.* stone.

Upalakkhaṇā, *f.* discrimination.

Upalakkhita, *pp.* of the following.

Upalakketi (upa + lakkh + e), to distinguish ; to discriminate. *aor.*—**esi.**

Upaladdha (*pp.* of **upalabhati**), acquired ; found.

Upaladdhi, *f.* acquisition ; view.

Upalabbhati (pass. of the following), to be found ; to exist.

Upalabhati (upa + labh + a), to acquire ; to get ; to find. *aor.*—**labhi.**

Upalāpana, nt. persuation ; humbug.

Upalāpeti (upa + lap + e), to persuade ; to coax. *aor.*—**esi.** *pp.*—**piṭa.**

Upalāleti (upa + lal + e), to caress ; to fondle. *aor.*—**esi.**

Upalitta, *pp.* of the following.

Upalimpati (upa + lip + ŋ - a), to smear ; to defile ; to taint. *aor.*—**limpi.**

Upalepa, *m.* coating ; defilement ; smearing.

Upavajja, *a.* blameworthy.

Upavattana, *a.* existing near.

Upavadati (upa + vad + a), to blame ; to insult. *aor.*—**vadi.**

Upavana, *nt.* a forest which is near by.

Upavasati (upa + vas + a), to dwell in or at ; to observe. *aor.* —**vasi.** *pp.* **upavuttha.**

Upavāda, *m.* blame ; insult.—**daka,** *a.* finding fault ; blaming.

Upavādī, *a.* one who blames or finds fault.

Upavāyati (upa + vā + a), to blow towards. *aor.*—**vāyi.**

Upavāsa, *m.* fasting ; abstaining from enjoyments.

Upavāsana, *nt.* perfuming.—

Upavāseti (upa + vas + e), to perfume. *aor.*—**esi.**

Upavisati (upa + vis + a), to come near ; to sit down. *aor.*—**upavisi.** *pp.* **upaviṭṭha.**

Upavīṇa, *m.* the neck of a lute.

Upavīta, *pp.* of the following.

Upavīyati (upa + vā + ī + ya), to be woven. *aor.*—**vīyi.**

Upavutta (*pp.* of **upavadati**), being blamed.

Upavuttha (*pp.* of **upavasati**), dwelt ; having kept a fast.

Upasaŋharaṇa, *nt.* **saŋhāra,** *m.* gathering ; folding ; comparison.

Upasaŋharati (upa + saŋ + har + a), to collect ; to focus ; to concentrate ; to compare. *aor.*—**hari.** *pp.*—**haṭa.**

Upasaṅkamati (upa + saŋ + + kam + a), to approach. *aor.* —**kami** *pp.*—**kanta.**

Upasaṅkamana, *nt.* approach ; going near.

Upasaṅkamma,—kamitvā, *abs.* having approached.

Upasagga, *m.* danger ; a prefix.

Upasanta (*pp.* of **upasammati**), being calmed, composed or at peace.

Upasama, *m.* calm ; appeasement.

Upasameti (upa + sam + e), to appease ; to calm. *aor.*—**esi.** *pp.* **upasamita.**

Upasampajja, *abs.* of the following.

Upasampajjati (upa + saŋ + pad + ya), to attain ; to enter on ; to become fully ordained. *aor.*—**pajji.**

Upasamapadā, *f.* acquisition ; higher ordination of a Buddhist monk.

Upasampanna, *pp.* possessed with ; attained ; ordained.

Upasampādeti, (*caus.* of—**pajjati**), to produce ; to ordain as a **bhikkhu.** *aor.*—**esi.** *pp.* —**pādita.**

Upasammati (upa + sam + ya), to be calmed ; to cease ; to appease.

Upasiṅghati (upa + siṅgh + a), to sniff at. *aor.*—**ghi.**

Upasussati (upa + sus + ya), to become dry. *aor.*—**sussi.**

Upasecana, *nt.* something sprinkled to relish food.

Upasevati (upa + sev + a), to practise ; to frequent ; to associate. *aor.*—**sevi.**

Upasevanā, *f.* practice ; frequency ; association.

Upasevita, *pp.* of **upasevati.**

Upasevī, *a.* one who associates, uses or practises.

Upasobhati (upa + subh + a), to appear beautiful. *aor.*—**sobhi.**

Upasobhita, (*pp.* of the above), embellished ; beautified ; possessed with.

Upasobheti (*caus.* of—**bhati**), to make beautiful. *aor.*—**esi.**

Upasoseti (upa + sus + e), to make dry or wither. *aor.*—**esi.** *pp.*—**sosita.**

Upassaṭṭha, *pp.* oppressed ; afflicted.

Upassaya, *m.* abode ; home.

Upassuti, *f.* listening to private conversation of others.—**tika**, 3. an eaves-dropper.

Upahacca, *abs.* (of **upahanati**), having touched, injured, or spoiled.

Upahaññati (*pass.* of **upahanati**), to be spoilt or injured. *aor.*—**haññi.**

Upahata, *pp.* of **upahanati.**

Upahattu, *m.* one who brings or conveys.

Upahanati (upa + han + a), to injure ; to destroy. *aor.*—**hani.**

Upahāra, *m.* a gift ; bringing forward.

Upāgata (*pp.* of **upāgacchati**), reached or attained.

Upādāna, *nt.* grasping ; attachment ; fuel.—**kkhandha**, *m.* the factors of clinging to existence.—**kkhaya**, *m.* extinction of attachment.

Upādāniya, *a.* connected with grasping.

Upādāya, *abs.* (of **upādāti**). having grasped ; compared with ; with reference to.

Upādi, *m.* fuel of life.—**sesa**, *a.* having some fuel of life left ; still dependent on existence.

Upādinna, *pp.* of the following.

Upādiyati (upa + ā + dā + i + ya), to grasp. *aor.*—**diyi.**

Upādhi, *m.* a title.

Upāya, *m.* way ; means ; resource. —**kusala**, *a.* clever in resources. —**kosalla**, *nt.* cleverness in expedient.

Upāyana, *nt.* a tribute ; gift.

Upāyāsa, *m.* tribulation ; grief.

Upārambha, *m.* reproof ; censure.

Upāvisi (*aor.* of **upavisati**), (he) took a seat.

Upāsaka, *m.* a lay devotee ; one who comes near.

Upāsati (upa + ās + a), to attend or serve. *pp.* **upāsita.**

Upāsana, *nt.* service ; attendance ; archery ; training (of some art).

Upāsikā, *f.* a female devotee.

Upāhana, *nt.* sandal ; shoe.

Upekkhaka, *a.* indifferent ; disinterested.

Upekkhati (upa + ikkh + a), to be indifferent. *aor.*—**kkhi.**

Upekkhanā, upekkhā, upekhā, *f.* neutrality ; equanimity ; indifference.

Upekkhiya,—khitvā, *abs.* being neutral or indifferent.

Upeta (*pp.* of the following), endowed with.

Upeti (upa + i + a), to approach ; to obtain. *aor.*—**upesi.**

Upetvā, upecca, *abs.* (of the above), having approached.

Uposatha, *m.* Sabbath day ; observance of 8 precepts ; biweekly recitation of the Vinaya rules by a chapter of Bud. monks.—**kamma**, *nt.* observance of the uposatha—**āgāra**, *nt.* a chapter house.

Uposathika, *a.* one who observes 8 precepts.

Uppakka, *a.* swollen ; scorched.

Uppajjati (u + pad + ya), to be born ; to arise. *aor.* **uppajji.**

Uppajjana, *nt.* arising ; birth ; —**naka,** *a.* being born; coming into existence.

Uppajjamāna, *pr. p.* see **uppajjanaka.**

Uppajjitabba, *pt. p.* fit to be born or arisen.

Uppaṭipāṭi, *f.* want of order ; irregularity.—**ṭiyā,** *ad.* against the order.

Uppaṇḍanā, *f.* ridicule ; mockery.

Uppaṇḍukajāta, *a.* having become pale.

Uppaṇḍeti (u + paṇḍ + e), to mock ; to deride. *aor.*—**esi.** *pp.* **uppaṇḍita.**

Uppatati (u + pat + a), to fly ; to jump up. *aor.* **uppati.**

Uppatana, *nt.* flying ; rising up ; jumping.

Uppatamāna, *pr. p.* flying ; jumping.

Uppatita, *pp.* of **uppatati.**

Uppatitvā, *abs.* having flown or jumped.

Uppatti, *f.* rebirth ; coming forth; origin.

Uppatha, *m.* wrong path or course.

Uppanna (*pp.* of **uppajjati**), reborn ; arisen.

Uppabbajati (u + pa + vaj + a), to leave the Order. *aor.* —**baji.** *abs.*—**jitvā.**

Uppabbajita, (*pp.* of the above), one who has left the community.

Uppabbājeti (*caus.* of the above), to turn out of the Order. *aor.* —**esi.** *pp.*—**bājita.** *abs.*—**bājetvā.**

Uppala, *nt.* waterlily.

Uppalinī, *f.* a pond or lake full of waterlilies.

Uppāṭana, *nt.* pulling or tearing out ; skinning ; uprooting.—**naka,** *a.* doing the work of uprooting or skinning.

Uppāṭita, *pp.* of the following.

Uppāṭeti (u + paṭ + e), to tear asunder ; to root out ; to skin. *abs.* **uppāṭetvā.**

Uppāta, *m.* flying up ; a meteor ; an unusual event.

Uppāda, *m.* rising ; coming into existence ; birth.—**daka,** *a.* producing ; generating ; producer.

Uppādana, *nt.* production ; raising ; generation.

Uppādeti (u + pad + e), to produce ; to make ; to give rise to. *aor.*—**esi.** *pp.* **uppādita.** *abs.*—**detvā.**

Uppādetu, *m.* producer ; generator.

Uppādetuṃ, *inf.* to produce or generate.

Uppīḷana, *nt.* pressing ; oppression.

Uppīḷita, *pp.* of the following.

Uppīḷeti (u + pīḷ + e), to press down ; to crush ; to oppress. *aor.*—**esi.** *abs.*—**ḷetvā.**

Uppoṭheti (u + poṭh + e), to beat ; to dust. *aor.*—**esi.** *pp.* —**ṭhita.**

Uplavana, *nt.* floating ; rising into the surface.

Uplavati (u + plav + a), to float ; to rise into the surface. *aor.* **uplavi.**

Ubbaṭṭana, *nt.* rubbing of one's body (while bathing) ; shampooing.

Ubbaṭṭita, *pp.* of the following

Ubbaṭṭeti (u + vaṭṭ + e), to rub ; to shampoo. *aor.*—**esi.**

Ubbatteti (u + vat + e), to tear out ; to cause to rise or swell ; to turn from a right course. *aor.*—**esi.** *pp.*—**ttita.**

Ubbandhati (u + bandh + a), to hang up ; to strangle. *aor.* **ubbandhi.**

Ubbandhana, *nt.* strangling ; hanging oneself up.

Ubbahati (u + vah + a), to pull out ; to take away ; to lift. *aor.* **ubbahi.**

Ubbahana, *nt.* lifting ; bearing ; pulling out.

Ubbāḷha, *pp.* troubled ; annoyed; harassed.

Ubbigga, *pp.* of the following.

Ubbijjati (u + vij + a), to be agitated ; to be frightened. *aor.* **ubbijji.**

Ubbijjanā *f.* agitation ; uneasiness.

Ubbega, *m.* excitement ; fright.

Ubbejeti (*caus.* of **ubbijjati**), to set into agitation ; to terrify. *aor.*—**esi.** *pp.* **ubbejita.**

Ubbedha, *m.* height.

Ubbhaṭṭhaka, *a.* standing upright.

Ubbhata, *pp.* withdrawn ; pulled out.

Ubbhava, *m.* origination ; production.

Ubbhāra, *m.* withdrawal ; removal.

Ubbhijja, (*abs.* of the following). having sprung or burst upwards.

Ubbhijjati (u + bhid + ya), to spring up ; to sprout. *aor.*—**jji.** *pp.* **ubbhinna.**

Ubbhida, *nt.* kitchen salt ; *m.* a spring. *adj.* bursting forth ; sprouting.

Ubbhujati (u + bhuj + a), to lift up ; to raise one's under garment up. *aor.*—**bhuji.**

Ubha, Ubhaya, *pron.* both.

Ubhato, *in.* in both ways or sides ; twofold.

Ubho, both. (This is an old remnant of the dual form in Pali).

Ummagga, *m.* a tunnel ; devious or wrong way.

Ummatta, *a.* mad ; out of one's mind.—**ka,** 3. one who is mad.

Ummā, *f.* linseed ; flax.

Ummāda, *m.* madness.—**dana,** *a.* that which is maddening.

Ummāra, *m.* threshold.

Ummi, *f.* wave.

Ummisati (u + mis + a), to open one's eyes. *aor.*—**misi.**

Ummihati (u + mih + a), to urinate. *aor.* **ummihi.**

Ummīlana, *nt.* opening of one's eyes.

Ummīleti (u + mil + e), to open one's eyes. *aor.*—**esi.**

Ummuka, *nt.* firebrand.

Ummukka, *pp.* fallen down.

Ummukha, *a.* having one's face upwards ; heedless.

Ummujjati (u + mujj + a), to emerge ; to rise out of water. *aor.* **ummujji.**

Ummujjana, emergence.—**jjanimujjā,** *f.* emerging and diving.—**jamāna,** *pr. p.* emerging from.

Ummūla, *a.* **Ummūlita,** *pp.* uprooted.—**lana,** *nt.* uprooting.

Ummūleti (u + mūla + e), to uproot ; to destroy. *aor.*—**esi.**

Uyyāna, *nt.* a park ; pleasure grove.—**kīḷā,** *f.* amusement in a park.—**pāla,** *m.* keeper of a park ; gardener.—**bhūmi,** *f.* pleasure ground.

Uyyāma, *m.* exertion ; effort.

Uyyuñjati (u + yuj + ŋ - a), to strive ; to be busy. *aor.*—**ñji.**

Uyyuñjana, *nt.* activity.—**janta,** *pr. p.* active ; busy.

Uyyutta (*pp.* of **uyyuñjati**), energetic ; parading.

Uyyoga, *m.* see **Uyyāma.**

Uyyojana, *nt.* instigation ; sending away.

Uyyojita, *pp.* of the following.

Uyyojeti (u + yuj + e), to instigate ; to dismiss ; to send off. *aor.*—**esi.**

Uyyodhika, *nt.* sham fight (of an army).

Ura, *m. nt.* the breast; chest.—**cakka,** *nt.* an iron wheel (put on the chest, as an instrument) of torture.—**cchada,** *m.* breastplate.—**ttāḷiŋ,** *ad.* beating one's own breast.

Uraga, *m.* a snake ; a creeping animal.

Urabbha, *m.* a ram.

Uru, *a.* large ; wide ; eminent.

Ulūka, *m.* an owl.—**pakkhika,** *a.* having a dress made of owl's feathers.

Ullaṅghana, *nt.*—**nā,** *f.* jumping over ; transgression.

Ullaṅgheti (u + lagh + e), to jump over ; to transgress. *aor.* —**esi.** *pp.* **ullaṅghita.**

Ullaṅghiya,—**ghetvā,** *abs.* of the above.

Ullapati (u + lap + a), to extol ; to speak in laudatory terms. *aor.* **ullapi.**

Ullapanā, *f.* enticement ; extolling.

Ullikhati (u + likh + a), to comb ; to scratch. *aor.* **ullikhi.** *pp.* **ullikhita.**

Ullikhana, *nt.* combing ; scratching.

Ullitta (*pp.* of **ullimpeti**), plastered ; covered with some kind of mortar.

Ullumpati (u + lup + ŋ - a), to raise up ; to help. *aor.*—**lumpi.**

Ullumpana, *nt.* raising up ; saving.

Ullokaka, *a.* looking at ; a spectator.

Ullokana, *nt.* looking up ; a window.

Ulloketi (u + lok + e), to look up or for. *aor.*—**esi.**

Ullola, *m.* commotion ; a big wave.

Ulloleti (u + lul + e), to agitate ; to make a commotion. *aor.*—**esi.** *pp.* **ullolita.**

Usabha, *m.* a leading bull ; a noble person ; the length of 140 cubits.

Usīra, *nt.* fragrant root of *Andropogon Muricantum.* සෑවැන්න.

Usu, *m.f.* an arrow.—**kāra,** *m.* arrow-maker ; fletcher.

Usūyaka, *a.* one who envies; jealous.

Usūyati (usūy + a), to be jealous ; to envy. *aor.* **usūyi.**

Usūyanā, usūyā, *f.* envy; jealousy.

Usmā, *m.* heat.

Ussaṅkī, *a.* distrustful ; full of fear.

Ussada, Ussanna, *a.* abundant ; excessive ; full of.

Ussannatā, *f.* abundance ; fullness.

Ussava, *m.* feast ; festival ; ceremony.

Ussahati (u + sah + a), to try; to strive ; to endeavour. *aor.* —**sahi.**

Ussahana, *nt.* striving ; effort.

Ussāpana, *nt.* lifting up ; raising.

Ussāpita, *pp.* of the following.

Ussāpeti (u + si + āpe), to lift up ; to hoist ; to raise. *aor.* —**esi.** *abs.* **ussāpetvā.**

Ussāraṇā, *f.* tumult ; rushing of a crowd.

Ussārita, *pp.* of the following.

Ussāreti (u + sar + e), to push aside. *aor.*—**esi.**

Ussāva, *m.* dew.—**bindu**, *nt.* a dew-drop.

Ussāha, *m.* endeavour ; effort.—**vantu**, *a.* energetic ; active.

Ussāhita, *pp.* of the following.

Ussāheti (*caus.* of **ussahati**), to encourage ; to incite. *aor.*—**esi.** *abs.* **ussāhetvā.**

Ussiñcati (u + sic + ŋ - a), to lave ; to bale ; to raise water. *aor.*—**ñci.**

Ussiñcana, *nt.* baling ; raising of water.

Ussita, *pp.* hoisted ; raised.

Ussīsaka, *nt.* the side where the head is laid ; a pillow.

Ussuka, *a.* zealous ; energetic.

Ussukka, *nt.* zeal ; energy.

Ussukkati (u + suk + a), to endeavour ; to try. *aor.*—**kki.**

Ussukkāpeti (*caus.* of the above), to entice ; to arouse. *aor.*—**esi.**

Ussussati (u + sus + ya), to dry up ; to evaporate. *aor.* **ussussi.**

Ussūra, *nt.* sunrise. (**ussūre**, when the sun is up).—**seyyā**, *f.* sleep after sunrise.

Ussoḷhi, *f.* exertion.

Uḷāra, *a.* lofty ; noble ; eminent. —**tā**, *f.*—**tta**, *nt.* greatness ; eminence.

Uḷu, *m.* star ; constellation.—**rāja**, *m.* the moon.

Uḷuṅka, *m.* a ladle.

Uḷumpa, *m.* a raft ; a float.

Ū

Ūkā, *f.* a louse.

Ūna, *a.* less ; minus ; wanting ; deficient.—**ka**, *a.* same as **ūna.**

Ūnatta, *nt.* **Ūnatā**, *f.* deficiency.

Ūmi, *f.* a wave.

Ūraṭṭhi, *nt.* the thigh-bone.

Ūru, *m.* the thigh.—**pabba**, *nt.* joint of the knee.

Ūsa, *m.* saline substance.

Ūsara, *a.* saline.

Ūhacca, (*abs.* of **ūhanati**), having pulled out or removed.

Ūhadati (u + had + a), to discharge ; to defecate. *aor.* **ūhadi.**

Ūhana, *nt.* consideration ; accumulation.

Ūhanati (u + han + a), to pull out ; to remove. *aor.* **ūhani.**

Ūhā, *f.* pondering ; consideration.

E

Eka, *a.* same ; certain ; unknown. (Used for the indefinite article). One, (only in the sing.) In plural it gives the meaning " some ".—**cara**, *a.*—**cāri**, *a.* one who lives alone.—**desa**, *m.* a portion ; a part.—**paṭṭa**, *a.* having a single lining.—**bhattika**, *a.* having one meal a day—**vāraŋ**, *ad.* once.

Ekaka, *a.* single ; solitary.

Ekakkhī, *a.* possessing only one eye.

Ekagga, *a.* calm ; tranquil.—**gatā**, *f.* tranquillity of mind ; onepointedness.

Ekacca, **ekacciya**, *a.* some ; certain ; a few.

Ekajjhaŋ, *ad.* together ; in the same place.

Ekato, *in.* together ; on one side.

Ekatta, *nt.* unity ; loneliness ; agreement.

Ekadā, *ad.* once ; at one time.

Ekanta, *a.* sure ; unfailing ; extreme. **Ekantaŋ**, *ad.*—**tena**, *ad.* surely ; certainly.

Ekantarika, *a.* alternate ; having one in between.

Ekapaṭalika, *a.* having a single skin for lining.

Ekapadika-magga, *m.* a foot-path.

Ekamantaŋ, *ad.* on one side ; aside.

Ekameka, **Ekeka**, *a.* one by one ; each.

Ekavidha, *a.* of one kind ; similar.

Ekaso, *ad.* singly ; one by one.

Ekaŋsa ; **Ekaŋsika**, *a.* definite ; sure ; pertaining to one shoulder.

Ekākī, 3. a lonely person. *f.* **ekākinī**.

Ekāyana, *m.* the only way or means.

Ekāsanika, 3. one who eats only once a day.

Ekāha, *nt.* one day.—**hika**, *a.* existing for a day.

Ekikā, *f.* a solitary woman.

Ekībhāva, *m.* unity ; solitude ; loneliness.

Ekībhūta, *a.* united ; connected; gathered together.

Ekūna, *a.* minus one.—**cattāḷīsati**, *f.* thirty-nine.—**tiŋsati**, *f.* twenty-nine.—**paññāsā**, *f.* forty-nine.—**vīsati**, *f.* nineteen.—**saṭṭhi**, *f.* fifty-nine.—**sattati**, *f.* sixty-nine.—**navuti**, *f.* eighty-nine.—**sata**, *nt.* ninety-nine.—**nāsīti**, *f.* seventy-nine.

Ekodibhāva, *m.* onepointedness ; concentration.

Ejā, *f.* craving ; motion.

Eṭṭhi, *f.* search ; seeking.

Eṇimiga, **Eṇeyya**, *m.* a kind of antelope.

Eṇeyyaka, *nt.* a kind of torture.

Eta (demons. pron.) that ; this. *mas. sing.* **eso**. *fem. sing.* **esā**.

Etarahi, *ad.* now ; at present.

Etādisa, *a.* such like ; of this kind.

Eti (i + a), to come.

Ettaka, *a.* this much ; so much.

Ettāvatā, *ad.* so far ; to that extent ; by this much.

Etto, *in.* from this ; here ; out of here.

Ettha, *ad.* here.

Edisa, **edisaka**, *a.* such ; such like.

Edha, *m.* fuel ; firewood.

Edhati (edh + a), to gain ; to succeed in. *aor.* **edhi**.

Ena, **eta** takes this form in some cases.

Enta, *pr. p.* (of **eti**), coming.

Eraka, *m.* a kind of grass used for making coverlets.—**dussa**, *nt.* a garment made of eraka-grass or fibre.

Eraṇda, *m.* the plant *Palma Christi* from the seeds of which castor oil is extracted.

Erāvaṇa, *m.* name of Indra's elephant.

Erāvata, *m.* mandarin orange.

Erita, *pp.* of the following.

Ereti (īr + e), to shake ; to set into motion *aor.* **eresi**.

Elā, *f.* saliva ; the seed or plant of cardamom.

Eva, emphatic particle.

Evarūpa, *a.* such ; of such form.

Evaŋ, *ad.* thus ; in this way ; (in reply :) yes.—**vidha**, *a.* such like.

Esa (euphonic form of **eso**), that person.

Esati (es + a), to seek ; to search. *aor.* **esi**. *abs.* **esitvā**.

Esanā, *f.* seeking ; longing.

Esanta, Esamāna, *pr. p.* seeking after.

Esikā, *f.* **Esikātthambha,** *m.* a strong post before a city gate.

Esita, *pp.* of **esati.**

Esitabba, *pt. p.* to be sought after.

Esī, 3. seeker. *f.* **esinī.**

Ehipassika, *a.* that which invites everyman to come and see ; open to all.

Ehi-bhikkhu, (the oldest formula of admission to the Order), come O monk.

Eḷaka, *m.* a wild goat.

Eḷagala, *a.* with oozing saliva.

Eḷagalā, *f.* the plant *Cassia Tora.*.

Eḷā, *f* saliva.

Eḷāluka, *nt.* cucumber.

O

Oka, *nt.* water ; abode ; habitation.

Okappaniya, *a.* trustworthy.

Okāra, *m.* lowliness ; degradation.

Okāsa *m.* room ; open space ; chance ; permission.—**kamma,** *nt.* permission.

Okiṇṇa, (*pp.* of **okirati**), strewn over.

Okiraṇa, *nt.* scattering ; casting out.

Okirati (ava + kir + a), to scatter ; to pour down. *aor.* **okiri.** *pr. p.* **okiranta.**

Okkanta, *pp.* of **okkamati.**

Okkanti, *f.* entry ; coming to be ; appearance.

Okkantika, *a.* recurring.

Okkamati (ava + kam + a), to enter ; to fall into ; to come on. *aor.* **okkami.** *abs.* **okkamitvā**

Okkamana, *nt.* entry or falling into.

Okkamanta,—mamāna, *pr. p.* entering or falling into.

Okkhitta, *pp.* of the following.

Okkhipati (ava + khip + a), to throw or cast down ; to drop. *aor.* **okkhipi.**

Ogacchati (ava + gam + a), to go down ; to sink down. *aor.* —**chi.** *pp.* **ogata.**

Ogadha, *a.* included ; immersed.

Ogayha, ogāhiya, (*abs.* of **ogāhati**), having plunged or absorbed.

Ogāha, *m.* **Ogāhana,** *nt.* diving or plunging into.

Ogāhati (ava + gāh + a), to plunge or enter into ; to be absorbed in. *aor.* **ogāhi.**

Ogāhamāna, *pr. p.* diving or plunging into.

Ogāḷha, *pp.* of **ogāhati.**

Ogilati (ava + gil + a), to swallow down. *aor.* **ogili.**

Oguṇṭheti (ava + guṇṭh + e), to cover ; to veil over. *aor.* —**esi.** *pp.* **oguṇṭhita.**

Ogha, *m.* a flood ; that which sweeps a man away from emancipation.—**tiṇṇa,** *a.* one who has overcome the flood.

Ocaraka, 3. an investigator ; informant ; of low behaviour.

Ociṇṇa, Ocita, *pp.* of **ocināti.**

Ocinana, *nt.* gathering ; picking.

Ocinanta, *pr. p.* of the following.

Ocināti (ava + ci + nā), to gather, collect, or pluck. *aor.* **ocini.** *abs.* **ocinitvā.**

Oja, *m. nt.* **Ojā,** *f.* nutritive essence ; juice.—**vantu,** *a.* rich in sap ; nourishing ; delicious.

Oṭṭha, *m.* a camel ; the lip.

Otaraṇa, *nt.* descent ; coming down.

Otarati (ava + tar + a), to descend; to go down to. *aor.* **otari.** *pr. p.* **otaranta.** *abs.* **otaritvā.**

Otāpeti (ava + tap + e), to expose to the sun. *aor.* **esi.** *pp.* **otāpita.**

Otāra, *m.* descent; access; chance; fault.—**gavesī,** *a.* -seeking an opportunity.—**rāpekka,** *a.* watching for a chance.

Otāraṇa, *nt.* lowering down.

Otāreti (ava + tar + e), to bring or lower down. *aor.*—**esi.** *pp.* **otārita.**

Otiṇṇa, (*pp.* of **otarati**), gone down; beset by; affected with.

Ottappa, *nt.* shrinking back from doing wrong.

Ottappati (ava + tap + ya), to feel a sense of guilt; to be afraid of evil. *aor.* **ottappi.**

Ottappī, ottāpī. *a.* afraid of wrong; scrupulous.

Otthaṭa, *pp.* of **ottharati.**

Ottharaṇa, *nt.* spreading over; submergence.

Ottharati (ava + thar + a), to spread over; to submerge. *aor.* **otthari.** *pr. p.* **ottharamāna.** *abs.* **ottharitvā.**

Odakantika, *nt.* neighbourhood of water. *adj.* having water as the final ablution.

Odana, *nt. m.* boiled rice.

Odanika, *m.* a cook.

Odahati (ava + dah + a), to put down; to insert; to be attentive *aor.* **odahi.** *abs.* **odahitvā.**

Odahana, *nt.* putting down; insertion; listening.

Odāta, *a.* white; clean. *m.* white colour.—**kasiṇa,** *nt.* object of meditation which is white. —**vasana,** *a.* clad in white.

Odissa, *abs.* having defined or separated.

Odissaka, *a.* definite; special.

Odhi, *m.* limit; boundary.—**so,** *ad.* limitedly; piece-meal.

Odhunāti (ava + dhu + nā), to shake off. *aor.* **odhini.**

Odhūta, *pp.* of the above.

Onaddha, *pp.* of the following.

Onandhati (ava + nadh + ŋ -a) to bind; to cover up; to wrap over. *aor.* **onandhi.**

Onata, *pp.* of the following.

Onamati (ava + nam + a), to bend down; to stoop. *aor.* **onami.** *pr. p.* **onamanta.** *abs.* **onamitvā.**

Onayhati (ava + nah + ya), to envelop; to cover over; to tie down. *aor.* **onayhi.**

Onahana, *nt.* covering; shrouding.

Onīta, *pp.* taken away; removed.

Onojana, *nt.* distribution; presentation.

Onojeti (ava + nuj + e), to dedicate; to distribute. *aor.* —**esi.** *pp.* **onojita.**

Opakkamika, *a.* caused by some contrivance.

Opanayika, *a.* leading to; bringing near.

Opapātika,—pātī, *a.* arisen without visible cause; born spontaneously.

Opamma, *nt.* simile; comparison.

Oparajja, *nt.* viceroyalty.

Opavayha, *a.* fit for riding.

Opāta, *m.* a pitfall.

Opāteti (ava + pat + e), to make fall; to interrupt. *aor.* —**esi.** *pp.* **opātita.**

Opāna, *nt.* a well; place where water is supplied free.

Opiya, *abs.* having put in.

Opilāpita, *pp.* of the following.

Opilāp(v)eti (ava + plav + e), to immerse; to make float. *aor.*—**esi.**

Opuṇāti (ava + pu + ṇā), to winnow; to sift. *aor.*—**opuṇi.** *abs.* **opuṇitvā.**

Obhagga, *pp.* broken; dragged down.

Obhāsa, *m.* light; lustre.

Obhāsati (ava + bhās + a), to shine. *aor.* **obhāsi.**

Obhāsana, *nt.* shining.

Obhāsita, *pp.* of the following.

Obhāseti (*caus.* of **obhāsati**), to make radiant; to illumine. *aor.*—**esi.** *abs.* **obhāsetvā.**

Obhāsenta,—sayamāna, (*pr. p.* of the above), radiating; illuminating.

Oma, Omaka, *a.* lower; inferior.

Omaṭṭha, (*pp.* of **omasati**), touched; made unclean.

Omaddati (ava + madd + a), to crush; to rub; to oppress. *aor.* **omaddi.**

Omasati (ava + mas + a), to touch; to handle. *aor.* **omasi.**

Omasanā, *f.* **Omasavāda,** *m.* insult; reproach.

Omukka (*pp.* of the following), cast off; undressed.

Omuñcati (ava + muc + ŋ - a) to take off; to unfasten; to undress. *aor.* —**ñci.**

Omuñcitvā, (*abs.* of the above), having taken off some kind of dress.

Omutteti (ava + mutt + e), to discharge urine. *aor.*—**esi.**

Ora, *nt.* the near shore; this world. *adj.* inferior.—**pāra,** *nt.* the below and the above; the near and the farther shore. —**mattaka,** *a.* trifling; insignificant.—**mbhāgiya,** *a.* belonging to the lower world. **Oraŋ, orena,** *ad.* under; within; below; on this side.

Oraka, *a.* inferior; low.

Orabbhika, *m.* a dealer or butcher of sheep.

Orasa, *a.* legitimate; self-begotten.

Orima, *a.* the lowest; one on this side.—**tīra,** *nt.* the near shore.

Oruddha *pp.* of the following.

Orundhati (ava + rudhi + ŋ - a), to obstruct; to imprison. *aor.* **orundhi.**

Oruyha, *abs.* of the following.

Oruhati (ava + ruh + a), to descend; to come down. *aor.* **oruhi.** *pr. p.* **oruhanta.**

Oruhana, *nt.* descent.

Orūḷha (*pp.* of **oruhati**), descended; climbed down.

Orodha, *m.* harem; seraglio; a harem-lady.

Oropana, *nt.* taking down; lowering; laying down.

Oropita, *pp.* of the following.

Oropeti (ava + rup + e), to take or lower down; to lay aside. *aor.*—**esi.** *pr. p.* **oropenta,—payamāna.**

Oropetvā, Oropiya, (*abs.* of the above), having lowered or laid aside.

Orohana, see **oruhana.**

Orohati, see **oruhati.**

Olaggeti (ava + lag + e), to hang down; to make stick to. *aor.*—**esi.** *pp.* **olaggita.**

Olamba,—baka, *a.* hanging down, *nt.* a support; a plummet.

Olambati (ava + lab + ŋ - a), to hang down; to rest on; to suspend. *aor.* **olambi.** *pp.* **olambita.**

Olambana, *nt.* suspension.

Olambamāna, *pr. p.* suspending.

Olambiya,—bitvā, *abs.* having suspended or hung down.

Olikhati (ava + likh + a), to scrape off; to comb. *aor.* **olikhi.**

Olikhiya, olikhitvā, *abs.* having combed or scraped off.

Oligalla, *m.* a cesspool.

Olīna, (*pp.* of the following), sluggish; inactive.

Olīyati (ava + lī + ya), to be inactive or sluggish; to stick to. *aor.* **olīyi.**

Olīyanā, *f.* sluggishness; infatuation.

Olīyamāna, *pr. p.* lagging behind.

Olugga (*pp.* of **olujjati**), fallen into pieces; rotting away.

Olubbha, *abs.* leaning on; holding on to.

Olokana, *nt.* looking at.—**naka.** *nt.* a window.

Olokiya, oloketvā, *abs.* of the following.

Oloketi (ava + lok + e), to look at; to inspect. *aor.*—**esi.** *pp.* **olokita.**

Oloketuŋ, *inf.* to look at.

Olokenta,—kayamāna, *pr. p.* looking at.

Ovaṭṭikā,*f.* waist-band; a pouch (formed with the waist clothe).

Ovadati (ava + vad + a), to give advice; to admonish. *aor.* **ovadi.** *pp.* **ovadita.**

Ovadana, *nt.* admonishing.

Ovadanta, ovadamāna, *pr. p.* exhorting; admonishing.

Ovaditabba, *pt. p.* fit to be admonished.

Ovaditvā, ovadiya, *abs.* having exhorted or advised.

Ovaraka, *m.* an inner chamber.

Ovariya, ovariyāna, (*abs.* of **ovarati**), holding back; preventing.

Ovassati (ava + vass + a), to rain down on. *aor.* **ovassi.** *pp.* **ovaṭṭha.**

Ovassāpeti (*caus.* of the above), to make wet through rain. *aor.* **—esi.**

Ovāda, *m.* advice; exhortation; instruction.—**ka,—dāyaka,** *a.* one who admonishes or exhorts. —**kkhama,** *a.* easy to be admonished.

Osakkati (ava + sakk + a), to draw back; to lag behind; to retreat. *aor.* **osakki.**

Osakkanā, *f.* drawing back; lagging.

Osakkita, *pp.* of **osakkati.**

Osakkitvā, osakkiya, *abs.* having retreated or moved aside.

Osaṭa, *pp.* of **osarati.**

Osadha, *nt.* medicine.

Osadhī, *f.* medicinal plant; name of a brilliant star.

Osaraṇa, *nt.* entry; meeting.

Osarati (ava + sar + a), to come into; to re-enter; to assemble. *aor.* **osari.**

Osāna, *nt.* the end; conclusion; ceasing.

Osāraṇā, *f.* reinstatement; crowding.

Osāreti (ava + sar + e), to reinstate; to expound. *aor.* **—esi.** *pp.* **osārita.** *abs.* **osāretvā.**

Osiñcati (ava + sic + ŋ - a), to pour down; to besprinkle. *aor.* **—ñci.** *pr. p.* **osiñcanta.**

Osñciya,—citvā, *abs.* having poured down or sprinkled.

Ositta, *pp.* of **osiñcati.**

Osīdati (ava + sid + a), to sink. *aor.* **osīdi.** *pr. p.* **osīdamāna.**

Osīdana, *nt.* sinking.

Osīdāpana, *nt.* causing to sink; immersion.

Osīdāpeti (*caus.* of **osīdati**), to immerse; to cause to sink. *aor.*—**esi**. *pp.*—**pita**. *abs.* **osīdāpetvā**.

Ossajati (ava + saj + a), to let loose; to give up; to release. *aor.* **ossaji**.

Ossajana, *nt.* release; sending off.

Ossajja,—**jjitvā**, *abs.* having given up or released.

Ossaṭṭha, *pp.* of **ossajati**.

Oharati (ava + har + a), to take off or down. *aor.* **ohari**. *pp.* **ohaṭa**.

Ohāya, (*abs.* of **ojahāti**), having left or given up.

Ohāraṇa, *nt.* removal; shaving (of hair).

Ohita ,(*pp.* of **oharati**), hidden; laid down.

Ohīna (*pp.* of **ohīyati**), left behind.

Ohīyaka, 3. one who remains or is left behind.

Ohīyati (ava + hi + ya), to stay behind; to remain. *aor.* **ohīyi**. *abs.* **ohīyitvā**.

Ohīyana, *nt.* staying behind.

Ohīyamāna, *pr. p.* lagging behind.

Oḷārika, *a.* gross; coarse; ample.

K

Ka (from *interrogative pron.* **kiŋ**), who; what; which.

Kakaca, *m.* a saw.

Kakaṇṭaka, *m.* chameleon.

Kaku, *m.* a knot; summit; projecting corner; hump.

Kakudha, *m.* hump (of a bull); cock's comb; the tree *Terminalia Arjuna.*—**bhaṇḍa**, *nt.* ensign of royalty; the five regalia, (*viz.* diadem, sword, canopy, slippers and yak's tail chowry).

Kakka, *nt.* a paste; sediment deposited by oily substances.

Kakkaṭa,—**ṭaka**, *m.* a crab.—**yanta**, *nt.* a ladder with hooks at one end for fastening it to a wall.

Kakkasa, *a.* rough; harsh.

Kakkārī, *f.* cucumber.

Kakkhaḷa, *a.* rough; harsh; hard.—**ḷatā**, *f.* harshness; rigidity.

Kaṅka, *m.* a heron.

Kaṅkaṇa, *nt.* bracelet.

Kaṅkhati (kakh + ŋ - a), to doubt; to be uncertain. *aor.* **kaṅkhi**.

Kaṅkhanā, **kaṅkhā**, **kaṅkhāyanā**, *f.* doubt; uncertainty.

Kaṅkhamāna, **Kaṅkhī**, *a.* being unsettled; one who is doubting or wavering.

Kaṅkhanīya, **Kaṅkhitabba**, *pt. p.* fit to be doubted.

Kaṅkhita, *pp.* of **kaṅkhati**.

Kaṅkhiya,—**khitvā**, *abs.* being doubtful.

Kaṅgu, *f.* millet (seed).

Kacavara, *m.* sweepings; rubbish.

Kacci, *an.* indefinite interrogative particle expressing doubt. (Often it is followed by some other particle such as **nu**, **nu kho**).

Kaccha, *m. nt.* marshy land; armpit.—**antara**, *nt.* below the armpit; interior of a royal palace.—**puṭa**, *m.* a hawker; *adj.* one who has a bundle hanging from one's shoulder.

Kacchaka, *m.* a kind of fig-tree.

Kacchapa, *m.* a turtle; tortoise.

Kacchā, *f.* loin-clothe; a belt for an elephant.

Kacchu, *f.* itch ; scab ; a plant the fruits of which cause itch when applied to the skin.

Kajjala, *nt.* soot.

Kañcana, *nt.* gold.—**vaṇṇa**, *a.* of the golden colour.

Kañcuka, *m.* a jacket ; an overcoat ; an armour; the slough of a snake.

Kañjika, **kañjiya**, *nt.* rice gruel.

Kaññā, *f.* girl ; maiden.

Kaṭa, *m.* a mat ; the cheek.—**sāra**, *m.* a mat made of some kind of stalks.

Kaṭa, (= **kata**), *pp.* of **karoti.**

Kaṭaka, *nt.* a bracelet ; a rocky cave.

Kaṭacchu, *m.* a spoon ;—**matta**, *a.* spoonful of.

Kaṭasi, *f.* cemetery.

Kaṭāha, *m.* receptacle ; cauldron; a nut-shell.

Kaṭi, *f.* the hip ; waist.

Kaṭuka, *a.* sharp ; severe, painful; pungent. *nt.* pungency.—**tta**, *nt.* pungency ; severity.—**bhaṇḍa**, *nt.* spices.—**pphala**, *a.* having severe results. *nt.* seeds of some aromatic plants. —**vipāka**, *a.* having bitter results.

Kaṭṭha, *nt.* timber ; a piece of wood.—**tthara**, *nt.* a bed of planks ; a mat made of twigs. —**maya**, *a.* made of wood.

Kaṭṭhaka, *m.* bamboo tree.

Kaṭṭhissa, *nt.* a silken coverlet embroidered with gems.

Kaṭhala, *nt.* potsherd.

Kaṭhina, *a.* rough ; hard ; stiff. *nt.* the cloth annually supplied to the monks for making robes. —**tthāra**, *m.* dedication of the **kaṭhina** robe.—**nuddhāra**, *m.* withdrawal of the **kaṭhina** robe.

Kaḍḍhati (kaḍḍh + a), to drag ; to pull. *aor.* **kaḍḍhi**. *pp.* **kaḍḍhita.**

Kaḍḍhana, *nt.* pulling ; dragging ; sucking.

Kaṇa, *m.* fine powder between the husk and the grain of rice ; broken rice.

Kaṇaya, *m.* a sort of spear ; a short lance.

Kaṇavīra, *m.* the oleander.

Kaṇājaka, *nt.* porridge of broken rice.

Kaṇikāra, *m.* the tree *Petrospermum Acerifolium* whose flowers are of golden colour.

Kaṇiṭṭha, **Kaṇiya**, *a.* the youngest ; younger born. *m.*—**ka**, *m.* the younger brother.

Kaṇiṭṭhā, **-ṭṭhikā**, **kaṇiṭṭhi**, *f.* the younger sister.

Kaṇeru, *m.* an elephant. *f.* a she-elephant. See **Kareṇu.**

Kaṇṭaka, *nt.* a thorn ; a bone; any instrument with a sharp point.—**āpassaya**, *m.* a bed made of an out-stretched skin, under which are iron spikes or thorns.—**ādhāna**, *nt.* a thorny hedge.

Kaṇṭha, *m.* the neck ; throat.—**ja**, *a.* produced in the throat ; guttural.—**nāḷa**, *m.* the throat.

Kaṇḍa, *m.* a portion or chapter ; an arrow or shaft.

Kaṇḍarā, *f.* tendon.

Kaṇḍu, **Kaṇḍuti**, *f.* itch.

Kaṇḍūyana,—**vana**, *nt.* itching ; scratching.

Kaṇḍūvati (*Deno.* from **kaṇḍu**), to itch ; to be irritated ; to suffer from itch. *aor.*—**ūvi.**

Kaṇṇa, *nt.* the ear ; an angle ; corner ; edge of a garment.—**kaṭuka**, *a.* disagreeable to hear. —**gūtha**,—**mala**, *nt.* ear-wax ; cerumen of the ear.—**cchidda**, *nt.* orifice of the ear.—**cchinna**, *a.* one whose ears are cut off.—**jappaka,** *a.* one who whispers. —**jappana,** *nt.* whispering.—**jalūkā,** *f.* a small kind of centipede.—**bila,** *nt.* orifice of the ear.—**bhūsā,** *f.* ear-ring; ornament for the ear.—**mūla,** *nt.* root of the ear.—**valli,** *f.* the lobe of the ear.—**vijjhana,** *nt.* perforation of the ear.—**veṭhana,** *nt.* a kind of ornament for the ear.—**sakkhalikā,** *f.* outer part of the ear.—**sukha,** *a.* pleasant to the ear. —**sūla,** *nt.* pain in the ear.

Kaṇṇadhāra, *m.* helmsman (of a vessel).

Kaṇṇikā, *f.* the pericap; a sheaf; house-top; an ornament for the ear.—**maṇḍala,** *nt.* the top of a roof where the rafters meet.—**baddha,** *a.* bound into sheafs.

Kaṇha, *a.* black; dark; evil; *m.* the black colour; god Vishṇu.—**vattanī,** *m.* fire.—**vipāka,** *a.* having evil results. —**sappa,** *m.* a venomous black snake.

Kata, (*pp.* of **karoti**), done; made; finished; fulfilled.—**kạmma,** *a.* practised; skilled, having done their own work.—**kalyāṇa,** *a.* one who has done good deeds.—**kicca,** *a.* having performed one's obligations.—**añjalī,** *a.* having raised one's hands in salutation.—**paṭisanthāra,** *a.* having (been) received kindly.—**paricaya,** *a.* having practised or made acquaintance with.—**pātarāsa,** *a.* having finished one's breakfast.—**puñña,** *a.* one who has performed meritorious actions. —**puññatā,** *f.* the fact of being meritorious.—**pubba,** *a.* done before.—**bhattakicca,** *a.* one who has fiinished his meal.—**bhāva,** *m.* the fact of having done.—**vedī,** *a.* grateful.—**veditā,** *f.* gratitude.—**sakkāra,** —**saṅgaha,** *a.* one who has received hospitality.—**saṅketa,** *nt.* an appointment or sign made beforehand.—**sikkha,** *a.* one who has practised.—**anuggaha,** *a.* assisted by.—**adhikāra,**—**abhinīhāra,**—**abhinivesa,** *a.* one who has formed a resolution or an aspiration.—**aparādha,** *a.* guilty; 3. a transgressor.—**abhiseka,** *a.* anointed; consecrated.

Kataññū, 3. grateful; obliging.—**utā,** *f.* gratitude.

Katatta, *nt.* the doing of; the fact of having done.

Katama, *a.* which; what; which of the many.

Katamatte, *loc.* as soon as something has done.

Katara, *a.* which (of the two).

Kati, (*interr.* particle), how many. —**vassa,** *a.* having how many years; how-old ?—**vidha,** *a.* of how many kinds ?

Katikā, *f.* talk; conversation; an agreement.—**vatta,** *nt.* a pact; an agreement.

Katipaya, *a.* some; several.

Katipāha, *nt.* a few days.—**haṃ,** *ad.* for a few days.

Katūpakāra, *a.* helped or assisted by. *m.* the help given to someone else.

Katupāsana, *a.* skilled in archery; dexterous.

Katokāsa, *a.* being permitted; given leave to.

Kattabba, *pt. p.* fit to be done. *nt.* duty; obligation.—**yuttaka,** *a.* fit to be done.—**batā,** *f.* fitness to be done.

Kattara, *a.* very small. **daṇḍa,** *m.*—**yaṭṭhi,** *f.* a walking stick; a staff.—**suppa,** *m.* small winnowing basket.

Kattari,—rikā, *f.* scissors; shears.

Kattikamāsa, *m.* name of a month; October-November.

Kattikā, *f.* the constellation of Pleiades.

Kattu, *m.* maker; doer; an author; the subject of a sentence.—**kāma,** *a.* willing to do.—**kāmatā,** *f.* desire to do.

Kattuŋ, *inf.* to do.

Kattha, *ad.* where ?

Katthaci, *in.* somewhere.

Katthati (kath + a), to boast. *aor.* **katthi.** *pp.* **katthita.**

Katthanā, *f.* boasting.

Katthī, *a.* boaster; boastful.

Katvā, *abs.* (of **karoti**), having done or made.

Kathaŋ, *ad.* how ?—**kathā,** *f.* doubt; uncertainty.—**kathī,** *a.* one who is doubtful.—**kara,** *a.* how acting.—**bhūta,** *a.* of what sort ? what like ?—**vidha,—pakāra,** *a.* of what kind ?—**sīla,** *a.* of what character ?

Kathana, *nt.* talk; conversation.

Kathā, *f.* speech; story; talk.—**pābhata,** *nt.* subject of conversation.—**magga,** *m.* a narrative; an account.—**vatthu,** *nt.* subject of a discussion; the 5th book of the Abhidhamma.—**sallāpa,** *m.* friendly conversation.

Kathāpeti (*caus.* of **katheti**), to make say; to send a message. *aor.*—**esi.**

Kathita, *pp.* of the following.

Katheti (kath + e), to say; to speak; to relate. *aor.* **kathesi.** *pr. p.* **kathenta.**

Kathetvā, *abs.* having said or spoken.

Kadanna, *nt.* spoiled rice; bad food.

Kadamba, *m.* the tree *Nauclea Cordifolia.*

Kadariya, *a.* miserly; stingy. *nt.* avarice; stinginess.—**yatā,** *f.* niggardliness.

Kadali, *f.* the plantain tree; a banner.—**phala,** *nt.* banana.—**miga,** *m.* a kind of deer whose hide is much valued.

Kadā, *ad,* when ?

Kadāci, *in.* sometimes.—**karahaci,** *in.* seldom; at times.

Kaddama, *m.* mud; mire.—**bahula,** *a.* full of mud.—**modaka,** *nt.* muddy water.

Kanaka, *nt.* gold.—**cchavī,—ttaca,** *a.* of golden complexion.—**ppabhā,** *f.* the colour of gold.—**vimāna,** *nt.* a golden palace.

Kanīnikā, *f.* the pupil of the eye.

Kanta, *a.* pleasant; lovely; agreeable. *m.* the beloved one; husband.

Kantati (kant + a), to spin; to cut; to shear; to incise. *aor.* **kanti,** *pr. p.* **kantanta.**

Kantana, *nt.* spinning; incision.

Kantā, *f.* a woman; the wife.

Kantāra, *m.* wilderness; desert. —**nittharaṇa,** *nt.* passing through a desert.

Kantita, *pp.* of **kantati.**

Kanda, *m.* a tuber; yam.

Kandati (kand + a), to cry; to wail; to lament. *aor.* **kandi.** *pp.* **kandita.**

Kandanta, *pr. p.* of the above.

Kandana, *nt.* crying; lamentation.

Kandara, *m.*—**rā,** *f.* a grotto on the slope of a mountain.

Kanduka, *m.* a ball (used in games).

Kapaṇa, *a.* poor; miserable; insignificant. *m.* a beggar.

Kapalla.—**laka,** *nt.* a frying pan; pot-sherd.—**pūva,** *m. nt.* pan-cake.

Kapāla,—**laka,** *m.* a shell (like that of a tortoise); frying pan; pan; beggar's bowl. **sīsa**—, the skull.

Kapi, *m.* monkey.—**kacchu,** *m.* the plant *Mucana pruritus,* කසාඹිලියා

Kapiñjala, *m.* a kind of partrige.

Kapittha, *m.* wood-apple.

Kapila, *a.* tawny. *m.* tawny colour; name of a sage.

Kapilavatthu, *nt.* the city where Prince Siddhartha was born.

Kapisīsa, *m.* the lintel of a door.

Kapota, *m.* a dove; pigeon.

Kapola, *m.* the cheek.

Kappa, *m.* a world cycle; an aeon; thought.—**ṭṭhāyī,**—**ṭṭhitika,** *a.* lasting a world cycle.—**rukkha,** *m.* a celestial tree fulfilling all wishes.—**vināsa,** *m.* destruction of the world.—**vināsaka,** *a.* consuming the world.

Kappa, *a.* suitable; proper; resembling. (In cpds.).

Kappaka, *m.* a barber; a chamberlain.

Kappaṭa, *m.* old rag; torn garment.

Kappati (kapp + a), to be fit, seeming, or proper.

Kappana, *nt.*—**nā,** *f.* fixing; harnessing; saddling; putting into order; thinking; (Preceded by **jīvita** :) livelihood.

Kappabindu, *nt.* a small black dot made on a monk's robe.

Kappara, *m.* the elbow.

Kappāsa, *nt.* cotton.—**paṭala,** *nt.* a layer of cotton.—**maya,**—**sika,** *a.* made of cotton.—**pāsī,** *m.* the cotton plant

Kappika, *a.* (in cpds.) belonging to a world cycle.

Kappita, *pp.* of **kappeti.**

Kappiya, *a.* appropriate; lawful; proper.—**kāraka,** *m.* an attendant of a monk; one who provides appropriate things.—**bhaṇḍa,** *nt.* things allowable to the monks.

Kappūra, *m. nt.* camphor.

Kappeti (kapp + e), to prepare; to harness; to trim; to consider; to make; to lead (one's life). *aor.*—**esi.** *pr. p.* **kappenta.**

Kappetvā, *abs.* having harnessed, trimmed, or prepared.

Kabara, *a.* spotted; variegated.

Kabala, *m. nt.* a lump; a morsel; a mouthful.—**liṅkāra,** *m.* lumping.—**liṅkārāhāra,** *m.* meterial food.

Kabba, *nt.* a poem; poetical composition.

Kama, *m.* order; manner; proceeding; way.

Kamati (kam + a), to go; to enter into. *aor.* **kami.** *pp.* **kanta.**

Kamaṇḍalu, *m. nt.* a water-pitcher.

Kamanīya, *a.* desirable; lovely; beautiful.

Kamala, *nt.* a lotus.—**dala,** *nt.* petal of a lotus.

Kamalāsana, *m.* the Brahmā; the creator.

Kamalinī, *f.* a lotus pond or lake.

Kamuka, *m.* arecanut tree.

Kampaka, *a.* one who shakes.

Kampati (kamp + a), to tremble; to waver. *aor.* **kampi.** *pr. p.* **kampamāna, kampanta.**

Kampana, *nt.* **kampā,** *f.* trembling; movement.

Kampita, (*pp.* of **kampeti** and **kampati**), shaken ; agitated.

Kampiya, *a.* movable ; shakable.

Kampeti (*caus.* of **kampati**), to shake ; to cause to tremble. *aor.*—**esi.** *pr. p.* **kampenta.**

Kampetvā, kampiya, *abs.* having shaken.

Kambala, *nt.* woollen stuff ; a blanket.—**balī,** *a.* one who has a woollen garment for his dress. —**līya,** *nt.* woollen garment.

Kambu, *m. nt.* gold ; a conch shell.—**gīva,** *a.* having a neck marked with three lines or folds.

Kamboja, *m.* name of a country.

Kamma, *nt.* deed ; action ; job ; work.—**kara,**—**kāra,** *m.* workman ; labourer.—**karaṇa,** *nt.* labour ; service ; working.—**kāraṇā,** *f.* bodily punishment.—**kāraka,** *nt.* the Objective case.—**kkhaya,** *m.* consummation of the previous actions and the results thereof.—**ja,** *a.* produced by karma.—**jāta,** *nt.* various actions or jobs.—**dāyāda,** *a.* inheriting the consequences of one's own deeds.—**nānatta,** *nt.* manifoldness of karma. —**nibbatta,** *a.* produced through karma.—**patha,** *m.* the ways of action.—**ppaccaya,** *a.* having karma as the basis.—**phala,** *nt.* the fruit or result of karma.—**bandhu,** *a.* having karma as one's relative.—**bala,** *nt.* the power of karma.—**yoni,** *a.* having karma as origin.—**vāda,** *m.* the view of the efficacy of karma.—**vādī,** *a.* believing in karma.—**vipāka,** *m.* the result of one's actions.—**vega,** *m.* the impetus of karma. —**samuṭṭhāna,** *a.* arising from karma.—**sambhava,** *a.* produced by karma.—**sarikkhaka,** *a.* similar in consequence to the deed done.—**saka,** *a.* one whose property is karma. —**ānurūpa,** *a.* according to one's karma.—**āyūhana,** *nt.* heaping of karmas.—**upacaya,** *m.* accumulation of kamma.

Kammañña, kammaniya, *a.* fit for work ; ready ; wieldy.—**ñatā,** *f.*—**bhāva,** *m.* readiness ; workableness ; fitness.

Kammaṭṭhāna, *nt.* a subject for meditation ; a branch of industry.—**ṭhānika,** 3. a person practising meditation.

Kammadhāraya, *m.* the adjectival compound.

Kammanta, *nt.* work ; business.—**ṭṭhāna,** *nt.* where the work is done ; place of business.—**ntika,** *a.* a labourer ; an artisan.

Kammappatta, *a.* those who have assembled to take part in an ecclesiastic act.

Kammavācā, *f.* the text of an official act.

Kammassāmī, 3. the owner of a business.

Kammādhiṭṭhāyaka, *m.* superintendent of a work.

Kammāra, *m.* a smith ; worker in metals.—**sālā,** *f.* smithy.

Kammārambha, *m.* commencement of an undertaking.

Kammāraha, *a.* entitled to take part in.

Kammārāma, *a.* delighting in activity.—**matā,** *f.* taking pleasure in worldly activities.

Kammāsa, *a.* spotted ; speckled ; inconsistent.

Kammika, kammī, 3. (in cpds.) doing ; one who performs or looks after.

Kamyatā, *f.* (in cpds.) wish ; longing.

Kaya, *m.* purchase.—**vikkaya,** *m.* trade ; buying and selling.—**vikkayī,** *m.* a trader or broker.

Kara, *m.* the hand ; a ray ; a tax ; the trunk of an elephant. *adj.* (in cpds), doing ; performing. —**gga,** tip of the hand.—**ja,** *m.* nail (of the hand).—**tala,** *nt.* the palm of the hand.—**puṭa,** *m.* the folded hand.—**bhūsā,** *f.* any kind of ornament for the hand ; a bracelet.

Karaka, *nt.* a drinking vessel ; *m.* pomegranate tree.

Karakā, *f.* hail ;—**vassa** *nt.* hail-storm.

Karajakāya, *m.* the body (which is born of impurity.)

Karañja, *m.* the tree *Pongamiya glabra.* කරඳ.

Karaṇa, *nt.* doing ; making ; production.—**attha,***m.*the sense of the instrumentality.—**vibhatti,** *f.* the instrumental case.

Karaṇīya, *a.* that ought to be done. *nt.* duty ; obligation.—**tā,** *f.* the fact that something has to be done.

Karaṇḍa,—**ḍaka,** *m.* casket ; a small box or receptacle.

Karabha, *m.* a camel ; the portion of the hand from the wrist to the root of the fingers.

Karamadda, *m.* the tree *Carissa carandas,* කරඹ.

Karamarānīta, *a.* one who is captured in a war.

Karavīka, *m.* the Indian cuckoo. —**bhāṇī,** *a.* speaking with a clear and melodious voice.

Karavīra, *m.* the oleander tree.

Karitvā, (*abs.* of **karoti**), having done.

Karī, *m.* an elephant.

Karīyati (*pass.* of **karoti**), to be done. *aor.* **karīyi.**

Karīyamāna, Kayiramāna (pr. p. of **Karīyati**) being done.

Karīsa, *nt.* dung ; excrement ; a square measure of land (which may be nearly an acre).—**magga,** *m.* the anus.

Karuṇā, *f.* compassion ; pity.—**yanā,** *f.* compassionateness.

Karuṇāyati (*Denm.* from **karuṇā**), to feel pity for. *aor.*—**nāyi.**

Kareṇu,—**ṇukā,** *f.* a she-elephant.

Kareri, *m.* the musk-rose tree.

Karoti (kar + o), to do ; to act ; to make ; to build. *aor.* **kari.** *abs.* **katvā.**

Karonta, *pr. p.* doing.

Kala, *m.* a sweet low sound.—**kala,** *m.* indistinct and confused noise.

Kalatta, *nt.* the wife.

Kalandaka, *m.* a squirrel.—**nivāpa,** *m.* a locality where the squirrels are fed.

Kalabha, *m.* a young elephant.

Kalala, *nt.* mud ; mire ;—**makkhita,** *a.* smeared or soiled with mud.—**rūpa,** *nt.* the first stage in the formation of the foetus.

Kalasa, *nt.* a small water-pot.

Kalaha, *m.* quarrel ; dispute.—**kāraka,** 3. one who quarrels.—**kāraṇa,** *nt.* the cause of a dispute.—**sadda,** *m.* a brawl ; squabble.

Kalaṅka, *m.* a spot ; mark ; fault.

Kalā, *f.* a fraction of a whole ; an art.

Kalāpa, *m.* a bundle ; sheaf ; a quiver ; a group of elementary particles.

Kalāpī, *m.* peacock ; one who has a quiver or a bundle.

Kali, *m.* defeat ; bad luck ; sin ; distress.—**ggaha,** *m.* a losing throw ; defeat ; evil consequence.—**yuga,** *m.* the age of vice and misery, i.e. the last of the four periods of an aeon.

Kaliṅgara, *m. nt.* a log ; rotten piece of wood ; chaff.

Kalīra, *nt.* the soft part above the stem of a palm tree.

Kalusa, *nt.* sin ; impurity. *adj.* impure ; dirty.

Kalebara, *nt.* the body.

Kalyāṇa, *a.* charming; morally good. *nt.* goodness ; merit ; virtue; welfare.—**kāma,** *a.* desiring what is good.—**kārī,** *a.* one who does good things; virtuous.—**dassana,** *a.* handsome ; lovely.—**dhamma,** *a.* virtuous ; *m.* good conduct or doctrine.—**paṭibhāṇa,** *a.* having quick understanding.—**mitta,** *m.* a good companion ; honest friend.—**ajjhāsaya,** *a.* having intention to do good.

Kalyāṇatā, *f.* goodness ; beauty.

Kalyāṇī, *f.* a beautiful woman ; name of a river and a town in Ceylon.

Kalla, *a.* clever ; able ; healthy ; sound ; ready ; proper.—**tā,** *f.* ability ; readiness.—**sarīra,** *a.* having a sound body.

Kallahāra, *nt.* white water lily.

Kallola, *m.* a billow.

Kavaca, *m.* a coat of mail ; armour.

Kav(b)andha, *m.* headless (trunk of the) body.

Kavāṭa, *m. nt.* window ; the shutters of a door.

Kavi, *m.* poet.—**tā,** *f.*—**tta,** *nt.* state of a poet.

Kaviṭṭha (= kapiṭṭha), *m.* elephant-apple tree.

Kasaṭa, *m.* the refuse ; dregs ; acrid taste. *adj.* nasty ; worthless.

Kasati (kas + a), to plough ; to till. *aor.* **kasi.** *pp.* **kasita, kaṭṭha.**

Kasana, *nt.* tilling.

Kasanta, kasamāna, *pr. p.* tilling ; ploughing.

Kasambu, *m.* filth ; rubbish .—**jāta,** *a.* impure ; of bad character.

Kasā, *f.* a whip.—**hata,** *a.* being whipped or flogged.

Kasāya, *nt.* a decoction ; a distillation.

Kasāva, *m. nt.* the acrid taste ; a cloth of orange colour. *adj.* of the orange colour.

Kasi, *f.* cultivation ; tilling.—**kamma,** *nt.* agriculture ; husbandry.—**bhaṇḍa,** *nt.* agricultural implements.

Kasiṇa, *a.* whole ; entire *nt.* an object for meditation.—**parikamma,** *nt.* the preliminary duties that should be performed before meditation.—**maṇḍala,** *nt.* the circular disk used as an object for meditation.

Kasitaṭṭhāna, *nt.* tilled ground.

Kasitvā, *abs.* having ploughed.

Kasira, *a.* miserable ; difficult. *nt.* misery ; trouble ; difficulty. —**rena,** *ad.* with difficulty.

Kasmīra, *m.* name of a country in Northern India.

Kassaka, *m.* farmer ; cultivator.

Kassati (kass + a), to drag. *aor.* **kassi.** see **kaḍḍhati.**

Kahaŋ, *ad.* where ?

Kahāpaṇa, *nt.* a coin whose value is about a half-crown.—**ṇaka,** *nt.* a torture which consisted in cutting off small pieces of flesh.

Kāka, *m.* a crow.—**pāda,** crow's foot ; cross mark.—**peyya,** *a.* full to the brim (that a crow can easily drink of it).—**vaṇṇa,** *a.* of the colour of a crow, i.e., black ; name of a king in Ceylon.

Kākacchati (kas + cha)* to snore. *aor.*—**cchi.** *pr. p.* **kākacchamāna.**

Kākaṇikā, *f.* a coin of very low value ; a farthing.

Kākasūra, *a.* clever as a crow ; a shameless fellow.

Kākassara, *a.* having the sound of a crow.

Kākī, *f.* she-crow.

Kākola, *m.* a raven.

Kāca, *m.* glass ; crystal ; cataract in the eye.—**tumba,** *m.* glass bottle.—**maṇi,** *m.* crystal. —**maya,** *a.* made of glass.

Kāja, *m.* a pingo ; carrying pole. **hāraka,** *m.* pingo-bearer.

Kāṭa, *m.* the male organ.

Kāṇa, *a.* blind (of one eye). *m.* one-eyed person.

Kātabba, *pt. p.* what ought to be done ; *nt.* duty.

Kātara, *a.* mean ; poor ; miserable.

Kātave, Kātuṃ, *inf.* to do.

Kātukāma, *a.* desirous of doing. —**kāmatā,—kamyatā,** *f.* desire to do or perform.

Kādamba, *m.* a kind of goose with grey wings.

Kānana, *nt.* forest ; grove.

Kāpilavatthava, *a.* belonging to Kapilavatthu.

Kāpurisa, *m.* a wretch ; contemptible person.

Kāpotaka, *a.* of a dull white.—**tikā,** *f.* a sort of liquor (which is of reddish colour).

Kāma, *m.* pleasure ; lust ; enjoyment ; an object of sensual enjoyment.—**giddha,** greedy of sensual pleasure.—**guṇa,** *m.* sensual pleasure.—**gedha,** *m.* attachment to s. pleasure.—**cchanda,** *m.* excitement of s. pleasure.—**taṇhā,** *f.* thirst after s. pleasure.—**da,—dada,** *a.* giving what is desired.—**dhātu,** *f.* the world of desire.—**paṅka,** *m.* the mire of lust.—**pariḷāha,** *m.* the fever of passion.—**bhava,** *m.* the sphere dominated by pleasures.—**bhogī,** *a.* enjoying the pleasures of the senses.—**mucchā,** *f.* sensual stupor.—**rati,** *f.* amorous enjoyment.—**rāga,** *m.* sensual passion.—**loka,** *m.* the world of pleasures. — **vitakka,** *m.* thought concerning s. pleasures. —**saṅkappa,** *m.* aspiration after pleasure.—**saññojana,** *nt.* hindrance formed by pleasures. —**sukha,** *nt.* happiness arising from sensual pleasures.—**sevanā,** *f.* (indulgence in) sexual intercourse.

Kāmatā, *f.* longing ; willingness.

Kāmī, *a.* one who possesses the objects of s. pleasures ; (in cpds.) desirous of.

Kāmuka, *a.* lustful ; lewd.

Kāmeti (kam + e), to crave ; to desire. *aor.*—**esi.** *pp.* **kāmita.**

Kāmetabba, *pt. p.* desirable.

Kāya, *m.* a heap ; a collection ; the body.—**kamma,** *nt.* bodily action.—**kammaññatā,** *f.* wieldiness of the body.—**gata,** *a.* relating to the body.—**gantha,** *m.* bodily fetter.—**gutta,** *a.* guarding one's own body ; calm in the bodily actions.—**ḍāha,** *m.* fever ; inflammation of the body.—**daratha,** *m.* bodily distress.—**duccarita,** *nt.* misconduct by the body.—**dvāra,** *nt.* the outlet of bodily senses.—**dhātu,** *f.* the faculty of touch.—**ppakopa,** *m.* misbehaviour.—**ppa-**

* ka is doubled and *s* is changed to *c* ; the vowel of the first *ka* is lengthened.

cālakaŋ, *ad.* swaying the body. —**paṭibaddha**, *a.* connected with the body.—**payoga**, *m.* instrumentality of the body.—**parihārika**, *a.* tending the body.—**ppasāda**, *m.* the sense of touch.—**passaddhi**, *f.* serenity of the senses.—**pāgabbhiya**, *nt.* immodesty.—**bandhana**, *nt.* waist-band; girdle.—**mudutā**, *f.* pliability of senses.—**lahutā**, *f.* buoyancy of senses. —**vaṅka**, *m.* crookedness of action.—**vikāra**, *m.* gesture.—**viññatti**, *f.* intimation through the body; a gesture.—**viññāṇa**, *nt.* consciousness by means of touch.—**viññeyya**, *a.* to be perceived by the sense of touch. —**viveka**, *m.* seclusion of the body.—**veyyāvacca**, *nt.* menial duties.—**saŋsagga**, *m.* bodily contact.—**sakkhī**, *a.* he who has realized the final truth (through the body).—**saṅkhāra**, *m.* substratum of the body.—**samācāra**, *m.* good conduct.—**samphassa**, *m.* the sense of touch.—**sucarita**, *nt.* good conduct in action.—**soceyya**, *nt.* purity of the body.

Kāyika, *a.* relating to or resulting from the body.—**dukkha**, *nt.* bodily pain.

Kāyujjukatā, *f.* straightness of the body.

Kāyūpaga, *a.* attached to the body; going to a new birth.

Kāyūra, *nt.* a bracelet worn on the upper arm.

Kāra, *m.* deed; service; act of homage.

Kāraka, *m.* the doer. *nt.* syntax (in gram.)

Kāraṇa, *nt.* reason; cause.—**ṇā**, *abl.* by means of; through; by. **Kiŋ kāraṇā** = why?

Kāraṇā, *f.* torture; bodily punishment.—**ṇika**, *m.* torturer.

Kārā, *f.* **Kārāghara**, *nt.* a prison; jail.

Kārāpaka, 3. a schemer; one who orders to do something. *f.* —**pikā**.

Kārāpana, *nt.* causing to do; ordering.

Kārāpeti, caus of **karoti**, *aor.*—**esi**, *pp.*—**pita**.

Kārābhedaka, *a.* one who has broken out of a jail.

Kārikā, *f.* a commentary.

Kāriya, *nt.* duty; action; what should be done.

Kārī, 3. doer. (Mostly in cpds. such as **sātaccakārī**).

Kāruñña, *nt.* compassion.

Kāruṇika, *a.* compassionate.

Kāreti (*caus.* of **karoti**), to cause to do, build or construct. *aor.* **kāresi**. *abs.* **kāretvā**. *pr. p.* **kārenta**.

Kāla, *m.* time. **Kālass 'eva**, early. **Kālena**, in proper time; at the right moment. **Kālena kālaŋ**, from time to time. **Kālaŋ karoti**, dies.—**kata**, *pp.* dead.—**kiriyā**, *f.* death.—**kaṇṇī**, *m.* an unfortunate person; a wretch.—**pavedana**, *nt.* announcement of time.—**vādī**, *a.* speaking at the proper time.

Kālaññū, *a.* one who knows the proper time.

Kālantara, *nt.* interval; period.

Kālika, *a.* temporal.

Kāliṅga, *m.* name of a country in East India.

Kālīya, *nt.* gallochum.

Kālusiya, *nt.* dirt; obscurity.

Kāveyya, *nt.* poetry.

Kāsa, *m.* a kind of reed; consumption.

Kāsāya, Kāsāva, *nt.* yellow robe. *adj.* dyed with orange colour.

Kāsi, *m.* name of a country (the capital of which was Benares). **Kāsika**, *a.* belonging to or made in **Kāsi**.

Kāsu, *f.* pit.

Kāḷa, *a.* black; dark. *m.* black colour.—**kūṭa**, *m.* name of a mountain in the Himalayas.—**kesa**, *a.* black-haired, i.e. young.—**tipu**, *nt.* black lead.—**pakkha**, *m.* the moonless fortnight.—**loṇa**, *nt.* black salt.—**sīha**, *m.* a kind of lion.—**sutta**, *nt.* carpenter's measuring line.—**haŋsa**, black swan.

Kāḷaka, *a.* black. *nt.* a black spot; a stain; black grain in the rice.

Kāḷāyasa, *nt.* (black) iron.

Kāḷāvaka, *m.* a kind of elephant.

Kāḷīya, see **Kālīya**.

Kikī, *m.* the blug jay. *f.* female of the jay.

Kiṅkara, 3. a servant; an attendant.

Kiṅkiṇī, *f.* a jingling bell.

Kiṅkiṇikajāla, *nt.* a net of tinkling bells.

Kicca, *nt.* duty; work; service; that which should be done.—**kārī**, *a.* doing one's own duty.

Kiccākicca, *nt.* what should be done and not to be done.

Kiccha, *a.* difficult; painful. *nt.* distress; difficulty.

Kicchati (kit + cha), to be troubled or wearied. *aor.*—**chi**.

Kiñcana, *nt.* something; a trifle; wordly attachment.

Kiñcāpi, *in.* whatever; however much; but.

Kiñjakkha, *nt.* filament; pollen.

Kiṭṭha, *nt.* growing corn.—**ṭhāda**, *a.* corn-eating.—**sambādha-samaya**, *m.* harvest-time; when corn is fully grown.

Kiṇanta, *pr. p.* of the fol.

Kiṇāti (ki + ṇā), to buy. *aor.* **kiṇi**, *abs.* **kiṇitvā**; **kītvā**. *inf.* **ketuŋ**; **kiṇituŋ**.

Kiṇṇa, (*pp.* of **kirati**), scattered. *nt.* yeast.

Kitava, *m.* a cheat.

Kittaka (*inter. pron.*), how much? to what extent? how many?

Kittana, *nt.* praising; expounding.

Kittāvatā, *ad.* how far? in what respect?

Kitti, *f.* fame; renown.—**ghosa**, —**sadda**, *m.* reputation.—**mantu**, *a.* famous.

Kittima, *a.* artificial.

Kitteti (kitt + e), to praise; to extol; to relate; to announce. *aor.*—**esi**. *pp.* **kittita**. *pr. p.* **kittenta**.

Kinnara, *m.* a bird with a human head; name of a forest-dwelling nation.—**rī**, *f.* a Kinnara woman.

Kipillikā, *f.* an ant.

Kibbisa, *nt.* wrong-doing; crime. —**kārī**, 3. a criminal.

Kimi, *m.* a worm; vermin—. **kula**, *nt.* a crowd or a kind of worms.

Kimakkhāyī, *a.* preaching what?

Kimatthaŋ, *ad.* for what purpose?—**tthiya**, *a.* to what purpose; purporting what.

Kimpakka,—**phala**, *nt.* a poisonous fruit in the shape of a mango.

Kimpurisa, see **Kinnara**.

Kira, *in.* really; truly; (refers to a report by hear-say.)

Kiraṇa, *m. nt.* ray; effulgence.

Kirati (kir + a), to scatter; *aor.* **kiri**. *pp.* **kiṇṇa**.

Kirāta, *m.* a kind of junglemen.

Kiriya, *nt.* **kriyā**, **kiriyā**, *f* action; deed; performance.—**vāda**, *m.* belief in the consequence of action.—**vādī**, 3. one who promulgates the view of **kiriyavāda.**

Kirīṭa, *nt.* a crown ; diadem.

Kilañja, *m.* mat of rushes.

Kilanta, (*pp.* of the following). tired ; weary ; exhausted.

Kilamati (kilam + a), to be wearied or fatigued. *aor.* **kilami.** *abs.* **kilamitvā.**

Kilamatha, *m.* fatigue ; weariness.

Kilamanta, (*pr. p.* of **kilamati**), becoming weary.

Kilamita, *pp.* of **kilameti.**

Kilamīyati (*pass.* of **kilameti**), to have been made weary. *aor.* —**mīyi.**

Kilamiyamāna (*pr. p.* of the above), being made weary.

Kilameti (*caus.* of **kilamati**), to make weary. *aor.*—**esi.** *pr. p.* **kilamenta.** *abs.* **kilametvā.**

Kilāsa, *m.* a cutaneous disease.

Kiliṭṭha, *pp.* of **kilissati.**

Kilinna (*pp.* of **kilijjati**), wet ; soiled ; moist.

Kilissati (kilis + ya), to become soiled or stained; to be impure. *aor.* **kilissi.** *pr. p.* **kilissanta.**

Kilissana, *nt.* getting dirty or stained.

Kilesa, *m.* passion ; lust ; depravity ; impurity.—**kāma,** *m.* lust.—**kkhaya,** *m.* destruction of passions.—**ppahāṇa,** *nt.* giving up of worldly passions.—**vatthu,** *nt.* objects of wordly attachment.

Kileseti (kilis + e), to cause to be soiled or defiled. *aor.*—**esi.** *pp.* **kilesita.**

Kilomaka, *nt.* the pleura.

Kisa, *a.* lean ; haggard ; emaciated.

Kiŋ (*rel.* or *inter. pron.*), what ? (*m.* **ko** = who ? *f.* **kā** = which woman ? *nt.* **kaŋ** = what thing ?)—**kāraṇā,** *ad.* by reason of what ?—**vādī,** *a.* holding what view ?

Kiŋsuka, *m.* the tree *Butea Frondosa* එරබදු.

Kīṭa, kīṭaka, *m.* an insect ; a moth.

Kīta, (*pp.* of **kiṇāti**), bought.

Kīdisa, *a.* of what kind ? what like ?

Kīra, *m.* a parrot.

Kīla, *m.* a stake.

Kīva, *in.* how much ? how long ? —**taka,** *a.* how many ? how much ?

Kīḷati (kīḷ + a), to play ; to sport ; to amuse oneself. *aor.* **kīḷi.** *pr. p.* **kīḷanta, kīḷamāna.** *abs.* **kīḷitvā.**

Kīḷanaka, *nt.* a toy ; *adj.* playing.

Kīḷanā, Keḷī, *f.* sport ; enjoyment.

Kīḷā, *f.* playing ; sport.—**goḷaka,** *nt.* a ball to play with. —**pasuta,** *a.* bent on play. —**bhaṇḍaka,** *nt.* a plaything ; toy.—**maṇḍala,** *nt.* playground.

Kīḷāpanaka, *a.* one who makes play.

Kīḷāpeti (*caus.* of **kīḷati**), to cause to play. *aor.*—**esi.** *pr. p* **kīḷāpenta.** *abs.* **kīḷāpetvā.**

Kīḷita (*pp.* of **kīḷati**), played. *nt.* sport ; play.

Kukutthaka, *m.* a kind of bird.

Kukku, *m.* a cubit.

Kukkucca, *nt.* remorse ; scruple ; worry.—**caka,** *a.* scrupulous.

Kukkuccāyati (*Denm.* from kukkucca), to feel remorse.

Kukkuṭa, *m.* a cock.

Kukkuṭī, *f.* a hen.

Kukkura, *m.* dog.—**vatika,** *a.* imitating a dog (in austerity).

Kukkuḷa, *m.* hot ashes ; name of a hell.

Kuṅkuma, *nt.* saffron.

Kucchi, *m.f.* the belly or womb ; interior.—**ṭṭha,** *a.* deposited in the womb.—**dāha,** *m.* inflammation in the stomach.

Kucchita, *pp.* contemptible ; vile.

Kuja, *m.* a tree ; the planet of Mars.

Kujjhati (kudh + ya), to be angry. *aor.* **kujjhi.** *pp.* **kuddha.** *pr. p.* **kujjhanta, kujjhamāna.**

Kujjhana, *nt.*—**nā,** *f.* anger ; irritation.

Kujjhitvā, kujjhiya, *abs.* being angry.

Kuñcanāda, *m.* trumpeting (of an elephant).

Kiñcikā, *f.* a key.—**vivara,** *nt.* key-hole.

Kuñcita (*pp.* of **kuñcati**), bent ; crooked ; curled.

Kuñja, *nt.* a glen ; dell.

Kuñjara, *m.* elephant.

Kuṭa, *m. nt.* a water pot.

Kuṭaja, *m.* a kind of medicinal herb.

Kuṭi, Kuṭikā, *f.* a hut.

Kuṭila, *a.* bent ; crooked.—**tā,** *f.* crookedness ; dishonesty.

Kuṭumba, *nt.* family.

Kuṭumbika, kuṭimbika, *m.* the head of a family ; a householder.

Kuṭṭha, *nt.* leprosy ; a kind of fragrant plant.

Kuṭṭhī, 3. a leper.

Kuṭhārī, *f.* an axe ; hatchet.

Kuḍumala, *m.* an opening bud.

Kuḍḍa, *nt.* a wall.

Kuṇapa, *m.* corpse ; carcase ; a loathesome thing.—**gandha,** *m.* smell of a rotting corpse.

Kuṇāla, *m.* the Indian cuckoo.

Kuṇī, *m.* a cripple.

Kuṇṭha, *a.* blunt.

Kuṇṭheti (kuṇṭh + e), to make blunt, bent or lame. *aor.*—**esi.** *pp.* **kuṇṭhita.**

Kuṇḍaka, *nt.* the powder obtained from the inner rind of rice.—**pūva,** *m. nt.* cake made of that powder.

Kuṇḍala, *nt.* an earring ; a curl.—**kesa,** *a.* having curled hair.—**āvatta,** *a.* twisting round (like a watch-spring).

Kuṇḍalī, *a.* having earrings or curls.

Kuṇḍikā, Kuṇḍī, *f.* a pitcher ; water-jug.

Kutūhala, *nt.* excitement ; curiosity.

Kuto, *ad.* where from ? whence ?

Kutta, *nt.* behaviour ; coquetry.

Kuttaka, *nt.* a carpet big enough for 12 women to dance on.

Kuttha, Kutra, *ad.* where ?

Kuthita, *pp.* boiling ; much heated.

Kudassu, *in.* when ?

Kudācana,—**naŋ,** *in.* sometimes ; at any time.

Kuddāla, *m.* a spade or hoe.

Kuddha (*pp.* of **kujjhati**), angry; irritated.

Kudrūsaka, *m.* a kind of grain. කුරක්කන්.

Kunta, *m.* sceptre lance ; a kind of bird.

Kuntanī, *f.* a curlew.

Kuntala, *m.* hair.

Kuntha, *m.* a sort of ant.

Kunda, *nt.* a kind of jasmine.

Kunnadī, *f.* rivulet.

Kupatha, *m.* wrong path.

Kupita, (*pp.* of **kuppati**), angry; offended.

Kupurisa, *m.* bad person.

Kuppa, *a.* unsteady ; movable.

Kuppati (kup + ya), to be angry or agitated ; to be changed. *aor.* **kuppi.** *pr. p.* **kuppamāna.**

Kuppana, *nt.* agitation ; anger ; disturbance.

Kubbati = karoti.

Kubbanaka, *nt.* a small forest ; brushwood.

Kubbanta, kubbamāna (*pr. p.* of **kubbati**), doing; performing.

Kubbara, *m.* pole of a carriage.

Kumati, *f.* a wrong view. *adj.* holder of a wrong view.

Kumāra, —raka, *m.* a boy ; a youngster.—**kīḷā,** *f.* amusement of a boy.

Kumārikā, kumārī, *f.* a girl ; virgin.

Kumina, *nt.* a fish-trap.

Kumuda, *nt.* white water-lily. —**ṇāla,** *nt.* the stalk of white water-lily.—**vaṇṇa,** *a.* of the colour of white lily.

Kumbha, *m.* waterpot.—**kāra,** *m.* potter.—**kārasālā,** *f.* pottery.—**dāsī.** *f.* a slave girl who brings water.

Kumbhaka, *nt.* the mast (of a ship).

Kumbhaṇḍa, *m.* pumpkin ; a kind of celestial beings.

Kumbhī, *f.* a pot.

Kumbhīla, *m.* crocodile.

Kumma, *m.* tortoise.

Kummagga, *m.* wrong path.

Kummāsa, *m.* junket.

Kura, *nt.* boiled rice.

Kuraṇḍaka, *m.* a flower plant ; a species of Amaranth.

Kurara, *m.* an osprey.

Kuruṅga, *m.* a kind of antelope.

Kurumāna (*pr. p.* of **karoti**), doing.

Kururaṭṭha, *nt.* the country of Kurus (in N. India).

Kurūra, *a.* cruel ; fierce.

Kula, *nt.* a family ; clan ; caste.—**geha,** *nt.* the house belonging to the family ; parents' house.—**tanti,** *f.* the line and tradition of a family.—**dūsaka,** 3. one who brings a family into bad repute.—**dhītu,** *f.* daughter of a respectable family.—**putta,** *m.* young man of a good family. —**vaṃsa,** *nt.* lineage ; progeny.

Kulaṅgāra, *m.* one who brings a family to ruin.

Kulattha, *m.* a kind of vetch.

Kulala, *m.* a hawk.

Kulāla, *m.* potter.—**cakka,** *nt.* potter's wheel.

Kulāvaka, *nt.* nest.

Kulisa, *nt.* thunder-bolt ; a mace.

Kulīna, *a.* having a recognized clan.

Kulīra, *m.* a crab.—**pāda,** *a.* (a bed), having the legs in the shape of a crab.

Kulla, *m.* a raft.

Kuvalaya, *nt.* water-lily.

Kavera, *m.* name of the deity who governs the North ; the king of Yakkhas.

Kusa, *m.* a kind of fragrant grass ; citronella ; a lot.—**agga,** *nt.* the point of a blade of **kusa**.—**cīra,** *nt.* garment made of kusa-grass. —**pāta,** *m.* casting of lots.

Kusala, *nt.* good action ; merit ; virtue. *adj.* clever.—**kamma,** *nt.* meritorious action ; right conduct.—**cetanā,** *f.* right volition.—**dhamma,** *m.* points of righteousness.—**vipāka,** *m.* fruit or result of good action.

Kusalatā, *f.* cleverness ; dexterity ; accomplishment.

Kusinārā, *f.* the chief city of the Mallas.

Kusīta, *a.* indolent ; lazy.—**tatā,** *f.*—**tatta,** *nt.* indolence ; laziness.

Kusuma, *nt.* a flower.

Kusumita, *a.* in flower; blooming.

Kusubbha, *m.* a small pit.

Kusumbha, *m.* the saf-flower (used for dying red).

Kusūla, *m.* a granary.

Kuha, kuhaka, *a.* deceitful; a cheat.

Kuhanā, *f.* deceit; hypocrisy; fraud.

Kuhara, *nt.* a hole; cavity.

Kuhiŋ, *ad.* where?

Kuheti (kuh + e), to deceive. *aor.*—**esi.**

Kūjati (kūj + a), to chirp. *aor.* **kūji.** *pp.* **kūjita.**

Kūjana, *nt.* chirping of birds.

Kūjanta, kūjamāna, *pr. p.* chirping.

Kūjita, *nt.* birds' singing. *pp.* resounded with the singing of birds.

Kūṭa, *a.* false; fraudulent; deceitful; untamed.—**goṇa**, *m.* an untamed bull.—**aṭṭa**, *nt.* false suit.—**aṭṭakāraka**, *m.* false suitor.—**jaṭila**, *m.* a fraudulent ascetic.—**vāṇija**, *m.* a dishonest trader.

Kūṭa, *m. nt.* the top; prominence; peak; ridge; pinnacle; a hammer. *nt.* falsehood; deceit.

Kūpa, *m.* a well; a cavity.

Kūpaka, *m.* the mast.

Kūla, *nt.* river-bank; embankment.

Kekara, *m.* a squint-eyed person

Kekā, *f.* the cry of a peacock.

Ketakī, *f.* screw-pine.

Ketu, *m.* flag; banner.—**kamyatā**, *f.* vainglory; desire for prominence.—**mantu**, *a.* adorned with flags.

Ketuŋ, *inf.* to buy.

Kedāra *m. nt.* arable land; a field.—**pāli**, *f.* a dam; narrow embankments in paddy fields.

Keṇipāta, *m.* rudder of a boat.

Keyūra, *nt.* a bracelet for the upper arm.

Keyya, *a.* fit to be bought; a thing to be bought.

Kerāṭika, *a.* deceitful; hypocritic. *m.* a dishonest person.

Kerāṭiya, *nt.* deceit; fraud.

Kelāsa, *m.* name of a mountain in the Himālayas.

Kevaṭṭa, *m.* a fisherman.

Kevala, *a.* lonely; unmixed; whole: entire.—**kappa**, *a.* almost the whole.—**paripuṇṇa**, *a.* complete in its entirety. —**laŋ**, *ad.* only.

Kesa, *m.* hair of the head. —**kambala**, *nt.* a blanket made of hair.—**kambalī**, *a.* having a blanket made of hair. —**kalāpa**, *m.* a tress of hair. —**kalyāṇa**, *nt.* beauty of hair. —**dhātu**, *f.* hair-relic.

Kesara, *nt.* hairy structures of flowers; mane (of animals.) —**sīha**, *m.* a maned lion.

Kesarī, *m.* a lion.

Kesava, *a.* of rich hair; *m.* the God Vishnu.

Kesoropana, *nt.* shaving of hair.

Kesohāraka, *m.* remover of hair, i.e. a barber.

Ko, *m.* (*sing.* of **kiŋ.**) who? which man?

Koka, *m.* a wolf.

Kokanada, *nt.* a red lotus.

Kokila, *m.* a cuckoo.

Koci, *in.* some one; whoever.

Koccha, *nt.* a brush; a rattan chair.

Kojava, *m.* a carpet.

Koñca, *m.* a heron.—**nāda**, *m.* see **Kuñcanāda.**

Koṭacikā, *f.* the female organ.

Koṭi, *f.* top: summit; point; the end; ten million.—**ppa-koṭi**, *f.* 10,000,000,000,000,000,-000,00.—**ppatta**, *a.* having reached the end; fully grasped.

Koṭilla, *nt.* crookedness.

Koṭisimbalī, **kūṭa**—, *m.* thorny red cotton tree.

Koṭṭana, *nt.* pounding.

Koṭṭita, *pp.* of the fol.

Koṭṭeti (kuṭṭ + e), to pound; to smash; to beat. *aor.*—**esi**. *pr. p.* **koṭṭenta**. *abs.* **koṭṭetvā**.

Koṭṭha, *m.* the abdomen; a cell; a store-room.—**āgāra**, *nt.* granary; treasury; storehouse. —**āgārika**, *m.* storekeeper. —**āsaya**, *a.* existing in the abdomen.

Koṭṭhaka, *m.* a stronghold; a gateway; place for concealment; closet.

Koṭṭhāsa, *m.* share; ration; portion.

Koṇa, *m.* corner; end; a bow.

Kotūhala, *nt.* excitement; curiosity.

Kotthu; **kotthuka**, *m.* a jackal.

Kodaṇḍa, *nt.* a bow.

Kodha, *m.* anger.

Kodhana, *a.* peevish; uncontrolled (of mind).

Konta, see. **Kunta**.

Kopa, *m.* anger; ill-temper. —**neyya**, *a.* apt to arouse anger.

Kopī, *a.* ill-tempered.

Kopīna, *nt.* the generative organ of either sex.*

Kopeti (*caus.* of **kuppati**), to make angry; to disturb; to shake; to trespass a law. *aor.* —**esi**. *pp.* **kopita**. *abs.* **kopetvā**.

Komala, *a.* soft; producing affection.

Komāra, *a.* juvenile.—**bhacca**, *nt.* the medical treatment of infants; brought up by a prince. —**brahmacariyā**, *f.* the vow of chastity beginning from the infancy.

Komudī, *f.* moonlight; the full-moon day in the month Kattika.

Koraka, *m.* a bud.

Korabya, **Koravya**, *a.* a descendant of Kuru; belonging to the country of the Kurus.

Kola, *m. nt.* jujube fruit.

Kolaka, *nt.* pepper.

Kolaṭṭhi, *nt.* the seed of jujube.

Kolamba, *m.* a big jar.

Kolāpa, *m.* a dead or hollow tree.

Koliya, *m.* name of a clan akin to Sākyas.

Koleyyaka, *a.* of good breed; (said of dogs).

Kovida, *a.* clever; well-versed.

Kosa, *m.* store-room; treasury; a sheath; a cocoon.

Kosaka, *m. nt.* a cup; drinking vessel; a small case or sheath.

Kosajja, *nt.* idleness; indolence.

Kosalla, *nt.* proficiency.

Kosātakī, *f.* a creeper the fruit of which is eaten; *Luffa acutangula*. වැටකොළු

Kosaphala, *nt* nutmeg.

Kosambī, *f.* name of the Capital of Vatsas.

Kosala, *m.* name of a country which was prominent at the time of Buddha.

Kosārakkha, *m.* keeper of a treasury.

*The P.T.S. Dictionary gives the meaning "loin cloth" for both kopīna and hirikopīna, then how to explain hirikopīna-paṭicchādanatthan?

Kosika, *m.* an owl.

Kosināraka, *a.* belonging to Kusinārā.

Kosī, *f.* a sheath.

Koseyya, *nt.* silk ; silk cloth . *adj.* silken.

Kosohita, *a.* ensheathed.

Kohañña, *nt.* hypocrisy ; deceit.

Kriyā, see **kiriyā.**

Kva, *in.* where ?—**ci,** *in.* somewhere.

Kh.

Kha, *nt.* space ; sky.

Khaga, *m.* a bird.

Khagga, *m.* a sword.—**kosa,** *m.* sheath for a sword.—**gāhaka,** *m.* swordbearer.—**tala,** *nt.* blade of a sword.—**dhara,** *a.* bearing a sword.—**visāṇa,** *m.* rhinoceros ; one who has a swordlike horn.

Khacati (khac + a), to inlay ; to adorn with. *aor.* **khaci.** *pp.* **khacita.**

Khajja, *a.* to be eaten or chewed. *nt.* solid food ; sweet-meat. —**ka,** *nt.* sweet-meat.—**antara,** *nt.* various kinds of sweets.

Khajju, *f.* itch.

Khajjūrī, *f.* date-palm.

Khajjopanaka, *m.* the fire-fly.

Khañja, *a.* lame.

Khañjati (khaj + ŋ - a), to hobble. *aor.* **khañji.**

Khañjana, *nt.* hobbling. *m.* a wagtail.

Khaṇa, *m.* a moment ; a minute ; an opportunity.—**ṇena,** *ad.* in a moment.—**ṇātīta,** *a.* having missed the opportunity.

Khaṇati (khan + a), to dig ; to uproot. *aor.* **khaṇi.** *pp.* **khata.** *pr. p.* **khaṇanta.** *abs.* **khaṇitvā.**

Khaṇana, *nt.* digging.

Khaṇika, *a.* momentary ; temporary ; changeable.

Khaṇittī, *f.* a crow-bar ; pick-axe.

Khaṇḍa, *m.* a bit ; broken piece ; candy. *adj.* broken.—**danta,** *a.* having broken teeth.—**phulla** *nt.* broken and shattered portions (of a building).

Khaṇḍana, *nt.* breakage.

Khaṇḍikā, *f.* a piece ; a broken bit.

Khaṇḍicca, *nt.* the state of being broken, (said of teeth).

Kaṇḍita, pp. of the foll.

Khaṇḍeti (khaṇḍ + e), to break into pieces ; to transgress. *aor.* —**esi.** *abs.* **khaṇḍetvā.**

Khata (*pp.* of **khaṇati**), dug up ; uprooted ; wounded ; devoid of virtue.

Khatta, *nt.* political science ; that which is belonging to Khattiyas.

Khattiya, *m.* a man of the warrior caste. *adj.* belonging to Khattiyas.—**kaññā,** *f.* a maiden of the Khattiya race.—**kula,** *nt.* the warrior caste.—**mahāsāla,** *m.* a millionaire of the Khattiya tribe.—**māyā,** *f.* the special knowledge of the Khattiyas. —**sukhumāla,** *a.* tender and delicate like a royal prince.

Khattiyā,—**yānī,** *f.* a woman of the Khattiya clan.

Khattu, *m.* charioteer ; a king's attendant adviser.

Khadira, *m.* acacia tree.—**aṅgāra,** *m.* embers of acacia wood.

Khanti, *f.* patience ; wish ; forbearance.—**bala,** *nt.* power of patience.—**mantu,** *a.* forbearing ; patient.

Khantika, *a.* (in cpds.) of such and such a belief. **aññakhantika** = of another belief.

Khantu, *m.* one who forbears ; gentle.

Khandha, *m.* bulk ; the trunk of the body or of a tree ; mass ; heap ; a section or chapter ; sensorial aggregates which condition the appearance of life in any form.—**pañcaka,** *nt.* the five aggregates, *viz.* material qualities, feeling, perception, coefficients of consciousness, and consciousness.

Khandhaka, *m.* a division or chapter.

Khandhāvāra, *m.* a camp.

Khama, *a.* forgiving ; enduring ; bearing.

Khamati (kham + a), to be patient ; to endure ; to forbear ; to pardon. *aor.* **khami.** *pp.* **khanta.** *pr. p.* **khamanta, khamamāna.**

Khamana, *nt.* **Khamā,** *f.* tolerance ; patience ; endurance.

Khamāpana, *nt.* asking for pardon.

Khamāpeti (kham + āpe), to ask one's pardon ; to apologize. *aor.*—**esi.** *pr. p.* **khamāpenta** *pp.* **khamapita.** *abs.* **khamāpetvā.**

Khamitabba, *pt. p.* fit to be forgiven.

Khamitvā, *abs.* having forgiven or endured.

Khambhakata, *a.* with one's arms akimbo.

Khaya, *m.* waste ; destruction ; decay ; consummation of. —**ānupassanā,** *f.* knowledge of the fact of decay.

Khara, *a.* rough ; hard ; sharp ; painful.—**tta,** *nt.*—**tā,** *f.* roughness.

Khala, *nt.* threshing floor (for corn) ;—**agga,** *nt.* the beginning of threshing.—**maṇḍala,** *nt.* threshing floor.

Khalati (khal + a), to stumble. *aor.* **khali.** *pp.* **khalita.** *abs.* **khalitvā.**

Khalita, *nt.* fault ; stumbling.

Khalīna, *m.* the bit (of a horse).

Khalu, *in.* indeed ; surely.

Khaluṅka, *m.* an inferior horse which is hard to manage.

Khallāṭa, *a.* bald.—**sīsa,** *a.* having a bald head.—**ṭiya,** *nt.* baldness.

Khalopī, *f.* a kind of pot.

Khaḷa, *a.* rough ; harsh. *m.* a rascal ; a vile person.

Khāṇu, *m. nt.* stump of a tree ; a post.—**ṇuka,** *m.* a stump ; stake ; a small post.

Khāta (*pp.* of **khaṇati**), dug.

Khādaka, *a.* one who eats ; living on.

Khādati (khād + a), to eat ; to chew ; to bite ; to gnash. *aor.* **khādi.** *pr. p.* **khādanta, khādamāna.**

Khādana, *nt.* the act of eating.

Khādanīya, *a.* fit for eating. *nt.* hard food ; sweetmeat.

Khādāpana, *nt.* the act of feeding ; causing to be eaten.

Khādāpeti (*caus.* of **khādati**), to make to eat or bite. *aor.*—**esi.** *pp.* **khādāpita.** *pr. p.* **khādāpenta.** *abs.* **khādāpetvā.**

Khādita (*pp.* of **khādati**), eaten ; bitten ; consumed.—**tatta,** *nt.* the fact of being eaten.

Khāditabba, *pt. p.* fit to be eaten.

Khādituṃ, *inf.* to eat.

Khāyati (khā + ya), seems to be ; appears like. *aor.* **khāyi.**

Khāyita, *a.* eaten up ; *nt.* something eaten.

Khāra, *m.* alkaline substance potash.—**ka,** *a.* alkaline. *m.* a fresh bud.—**rika,** *a.* alkaline

Khāri, *f.* 16 measures of grain; a basket suspended from a pingo.

Khāri-kāja, Khāri-vidha, *m. nt.* pingo basket and the pingo.

Khāḷeti (khaḷ + e), to wash; to rinse. *aor.*—**esi.** *pp.* **khāḷita.** *abs.* **khāḷetvā.**

Khiḍḍā, *f.* play; amusement. —**dasaka,** *nt.* decad of play. —**rati,** *f.* enjoyment.

Khitta (*pp.* of **khipati**), thrown; overthrown; cast away; upset. —**citta,** *a.* one whose mind is deranged.

Khipa, *m.* anything thrown over; a fish trap; a cloak.

Khipati (khip + a), to cast; to throw out; to sneeze. *aor.* **khipi.** *pr. p.* **khipanta, khipamāna.** *abs.* **khipitvā.**

Khipana, *nt.* throwing; casting away.

Khipita (*pp.* of **khipati**), thrown out. *nt.* sneezing.—**sadda,** *m.* the sound of sneezing.

Khipituŋ, *inf.* to throw; to sneeze.

Khippa, *a.* quick.—**taraŋ,** *ad.* very soon; very quickly. —**paŋ,** *ad.* quickly.

Khila, *nt.* callosity; hardness.

Khīṇa (*pp.* of **khīyati**), exhausted; wasted.—**tta,** *nt.*—**tā,** *f.* the fact of being wasted or exhausted.—**maccha,** *a.* without fish.—**bīja,** *a.* one who is without the seed of existence. —**āsava,** *a.* whose mind is free from mental obsessions.

Khīyati (khī + ya), to be exhausted; to waste away; to become dejected. *aor.* **khīyi.** *pr. p.* **khīyamāna.** *abs.* **khīyitvā.**

Khīra, *nt.* milk.—**aṇṇava,** *m.* the white see.—**paka,** *a.* sucking the milk.—**odana,** *nt.* milk-rice.

Khīrikā, *f.* the tree *Buchanania Latifolia.* කිරිපළු.

Khīla, *m.* a peg; a stake; a post.

Khujja, *a.* humpbacked (person).

Khudā, *f.* hunger.

Khudda,—**ka,** *a.* small; inferior; insignificant. *nt.* honey made by a kind of small bees. —**kanikāya,** *m.* name of a collection of canonical books. —**kapāṭha,** *m.* name of the first book in the Khuddaka-group.

Khuddā, *f.* a kind of small bees.

Khuddānukhuddaka, *a.* the lesser and minor (duties or precepts).

Khuppipāsā, *f.* hunger and thirst.

Khubhati (khubh + a), to be agitated or disturbed. *aor.* **khubhi.** *pp.* **khubhita.**

Khura, *nt.* a razor; hoof (of an animal).—**agga,** *nt.* the hall of tonsure.—**kosa,** *m.* sheath for a razor.—**cakka,** *nt.* a wheel sharp as razor.—**dhārā,** *f.* the blade of a razor.—**bhaṇḍa,** *nt.* the outfit of a barber.—**muṇḍa,** a close-shaven.

Khurappa, *m.* a kind of arrow.

Kheṭa, kheṭaka, *nt.* a shield.

Khetta, *nt.* field; plot of land; suitable place; a place where something is produced or found.—**kamma,** *nt.* work in the field.—**gopaka,** *m.* field watcher.—**sāmika,** *m.* owner of a field.—**tājīva,** *m.* cultivator; farmer.—**tūpama,** *a.* to be likened to a field.

Kheda, *m.* regret; distress; affliction.

Khepa, *m.* a throw; casting; loss (of mind.)

Khepana, *nt.* passing of (time); wasting; annihilation.

Khepita, *pp.* of the foll.

Khepeti (khip + e), to spend (time or wealth); to cause to be wasted. *aor.* —**esi.** *pr. p.* **khepenta.** *abs.* **khepetvā.**

Khema, *a.* safe; calm; full of peace.—**ṭṭhāna,** *nt.* secure place; place of shelter.—**ppatta,** *a.* having attained tranquillity. —**bhūmi,** *f.* a peaceful place.

Khemī, 3. one who enjoys security.

Kheḷa, *m.* saliva.—**mallaka,** *m.* a spittoon.

Khelāsika, *a.* phelm-eater; an abusive term.

Kho, *in.* indeed; really; surely; (an enclictic particle).

Khobha, *m.* shock; agitation.

Khoma, *nt.* linen cloth. *adj.* flaxen.—**dussa,** *nt.* linen cloth; name of a village in the Sākyan territory.

G

Gagana, *nt.* the sky.—**gāmī,** *a.* flying through the sky.

Gaggarā, *f.* name of a lake.

Gaggarāyati (*Denm.* from **gaggarī**), to bellow; to roar.

Gaggarī, *f.* blacksmith's bellows.

Gaṅgā, *f.* river; the Ganges. —**tīra,** *nt.* riverbank.—**dvāra,** *nt.* mouth of a river.—**dhāra,** *m.* a river-basin.—**pāra,** *nt.* further bank of a river.—**sota,** *m.* riverstream; torrent.

Gaṅgeyya, *a.* belonging to the Ganges.

Gaccha, *m.* a plant; a shrub.

Gacchati (gam + a), to go; to move; to walk. *aor.* **gacchi.** *pr. p.* **gacchanta; gacchamāna,** *pp.* **gata.** *abs.* **gantvā.** *inf.* **gantuṃ.**

Gaja, *m.* an elephant.—**kumbha,** *m.* the forehead of an elephant. —**potaka,** *m.* a young elephant.

Gajjati (gajj + a), to roar; to thunder. *aor.* **gajji.** *pr. p.* **gajjanta, gajjamāna.** *abs.* **gajjitvā.**

Gajjanā, *f.* roaring.

Gajjita (*pp.* of **gajjati**), *nt.* roar; thunder.

Gajjitu, *m.* one who roars or thunders.

Gaṇa, *m.* a gang; crowd; a chapter of monks.—**pūraka,** *a.* one who completes the quorum. —**bandhana,** *nt.* co-operation. —**saṅgaṇikā,** *f.* desire to be in a crowd.—**ācariya,** *m.* a teacher of many; one who has many followers.—**ārāmatā,** *f.* desire to be in a crowd.

Gaṇaka, *m.* an accountant; one skilled in arithmetic.

Gaṇanapathātīta, *a.* gone beyond the calculation; unaccountable.

Gaṇanā, *f.* number; counting; arithmetic.

Gaṇikā, *f.* harlot; courtesan.

Gaṇita (*pp.* of **gaṇeti**), counted. *nt.* arithmetic.

Gaṇī, 3. one who has a following.

Gaṇeti (gaṇ + e), to count; to reckon. *aor.* **gaṇesi.** *pr. p.* **gaṇenta,** *abs.* **gaṇetvā.** *pt. p.* **gaṇetabba.**

Gaṇṭhi,—**kā,** *f.* a knot; a tie; a wooden block;—**ṭṭhāna,** *nt.* a difficult and obscure passage.—**pada,** *nt.* an obscure word; a glossary.

Gaṇḍa, *m.* a boil; a swelling; a protuberance.

Gaṇḍaka, *m.* a rhinoceros.

Gaṇḍikā, *f.* a hollowed block of wood which is used to serve the purpose of a bell; a gong.

Gaṇḍī, *f.* a gong; the executioner's block. *adj.* having boils.

Gaṇḍuppāda, *m.* an earth-worm.

Gaṇḍūsa, *m.* a mouthful.

Gaṇhanta (*pr. p.* of **gaṇhāti**), taking; catching; holding.

Gaṇhāti (gah + ṇhā), to take; to hold of; to seize. *aor.* **gaṇhi.** *pp.* **gahita.** *abs.* **gahetvā, gaṇhitvā.**

Gaṇhāpeti (*caus.* of the above), to cause to be taken or seized. *aor.*—**esi.** *pp.*—**pita, gāhāpita.** *abs.*—**petvā.**

Gaṇhituŋ, *inf.* to take.

Gaṇhiya, *abs.* (of **gaṇhāti**), having taken or held.

Gata (*pp.* of **gacchati**), gone; passed; arrived at; having come to a condition.—**ṭṭhāna,** *nt.* the place where one has gone.— **tta,** *nt.* the fact of having gone. —**ddha,—ddhī,** *a.* one who has completed his journey.—**bhāva,** *m.* see **gatatta.**—**yobbana,** *a.* one who has passed his youth.

Gati, *f.* going; career; course; passing on to another existence; destiny; behaviour.—**mantu,** *a.* of perfect behaviour.

Gatta, *nt.* the body.

Gathita, *pp.* bound; fettered; greedy for.

Gada, *m.* sickness; sound; speech.

Gadati (gad + a), to say; to speak. *aor.* **gadi.** *pp.* **gadita.**

Gaddula, *m.* a leash; leather strap.

Gadduhana, *nt.* milking (of a cow);—**mattaŋ,** *ad.* a short time as that of pulling once a cow's teat.

Gadrabha, *m.* an ass; donkey.

Gadhita, see **gathita.**

Gantabba, *pt. p.* fit to be gone.

Gantu, *m.* one who goes.

Gantuŋ, *inf.* to go.

Gantha, *m.* bond; fetter; a composition; a text.—**kāra,** *m.* an author; compiler of a book. —**dhura,** *nt.* the burden of studying Scriptures.—**ppamocana,** *nt.* releasing from the fetters of the body.

Ganthana, *nt.* knitting; twisting; composition.

Ganthita, *pp.* of the foll.

Gantheti (ganth + e), to tie to bind or fasten together; to knit. *aor.*—**esi.** *pr. p.* **ganthenta.** *abs.* **ganthetvā.**

Gandha, *m.* odour; smell; scent. —**karaṇḍaka,** a perfume chest. —**kuṭi,** *f.* perfumed chamber; the room occupied by the Buddha.—**cuṇṇa,** *nt.* scented powder.—**jāta,** *nt.* kinds of perfumes.—**tela,** *nt.* scented oil. —**pañcaṅgulika,** *nt.* the five-finger-mark made after the fingers have been immersed in some scented solution.—**sāra,** *m.* sandal-wood tree.—**āpaṇa,** *m.* a perfumery.

Gandhabba, *m.* a musician; a heavenly musician belonging to the demigods; a being ready to take a new existence.

Gandhamādana, *m.* name of a mountain in the Himālayas.

Gandhāra, *m.* the country (now called) Kandahar.

Gandhārī, *f.* (a magical charm) belonging to Gandhāra.

Gandhika, Gandhī, *a.* having fragrance.

Gandhodaka, *nt.* scented water.

Gabbita, *a.* proud; arrogant.

Gabbha, *m.* interior; the womb; an inner chamber.—**gata,** *a.* gone to the womb; conceived. —**pariharaṇa,** *nt.* protection of the embryo.—**pātana,** *nt.* an abortive preparation; destruction of the embryo.—**mala,** *nt.* accompanying dirty matter of child-birth.—**vuṭṭhāna,** *nt.* child-birth; delivery.—**seyyaka,** *a.* one who is born in an uterus; viviparous.—**seyyā,** *f.* conception in a womb.—**āvakkanti,** *f.* conception.

Gabbhāsaya, *m.* the uterus.

Gabbhinī, *f.* a pregnant woman.

Gambhīra, *a.* deep. *nt.* depth.

Gamana, *nt.* going; walk; journey; pursuit. *adj.* leading to; conducive to.—**antarāya,** *m.* obstacle to one's departure. —**āgamana,** *nt.* going and coming.—**kāraṇa,** *nt.* reason for going.

Gamanīya, *a.* ought to go; fit to be gone.

Gamika, *a.* going away; setting out for a journey. *m.* a traveller.—**vatta,** *nt.* preparation for a journey.

Gameti (gam + e), to make go; to send; to understand. *aor.* **gamesi.**

Gambhīra, *a.* deep; profound; hard to perceive.—**tā,** *f.* depth. —**āvabhāsa,** *a.* having the appearance of depth or profundity.

Gamma, *a.* vulgar; what should be understood or attained.

Gayha, *a.* fit to be taken, seized or gripped. *nt.* that which comes into one's grasp.

Gayhati (gah + ya), to be taken or seized. *aor.* **gayhi.** *pr.p.* **gayhamāna.**

Garahati (garah + a), to reproach; to blame; to scold. *aor.* **garahi.** *pp.* **garahita.** *pr.p.* **garahanta, garahamāna.**

Garahana, *nt.* **Garahā,** *f.* reproach; reproof.

Garahitvā, garahiya, *abs.* having reproached.

Garahī, *a.* one who blames or censures.

Garu, *a.* heavy; serious; grave; venerable; honoured. *m.* a teacher; instructor.—**kātabba,** *a.* worthy of esteem; fit to be respected.—**kāra,** *m.* esteem; honour; respect.—**gabbhā,** *f.* a pregnant woman—**ṭṭhānīya,** *a.* one who takes the place of a teacher; respectable.

Garuka, *a.* heavy; serious; grave.

Garutta, *nt.* **Garutā,** *f.* heavyness; honourableness.

Garukaroti (garu + karoti), to respect; to revere. *aor.*—**kari.** *pp.*—**kata.** *pr.p.* **garukaronta.**

Garuḷa, *m.* a mythical bird; a harpy.

Gala, *m.* the neck; the throat. —**ggāha,** *m.* taking by the neck; throttling.—**nāḷi,** *f.* the larynx. —**ppamāṇa,** *a.* going up to the neck.—**vāṭaka,** *m.* the bottom of the throat.

Galati (gal + a), to drip; to flow; to trickle. *aor.* **gali.** *pr.p.* **galanta; galamāna.** *pp.* **galita,** *abs.* **galitvā.**

Gava, the substantive **go** takes this form in cpds. such as **puṅgava.**

Gavaja, gavaya, *m.* the gayal.

Gavesaka, *a.* one who seeks or looks for.

Gavesati (gaves + a), to seek; to search for; to strive after. *aor.* **gavesi.** *pp.* **gavesita.** *pr.p.* **gavesanta, gavesamāna.** *abs.* **gavesitvā, gavesiya.**

Gavesana, *nt.*—**nā,** *f.* search; seeking.

Gavesī, 3. one who seeks.

Gaha, *m.* one who catches or takes possession of.

Gaha, *nt.* house.—**kāraka**, *m.* house-builder.—**kūṭa**, *nt.* the peak of a house.—**ṭṭha**, *m.* a layman ; householder.—**patānī**, *f.* mistress of a house.—**pati**, *m.* master of a house.—**pati-mahāsāla**, *m.* a very wealthy householder.

Gahaṇa, *nt.* taking ; seizing ; acquisition ; grasp.

Gahaṇika, *a.* having a good digestion.

Gahaṇī, *f.* gestation ; digestion.

Gahana, *nt.* a thicket ; a jungle ; impenetrable place. *adj.* thick ; impervious.—**ṭṭhāna**, *nt.* impenetrable place in a jungle.

Gahita (*pp.* of **gaṇhāti**), taken ; seized ; grasped. *nt.* grip. —**bhāva**, *m.* the fact of being taken or held.

Gaḷagaḷāyati (*Denm.* from **gaḷa-gaḷa**), to rain heavily making the sound gala-gala ; to roar. *aor.*—**ḷāyi**.

Gaḷocī, *f.* a medicinal creeper, *Tinospora Cordifolia* රසකිඳ.

Gāthā, *f.* a verse ; stanza ; a line of poetry.—**pada**, *m.* a line of a stanza.—**bhigīta**, *a.* gained by reciting verses.

Gādha, *a.* deep. *m.* depth ; a safe stand ; foothold.

Gādhati (gādh + a), to stand fast ; to have a firm footing. *aor.* **gādhi**.

Gāna, *nt.* singing ; a song.

Gāma, *m.* village.—**ka**, *m.* small village.—**ghāta**, *m.* sacking or plundering of a village.—**ghātaka**, 3. those who sack villages ; a dacoit.—**jana**, *m.* people of a village.—**jeṭṭha**, *m.* village headman.—**ṭṭhāna**, *nt.* a ruined village.—**dāraka**, *m.* a youngster of a village.—**dārikā**, *f.* a village damsel.—**dvāra**, *nt.* the entrance to a village. —**dhamma**, *m.* vile conduct ; sexual intercourse.—**vāsī**, 3. a villager.—**sīmā**, *f.* the boundary of a parish.

Gāmaṇī, *m.* the head of a village.

Gāmika, *m.* villager.

Gāmī, (in cpds.) *a.* one who goes ; leading to.

Gāyaka, *m.* a singer.

Gāyati (ge + a), to sing ; to recite. *aor.* **gāyi**. *pr.p.* **gāyanta**, **gāyamāna**. *pp.* **gāyita**, **gīta**. *abs.* **gāyitvā**.

Gāyana, *nt.* singing.

Gāyikā, *f.* a female singer.

Gārayha, *a.* contemptible ; low.

Gārava, *m.* respect; reverence ; esteem.—**tā**, *f.* respect.

Gāvī, *f.* a cow.

Gāvuta, *nt.* a league ; a measure little less than two miles.—**tika**, *a.* reaching a league in extent.

Gāvo, *m.* (Nom. pl.) cattle.

Gāha, *m.* seizure ; grip ; obsession ; an idea ; a view.

Gāhaka, *a.* a holder ; taker ; bearer.

Gāhati (gāh + a), to immerse ; to penetrate ; to plunge into.

Gāhana, *nt.* submersion ; plunging.

Gāhāpaka, *a.* one who causes to take or hold.

Gāhāpeti (*caus.* of **gaṇhāti**), to cause to take or to be seized. *aor.*—**esi**. *pp.* **gāhāpita**. *pr.p.* **gāhāpenta**. *abs.* **gāhāpetvā**.

Gāhī, *a.* see **Gāhaka**.

Gāheti (*caus.* of **gaṇhāti**), see **gāhāpeti**. *pp.* **gāhita**. *abs.* **gāhetvā**, **gāhiya**.

Gāḷha, *a.* strong ; tight ; serious. —**aṃ**, *ad.* tightly ; strongly.

Gijjha, *m.* a vulture.—**kūṭa,** *m.* the Vulture's peak near **Rājagaha.**

Gijjhati (gidh + ya), to long for; to desire much. *aor.* **gijjhi.** *pr.p.* **gijjhamāna.**

Giñjakā, *f.* brick.—**āvasatha,** *m.* a house made of bricks.

Giddha (*pp.* of **gijjhati**), greedy.

Giddhi, *f.* greed; attachment.

Giddhī, *a.* greedy for; desirous after.

Gini, *m.* fire.

Gimha, *m.* heat; hot season.

Gimhāna, *m.* summer.

Gimhika, *a.* belonging to the summer.

Girā, *f.* word; utterance.

Giri, *m.* mountain.—**kaṇṇikā,** *f.* the plant *Clitoria Ternatea.* කටරොළු.—**gabbhara,** *nt.* —**guhā,** *f.* a mountain cleft; a gorge or cave.—**bbaja,** *nt.* name of a former capital of Magadha. —**rāja,** *m.* the Mount Meru. —**sikhara,** *nt.* a peak; top of a mountain.

Gilati (gil + a), to swallow; to devour. *aor.* **gili.** *pp.* **gilita.** *pr.p.* **gilanta.** *abs.* **gilitvā.**

Gilana, *nt.* swallowing.

Gilāna,—**naka,** *a.* sick; unwell; a sick person.—**paccaya,** *m.* support for the sick.—**bhatta,** *nt.* food for the sick.—**sālā,** *f.* a hall for the sick.—**ālaya,** *m.* pretence of illness.—**nupuṭṭhāka,** 3. one who attends the sick.—**nupaṭṭhāna,** *nt.* tending or nursing of the sick.

Gihī, *m.* a layman; one who leads a domestic life.—**bandhana,** *nt.* layman's fetters. —**vyañjana,** *nt.* characteristic of a layman.—**saŋsagga,** *m.* association with laymen.

Gīta, *nt.* a song; singing. (*pp.* of **gāyati**), sung.—**rava,**—**sadda,** *m.* sound of a song.

Gītikā, *f.* a song.

Gīvā, *f.* the neck.

Gīveyyaka, *nt.* an ornament for the neck.

Guggulu, *m.* a medicinal resin; bdellium.

Guñjā, *f.* the medicinal creeper *Abrus Precatorius.* ඔලිද.

Guṇa, *m.* virtue; quality; a cord or string; a bow-string; (with numerals; **diguṇa** = twofold). —**kathā,** *f.* praise.—**kittana,** *nt.* telling about one's virtues. —**gaṇa,** *m.* accumulation of good qualities.—**vantu,** *a.* virtuous.—**ṇūpeta,** *a.* endowed with good qualities.

Guṇī, *a.* possessed of good qualities.

Guṇṭhikā, *f.* a ball of strings.

Guṇṭhita, *pp.* of the foll.

Guṇṭheti (guṇṭh + e), to wrap; to cover; to hide. *aor.*—**esi.**

Gutta (*pp.* of **gopeti**), guarded; protected; watchful.—**dvāra,** *a.* with well-guarded senses. —**dvāratā,** *f.* control over one's senses.—**tindriya,** *a.* having guarded senses.

Gutti, *f.* protection; guard; watchfulness.—**ka,** 3. a guardian.

Guda, *nt.* the anus.

Gundā, *f.* the bulbous grass *Cyperus Rotundus.* කලාදුරු.

Gumba, *m.* a bush; a thicket; a troop or swarm.—**antara,** *nt.* interior of a bush.

Guyha, *a.* fit to be hidden. *nt.* a secret; that which is to be hidden.—**bhaṇḍaka,** *nt.* the male or female organ.

Guru, *m.* a teacher. *adj.* heavy; venerable.—**dakkhiṇā,** *f.* teacher's fee.

Guhā, *f.* a cave ; cavern.

Guḷa, *nt.* sugar ; molasses ; a ball; a globe.—**kīḷā,** *f.* a play at ball.

Guḷā, *f.* a kind of bird whose nest is much entangled.

Guḷikā, *f.* a pill.

Gūtha, *m.* faeces ; dung ; excrement.—**kaṭāha,** *m.* a pot for defecation.—**kūpa,** *m.* a pit for defecation.—**gata,** *nt.* a heap of dung.—**pāṇaka,** *m.* an insect living on excrement. —**bhakkha,** *a.* feeding on dung. —**bhāṇī,** 3. of foul speech.

Gūhati (gūh + a), to hide ; to conceal. *aor.* **gūhi.** *pr.p.* **gūhamāna.** *abs.* **gūhitvā.**

Gūhana, *nt.* concealment.

Gūhita, Gūḷha (*pp.* of **gūhati**), hidden ; concealed ; secret.

Geṇḍuka, *m.* a playing ball.

Gedha, *m.* greed.

Gedhita, *pp.* greedy. *nt.* greed.

Geyya, *a.* that which is to be sung. *nt.* a poem ; a certain style of literature.

Geruka, *nt.* red chalk used for colouring.

Gelañña, *nt.* sickness.

Geha, *m.* *nt.* house ; dwelling place.—**aṅgana,** *nt.* the yard in front of a house.—**jana,** *m.* members of a household. —**ṭṭhāna,** *nt.* site for a house. —**dvāra,** *nt.* the gate or the front of a house.—**nissita,** *a.* connected with the family life. —**ppavesana,** *nt.* (the ceremony of), entering a new building. —**sita,** see—**nissita.**

Go, *m.* an ox ; cattle in general. —**kaṇṭaka,** *nt.* the hoof of cattle; a thorny medicinal plant *Ruellia Longifolia*.—**kula,** *nt.* a cow-shed.—**gaṇa,** *m.* a herd of cattle.—**ghātaka,** *m.* a butcher.

Gokaṇṇa, *m.* en elk.

Gocara, *m.* pasture ; fodder ; food (in common) ; sense object; suitable place.—**gāma,** *m.* a village from where a monk obtains his food.

Gocchaka, *m.* a cluster or bunch.

Goṭṭha, *nt.* cow-shed.

Goṇa, *m.* an ox ; a bull.

Goṇaka, *m.* a woollen carpet with long fleece.

Gotama, *a.* belonging to the Gotama clan.

Gotamī, *f.* a woman of the Gotama clan.

Gotta, *nt.* clan ; ancestry.

Gotrabhū, *a.* one who destroys the lineage.

Godhā, *f.* iguana ; a large kind of lizard.

Godhuma, *m.* wheat.

Gonasa, *m.* a viper.

Gopaka, 3. a guardian ; watchman.

Gopakhuma, *a.* having eyelashes like that of a heifer.

Gopana, *nt.*—**nā,** *f.* protection ; care ; watchfulness.

Gopānasī, *f.* a bent beam supporting the framework of a roof.—**vaṅka,** *a.* as crooked as a **gopānasī.**

Gopāla,—**laka,** *m.* a cowherd.

Gopita, *pp.* of **gopeti.**

Gopī, *f.* a woman herding the cows or the wife of a cowherd.

Gopura, *nt.* gateway.

Gopeti (gup + e), to guard ; to protect ; to watch. *aor.* **gopesi.** *pr.p.* **gopenta.** *abs.* **gopetvā, gopiya.** *pt.p.* **gopetabba.**

Gopetu, *m.* protector.

Gopphaka, *nt.* the ankle.

Gomaya, *nt.* cow-dung.

Gomika, Gomī, *a.* owner of cattle.

Gomutta, *nt.* urine of the cows.

Goyūtha, *m.* a herd of cattle.

Gorakkhā, *f.* cow-keeping.

Golomī, *f.* orris root.

Govinda, *m.* an epithet of Krishṇa.

Gosīsa, *m.* the yellow sandal-wood.

Goḷa, Goḷaka, *m. nt.* a ball.

Gh.

Ghaṭa, *m.* a water-pot.

Ghaṭaka, *m. nt.* a small jar; capital of a pillar; a knot of wood.

Ghaṭati (ghaṭ + a), to try; to strive; to exert oneself. *aor.* **ghaṭi,** *pp.* **ghaṭita.** *pr.p.* **ghaṭamāna.**

Ghaṭana, *nt.*—**nā,** *f.* fixing; combination.

Ghaṭā, *f.* a cluster; a swarm; a crowd.

Ghaṭikā, *f.* a small bowl; knot; an hour; a ball; a game of sticks.—**yanta,** *nt.* a clock; any contrivance to measure time.

Ghaṭī, *f.* water-pot.—**kāra,** *m.* a potter.—**yanta,** *nt.* a contrivance to raise water.

Ghaṭīyati (*pass.* of **ghaṭati**), to be combined or connected. *aor.*—**ṭīyi.**

Ghaṭeti (ghaṭ + e), to connect; to unite; to strive. *aor.*—**esi** *pr. p.* **ghaṭenta.** *pp.* **ghaṭita,** *abs.* **ghaṭetvā.**

Ghaṭṭana, *nt.* striking; knocking against; insult.

Ghaṭṭita, *pp.* of the following.

Ghaṭṭeti (ghaṭṭ + e), to strike; to knock against; to offend. *aor.*—**esi.** *pr.p.* **ghaṭṭenta.** *abs.* **gaṭṭetvā.**

Ghaṇṭā, *f.* a bell.

Ghata, *nt.* ghee; clarified butter. —**sitta,** *a.* sprinkled with ghee.

Ghana, *a.* thick; solid; dense; compact. *nt.* a club; a hammer; a musical instrument played by striking. *m.* a cloud. —**tama,** *a.* very thick. *m.* a thick darkness.—**puppha,** *nt.* a woollen coverlet embroidered with flowers.

Ghanasāra, *m.* camphor.

Ghanopala, *nt.* hailstorm.

Ghamma, *m.* heat; the hot season.—**jala,** *nt.* sweat; perspiration.—**mābhibhūta,**—**mābhitatta,** *a.* overpowered by heat.

Ghara, *nt.* house.—**goḷikā,** *f.* a house lizard.—**dvāra,** *nt.* house-door; a gate.—**bandhana,** *nt.* establishing of marriage.—**mānusa,** *m.* members of a house.—**sappa,** *m.* a rat-snake.—**rājira,** *nt.* house-yard. —**rāvāsa,** *m.* the household life.

Gharaṇī, *f.* a house-wife; mistress of a house.

Ghasa (in cpds.), *a.* one who eats.

Ghasati (ghas + a), to eat; to consume. *aor.* **ghasi.** *pr.p.* **ghasanta, ghasamāna.** *abs.* **ghasitvā.**

Ghāta, *m.* **Ghātana,** *nt.* killing; slaughter; destruction; robbery; brigandage.

Ghātaka, Ghātī, 3. one who kills, robs, or destroys.

Ghātita, *pp.* of the foll :

Ghāteti (han + e), to kill; to slay; to destroy. *aor.*—**esi.** *pr.p.* **ghātenta.** *abs.* **ghātetvā, ghātiya.** *pt.p.* **ghātetabba.**

Ghāṇa, *nt.* the nose.—**viññāṇa**, *nt.* perception of smell.—**ṇindriya**, *nt.* the sense of smell.

Ghāyati (ghā + ya), to smell. *aor.* **ghāyi**. *pr.p.* **ghāyanta**, **ghāyamāna**. *abs.* **ghāyitvā**.

Ghāyita (*pp.* of the above), the smell.

Ghāsa, *m.* food ; fodder ; a kind of grass.—**sacchādana**, *nt.* food and clothing.—**hāraka**, *a.* one who fetches the fodder or ghāsa-grass.

Ghuṭṭha (*pp.* of **ghoseti**), proclaimed ; announced.

Ghoṭaka, *m.* an untamed horse.

Ghora, *a.* terrible ; awful.—**tara**, *a.* most terrible.

Ghosa, *m.* sound ; shout ; utterance.—**ka**, 3. one who shouts or proclaims.

Ghosanā, *f.* shouting.

Ghosāpeti (*caus.* of the following), to make proclaim.

Ghoseti (ghus + e), to shout ; to announce ; to proclaim. *aor.* —**esi**. *pp.* **ghosita**, **ghuṭṭha**. *pr.p.* **ghosenta**. *abs.* **ghosetvā**.

C

Ca, (copulative or disjunctive particle), and; then ; now.

Cakita, *a.* disturbed ; afraid.

Cakora, *m.* the francolin partridge.

Cakka, *nt.* a wheel ; circle ; disc ; cycle ; command.—**aṅkita**, *a.* having a wheelmark. —**pāṇī**, *m.* the God Vishnu (in whose hand is a disc). —**yuga**, *nt.* a pair of wheels. —**ratana**, *nt.* jewel wheel of a universal monarch.—**vattī**, *m.* a universal monarch.—**samārūḷha**, *a.* having mounted their vehicles (in an emergency).

Cakkavāka, *m.* the ruddy goose.

Cakkavāḷa, *m.* *nt.* a world-circle ; a solar system.—**gabbha**, *m.* the interior of a world-circle. —**pabbata**, *m.* the (circular) rock supposed to encircle the earth.

Cakkhu, *nt.* the eye.—**ka**, *a.* having eyes.—**da**, *a.*—**dada**, *a.* one who gives the eye (of understanding).—**dhātu**, *f.* the element of vision.—**patha**, *m.* the range of vision.—**bhūta**, *a.* possessor of right understanding. —**mantu**, *a.* endowed with eyes.—**lola**, *a.* greedy to see many things.—**viññāṇa**, *nt.* visual cognition.—**viññeyya**, *a.* to be apperceived by the sense of sight.—**samphassa**, *m.* contact with the vision.

Cakkhussa, *a.* good for the eyes.

Caṅkama, *m.*—**mana**, *nt.* a terraced walk : walking up and down.

Caṅkamati (kam + ṇ-a ; **kam** is doubled and the former **k** is changed to **c**), to walk up and down. *aor.* **caṅkami**. *pr.p.* **caṅkamanta**. *abs.* **caṅkamitvā**.

Caṅgoṭaka, *m.* a casket.

Caccara, *nt.* a courtyard ; a cross road.

Cajati (caj + a), to let loose ; to abandon ; to give up. *aor.* **caji**. *pp.* **catta**. *pr.p.* **cajanta**, **cajamāna**. *abs.* **cajitvā**.

Cañcala, *a.* unsteady ; moving.

Caṭaka, *m.* a sparrow.

Caṇaka, *m.* gram.

Caṇḍa, *a.* fierce ; violent ; passionate.—**sota**, *m.* violent stream. —**hatthī**, *m.* a fierce elephant.

Caṇḍāla, *m.* an outcaste or untouchable.—**kula**, *nt.* the lowest caste.

Caṇḍālī, *f.* a caṇḍāla woman.

Caṇḍikka, *nt.* ferocity.

Catu, *a.* four.—**kkaṇṇa,** ractangular; having four corners. —**kkhattuŋ,** *ad.* four times. —**gguṇa,** *a.* four-fold; quadruple.—**cattāḷīsati,** *f.* forty-four. —**jjātigandha,** *m.* four kinds of perfumes, *viz.* saffron, jasmine, Turkish plant named *Turukkha,* and a kind of Greek flower.—**ttiŋsati,** *f.* thirty-four. —**ddasa,** 3. fourteen.—**ddisā,** *f.* the four quarters of the globe. —**dvāra,** *a.* having four gates. —**navuti,** *f.* ninety-four.—**paccaya,** *m.* the four requisites. *viz.* food, clothing, medicine and lodgings.—**paṇṇāsā,**—**paññāsā,** *f.* fifty-four.—**parisā,** *f.* the fourfold assembly, *viz.* monks, nuns, laymen, and laywomen.—**bhūmaka,** *a.* having four storeys or stages. —**madhura,** *nt.* the four sweets; ghee, honey, sugar and sesemum oil.—**raṅgika,** *a.* consisting of four divisions. —**ranginī,** *f.* (an army) consisting of elephants, chariots, cavalry, and infantry.—**raṅgula,** *a.* measuring four inches. —**rassa,** *a.* quadrangular. —**raŋsa,** *a.* having four edges. —**rāsīti,** *f.* eighty-four.—**vīsati,** *f.* twenty-four.—**saṭṭhi,** *f.* sixty-four.—**sattati,** *f.* seventy-four.

Catukka, *nt.* a set of four; a cross road.

Catuttha, *a.* fourth.

Cattutthī, *f.* the fourth day of a fortnight; the fourth case, i.e. Dative.

Catudhā, *ad.* in four ways.

Catuppada, *m.* a quadruped.

Catubbidha, *a.* fourfold.

Catura, *a.* clever; skilled; shrewd.

Catta (*pp.* of **cajati**), given up; sacrificed.

Cana, Canaŋ, a particle used to express a portion of a whole: **Kudācana,** sometimes.

Canda, *m.* the moon.—**ggāha,** *m.* eclipse of the moon.—**maṇḍala,** *nt.* the disc of the moon.

Candana, *m.* sandal-wood tree: *nt.* sandal-wood.—**sāra,** *m.* the essence of sandal-wood.

Candanikā, *f.* a cesspool.

Candikā, *f.* moonlight.

Candimā, *m.* the moon.

Capala, *a.* fickle; wavering; unsteady.—**tā,** *f.* fickleness.

Capu-capu-kāraka, *m.* making such a sound while eating or drinking.

Camara, Camarī, *m.* the yak ox (in the Himalayan regions).

Camū, *f.* an army.—**pati,**—**nātha,** *m.* a general of an army.

Campaka, *m.* the tree *Michelia Champaka,* සපු.

Campā, *f.* name of a town in India; present Bhagalpore.

Campeyyaka, *a.* belonging to **Campā.**

Camma, *nt.* a hide; leather. —**kāra,** *m.* a tanner.—**khaṇḍa,** *m.* a piece of leather used as a rug.—**pasibbaka,** *m.* a leather bag.

Caya, *m.* piling; heaping; a mass.

Cara, 3. one who walks or frequents; *m.* a spy.

Caraka, see **Cara.**

Caraṇa, *nt.* walking about; the foot; conduct; behaviour.

Carati (car + a), to walk or roam about; to behave; to practise; to perform. *aor.* **cari.** *pp.* **carita.** *pr.p.* **caranta, caramāna.** *abs.* **caritvā.**

Carāpeti (*caus.* of the above), to cause to move or practise; to circulate. *aor.*—**esi.**

Carita, *nt.* character; behaviour; life.

Caritu, *m.* performer; observer.

Carima,—maka, *a.* the last; subsequent.

Cariyā, *f.* conduct; behaviour.

Cala, *a.* moving; quivering; unsteady.—**citta,** having a fickle mind.

Calati (cal + a), to move; to stir; to tremble; to be agitated. *aor.* **cali.** *pp.* **calita.** *pr.p.* **calanta, calamāna,** *abs.* **calitvā.**

Calana, *nt.* movement; trembling; agitation.

Cavati (cu + a), to fall away; to shift; to pass from one state of existence into another. *aor.* **cavi.** *pp.* **cuta.** *pr. p.* **cavanta, cavamāna,** *abs.* **cavitvā.**

Cavana, *nt.* shifting; falling away; death.

Cāga, *m.* gift; abandoning; giving up; generosity.

Cāgānussati, *f.* remembrance of one's generosity.

Cāgī. *a.* one who abandons or donates.

Cāṭi, *f.* a jar; a pot.

Cāṭukamyatā, *f.* flattery.

Cātaka, *m.* a hornbill.

Cātuddasī, *f.* the 14th day of a fortnight.

Cātuddisa, *a.* belonging to the four directions.

Cātuddīpaka, *a.* covering the four continents or sweeping over the whole earth.

Cātummahāpatha, *m.* the place where four roads meet.

Cātummahābhūtika, *a.* consisting of the four great elements.

Cātummahārājika, *a.* belonging to the retinue of four Deva kings, inhabiting the lowest Deva heaven.

Cāturiya, *nt.* skill; shrewdness.

Cāpa, *m.* a bow.

Cāpalla, *nt.* fickleness.

Cāmara, *nt.* a chowrie; the tail of the yak used as a whisk.

Cāmīkara, *nt.* gold.

Cāra, *m.* motion; action; process; going.

Cāraka, *a.* one who causes to move or act. *m.* a prison.

Cāraṇa, *nt.* causing to move or act; management.

Cārikā, *f.* a journey; wandering.

Cāritta, *nt.* custom; conduct; practice; calling on.

Cārī, *a.* (in cpds.) acting; practising; living; behaving.

Cāru, *a.* charming; beautiful; pleasant.—**dassana,** *a.* lovely to behold.

Cāreti (*caus.* of **carati**), to set going; to pasture; to feast one's senses. *aor.* **cāresi.** *pp.* **cārita.** *pr.p.* **cārenta.** *abs.* **cāretvā.**

Cāla, *m.* a shock; a sudden agitation.

Cāleti (*caus.* of **calati**), to shake; to agitate. *aor.* **esi.** *pp.* **cālita.** *pr.p.* **cālenta, cālayamāna.** *abs.* **cāletvā.**

Cāvanā, *f.* making to shift.

Cāveti (*caus.* of **cavati**), to bring to fall; to drive away; to distract. *aor.*—**esi.** *pp.* **cāvita.** *pr.p.* **cāventa.** *abs.* **cāvetva.**

Ci, an indefinite interrogative particle: **koci**=some one.

Cikkhalla, *nt.* mire mud; swamp.

Ciccitāyati (onom.) to hiss; to fizz; to make the sound chit chit.

Ciñcā, *f.* tamarind.

Ciṇṇa (*pp.* of **cināti**), practised; made a habit of; accomplished.

Cita (*pp.* of **cināti**), heaped; lined or faced with.

Citaka, *m.* funeral pile.

Citi, *f.* a heap; a cairn.

Citta, *nt.* mind; thought; *m.* name of a month : March-April. —**kkhepa**, *m.* derangement of the mind.—**passaddhi**, *f.* serenity of mind.—**mudutā**, *f.* plasticity of mind.—**vikkhepa**, *m.* madness.—**santāpa**, *m.* sorrow.—**samatha**, *m.* collectedness of thought.—**tānupassanā**, *f.* a critique of heart.—**tābhoga**, *m.* consideration.—**tujjukatā**, *f.* rectitude of mind.—**uttrāsa**, *m.* terror; fear.—**tuppāda**, *m.* rise of a thought.—

Citta, *a.* variegated; manifold; beautiful. *nt.* a painting; picture.—**kata**, *a.* adorned; made by the mind.—**kathika**.—**kathī-**, *a.* a brilliant speaker; an orator.—**kamma**, *nt.* painting; the art of painting; ornamentation.—**kāra**, *m.* a painter; decorator.—**tara**, *a.* more varied or diversified. —**tāgāra**, *nt.* a picture gallery.

Cittaka, *nt.* a sectarian mark on the forehead.

Cittatā, *f.* variegation; (in cpds:) being of such a mind.

Cittīkāra, *m.* respect; consideration.

Citra, see **Citta 2.**

Cināti (ci + nā), to heap up; to collect; to accumulate. *aor.* **cini.** *pp.* **cita.** *pr.p.* **cinanta, cinamāna.** *abs.* **cinitvā.**

Cintaka, **Cintanaka**, *a.* considerate; thoughtful; a thinker.

Cintā, *f.* (**Cintana**, *nt.*) thinking; thought; consideration. —**maṇi**, *m.* a wish-fulfilling gem.—**maya**, *a.* consisting of thought.

Cintita (*pp.* of **cinteti**), thought out; invented; devised.

Cintī, *a.* (in cpds.) thinking of.

Cintetabba, *pt.p.* fit to be considered.

Cinteti (cint + e), to think; to reflect; to consider. *aor.* **cintesi.** *pr.p.* **cintenta, cintayamāna,** *abs.* **cintetvā, cintiya.**

Cinteyya, *a.* what should be considered.

Cimilikā, *f.* a case for pillow, etc.

Cira, *a.* lasting long.—**kālaŋ**, *ad.* a long time.—**ṭṭhitika**, *a.* lasting long; perpetual.—**taraŋ**, *ad.* a further long time. —**nivāsī**, *a.* dweller for a long time.—**pabbajita**, *m.* having long since become a monk. —**ppavāsī**, *a.* a person long absent from his home.—**rattaŋ**, *ad.* a long time.—**rattāya**, *ad.* for a long time.

Ciraŋ, *ad.* (for) a long time.

Cirassaŋ, *ad.* a very long time; at last.

Cirāya, *ad.* for a long time.

Cirāyati (Denm. from **cira**), to tarry; to delay. *aor.* **cirāyi.** *pp.* **cirāyita.** *pr. p.* **cirāyanta.** *abs.* **cirāyitvā.**

Cirena, *ad.* after a long time.

Cīnapiṭṭha, *nt.* red lead.

Cīnaraṭṭha, *nt.* China.

Cīra, Cīraka, *nt.* fibre; a strip; a bark dress.

Cīrī, *f.* a cricket.

Cīvara, *nt.* the yellow robe (of a Buddhist monk).—**kaṇṇa**, *nt.* the lappet of a robe.—**kamma**, *nt.* robe-making.—**kāra**, *m.* deviser of a robe; robe-maker. —**dāna**, *nt.* donation of robes.

—**dussa,** *nt.* cloth for robes. —**rajju,** *f.* a rope for hanging the robes.—**vaŋsa,** *m.* a bamboo for hanging up robes.

Cuṇṇa, *nt.* powder; chunam; soap-powder.—**vicuṇṇa,** *a.* crushed to bits; smashed.

Cuṇṇaka, *nt.* scented powder. —**jāta,** *a.* reduced to powder. —**cālanī,** *f.* a sieve.

Cuṇṇita, *pp.* of the following.

Cuṇṇeti (cuṇṇ + e), to grind; to powder; to crush. *aor.* —**esi.** *pr.p.* **cuṇṇenta.** *abs.* **cuṇṇetvā.** *pass.* **cuṇṇīyati.**

Cuta, *pp.* of **cavati.**

Cuti, *f.* shifting; passing away; vanishing.

Cudita, *pp.* of **codeti.**

Cuditaka, 3. an accused; being reproved.

Cuddasa, 3. fourteen.

Cundakāra, *m.* a turner.

Cubuka, *nt.* the chin.

Cumbaṭa,—**ṭaka,** *nt.* a pad; a coil.

Cumbati (cumb + a), to kiss. *aor.* **cumbi.** *pp.* **cumbita.** *pr.p.* **cumbanta; cumbamāna.** *abs.* **cumbitvā.**

Culla, *a.* small; minor.—**antevāsika,** *m.* a page.—**pitu,** *m.* uncle.—**lupaṭṭhāka,** *m.* a personal attendant; page boy.

Cūcuka, *nt.* the nipple; teat.

Cūla, see **culla.**

Cūḷā, *f.* crest; a lock of hair left on the crown of the head; cockscomb.—**maṇi,** *m.* diadem; a jewel worn in the crest.

Cūḷikā, *f.* a knot of hair.

Ce, (conditional particle), if.

Ceṭa, Ceṭaka, *m.* a servant boy.

Ceṭikā, Ceṭī, *f.* a maid servant.

Ceta, *m.* *nt.* (**mano**-group), thought; intention; purpose.

Cetanā, *f.* intention.

Cetayati (cit + aya), to perceive; to think. *aor.* **cetayi.** *pp.* **cetayita.** *abs.* **cetetvā, cetayitvā.**

Cetasa, *a.* (in cpds.), having the purpose of. **Pāpacetasa**=evil-minded.

Cetasika, *a.* mental; *nt.* a mental property.

Cetiya, *nt.* a sepulchral monument; a pagoda.—**aṅgaṇa,** *nt.* the open space around a pagoda. —**gabbha,** *m.* the dome of a pagoda.—**pabbata,** *m.* name of a mountain in Ceylon, present Mihintale.

Ceteti, see **Cetayati.**

Ceto, is the form that **ceta** takes in cpds.—**khila,** *nt.* fallowness; waste of mind.—**paṇidhi,** *f.* resolution; aspiration.—**pariyañāṇa,** *nt.* understanding the ways of others' thought. —**pasāda,** *m.* gladdening of heart.—**vimutti,** *f.* emancipation of heart.—**samatha,** *m.* calmness of mind.

Cela, *nt.* cloth; garment.—**vitāna,** *nt.* an awning.—**lukkhepa,** *m.* waving of garments (as a sign of applause).

Coca, *m.* banana.—**pāna,** *nt.* a sweet drink made of banana.

Codaka, *m.* a plaintiff; one who censures or complains.

Codanā, *f.* reproof; accusation; plaint.

Codita, *pp.* of the foll.

Codeti (cud + e), to incite; to reprove; to accuse. *aor.* **codesi.** *pr.p.* **codenta, codayamāna.** *abs.* **codetvā, codiya.**

Codetu, *m.* see **Codaka.**

Copana, *nt.* stirring

Cora, *m.* a thief; robber.—**ghātaka,** *m.* executioner of robbers.—**rupaddava,** *m.* an attack from robbers.

Corikā, *f.* theft.

Corī, *f.* a female thief.

Coḷa, *m.* cloth.—**raṭṭha**, *nt.* the country of **Coḷa** in South India.

Coḷaka, *nt.* a piece of cloth ; a rag.

Coḷiya, *a.* belonging to the Coḷa country.

Ch.

Cha, 3. six.—**kkhattuŋ**, *ad.* six times.—**cattāḷīsati**, *f.* forty-six.—**dvārika**, *a.* belonging to the six outlets of the senses. —**navuti**, *f.* ninety-six.—**paññāsā**, *f.* fifty-six.—**bbaggiya**, *a.* belonging to the group of six.—**bbaṇṇa**, *a.* consisting of six colours.—**bbassika**, *a.* existing throughout six years ; six years old.—**bbidha**, *a.* sixfold.—**bbīsati**, *f.* twenty-six.—**saṭṭhi**, *f.* sixty-six.—**sattati**. *f.* seventy-six.

Chakana,—**naka**, *nt.* the dung of animals.

Chakalaka, **Chagalaka**, *m.* a he-goat.

Chakka, *nt.* a set of six.

Chaṭṭha, *a.* sixth.

Chaṭṭhī, *f.* the sixth case, i.e., Genitive.

Chaḍḍaka, *a.* thrower ; remover.

Chaḍḍana, *nt.* throwing away ; rejection.

Chaḍḍanīya, *a.* fit to be thrown away.

Chaḍḍāpeti (*caus.* of **chaḍḍeti**), *aor.*—**esi**. *pp.* **chaḍḍāpita**. *abs.* **chaḍḍāpetvā**.

Chaḍḍita, *pp.* of **chaḍḍeti**.

Chaḍḍiya, *a.* to be rejected or thrown away.

Chaḍḍīyati (*pass.* of **chaḍḍeti**).

Chaḍḍeti (chaḍḍ + e), to throw away ; to abandon ; to reject ; to leave. *aor.*—**esi**. *pr.p.* **chaḍḍenta**. *abs.* **chaḍḍetvā**. *pt.p.* **chaḍḍetabba**.

Chaṇa, *m.* a festival.

Chatta, *nt.* umbrella ; sunshade ; the royal canopy.—**kāra**, *m.* maker of sunshades.—**gāhaka**, 3. one who carries his master's sunshade.—**nāḷi**, *f.* —**daṇḍa**, *m.* the handle of a sunshade.—**pāṇī**, *m.* one who carries an umbrella.—**maṅgala**, *nt.* coronation festival ; pinnacle raising of a pagoda. —**tussāpana**, *nt.* raising of the royal canopy, i.e., to occupy the throne.

Chattiŋsā,—**sati**, *f.* thirty-six.

Chada (in cpds.) *m.* anything that covers ; a veil.

Chadana, *nt.* a thatch ; a roof ; a cover.

Chaddanta, *a.* having six tusks. *m.* name of a great lake and a race of elephants.

Chaddikā, *f.* vomiting.

Chaddhā, **Chadhā**, *ad.* in six ways.

Chanda, *m.* impulse ; will ; wish.

Chanda (**mano**-group), *m.* *nt.* metrics ; prosody.

Chandaka, *nt.* vote ; a voluntary collection.

Chandatā, *f.* (in cpds.), impulse ; desire for.

Chandāgati, *f.* wrong way of behaviour under an impulse.

Channa, *pp.* of **chādeti**.

Channa, *a.* proper ; suitable.

Chappada, *m.* a bee.

Chamā, *f.* the earth; ground.

Chambhitatta, *nt.* stupefaction; consternation.

Chambhī, *a.* terrified ; paralysed with fear.

Chava, *m.* a corpse. *adj.* low ; miserable.—**kuṭikā**, *f.* charnel-house.—ṭṭhika, *nt.* a bone separated from a skeleton. —ḍāhaka, *m.* one who officially burns the dead.—ālāta, *nt.* fire brand from a pyre.

Chavi, *f.* the outer skin; tegument.—**kalyāṇa,** *nt.* beauty of complexion.—**vaṇṇa,** *m.* colour of the skin; complexion.

Chaḷaṅga, *a.* consisting of six parts.

Chaḷabhiññā, *a.* possessing the six branches of higher knowledge.—**ññā,** *f.* the six branches of super-human knowledge.

Chaḷaŋsa, *a.* having six sides or corners.

Chāta, *a.* hungry.—**jjhatta,** *a.* hungry.—**tā,** *f.* the state of being hungry

Chātaka, *nt.* hunger; famine.

Chādana, *nt.*—**danā,** *f.* covering; clothing; concealment.

Chādanīya, chādetabba, *pt. p.* fit to be covered.

Chādeti (chad + e), to cover; to conceal; to thatch; to give pleasure; to relish. *aor.*—**esi.** *pp.* **chādita,** *pr.p.* **chādenta, chādayamāna.** *abs.* **chādetvā, chādiya.**

Chāpa, chāpaka, *m.* the young one of an animal.

Chāyā, *f.* shade; shadow.—**māna,** *nt.* the measuring of shadow.—**rūpa,** *nt.* a photograph; portrait.

Chārikā, *f.* ashes.

Chāha, *nt.* six days.

Chiggala, *nt.* a hole.

Chijjati (*pass.* of **chindati**), to be cut, broken or severed. *aor.* **chijji,** *pr.p.* **chijjanta, chijjamāna,** *abs.* **chijjitvā, chijjiya.**

Chida, *a.* (in cpds.) breaking; cutting; destroying: **Bandhanacchida**=one who breaks or cuts the bond.

Chidda, *nt.* a hole; a fissure; fault; defect. *adj.* having fissures; perforated; faulty.—**ka,** *a.* having holes or pores.—**gavesi,** *a.* looking for others' faults or weak points.—**āvacchiddaka,** *a.* full of breaches and holes.

Chiddita, *a.* perforated; bored through.

Chindati (chid + ŋ-a), to cut; to sever; to destroy. *aor.* **chindi.** *pp.* **chinna.** *pr.p.* **chindanta, chindamāna.** *abs.* **chinditvā, chindiya.**

Chindiya, *a.* breakable.

Chinna (*pp.* of **chindati**), —**āsa.** *a.* without hope.—**nāsa,** *a.* one whose nose is cut off. —**bhatta,** *a.* famished; starved.—**vattha,** *a.* one whose garments are taken by force. —**hattha,** *a.* one whose hands are cut off.—**niriyāpatha,** *a.* unable to walk; a cripple.

Chuḍḍha, *pp.* thrown away; rejected; contemptible.

Chupati (chup + a), to touch. *aor.* **chupi.** *abs.* **chupitvā.**

Chupana, *nt.* touching.

Chūrikā, *f.* a dagger.

Cheka, *a.* clever; skilful.—**tā,** *f.* cleverness; skill.

Chejja, *a.* fit to be cut off; liable to break. *nt.* punishment by cutting off one's limbs.

Chettabba, *pt.p.* ought to be cut off.

Chettu, *m.* one who cuts.

Chetvā, chetvāna, *abs.* having cut off or severed.

Cheda, *m.* cutting off; severence. —**ka,** 3. cutter; breaker.

Chedana, *nt.* cutting; severing.

Chedāpana, *nt.* causing to cut or break.

Chedāpeti (*caus.* of **chindati**), to cause to cut or break. *aor.* —**esi**. *pp.* **chedāpita**. *abs.* **chedāpetvā**.

J.

Jagati, *f.* the earth; the world. —**ppadesa**, *m.* a spot on the earth—**ruha**, *m.* a tree.

Jaggati (jagg + a), to watch over ; to nourish ; to lie awake. *aor.* **jaggi**. *abs.* **jaggitvā**.

Jaggana, *nt.*—**nā**, *f.* tending ; bringing up ; watchfulness.

Jagghati (jaggh + a), to laugh ; to deride. *aor.*—**ghi**.

Jagghanā, *f.* **jagghita**, *nt.* laughter.

Jaghana, *nt.* the loins ; the buttocks.

Jaṅgama, *a.* movable.

Jaṅgala, *nt.* jungle ; a sandy and waterless place.

Jaṅghamagga, *m.* foot-path.

Jaṅghapesanika, *nt.* carrying messages on foot ; *m.* one who carries messages.

Jaṅghā, *f.* the lower leg ; the calf of the leg.—**bala**, *nt.* strength of the leg.—**vihāra**, *m.* a walk.

Jaṅgheyya, *nt.* a knee-piece.

Jacca, *a.* (in cpds.), having such a birth.—**ndha**, *a.* blind from birth.

Jaccā = **jātiyā**.

Jajjara, *a.* feeble with age ; old ; withered.

Jajjarita, *pp.* weakened.

Jañña, *a.* pure ; noble ; charming ; of good birth.

Jaṭa, *nt.* the handle (of a knife etc.)

Jaṭā, *f.* tangle ; plaiting ; matted hair.—**dhara**, *m.* an ascetic wearing matted hair.

Jaṭita, *pp.* entangled ; plaited.

Jaṭiya, Jaṭila, *m.* a kind of ascetics with matted hair.

Jaṭhara, *m.* *nt.* the belly ; the stomach.—**aggi**, *m.* gestation.

Jaṇṇu, *nt.*—**kā**, *f.* the knee. —**matta**, *a.* knee-deep.

Jatu, *nt.* the lac ; sealing wax. —**maṭṭhaka**, *nt.* something encased with lac.

Jattu, *nt.* the shoulder.

Jana, *m.* a person ; a man ; the people.—**kāya**, *m.* a crowd of people.—**tā**, *f.* a gathering of people.—**pada**, *m.* a province ; a county ; country-side.—**pad-akalyāṇī**, *f.* the most beautiful girl in a country.—**pad-acārikā**, *f.* travelling in a country.—**sammadda**, *m.* crowding of the people.

Janaka, *m.* a producer ; father. *adj.* producing ; generating.

Janana, *nt.* production ; causing.

Jananī, *f.* the mother.

Janādhipa, Janinda, *m.* a king (of men).

Janikā, *f*, the mother ; genetrix.

Janita, *pp.* of the foll.

Janeti (jan + e), to generate ; to produce ; to give birth. *pr.p.* **janenta**. *abs.* **janetvā**.

Janetu, *m.* producer ; generator.

Janettī, *f.* the mother.

Jantāghara, *nt.* a hot room for steam bath.

Jantu, *m.* a creature ; living being.

Japa, *m.* muttering.

Japati (jap + a), to utter ; to mumble ; to recite. *aor.* **japi**. *pp.* **japita**. *abs.* **japitvā**.

Japana, jappana, *nt.* mumbling ; whispering.

Japā, *f.* China-rose.

Jappā, jappanā, *f.* greed ; talk for gain.

Jambālī, *f.* a dirty pool.

Jambu (ū), *f.* the rose-apple tree.—**dīpa,** *m.* the country of the rose-apples. i.e., India. —**pakka,** *nt.* the fruit of *Eugenia Jambolana.*—**saṇḍa,** *m.* rose-apple grove.

Jambuka, *m.* a jackal.

Jambonada, *nt.* a sort of gold coming from the Jambu river.

Jambhati (jabh + ŋ-a), to yawn ; to arouse oneself. *aor.* **jambhi.**

Jambhanā, *f.* yawning ; arousing.

Jambhīra, *m.* the orange tree ; *nt.* orange.

Jamma, *a.* vulgar ; contemptible.

Jaya, *m.* victory ; conquest.—**ggaha,**—**gāha,** *m.* conquest ; the lucky throw or lot.—**pāna,** *nt.* the drink of victory.—**sumana,** *nt.* the red China-rose.

Jayati (ji + a), to conquer ; to surpass ; to defeat. *aor.* **jayi.** *pp.* **jita.** *pr.p.* **jayanta.** *abs.* **jayitvā.**

Jayampati, *m.* the husband and wife.

Jara, *m.* fever. *adj.* old ; decayed ; decrepit.—**ggava,** *m.* an old bull.—**sakka,** *m.* the old **sakka,** (the deva-king).

Jaratā, *f.* decay ; old age.

Jarā, *f.* decay ; old age.—**jajjara,**—**jiṇṇa,** *a.* feeble and decrepit with age.—**dukkha,** *nt.* suffering through the old age.—**dhamma,** *a.* subject to growing old or decaying. —**bhaya,** *nt.* fear of old age or decay.

Jala, *nt.* water.—**gocara,**—**cara,** *a.* living in the water ; aquatic. *m.* a fish.—**ja,** *a.* born or sprung from the water. *nt.* a lotus. *m.* a fish.—**da,** —**dhara,** *m.* a raincloud.—**niggama,** *m.* an outlet for water ; a drain. —**ādhāra,** *m.* deposit of water ; reservoir.—**ālaya,**—**āsaya,** *m.* a lake ; an artificial tank.

Jalati (jal + a), to shine ; to burn. *aor.* **jali.** *pp.* **jalita.** *pr.p.* **jalanta, jalamāna.** *abs.* **jalitvā.**

Jaladhi, jalanidhi, *m.* the ocean.

Jalana, *nt.* shining ; burning.

Jalābu, *m.* the placenta.—**buja,** *a.* born in a placenta ; viviparous.

Jalūkā, *f.* a leech.

Jalla, *nt.* wet dirt.

Jallikā, *f.* dirt (on the body); decayed outer bark of a tree.

Java, *m.* speed ; strength.

Javati (ju + a), to run ; to hasten ; to hurry. *aor.* **javi.** *pp.* **javita.** *pr.p.* **javamāna.** *abs.* **javitvā.**

Javana, *nt.* impulse ; alacrity ; swift understanding ; running. *adj.* swift.—**pañña,** *a.* having swift understanding.

Javanikā, *f.* a screen ; curtain.

Jaha, *a.* (in cpds.), leaving behind ; giving up.

Jahati, Jahāti (hā + a ; **hā** is duplicated and the first is changed to **ja**), to leave ; to abandon; to give up ; to forsake. *aor.* **jahi.** *pp.* **jahita.** *pr.p.* **jahanta.** *abs.* **jahitvā.** *pt.p.* **jahitabba.**

Jaḷa, *a.* slow ; stupid. *m.* a stupid person.

Jāgara, *a.* awake ; vigilant ; watchful.

Jāgaraṇa, *nt.* keeping awake.

Jāgarati (jāgar + a), to be awake or watchful. *aor.* **jāgari.** *pr.p.* **jāgaranta.**

Jāgariya, *nt.* vigil; waking. —**yānuyoga,** *m.* vigilance; practice of watchfulness.

Jāṇu, *m.* the knee.—**maṇḍala,** *nt.* the knee-cap.—**matta,** *a.* knee-deep.

Jāta (*pp.* of **jāyati**), born; arisen; become; occurred; happened. *nt.* a collection or variety.—**divasa,** *m.* birthday.—**rūpa,** *nt.* gold.—**veda,** *m.* fire.—**ssara,** *m. nt.* a natural lake.

Jātaka, *nt.* a birth story. *adj.* born; arisen.—**bhāṇaka,** 3. a repeater of the Jātakas.

Jātatta, *nt.* the fact of being born.

Jāti, *f.* birth; rebirth; race; nation; genealogy; a sort of; a kind of.—**kosa,** *m.* mace (of nutmeg).—**kkhaya,** *m.* destruction of the chance of being reborn.—**kkhetta,** *nt.* birthplace; the realm of rebirth. —**tthaddha,** *a.* proud of (one's own) birth.—**nirodha,** *m.* extermination of rebirth.—**phala,** *nt.* nutmeg.—**mantu,** *a.* of good birth; having genuine qualities.—**vāda,** *m.* discussion about the parentage.—**sampanna,** *a.* of good birth or a noble family.—**sumanā,** *f.* jasmine.—**ssara,** *a.* remembering former births.—**hiṅgulaka,** *nt.* natural vermillion.

Jātika, *a.* descended from; belonging to the class, clan, or nation of.

Jātu, *in.* surely; undoubtedly.

Jānana, *nt.* knowledge; recognition.

Jānanaka, *a.* knowing.

Jānanīya, *a.* what should be known.

Jānapada,—padika, *a.* belonging to the country; *m.* a rustic. *pl.* country-folk.

Jānāti (ñā + nā), to know; to find out; to be aware. *aor.* **jāni.** *pr.p.* **jānanta, jānamāna.** *pp.* **ñāta.** *abs.* **jānitvā, ñatvā.** *inf.* **jānituŋ; ñātuŋ.**

Jānāpeti (*caus.* of the above), to make known; to inform; to reveal oneself. *aor.*—**esi.** *pp.* **jānāpita, ñāpita.** *pr.p.* **ñāpenta.** *abs.* **jānāpetvā, ñāpetvā.**

Jāni, *f.* loss; deprivation; the wife.—**pati,** *m.* the wife and husband.

Jāmātu, *m.* son-in-law.

Jāyati (jan + ya), to be born; to arise. *aor.* **jāyi.** *pp.* **jāta.** *pr.p.* **jāyanta, jāyamāna,** *abs.* **jāyitvā.**

Jāyattana, *nt.* the state of a wife.

Jāyana, *nt.* birth; arising.

Jāyā, *f.* wife.—**pati,** *m.* wife and husband.

Jāra, *m.* a paramour.—**ttana,** *nt.* the state of a paramour.

Jārī, *f.* an adultress.

Jāla, *nt.* a net; entanglement. -**pūva,** *m.* pancake.

Jālaka, *m.* a bud; a small net.

Jālakkhika, *nt.* a mesh of a net.

Jālā, *f.* flame.—**kula,** *a.* surrounded by flames.

Jālika, *m.* a fisherman who uses a net.

Jālikā, *f.* an armour made of chain.

Jālinī, *f.* lust; desire; craving.

Jāleti, (jal + e), to kindle; to light; to cause to burn. *aor.* —**esi.** *pp.* **jālita.** *pr. p.* **jālenta; jālayamāna.** *abs.* **jāletvā.**

Jigiŋsaka, *a.* desirous of.

Jigiŋsati (har + sa. **har** becomes **giŋ**; it is doubled and the former **gin** becomes **ji**). to desire. *aor.*—**ŋsi.** *pp.*—**sita.** *pr.p.* **jigiŋsamāna.**

Jigiŋsanā, jigiŋsā, *f.* covetousness; desire for.

Jigucchaka, *a.* one who disapproves of or dislikes.

Jigucchati (gup + cha; **gu** is doubled and the first **gu** becomes **ji**), to shun; to loathe; to be disgusted at. *aor.*—**chi.** *pp.*—**chita.** *pr.p.*—**chanta,** —**chamāna.** *abs.*—**chitvā,** —**chiya.**

Jigucchana, *nt.*—**nā,** *f.*—**chā,** *f.* disgust for; dislike; detestation.

Jighacchati (ghas + cha; **g** is doubled and the first **g** is changed to **ji.** the **s** of the root becomes **c.**), to be hungry; to have a desire to eat. *aor.* —**chi.** *pp.*—**chita.**

Jighacchā, *f.* hunger.

Jiñjuka, *m.* wild liquorice.

Jiṇṇa (*pp.* of **jīrati**), decayed; old; digested.—**ka, 3.** an old person.—**tā,** *f.* decrepitude.

Jita (*pp.* of **jināti**), conquered; subdued; *nt.* victory.—**tta,** *nt.* mastery.

Jitatta (jita + atta), one who has subdued the mind.

Jina, *m.* the conqueror; the victor; the Buddha.—**cakka,** *nt.* the doctrine of the Buddha. —**putta,** *m.* a disciple of the Buddha.—**sāsana,** *nt.* the Buddha's teaching.

Jināti (ji + nā), to conquer; to subdue. *aor.* **jini.** *pp.* **jita.** *pr.p.* **jinanta.** *abs.* **jinitvā, jitvā.**

Jimha, *a.* crooked; slant; dishonest.—**tā,** *f.* crookedness; dishonesty.

Jiyā, *f.* a bow string.

Jivhā, *f.* the tongue.—**hagga,** *nt.* the tip of the tongue.—**yatana,** *nt.* the organ of taste. —**viññāṇa,** *nt.* the cognition of taste.—**hindriya,** *nt.* the sense of taste.

Jīna, *a.* diminished; wasted; deprived of.

Jīmūta, *m.* rain-cloud.

Jīyati (ji + ya), to become diminished; to lose; to become old; to decay. *aor.* **jīyi.** *pr.p.* **jīyamāna.** *pp.* **jīna.**

Jīraka, *nt.* cummin seed.

Jīrati (jir + a), to become old; to decay. *aor.* **jīri.** *pp.* **jiṇṇa.** *pr.p.* **jīramāna.**

Jīraṇa, *nt.* decaying; getting old; digestion.

Jīrāpeti, Jīreti (*caus.* of **jīrati**), to cause to decay or digest. *aor.*—**esi.** *pp.* **jīrāpita.** *pr.p.* **jīrāpenta.**

Jīva, *m.* the life.—**danta,** *m.* the tusks of a living animal.

Jīvaka, 3. one who lives; a personal name.

Jīvati (jīv + a), to live; to subsist on. *aor.* **jīvi.** *pr.p.* **jīvanta; jīvamāna.** *abs.* **jīvitvā.**

Jīvana, *nt.* living; means of subsistence; livelihood.

Jīvikā, *f.* livelihood.

Jīvita, *nt.* life; span of life. —**kkayha,** *m.* the dissolution of life; death.—**dāna,** *nt.* saving of life.—**pariyosāna,** *nt.* the end of life.—**mada,** *m.* the pride of life.—**vutti,** *f.* livelihood.—**saṅkhaya,** *m.* the solution of life.—**āsā,** *f.* desire for life.—**tindriya,** *nt.* the faculty of life; vitality.

Jīvī, 3. one who lives. (in cpds:) leading a life of.

Juṇha, *a.* bright.—**pakkha,** *m.* the bright half of the month.

Juṇhā, *f.* moonlight; a moonlit night.

Juti, *f.* effulgence ; brightness. —**ka,** *a.* having brightness. —**ndhara,** *a.* resplendent ; brilliant.—**mantu,** *a.* brilliant.

Juhati (hu + a ; **hu** is doubled and the first **h** becomes **j**), to pour into fire ; to dedicate. *aor.* **juhi.**

Juhana, *nt.* a sacrifice ; an offering.

Jūta, *nt.* gambling.—**kāra,** *m.* a gambler.

Je, a particle used to address a slave woman or a woman of low grade.

Jeguccha, *a.* contemptible ; loathsome.

Jegucchī, *a.* one who detests or avoids.

Jeṭṭha, *a.* elder ; supreme ; foremost.—**bhaginī,** *f.* the elder sister.—**bhātu,**—**bhātika,** *m.* the elder brother.—**māsa,** *m.* name of a month, May-June. —**ṭhāpacāyana,** *nt.* respect to the elders.—**ṭhāpacāyī,** 3. paying respect for the elders.

Jeti (ji + e), to conquer ; to subdue. *aor.* **jesi.** *pr.p.* **jenta.** *abs.* **jetvā.**

Jeyya, jetabba, *pt.p.* fit to be conquered.

Jotati (jut + a), to shine ; to become bright. *aor.* **joti.** *pr.p.* **jotanta.**

Jotana, *nt.*—**nā,** *f.* shining ; explanation.

Joti, *f.* light ; radiance. *nt.* a star. *m.* fire.—**pāsāṇa,** *m.* a crystal generating heat.—**sattha,** *nt.* astronomy.

Joteti (*caus.* of **jotati**), to illuminate ; to make clear ; to explain. *aor.* **jotesi.** *pp.* **jotita.** *pr.p.* **jotenta, jotayamāna.** *abs.* **jotetvā.** *inf.* **jotetuṃ.**

Jh

Jhatvā(=**jhāpetvā**), *abs.* having burnt.

Jhasa, *m.* a fish.

Jhāna, *nt.* concentration of mind ; meditation (on a religious subject).—**aṅga,** *nt.* a constituent of meditation.—**rata,** *a.* fond of meditation.—**vimokkha,** *m.* emancipation through **jhāna.**

Jhānika, *a.* one who has attained a **jhāna.**

Jhāpaka, 3. one who sets fire to.

Jhāpana, *nt.* setting fire to.

Jhāpīyati (*pass.* of **jhāyati**), to be burnt.

Jhāpita, *pp.* of the foll.

Jhāpeti (*caus.* of **jhāyati**), to burn ; to set fire to. *aor.* **jhāpesi.** *pr.p.* **jhāpenta.** *abs.* **jhāpetvā, jhāpiya.**

Jhāma, —**maka,** *a.* burnt.

Jhāyaka, 3. one who meditates.

Jhāyati (jhe + a), to meditate or contemplate. *aor.* **jhāyi.** *pr.p.* **jhāyanta.** *abs.* **jhāyitvā.**

Jhāyati (jhā + ya), to burn ; to be on fire.

Jhāyana, *nt.* burning ; meditation.

Jhāyī, 3. one who meditates.

Ñ.

Ñatta, *nt.* learning ; something known.

Ñatti, *f.* announcement ; declaration.

Ñatvā (*abs.* from **jānāti**), having known, understood, or learnt.

Ñāṇa, *nt.* wisdom ; insight. —**karaṇa,** *a.* enlightening. —**cakkhu,** *nt.* the eye of knowledge.—**jāla,** *nt.* the net of knowledge.—**dassana,** *nt.* perfect knowledge.—**vippayutta,** *a.* void of knowledge.—**sampayutta,** *a.* associated with knowledge.

Ñāṇī, *a.* possessed of knowledge; a wise person.

Ñāta (*pp.* of **jānāti**), known; well-known; realized.

Ñātaka, *m.* a relation; kinsman.

Ñāti, *m.* a kinsman.—**kathā,** *f.* talk about relatives.—**dhamma,** *m.* the duties of relatives.—**parivaṭṭa,** *nt.* the circle of relations.—**peta,** *m.* a deceased relation.—**vyasana,** *nt.* misfortune of relatives.—**saṅgaha,** *m.* good treatment towards kinsmen.—**saṅgha,** *m.* congregation of kinsmen.—**sālohita,** *m.* relations and blood-relations.

Ñāpana, *nt.* announcement; information.

Ñāpeti (ñā + āpe), to make known; to announce. *aor.* **ñāpesi.** *pp.* **ñāpita.** *pr.p.* **ñāpenta.** *abs.* **ñāpetvā.**

Ñāya, *m.* method; system; right manner.—**paṭipanna,** *a.* walking in the right path.

Ñeyya, *a.* what should be understood.—**dhamma,** *m.* anything that should be learnt or understood.

Ṭ.

Ṭanka, *m.* an instrument to cut stones.

Ṭīkā, *f.* sub-commentary.—**cariya,** *m.* a sub-commentator.

Ṭh.

Ṭhatvā, *abs.* (from tiṭṭhati), having stood.

Ṭhapana, *nt.*—**nā,** *f.* setting up; placing; keeping.

Ṭhapāpeti (*caus.* of **ṭhapeti**), to cause to be placed. *aor.* —**esi.** *abs.* **ṭhapāpetvā,**

Ṭhapita, *pp.* of the foll.

Ṭhapeti (ṭhā + āpe), to place; to set up; to fix (a date); to establish; to set aside. *aor.* **ṭhapesi.** *pr.p.* **ṭhapenta.**

Ṭhapetvā (*abs.* of the above), having placed; set aside, or left.

Ṭhāna, *nt.* place; locality; condition; reason; office; cause; standing up; stay.—**so,** *ad.* with reason and cause.

Ṭhānīya, *nt.* a metropolis. *adj*: fit to be placed.

Ṭhāyaka, *a.* one who stands.

Ṭhāpaka, *a.* one who places or keeps.

Ṭhāyī, *a.* standing. (in cpds.) being in a state of; lasting.

Ṭhita (*pp.* of **tiṭṭhati**), stood; stationary; immovable; one who stays.—**ka,** *a.* one who stands.—**ṭṭhāna,** *nt.* the place where one was (standing) —**tta,** *nt.* the fact of standing.

Ṭhitatta (ṭhita + atta), *a.* self-controlled.

Ṭhiti, *f.* stability; duration; continuance.—**bhāgiya,** *a.* lasting; connected with duration.

Ṭhitika, *a.* (in cpds.) lasting; enduring; living on; dependent on.

Ṭhitikā, *f.* place in a list at which the distribution of lots was stopped.

Ḍ

Ḍasati (ḍaṃs + a), to bite. *aor.* **ḍasi.** *pp.* **daṭṭha,** *pr.p.* **ḍa-**

santa, **ḍasamāna**. *abs.* **ḍasitvā**.

Ḍasana, *nt.* biting.

Ḍayhati (*pass.* of **ḍahati**), to be burnt. *aor.* **ḍayhi**. *pr.p.* **ḍayhamāna**.

Ḍahati (dah + a), to burn; to set fire to. *aor.* **ḍahi**. *pp.* **daḍḍha**. *pr.p.* **ḍahanta, ḍahaṃāna,** *abs.* **ḍahitvā**.

Ḍaŋsa, *m.* a gadfly.

Ḍāka, *m. nt.* edible herbs.

Ḍāha, *m.* glow; heat; inflammation; burning.

Ḍīyana, *nt.* flying.

Ḍeti (ḍī + a), to fly. *aor.* **ḍesi**. *pr.p.* **ḍenta**.

T.

Ta (*demonstrative pron.*), that; (**so**=he; **sā**=she; **taŋ**=that thing, are some forms of this).

Takka, *m.* thought; reasoning; logic. *nt.* butter-milk.

Takkana, *nt.* thinking; reasoning.

Takkara, *a.* a doer thereof. *m.* a thief.

Takkasilā, *f.* name of a city in Gandhāra, where was a well-known university.

Takkika, Takkī, 3. a sophist; a logician.

Takketi (takk + e), to think: to reason; to argue; to trust. *aor.*—**esi**. *pp.* **takkita**. *abs.* **Takketvā**.

Takkola, *nt.* a kind of perfume.

Tagara, *nt.* a fragrant shrub.

Taggaruka, *a.* bent thereon.

Taggha (*an affirmative particle*), truly; surely; if it is so.

Taca, *m.* skin; bark; hide. —**gandha,** *m.* the scent of bark. —**pañcaka,** *nt.* the five constituents ending with **taca,** *viz:* kesā, lomā, nakhā, dantā, taco. —**pariyosāna,** *a.* limited by the skin.

Taccha, *a.* true; real; *nt.* the truth.

Tacchaka, *m.* a carpenter; chipper of wood.

Tacchati (tacch + a), to chip; to chop; to make thin. *aor.* **tacchi**. *pp.* **tacchita**. *abs.* **tacchitvā**.

Tacchana, *nt.* chipping off.

Tacchanī, *f.* chip-axe.

Taccheti (tacch + e), to chip. *aor.* **esi**. *pp.* **tacchita**. *pr.p.* **tacchenta,** *abs.* **tacchetva**.

Tajja, *a.* arising from that.

Tajjanā, *f.* threat; menace.

Tajjaniya, *a.* to be blamed or censured.

Tajjanī, *f.* the forefinger.

Tajjeti (tajj + e), to frighten; to threaten. *aor.* **esi**. *pp.* **tajjita**. *pr.p.* **tajjenta**. *abs.* **tajjetvā**.

Taṭa, *nt.* side of a river; a river bank; *m.* a precipice.

Taṭa-taṭāyati (*Onom.* from **taṭa**), to make the sound **ṭat ṭat**. *aor.*— **āyi,** *pr.p.* **taṭataṭāyamāna**.

Taṭṭaka, *nt.* a tray; a porringer.

Taṭṭikā, *f.* a small mat; a piece of hide to sit on.

Taṇḍula, *nt.* rice-grain.—**muṭṭhi,** *m.* a handful of rice.

Taṇhā, *f.* craving; thirst; lust; attachment.—**kkhaya,** *m.* the destruction of craving.—**jāla,** *nt.* the snare of craving. —**dutiya,** *a.* having craving as one's companion.—**paccaya,** *a.* caused by craving.—**vicarita,** a thought of craving.—**saṅkhaya,** *m.* complete destruction of craving.—**saŋyojana,**

nt. the fetter of craving.—**salla**, *nt.* the dart of craving.

Taṇhīyati (*deno* from **taṇhā**); to have thirst for. *aor.* — **hīyi.**

Tata (*pp.* of **tanoti**), extended; spread out.

Tatiya, *a.* third.—**yā,** *f.* the third case, i.e., *instrumental.* —**yaŋ.** *ad.* for the third time.

Tato, *in.* from there; from that; thence; therefore; thereupon. —**paṭṭhāya,** *in.* henceforth; since.—**nidānaŋ,** *ad.* on account of that.—**paraŋ,** *in.* beyond that.

Tatta, *nt.* the real nature; reality.—**to** *in.* accurately.

Tatta (*pp.* of **tapati**), heated; hot; glowing.

Tattaka, *a.* that much; of such size.

Tattha, Tatra, *ad.* there; in that place.

Tatha, *a.* true; real. *nt.* the truth.—**tā,** *f.* reality; such likeness.—**tta,** *nt.* the state of being so; the truth.—**vacana,** *a.* speaking the truth.

Tathā, *ad.* thus; so; in that way; likewise.—**kārī,** *a.* acting so.—**gata,** *a.* one who has gone so; the Enlightened One. —**bhāva,** *m.* suchness; such a condition.—**rūpa,** *a.* such; like that.—**th'eva,** *ad.* in the same way.

Tathāgata-bala, *nt.* the supreme intellectual powers of a **Tathāgata.**

Tadagge, *ad.* henceforth.

Tadaṅga, *a.* temporal (?); *nt.* that portion.

Tadanurūpa, *a.* conforming with that.

Tadaha, -hu *nt.* the same day. —**huposathe,** *loc.* on the fast day.

Tadupiya, *a.* agreeing with that; befitting.

Tadupeta, *a.* endowed with that.

Tanaya, Tanuja, *m.* a son; offspring.—**yā,-jā,** *f.* a daughter.

Tanu, *a.* thin; slender.—**ka,** *a.* thin.—**kata,** *a.* made thin; reduced—**karaṇa,** *nt.* making thin; reduction.—**tara,** *a.* thinner.—**tā,—tta,** *nt.*—**bhāva,** *m.* thinness; diminution; reduction.

Tanu, *f. nt.* the body.—**ruha,** *nt.* hair on the body.

Tanoti (tan + o), to extend; to stretch. *aor.* **tani.** *pp.* **tata.**

Tanta, *nt.* thread; string; a loom.—**vāya,** *m.* a weaver. —**tākulakajāta,** *a.* entangled like a ball of string.

Tanti, *f.* a cord of a lute; a line; lineage; tradition; a sacred text.—**dhara,** *a.* bearer of tradition.—**ssara,** *m.* string music; sound of a lute.

Tantu, *m.* a string; cord; thread.

Tandita, *a.* weary; lazy; inactive.

Tandī, *f.* weariness; sloth.

Tapa, *m. nt.* (mano-group), penance; religious austerity; morality. (In cpds. this changes its last vowel **a** to **o.** and stands as **tapo.**) **tapokamma,** *nt.* ascetic practice. —**dhana,** *a.* one whose wealth is self-control; an ascetic. —**vana,** *nt.* a place suitable for religious practices.

Tapati (tap + a), to shine; to be bright. *aor.* **tapi.** *pr.p.* **tapanta, tapamāna.**

Tapana, *nt.* shining; brightness.

Tapanīya, *a.* causing remorse. *nt.* gold.

Tapassī, *a.* devoted to religious austerities. *m.* a hermit.—**sinī,** *f.* a female ascetic.

Tappaṇa, *nt.* satiation ; refreshment.

Tappati (*pass.* of **tapati**), to burn ; to shine ; to be tormented by remorse. *aor.* **tappi.** *pr.p.* **tappamāna.**

Tappara, *a.* devoted to ; quite given to.

Tappita, *pp.* of **tappeti.**

Tappiya, *a.* satiable. *abs.* having satiated.

Tappeti (tapp + e), to satiate ; to satisfy ; to please. *aor.* —**esi.** *pr.p.* **tappenta.** *abs.* **tappetvā, tappiya.**

Tappetu, *m.* one who satiates.

Tabbahula, *a.* having abundantly or often.

Tabbipakkha, *a.* antagonistic to that.

Tabbiparīta, *a.* different from that.

Tabbisaya, *a.* having that as an object.

Tabbhāva, *m.* that state ; the real nature.

Tama, *m. nt.* (mano-group), darkness, ignorance. (In cpds. it becomes **tamo.**)—**khandha,** *m.* great darkness.—**naddha,** *a.* enveloped in darkness.—**nuda,** *a.* dispeller of darkness. —**parāyaṇa,** *a.* having a state of darkness for his destiny.

Tamāla, *m.* the tree *Xantochymus pictorius.*

Tamba, *a.* copper-coloured ; brown. *nt.* copper.—**kesa,** *a.* having tawny hair.—**cūla,** *m.* a cock.—**nakha,** *a.* having brown finger-nails.—**netta,** *a.* having brown eyes.—**bhājana,** *nt.* a copper vessel.

Tambūla, *nt.* betel-leaf.—**pasibbaka,** *m.* a purse to keep betel.—**peḷā** *f.* a betel-box.

Taya, *nt.* a triad.

Tayo (*Nom. pl.* of **ti**), three (persons).

Tara, *a.* (in cpds.), crossing; passing over.

Taraṅga, *m.* a wave.

Taraccha, *m.* a hyaena.

Taraṇa, *nt.* going across ; passing over.

Taraṇī, *f.* a ship ; a boat.

Tarati (tar + a), to cross or pass over ; to be in a hurry. *aor.* **tari.** *pp.* **tarita.** *pr.p.* **taranta, taramāna.** *abs.* **taritvā.**

Taramāna-rūpa, *a.* being in a hurry.

Taritu, *m.* one who passes or crosses over.

Taru, *m.* a tree.—**saṇḍa,** *m.* a grove of trees.

Taruṇa, *a.* young ; of tender age. *m.* a young man.—**ṇī,** *f.* a young woman ; maiden.

Tala, *nt.* a flat surface ; level ground ; a base ; a flat roof ; a stage ; the blade of a weapon ; the palm or sole.—**ghātaka,** *nt.* a slap with the palm of the hand.—**sattika,** *nt.* lifting the hand in a threatening form.

Taluṇa, see **Taruṇa.**

Tasa, *a.* movable ; trembling.

Tasati (tas + a), to tremble ; to be frightened ; to be thirsty ; to crave for. *aor.* **tasi.** *pp.* **tasita.** *pr.p.* **tasanta.** *abs.* **tasitvā.**

Tasinā, *f.* craving ; thirst.

Taḷāka, *m. nt.* a lake.

Tahaŋ, tahiŋ, *ad.* there ; on it ; in that place.

Tāṇa, *nt.* protection ; refuge ; shelter.—**tā,** *f.* protection.

Tāta, *m.* father ; son. (Used as a term of affectionate address to persons both younger and older).

Tādisa, -saka, tādī, *a.* such; of such quality.

Tāpana, *nt.* scorching; self-mortification; tormenting.

Tāpasa, *m.* a hermit.—**sī** *f.* a female ascetic.

Tāpeti (*caus.* of **tapati**), to scorch; to torment; to heat. *aor.* **tāpesi.** *pp.* **tāpita.** *pr.p.* **tāpenta, tāpayamāna.** *abs.* **tāpetvā.**

Tāmbūlī, *f.* the betel creeper.

Tāyati (tā + ya), to protect; to preserve; to nourish. *aor* **tāyi.** *pp.* **tāyita.** *abs.* **tāyitvā.** *inf.* **tāyituŋ.**

Tārakā, Tārā, *f.* a star.—**gaṇa,** *m.* the host of stars.—**pati,** *m.* the moon.—**patha,** *m.* the sky.

Tāreti (*caus.* of **tarati**), to make cross; to help over; to assist. *aor.* **tāresi.** *pp.* **tārita,** *pr.p.* **tārenta, tārayamāna.** *abs.* **tāretvā.**

Tāretu, *m.* one who helps to cross; a saviour.

Tāla, *m.* the palmyra tree. —**ṭṭhika,** *nt.* the inner shell of a palm nut.—**kanda,** *m.* the sprout coming out of a palm nut, (which is eaten when boiled and dried).—**kkhandha,** *m.* the trunk of a palm tree.—**pakka,** *nt.* palm nut. —**paṇṇa,** *nt.* palm-leaf (used for writing).—**patta,** *nt.* a whole palm-leaf (used for thatching, etc.).—**vaṇṭa,** *nt.* a fan. (*lit.* the stem of a palm-leaf; this is a corruption of **tālavaṭṭa**= a circle made of palm-leaf).

Tālāvatthukata, *a.* rendered groundless; uprooted.

Tālu, *m.* the palate.—**ja,** *a.* palatel.

Tāva, *in.* so much; so long; as far as.—**kālika,** *a.* temporary; for the time being. —**taka,** *a.* just so much; just so long.

Tāvatā, *ad.* so long; on that account; by that much.

Tāvatiŋsa, *m.* name of a heavenly abode.—**bhavana,** *nt.* the realm of the 33 gods.

Tāvade,-deva, *in.* at that moment; instantly.

Tāḷa, *m.* a key; a cymbal; music (in general).—**cchidda, -cchiggla,** *nt.* key-hole.— **āvacara,** *nt.* music. *m.* a musician.

Tāḷana, *nt.* beating; striking.

Tāḷeti (tal + e), to strike; to beat; to flog. *aor.* **tāḷesi.** *pp.* **tāḷita.** *pr.p.* **tāḷenta.** *abs.* **tāḷetvā.**

Tāsa, *m.* terror; fear; trembling.

Tāsana, *nt.* frightening; impalement.

Tāseti (*caus.* of **tasati**), to make tremble; to frighten; to impale. *aor.* **tāsesi.** *pp.* **tāsita.** *pr.p.* **tāsenta, tāsayamāna.** *abs.* **tāsetvā.**

Ti, *a.* three. (Declined in the plural of all genders).—**kaṭuka,** *nt.* the threefold spices. —**kkhattuŋ,** *ad.* thrice.—**gāvuta,** *a.* measuring 3 gāvutas. —**cīvara,** the 3 robes of a monk, *viz.* the inner, under, and the upper robes.—**piṭaka,** *nt.* the 3 divisions of the Buddhist Canon.—**peṭaka.**—**peṭakī,** *a.* master of the three Piṭakas. —**yāmā,** *f.* the night.—**yojana,** *nt.* a distance of 3 leagues. *adj.* measuring three leagues. —**liṅgika,** *a.* belonging to the 3 genders.—**loka,** *m.* the 3 worlds.—**vagga,** *a.* consisting of 3 divisions.—**vaṅgika,** *a.* having 3 constituents.—**vassika,** *a.* three years old. —**vidha,** *a.* threefold.

Tika, *nt.* a triad. *adj.* consisting of three.

Tikicchaka, *m.* a physician.

Tikicchati (kit + cha ; **ki** is doubled and the former **k** is changed to **t**), to cure ; to treat medically. *aor.*— **chi.** *pp.* — **chita.** *pr.p.*—**chanta.** *abs.* **tikicchitvā.**

Tikicchā, *f.* the art of healing ; practice of medicine.

Tikkha, *a.* sharp ; acute ; quick in deciding.—**pañña,** *a.* having sharp intellect.

Tikhiṇa, *a.* sharp ; pointed ; pungent ; acrid.

Tiṭṭhati (ṭhā + a ; **ṭhā** is changed to **tiṭṭha**), to stand ; to stay ; to abide ; to last, to remain. (comparative **tiṭṭhatu** has the meaning ; leave it alone or let it be so.) *aor.* **aṭṭhāsi.** *pp.* **ṭhita.** *pr.p.* **tiṭṭhanta, tiṭṭhamāna,** *abs.* **ṭhatvā.**

Tiṇa, *nt.* grass.—**gahaṇa,** *nt.* a thicket of grass.—**jāti,** *f.* a variety of grass.—**bhakkha,** *a.* subsisting on grass.—**bhisi,** *f.* a mattress of grass.—**santhāra,** *m.* a mat of grass.— **sūla,** *nt.* a kind of jasmine.—**aṇḍūpaka,** *nt.* a pad of grass. —**āgāra,** *nt.* a cottage thatched with grass.—**ṇukkā,** *f.* a torch made of grass.

Tiṇṇa (*pp.* of **tarati**), crossed over ; gone through ; one who has reached the final end.

Tiṇha, *a.* sharp.

Titikkhati (tij + kha ; **ti** is doubled and **j** is changed to **k**.), to endure ; to forebear. *aor.*—**khi.** *pr.p.*—**khanta,** —**khamāna,** *abs.*—**khitvā.**

Titikkhā, *f.* endurance ; forgiveness.

Titta, tittaka, *a.* bitter. *nt.* bitter taste.

Titta (*pp.* of **tappati**), contented ; satisfied.

Titti, *f.* satisfaction ; the brim.

Tittira, *m.* a partridge.

Tittha, *nt.* a fording or landing place ; a harbour ; a belief.—**kara,** *m.* founder of a religious order.—**thāyatana,** *nt.* the sphere of a religious sect ; the fundamental doctrine (of any religion.)

Titthiya, *m.* a heretical teacher ; an adherent of another religion. —**sāvaka,** *m.* a follower of a heretical teacher.—**yārāma,** *m.* an abode of heretics.

Tithi, *f.* a lunar day.

Tidasa, *m.* a deity (in general). —**pura,** the city of the devas. —**sinda,** *m.* the king of the devas.

Tidaṇḍa, *nt.* a tripod (to place something on).

Tidiva, *m.* the celestial abode.

Tidhā, *ad.* in three ways.

Tinta, *a.* wet ; moist.

Tintinī, *f* tamarind.

Tinduka, *m.* the tree *Diospyros embryopteris.*

Tipu, *nt.* lead.

Tipusa, *nt.* a species of cucumber.

Tippa, Tibba, *a.* sharp ; piercing ; acute.

Timi, *m.* name of an enormous fish.—**ṅgala,** a kind of fish.

Timira, Timisa, *nt.* darkness. *adj.* dark.

Timirāyitatta, *nt.* gloom ; darkness.

Timīsikā, *f.* a very dark night.

Timbaru,-rūsaka, see **Tinduka.**

Tiracchāna, *m.* an animal ; a beast.—**kathā,** *f.* talk about animals ; a childish talk. —**gata,**—*m.* an animal.—**yoni,** *f.* the realm of the brute creation.

Tiriyaŋ, *ad.* across; transversely.—**taraṇa**, *nt.* ferrying across.

Tirīṭaka, *nt.* a garment made of bark; the strips used for that purpose.

Tiro, *in.* across; beyond; outside.—**karaṇī**, *f.* a curtain; veil.—**kuḍḍa**, *nt.* outside the wall.—**dhāna**, *nt.* a lid; a screen.—**bhāva**, *m.* concealment; disappearance.

Tirokkāra, *m.* insult.

Tila, *nt.* the sesamum seed. —**kakka**, *nt.* sesame paste. —**piṭṭha**,—**piññāka**, *nt.* sesamum-grinding.—**muṭṭhi**, *m.* a handful of sesame.—**vāha**, *m.* a cartload of sesame.—**saṅgulikā**, *f.* sesamum cake.

Tiŋsati, **Tiŋsā**, *f.* thirty.

Tīra, *nt.* shore; riverbank. —**dassī**, 3. seeing the shore.

Tīreti (tīr + e), to decide; to judge; to finish; to execute. *aor.* **tīresi**. *pp.* **tīrita**. *pr.p.* **tīrenta**, **tīrayamāna**, *abs.* **tīretvā**.

Tīha, *nt.* a period of three days.

Tu, *in.* however; but; yet; now; then.

Tuṅga, *a.* high; prominent.—**nāsika**, *a.* having a prominent nose.

Tuccha, *a.* empty; vain; deserted.

Tujjati (*pass.* of **tudati**), to be pierced or struck.

Tuṭṭha (*pp.* of **tussati**), glad; satisfied.—**citta**,—**mānasa**, *a.* with gladdened mind.

Tuṭṭhi, *f.* pleasure; joy.

Tuṇḍa, **-ka**, *nt.* the beak; snout.

Tuṇṇakamma, *nt.* needle-work; tailoring.

Tuṇṇavāya, *m.* a tailor.

Tuṇhī, *in.* silent; silently. —**bhāva**, *m.* silence.—**bhūta**, *a.* silent.

Tutta, *nt.* a pike for guiding elephants.

Tudati (tud + a), to prick; to peck; to pierce; to instigate. *aor.* **tudi**. *pp.* **tudita**, **tunna**. *pr.p.* **tudanta**, **tudamāna**. *abs.* **tuditvā**.

Tudana, *nt.* pricking; piercing.

Tumula, *a.* great; big; grand.

Tumba, *m.* *nt.* a kind of water-vessel; a measure used for grain.—**kaṭāha**, *m.* a vessel made of calabash or gourd.

Tumbī, *f.* long gourd.

Tumha (*the second personal pron.*), you.—**hādisa**, *a.* of your kind.

Turaga, **turaṅga**,—**ṅgama**, *m.* a horse.

Turita, *a.* speedy; quick.—**taŋ**, *ad.* quickly; in a hurry.—**turitaŋ**, *ad.* very quickly; in a great haste.

Turiya, **tūriya**, *nt.* musical instrument.

Turukkha, *a.* belonging to Turkey. *m.* a kind of incense.

Tulana, *nt.*—**nā**. *f.* weighing; rating; deliberation.

Tulasī, *f.* the basil plant.

Tulā, *f.* a balance; scales; a rafter.—**kūṭa**, *nt.* false weighing.—**daṇḍa**, *m.* the beam of a balance.

Tuliya (**tūliya** ?), *m.* flying fox.

Tuleti (tul + e), to weigh; to examine; to compare. *aor.* **tulesi**. *pp.* **tulita**. *pr.p.* **tulenta**. *abs.* **tuletvā**.

Tulya, *a.* equal; measurable. —**tā**, *f.* equality.

Tuvaŋ, **Tvan** (*nom.* *sing.* of **tumha.**) thou.

Tuvaṭaŋ, *ad.* quickly.

Tussati (tus + ya), to be glad

or satisfied. *aor.* **tussi.** *pp.* **tuṭṭha.** *pr.p.* **tussanta, tussamāna.** *abs.* **tussitvā.**

Tuhina, *nt.* dew.

Tūṇa, tūṇīra, *m.* a quiver.

Tūla, *nt.* cotton.—**picu,** *m.* cotton-wool.

Tūlikā, *f.* a painter's brush ; a cotton-mattress.

Te-asīti, *f.* eighty-three.

Tekiccha, *a.* curable ; one who can be pardoned.

Te-cattāḷīsati, *f.* forty-three.

Te-cīvarika, *a.* using three robes only.

Teja, *m. nt.* (**mano**-group), heat ; radiance ; glory ; power. (This becomes **tejo** in cpds.)—**dhātu,** *f.* the element of heat.—**kasiṇa,** *nt.* fire-contemplation.

Tejana, *nt.* an arrow.

Tejavantu, *a.* majestic ; glorious ; generating heat.

Tejeti (tij + e), to heat ; to sharpen. *aor.*—**esi.** *pp.* **tejita.** *pr.p.* **tejenta.** *abs.* **tejetvā.**

Tettiŋsā,-sati, *f.* thirty-three.

Tenavuti, *f.* ninety-three.

Tepaññasati, *f.* fifty-three.

Temana, *nt.* wetting ; moistening.

Temīyati (*pass.* of **temeti**), to become wet ; to be showered on. *pr.p.* **temiyamāna.**

Temeti (tim + e), to make wet ; to moisten. *aor.*—**esi.** *pp.* **temita.** *pr.p.* **tementa, temayamāna,** *abs.* **temetvā.**

Terasa, teḷasa, 3. thirteen.

Terovassika, *a.* three or four years old.

Tela, *nt.* oil.—**ghaṭa,** *m.* oil jar.—**cāṭi,** *f.* a pot of oil.—**dhūpita,** *a.* flavoured with oil.—**padīpa,** *m.* oil lamp.—**makkhana,** *nt.* anointing with oil.

Telika, *m.* a dealer in oil.

Tesaṭṭhi, *f.* sixty-three.

Tesattati, *f.* seventy-three.

Tomara, *m. nt.* a spear ; a lance (for driving elephants).

Toya, *nt.* water.

Toraṇa, *nt.* an arched gateway ; a decorative pandal.

Tosa, *m.* joy ; satisfaction.

Tosanā, *f.* **tosāpana,** *nt.* the act of making joyful or giving pleasure.

Tosāpeti (*caus.* of **tussati**), to make joyful ; to please. *aor.* —**esi.** *pp.* **tosāpita.**

Toseti, (see the above), *aor.* **tosesi.** *pp.* **tosita,** *pr.p.* **tosenta, tosayamāna.** *abs.* **tosetvā.**

Tvaŋ, see **tuvaŋ.**

Th.

Thakana, *nt.* closing up ; a lid.

Thaketi (thak + e), to close ; to shut ; to cover. *aor.*—**esi.** *pp.* **thakita.** *pr.p.* **thakenta.** *abs.* **thaketvā.**

Thañña, *nt.* mother's milk.

Thaṇḍila, *nt.* a hard stony ground ; a mound.—**sāyikā,** —**seyyā,** *f.* lying on the bare ground.

Thaddha, *a.* hard ; stiff ; callous. —**maccharī,** 3. a great miser.

Thana, *nt.* the breast of a woman ; the udder of a cow. —**gga,** *nt.* the nipple.—**pa,** *m. nt.* a suckling ; an infant.

Thanayati (than + aya), to roar ; to thunder. *aor.* **thanayi.** *pr.p.* **thanayanta.**

Thanita, *nt.* the thunder.

Thaneti (than + e), to roar ; to thunder. *aor.*—**esi.** *pp.* **thanita.** *pr.p.* **thanenta.** *abs.* **thanetvā.**

Thapati, *m.* a carpenter.

Thabaka, *m.* a bunch.

Thambha, *m.* a pillar ; post ; a clump of grass ; obduracy. —**bhaka,** *m.* a clump of grass.

Tharu, *m.* the hilt or handle of a weapon.

Thala, *nt.* land ; dry ground. —**gocara,** *a.* living on land. —**ja,** *a* sprung from land. —**ṭṭha,** *a.* situated on land. —**patha,** *m.* land-route.

Thava, *m.* praise ; eulogy.

Thavati (thu + a), to praise ; to extol. *aor.* **thavi.** *pp.* **thuta, thavita.** *pr.p.* **thavamāna.** *abs.* **thavitvā.**

Thavikā, *f.* a purse ; knapsack.

Thāma, *m.* strength ; power ; vigour.—**vantu,** *a.* strong ; powerful.

Thāla, *m. nt.* **thāli,** *f.* a plate ; a dish.

Thālaka, *nt.*—**likā,** *f.* a small bowl ; a beaker.

Thālipāka, *m.* a pot of boiled rice.

Thāvara, *a.* immovable ; long-lasting.—**riya,** *nt.* immobility ; firmness ; solidity.

Thira, *a.* firm ; solid ; lasting. —**tara,** *a.* more firm, solid or lasting.—**tā,** *f.* firmness ; immobility.

Thī, *f.* a woman.—**raja,** *m. .nt.* menstrual flux.

Thīna, *nt.* unwieldliness ; impliability.

Thuti, *f.* praise.—**pāṭhaka,** *m.* a panegyrist ; a bard.

Thunāti (thu + nā), to moan ; to groan. *aor.* **thuni.** *pr.p.* **thunanta, thunamāna.** *abs.* **tyunitvā.**

Thulla, *a.* massive ; fat ; grave ; gross.—**ccaya,** *m.* a grave offence.—**kumārī,** *f.* a fat girl ; an unmarried (but grown up) woman.—**phusitaka,** *a.* that which has big drops.—**sarīra,** *a.* corpulent.

Thusa, *m.* chaff ; husk of grain; —**ggi,** *m.* fire of husks. —**pacchi,** *f.* a basket to keep chaff.—**sodaka,** *nt.* a kind of vinegar.

Thūṇa, *m.* **-ṇā,** *f.* sacrificial post.

Thūpa, *m.* a tope ; pagoda ; a cairn ; a monument erected over the ashes of a holy person.—**pāraha,** *a.* one who should be honoured by erecting a tope.

Thūpikā, *f.* a pinnacle ; spire.

Thūpīkata, *a.* heaped so as to have a pointed top.

Thūla, *a.* gross ; rough ; fat ; massive.—**tā,** *f.* coarseness. —**sāṭaka,** *m.* coarse cloth.

Theta, *a.* reliable ; trustworthy.

Thena, thenaka, *m.* a thief.

Thenana, *nt.* theft.

Theneti (then + e), to steal. *aor.* **thenesi.** *pp.* **thenita.** *pr.p.* **thenenta,** *abs.* **thenetvā.**

Theyya, *nt.* theft.—**citta,** *nt.* intention to steal. *adj* :- intending to steal.—**saŋvāsaka,** *a.* one who lives clandestinely (with bhikkhus).

Thera, *m.* an elder; a senior ; a monk who has spent 10 years from his **upasampadā.** *adj* : old ; elder.—**gāthā,** *f.* hymns of the Elders.—**vāda,** *m.* the doctrine of the Theras ; the Southern Buddhism.

Therī, *f.* a senior nun ; an old woman.

Theva, *m.* a drop.

Thoka,-kaka, *a.* small ; little ; a few.—**thokaŋ,** *ad.* little by little.

Thomana, *nt.* **-nā,** *f.* see **thuti.**

Thometi (thom + e), to praise; to extol. *aor.* **—esi.** *pp.* **thomita.** *pr.p.* **thomenta, thomayamāna,** *abs.* **thometvā**

D.

Daka, *nt.* water.—**rakkhasa,** *m.* a water-sprite.

Dakkha, *a.* clever; able; skilled; dexterous. **-tā,** *f.* skill; ability; cleverness.

Dakkhaka, *a.* one who sees.

Dhakkhati (dis + a; **dis** is changed to **dakkh**), to see. *aor.* **addakkhi.** *inf.* **dakkhituŋ, dakkhitāye.**

Dakkhiṇa, *a.* southern; right (side).—**akkhaka,** *nt.* the right collar-bone.—**disā,** *f.* the south.—**desa,** *m.* the southern country.—**ṇāpatha,** *m.* the southern route (in India); the country in the south, now called Dekkan.—**ṇāyana,** *nt.* the southern course of the sun. —**ṇāraha,** *a.* worthy of a dedicatory gift.—**ṇāvatta,** *a.* winding to the right.

Dakkhiṇā, *f.* the south; a gift; donation (to a holy person). —**visuddhi,** *f.* purity of a gift. —**ṇodaka,** *nt.* water of dedication.

Dakkhiṇeyya, *a.* worthy of an offering.—**puggala,** *m.* an individual deserving a donation.

Dakkhī, 3. one who sees or perceives.

Daṭṭha (*pp.* of **ḍasati**), bitten. —**ṭṭhāna,** *nt.* the place where one is bitten.—**bhāva,** *m.* the fact of being bitten.

Daḍḍha (*pp.* of **dahati**), burnt; consumed by fire.—**ṭṭhāna,** *nt.* the place burnt by fire.—**geha,** *a.* one whose house is burnt.

Daṇḍa, *m.* 1. a stem; stick; cudgel; walking stick; timber (in general); 2. a fine; punishment.—**ka,** *nt.* a stick; twig; rod; a handle.—**kamadhu,** *nt.* a bee-hive hanged on a branch.—**kamma,** *nt.* punishment; penalty; atonement. —**koṭi,** *f.* the tip of a stick. —**dīpikā,** *f.* a torch.—**nīya,** *a.* liable to punishment.—**ppatta,** *a.* one who is prosecuted. —**parāyaṇa,** *a.* leaning on a stick; supported by a staff. —**pāṇī,** *a.* carrying a staff in one's hand.—**bhaya,** *nt.* fear of punishment.—**hattha,** *a.* one who has a stick in hand.

Datta, *pp.* given.

Datti, *f.* a small vessel to keep food in.

Dattika,-tiya, *a.* (in cpds.) given by.

Dattu, *m.* a stupid person.

Dada, *a.* (in cpds.) giving; bestowing.

Dadāti (dā + a; **dā** is doubled and the former **ā** is shortened), to give; to offer; to allow; to grant; to hand over. *aor.* **dadi, adadi.** *pp.* **dinna.** *pr.p.* **dadanta, dadamāna.** *abs.* **datvā, daditvā.** *inf.* **dātuŋ, dadituŋ.**

Daddu, *f.* a kind of cutanious eruption.

Dadhi, *nt.* curds.—**ghaṭa,** *m.* a pot of curds.—**maṇḍa,** *nt.* whey.

Danta, *nt.* a tooth; tusk; fang. —**kaṭṭha,** *nt.* a tooth-brush; tooth-cleaner.—**kāra,** *m.* an artisan in ivory.—**panti,** *f.* row of teeth.—**poṇa,** *m.* tooth-cleaner.—**valaya,** *nt.* an ivory bangle.—**vidaŋsaka,** *a.* showing one's teeth.—**tāvaraṇa,** *nt.* the lip.

Danta (*pp.* of **dameti**), tamed; controlled; restrained.—**tā**, *f.* —**bhāva**, *m.* tameness; control; state of being restrained.

Dantasaṭha, *m.* lime tree; *nt.* lime fruit.

Dandha, *a.* slow; silly; stupid. —**tā**, *f.* stupidity; sluggishness.

Dappa, *m.* arrogance; wantonness.

Dappaṇa, *nt.* a mirror; looking glass.

Dappita, *a.* arrogant; haughty.

Dabba, *a.* wise; able. *nt.* timber; wealth; substance.—**jātika**, *a.* intelligent.—**sambhāra**, *m.* a collection of wood-work or building material.

Dabbatiṇa, *nt.* a kind of grass.

Dabbimukha, *m.* a kind of bird.

Dabbī, *f.* a spoon; ladle.

Dabbha, *m.* kusa-grass.

Dama,-matha, *m.* **damana**, *nt.* taming; subjugation; restraint; mastery.

Damaka, *a.* tamer; controller; trainer.

Dameti (dam + e), to tame; to train; to master; to convert. *aor.*— **esi**. *pp.* **damita**, **danta**. *pr.p.* **damenta**. *abs.* **dametvā**. *pt.p.* **dametabba**, **damanīya**.

Dametu, see **damaka**.

Dampati, *m.* wife and husband.

Damma, *a.* to be tamed or trained.

Dayā, *f.* sympathy; compassion; kindness.—**lu**, *a.* kind; compassionate.

Dayita, *pp.* being sympathized. —**tabba**, *pt.p.* fit to be sympathized or helped.

Dayitā, *f.* a woman.

Dara, **Daratha**, *m.* sorrow; anxiety; distress.

Darī, *f.* a cleavage; cleft; cavern.

Dala, *nt.* a blade; leaf; petal.

Dava, *m.* play; sport.—**kamyatā**, *f.* fondness for joking. —**tthāya**, **davāya**, (*dat. sing.*) for fun.

Davaḍāha, *m.* forest fire.

Dasa, 3. ten.—**ka**, *nt.* a decade; a group of ten.—**kkhattuṃ**, *ad.* ten times.—**dhā**, *ad.* in ten ways.—**bala**, *a.* endowed with ten supernormal powers; the Buddha.—**vidha**, *a.* tenfold. -**sata**, *nt.* a thousand.—**satanayana** *a.* having one thousand eyes, i.e. the Sakka. —**sahassa**, *nt.* ten-thousand.

Dasa, *a.* (in cpds.) one who sees. **duddasa**=difficult to be seen.

Dasana, *nt.* tooth.—**cchada**, *m.* the lip.

Dasā, *f.* 1. fringe, edge, or border of a garment; 2. condition.

Dasikasutta, *nt.* a loose thread of a fringe.

Dassaka, *a.* one who shows.

Dassati (future of **dadāti**), he will give.

Dassana, *nt.* sight; intuition; insight.

Dassanīya,-neyya, *a.* fair to behold; beautiful; handsome.

Dassāvī, **Dassī**, 3. one who sees.

Dassu, *m.* a robber.

Dasseti (dis + e; **dis** is changed to **das**), to show; to exhibit. *aor.*—esi. *pp.* **dassita**. *pr.p.* **dassenta**. *abs.* **dassetvā**; **dassiya**.

Dassetu, *m.* one who points out or shows.

Daha, *m.* a lake.

Dahana, *nt.* burning. *m.* fire.

Dahara, *a.* young in years. *m.* a boy.—**rā**, *f.* a girl.

Daḷidda, *a.* poor; needy; a poor person.

Daḷha, *a.* firm ; strong ; steady. —**parakkama,** *a.* of strong effort ; energetic.—**haŋ,** *ad.* firmly ; strongly.

Daḷhīkamma,—karaṇa, *nt.* strengthening ; making firm.

Dāṭhā, *f.* a fang ; the canine tooth.—**dhātu,** *f.* the tooth relic (of the Buddha).—**vudha,** *a.* using tusks as his weapon. —**balī,** *a.* one whose strength lies in his tusks.

Dātu, *m.* giver ; a generous person.

Dātuŋ, *inf.* to give.

Dātta, *nt.* a sickle ; scythe.

Dāna, *nt.* gift ; charity ; alms ; alms-giving.—**kathā,** *f.* talk about charity.—**gga,** *nt.* a place where alms are given. —**pati,** *m.* master in liberality. —**phala,** *nt.* the fruit of munificence.—**maya,** *a.* consisting of giving alms.—**vaṭṭa,** *nt.* constant giving of alms.—**vatthu,** *nt.* things to be given. —**veyyāvaṭika,** *a.* a distributor of alms or one who serves in feeding.—**sālā,** *f.* alms-hall. —**sīla,** *a.* of liberal disposition. —**soṇḍa,** *a.* fond of giving. —**nāraha,** *a.* worthy of receiving gifts.

Dānava, *m.* a Titan.

Dāni, see **Idāni.**

Dāpana, *nt.* inducement to give.

Dāpeti (*caus.* of **deti**), to induce to give. *aor.* **dāpesi.** *pp.* **dāpita.** *pr.p.* **dāpenta.** *abs.* **dāpetvā.**

Dāpetu, *m.* one who induces to give.

Dāma, *m.* a wreath ; rope ; chain ; a garland.

Dāya, *m.* forest ; grove ; a gift. —**pāla,** *m.* a grove-keeper.

Dāyaka, Dāyī, 3. giver ; supporter.

Dāyajja, *nt.* inheritance. *adj.* one who inherits.

Dāyati (dā + ya), to mow ; to reap. *aor.* **dāyi.** *pp.* **dāyita.**

Dāyana, *nt.* mowing.

Dāyāda, *m.* inheritance ; *a.* (in cpds.) inheriting.—**daka,** *a.* one who inherits.

Dāyikā, *f.* a female donor.

Dāra, *m.* wife.—**bharana,** *nt.* maintenance of a wife.

Dāraka, *m.* a boy ; youngster.

Dārikā, *f.* a girl.

Dāreti (dāl + e), to split ; to burst open. *aor.* **dāresi.** *pp.* **dārita.** *pr.p.* **dārenta.** *abs.* **dāretvā.**

Dāru, *nt.* wood ; timber ; fire-wood.—**khaṇḍa,** *nt.* a piece of wood.—**kkhandha,** *m.* a log of wood.—**bhaṇḍha,** *nt.* furniture ; wooden articles. —**maya,** *a.* made of wood. —**saṅghāṭa,** *m.* a raft made of wood.

Dāruṇa, *a.* severe ; harsh ; cruel.

Dālana, *nt.* splitting.

Dāleti, see **dāreti.** *aor.* **dālesi.** *pp.* **dālita.** *pr.p.* **dālenta, dālayamāna.** *abs.* **dāletvā.**

Dāvaggi, *m.* forest-fire.

Dāsa, *m.* a slave.—**ka,** *m.* slave. —**gaṇa,** *m.* a group of slaves. **tta,—vya,** *nt.* slavery ; the condition of a slave.

Dāsitta, *nt.* status of a female slave.

Dāsī, *f.* a female slave.

Dāha, *m.* burning ; inflammation; heat.

Dāḷima, dāḍima, *nt.* pomegranate.

Dāḷiddiya, *nt.* poverty.

Dikkhati (dis + a), to see ; to become a monk.

Dikkhita (*pp.* of the above), initiated ; consecrated.

Digambara, *m.* a naked ascetic.

Diguṇa, *a.* twofold; double.

Digghikā, *f.* a ditch.

Dija, *m.* a brahman; a twice-born; a bird.—**gaṇa,** *m.* a group of brahmans or birds.

Diṭṭha (*pp.* of. **passati**), seen. *nt.* vision.—**dhamma,** *m.* this world. *adj.* one who has realized the final truth.—**dhammika,** *a.* belonging to this world. —**maṅgalika,** *a.* one who believes in auspicious things seen. —**sansandana,** *nt.* to compare one's views on things seen or known.—**ānugati,** *f.* imitation of what one sees.

Diṭṭhi, *f.* dogma; theory; belief. —**ka,** *a.* (in cpds.) believing in; having the theory of.—**kantāra,** *m.* the wilderness of dogmas.—**gata,** *nt.* a belief; wrong view.—**gahana,** *nt.* the thicket of speculation.—**jāla,** *nt.* the net of sophistry. —**vipatti,** *f.* failure in theory. —**vipallāsa,** *m.* contortion of views.—**visuddhi,** *f.* clear vision; right understanding. —**sampanna,** *a.* endowed with right views.—**saŋyojana,** *nt.* the fetter of empty speculation.

Diṭṭhī, *a.* see **Diṭṭhika.**

Ditta (*pp.* of **dippati**), blazing.

Ditti, *f.* light; brightness.

Diddha, *a.* smeared with; poisoned.

Dina, *nt.* day.—**kara,** *m.* the sun.—**ccaya,** *m.* exhaustion of the day; evening.—**pati,** *m.* the sun.

Dindibha, *m.* a lap-wing.

Dinna (*pp.* of=**deti**), given; granted.—**ādāyī,** *a.* taking what is given.

Dinnaka, *m.* an adopted son. *nt.* the thing given.

Dipada, *m.* a biped; a man. —**dinda,**—**duttama,** *m.* the most noble of the bipeds, i.e. the Enlightened One.

Dippati (dip + ya), to shine. *aor.* **dippi.**

Dippana, *nt.* shining.

Dibba, *a.* divine; celestial. —**cakkhu,** *nt.* the divine eye. —**cakkhuka,** *a.* endowed with the superhuman eye.—**vihāra,** *m.* the supreme condition of heart.—**sampatti,** *f.* heavenly bliss.

Dibbati (div + ya), to sport; to amuse oneself. *aor.* **dibbi.**

Diyaḍḍha, *m.* one and a half.

Diva, *m.* heaven.

Divasa, *m.* day.—**kara,** *m.* the sun.—**bhāga,** *m.* daytime.

Divā, *in.* day; by day.—**kara,** *m.* the sun.—**ṭhāna,** *nt.* place where the daytime is spent. —**vihāra,** *m.* rest during the heat.—**seyyā,** *f.* lying on at midday; siesta.

Diviya, divya, *a.* see **Dibba.**

Disa, *m.* enemy.

Disampati, *m.* king.

Disā, *f.* a direction; a point of the compass.—**kāka,** *m.* a crow kept on board a ship in order to search a land.—**kusala,** *a.* one who knows the directions. —**pāmokkha,** *a.* world-famed. **bhāga,** *m.* a direction.—**mūḷha,** *a.* one who has lost his bearings.—**vāsī,**—**vāsika,** *a.* living in another country or in different parts of a country.

Dissati (dis + ya), it seems; appears. *pr.p.* **dissanta, dissamāna,** (=visible).

Dīgha, *a.* long.—**aṅguli,** *a.* having long fingers.—**jātika,** *m.* a being of the snake kind. —**tā,** *f.*—**tta,** *nt.* length.—**dassī,** *a.* far-seeing.—**nikāya,**

m. the collection of long suttas. —**bhāṇaka,** *m.* a repeater or expounder of the **Dīghanikāya.**—**rattaŋ,** *ad.* a long time. —**lomaka,** *a.* having long fleece.—**sotthiya,** *nt.* long sleep; sluggishness.

Dīghavaṇṭa, *m.* the tree *Oroflylum indicum,* තොටිල.

Dīdhiti, *f.* light; radiance.

Dīna, *a.* miserable; base; mean. —**tā,** *f.*—**tta,** *nt.* wretchedness.

Dīpa, *m.* a lamp; an island; help; support.—**ka,** *nt.* a small island. *adj.* showing; explaining.—**ṅkara,** *a.* one who lights a lamp; name of a former Buddha.—**cci,** *f.* flame of a lamp.—**rukkha,** *m.* a lamp-post.—**sikhā,** *f.* flame of a lamp.—**pāloka,** *m.* light of a lamp.

Dīpanā, *f.* illustration; explanation.

Dīpanī, *f.* an explanatory work.

Dīpi, Dīpika, *m.* a panther.

Dīpita (*pp.* of **dīpeti**), illustrated; explained; shown.

Dīpikā, *f.* a torch; a commentary.

Dīpinī, *f.* a female panther.

Dīpeti (dip + e), to light; to make clear; to explain. *aor.* - **esi.** *pp.* **dīpita,** *pr.p.* **dīpenta, dīpayamāna.** *abs.* **dīpetvā.** *pt. p.* **dīpetabba.**

Du, *antithetic prefix* implying badness, perverseness, and difficulty.

Duka, *nt.* a dyad; a pair.

Dukūla, *nt.* a kind of very fine cloth.

Dukkata,-ṭa, *a.* badly done. *nt.* wrong action.

Dukkara, *a.* difficult to do. —**tā,** *f.*—**tta,** *nt.*—**bhāva,** *m.* difficulty.

Dukkha, *nt.* suffering; pain; misery; agony; discomfort. —**kkhaya,** *m.* extinction of misery.—**kkhandha,** *m.* aggregate of suffering.—**nidāna,** *nt.* source of misery. *adj.* causing pain.—**nirodha.** *m.* destruction of suffering.—**nirodhagāminī,** *f.* (the practice) leading to the extinction of suffering.—**ntagū,** *a.* one who has conquered suffering.—**paṭikkūla,** *a.* averse to pain.—**pareta,** *a.* afflicted by misery.—**ppatta,** *a.* being in pain.—**ppahāṇa,** *nt.* removal of misery. —**vipāka,** *a.* having pain as its fruit; creating misery.—**sacca,** *nt.* the truth of misery. —**samudaya,** *m.* the origin of suffering.—**samphassa,** *a.* having an unpleasant touch. —**seyyā,** *f.* an uncomfortable sleep.—**ānubhavana,** *nt.* undergoing punishment.—**āpagama,** *m.* removal of pain.

Dukkhaŋ, *ad.* with difficulty.

Dukkhāpana, *nt.* hurting.

Dukkhāpeti (*Deno.* from **dukkha**), to afflict; to cause pain; to hurt. *aor.*—**esi.** *pp.* - **pita.** *pr.p.*- **penta.** *abs.* - **petvā.**

Dukkhī, Dukkhita, *a.* afflicted; grieved; unhappy; dejected; ailing.

Dukkhīyati (*Deno.* from **dukkha**), to feel pain; to be distressed. *aor.*- **khīyi.** *pp.* **dukkhita.**

Dukkhudraya, *a.* causing pain; resulting in ill.

Dukkhūpasama, *m.* alleviation of suffering.

Dukkhotiṇṇa, *a.* fallen into misery.

Dugga, *nt.* a place difficult to access; a fortress.

Duggata, *a.* poor; miserable.

Duggati, *f.* a realm of miserable existence.

Dugganda, *a.* having a bad smell.—*m.* a bad smell.

Duggama, *a.* difficult to go.

Duggahita, *a.* held or taken wrongly. *nt.* a wrong view.

Duccaja, *a.* difficult to leave or give up.

Duccarita, *nt.* bad conduct; wrong action.

Dujivha, *m.* a serpent.

Dujjaha, *a.* difficult to give up or remove.

Dujjāna, *a.* difficult to know.

Dujjīvita, *nt.* wrong livelihood.

Duṭṭha, *a.* spoilt; corrupt; wicked; bad.—**citta**, *nt.* evil-minded; malignant.

Duṭṭhu, *ad.* badly.

Duṭṭhulla, *nt.* lewd talk. *adj.* inferior.

Dutappaya, *a.* not easily satiable.

Dutiya, *a.* second; having as the second.—**yaka**, *a.* a companion.—**yaŋ**, *ad.* for the second time.

Dutiyā, *f.* the wife; the second case, i.e., accusative.

Dutiyikā, *f.* the wife.

Duttara, *a.* difficult to cross over.

Duddama, *a.* difficult to manage or tame.

Duddasa, *a.* difficult to see or understand.—**tara**, *a.* more difficult to see.

Duddasā, *f.* misfortune; unlucky period.—**panna**, *a.* come to misfortune.

Duddasika, *a.* having ugly features.

Duddina, *nt.* a cloudy or unlucky day.

Duddha, *nt.* milk.

Dundubhi, *f.* a drum.

Dunnāmaka, *nt.* piles; haemorrhoids.

Dunnikkhitta, *a.* badly or wrongly placed.

Dunniggaha, *a.* difficult to subdue or control.

Dunnimitta, *nt.* bad omen.

Dunnīta, *a.* wrongly carried or applied.

Dupaṭṭa, *a.* having two folds.

Duppañña, *a.* foolish. *m.* a fool.

Duppaṭinissaggiya, *a.* difficult to give up or abstain from.

Duppaṭivijjha, *a.* difficult to understand.

Duppamuñca, *a.* difficult to be freed.

Dupparihāriya, *a.* difficult to use or manage.

Duphassa, *m.* the nettle plant; disagreeable touch.

Dubbaca, *a.* obstinate; disobedient.

Dubbaṇṇa, *a.* of bad colour; discoloured; ugly.

Dubbala, *a.* feeble; weak. —**tta**, *nt.* **tā**, *f.*—**bhāva**, *m.* feebleness.

Dubbā, *f.* panic grass.

Dubbijāna, *a.* difficult to understand.

Dubbinīta, *a.* obstinate; badly trained.

Dubbuṭṭhika, *a.* rainless. *nt.* a famine; scarcity of rain.

Dubbhaka, *a.* treacherous; insidious person.

Dubbhati (dubh + a), to be treacherous or unfaithful; to plot against. *aor.* **dubbhi**, *abs.* **dubbhitvā**.

Dubbhana, *nt.* treachery.

Dubbhara, *a.* difficult to bring up or nourish.

Dubbhāsita, *nt.* an insulting word ; bad speech.

Dubbhikkha, *nt.* a famine ; scarcity of food.

Dubbhī, *a.* plotting against ; seeking to injure.

Duma, *m.* a tree.—**gga,** *nt.* tree-top.—**ntara,** *nt.* variety of trees ; interval of trees.—**minda,**—**muttama,** *m.* the king of trees, i.e., the Bo-tree.

Dumuppala, *m.* a tree producing yellow flowers. කිණිහිරිය. see **Kaṇikāra.**

Dummaṅku, *a.* one who is difficult to make silent ; obstinate person.

Dummatī, 3. an evil-minded person ; a fool.

Dummana, *a.* unhappy ; sorrowful.

Dummedha, *a.* foolish.

Duyhati (*pass.* of **duhati**), to be milked. *aor.* **duyhi.**

Durakkha, *a.* difficult to protect.

Duraccaya, Duratikkama *a.* difficult to pass over.

Duranubodha, Durājāna, *a.* difficult to know or understand.

Durāsada, *a.* difficult to be approached.

Durutta, *a.* badly spoken. *nt.* bad speech.

Durita, *nt.* sin ; bad action.

Dulladdha, *a.* obtained with difficulty.

Dulladdhi, *f.* a wrong view.

Dullabha, *a.* difficult to obtain.

Duvaṅgika, *a.* consisting of two portions.

Duvidha, *a.* twofold.

Duve (*Nom. pl.* of **dvi**), two ; two persons or things.

Dussa, *nt.* cloth.—**karaṇḍaka,** *m.* clothes-chest.—**koṭṭhāgāra,** *nt.* a store-room for clothes.—**yuga,** a suit of garments.—**vaṭṭi,** *f.* a roll of cloth ; fringe of a cloth.

Dussati (dus + ya), to offend against ; to become corrupted or angry. *aor.* **dissi.** *pp.* **duṭṭha.** *abs.* **dussitvā.**

Dussana, *nt.* offending; corruption ; anger.

Dussaha, *a.* difficult to bear on.

Dussīla, *a.* of bad character ; void of morality.

Duha, *a.* (in cpds.) milking ; yielding ; granting.

Duhati (duh + a), to milk. *aor.* **duhi.** *pp.* **duddha.** *abs.* **duhitvā.** *pr.p.* **duhamāna.**

Duhana, *nt.* milking.

Duhitu, *f.* daughter.

Dūta, *m.* a messenger; envoy. *f.* **Dūtī.**—**teyya,** *nt.* errand ; commission ; carrying of messages.

Dūbhaka, *a.* a treacherous person.

Dūra, *nt.* distance. *adj.* distant ; far.—**ṅgama,** *a.* going afar.—**to,** *in.* from afar.—**tta,** *nt.* the fact of being distant.

Dūsaka, *a.* one who defiles or defames ; corrupting ; spoiling.

Dūsana, *nt.* corruption ; defilement.

Dūsita, *pp.* of the foll.

Dūseti (dus + e), to spoil ; to pollute ; to defame ; to ill-treat. *aor.* - **esi.** *pr.p.* **dūsenta, dūsayamāna.** *abs.* **dūsetvā.**

Dūhana, *nt.* pollution ; robbery ; infestation.

Deḍḍubha, *m.* a water-snake.

Deṇḍima, *m.* a kettle-drum.

Deva, *m.* a deity ; the sky ; a rain cloud ; a king.—**kaññā,** *f.* a heavenly maiden.—**kāya,** *m.* a group of gods.—**kumāra,** *m.* a divine prince.—**kusuma,**

nt. cloves.—**gaṇa,** *m.* a troop of gods.—**cārikā,** *f.* a journey in heaven.—**ccharā,** *f.* a nymph.—**ññatara,** *a.* an inferior deity.—**ṭṭhāna,** *nt.* a temple dedicated to a deity.—**ttabhāva,** *m.* divine condition or body.—**dattika,**—**dattiya,** *a.* given by a deity.—**dundubhi,** *f.* thunder.—**dūta,** *m.* gods' messenger.—**deva,** *m.* the god of gods.—**dhamma,** *m.* divine virtue; fear to sin.—**dhītu,** *f.* a young nymph.—**nagara,** *nt.* the city of the devas.—**nikāya,** *a.* a community of devas.—**parisā,** *f.* an assembly of devas.—**putta,** *m.* son of a god.—**pura,** *nt.* the celestial city.—**bhavana,** *nt.* abode of a deity.—**yāna,** *nt.* the path to heaven; an air-ship.—**rāja,** *m.* the king of devas.—**rukkha,** *m.* a celestial tree.—**rūpa,** *nt.* an image of a deity.—**loka,** *m.* heaven.—**vimāna,** a heavenly mansion.

Devatā, *f.* a deity.

Devatta, *nt.* divinity.

Devadāru, *m.* a kind of pine, *Uvaria longifolia.*

Devara, *m.* brother-in-law; husband's brother.

Devasika, *a.* occurring daily. —**kaŋ,** *ad.* daily.

Devātideva, *m.* the god of gods.

Devānubhāva, *m.* **Deviddhi,** *f.* divine power.

Devisi, *m.* a divine seer.

Devī, *f.* a goddess; a queen.

Devūpapatti, *f.* rebirth among gods.

Desa, *m.* region; country; a district.

Desaka, Desetu, *m.* a preacher; one who expounds.

Desanā, *f.* discourse, sermon, preaching.—**vilāsa,** *m.* beauty of instruction.

Desika, *a.* belonging to a country or province.

Desita, *pp.* of the foll.

Deseti (dis + e), to point out; to preach; to expound. *aor.* **desesi.** *pr.p.* **desenta.** *abs.* **desetvā.**

Dessa, Dessiya, *a.* disagreeable; detestable; odious.

Deha, *m.* *nt.* the body.—**nikkhepana,** *nt.* laying down the body; death.—**nissita,** *a.* connected with or belonging to the body.

Dehī, *a.* & *n.* that which has a body; a creature.

Doṇa, *m.* *nt.* a measure of capacity; $\frac{1}{8}$th of a bushel.

Doṇi, Doṇikā, *f.* a boat; a canoe; a trough.

Domanassa, *nt.* displeasure; melancholy; grief.

Dolā, *f.* a swing; palanquin. —**yati,** (*Deno.* from **dolā**), to swing; to move to and fro. *aor.* **dolāyi.**

Dovārika, *m.* gatekeeper.

Dosa, *m.* anger; corruption; defect; fault; —**kkhāna,** *nt.* blaming. —**ggi,** *m.* the fire of anger.—**sāpagata,** *a.* free from fault or defect.—**sāropaṇa,** *nt.* blaming; finding fault.

Dohaka, *m.* one who milks.

Dohaḷa, *m.* longing of a pregnant woman; strong desire. —**ḷinī,** *f.* the woman who has some longing.

Dohī, 3. one who milks; an ungrateful person.

Dvaṅgula, *a.* measuring two inches. *nt.* two inches.

Dvattikkhattuŋ, *ad.* twice or thrice.

Dvattipatta, *nt.* two or three bowls.

Dvattiŋsati, *f.* thirty-two.

Dvanda, *nt.* a pair; couple; dyad. *m.* the Collective Compound.

Dvaya, *nt.* a pair; couple; dyad.

Dvācattāḷīsati, *f.* forty-two.

Dvādasa, 3. twelve.

Dvānavuti, *f.* ninety-two.

Dvāra, *nt.* door; entrance; gate. —**kavāṭa,** *nt.* the shutter of a door; doors and windows. —**koṭṭhaka,** *nt.* the gateway; room over a gate.—**gāma,** *m.* village outside the city-gates. —**pāla,** —**ṭṭha,** *m.* gate-man; gatekeeper.—**bāhā,** *f.* doorpost. —**sālā,** *f.* a hall near the gate.

Dvārika, *a.* belonging to a gate. *noun* : a doorkeeper, *m.*

Dvāvīsati, *f.* twenty-two.

Dvāsaṭṭhi, *f.* sixty-two.

Dvāsattati, *f.* seventy-two.

Dvāsīti, *f.* eighty-two.

Dvi, 3. (the numeral) two. —**ka,** *nt.* a dyad; pair; couple. —**kkhattuŋ,** *ad.* twice.—**guṇa,** *a.* twofold; double. —**cattāḷīsati,** *f.* forty-two. —**jivha,** *a.* a serpent, (having two tongues). —**navuti,** *f.* ninety-two.—**paññāsati,** *f.* fifty-two. —**māsika,** *a.* two months old *or* existing two months. —**saṭṭhi,** *f.* sixty-two.—**sata,** *nt.* two hundred. —**sattati,** *f.* seventy-two. —**sahassa,** *nt.* two-thousand.

Dvija, *m.* a brahmin; a bird; a tooth; (a twice-born).

Dvidhā, *ad.* in two ways; in two parts.—**patha,** *m.* crossing of roads.

Dvipa, *m.* an elephant.

Dvīha, *nt.* two days.—**tīhaŋ,** *ad.* two or three days.

Dve (*Nom. pl.* of **dvi.**) the two —**bhāva,** *m.* twofoldness. —**vācika,** *a.* having only two words (to repeat).

Dvejjha, *nt.* doubt; contradiction. *adj.* doubtful.

Dvedhā, *ad.* in two ways; in two.—**patha,** *m.* a cross road.

Dveḷhaka, *nt.* doubt.—**jāta,** *a.* being in doubt.

Dh.

Dhaṅka, *m.* a crow.

Dhaja, *m.* a flag; emblem; symbol.—**gga,** the top of a standard.—**ālu,** *a.* adorned with flags.—**āhaṭa,** *a.* captured in war; taken as a booty.

Dhajinī, *f.* an army.

Dhañña, *nt.* grain; corn.—**rāsi,** *m.* a heap of grain.—**āgāra,** a granary.

Dhañña, Dhaññavanta, *a.* fortunate; lucky.

Dhata, (*pp.* of **dhāreti**), kept in mind; known by heart.

Dhana, *nt.* wealth, riches. —**kkhaya,** *m.* exhaustion of wealth.—**kkīta,** *a.* bought for money.—**tthaddha,** *a.* proud of wealth.—**tthika,** *a.* desiring wealth.—**lola,** *a.* greedy of wealth.—**vantu,** *a.* rich, wealthy.—**hetu,** *ad.* for the sake of wealth.—**āsā,** *f.* craving for wealth.

Dhanāyati (*Deno.* from **dhana**), to consider something as one's wealth.

Dhanika, 3. a creditor.

Dhanita, *nt.* sound. *adj* : sounded; sonant.

Dhanī, *a.* wealthy. *noun* : wealthy person.

Dhanu, *nt.* a bow.—**ka,** *nt.* a small bow.—**kāra,** *m.* bow-maker.—**ketakī,** *m.* the screw-pine.—**ggaha,** *m.* an archer.

—**sippa,** *nt.* the art of shooting.

Dhanta, *pp.* of **dhamati.**

Dhama, Dhamaka, *a.* and *n.* one who blows; a player (of a trumpet etc.).

Dhamati (dham + a), to blow; to sound; to kindle. *aor.* **dhami.** *pr. p.* **dhamanta.** *abs.* **dhamitvā.** *ger.* **dhamana.**

Dhamani, *f.* a vein.—**santhatagatta,** *a.* having veins showing all over the body (for lack of flesh).

Dhameti (dham + e), to blow; to sound. *aor* —**esi.** *pp.* **dhamita.** *pr. p.* **dhamenta.** *caus.* **dhamāpeti.**

Dhamma, *m.* doctrine; nature; truth; the Norm; morality; good conduct.—**kkhāna,** *nt.* preaching of the doctrine. —**kathā,** *f.* religious talk; ethical discussion. —**kathika,** 3. one who preaches the Norm. —**kamma,** *nt.* a legally valid act; procedure in accordance with Vinaya rules.—**karaka,** *m.* a filter or water-strainer. —**kāma,** *a.* lover of the truth. —**kāya,** *a.* the Normal body. —**kkhandha,** *m.* a portion of the Norm.—**gaṇḍikā,** *f.* the block of justice. i.e., of execution.—**garu,** *a.* respecting the Norm.—**gutta,** *a.* protected by the Norm.—**ghosaka,** *m.* one who announces about the preaching of the Norm. —**cakka,** *nt.* the wheel of Norm. —**cakkappavattana,** *nt.* preaching of the universal righteousness.—**cakkhu,** *nt.* the eye of wisdom.—**cariyā,** *f.* observance of righteousness.—**cārī,** 3.one who walks in the righteousness. *adj*: virtuous.—**cetiya,** *nt.* a shrine in which sacred texts are enshrined.—**jīvī,** *a.* living righteously. —**ññū,** *a.* one who knows the doctrine.—**ṭṭha,** *a.* just; righteous.—**ṭṭhiti,** *f.* the real nature of the Norm.—**takka,** *m.* right reasoning.—**dāna,** *nt.* the gift of the Norm.—**dāyāda,** *a.* having dhamma as one's inheritance; spiritual heir.—**dīpa,** *a.* having the Norm as a sound footing.—**desanā,** *f.* exposition of the Norm.—**dessī,** 3. a hater of the Norm.—**dhaja,** *a.* having dhamma as one's banner.—**dhara,** *a.* one who knows the Norm by heart. —**niyāma,** *m.* the order of the Norm.—**paṇṇākāra,** *m.* a present consisting of dhamma. —**pada,** *nt.* a line or stanza of the Norm.—**ppamāṇa,** *a.* measuring by the teaching. —**bhaṇḍāgārika,** *m.* the treasurer of the Norm.—**bheri,** *f.* the drum of the Norm.—**rakkhita,** *a.* protected by the Norm.—**rata,** *a.* fond of the Law.—**rati,** *f.* delight in the Law.—**rasa,** *m.* taste of the Norm.—**rāja,** *m.* the king of righteousness. — **laddha,** *a.* righteously acquired. — **vara,** *m.* the excellent doctrine. —**vādī,** 3. speaking according to the Law.—**vicaya,** *m.* investigation of doctrine. — **vidū,** *a.* one who understands the Law. —**vinicchaya,** *m.* righteous decision.—**vihārī,** *a.* living according to the Law.—**saŋvibhāga,** *m.* distribution of the Law. —**saṅgīti,** *f.* recital of sacred scriptures.—**saṅgāhaka,** compiler of the scriptures.—**samādāna,** *nt.* acquisition of the Norm.—**saraṇa,** *nt.* putting one's faith on the Norm. —**savaṇa,** *nt.* hearing of the Norm.—**sākacchā,** *f.* discussion about the Law.—**sālā,** *f.* preaching hall.—**senāpati,** *m.* generalissimo of the Law.

—soṇḍa, *a.* fond of the Norm. —ssāmī, *m.* the lord of the Norm.—ādhipati, *a.* respecting the Law as one's guide. —ānudhamma, *m.* lawfulnes ; conformity with the Norm. —ānuvattī—ānusārī, *a.* acting in conformity with the Law. —ābhisamaya, *m.* understanding of the Truth.—āmata, *nt.* the nectar of the Norm.—ādāsa, *m.* the mirror of the Norm.—ādhāra, *a.* being a support to the Norm. —āsana, *nt.* a pulpit.

Dhammatā, *f.* a general rule ; nature.

Dhammani, *m.* rat-snake.

Dammika, *a.* righteous.

Dhammilla, *m.* a knot of hair ; braided hair.

Dhammīkathā, *f.* religious talk.

Dhara, *a.* (in cpds.) bearing ; holding ; keeping in mind ; wearing.

Dharaṇa, *nt.* a weight comprising about ⅜ of an ounce.

Dharaṇī, *f.* the earth.—**ruha,** *m.* a tree.

Dharati (dhar + a), to last ; to continue; to live. *aor.* **dhari.** *pr. p.* **dharanta, dharamāna.**

Dharā, *f.* the earth.

Dhava, *m.* husband ; the acacia tree.

Dhavala, *a.* white ; clean. *noun.* white colour.

Dhāta, *pp.* fed ; satiated.

Dhātī, *f.* a nurse ; foster-mother.

Dhātu, *f.* an element ; natural condition ; a relic ; root of a word ; humour of the body ; faculty of senses.—**kathā,** *f.* an explanation about elements ; the 3rd book of the **Abhidhamma.**—**kusala,** skilled in the elements.—**ghara,** *nt.* a relic chamber.—**nānatta,** *nt.* diversity of natures or elements.—**vibhāga,** *m.* separation of elements ; distribution of relics.

Dhātuka, *a.* (in cpds.) having the nature of.

Dhāra, Dhāraka, Dhārī *a.* (in cpds.) bearing ; holding ; wearing.

Dhārā, *f.* a torrent ; stream ; shower ; the edge of a weapon.

Dhāreti (dhar + e), to bear ; to hold ; to wear. *aor.*—**esi.** *pp.* **dhārita.** *pr. p.* **dhārenta** *abs.* **dhāretvā.**

Dhāretu, *m.* bearer ; holder ; wearer.

Dhāvati (dhāv + a), to run ; to run away. *aor.* **dhāvi.** *pp.* **dhāvita.** *pr. p.* **dhāvanta.** *abs.* **dhāviya, dhāvitvā.**

Dhāvī, *a.* one who runs.

Dhi, *in.* fie! shame! woe !

Dhikkata, *a.* despised ; detested ; reviled.

Dhiti. *f.* energy; courage.--**mantu,** *a.* energetic ; resolute.

Dhī, *f.* wisdom.—**mantu,** *a.* wise.

Dhītalikā, *f.* a doll.

Dhītu, *f.* daughter.—**pati,** *m.* son-in-law.

Dhīyati (dhā + ī + ya), to be borne. *aor.* **dhīyi.** *pr. p.* **dhīyamāna.**

Dhīra, *a.* wise ; the wise.

Dhīvara, *m.* a fisher-man.

Dhuta, Dhūta (*pp.* of **dhunāti**), shaken off ; removed.—**aṅga,** *nt.* an ascetic practice.—**dhara,** *a.* and *n.* one who practises dhutaṅgas.—**vādī,** *m.* one who inculcates dhutaṅgas.

Dhutta, -ka, *m.* one who leads a corrupted life, a scoundrel ; a cheat.

Dhuttī, -tikā, *f.* of the above.

Dhunana, *nt.* shaking off; doing away with.

Dhunāti (dhu + nā), to toss; to shake off; to remove. *aor.* **dhuni.** *pr. p.* **dhunanta.** *pt. p.* **dhunitabba,** *abs.* **dhunitvā.**

Dhura, *nt.* an office; responsibility; a charge; a yoke; the shaft of a carriage; the forepart *adj.* foremost; near. —**gāma,** *m.* neighbouring village.—**ndhara,** *a.* bearing the office or taking the responsibility.—**nikkhepa,** *m.* giving up of a charge or responsibility.—**bhatta,** *nt.* regularly given meal.—**vahana,** *nt.* bearing of the yoke or office. —**vihāra,** *m.* neighbouring monastery.

Dhuva, *a.* stable; permanent; regular; constant.—**vaŋ,** *ad.* regularly; constantly.

Dhūpa, *m.* incense.

Dhūpana, *nt.* fumigation; incensing; flavouring; seasoning (of curry).

Dhūpāyati (*Deno.* from **dhūpa**) to emit smoke; to fumigate. *aor.* **dhūpāyi.** *pr. p* .**dhūpāyanta.**

Dhūpeti (dhūp + e), to flavour or season with oil; to fumigate. *aor* —**esi.** *pp.* —**pita.** *abs.* **dhūpetvā.**

Dhūma, *m.* smoke; fumes. —**ketu,** *m.* a comet; fire.—**jāla,** *nt.* a mass of smoke.—**netta,** *nt.* an outlet for smoke; a tobacco pipe.—**sikha,** *m.* fire. —**māyitatta,** *nt.* obscuration; clouding over; becoming like smoke.

Dhūmāyati (*Deno.* from **dhūma**), to smoke; to smoulder; to cloud over. *aor* — **māyi.**

Dhūli, *f.* dust.

Dhūsara, *a.* dust-coloured; yellowish.

Dhenu, *f.* a cow; a female animal in general.—**pa,** *m.* a suckling calf.

Dhota, *pp.* of **dhovati.**

Dhona, *a.* wise.

Dhorayha, *a.* able to bear a burden or to carry the yoke; *m.* a beast of burden.

Dhovati (dhov + a), to wash; to rinse; to cleanse. *aor.* **dhovi.** *pp.* **dhota.** *pr. p.* **dhovanta.** *pt. p.* **dhovitabba.** *abs.* **dhovitvā, dhoviya.** *ger.* **dhovana,** *nt.*

N.

Na, *in.* (negative particle), no; not.

Nakula, *m.* mungoose.

Nakka, *m.* a turtle.

Nakkhatta, *nt.* a constellation; star; celebration.—**kīḷā,** *f.* —**kīḷana,** *nt.* a festival celebrated at the appearance of some constellations.—**pāṭhaka,** *m.* an astrologer. —**yoga.** *m.* conjunction of the planets; horoscope.—**rāja,** *m.* the moon.

Nakha, *m. nt.* nail (of finger or toe); a claw.

Nakhī, *a.* having claws.

Naga, *m.* mountain.

Nagara, *nt.* town; a citadel. —**guttika,** *m.* mayor.—**vara,** *nt.* a noble city.—**vāsī,** *m.* a citizen.—**sodhaka,** *m.* a town-cleaner.—**sobhinī,** *f.* the city-belle; town courtesan.

Nagga, *a.* naked; nued.—**cariyā,** *f.* nudity.—**samaṇa,** *m* a naked ascetic.

Naggiya, *nt.* nudity.

Naṅgala, *nt.* a plough.—**phāla,** *m.* ploughshare.—**līsā,** *f.* the beam of a plough.

Naṅguṭṭha, *nt.* tail.

Na cirassaŋ, *ad.* shortly ; before long.

Nacca, *nt.* dancing ; a play. —**ṭṭhāna**, *nt.* a theatre ; dancing place.

Naccaka, *m.* dancer , actor.

Naccati (naṭ + ya), to dance ; to perform as a dramatist. *aor.* **nacci.** *pr. p.* **naccanta.** *abs.* **naccitvā.** *ger.* **naccana.**

Naṭa, Naṭaka, Naṭṭaka, Nattaka, *m.* dancer ; actor.

Naṭṭa, Natta, Nattana, *nt.* a dance ; a play.

Naṭṭha, (*pp.* of **nassati**), lost ; perished.

Nata, (*pp.* of **namati**), bent ; stooping ; inclined.

Nati, *f.* bending ; inclination ; bowing down.

Nattamāla, *m.* the tree *Pongamia Glabra.* කරද.

Nattu, *m.* grand-son.

Natthi (na + atthi), no ; not ; not present.—**kadiṭṭhi**, nihilistic view.—**kavādī**, *m.* one who professes a nihilistic view. —**tā**, *f.* —**bhāva**, *m.* absence.

Natthu, *f.* the nose.—**kamma**, *nt.* nose-treatment, consisting application of oil etc.

Nadati (nad + a), to roar ; to make a noise. *aor.* **nadi.** *pr. p.* **nadanta.** *pp.* **nadita.** *abs.* **naditvā.**

Nadana, *nt.* roaring.

Nadī, *f.* river.—**kūla**, *nt.* river-bank.—**dugga**, *nt.* a place inaccessible because of rivers. —**mukha**, *nt.* mouth of a river.

Naddha, (*pp.* of **nandhati**), tied; wrapped ; twisted with.

Naddhi, *f.* a thong.

Nanandā, *f.* husband's sister.

Nanu, *in.* (*particle of affirmation*), is it not ? certainly ; surely.

Nanda, -ka, *a.* rejoicing.

Nandati (nand + a), to be glad ; to rejoice ; to find delight in. *aor.* **nandi.** *pp.* **nandita.** *pr. p.* **nandamāna.** pt. p. **nanditabba.** *abs.* **nanditvā.**

Nandana, *nt.* rejoicing ; name of a garden in Indra's city.

Nandanā, *f.* rejoicing.

Nandi, *f.* pleasure ; joy ; delight ; craving.—**kkhaya**, *m.* consummation of craving.—**rāga**, *m.* passionated delight.—**saŋyojana**, *nt.* the fetter of craving.

Nandhati (nadh + ŋ - a), to wrap ; to twist with ; to tie. *aor.* **nandhi.** *abs.* **nandhitvā.** see **Vinandhati.**

Nandhi, *f.* see **Naddhi.**

Napuŋsaka, *m.* eunuch ; the neuter gender.

Nabha, *m. nt.* the sky. This takes the form **nabho** in cpds. e.g., **nabhogata**=existing in the sky.

Namakkāra, *m.* homage ; veneration ; bowing down.

Namati (nam + a), to bend ; to bow down. *aor.* **nami.** *pp.* **nata.** *pr. p.* **namanta.** *abs.* **namitvā.** *pt. p.* **namitabba.** *ger.* **namana,** *nt.*

Namassati (namas + a),to pay honour ; to venerate. *aor.* **namassi.** *pp.* —**sita.** *pr. p.* —**santa.** *abs.* —**sitvā, namassiya.** *inf.* —**situŋ.**

Namassana, *nt.*—**nā**, *f.* veneration ; worship.

Namuci, *m.* the destroyer ; the Death.

Namo, *in.* be my adoration to.

Nammadā, *f.* name of an Indian river.

Naya, *m.* method ; plan ; manner ; inference ; right conclusion.

Nayati (ni + a), to lead; to guide; to conduct. *aor.* **nayi.** see **Neti.**

Nayana, *nt.* the eye. *ger.* carrying.—**āvudha,** *m.* one whose weapon is the eye, i.e. King Yama.

Nayhati (nah + ya), to tie; to bind; to wrap; to twist. *aor.* **nayhi.** *pp.* **naddha.** *ger.* **nayhana.** *abs.* **nayhitvā.**

Nara, *m.* man; a human being. —**deva,** *m.* a king.—**vīra,** *m.* a hero; the Buddha.—**sīha,** *m.* a lion of man; the Buddha. —**rāsabha,** *m.* the lord of men. —**ruttama,** *m.* the best of men.—**rādhama,** *m.* a wicked or vile man.

Naraka, purgatory; the hell. —**ggi,** *m.* hell-fire.

Nalāṭa, *m.* the forehead.

Nalinī, *f.* a lotus pond.

Nava, *a.* new; nine.—**kamma,** *nt.* new work.—**kammika,** *a.* an expert in building.—**ṅga,** *a.* having nine portions. —**navuti,** *f.* ninety-nine.

Navaka, 3. a new comer; a young person. *nt.* a group of nine. —**tara,** *a.* younger.

Navanīta, *nt.* fresh butter.

Navama, *a.* ninth.—**mī,** *f.* the ninth day of a lunar month.

Navuti, *f.* ninety.

Nassati (nas + a), to perish; to disappear. *aor.* **nassi.** *pp.* **naṭṭha,** *pr. p.* **nassanta.** *abs.* **nassitvā.**

Nassana, *nt.* disappearance; loss; destruction.

Nahāta, nhāta (*pp.* of **nahāyati**), one who has bathed.

Nahāna, Nhāna, *nt.* bathing; bath.—**niya,** *nt.* bath-powder or anything useful for a bath.

Nahāpaka, *m.* a bath attendant.

Nahāpana, *nt.* bathing or washing (someone else).

Nahāpeti (nah + āpe), to give a bath. *aor.* —**esi.** *pp.* **nahāpita.** *pr. p.* **nahāpenta.** *abs.* **nahāpetvā.**

Nahāyati (nhā + ya), to take a bath. *aor.* **nahāyi.** *pr. p.* **nahāyanta.** *abs.* **nahāyitvā.** *inf.* **nahāyituṃ.** *ger.* **nahāyana,** *nt.*

Nahāru, Nhāru, *m.* a sinew; a tendon.

Nahuta, *nt.* ten thousand; a myriad.

Naḷa *m.* a reed; a tube.—**kāra,** *m.* basket-maker; a worker in reeds.—**kalāpa,** *m.* a bundle of reeds.—**mīṇa,** *m.* a shrimp. —**āgāra,** *nt.* a hut made of reeds.

Nāka, *m.* the heaven.

Nāga, *m.* a cobra; an elephant; the iron-wood tree; a noble person.—**danta,**—**taka,** *nt.* an ivory peg; a peg on a wall. —**bala,** *a.* having the strength of an elephant.—**balā,** *f.* a kind of creeping plant.—**bhavana,** *nt.* the region of the nāgas. —**māṇavaka,** *m.* a young man of the Nāga race.—**māṇavikā,** *f.* a. Nāga maiden.—**rāja,** *m.* king of the Nāgas.—**rukkha,** *m.* the iron-wood tree. —**latā,** *f.* the betel creeper. —**loka,** *m.* the Nāga-world. —**vana,** *nt.* an iron-wood grove *or* a forest where there are elephants.

Nāgara, -garika, *a.* & *n.* belonging to a city; urbane; polite; a citizen.

Nāṭaka, *nt.* a drama.

Nāṭakitthī, Nāṭikā, *f.* a dancing girl.

Nātha, *m.* protection; protector.

Nāda, *m.* roar; sound.

Nānatā, *f.* see the foll.

Nānatta, *nt.* diversity, variety ; manifoldness.—**kāya,** *a.* having a variety of bodily states.

Nānā, *in.* different ; differently. —**karaṇa,** *nt.* diversity ; difference.—**gotta,** *a.* of many kinds of descent.—**jacca,** *a.* of many nations. —**jana,** *m.* many kinds of folk. --**titthiya,** *a.* of various religions.—**pakāra,** *a.* various ; manifold.—**ratta,** *a.* of various colours.—**vāda,** *a.* and *n.* having different views ; the different views.—**vidha,** *a.* various ; divers.—**saŋvāsaka,** *a.* living in different parties.

Nābhi, *f.* the naval ; the nave of a wheel.

Nāma, *nt.* name ; the immaterial factors such as consciousness, perception. *adj.* (in cpds) having the name of.—**karaṇa,** *nt.* naming.—**gahaṇa,** *nt.* receiving a name.—**dheya,** —**dheyya,** *nt.* name. *aj.* having the name. —**pada,** *nt.* a noun.

Nāmaka, *a.* (in cpds.) by name.

Nāmeti (caus. of **namati**), to bend ; to wield. *aor.* —**esi.** *pp.* **nāmita.** *abs.* **nāmetvā.**

Nāyaka, *m.* leader ; master. —**yikā,** *f.* a female leader ; mistress

Nāraṅga, *m.* the mandarin orange tree.

Nārāca, *m.* an iron bar.

Nārī, *f.* a woman.

Nālaŋ (na + alaŋ), *in.* not enough ; unsuitable.

Nāvā, *f.* ship ; boat.—**tittha,** *nt.* a harbour ; ferry. —**sañcāra,** *m.* the traffic of boats.

Nāvika, *m.* a sailor.—**vikī,** *f.* a woman sailor.

Nāvutika, *a.* ninety years old.

Nāsa, *m.* ruin ; destruction ; death.

Nāsana, *nt.* killing ; destruction ; expulsion.

Nāsā, *f.* the nose.—**rajju,** *f.* a nose-rope (to curb an ox etc.).

Nāsikā, *f.* the nose.

Nāseti (nas + e), to kill ; to ruin ; to destroy ; to expel. *aor.* **nāsesi.** *pp.* **nāsita.** *pr. p.* **nāsenta.** *abs.* **nāsetvā.** *pt. p.* **nāsetabba.**

Nāḷa, *m.* a stalk ; tube.

Nāḷi, *f.* a measure of capacity ; a tube.—**matta,** *a.* about a measure.

Nāḷikā, *f.* a tube ; a bottle. —**yanta,** *nt.* a clock ; an instrument to measure time.

Nāḷikera, *m.* the coconut tree. *nt.* coconut.

Nāḷipaṭṭa, *m.* a cap ; hat.

Nikaṭa, nikaṭṭha, *nt.* neighbourhood ; *adj.* near.

Nikati, *f.* fraud ; cheating.

Nikanta, Nikantita, *pp.* of the foll.

Nikantati (ni + kant + a), to cut down ; to cut off. *aor.* **nikanti.** *abs.* **nikantitvā.**

Nikara, *m.* multitude.

Nikasa, *m.* whetstone.

Nikāmanā, *f.* desire.

Nikāmalābhī, *a.* one who has obtained something without difficulty.

Nikāmeti (ni + kam + e), to crave ; to desire. *aor.* —**esi.** *pp.* —**mita.** *pr. p.* **nikāmenta.**

Nikāya, *m.* a group ; sect ; a collection.

Nikāsa, *m.* neighbourhood.

Nikiṭṭha, *a.* low ; vile.

Nikuñja, *m. nt.* a glen ; a thicket.

Nikūjati (ni + kūj + a), to chirp ; to warble. *aor.* **nikūji.** *pp.* —**jita.** *pr. p.* **nikūjamāna.**

Niketa, Niketana, *nt.* abode; home.

Nikkaṅkha, *a.* confident; doubtless.

Nikkaḍḍhati (ni + kaḍḍh + a), to throw or drag out; to expel. *aor.* **—ḍḍhi.** *pp.* **—ḍhita.** *pt. p.* **—ḍhitabba.** *abs.* **—ḍhitvā, —ḍhiya.**

Nikkaṇṭaka, *a.* free from thorns or enemies.

Nikkaddama, *a.* free from mud.

Nikkama, *m.* exertion.

Nikkaruṇa, *a.* merciless, heartless.

Nikkasāva, *a.* free from impurity.

Nikkāma, *a.* without craving or lust.

Nikkāraṇa, *a.* groundless; causeless.—**ṇā,** *ad.* without reason, cause or purpose.

Nikkilesa, *a.* free from depravity; unstained.

Nikkujja, *a.* upset; thrown over.

Nikkujjeti (ni + kuj + e), to turn upside down. *aor.* **—esi.** *pp.* **—jita.** *abs.* **—jetvā, nikkujjiya.**

Nikkuha, *a.* not deceitful

Nikkodha, *a.* free from anger.

Nikkha, *m.* a big gold coin; a weight equal to 25 dharaṇas.

Nikkhanta (*pp.* of **nikkhamati**), gone out; departed from.

Nikkhama, *m.*—**mana,** *nt.* going out; departure.

Nikkhamati (ni. + kam + a), to go out; to go forth from; to leave the household life. *aor.*—**mi.** *pr. p.* **—manta.** *abs.* **—mitvā, nikkhamma.** *pt.p.* **—mitabbha.** *inf.* **—mituṃ.**

Nikkhamanīya, *m.* name of a month; July-August.

Nikkhāmeti (caus. of **nikkhamati**), to make to go out; to bring forth or out. *aor*—**esi.** *pp.* **—mita.** *pr. p.* **—menta.** *abs.* **—metvā.**

Nikkhitta, *pp.* of the foll.

Nikkhipati (ni + khip + a), to lay down or aside; to put down; to give up. *aor.* **—khipi.** *pr. p.* **—panta.** *abs.* **—pitvā.** *pt. p.* **—pitabba.**

Nikkhepa, *m.*—**pana,** *nt.* putting down; casting off; discarding; summary treatment.

Nikhaṇati (ni + khan + a), to dig into; to bury. *aor.* **nikhaṇi.** *pp.* **nikhāta.** *pr. p.* **nikhaṇanta.** *abs.* **nikhaṇitvā.**

Nikhādana, *nt.* a chisel.

Nikhila, *a.* all; entire; whole.

Nigacchati (ni + gam + a), to undergo; to come to. *aor.* **—chi.**

Nigaṇṭha, *m.* a member of the Jain Order.

Nigama, *m.* a market town.

Nigamana, *nt.* conclusion; explanation.

Nigaḷa, *m.* a chain for the feet of an elephant.

Nigūhati (ni + gūh + a), to cover up; to conceal; to hide. *aor.* **nigūhi.** *pp.* **—hita, nigūḷha.** *abs.* **nigūhitvā.**

Niggacchati (ni + gam + a), to go out; to proceed from. *aor.* **—chi.** *pp.* **niggata.** *abs.* **niggantvā.**

Nigganhāti (ni + gah + ṇhā) to rebuke; to censure; to restrain. *aor.* **—ṇhi.** *pp.* **niggahita.** *pr. p.* **—ṇhanta.** *abs.* **niggayha, —ṇhitvā.**

Niggama, *m.*—**mana,** *nt.* going out; departure; outcome.

Niggayha-vādī, 3. one who speaks reprovingly

Niggaha, *m.* censure; blame; reproach.

Niggahīta, *nt.* the nasal consonant 'ŋ.'

Niggahetabba, *pt. p.* fit to be reproved or checked.

Niggāhaka, 3. one who rebukes or restrains.

Niggunḍī, *f.* a medicinal shrub. ඕිකා.

Niggumba, *a.* free from bushes; clear.

Nigghātana, *nt.* killing; destruction.

Nigghosa, *m.* shouting.

Nigrodha, *m.* the banyan tree. —**pakka,** *nt.* the ripe fruit of the banyan.—**parimaṇḍala,** *a.* having proportionate limbs like the circumference of a banyan tree.

Nighaŋsa, *m.*—**sana,** *nt.* rubbing against; chafing.

Nighaŋsati (ni + ghaŋs + a), to rub; to chafe; to graze. *aor.* —**si.** *pp.* —**sita.** *abs.* —**sitvā.**

Nighaṇḍu, a dictionary of synonyms.

Nighāta, *m.* striking down; destroying.

Nicaya, *m.* accumulation; heaping up.

Nicita (*pp.* of **nicināti**), accumulated.

Nicca, *a.* constant; continuous; permanent.—**kālaŋ,** *ad.* always; constantly.—**dāna,** *nt.* perpetual gift.—**bhatta,** *nt.* a continuous food-supply.—**sīla,** *nt.* uninterrupted observance of virtue.

Niccatā, *f.* continuity; permanence.

Niccamma, *a.* skinless; flogged off.

Niccala, *a.* motionless.

Niccaŋ, *ad.* constantly; always; perpetually.

Niccola, *a.* clotheless; naked.

Nicchaya, *m.* resolution; determination; discrimination.

Niccharaṇa, *nt.* emanation; sending out.

Niccharati (ni + car + a), to go out or forth from; to emanate. *aor.*—**chari** *pp.*—**charita.** *abs.* —**ritvā.**

Nicchāta, *a.* having no hunger; satisfied.

Nicchāreti (caus. of **niccharati**), to emit; to send out; to speak. *aor.* —**esi.** *pp.*—**rita.** *abs.* —**retvā.**

Nicchita, *pp.* of the foll.

Nicchināti (ni + chi + nā), to discriminate; to consider; to investigate. *aor.* —**chinitvā.**

Nija, *a.* one's own.—**desa,** *m.* one's own country.

Nijjaṭa, *a.* disentangled.

Nijjara, *a.* free from old age or decay. *m.* a deity.

Nijjareti (ni + jar + e), to destroy; to annihilate. *aor.* —**esi.**

Nijjiṇṇa, pp. exhausted.

Nijjivha, *a.* tongueless; *m.* a jungle cock.

Nijjīva, *a.* lifeless.

Nijjhāna, *nt.* insight.

Nijjhāyati (ni + jhā + ya), to meditate; to fret; to reflect. *aor.* —**yi.** *pp.* —**yita.**

Niṭṭhā, *f.* the end; conclusion; perfection.

Niṭṭhāti (ni + ṭhā + a), to be at an end; to be finished. *aor.* **niṭṭhāsi.** *pp.* **niṭṭhita.**

Niṭṭhāna, *nt.* completion; ending.

Niṭṭhāpeti (caus. of **niṭṭhāti**), to accomplish; to finish; to carry out. *aor.* —**esi.** *pp.* —**pita.** *pr. p.* —**penta.** *abs.* —**petvā.**

Niṭṭhubhati (ni + ṭhubh + a), to spit out; to expectorate. *aor.* – **bhi.** *pp.* —**bhi a.** *abs.* —**bhitvā.**

Niṭṭhubhana, *nt.* spitting; spittle.

Niṭṭhura, *a.* rough; hard; cruel. --**riya,** *nt.* harshness; roughness.

Niḍḍa, *nt.* nest; resting place.

Niḍḍeti (ni + ḍi + e), to weed. *aor.* — **esi.**

Niṇṇaya, *m.* decision; discrimination.

Nitamba, *m.* the hip; the ridge of a mountain.

Nittaṇha, *a.* free from desire.

Nittiṇṇa, *pp.* got out of; having crossed over.

Nittudana, *nt.* pricking; piercing.

Nitteja, *a.* powerless, abashed.

Nittharaṇa, *nt.* getting across; traversing; overcoming; finishing.

Nittharati (ni + thar + a), to cross over; to get over. *aor.* **nitthari.** *pp.* —**rita.** *abs.* —**ritvā.**

Nitthāreti (*caus.* of the above), to finish; to complete. *aor.* —**esi.** *pp.* —**rita.** *abs.* —**retvā.**

Nitthunana, *nt.* a moan ; a groan.

Nitthunāti (ni + thu + nā), to moan; to groan. *aor.* —**thuni.** *pr. p.* **nitthunanta.** *abs.*--**nitvā.**

Nidassana, *nt.* an example; evidence; comparison.

Nidasseti (ni + dis + e), to point out; to explain; to define. *aor.* —**esi.** *pp.* —**ssita.** *abs.* —**setvā, nidassiya,** *pt. p.* —**sitabba.**

Nidahati (ni + dah + a), to deposit; to bury some treasure. *aor.* **nidahi.** *pp.* **nidahita** or **nihita.** *abs.* —**hitvā.**

Nidāgha, *m.* drought; heat; summer.

Nidāna, *nt.* source; cause; origin;—**kathā,** *f.* introduction (to a book.)

Nidānaŋ, *ad.* (in cpds.) by means of; in consequence of.

Niddaya, *a.* merciless; cruel.

Niddara, *a.* free from anguish, pain or fear.

Niddā, *f.* sleep.—**yana,** *nt.* sleeping.—**lu,**—**sīlī,** *a.* fond of sleep; of drowsy habits.—**rāmatā,** *f.* fondness of sleep.

Niddāyati (*Deno.* from **niddā**), to sleep. *aor.* —**yi.** *pr. p.* **niddāyanta.** *abs.* —**yitvā.**

Niddiṭṭha, *pp.* of the foll.

Niddisati (ni + dis + a), to point out; to explain; to define. *aor.* **niddisi.** *abs.* **niddisitvā.** *pt. p.* —**sitabba.**

Niddukkha, *a.* free from pain or misery.

Niddesa, *m.* description; analytic explanation.

Niddosa, *a.* faultless; undefiled.

Niddhana, *a.* poor; without property.

Niddhanta. *pp.* of the foll.

Niddhamati (ni + dham + a), to blow off; to eject. *aor.* —**mi.** *abs.* —**mitvā.**

Niddhamana, *nt.* a drain; canal; ejection.

Niddhāraṇa, *nt.* specification.

Niddhāreti (ni + dhar + e), to specify. *aor.* —**esi.** *pp.* **rita.** *abs.* —**retvā.**

Niddhunana, *nt.* shaking off.

Niddhunāti (ni + dhu + nā), to shake off. *aor.* —**dhuni.** *pp.* **niddhūta,** *abs.* —**nitvā.**

Niddhota, *pp.* washed; cleansed; sharpened.

Nidhāna, *nt.* a deposit; a hidden treasure.

Nidhāya, *abs.* (of **nidahati**), having deposited or kept aside.

Nidhāpeti (*caus.* of **nidahati**), to cause to deposit. *aor.* **—esi.** *pp.* **nidhāpita.**

Nidhi, *m.* hidden treasure. **—kumbhi,** *f.* a treasure-pot.

Nidhīyati, *pass.* of the foll.

Nidheti (ni + dah + e), to deposit; to hide or put aside. *aor.* **nidhesi.** see **nidahati.**

Nindati (nind + a), to blame; to disparage; to insult. *aor.* **nindi.** *pp.* **nindita.** *pr. p.* **nindanta.** *abs.* **ninditvā.** *pt.p.* **ninditabba.**

Nindiya, *a.* blameworthy; faulty.

Ninna, *a.* low-lying; bent down. *nt.* low ground.

Ninnatā, *f.* lowliness; inclination.

Ninnāda, *m.* melody; tune; sound. **—dī.** *a.* sounding loud; having a melodious voice.

Ninnāmeti (ni + nam + e), to bend down; to put out. *aor.* **—esi.** *abs.* **—metvā.** *pp.* **—mita.**

Ninnetu, *m.* one who leads down to; one who decides.

Nipaka, *a.* clever; prudent; wise.

Nipacca, *abs.* (of **nipatati**), having fallen down or bowed down.**—kāra,** *m.* humbleness; obedience; respect.

Nipajjati (ni + pad + ya), to lie down; to sleep. *aor.* **nipajji.** *pp.* **nipanna.** *pr. p.* **nipajjanta.** *abs.* **nipajja, nipajjiya, —jitvā.** *caus.* **—jāpeti.**

Nipajjana, *nt.* lying down.

Nipatati (ni + pat + a), to fall down. *aor.* **nipati.** *pp.* **nipatita.** *abs.* **—titvā.**

Nipāta, *m.* falling (down); descent; an indeclinable particle.

Nipātana, *nt.* falling upon; throwing down.

Nipātī, *a.* one who falls upon; going to bed.

Nipāteti (ni + pat + e), to let fall; to throw down into. *aor.* **—esi.** *pp.* **nipātita.** *pr.p.* **—tenta.** *abs.* **—tetvā.**

Nipāna, *nt.* a watering place or a trough for cattle etc.

Nipuṇa, *a.* clever; skilful; accomplished.

Nippakka, *a.* boiled; infused.

Nippadesa, *a.* all-embracing; not leaving a portion aside.

Nippapañca, *a.* free from defilement or diffuseness.

Nippabha, *a.* without splendour or lustre.

Nippariyāya, *a.* without distinction or difference.

Nippalāpa, *a.* free from chaff or prattle.

Nippāpa, *a.* sinless.

Nippitika, *a.* fatherless

Nippīḷana, *nt.* squeezing; pressing.

Nippīḷeti (ni + pīl + e), to squeeze; to press. *aor.* **—esi.** *pp.* **—ḷita.** *abs.***—ḷetvā.**

Nippurisa, *a.* composed entirely of women.

Nippoṭhana, *nt.* beating; shaking off.

Nipphajjati (ni + pad + ya), to be produced; to spring forth; to result; to happen. *aor.* **—jji.** *pp.* **nipphanna.** *pr. p.* **—jamāna.** *abs.* **—jitvā.**

Nipphajjana, *nt.* **Nipphatti,** *f.* result; effect; achievement; accomplishment.

Nipphala, *a.* fruitless; useless; vain.

Nipphādaka, *a.* producing; one who produces.

Nipphādana, *nt.* production; accomplishment.

Nipphādeti (ni + pad + e), to produce; to bring forth; to accomplish. *aor.* **—esi.** *pp.* **—dita.** *pr. p.* **—denta.** *abs.* **—detvā.**

Nipphādetu, *m.* producer.

Nipphoṭana, *nt.* beating.

Nipphoṭeti (ni + phuṭ + e), to beat down; to smother; to crush. *aor.* **—esi.** *pp.* **—ṭita.** *pr. p.* **—ṭenta.** *abs.* **—ṭetvā.**

Nibaddha, *a.* regular; continuous; constant; *pp.* being importuned.

Nibandha, *m.*—**dhana,** *nt.* binding; fastening; importunity.

Nibandhati (ni + bandh + a), to bind; to urge; to importune. *aor.* **nibandhi.** *pp.* **nibaddha.** *abs.* **—dhitvā.**

Nibbaṭṭa, *a.* freed from seed.

Nibbaṭṭeti (ni + vaṭ + e), to remove. *aor.* **—esi.** *pp.* **—ṭita.** *abs.* **—ṭetvā.**

Nibbatta (*pp.* of **nibbattati**), being reborn; arisen.

Nibbattaka,-tanaka, *a.* producing; bringing forth.

Nibbattati (ni + vat + a), to be born; to result; to arise. *aor.* **nibbatti.** *pp.* **nibbatta.** *pr. p.* **—tanta.** *abs.* **—titvā.**

Nibbattana, *nt.* **Nibbatti,** *f.* birth; rebirth; product; coming forth.

Nibbattāpana, *nt.* reproduction.

Nibbatteti (ni + vat + e), to produce; to bring forth. *aor.* **—esi.** *pp.*—**tita.** *pr. p.* **tenta.** *pt. p.* **—tetabba.** *abs.* **—tetvā.**

Nibbana,-banatha, *a.* free from craving.

Nibbasana, *nt.* cast-off cloth.

Nibbāti (ni + vā + a), to get cold; to become passionless. to be extinguished. *aor.* **nibbāyi.** *pp.* **nibbuta.** *pr. p.* **nibbāyanta.** *abs.* **nibbāyitvā.**

Nibbāna, *nt.* cooling; extinction (of a fire); emancipation; the final bliss.—**gamana,** *a.* leading to nibbāna.—**dhātu,** *f.* the sphere of nibbāna.—**patti,** *f.* attainment of nibbāna. —**sacchikiriyā** *f.* realisation of nibbāna.—**sampatti,** *f.* the bliss of nibbāna. —**ābhirata,** *a.* finding delight in nibbāna; fond of nibbāna.

Nabbāpana, *nt.* cooling; quenching; extinction.

Nibbāpeti (ni + vā + e), to put out; to cool; to extinguish. *aor.* **—esi.** *pp.* **—pita.** *pr. p.* **—penta.** *abs.* **—bāpetvā.**

Nibbāyati (ni + vā + ya), to cease to exist; to become cool. *aor.* **nibbāyi.** see **nibbāti.**

Nibbāyituŋ, nibbātuŋ, *inf.* to cease to exist.

Nibbāhana, *nt.* removal; clearance. *adj.* leading out.

Nibbikāra, *a.* unchanging; steadfast.

Nibbicikiccha, *a.* doubtless; sure; trusting.

Nibbijja, *abs.* of the foll.

Nibbijjati (ni + vij + ya), to be disheartened or disgusted. *aor.* **—jji.** *pp.* **nibbinna.** *abs.* **nibbijjitvā.**

Nibbijjhati (ni + vidh + ya), to pierce; to break through. *aor.* **—jhi.** *pp.* **nibbiddha.**

Nibbidā, *f.* aversion; disgust; weariness.

Nibbindati (ni + vid + ŋ-a), to get wearied of; to be disgusted with. *aor.* **—ndi.** *pp* **nibbinna.** *abs.* **—ditvā.**

Nibbisa, *nt.* wages. *adj.* poisonless.

Nibbisati (ni + vis + a), to seek after. *aor.* **nibbisi.** *pr.p.* **—santa.**

Nibbisesa, *a.* similar; showing no difference.

Nibbuti, *f.* peace; happiness; allayment; the final bliss.

Nibbeṭhana, *nt.* unwinding; explanation.

Nibbeṭheti (ni + veṭh + e), to unravel; to untwist; to explain. *aor.* **—esi.** *pp.* **—ṭhita.** *abs.* **—ṭhetvā.**

Nibbedha, *m.* penetration; piercing.

Nibbematika, *a.* of one accord; unanimous.

Nibbhaya, *a.* fearless; brave.

Nibbhoga, *a.* useless; deserted.

Nibha, *a.* equal to; resembling.

Nibhā, *f.* lustre; light.

Nibhāti (ni + bhā + a), to shine. *aor.* **nibhāsi.**

Nimantaka, *a.* one who invites.

Nimantana, *nt.* invitation.

Nimanteti (ni + mant + e), to invite. *aor.* **—esi.** *pp.* **—tita.** *abs.* **—tetvā, nimantiya.** *pr.p.* **—tenta.**

Nimitta, *nt.* sign; omen; portent; cause. **—ggāhī,** *a.* sensuously attracted; led away by outward signs. **—pāṭhaka,** *m.* one who prognosticates.

Nimināti (ni + mā + nā), to exchange for; to barter. *aor.* **nimini.** *pp.* **niminita.**

Nimisa, Nimesa, *m.* winking.

Nimisati (ni + mis + a), to wink. *aor.* **nimisi.** *pr.p.* **nimisanta.**

Nimīleti (ni + mil + e), to wink; to shut; to close. *aor.* **—esi.** *pp.* **nimīlita.** *abs.* **—letvā.**

Nimīlana, *nt.* winking.

Nimugga, *pp.* of the foll.

Nimujjati (ni + mujj + a), to sink down; to dive in; to plunge into. *aor.* **nimujji.** *abs.* **—jjitvā.** *inf.* **—jituṃ.**

Nimujjā, *f.* **-jjana,** *nt.* diving; sinking; ducking.

Nimesa, *m.* a wink.

Nimba, *m.* the margosa tree.

Nimmakkhika, *a.* free from flies or larvae.

Nimmajjana, *nt.* squeezing.

Nimmathana, *nt.* crushing.

Nimmathati (ni + math + a), to suppress; to destroy; to squeeze. *aor.* **—thi.** *pp.* **—thita.** *abs.* **—thitvā.**

Nimmanthati (ni + manth + a), see the above.

Nimmaddana, *nt.* crushing; subduing.

Nimmala, *a.* clean; pure; free from impurity.

Nimmaṃsa, *a.* free from flesh.

Nimmātāpitika, *a.* orphan.

Nimmātika, *a.* motherless.

Nimmātu, *m.* the creator; maker; builder.

Nimmāṇa, *nt.* creation; production.

Nimmāna, *a.* free from pride.

Nimmita, *pp.* of the foll.

Nimmiṇāti (ni + mi + nā), to create; to fashion; to build; to produce. *aor.* **—miṇi.** *pr.p.* **—ṇanta.** *abs.* **—ṇitvā, nimmāya.**

Nimmoka, *m.* the slough of a serpent.

Niya, Niyaka, *a.* one's own. See **nija.**

Niyata, *a.* sure; certain; constant.

Niyati, *f.* fate; destiny.

Niyama, *m.* limitation; certainty; definiteness.

Niyamana, *nt.* fixing ; settling ; definition.

Niyameti (ni + yam + e), to fix ; to command ; to control ; to define. *aor.* **—esi.** *pp.* **niyamita.** *abs.* **—metvā.**

Niyāma, *m.* **-matā,** *f.* certainty ; fixed method ; regular order.

Niyāmaka, *m.* a ship's captain ; commander ; regulator.

Niyuñjati (ni + yuj + a), to engage in. *aor.* **—ñji.**

Niyutta (*pp.* of the above), appointed to ; engaged in ; commissioned.

Niyoga, *m.* command ; order.

Niyojana, *nt.* urging ; ordering ; committing.

Niyojita (*pp.* of the foll.), a representative.

Nijojeti (ni + yuj + e), to urge; to incite ; to commit. *aor.* **—esi.** *pr. p.* **—jenta.** *abs.* **—jetvā.**

Niyyati (or **Nīyati**), pass. of **nayati.** to be led, guided or conducted ; to be carried.

Niyyātana, *nt.* giving in charge; dedication; returning (of something).

Niyyāti (ni + yā + a), to go out ; to get out of. *aor.* **niyyāsi.** *pp.* **niyyāta.**

Niyyātu, *m.* a leader ; guide; one who goes out.

Niyyāteti, Niyyādeti (ni + yat + e), to give into charge ; to give over ; to assign ; to dedicate. *aor.* **—esi.** *pp.* **—tita, —dita.** *abs.* **tetvā, —detva.**

Niyyāna, *nt.* going out ; departure ; release ; deliverance.

Niyyānika, *a.* leading out to salvation ; profitable.

Niyyāsa, *m.* gum ; exudation of trees.

Niyyūha, *m.* a turret ; pinnacle.

Niraṅkaroti, Nirākaroti (ni + ā + kar + o), to repudiate ; to disregard. *aor.* **—kari.** *pp.* **—kata.** *abs.* **—katvā.**

Niraggala, *a.* unobstructed ; free.

Nirata, *a.* fond of ; attached to.

Nirattha,-thaka, *a.* useless ; unproficient ; vain.—**kaŋ,** *ad.* in vain.

Nirantara, *a.* continuous ; uninterrupted.—**raŋ,** *ad.* always ; continuously.

Niraparādha, *a.* guiltless ; innocent.

Nirapekka,-khaka, *a.* indifferent ; heedless ; disregarding.

Nirabbuda, *a.* free from trouble or tumours. *nt.* a vast number. *m.* name of a hell.

Niraya, *m.* the purgatory; hell. **—gāmī,** *a.* leading to hell. **—dukkha,** *nt.* the pain of hell. **—pāla,** *m.* a guardian in hell. **—bhaya,** *nt.* the fear of hell. **—saŋvattanika,** *a.* conducive to hell.

Niravasesa, *a.* inclusive ; without remainder.

Nirassāda, *a.* insipid ; tasteless ; dull.

Nirākula, *a.* unconfused ; undisturbed.

Nirātaṅka, *a.* free from disease ; healthy.

Nirāmaya, *a.* see the above.

Nirāmisa, *a.* having no meat ; free from sensual desires ; non-material.

Nirārambha, *a.* without killing of animals.

Nirālamba, *a.* unsupported ; groundless.

Nirālaya, *a.* free from desire ; regardless ; houseless.

Nirāsa, *a.* desireless.

Nirāsaṅka, *a.* unsuspicious ; not doubting.

Nirāsaŋsa, *a.* without wishes or expectations.

Nirāhāra, *a.* foodless; fasting.

Nirindhana, *a.* fuel-less.

Nirujjhati (ni + rudh + ya), to cease; to dissolve; to vanish. *aor.* **—jjhi.** *pp.* **niruddha.** *abs.* **—jhitvā.**

Niruttara, *a.* not answerable; making no reply; one who has no superior; the most noble.

Nirutti, *f.* language; philology. **—paṭisambhidā,** *f.* knowledge of dialects or philological analysis.

Nirudaka, *a.* waterless.

Niruddha (*pp.* of **nirujjhati**), ceased to exist.

Nirupaddava, *a.* harmless; secure; without mishap.

Nirupadhi, *a.* free from passions or attachment.

Nirupama, *a.* incomparable.

Niroga, *a.* healthy.

Niroja, *a.* insipid; sapless.

Nirodha, *m.* cessation; the final truth.**—dhamma,** *a.* subject to destruction.**—samāpatti,** *f.* attainment of cessation of consciousness.

Nirodheti (ni + rudh + e), to destroy; to dissolve; to annihilate. *aor.* **—esi.** *pp.* **nirodhita.** *abs.* **—dhetvā.**

Nilaya, *m.* home; lair; habitation; dwelling place.

Nilīyati (ni + lī + ya), to hide; to lurk; to keep oneself hidden. *aor.* **nilīyi.** *pp.* **nilīna.** *abs.* **nilīyitvā.**

Nillajja, *a.* shameless.

Nillehaka, *a.* licking or one who licks.

Nillopa, *m.* plundering.

Nillolupa, *a.* free from greed.

Nivatta (*pp.* of the foll.), stopped; remaining behind.

Nivattati (ni + vat + a), to turn back; to turn away from; to stay; to remain behind. *aor.* **nivatti.** *pr.p.* **—tanta.** *abs.* **—titvā, nivattiya.** *inf.* **—tituŋ.**

Nivattana, *nt.* **Nivatti,** *f.* stoppage; return; turning back; remaining behind.

Nivatteti (ni + vat + e), to stop; to make go back; to bar; to make remain behind. *aor.* **—esi.** *pp.* **—tita.** *pr.p.* **—tenta.** *abs.* **—tetvā.**

Nivattha (*pp.* of **nivāseti**), clothed in or with; dressed.

Nivasati (ni + vas + a), to live; to dwell; to inhabit; to stay. *aor.* **nivasi.** *pp.* **nivuttha.** *pr.p.* **nivasanta.** *abs.* **nivasitvā.**

Nivaha, *m.* a heap; multitude.

Nivātaka, *nt.* a sheltered place; opportunity for hiding.

Nivātavuttī, *a.* humble; obedient.

Nivāpa, *m.* fodder; bait; food thrown for feeding.

Nivāraṇa, *nt.* prevention; warding off; refusal.

Nivāriya, *a.* what should be prevented or checked.

Nivāreti (ni + var + e), to prevent; to keep back; to forbid; to obstruct. *aor.* **—esi.** *pp.* **—rita.** *abs.* **—retvā.**

Nivāretu, *m.* one who prevents, forbids or obstructs.

Nivāsa, *m.* abode; resting place; living.**—bhūmi,** *f.* dwelling place.

Nivāsana, *nt.* undergarment; clothing; dress.

Nivāsika, Nivāsī, 3. one who dwells, lives or stays.

Nivāseti (ni + vas + e), to dress oneself; to get clothed or dressed. *aor.* **—esi.** *pp.* **nivāsita, nivattha.** *pr. p.*

—senta. *abs.* —setvā. *inf.* —setuṃ.

Niviṭṭha (*pp.* of the foll.), settled; established in; devoted to.

Nivisati (ni + vis + a), to settle down; to enter; to establish oneself. *aor.* **nivisi.**

Nivuta, *pp.* enveloped; hammed in; surrounded.

Nivuttha, *pp.* of **nivasati.**

Nivedaka, *a.* one who announces or informs.

Nivedana, *nt.* announcement; information; report.

Nivedeti (ni + vid + e), to make known; to communicate; to report; to announce. *aor* —**esi.** *pp.* —**dita.** *abs.* —**detvä, nivediya.**

Nivesa, *m.*—**sana,** *nt.* settlement; abode; house.

Niveseti (ni + vis + e), to establish in; to settle; to arrange. *aor.* —**esi.** *pp.* —**sita.** *abs.* —**setvā.**

Nisajja, *abs.* (of **nisīdati**), having sat down.

Nisajjā, *f.* sitting down.

Nisada, *m.* a grindstone.—**pota,** *m.* the upper stone for grinding.

Nisabha, *m.* a leading ox; the best of men.

Nisamma, *abs.* (of **nisāmeti**), having considered. *ad.* considerately.—**kārī,** *a.* acting considerately.

Nisā, *f.* night.—**kara,**—**nātha,** *m.* the moon.

Nisāṇa, *m.* whetstone.

Nisādī, *a.* lying down.

Nisāmaka, *a.* observant; listening to.

Nisāmeti (ni + sām + e), to listen to; to observe; to attend to. *aor.* —**esi.** *pp.* —**mita.** *pr.p.* —**menta.** *abs.* — **metvā.**

Nisita, *a.* sharp; whetted; sharpened.

Nisinna, *pp.* of **nisīdati.**

Nisinnaka, *a.* sitting down.

Nisītha, *m.* midnight.

Nisīdati (ni + sad + a), to sit down. *aor.* **nisīdi.** *pr.p.* **nisīdanta.** *pt. p.* **nisīditabba.** *abs.* —**ditvā, nisīdiya.**

Nisīdana, *nt.* sitting down; a seat; a mat to sit on.

Nisīdāpana, *nt.* causing to sit down.

Nisīdāpeti (caus. of **nisīdati**), to cause to sit down. *aor.* —**esi.** *p.p* —**pita.** *abs.* —**petvā.**

Nisedha, *m.*—**dhana,** *nt.* prevention; prohibition; holding back.—**dhaka,** *a.* prohibiting; one who prevents or obstructs.

Nisedheti (ni + sidh + e), to prevent; to prohibit; to keep off. *aor.* —**esi.** *pp.* —**dhita.** *pr. p.* **dhenta.** *pt. p.* —**dhetabba.** *abs.* —**dhetvā,** —**dhiya.**

Nisevati (ni + sev + a), to associate; to pursue; to indulge in. *aor.* **nisevi.** *pp.* **nisevita.** *abs.* —**vitvā.**

Nissagga, *m,* giving up.—**ggiya,** *a.* what ought to be rejected or abandoned.

Nissaṅga, *a.* unattached; unselfish.

Nissajati (ni + saj + a), to give up; to let loose. *aor.* **nissaji.** *pp.* **nissaṭṭha.** *abs.* **nissajja,**—**jitvā.**

Nissaṭa, *p.p.* (of **nissarati**), come out from; rejected; let loose.

Nissaṭṭha, (*pp.* of **nissajati**), dismissed; given up; handed over.

Nissatta, *a.* soulless.

Nissadda, *a.* silent; noiseless.

Nissanda, *m.* result ; outcome ; discharge ; trickling down.

Nissaya, *m.* support ; protection ; that on which anything depends.

Nissayati (ni + si + ya), to lean on ; to rely on ; to associate. *aor.* **nissayi.**

Nissaraṇa, *nt.* going out ; departure ; outcome ; escape.

Nissarati (ni + sar + a), to depart ; to escape from. *aor.* **—sari.** *pp.* **nissaṭa.** *abs.* **—ritvā.**

Nissāya, *in.* by means of ; by one's support ; near by.

Nissāra, *a.* worthless ; sapless ; unsubstantial.

Nissārajja, *a.* without diffidence; confident on one's own power.

Nissāraṇa, *nt.* driving out.

Nissita (*pp.* of **nissayati**), dependent on; hanging on ; living by means of.

Nissitaka, *a.* and *n.* an adherent ; one who is supported by.

Nissirīka, *a.* unfortunate ; miserable.

Nisseṇī, *f.* ladder ; a flight of steps.

Nissesa, *a.* entire ; whole. **—saŋ** *ad.* entirely.

Nissoka, *a.* free from sorrow.

Nihata, *pp.* of the foll.

Nihanati (ni + han + a), to slay ; to put down ; to humiliate ; to destroy. *aor.* **nihani.** *abs.* **nihantvā.**

Nihita (*pp.* of **nidahati**), kept ; put into ; settled.

Nihīna, *a.* low ; vile ; base. **—kamma,** *nt.* sinful action. *adj.* sinful ; of low action. **—pañña,** *a.* of inferior wisdom. **—sevī,** *a.* having bad association ; of vile pursuit.

Nihīyati (ni + hā + ī + ya), to come to ruin ; to be destroyed. *aor.* **nihīyi.** *pp.* **nihīna.** *pr. p.* **nihīyamāna.**

Nīgha, *m.* misery ; confusion.

Nīca, *a.* low ; humble ; inferior. **—kula,** *nt.* low caste.**—kulīnatā,** *f.* state of having a low birth.**—āsana,** *nt.* a low seat.

Nīta (*pp.* of **neti**), carried ; guided ; inferred ; led by. **—attha,** *m.* inferred meaning.

Nīti, *f.* law ; guidance.**—sattha,** *nt.* the science of statecraft; law-book.

Nīpa, *m.* the tree *Nauclea Cadamba.*

Nīyati (*pass.* of **neti**), to be led or carried.

Nīyāti (ni + yā + a), see **niyyāti.**

Nīyādeti, see **niyyādeti.**

Nīyānika, see **niyyānika.**

Nīra, *nt.* water.

Nīla, *a.* blue. *m.* the blue colour. **—kasiṇa,** *nt.* a blue disk used for meditation.**—gīva,** *m.* a peacock.**—maṇi,** *m.* a sapphire.**—vaṇṇa,** *a.* having the blue colour.**—vallī,** *f.* a kind of medicinal creeper.**—sappa,** *m.* the whip snake.

Nīlinī, Nīlī, *f.* the indigo plant.

Nīluppala, *nt.* blue water-lily.

Nīvaraṇa, *nt.* obstacle or hindrance (to the progress of mind).**—ṇiya,** *a.* forming a hindrance.

Nīvāra, *m.* a kind of grain.

Nīhaṭa, *pp.* of **niharati.**

Nīharaṇa, *nt.* taking out ; carrying away.

Nīharati (ni + har + a), to take out ; to drive away ; to stretch out. *aor.* **nīhari.** *pr. p.* **nīharanta.** *abs.* **nīharitvā.**

Nīhāra, *m.* ejection ; carrying out ; the way ; manner.

Nīḷa, *nt.* a nest.—**ja**, *m.* a bird.

Nu, an affirmative indefinite particle, frequently combined with interrogative pronouns.

Nuda, Nudaka, *a.* expelling; dispelling.

Nudati (nud + a), to drive away; to expel; to reject. *aor.* **nudi.** *abs.* **nuditvā.**

Nuṇṇa (*pp.* of the above), driven away; removed.

Nūtana, *a.* new; fresh.

Nūna, *in.* indeed; surely; certainly.

Nūpura, *nt.* anklet.

Neka, *a.* several; many.

Nekākāra, *a.* various; divers.

Nekatika, *m.* a cheat. *adj.* deceitful; fraudulent.

Nekāyika, *a.* versed in the five collections of the scriptures; belonging to a sect.

Nekkha, *nt.* a big gold coin.

Nekkhamma, *nt.* giving up the world; renunciation.—**vitakka**, —**saṅkappa**, *m.* thought of self-abnegation.—**sukha**, *nt.* the happiness of leading a holy life.—**ābhirata**, *a.* fond of renunciation.

Negama, *a.* belonging to a market-town. *m.* a town-council.

Neti (ni + a), to lead; to guide; to carry away. *aor.* **nesi.** *pp.* **nīta.** *pr.* *p.* **nenta.** *pt.* *p.* **netabba.** *abs.* **netvā.**

Netu, *m.* leader.

Netta, *nt.* the eye.—**tārā**, *f.* pupil of the eye.

Netti, *f.* craving; conduit.

Nettika, *m.* one who makes conduits for irrigation.

Nettiŋsa, *m.* a sword.

Nepakka, *nt.* prudence.

Nepuñña, *nt.* skill.

Nemi, *f.* the rim of a wheel.

Nemittika, *m.* a fortune-teller; soothsayer.

Nemindhara, *m.* name of a mountain.

Neyya, *a.* to be led or carried; to be inferred or understood.

Nerayika, *a.* born in the hell; one doomed to suffer in the hell.

Neru, *m.* name of the highest mountain. see **Meru.**

Nevāsika, 3. an inmate; a residant.

Nesajjika, *a.* remaining in a sitting position.

Nesāda, *m.* a hunter.

No, negative and adversative particle.

Nonīta, *nt.* fresh butter.

Nyāsa, *m.* a mortgage; pawn.

P.

Pakaṭṭha, *a.* most noble.

Pakata, *a.* done; made.—**atta**, *a.* of good behaviour; of a sound state.

Pakati, *f.* original or natural form; nature.—**gamana**, *nt.* usual walk. —**citta**, *nt.* normal consciousness. *adj.* of sound mind.—**sīla**, *nt.* natural virtue.

Pakatika, *a.* (in cpds.) having the nature of; being by nature.

Pakappanā, *f.* reasoning; planning; arrangement.

Pakappeti (pa + kapp + e), to consider; to design; to arrange; to think over. *aor.* —**esi.** *pp.* —**pita.** *abs.* —**petvā.**

Pakampati (pa + kamp + a), to tremble; to quake. *aor.* —**mpi.** *pp.* —**mpita.** *ger.* —**mpana.**

Pakaraṇa, *nt.* an occasion; a literary work or exposition.

Pakāra, *m.* mode; method; manner; way.

Pakāsa, *m.* brightness; annunciation; explanation. **—saka,** 3. a publisher; one who announces or explains.

Pakāsati (pa + kās + a), to be visible; to become known; to shine forth. *aor.* **pakāsi.** *pp.* **pakāsita.**

Pakāsana, *nt.* shining; announcement; publicity.

Pakāsetī (pa + kās + e), to make known; to illustrate; to publish. *aor.* **—esi.** *pp.* **—sita.** *pr. p.* **—senta.** *abs.* **—setvā.**

Pakiṇṇaka, *a.* scattered about; miscellaneous.

Pakitteti (pa + kitt + e), to speak highly; to praise; to explain. *aor.* **—esi.** *pp.* **pakittita,** *pr. p.* **—tenta.** *abs.* **—tetvā.**

Pakirati (pa + kir + a), to scatter; to let fall; to throw down. *aor.* **pakiri.** *pp.* **pakiṇṇa.**

Pakuppati (pa + kup + ya), to be angry. *aor.* **—ppi.**

Pakubbati (pa + kar + o; **karo** is changed to **kubba**), to do; to make; to perform. *pr. p.* **—bbamāna.**

Pakopa, *m.* anger; fury; agitation.

Pakopana, *a.* making turbulent; agitating.

Pakka (*pp.* of **pacati**), ripe; boiled, cooked; decaying. *nt.* ripe fruit.

Pakkaṭṭhita, *pp.* much heated; smouldering; boiled up.

Pakkama, *m.*—**mana,** *nt.* departure; going away.

Pakkamati (pa + kam + a), to step forward; to go away. *aor.* **pakkami.** *pp.* **pakkanta.** *pr. p.* **pakkamanta.** *abs.* **pakkamitvā.**

Pakkāmi (pret. of the above), went forth.

Pakkosati (pa + kus + a), to call; to summon. *aor.* **—kosi.** *pp.* **—sita.** *abs.* **—sitvā.**

Pakkosana, *nt.*—**sanā,** *f.* calling.

Pakkha, *m.* side; party; faction; side of the body; a flank; a wing, a fortnight. *adj.* adherent; associated with.

Pakkha, *m.* a cripple; a lame person.

Pakkhandati (pa + khandh + a), to spring forward; to jump on to. *aor.* **—ndi.** *pp.* **pakkhanta.** *abs.* **—nditvā.**

Pakkhandana, *nt.* leaping; springing; chasing.

Pakkhandikā, *f.* dysentery; diarrhoea.

Pakkhandī, *m.* one who jumps on; a braggart.

Pakkhabilāla, *m.* a flying-fox.

Pakkhalati (pa + hkal + a), to stumble; to stagger. *aor.* **—khali,** *pp.* **—lita.** *abs.* **—litvā.**

Pakkhalana,—lita, *nt.* stumbling.

Pakkhāleti (pa + khal + e), to wash; to cleanse; to rinse. *aor.* **—esi.** *pp.* **—lita.** *abs.* **—letvā.**

Pakkhika, *a.* belonging to a faction; siding with; fortnightly. **—bhatta,** *nt.* food given once a fortnight.

Pakkhipati (pa + khip + a), to put in; to enclose in; to throw into. *aor.* **—khipi.** *pp.* **—khitta.** *pr. p.* **—panta.** *abs.* **—pitvā.**

Pakkhipana, *nt.* putting in; throwing into.

Pakkhiya, *a.* see **pakkhika.**

Pakkhī, *m.* a bird ; the winged one.

Pakkhepa, *m.* see **pakkhipana.**

Pakhuma, *nt.* the eyelash.

Pagabbha, *a.* bold ; daring; reckless.

Pagāḷha, *pp.* of the foll.

Pagāhati (pa + gāh + a), to dive into ; to sink ; to plunge. *aor.* **pagāhi.** *pr. p.* **pagāhanta.** *abs.* **pagāhitvā.**

Pagiddha (*pp.* of **pagijjhati**), greedy after ; clinging to.

Paguṇa, *a.* well-practised ; well-acquainted ; familiar ; learnt by heart.—**ṇatā,** *f.* competence.

Pagumba, *m.* a bush ; thicket.

Pageva, *in.* too early ; not to be said of.

Paggaṇhāti (pa + gah + ṇhā), to hold up ; to take up ; to support ; to favour ; to stretch forth. *aor.* —**ṇhi.** *pp.* **paggahita.** *pr. p.* **paggaṇhanta.** *abs.* **paggahetvā, paggayha.** *pt. p.* **paggahetabba.**

Paggaha,—gāha, *m.*—**gahana,** *nt.* exertion ; energy ; lifting ; holding up ; support ; patronage.

Paggharaṇa, *nt.* trickling ; oozing ; dripping.—**ṇaka,** *a.* flowing ; oozing out ; trickling.

Paggharati (pa + ghar + a), to flow forth ; to ooze ; to drip ; to trickle. *aor.* —**ghari.** *pp.* —**rita.** *pr. p.* —**raṇta.** *abs.* —**ritvā.**

Paghaṇa, *m.* a covered terrace before a house.

Paṅka, *m.* mud ; mire ; impurity ; defilement.

Paṅkaja, Paṅkeruha, *nt.* a lotus; that which is risen from the mud.

Paṅgu,—gula, *a. & n.* lame ; a cripple.

Pacati (pac + a), to cook. *aor.* **paci.** *pp.* **pacita,.pakka.** *pr. p.* **pacanta.** *pt. p.* **pacitabba.** *abs.* **pacitvā.**

Pacana, *nt.* cooking.

Pacarati (pa + car + a), to practise ; to observe ; to walk. *aor.* **pacari.**

Pacalāyati (pa + cal + āya), to be sleepy ; to nod ; to begin to doze. *aor.* —**lāyi.**

Pacalāyikā, *f.* nodding ; dozing.

Pacāpeti (*caus.* of **pacati**) to cause to cook. *aor.* —**esi.** *abs.* **pacāpetvā.**

Pacāraka, 3. one who manages or makes known ; a publisher.

Pacāreti (pa + car + e), to manage ; to broadcast ; to publish. *aor.* —**esi.** *pp.* —**rita.** *abs.* —**retvā.**

Pacālaka, *a.* swinging ; shaking. —**kaŋ,** *ad.* swaying.

Pacināti (pa + ci + nā), to pick; to pluck ; to collect ; to accumulate. *aor.* **pacini.** *pr. p.* **pacinanta.**

Pacura, *a.* abundant ; various ; many.

Paccakkosati (pati + ā + kus + a), to curse in return. *aor.*—**kosi.**

Paccakkha, *a.* evident ; realised ; perceptible to the senses. —**kamma,** *nt.* realization.

Paccakkhāti (pati + ā + khā + a), to reject ; to refuse ; to disavow ; to give up. *aor.* —**khāsi.** *pp.* —**khāta.** *abs.* —**khāya.**

Paccakkhāna, *nt.* refusal ; rejection ; giving up.

Paccaggha, *a.* costly.

Paccaṅga, *nt.* a sub-limb.

Paccati (*pass.* of **pacati**), to be cooked ; to suffer. *aor.* **pacci.** *abs.* **paccitvā.** *pr. p.* **paccamāna.**

Paccatta, *a.* separate ; individual. —**ttaŋ,** *ad.* separately ; individually.

Paccattharaṇa, *nt.* a cover ; something spread against ; a bed-sheet.

Paccatthika, *m.* enemy ; an opponent. *adj.* opposed ; adverse.

Paccana, *nt.* boiling ; undergoing; suffering.

Paccanika, *a.* contrary ; reverse ; negative ; adverse. *m.* an enemy ; opponent.

Paccanubhavati,—bhoti (pati + anu + bhū + a), to undergo ; to experience. *aor.* —**bhavi.** *pp.* —**bhūta.** *abs.*—**bhavitvā.**

Paccanta, *m.* the border of a country ; countryside.—**desa,** *m.* the outskirts of a country. —**vāsī,** *m.* a villager ; a rustic. —**visaya,** *m.* see—**desa.**

Paccantima, *a.* bordering ; situated far away.

Paccaya, *m.* cause ; motive ; requisite ; means ; support. —**yatā,** *f.* causation.—**yākāra,** *m.* the mode of causes ; the causal genesis.—**yuppanna,** *a.* arisen from a cause.

Paccayika, *a.* trustworthy.

Paccavekkhati (pati + ava + ikkh + a), to consider ; to review ; to contemplate. *aor.* —**kkhi.** *pp.* —**kkhita.** *abs.* —**khitvā,** —**vekkhiya.**

Paccavekkhana, *nt.*—**nā,** *f.* consideration ; reviewing ; reflection.

Paccassosi (*aor.* of **paṭissuṇāti**), he assented or promised.

Paccākata, *pp.* rejected.

Paccākoṭita, *pp.* smoothed out ; ironed.

Paccāgacchati (pati + ā + gam + a), to return ; to come back; to withdraw. *aor.* —**chi.** *pp.* **paccāgata.** *abs.* —**āgantvā.**

Paccāgamana, *nt.* return ; coming back.

Paccājāyati (pati + ā + jan + ya), to be reborn. *aor.* —**jāyi.** —**jāta.** *abs.* —**jāyitvā.**

Paccāmitta, *m.* enemy ; adversary.

Paccāsiŋsati (pati + ā + siŋs + a), to expect ; to desire ; to wait for. *aor.* —**siŋsi.** *pp.* —**siŋsita.**

Paccāharati (pati + ā + har + a), to bring back. *aor.* —**hari.** *pp.* —**cāhaṭa.** *abs.* —**haritvā.**

Paccuggacchati (pati + u + gam + a), to go out to meet. *abs.* —**ggantvā.**

Paccuggamana, *nt.* going out to meet.

Paccuṭṭhāti (pati + u + ṭhā + a), to rise from one's seat as a token of respect. *aor.* —**ṭhāsi.** *pp.* —**ṭhita.** *abs.* —**ṭṭhāya.**

Paccuṭṭhāna, *nt.* reverence ; rising from one's seat.—**naka,** *a.* arising or producing.

Paccupaṭṭhāti (pati + upa + ṭhā + a), to be present. *aor.* —**ṭhāsi.** *pp.* —**ṭhita.** *abs.* —**ṭhitvā.**

Paccupaṭṭhāna, *nt.* understanding ; appearance ; coming on ; attending.

Paccupaṭṭhāpeti (pati + upa + ṭhā + āpe), to bring before ; to provide ; to arrange.

Paccuppanna, *a.* existing ; present.

Paccūsa, *m.* early morning. —**kāla,** *m.* dawn.

Pacceka, *a.* separate ; each ; various ; single.—**buddha,** *m.* one who is enlightened but does not preach the truth to the world.—**kaŋ**, *ad.* separately; individually.

Pacceti (pati + i + a), to come on to; to realize; to fall back on. *aor.* **paccesi.**

Paccorohati (pati + ava + ruh + a), to come down; to descend. *aor.* **—rohi.** *pp.* **—corūḷha.** *abs.* **—rohitvā. —oruyha.**

Paccosakkati (pati + ava + sakk + a), to retreat; to withdraw. *aor.* **—sakki.** *pp.* **—kita.** *abs.* **—kitvā.**

Paccosakkanā, *f.* retreating; shrinking from.

Pacchato, *in.* from behind; behind.

Pacchanna (*pp.* of **pacchādeti**), covered with; hidden; wrapped with.

Pacchā, *in.* afterwards.—**jāta,** *a.* born or arisen afterwards. **—nipātī,** 3. one who retires later than others.—**nutāpa,** *m.* remorse; repentance.—**bāhaŋ,** *ad.* with hands tied behind one's back.—**bhattaŋ,** *ad.* afternoon.—**bhāga,** *m.* the hind part. *loc.* afterwards. **—samaṇa,** *m.* a junior monk who walks behind a senior on his rounds.

Pacchāda, *m.* a cover.

Pacchānutappati (pacchā + anu + tap + a), to feel remorse. *aor.* **—tappi.**

Pacchāyā, *f.* shaded part; a place in the shade.

Pacchi, *f.* a hand-basket.

Pacchijjati (pa + chid + ya), to be cut short; to be interrupted. *aor.* **—jji.** *pp.* **pacchinna.** *abs.* **—jitvā.**

Pacchijjana, *nt.* interruption; stoppage.

Pacchindati (pa + chid + ŋ - a), to cut short; to break up; to put an end to. *aor.* **—ndi.** *pp.* **—chinna.** *abs.* **—nditvā.**

Pacchima, *a.* latest; hindmost; lowest; western. **—maka,** *a.* last; meanest.

Pacchedana, *nt.* cutting off; breaking.

Pajagghati (pa + jaggh + a), to laugh loud. *aor.* **—ghi.** *ger.* **—ghana.**

Pajappati (pa + japp + a), to prattle; to crave. *aor.* **—ppi.**

Pajahati (pa + hā + a; *hā* is doubled and the former *h* is changed to *j.*), to give up; to renounce; to forsake; to abandon. *aor.* **pajahi.** *pp.* **—hita.** *abs.* **—hitvā, pahāya.** *pr. p.* **pajahanta.**

Pajā, *f.* progeny; offspring; generation; mankind. **—pati,** *m.* the lord of creation.

Pajānanā, *f.* knowledge; understanding; discernment.

Pajāyati (pa + jan + ya), to be born or produced. *aor.* **pajāyi.**

Pajāyana, *nt.* birth; coming into existence.

Pajja, *nt.* a verse; a poem; something good for feet. *m.* road; path.

Pajjalati (pa + jal + a), to blaze up; to burn forth. *aor.* **—jali.** *pp.* **—lita.** *pr. p.* **—lanta.** *abs.* **—litvā.**

Pajjalana, *nt.* blazing.

Pajjunna, *m.* rain-cloud; Rain-God.

Pajjota, *m.* a lamp; a light; lustre.

Pajjhāyati (pa + jhā + ya), to overcome with grief or remorse; to ponder over. *aor.* **—āyi.** *pr. p.* **—yanta.**

Pañca, 3. five.—**kalyāṇa,** *nt.* the five beauty marks (of hair, flesh, teeth, skin, and age). —**kāmaguṇa,** *m.* pleasures of five senses.—**kkhandha,** *m.* the five aggregates, *viz* : material qualities, feeling, perception, coefficients of consciousness, and consciousness.—**gorasa,** *m.* five products of the cow, *viz* : milk, curd, ghee, fresh butter, and sour milk.—**ṅga,**—**ṅgika,** *a.* consisting of five parts. —**ṅgulika,** the five-finger mark made after the fingers have been emersed in some scented solution.—**cakkhu,**—**netta,** *a.* having five sorts of visions. —**cattāḷīsati,** *f.* forty-five. —**cūḷaka,** *a.* having five knots of hair.—**tiŋsati,** *f.* thirty-five. —**dasa,** 3. fifteen. —**navuti,** *f.* ninety-five. —**nīvaraṇa,** five-fold obstacles for the progress of mind, *viz* : sensuality, ill-will, toper of mind, worry, and wavering.—**paññāsati,** *f.* fifty-five.—**patiṭṭhita,** *nt.* fivefold prostration (with forehead, waist, elbows, knees, and feet). —**bandhana,** *nt.* fivefold bondage.—**bala,** *nt.* five mental forces.—**mahāpariccāga,** *m.* fivefold great liberalities, *viz* : of the most valued things, sons, wives, kingdoms, and limbs. —**mahāvilokana,** *nt.* fivefold investigation of a Bodhisatta, *viz:* of time, continent, place, clan, and mother.—**vaggiya,** *a.* belonging to a group of five. (The five monks, who accompanied Gotama when he became an ascetic, are called **pañca-vaggiyā**).—**vaṇṇa,** *a.* of five colours, *viz* : blue, yellow, red, white, and brown.—**vīsati,** *f.* twenty-five.—**saṭṭhi,** *f.* sixty-five.—**sata,** *nt.* five hundred —**sattati,** *f.* seventy-five.—**sahassa,** *nt.* five thousand. —**sīla,** *nt.* the five moral precepts.—**hattha,** *a.* measuring five cubits.

Pañcaka, *nt.* a pentad ; a group of five.

Pañcakkhattuŋ, *ad.* five-times.

Pañcadhā, *ad.* in five ways.

Pañcavidha, *a.* fivefold.

Pañcaso, *in.* by fives or in five ways.

Pañcānantariya, *nt.* the five acts that have immediate retribution, *viz* : matricide, patricide, murdering of a holy person, wounding a Buddha, and making a schism in the community of monks.

Pañcābhiññā, *f.* five psychic powers, *viz* : power of performing miracles, clair-audience, clairvoyance, knowing others' thoughts, and recollecting one's previous births.

Pañcāvudha, *nt.* a set of five weapons, *viz* : sword, spear, battle-axe, bow, and mace.

Pañcāsīti, *f.* eighty-five.

Pañcāha, *nt.* five days.

Pañjara, *m.* a cage.

Pañjalika, *a.* holding up the clasped hands as a token of salutation.

Pañña, *a.* wise ; endowed with knowledge.

Paññatā, *f.* (in cpds.) the fact of having wisdom.

Paññatta, *pp.* of **paññāpeti.**

Paññatti, *f.* designation ; name ; concept ; idea ; a regulation.

Paññavantu, *a.* wise ; intelligent.

Paññā, *f.* wisdom ; knowledge ; insight.—**kkhandha,** *m.* the code of intellectual duties ; practice of the attainment of highest knowledge.—**cakkhu,** *nt.* the eye of wisdom.—**dhana,** *nt.* the treasure of wisdom.

—**bala,** *nt.* the power of insight. —**vimutti,** *f.* emancipation through insight.—**vuddhi,** *f.* increase of knowledge.—**sampadā,** *f.* the blessing of higher knowledge.

Paññāṇa, *nt.* a mark ; sign ; token.

Paññāta, *pp.* of **paññāyati.**

Paññāpaka, *a.* one who advises, assigns or appoints.

Paññāpana, *nt.* declaration ; preparation (of seats, etc.)

Paññāpeti (pa - ñā + āpe), to regulate or make a rule ; to make known ; to declare ; to prepare (a seat, etc.) *aor.* —**esi.** *pp.* —**pita** or **paññatta.** *pr. p.* —**penta.** *abs.* —**petvā.**

Paññāyati (pa + ñā + ya), to appear ; to be clear or evident *aor.*—**āyi.** *pp.*—**paññāta.** *pr. p.* —**yamāna.** *abs.* —**yitvā.**

Pañha, 3. a question ; an inquiry. —**vissajjana,** —**vyākaraṇa,** *nt.* answering questions.

Paṭa, *m. nt.* a cloth ; garment.

Paṭaggi, *m.* a counter fire.

Paṭaṅga, *m.* a grasshopper.

Paṭala, *nt.* a covering ; a membrane ; envelope ; lining ; film.

Paṭalikā, *f.* a woollen coverlet embroidered with flowers.

Paṭaha, *m.* a kettle-drum ; a war drum.

Paṭākā, *f.* a flag.

Paṭi, Pati, a prefix having the meanings : against, opposite, towards, in opposition to.

Paṭikaṅkhati (paṭi + kakh + ŋ - a), to wish or long for. *aor.* —**khi.** *pp.* —**khita.**

Paṭikaṇṭaka, *a.* adverse; opposing ; hostile ; inimical. *m.* an enemy.

Paṭikamma, *nt.* redress ; atonement.

Paṭikara, *a.* counteracting ; redressing ; expiating.

Paṭikaroti (paṭi + kar + o), to redress ; to expiate ; to act against. *aor.* —**kari.** *pp.* —**kata.** *pr. p.* —**karonta.**

Paṭikassati (paṭi + kas + a), to draw back ; to throw back. *aor.* —**kassi.** *pp.* —**kassita.**

Paṭikāra, *m.* counteraction ; remedy ; requital.

Paṭikujjana, *nt.* covering or bending over ; turning upside down.

Paṭikujjeti (paṭi + kuj + e), to cover over ; to turn upside down. *aor.* —**esi.** *pp.* —**kujjita.** *abs.* —**jetvā,** —**jitvā,** —**kujjiya.**

Paṭikujjhati (paṭi + kudh + ya), to be angry in return.

Paṭikuṭṭha, *pp.* scorned defamed ; blameworthy.

Paṭikkanta, *pp.* of **paṭikkamati.**

Paṭikkama, *m.* going aside going back.

Paṭikkamati (pa i + kam + a), to step backwards ; to go back or aside. *aor.* —**kami.** *pr. p.* —**manta.** *abs.* —**mitvā, paṭikkamma.**

Paṭikkamana, *nt.* going back ; retiring.—**sālā,** *f.* retiring hall.

Paṭikkūla, *a.* loathsome ; disagreeable ; objectionable.—**tā,** *f.* reluctance ; loathsomeness. —**saññā,** *f.* the consciousness of impurity.

Paṭikkosana, *f.* protest.

Paṭikkosati. (paṭi + kus + a), to blame ; to reject ; to scorn ; to revile. *aor.* —**kosi.** *pp.* **paṭikkuṭṭha.** *abs.*—**kositvā.**

Paṭikkhipati (paṭi + khip + a), to reject ; to refuse ; to oppose. *aor.* —**khipi**. *pp.* —**khitta**. *abs.* —**pitvā**, —**khippa**.

Paṭikkhepa, *m.* refusal ; denial ; objection ; negation.

Paṭigacca, *in.* beforehand.

Paṭigijjhati (paṭi + gidh + ya), to long for ; to desire ; to become greedy. *aor.* —**jhi**. *pp.* —**giddha**. See **Gijjhati**.

Paṭigūhati (paṭi + gūh + a), to conceal ; to keep back. *aor.* —**gūhi**. *pp.* —**gūhita**. *abs.* —**gūhitvā**.

Paṭigganhana, *nt.* acceptance ; reception ; taking.—**naka**, *a.* receiving ; a receiver ; able to hold in.

Paṭigganhāti (paṭi + gah + ṇhā), to take ; to receive ; to accept. *aor.* —**ganhi**. *pp.* —**gahita**. *pr. p.* —**ganhanta**. *abs.* —**gahetvā**, —**ganhiya**, **paṭiggayha**.

Paṭiggahaṇa, see —**ganhana**.

Paṭiggahetu, *m.* —**gāhaka**, 3. one who accepts, receives or takes ; a recipient.

Paṭigha, *m.* anger ; repulsion ; collision.

Paṭighāta, *m.* collision ; knocking against ; repulsion.

Paṭighosa, *m.* an echo.

Paṭicarati (paṭi + car + a), to go about ; to evade a question ; to obscure a matter of discussion. *aor.* —**cari**.

Paṭicodeti (paṭi + cud + e), to blame in return ; to reprove *aor.* —**esi**. *pp.* —**dita**. *abs.* —**detvā**.

Paṭicca, *in.* & *abs.* on account of ; because of ; concerning. —**samuppanna**, *a.* evolved by reason of the law of causation. —**samuppāda**, *m.* causal genesis ; dependent origination.

Paṭicchati (paṭi + isu + a), to accept ; to receive. *aor.*—**cchi**. *pp.* —**chita**. *abs.* —**chitvā**, —**chiya**.

Paṭicchanna, *pp.* of **paṭicchādeti**.

Paṭicchādaka, —**chādī**, *a.* hiding ; covering ; concealing ; obscuring.—**dana**, *nt.* concealment ; covering.

Paṭicchādaniya, *nt.* meat broth or gravy.

Paṭicchādeti (paṭi + chad + e), to cover over ; to conceal. *aor.* —**esi**. *pp.* —**dita**, —**channa**. *pr. p.* —**denta**. *abs.* —**detvā**, —**chādiya**.

Patijaggaka, 3. one who rears, brings up, nurses, or fosters.

Paṭijaggati (paṭi + jag + a), to watch over ; to look after ; to tend ; to nourish ; to repair. *aor.* —**ggi**. *pp.* —**gita**. *abs.* —**gitvā**, —**ggiya**.

Paṭijaggana, *nt.* rearing ; fostering ; tending ; care ; repair. —**naka**, *a.* nursing ; taking care.

Paṭijaggiya, *a.* fit to be nursed or repaired.

Paṭijānāti (paṭi + ñā + nā), to acknowledge, to promise; to consent. *aor.* —**jāni**. *pp.* **paṭiññāta**. *pr. p.* —**jānanta**. *abs.* —**jānitvā**.

Paṭiñña, *a.* (in cpds. such as **samaṇapaṭiñña**), making belief ; pretending to be.

Paṭiññā, *f.* promise ; vow ; consent ; permission.

Paṭidadāti (paṭi + dā + a), to give back ; to restore. *aor* —**dadi**. *pp.* —**dinna**. *abs.* —**datvā**.

Paṭidaṇḍa, *m.* retribution ; recompense.

Paṭidasseti (paṭi + dis + e), to show oneself; to appear again. *aor.* **—esi.** *pp.* **—dassita.** *abs.* **—setvā.**

Paṭidāna, *nt.* reward; restitution.

Paṭidissati (paṭi + dis + ya), to be seen; to appear. *aor.* **—dissi.**

Paṭideseti (paṭi + dis + e), to confess. *aor.* **—esi.** *pp.* **—desita.** *abs.* **—setvā.**

Paṭidhāvati (paṭi + dhāv + a), to run back to; to run near. *aor.* **—dhāvi.** *abs.* **—vitvā.**

Paṭinandati (paṭi + nand + a), to be glad; to accept gladly. *aor.* **—nandi.** *pp.* **—dita.** *abs.* **ditvā.**

Paṭinandanā, *f.* rejoicing.

Paṭināsikā, *f.* a false nose.

Paṭinivattati (pati + ni + vat + a), to turn back again. *aor.* **—tti.** *pp.* **—vatta.** *abs.* **—titvā.**

Paṭinissagga, *m.* giving up; rejection; forsaking.

Paṭinissajjati (paṭi + ni + saj + ya), to give up; to renounce; to forsake. *aor.* **—jji.** *pp.* **—nissaṭṭha.** *abs.* **—jitvā, —jjiya.**

Paṭineti (paṭi + ni + a), to lead back to. *aor.* **—esi.** *pp.* **—nīta.** *abs.* **—netvā.**

Paṭipakkha, *a.* opposed; opposite. *m.* an onemy; opponent. **—khika,** inimical; of an opponent party.

Paṭipajjati (paṭi + pad + ya), to enter upon a path or course; to go along; to follow a method. *aor.* **—jji.** *pp.* **—panna.** *pr. p.* **—pajjamāna.** *abs.* **—jitvā.**

Paṭipajjana, *nt.* procedure; practice; observance.

Paṭipaṇṇa, *nt.* a letter in reply.

Paṭipatti, *f.* conduct; practice; behaviour; religious practice.

Paṭipatha, *m.* the opposite way; way in front.

Paṭipadā, *f.* line of conduct; mode of progress.

Paṭipanna, *pp.* of **patipajjati.**

Paṭipaharati (paṭi + pa + har + a), to strike in return. *aor.* **—hari.** *pp.* **—pahaṭa.** *abs.* **—ritvā.**

Paṭipahiṇāti (paṭi + pa + hi + ṇā), to send back. *aor.* **—hiṇi.** *pp.* **—pahita.** *abs.* **—hiṇitvā.**

Paṭipāṭi, *f.* the order; successsion.—**pāṭiyā,** *ad.* in order; successively; in succession.

Paṭipādaka, 3. one who arranges or supplies. *m.* the supporter of a bed.

Paṭipādeti (paṭi + pad + e), to bring into; to arrange; to supply. *aor.* **—esi.** *pp.* **—dita.** *abs.* **—detvā.**

Paṭipīḷana, *nt.* oppression.

Paṭipīḷeti (paṭi + pīḷ + e), to oppress. *aor.* **—esi.** *pp.* **—ḷita.** *abs.* **—ḷetvā.**

Paṭipuggala, *m.* a rival; a compeer; a match.

Paṭipucchati (paṭi + pucch + a), to ask in return; to put a question to. *aor.* **—cchi.** *pp.* **—cchita.**

Paṭipucchā, *f.* a question in return.

Paṭipūjanā, *f.* reverence; honour.

Paṭipūjeti (paṭi + pūj + e), to honour; to revere. *aor.* **—esi.** *pp.* **—jita.** *abs.* **—jetvā.**

Paṭipeseti (paṭi + pes + e), to send back; to send out to.

Paṭippassaddha, *pp.* of **—passambhati.**

Paṭippassaddhi, *f.* calming; allaying; quieting down; complete ease.

Paṭippassambhati (paṭi + pa + sambh + a), to be eased or calmed; to be allayed. *aor.* **—mbhi.**

Paṭippassambhanā, *f.* see **—passaddhi.**

Paṭibaddha, (*pp.* of **paṭibandhati**), bound to; dependent on; attracted to or by.**—citta,** *a.* enamoured; bound in love.

Paṭibala, *a.* able; adequate; competent.

Paṭibāhaka, *a.* repelling; preventing; one who prevents.

Paṭibāhati (paṭi + vah + a), to ward off; to evade; to keep off; to refuse. *aor.* **—bāhi.** *pp.* **—bāhita.** *pr. p.* **—bāhanta.** *abs.* **—bāhitvā, —bāhiya.**

Paṭibimba, *nt.* counterpart; image; reflection.**—bimbita,** *a.* reflected.

Paṭibujjhati (paṭi + budh + ya), to understand; to wake up. *aor.* **—jjhi.** *pp.* **—buddha.** *abs.* **—jhitvā.**

Paṭibhaya, *nt.* fear; terror; fright.

Paṭibhāga, *a.* equal; similar; *m.* likeness; resemblance.

Paṭibhāti (paṭi + bhā + a), to come into one's mind; to be evident. *aor.* **—bhāsi.**

Paṭibhāna, *nt.* ready wit; promptitude; readiness of speech; intelligence. **—vantu,** *m. f. a.* possessed of ready wit.

Paṭibhāsati (paṭi + bhās + a), to address in return; to reply. *aor.* **—bhāsi.**

Paṭimagga, *m.* the way against; confronting road.

Paṭimaṇḍita (*pp.* of **paṭimaṇḍeti**), adorned with; consisting of.

Paṭimalla, *m.* a rival; rival wrestler.

Paṭimā, *f.* an image; figure.

Paṭimāneti (paṭi + mān + e), to honour; to wait for. *aor.* **—esi.** *pp.* **—mānita.** *abs.* **—netvā.**

Paṭimukka (*pp.* of the foll.), clothed in; fastened on; tied to.

Paṭimuñcati (paṭi + muc + ŋ - a), to put on a dress; to fasten; to bind. *aor.* **—muñci.** *abs.* **—citvā.**

Paṭiyādeti (paṭi + yat + e), to prepare; to arrange; to give over; to supply. *aor.* **—esi.** *pp.* **—dita, —yatta.** *abs.* **—detvā.**

Paṭiyodha, *m.* a hostile warrior; a counter fight.

Paṭirāja, *m.* a hostile king.

Paṭi (ti) rūpa, *a.* fit; proper; suitable; befitting.

Paṭi (ti) rūpaka, *a.* resembling; disguised as; in the appearance of.

Paṭirūpatā, *f.* semblance; likeness; fitness.

Paṭiladdha, *pp.* of the following.

Paṭilabhati (paṭi + labh + a), to obtain; to receive; to get. *aor.* **—labhi.** *pr. p.* **—bhanta.** *abs.* **—bhitvā, —laddhā.**

Paṭilābha, *m.* attainment; acquisition; obtaining.

Paṭilīyati (paṭi + lī + ya), to draw back; to keep away from. *aor.* **—līyi.** *pp.* **paṭilīna.** *abs.* **—līyitvā.**

Paṭilīyana, *nt.* keeping away; drawing back.

Paṭiloma, *a.* reverse; opposite; contrary.**—pakkha,** *m.* opposing party; opposition.

Paṭivacana, *nt.* answer; reply.

Paṭivattana, *nt.* moving backwards; turning back.

Paṭivattiya, *a.* to be turned or rolled back.

Paṭivattu, *m.* one who speaks against or contradicts.

Paṭivatteti (paṭi + vat + e), to roll or turn back. *aor.* **—esi.** *pp.* **—vattita,** *abs.* **—tetvā, —vattiya.**

Paṭivadati (paṭi + vad + a), to answer; to reply; to speak against. *aor.* **—vadi.** *pp.* **—vutta.** *abs.* **—vatvā, —vaditvā.**

Paṭivasati (paṭi + vas + a), to live; to dwell. *aor.* **—vasi.** *pp.* **—vuttha.** *abs.* **—sitvā.**

Paṭivātaŋ, *ad.* against the wind.

Paṭivāda, *m.* retort; recrimination.

Paṭiviŋsa, *m.* a share; a portion.

Paṭivijānāti (paṭi + vi + ñā + nā), to recognize; to know. *aor.* **—jāni.**

Paṭivijjhati (paṭi + vidh + ya), to penetrate; to comprehend. *aor.* **—jhi.** *pp.* **—viddha.** *abs* **—vijjha, —vijjhitvā.**

Paṭividita (*pp.* of **paṭivijānāti**), known; ascertained.

Paṭivinodana, *nt.* removal; expulsion; driving out.

Paṭivinodeti (paṭi + vi + nud + e), to dispel; to remove; to get rid of. *aor.* **—esi.** *pp.* **—dita.** *abs.* **—detvā.**

Paṭivibhajati (paṭi + vi + bhaj + a), to divide; to define. *aor.* **—bhaji.** *pp.* **—vibhatta.** *abs.* **—bhajitvā.**

Paṭivirata, *pp.* of the following.

Paṭiviramati (paṭi + vi + ram + a), to abstain from. *aor.* **—rami.** *pr. p.* **—manta.** *abs.* **—mitvā.**

Paṭivirujjhati (paṭi + vi + rudh + ya), to be hostile; to contradict. *aor.* **—jhi.** *abs.* **—jhitvā.**

Paṭiviruddha (*pp.* of the above), opposing; contrary.

Paṭivirūhati (paṭi + vi + ruh + a), to grow again. *aor.* **—rūhi.** *pp.* **—virūḷha.** *abs.* **—rūhitvā.**

Paṭivirodha, *m.* opposition; hostility.

Paṭivissaka, *m.* a neighbour. *adj.* neighbouring; dwelling near.

Paṭivedeti (paṭi + vid + e), to make known; to inform; to announce. *aor.* **—esi.** *pp.* **—vedita.** *abs.* **—detvā.**

Paṭivedha, *m.* penetration; attainment; comprehension.

Paṭisaŋyutta (*pp.* of **—saŋyujjati**), connected with; belonging to.

Paṭisaŋvedī, *a.* one who feels, experiences, suffers, or enjoys.

Paṭisaŋvedeti (paṭi + saŋ + vid + e), to undergo; to feel; to experience. *aor.* **—esi.** *pp.* **—vidita** or **—vedita.** *abs.* **—detvā.**

Paṭisaŋharaṇa, *nt.***—hāra,** *m.* folding; removal.

Paṭisaŋharati (paṭi + saŋ + har + a), to withdraw; to remove; to fold. *aor.* **—hari.** *pp.* **—harita** or **—haṭa.** *abs.* **—haritvā.**

Paṭisaṅkharaṇa, *nt.* restoration; mending.

Paṭisaṅkharoti (paṭi + saŋ + kar + o), to repair; to restore; to mend. *aor.* **—khari.** *pp.* **—khata.** *abs.* **—kharitvā.**

Paṭisaṅkhā, —khāya, *abs.* having considered or discriminated.

Paṭisaṅkhāna, *nt.* discrimination; consideration; mindfulness.

Paṭisaṅkhāra, *m.* see **—kharaṇa.**

Paṭisañcikkhati (paṭi + saŋ + cikkh + a), to discriminate; to consider. *aor.* **—khi.** *pp.* **—khita.**

Paṭisanthāra, *m.* friendly welcome; kind reception.

Paṭisandahati (paṭi + saŋ + dah + a), to reunite. *aor.* **—dahi.** *pp.* **—sandhita** or **—sandahita.**

Paṭisandhātu, *m.* one who reunites; a peace-maker.

Paṭisandhāna, *nt.* reunion.

Paṭisandhi, *f.* reincarnation; conception; reunion

Paṭisambhidā, *f.* analytic insight; discriminating knowledge.

Paṭisammodati (paṭi + sam + mud + a), to talk or greet friendly. *aor.* **—modi.** *pp.* **—modita.** *abs.* **—ditvā.**

Paṭisaraṇa, *nt.* shelter; help; protection.

Paṭisallāna, *nt.* retirement; seclusion.— **sāruppa,** *a.* suitable for seclusion.

Paṭisallīyati (paṭi + saŋ + lī + ya), to be in seclusion. *aor.* **—līyi.** *pp.* **—līna.** *abs.* **—līyitvā.**

Paṭisāmeti (paṭi + sam + e), to set in order; to keep away. *aor.* **—esi.** *pp.* **—mita.** *abs.* **—metvā.**

Paṭisāsana, *nt.* reply; counter-message.

Paṭisedha, *m.* **—dhana,** *nt.* prohibition; warding off; refusal.—**ka,** *a.* prohibiting; preventing; warding off; refusing.

Paṭisedheti (paṭi + sidh + e), to ward off; to prevent; to refuse; to prohibit. *aor.*—**esi.** *pp.* **—dhita.** *abs.* **—dhetvā. —dhiya.**

Paṭisevati (paṭi + sev + a), to follow; to pursue; to practise; to indulge in; to use a medicine, etc. *aor.* **—sevi.** *pp.* **—vita.** *pr. p.* **—sevanta.** *abs.* **—sevitvā, —seviya.**

Paṭisevana, *nt.* practising; using; following.

Paṭisotaŋ, *ad.* against the stream.

Paṭissava, *m.* promise; assent.

Paṭissuṇāti (paṭi + su + ṇā), to assent; to promise; to agree. *aor.* **—suṇi.** *pp.* **—suta.** *abs.* **—suṇitvā.**

Paṭihaññati (paṭi + han + ya), to be struck against; to be afflicted. *aor.* **—haññi.** *pp.* **—hata.** *abs.* **—haññitvā.**

Paṭihata (*pp.* of the above), smitten; stricken.

Paṭihanana, *nt.* striking; repulsion; dashing.

Paṭihanati (paṭi + han + a), to strike against; to ward off; to collide. *aor.* **—hani.** *pp.* **paṭihata.** *abs.* **—hantvā.**

Paṭu, *a.* clever; skilful; a clever person.—**tā,** *f.*—**tta,** *nt.* cleverness; skill.

Paṭola, *m.* the snake-gourd.

Paṭṭa, Paṭṭaka, *nt.* a sheet; slab; plate; a strip.

Paṭṭa, *nt.* silk cloth; a bandage; a strip of cloth. *adj.* silken.

Paṭṭana, *nt.* a port; a town near a port.

Paṭṭikā, *f.* a strip of cloth; bandage; waist-band; a girdle.

Paṭṭhapeti (pa + ṭhā + āpe), to establish; to begin; to start. *aor.* **—esi.** *pp.* **—pita.** *abs.* **—petvā.**

Paṭṭhāna, *nt.* setting forth; putting forward; starting point.

Paṭṭhāya, *in.* beginning with; henceforth; from the time of.

Paṭhati (paṭh + a), to read; to recite. *aor.* **paṭhi.** *pp.* **paṭhita.** *abs.* **paṭhitvā.**

Paṭhana, *nt.* reading.

Paṭhama, *a.* first; foremost; former.—**maŋ,** *ad.* at first; for the first time.—**taraŋ,** *ad.* first of all; as early as possible.

Paṭhavī, *f.* the earth.—**kampana,** *nt.* an earthquake. —**kasiṇa,** *nt.* the earth artifice (used for meditation).—**calana,** *nt.*—**cāla,** *m.* an earthquake. —**dhātu,** *f.* the earth element. —**sama,** *a.* like the earth. —**vojā,** *f.* the sap or essence of the earth.

Paṇamati (pa + nam + a), to bow down; to adore; to worship. *aor.* **paṇami.** *pp.* **paṇamita, paṇata.** *abs.* —**mitvā**

Paṇāma, *m.* salutation; bending; adoration; bowing down.

Paṇāmeti (pa + nam + e), to dismiss; to eject; to shut; to stretch out. *aor.* —**esi.** *pp.* —**mita.** *pr. p.* —**menta.** *abs.* —**metvā.**

Paṇidahati (pa + ni + dah + a), to aspire to; to long for; to put forth; to direct. *aor.* —**dahi.** *pp.* **paṇihita,** —**dahita.** *abs.* **paṇidhāya,** —**dahitva.**

Paṇidhāna, *nt.* **Paṇidhi,** *m.* aspiration; determination.

Paṇipāta, *m.* adoration; prostration.

Paṇiya, *nt.* article of trade; *m.* a trader.

Paṇihita, (*pp.* of **paṇidahati**), directed; bent on; intent.

Paṇīta, *a.* excellent; delicious. —**tara,** *a.* more exalted; much delicious.

Paṇeti (pa + ni + e), to decree (a fine or punishment). *aor.* —**esi.** *abs.* **paṇetvā.**

Paṇḍaka, *m.* an eunuch.

Paṇḍara, *a.* white.

Paṇḍicca, *nt.* wisdom; erudition.

Paṇḍita, *a.* wise. *m.* a wise man. —**ka,** *m.* a pedant.

Paṇḍu, *a.* pale-yellow; yellowish. —**kambala,** *nt.* an orange-coloured blanket; name of the Sakka's throne.—**palāsa,** *m.* a withered leaf; one who is ready to leave household life. —**roga,** *m.* jaundice.—**rogī,** *m.* one who suffers from jaundice.

Paṇṇa,—**ṇaka,** *nt.* a leaf; a leaf for writing upon; a letter. —**kuṭi,** *f.* a hut of leaves. —**cchatta,** *nt.* a sunshade made of leaves.—**santhara,** *m.* a mattress of leaves.—**sālā,** *f.* a hermitage.

Paṇṇatti, see **Paññatti.**

Paṇṇarasa, 3. fifteen.

Paṇṇākāra, *m.* a present.

Paṇṇāsā, *f.* fifty.

Paṇṇika, *m.* a green-grocer; vendor of green leaves.

Paṇya, see **Paṇiya.**

Paṇhi, *m.* the heel.

Patati (pat + a), to fall down; to alight on. *aor.* **pati.** *pp.* **patita.** *pr. p.* **patanta.** *abs.* **patitvā.**

Patana, *nt.* falling.

Patanu, *a.* very thin.

Patākā, *f.* a flag; banner.

Patāpa, *m.* splendour; majesty. —**vantu,** *a.* majestic; splendid.

Patāpeti (pa + tap + e), to scorch; to heat. *aor.* —**esi.** *pp.* **patāpita.**

Pati, *m.* lord; husband; master. —**kula,** *nt.* husband's family.

Patiṭṭhahati,—**ṭṭhāti** (pati + ṭhā + a), to be established; to stand firmly; to find a support. *aor.* 1. —**ṭhahi,** 2. —**ṭhāsi**

pp. **patiṭṭhita.** *pr. p.* **—hanta.** *abs.* **—ṭhahitvā, patiṭṭhāya.** *inf.* **—ṭhituŋ, —ṭhātuŋ.**

Patiṭṭhā, *f.* help ; support ; resting place.

Patiṭṭhātabba, —ṭhitabba, *pt. p.* fit to be established.

Patiṭṭhāna, *nt.* fixing ; setting up ; support.

Patiṭṭhāpeti (*caus.* of **patiṭṭhāti**), to establish ; to set up ; to install. *aor.* **—esi.** *pp.* **—pita.** *pr. p.* **—penta,** *abs.* **—petvā, —piya.**

Patiṭṭhāpetu, *m.* founder ; one who establishes.

Patita, *pp.* of **patati.**

Patitiṭṭhati (pati + ṭhā + a), to stand up again.

Patibbatā, *f.* a devoted wife.

Patirūpa, see **Paṭirūpa.**

Patissata, *a.* thoughtful ; mindful.

Patīci, *f.* the west.

Patīta, *a.* delighted.

Patoda, *m.* a goad ; driving stick. **—ka,** *nt.* an spur ; nudging with one's fingers.**—laṭṭhi,** *f.* a driver's stick.

Patta (*pp.* of **pāpuṇāti**), reached; attained ; obtained.

Patta, *m.* an alms bowl. *nt.* a leaf ; a feather ; the wing of a bird.**—kkhandha,** *a.* downcast ; dejected ; with drooping shoulders.**—gata,** *a.* that which is in the bowl.**—gandha,** *m.* the odour of leaves.**—gāhaka,** *m.* one who carries another's bowl.**—thavikā,** *f.* case for a bowl.**—pāṇī,** *a.* bowl in hand. **—piṇḍika,** *a.* eating from one vessel only.

Pattabba (*pt. p.* of **pāpunāti**), what should be gained, attained or reached.

Pattādhāraka, *m.* a stand for a bowl.

Pattānumodanā, *f.* transference of merit.

Patti, *m.* a foot-soldier ; an infantry ; *f.* arrival ; attainment ; merit ; profit ; a share. **—ka,** *a.* having a share ; a partner.**—dāna,** *nt.* transference of merit or a share.

Pattika (=**Padika**), *a.* on foot. 3. a pedestrian ; a soldier on foot.

Pattuṇṇa, *nt.* a kind of cloth.

Pattuŋ, *inf.* to reach ; to attain ; to obtain.

Pattha, *m.* a measure of grain or liquid, four of which make a seer. See **Pasata.**

Patthaṭa (*pp.* of **pattharati**), spread out; widely known.

Patthaddha, *a.* very stiff.

Patthanā, *f.* aiming at ; aspiration ; desire.

Patthayati (pa + atth + aya), to wish for ; to desire ; to aspire. *aor.* **—thayi.** *pr. p.* **—yanta.** *pp.* **patthita.** *abs.* **—yitvā.**

Patthayāna, *a.* desiring.

Patthara, *m.* a slab ; a flat stone.

Pattharati (pa + thar + a), to spread out ; to extend. *aor.* **—thari.** *pp.* **patthaṭa.** *pr. p.* **—ranta.** *abs.* **—ritvā.**

Patthiva, *m.* a king.

Pattheti (pa + atth + e), to aspire ; to desire. *aor.* **—esi.** *pp.* **—thita.** *pr. p.* **—thenta.** *abs.* **—thetvā.**

Patvā, *abs.* (from **pāpuṇāti**), having reached, attained or obtained.

Patha, *m.* path ; way ; road. (In cpds.) range of, e.g. **gaṇanapatha** = range of calculation.

Pathavī, see **Paṭhavī.**

Pathāvī, Pathika, *m.* a pedestrian ; traveller.

Pada, *nt.* foot ; foot-step ; a word ; position ; place ; reason ; cause ; a line of stanza ; the final rest.—**ṭṭhāna,** *nt.* a proximate cause.—**cetiya,** *nt.* a holy foot-print.—**jāta,** *nt.* various kinds of foot-prints. —**pūraṇa,** *nt.* an expletive particle.—**bhājana,** *nt.* dividing of words ; treating each word separately.—**bhāṇaka,** *a.* one who recites the words of the Scriptures.—**vaṇṇanā,** *f.* explanation of words.—**valañja,** *nt.* a track or foot-print. —**vibhāga,** *m.* separation of words ; parsing.—**sadda,** *m.* sound of foot-steps.

Padakkhiṇā, *f.* to go round, keeping the right side turned towards a respectful person or an object of veneration ; circumambulation.

Padatta (*pp.* of **padāti**), given over ; distributed.

Padara, *nt.* a board.

Padahati (pa + dah + a), to strive ; to take up ; to confront. *aor.* **padahi.** *pp.* —**hita.** *abs.* —**hitvā.**

Padātave, *inf.* to give.

Padātu, *m.* giver ; distributer.

Padāna, *nt.* giving ; bestowing.

Padāḷana, *nt.* splitting ; cleaving; tearing.

Padāḷeti (pa + dār + e), to cleave ; to split ; to burst open. *aor.* —**esi.** *pp.* —**ḷita.** *pr. p.* —**ḷenta.** *abs.* —**ḷetvā.**

Padāḷetu, *m.* one who splits or breaks open.

Padika, *a.* consisting of poetical lines. *m.* a pedestrian.

Paditta, *pp.* of the following.

Padippati (pa + dip + ya), to blaze ; to flame forth. *aor.* —**ppi.** *pr. p.* —**pamāna.**

Padissati (pa + dis + ya), to be seen ; to appear. *aor.* —**dissi.** *pp.* **padiṭṭha.** *pr. p.* —**samāna.**

Padīpa, *m.* a lamp ; a light. —**peyya,** *nt.* material for lighting.—**kāla,** *m.* lighting time.

Padīpeti (pa + dip + e), to light a lamp ; to explain ; to make keen. *aor.* —**esi.** *pp.* —**pita.** *pr. p.* —**penta.** *abs.* —**petvā.**

Padīyati (pa + dā + ī + ya), to be given out or presented. *aor.* **padīyi.** *pp.* **padinna.**

Paduṭṭha (*pp.* of **padussati**), wicked ; corrupt.

Padubbhati (pa + dubh + ya), to plot against. *aor.* —**bhi.** *pp.* —**bhita.** *abs.* —**bhitvā.**

Paduma, *nt.* a lotus ; name of a purgatory and that of an enormous number.—**kaṇṇikā,** *f.* the pericarp of a lotus.—**kalāpa,** *m.* a bundle of lotuses. —**gabbha,** *m.* inside of a lotus. —**patta,** *nt.* a petal of lotus. —**rāga,** *m.* a ruby.—**sara,** *m. nt.* a lotus pond or lake.—**minī,** *f.* a lotus plant.—**minīpatta,** *nt.* leaf of a lotus plant.

Padumī, *a.* having lotuses ; a spotted (elephant).

Padussati (pa + dus + ya), to do wrong ; to offend against ; to be corrupted. *aor.* —**ssi.** *pp.* **paduṭṭha.** *abs.* —**ssitvā.**

Padussana, *nt.* offending or plotting against.

Padūseti (pa + dus + e), to defile ; to pollute ; to spoil ; to corrupt. *aor.* —**esi.** *pp.* **padūsita.** *abs.* —**setvā.**

Padesa, *m.* region ; place ; district ; location ; spot.—**ñāṇa,** *nt.* limited knowledge.—**rajja,**

nt. principality over a district. —**rāja,** *m.* a sub-king.

Padosa, *m.* the nightfall ; anger ; defect ; blemish.

Padma, see **Paduma.**

Padhaŋsa, *m.*—**sana,** *nt.* destruction ; violation ; offending; plunder.

Padhaŋsiya, *a.* liable to be violated, assaulted, or plundered.

Padhaŋseti (pa + dhaŋs + e), to destroy ; to assault ; to plunder ; to offend. *aor.* —**esi.** *pp.* —**sita.** *abs.* —**setvā.** *pr. p.* —**senta.**

Padhāna, *a.* chief ; foremost.

Padhāna (= **padahana**), *nt.* exertion; effort; striving.—**ghara,** *nt.* a house prepared for meditation.—**nika,** *a.* exerting in meditation.

Padhāvati (pa + dhāv + a), to run out or forth. *aor.* **padhāvi.**

Padhāvana, *nt.* running out.

Padhūpeti (pa + dhup + e), to fumigate ; to smoke. See **dhūpeti.** *pp.* **padhūpita.**

Padhota (*pp.* of **padhovati**), well-washed or sharpened.

Pana, *in.* (*Adversative and interrogative particle*), and ; yet ; but ; on the contrary ; and now ; more over.

Panasa, *m.* jack tree. *nt.* jack fruit.

Panassati (pa + nas + ya), to be lost ; to disappear ; to go to ruin. *aor.* —**ssi.** *pp.* **panaṭṭha.**

Panāḷikā, *f.* a pipe ; tube ; channel ; water course.

Panudati (pa + nud + a), to dispel ; to remove ; to push away. *aor.* —**nudi.** *pp.* —**dita.** *abs.* —**ditvā,** —**diya.** *pr. p.* —**damāna.**

Panu (ū) dana, *nt.* removal ; dispelling ; rejection.

Panta, *a.* distant ; remote ; secluded ; solitary.—**senāsana,** *nt* a secluded resting place.

Panti, *f.* a row ; range ; line.

Pantha, *m.* a path ; road.—**ka,** —**thika,** *m.* a wayfarer ; traveller.—**ghāta,** *m.*—**dūhana,** *nt.* waylaying ; robbery.—**ghātaka** *m.* a waylayer.

Panna, *a.* fallen ; gone down. —**bhāra,** *a.* one who has put down his burden.—**loma,** *a.* one whose hairs have fallen, i.e. subdued.

Pannaga, *m.* a serpent.

Papa, *nt.* water.

Papañca, *m.* an obstacle ; impediment ; delay ; illusion ; hindrance to spiritual progress.

Papañceti (pa + pac + e), to explain ; to delay on. *aor.* —**esi.** *pp.* —**ñcita.** *abs.* —**cetvā.**

Papaṭikā, *f.* the outer dry bark or crust of a tree.

Papatati (pa + pat + a), to fall down, off or into. *aor.* **papati.** *pp.* —**tita.** *abs.* —**titvā.**

Papatana, *nt.* falling down.

Papada, *m.* tip of the foot.

Papā, *f.* a shed by the roadside to provide travellers with water.

Papāta, *m.* a precipice ; steep rock.—**taṭa,** *m.* a steep declivity.

Papitāmaha, *m.* paternal great-grandfather.

Paputta, *m.* grandson.

Pappaṭaka, *m.* a mushroom.

Pappoṭheti (pa + poth + e), to flap,; to beat. *aor.* —**esi.** *pp.* —**ṭhita.** *abs.* —**ṭhetvā.**

Pappoti (pa + ap + o), to reach; to arrive ; to obtain ; to attain. *abs.* **pappuyya.**

Papphāsa, *m.* the lungs.

Pabandha, *m.* continuity; a treatise or poem.

Pabala, *a.* mighty.

Pabujjhati (pa + budh + ya), to awake; to understand. *aor.* **—jjhi.** *pp.* **pabuddha.** *abs.* **—jjhitvā.**

Pabodhana, *nt.* awakening; arousing; enlightenment.

Pabodheti (pa + budh + e), to arouse; to awaken; to enlighten. *aor.* **—esi.** *pp.* **—dhita.** *abs.* **—dhetvā.** *pr. p.* **—dhenta.**

Pabba, *nt.* knot of a stalk; joint; section; division.

Pabbajati (pa + vaj + a), to go forth; to become a monk; to leave household life. *aor.* **—baji.** *pp.* **—jita.** *abs.* **—jitvā.** *pr. p.* **—janta.**

Pabbajana, *nt.* **Pabbajjā,** *f.* taking up of the ascetic life; becoming a monk.

Pabbajita, *m.* a monk.

Pabbata, *m.* a mountain; rock. **—kūṭa,** *nt.* peak of a mountain. **—gahana,** *nt.* a district full of mountains.**—ṭṭha,** *a.* standing or situated on a mountain. **—pāda,** *m.* the foot of a mountain.**—sikhara,** *nt.* mountain-crest.**—teyya,** *a.* used to walk in mountains.

Pabbājana, *nt.* exile; banishment.**—janiya,** *a.* deserving to be expelled or exiled.

Pabājeti (pa + vaj + e), to exile; to banish; to make a monk. *aor.* **—esi.** *pp.* **—jita.** *abs.* **—jetvā.**

Pabbhāra, *m.* an incline of a mountain. *adj.* sloping; inclining; leading to.

Pabhagga (*pp.* of **pabhañjati**), broken up; destroyed; defeated.

Pabhaṅkara, *m.* light-bringer, i.e. the sun.

Pabhaṅgu, —ṅgura, *a.* brittle; frail; perishable.

Pabhava, *m.* origin; source; *adj.* (in cpds.) having as the origin.

Pabhavati (pa + bhū + a), to flow down; to originate. *aor.* **—vi.** *pp.* **—vita.** *abs.* **—vitvā.**

Pabhassara, *a.* very bright; resplendent.

Pabhā, *f.* light; radiance.

Pabhāta, *m.* daybreak; dawn. *adj.* become clear or shining.

Pabhāva, *m.* power; strength; dignity.

Pabhāveti (pa + bhū + e), to increase; to augment; to foster. *aor.* **—esi.** *pp.* **—vita.** *abs.* **—vetvā.**

Pabhāsa, *m.* light; splendour.

Pabhāsati (pa + bhās + a), to shine. *aor.* **—āsi.** *abs.* **—sitvā.** *pr. p.* **—santa.**

Pabhāseti (*caus.* of the above), to illumine; to pervade with light. *aor.* **—esi.** *pp.* **—sita.** *pr. p.* **—senta.** *abs.* **—setvā.**

Pabhijjati (pa + bhid + ya), to be broken; to burst open. *aor.* **—jji.** *pp.* **pabhinna.** *pr. p.* **—jamāna.** *abs.* **—jitvā.**

Pabhijjana, *nt.* separation; cleavage.

Pabhuti, *in.* beginning from; since; subsequently. **(Tato pabhuti** = thenceforth).**—ka,** *a.* dating from; derived or coming from.

Pabhū, *m.* overlord; ruler.

Pabheda, *m.* variety; cleavage. **—na,** *nt.* dividing; breaking up. *adj.* destructive.

Pamajjati (pa + mad + ya), to become intoxicated; to be careless, slothful or negligent;

to neglect. *aor.* **—jji.** *pp.* **pamatta.** *abs.* **—jitvā, pamajja, —jiya.** *inf.* **—jituṃ.**

Pamajjanā, *f.*—**na,** *nt.* delay; negligence.

Pamattabandhu, *m.* friend of the careless; i.e. the Evil One.

Pamathati (pa + math + a), to crush; to subdue. *aor.* **—thi.** *pp.* **—thita.** *abs.* **—thitvā.**

Pamadavana, *nt.* garden near a royal palace.

Pamadā, *f.* a woman.

Pamaddati (pa + mad + a), to crush down; to defeat; to overcome. *aor.* **—addi.** *pp.* **—dita.** *abs.* **—ditvā.**

Pamaddana, *nt.* crushing; overcoming.

Pamaddī, *m.* one who crushes or defeats.

Pamāṇa, *nt.* measure; size; amount.—**ṇaka,** *a.* measuring by; of the size of.—**ṇika,** *a.* according to the regular measurements.

Pamāda, *m.* negligence; indolence; remissness.—**pāṭha,** *nt.* a corrupt reading in a book.

Paminṇāti (pa + mi + nā), to measure; to estimate; to define. *aor.* **—miṇi.** *pp.* **pamita.** *abs.* **paminṇitvā** or **pamitvā.**

Pamukha, *a.* foremost; chief; prominent. *nt.* the front; a house-front.

Pamuccati (pa + muc + ya), to be delivered or freed. *aor* **—cci.** *pp.* **pamutta.** *abs.* **—citvā.**

Pamucchati (pa + mucch + a), to swoon; to faint. *aor.* **—chi.** *pp.* **—chita.** *abs.* **—chitvā.**

Pamuñcati (pa + muc + ṃ - a), to let loose; to emit; to liberate. *aor.* **—ñci.** *pp.* **—ñcita, pamutta.** *abs.*—**ñciya.—citvā.** *pr. p.* **—canta.**

Pamuṭṭha, *pp.* of **pamussati.**

Pamutta, see under **pamuñcati.** **—tti.** *f.* freedom; release.

Pamudita (*pp.* of **pamodati**), greatly delighted.

Pamuyhati (pa + muh + ya), to become bewildered or infatuated. *aor.* **—yhi.** *pp.* **pamūḷha.** *abs.*—**hitvā, pamuyha.**

Pamussati (pa + mus + ya), to forget. *aor.* **—ssi.** *pp.* **pamuṭṭha.** *abs.* **—ssitvā.**

Pameyya, *a.* measurable; limitable; fathomable.

Pamokkha, *m.* release; deliverance; letting loose; discharge.

Pamocana, *nt.* setting free; loosening; deliverance.

Pamoceti (pa + muc + e), to set free; to release. *aor.* **—esi.** *pp.* **—cita.** *abs.* **—cetvā.**

Pamoda, *m.* delight; joy.

Pamodati (pa + mud + a), to rejoice; to enjoy; to be glad. *aor.* **pamodi.** *pp.* **—dita.** *pr. p.* **—damāna.** *abs.* **—ditvā.**

Pamodanā, *f.* see **Pamoda.**

Pamohana, *nt.* deception; delusion.

Pamoheti (pa + muh + e), to deceive; to bewilder; to fascinate. *aor.* **—esi.** *pp.* **—hita.** *abs.* **—hetvā.**

Pampaka, *m.* a loris.

Pamha, *nt.* the eye-lash.

Paya, *m. nt.* (mano-group), milk; water.

Payata, *a.* purified; restrained.

Payatana, *nt.* striving; effor; endeavour.

Payāti (pa + yā + a), to go forward; to set out; to proceed. *aor.* **payāsi.** *pp.* **payāta.**

Payirupāsati (pari + upa + ās + a), to attend on; to associate; to honour. *aor.* —**pāsi.** *pp.* —**sita.** *abs.* —**sitvā.**

Payirupāsanā, *f.* attending on; associating.

Payuñjati (pa + yuj + ŋ - a), to harness; to employ; to apply. *aor.* —**ñji.** *pp.* —**payutta.** *pr. p.* —**ñjamāna.** *abs.* —**jitvā.**

Payuttaka, *a.* one who is put to a task; a spy.

Payoga, *m.* means; undertaking; action; practice; business. —**karaṇa,** *nt.* exertion; pursuit. —**vipatti,** *f.* failure of means; wrong application.—**sampatti,** *f.* success of means.

Payojaka, —**jetu,** *m.* one who directs or manages; a manager.

Payojana, *nt.* application; use; undertaking; appointment.

Payojeti (pa + yuj + e), to engage in; to undertake; to apply; to prepare; to employ; to take into service; to challenge. *aor.* —**esi.** *pp.* —**jita.** *pr. p.* —**jenta.** *abs.* —**jetvā,** —**jiya.**

Payodhara, *m.* a rain cloud; the breast of a woman.

Payyaka, *m.* paternal great-grandfather.

Para, *a.* other; another; foreign; alien; outsider.—**kata,** *a.* done by others.—**kāra,** *m.* actions of others.—**jana,** *m.* stranger; outsider.—**attha,** *m.* the welfare of others.—**dattūpajīvī,** *a.* living on what is given by others.—**neyya,** *a.* to be led by another. —**paccaya,**—**pattiya,** *a.* relying or dependent on someone else.—**puṭṭha,** *a.* brought up by another. —**pessa,** *a.* serving others. —**bhāga,** *m.* hinder portion; the outer part.—**loka,** *m.* the world beyond.—**vambhana,** *nt.* contempt of others.—**vāda,** *m.* a contrary view.—**vādī,** 3. the opponent in a controversy. —**visaya,** *m.* a foreign country; realm of another.—**senā,** *f.* a hostile army.—**hatthagata,** *a.* seized by the enemy.—**hita,** *m.* welfare of others.—**hetu,** *ad.* on account of others.

Parakkama, *m.*—**mana,** *nt.* exertion; endeavour; effort.

Parakkamati (parā + kam + a), to exert; to show courage, *aor.* —**kami.** *pp.* **parakkanta.** *pr. p.* —**kamanta.** *abs.* —**mitvā, parakkamma.**

Parattha, *in.* in another place; hereafter.

Paradāra, *m.* somebody else's wife.—**kamma,** *nt.* adultery; unlawful intercourse with others' wives.—**dārika,** *m.* an adulterer.

Parama, *a.* superior; best; excellent.—**matā,** *f.* (in cpds.) the highest quantity; at the most. **Nāḷikodanaparamatāya** = on a seer of boiled rice at the most.—**mattha,** *m.* the highest ideal; truth in the ultimate sense.—**māyu,** *nt.* the age limit.

Paramāṇu, *m.* the 36th part of an **aṇu.**

Paramparā, *f.* lineage; succession; series.

Parammukha, *a.* with face turned away.—**khā,** *ad.* in one's absence.

Parasuve, *ad.* day after tomorrow.

Paraŋ, *ad.* after; beyond; further; on the other side of. —**maraṇā,** after the death.

Parājaya, *m.* defeat; losing at play.

Parājīyati (*pass.* of the foll.), to be defeated. *aor.* —**jīyi.**

Parājeti (parā + ji + e), to defeat; to conquer; to subdue; to beat in a game. *aor.* —**esi.** *pp.* —**jita.** *pr. p.* —**jenta.** *abs.* —**jetvā.**

Parādhīna, *a.* dependent on others; belonging to others.

Parābhava, *m.* ruin; disgrace; degeneration.

Parābhavati (parā + bhū + a), to decline; to go to ruin. *aor.* —**bhavi.** *pp.* —**bhūta.** *pr. p.* —**bhavanta.**

Parāmaṭṭha, *pp.* of the following.

Parāmasati (pari + ā + mas + a), to touch; to hold on to; to be attached; to caress. *aor.* —**masi.** *pp.* —**masita,** —**maṭṭha.** *pr. p.* —**santa.** *abs.* —**masitvā.**

Parāyaṇa, *nt.* support; rest; relief; the final end; (In cpds.) aiming at; ending in; destined to; finding one's support in. **Saggaparāyaṇa** = destined to be born in heaven.

Parāyatta, *a.* belonging to others.

Pari, (*a prefix* denoting completion), all round; altogether; completely.

Parikaḍḍhana, *nt.* drawing over; dragging.

Parikaḍḍhati (pari + kaḍḍh + a), to draw over or towards oneself; to drag. *aor.* —**ḍhi.** *pp.* —**ḍhita.** *abs.* —**ḍhitvā.**

Parikathā, *f.* exposition; an introduction; round-about talk.

Parikantati (pari + kant + a), to cut open or through. *aor.* —**nti.** *pp.* —**ntita.** *abs.* —**ntitvā.**

Parikappa, *m.* intention; assumption; supposition.

Parikappeti (pari + kap + e), to intend; to surmise; to suppose. *aor.* —**esi.** *pp.* —**pita.** *abs.* —**petvā.**

Parikamma, *nt.* arrangement; preparation; preliminary action; plastering.—**kata,** *a.* plastered with.—**kāraka,** 3. one who makes preparations.

Parikassati (pari + kas + a), to drag about; to sweep away; to move back. *aor.* —**ssi.** *pp.* —**sita.**

Parikiṇṇa, *pp.* of **parikirati.**

Parikitteti (pari + kitt + e), to expound; to praise; to make public. *aor.* —**esi.** *pp.* —**kittita.**

Parikirati (pari + kir + a), to scatter about; to surround. *aor.* —**kiri.** *pp.* —**kiṇṇa.** *abs.* **parikiriya,** —**kiritvā.**

Parikilanta, *pp.* of the following.

Parikilamati (pari + kilam + + a), to get tired out; to be exhausted or fatigued. *aor.* —**lami.** *abs.* —**mitvā.**

Parikiliṭṭha, *pp.* of the foll.

Parikilinna, *pp.* stained; soiled; dirty; wet.

Parikilissati (pari + kilis + ya), to get stained or soiled; to get into trouble. *aor.* —**ssi.** *abs.* —**sitvā.**

Parikilissana, *nt.* impurity.

Parikuppati (pari + kup + ya) to be excited or much agitated. *aor.* —**ppi.** *pp.* —**kupita.**

Parikopeti (pari + kup + e), to excite violently; to make angry. *aor.* —**esi.** *pp.* —**kopita.** *abs.* —**petvā.**

Parikkamana, *nt.* the space around; going round; walking about.

Parikkhaka, 3. investigator; examiner; inspector.—**khaṇa,** *nt.* investigation; putting to the test.

Parikkhata (*pp.* of **parikhaṇati**). dug out; wounded; prepared; equipped.

Parikkhati (pari + ikkh + a), to inspect; to investigate. *aor.* —**kkhi.** *pp.* —**khita.** *abs.* —**khitvā.**

Parikkhaya, *m.* exhaustion; waste; decay; loss.

Parikkhā, see **parikkhaṇa.**

Parikkhāra, *nt.* requisite; accessory; equipment; utensil.

Parikkhitta, *pp.* of the foll.

Parikkhipati (pari + khip + a) to encircle; to surround. *aor.* —**khipi.** *pr. p.* —**panta.** *abs.* —**khipitvā.** *pt. p.* —**pitabba.** *caus.* —**pāpeti.**

Parikkhīṇa, (*pp.* of **parikhīyati**), wasted; exhausted.

Parikkhepa, *m.* enclosure; closing round; circumference.

Pariklesa, *m.* hardship: impurity.

Parikhaṇati, Paḷikhaṇati (pari + khan + a), to dig around. *aor.* —**khaṇi.** *pp.* —**khata.** *abs.* —**ṇitvā.**

Parikhā, *f.* a ditch; a moat.

Pariganhana, *nt.* investigation; comprehension.

Pariganhāti (pari + gah + ṇā), to explore; to examine; to search; to take possession of; to comprehend. *aor.* —**ganhi.** *pp.* —**ggahita.** *pr. p.* —**ganhanta.** *abs.* —**ganhitvā,** —**gahetvā,** —**ggayha.**

Parigilati (pari + gil + a), to swallow. *aor.* —**gili.** *pp.* —**gilita.** *abs.* —**gilitvā.**

Parigūhati (pari + gūh + a), to hide; to conceal. *aor.* —**gūhi.** *pp.* —**gūhita,** —**gūḷha.** *abs.* —**gūhitvā,**—**gūhiya.**

Pariggaha, *m.* taking up; possession; acquirement; grasping; belongings; a wife.

Pariggahita (*pp.* of **pariganhāti**), owned; taken possession; occupied.

Paricaya, *m.* practice; familiarity; acquaintance.

Paricaraṇa, *nt.* attending to; looking after; enjoyment.

Paricarati (pari + car + a), to move about; to attend; to look after; to feast one's senses. to observe or practise. *aor.* —**cari.** *abs.* —**caritvā.**

Paricāraka, *a.* serving; attending; *m.* a servant; an attendant.

Paricāraṇā, *f.* care; looking after; feasting.

Paricārikā, *f.* a maid-servant; a wife.

Paricāreti (*caus.* of **paricarati**), to serve; to wait on; to amuse oneself. *aor.* —**esi.** *pp.* —**rita.** *abs.* —**retvā.**

Paricinna, Paricita (*pp.* of **paricināti**), practised; attended; acquainted with; accumulated; accustomed.

Paricumbati (pari + cub + ŋ - a), to cover with kisses. *aor.* —**mbi.** *pp.* —**bita.** *abs.* —**bitvā.**

Paricca, *abs.* having distinguished or understood.

Pariccajati (pari + caj + a), to give up; to abandon; to leave behind; to bestow. *aor.* —**caji.** *pp.* —**ccatta.** *pr. p.* —**cajanta.** *abs.* —**cajitvā.** *inf.* —**cajituŋ.**

Pariccajana, *nt.* **Pariccāga,** *m.* giving up; abandonment; bestowal; renunciation.

Paricchanna (*pp.* of **paricchādeti**), covered over; wrapped. round.

Paricchādanā, *f.* covering all over.

Paricchindati (pari + chid + ŋ - a), to mark out; to limit; to define. *aor.* —**ndi.** *pp.* —**chinna.** *abs.* —**chindiya,** —**cchijja.**

Paricchindana, *nt.* definition; marking out; limitation; analysis.

Paricchedа, *m.* measure; limit; boundary; division; a chapter (in a book).

Parijana, *m.* retinue; followers; attendants.

Parijānana, *nt.* —**nā**, *f.* knowledge; cognition.

Parijānāti (pari + ñā + nā), to know for certain; to comprehend; to know accurately. *aor.* —**jāni.** *pp.* **pariññāta.** *pr. p.* —**jānanta.** *abs.* —**jānitvā, pariññāya.**

Parijiṇṇa, (*pp.* of **parijīyati**), worn out; decayed.

Pariññā, *f.* exact knowledge; full understanding.

Pariññāta, see under **parijānati.**

Pariññāya, *abs.* of **parijānāti.**

Pariññeyya, *nt.* what should be known accurately.

Pariḍayhati (pari + dah + ya), to be burnt or scorched. *aor.* —**yhi.** *pp.* —**daḍḍha.** *abs.* —**ḍayhitvā.**

Pariḍayhana, *nt.* burning.

Pariṇata, *pp.* of the following.

Pariṇamati (pari + nam + a), to be transformed into; to ripen; to mature. *aor.* —**ṇami.**

Pariṇaya, *m.* marriage.

Pariṇāma, *m.* ripening; change; development; digestion.

Pariṇāmana, *nt.* diverting to somebody's use.

Pariṇāmeti (pari + nam + e), to change into; to appropriate; to turn to somebody's use. *aor.* —**esi.** *pp.* —**ṇāmita.** *abs.* —**metvā.**

Parināyaka, *m.* a guide; leader; adviser.—**ratana**, *nt.* the chief of the army of a universal monarch.—**nāyikā**, *f.* a woman leader; insight.

Pariṇāha, *m.* girth; dimensions; circumference.

Paritappati (pari + tap + ya), to grieve; to worry; to be sorrowful. *aor.* —**tappi.**

Paritassati (pari + tas + ya), to be excited or worried; to show a longing after. *aor.* —**ssi.** *pp.* —**sita.**

Paritassanā, *f.* worry; excitement; longing.

Paritāpa, *m.*—**tāpana**, *nt.* tormenting; affliction; mortification.

Paritāpeti (pari + tap + e), to scorch; to molest; to torment. *aor.* —**esi.** *pp.* —**pita.** *abs.* —**petvā.**

Parituleti (pari + tul + e), to weigh; to consider; to estimate. *aor.* —**esi.** *pp.* —**tulita.** *abs.* —**tuletvā.**

Parito, *ad.* round about; on every side; everywhere.

Paritoseti (pari + tus + e), to please; to make happy. *aor.* —**esi.** *pp.* —**sita.** *abs.* —**setvā.**

Paritta,—**taka**, *a.* small; insignificant; little; trifling.

Paritta, *nt.* a little; protection; protective charm.—**sutta**, *nt.* enchanted thread.

Parittāṇa, *nt.* protection ; refuge; safety.

Parittāyaka, *a.* protecting ; safeguarding against.

Paridahati (pari + dah + a), to put on ; to clothe ; to dress oneself. *aor.* **—dahi.** *pp.* **—dahita.** *abs.* **—dahitvā.**

Paridahana, *nt.* putting on ; dressing oneself.

Paridīpaka, *a.* explanatory ; illuminating.

Paridīpana, *nt.* **—nā,** *f.* explanation ; illustration.

Paridīpeti (pari + dīp + e), to make clear ; to explain ; to illumine. *aor.* **—esi.** *pp.* **pita.** *pr. p.* **—penta.** *abs.* **—petvā.**

Paridūseti (pari + dūs + e), to spoil altogether. *aor.* **—esi.** *pp.* **—sita.** *abs.* **—setvā.**

Parideva, *m.* **—vanā,** *f.* wailing ; lamentation.

Paridevati (pari + dev + a), to wail ; to lament. *aor.* **—devi.** *pp.* **—vita.** *abs.* **—vitvā.** *pr. p.* **—devanta.** **—devamāna.**

Paridhaṇsaka, *a.* destructive ; ruinous ; one who speaks destructively.

Paridhāvati (pari + dhāv + a), to run about. *aor.* **—dhāvi.** *pp.* **—vita.** *abs.* **—vitvā.**

Paridhota, *pp.* of the following.

Paridhovati (pari + dhov + a), to wash all round ; to cleanse. *aor.* **—dhovi.**

Pariniṭṭhāna, *nt.* the end ; accomplishment.

Pariniṭṭhāpeti (pari + ni + ṭhā + āpe), to bring to an end ; to accomplish. *aor.* **—esi.** *pp.* **—pita.** *abs.* **—petvā.**

Parinibbāna, *nt.* final release from transmigration ; death after the last lifespan of an Arahant. **—bāpana.** *nt.* complete extinction or cooling.

Parinibbāti (pari + ni + vā + a), to die without being reborn. *aor.* **—nibbāyi.** *pp.* **—nibbuta** *abs.* **—bāyitvā.**

Parinibbāyī, *a.* one who has attained the final release.

Paripakka (*pp.* of **paripaccati**), quite ripe ; well-matured.

Paripat(ṭ)ati (pari + pat + a), to fall down ; to go to ruin. *aor.* **—pati.** *pp.* **—patita.**

Paripantha, *m.* danger ; obstacle. **—thika,** *a.* obstructing ; opposing.

Paripāka, *m.* ripeness ; maturity ; digestion.

Paripācana, *nt.* ripening ; maturing ; development.

Paripāceti (pari + pac + e), to bring to maturity ; to ripen ; to develop. *aor.* **—esi.** *pp.* **—cita.**

Paripāteti (pari + pat + e), to attack ; to fell down ; to kill ; to bring to ruin. *aor.* **—esi.** *pp.* **—tita.** *abs.* **—tetvā.**

Paripāleti (pari + pāl + e), to protect ; to guard ; to watch. *aor.* **—esi.** *pp.* **—lita.** *abs.* **—letvā.**

Paripīḷeti (pari + piḷ + e), to oppress. *aor.* **—esi.** *pp.* **—ḷita.**

Paripucchaka, *a.* one who asks a question or investigates.

Paripucchati (pari + pucch + a), to interrogate ; to inquire. *aor.* **—cchi.** *pp.* **—chita, —puṭṭha.** *abs.* **—chitvā.**

Paripucchā, *f.* a question ; interrogation.

Paripuṇṇa (*pp.* of **paripūrati**), quite full ; fulfilled ; complete ; perfect. **—tā,** *f.* fullness ; completeness.

Paripūra, *a.* full; complete. **—ka**, *a.* one who fills or fulfils. **—kāritā**, *f.* completion. **—kārī**, *m.* one who completes or fulfils. **—raṇa**, *nt.* fulfilment; completion.

Paripūrati (pari + pūr + a), to become full or perfect. *aor.* **—pūri**. *pp.* **—puṇṇa**. *abs.* **—pūritvā**.

Paripūreti (*caus.* of the above). to fill; to fulfil; to accomplish. *aor.* **—esi**. *pp.* **—pūrita**. *pr. p.* **—renta**. *abs.* **—retvā**, **—pūriya**. *pt. p.* **—retabba**.

Paripphuṭa, *pp.* filled; pervaded.

Pariplava, *a.* unsteady; wavering; swerving.

Pariplavati (pari + plav + a), to quiver; to swerve; to roam about. *aor.* **—plavi**. *pp.* **—vita**.

Pariphandati (pari + phand + a), to tremble; to throb. *aor.* **—ndi**.

Paribāhira, *a.* external; alien to; an outsider.

Paribbajati (pari + vaj + a), to wander about. *aor.* **—baji**.

Paribbaya, *m.* expenses; expenditure; wages.

Paribbājaka, *m.* a wandering religious mendicant. **—jikā**, *f.* a wandering nun.

Paribbūḷha, *pp.* encompassed; surrounded.

Paribbhamati (pari + bham + a), to walk or roam about. *aor.* **—bhami**. *pp.* **—bhanta**. *pr.p.* **—bhamanta**. *abs.* **—bhamitvā**.

Paribbhamana, *nt.* roaming or reeling about.

Paribbhameti (*caus.* of **—mati**), to make reel round. *aor.* **—esi**. *pp.* **—bhamita**. *abs.* **—bhametvā**.

Paribhaṭṭha, *pp.* fallen; dropped.

Paribhaṇḍa, *m.* plastered flooring; an encircling. **—kata**, *a.* plastered.

Paribhava, *m.* **—vana**, *nt.* contempt; abuse.

Paribhavati (pari + bhū + a), to treat with contempt; to despise; to abuse; to revile. *aor.* **—bhavi**. *pp.* **—bhūta**. *pr. p.* **—bhavanta**, **—vamāna**. *abs.* **—bhavitvā**.

Paribhāvita (*pp.* of **paribhāveti**), trained; penetrated; practised; mixed or filled with; fostered.

Paribhāsa, *m.* **—sana**, *nt.* abuse; blame; censure. **—saka**, *a.* one who abuses or reviles; abusive.

Paribhāsati (pari + bhās + a), to abuse; to scold; to defame. *aor.* **—bhāsi**. *pp.* **—sita**. *pr. p.* **—bhāsamāna**. *abs.* **—sitvā**.

Paribhinna (*pp.* of **paribhindati**), broken; split; set at variance.

Paribhuñjati (pari + bhuj + ŋ - a), to eat; to use; to enjoy. *aor.* **—ñji**. *pp.* **—bhutta**. *pr. p* **— janta**, **— jamāna**. *abs.* **—jitvā**, **—bhutvā**, **—ñjiya**. *pt. p.* **—jitabba**.

Paribhutta, *pp.* see the above.

Paribhūta, *pp.* of **paribhavati**.

Paribhoga, *m.* use; enjoyment; feeding; material for enjoyment. **—cetiya**, *nt.* something used by the Buddha and consequently sacred.

Paribhojanīya, *a.* fit to be used. **—udaka**, *nt.* water for washing only.

Parimajjati (pari + maj + a), to stroke; to rub; to polish; to wipe off or out. *aor.* **—majji**. *pp.* **—majjita** or **—maṭṭha**. *abs.* **—jitvā**.

Parimajjana, *nt.* rubbing; wiping off; massaging.

Parimaṇḍala, *a.* round; circular; well sounding. **—laŋ**, *ad.* all round.

Parimaddati (pari + mad + a), to rub; to crush; to massage. *aor.* **—maddi.** *pp.* **—dita.** *abs.* **—ditvā.**

Parimaddana, *nt.* rubbing; crushing; subduing; massaging.

Parimāṇa, *nt.* measure; extent; limit. *adj.* (in cpds.) measuring; comprising; extending over.

Parimita (*pp.* of **parimiṇāti**), measured; limited; restricted.

Parimukhaŋ, *ad.* in front of.

Parimuccati (pari + muc + ya), to be released; to escape. *aor.* **—mucci.** *p p.*—**mutta.** *abs.* **—muccitvā.**

Parimuccana, *nt.* release; escape.

Parimutta, *pp.* of **parimuccati.**

Parimutti, *f.* release; deliverance.

Parimoceti (pari + muc + e), to set free; to deliver. *aor.* **—esi.** *pp.* **—mocita.** *abs.* **—cetvā.**

Pariyatti, *f.* the Scriptures. **—dhara**, *a.* knowing the Scriptures by heart. **—dhamma**, *m.* **—sāsana**, *nt.* code of the Holy Texts.

Pariyanta, *m.* the end; limit; climax; border. **—kata.** *a.* limited; restricted. **—yantika**, *a.* (in cpds.) ending in; bounded by.

Pariyādāti (pari + ā + dā + a), to exhaust; to take up in an excessive degree. *pp.* **—yādinna.** *abs.* **pariyādāya.**

Pariyādiyati (*pass.* of the above), to overpower; to control; to become exhausted. *aor.* **—diyi.** *pp.* **—dinna.** *abs.* **—diyitvā.**

Pariyāpanna, *pp.* included in; belonging to; got into.

Pariyāpuṇana, *nt.* learning; studying.

Pariyāpuṇāti (pari + ā + pu + nā), to learn thoroughly; to master. *aor.* **—puṇi.** *pp.* **—yāputa.** *abs.* **—puṇitvā.**

Pariyāya, *m.* order; course; quality; method; figurative language; a synonym; a turn. **—kathā**, *f.* round-about talk.

Pariyāhata, *pp.* of the following.

Pariyāhanati (pari + ā + han + a), to strike; to knock against. *aor.* **—hani.** *ger.* **—hanana**, *nt.*

Pariyuṭṭhāti (pari + u + ṭhā + a), to arise; to pervade. *aor.* **—ṭhāsi.** *pp.* **—ṭṭhita.**

Pariyuṭṭhāna, *nt.* outburst; prepossession.

Pariyeṭṭhi *f.* search for.

Pariyesati (pari + es + a), to seek for; to search; to investigate. *aor.* **—yesi.** *pp.* **—sita.** *pr. p.* **—santa.** **—samāna.** *abs.* **—sitvā.**

Pariyesanā, *f.* search; quest.

Pariyogāḷha, *pp.* of the following.

Pariyogāhati (pari + ava + gāh + a), to dive into; to fathom; to penetrate; to scrutinise. *aor.* **—gāhi.** *abs.* **—gāhitvā.**

Pariyogāhana, *nt.* plunging into; penetration.

Pariyodapanā, *f.* purification.

Pariyodapeti (pari + ava + dā + āpe), to cleanse; to purify. *aor.* **—esi.** *pp.* **—dapita.**

Pariyodāta, *a.* very clean; pure.

Pariyonaddha, *pp.* of the following.

Pariyonandhati (pari + ava + nah + ŋ - a), to tie down ; to envelope ; to cover up. *aor.* **—ndhi.**

Pariyonahana, *nt.* **—nāha,** *m.* covering ; enveloping.

Pariyosāna, *nt.* the end ; conclusion ; perfection.

Pariyosāpeti (pari + ava + sā + āpe), to bring to an end ; to finish ; to conclude. *aor.* **—esi.** *pp.* **—sāpita.** *abs.* **—petvā.**

Pariyosita, *pp.* finished ; concluded ; satisfied.

Parirakkhati (pari + rakkh + a), see **rakkhati.**

Parirakkhana, *nt.* guarding ; protection.

Parivaccha, *nt.* preparation ; outfit.

Parivajjana, *nt.* avoidance.

Parivajjeti (pari + vaj + e), to shun ; to avoid ; to keep away from. *aor.* **—esi.** *pp.* **—vajjita.** *pr. p.* **—jenta.** *abs.* **—jetvā.**

Parivaṭṭa, *nt.* a circle.

Parivattaka, *a.* rolling ; turning ; twisting ; one who rolls.

Parivattati (pari + vat + a), to turn round ; to roll ; to change about. *aor.* **—vatti.** *pp.* **—vatta.** *abs.* **—ttitvā.** *pr. p* **—vattamāna.**

Parivatteti (*caus.* of the above), to turn round ; to roll ; to recite ; to exchange ; to translate. *aor.* **—esi.** *pp.* **—tita.** *abs.* **—tetvā, —vattiya.** *pr. p.* **—tenta.**

Parivasati (pari + vas + a), to live under probation. *aor.* **—vasi.** *pp.* **parivuttha.**

Parivāra, *m.* retinue ; suite ; pomp ; followers. **—raka,** *a.* accompanying.

Parivāreti (pari + var + e), to surround ; to follow. *aor.* **—esi.** *pp.* **—vārita.** *abs.* **—retvā.**

Parivāsita (*pp.* of **parivāseti**), perfumed ; scented.

Parivitakka, *m.* reflection ; consideration.

Parivitakketi (pari + vi + tak + e), to reflect; to consider. *aor.* **—esi.** *pp.* **—kkita.** *abs.* **—ketvā.**

Parivisati (pari + vis + a), to serve with food ; to wait upon when food is taken. *aor.* **—visi.** *abs.* **—visitvā.**

Parivīmaŋsati (pari + vi + mas + ŋ - a), to think over ; to consider thoroughly. *aor.* **—ŋsi.**

Parivuta, *pp.* of **parivāreti.**

Pariveṇa, *nt.* a separated residence of monks. (Now it means a place for religious learning).

Parivesaka, 3. one who serves up meals. **—sanā,** *f.* feeding ; serving meals.

Parisakkati (pari + sakk + a), to endeavour ; to try. *aor.* **—sakki.** *pp.* **—sakkita.** *ger.* **—sakkana,** *nt.*

Parisagata, *a.* having entered a company.

Parisaṅkati (pari + sak + ŋ - a), to suspect ; to have apprehension. *aor.* **—saṅki.** *pp.* **—kita.** *abs.* **—kitvā.**

Parisaṅkā, *f.* suspicion.

Parisadūsaka, 3. a black sheep in an assembly.

Parisappati (pari + sap + a), to crawl about. *aor.* **—sappi.** *pp.* **—pita.**

Parisappanā, *f.* crawling about ; trembling ; doubt ; hesitation.

Parisamantato, *ad.* from all sides ; all-around.

Parisahati (pari + sah + a), to overcome; to master. *aor.* **—sahi.**

Parisā, *f.* a company; an assembly; association. **—vacara,** *a.* one who moves in society.

Parisiñcati (pari + sic + ŋ - a), to sprinkle all over. *aor.* **—siñci.** *pp.* **—sitta.** *abs.* **—ñcitvā.**

Parisujjhati (pari + sudh + ya), to become clean; to be purified. *aor.* **—jjhi.** *pr. p.* **—jhanta.** *abs.* **—jhitvā.**

Parisuddha (*pp.* of the above), clean; pure; perfect.

Parisuddhi, *f.* purity.

Parisussati (pari + sus + ya), to dry up; to waste away. *aor.* **—sussi.** *pp.* **—sukkha.** *abs.* **—sitvā.**

Parisussana, *nt.* drying up completely; withering.

Parisedita (*pp.* of **parisedeti**), heated with steam; hatched.

Parisodhana, *nt.* purification; cleansing.

Parisodheti (pari + sudh + e), to cleanse; to purify. *aor.* **—esi.** *pp.* **—sodhita.** *abs.* **—dhetvā.** **—sodhiya.**

Parisoseti (pari + sus + e), to make dry up or evaporate. *aor.* **—esi.** *pp.* **—sosita.**

Parissajati (pari + saj + a), to embrace. *aor.* **—saji.** *pp* **—jita.** *pr. p.* **– sajanta.** *abs.* **—sajitvā.**

Parissajana, *nt.* embracing.

Parıssanta, *pp.* tired; fatigued.

Parissama, *m.* effort; toil; fatigue; exhaustion.

Parissaya, *m.* danger; risk; trouble.

Parissāvana, *nt.* a water strainer; a filter; filtering (of).

Parissāveti (pari + sav + e), to strain; to filter. *aor.* **—esi.** *pp.* **—sāvita.** *abs.* **—vetvā.**

Pariharaṇa, *nt.* **—ṇā,** *f.* keeping on; protection; attention.

Pariharati (pari + har + a), to keep up; to protect; to carry about; to avoid. *aor.* **—hari.** *pp.* **—harita** or **—haṭa,** *abs.* **—haritvā.** *pt. p.* **—ritabba.**

Parihasati (pari + has + a), to laugh at; to mock; to deride. *aor.* **—hasi.** *abs.* **—sitvā.**

Parihāni, *f.* loss; decrease; wasting away; ruin. **—niya,** *a.* causing loss or ruin.

Parihāpeti (pari + hā + āpe), to cause to dwindle; to bring ruin; to neglect; to omit. *aor.* **—esi.** *pp.* **—hāpita.** *abs.* **—petvā.**

Parihāyati (pari + hā + ya), to dwindle; to waste away; to fall away from. *aor.* **—hāyi.** *pp.* **parihīna.** *pr. p.* **—hāyamāna.** *abs.* **—hāyitvā.**

Parihāra, *m.* care; attention; protection; avoidance; dignity; keeping away. **—raka,** *a.* protecting; guarding. **—patha,** *m.* a round about way, circular road. **—rika,** *a.* sustaining; keeping up.

Parihāsa, *m.* laughter; mockery.

Parihīna (*pp.* of **parihāyati**), fallen away from; destitute; emaciated.

Parūpakkama, *m.* aggression of an enemy.

Parūpaghāta, *m.* injurying others.

Parūpavāda, *m.* censuring by others; reproach of others.

Parūḷha (*pp.* of **parūhati**), grown long. **—kesa,** *a.* with hair grown long.

Pareta, *a.* afflicted with; overcome by; gone on to.

Paro, *in.* beyond ; further ; above; upwards ; more than. **—vara, —variya,** *a.* high and low. **—sata,** *a.* more than a hundred. **—sahassa,** *a.* more than a thousand.

Parokkha, *a.* beyond the eye ; out of sight. **—khe** (loc.), in the absence ; behind one's back.

Parodati (pa + rud + a), to cry out ; to wail. *aor.* **parodi.** *abs.* **—ditvā.**

Pala, *nt.* a certain weight (of about 4 ounces).

Palagaṇḍa, *m.* a mason.

Palaṇḍu, —ḍuka, *m.* onion.

Palapati (pa + lap + a), to talk nonsense. *aor.* **palapi.** *pp.* **—pita.** *abs.* **—pitvā.**

Palapana, palapita, *nt.* useless talk.

Palāta, *pp.* of **palāyati.**

Palāpa, *m.* chaff (of corn) ; prattle ; nonsense ; void of essence.

Palāpī, 3. one who talks nonsense.

Palāpeti (*caus.* of **palāyati**), to put to flight. *aor.* **—esi.** *pp.* **—pita.** *abs.* **—petvā.**

Palāyati (pal + aya), to run away ; to escape. *aor.* **palāyi.** *pp.* **palāta.** *pr. p.* **—yanta.** *abs.* **—yitvā.**

Palāyana, *nt.* running away. **—naka,** *a.* fleeing.

Palāyī, 3. one who runs away.

Palāla, *nt.* straw. **—puñja,** *m.* a heap of straw.

Palāsa, *m.* leaf ; foliage ; malice ; spite. **—sāda,** *a.* feeding on foliage. *m.* a rhinoceros.

Palāsī, *a.* spiteful ; malicious.

Palita, *a.* matured. *nt.* grey hair.

Palipa, *m.* a marsh.

Palipatha, *m.* a dangerous or difficult path.

Palipanna, *pp.* fallen or sunk into.

Palugga, *pp.* of the following.

Palujjati (pa + luj + ya), to fall down ; to crumble ; to be dissolved. *aor.* **—jji.** *pr. p.* **—jamāna,** *abs.* **—jitvā.**

Palujjana, *nt.* crumbling.

Paluddha (*pp.* of **palubbhati**), much attached ; enticed.

Paleti, see **palāyati.**

Palobhana, *nt.* enticement.

Palobheti (pa + lubh + e), to entice ; to seduce. *aor.* **—esi.** *pp.* **—bhita.** *abs.* **—bhetvā.**

Pallaṅka, *m.* a sofa ; a couch ; a cross-legged sitting.

Pallatthikā, *f.* a palanquin with sitting accommodation.

Pallala, *nt.* a small lake.

Pallava, *m.* a young leaf ; sprout ; name of a country.

Pavakkhati (Future of **pavadati**), he will tell.

Pavaḍḍha, pavaddha, *a.* grown up ; strong.

Pavaḍḍhati (pa + vaḍḍh + a), to grow ; to increase. *aor.* **—ḍḍhi.** *pp.* **—ḍhita.** *abs.* **—ḍhitvā.**

Pavaḍḍhana, *nt.* growing up ; increase.

Pavatta, *a.* going on ; fallen down. *nt.* the circle of existence.

Pavattati (pa + vat + a), to move on ; to proceed ; to exist ; to be. *aor.* **pavatti.** *pp.* **—ttita.** *abs.* **—titvā.**

Pavattana, *nt.* existence ; carrying out ; moving forward.

Pavattāpana, *nt.* making continue ; upkeep ; preservation.

Pavatti, *f.* happening ; incident ; news.

Pavatteti (pa + vat + e), to set going ; to keep on ; to wield ; to behave. *aor.* **—esi.** *pp.*

—ttita. *pr. p.* —tenta. *abs.* —tetvā. *inf.* —tetuŋ.

Pavattetu, *m.* one who keeps on or continues.

Pavana, *m.* the wind. *nt.* a big forest.

Pavara, *a.* noble ; excellent.

Pavasati (pa + vas + a), to dwell abroad ; to be away from home. *aor.* **pavasi.** *pp.* **pavuttha.** *abs.* —**sitvā.**

Pavassati (pa + vass + a), to shed rain. *aor.* —**ssi.** *pp.* **pavuṭṭha.**

Pavassana, *nt.* raining.

Pavāta, *nt.* a windy place.

Pavāti (pa + vā + a), to diffuse a scent ; to blow forth.

Pavāyati (pa + vā + ya), to blow forth ; to diffuse. *aor.* **pavāyi.** *pp.* —**yita.** *abs.* —**yitvā.**

Pavāraṇā, *f.* invitation ; a ceremony at the end of the rainy retreat.

Pavāreti (pa + var + e), to invite ; to satisfy ; to give in charge ; to celebrate the Pavāraṇā. *aor.* —**esi.** *pp.* —**rita.** *abs.* —**retvā.**

Pavāsa, *m.* sojourning abroad.

Pavāsī, *m.* one who lives abroad or away from home.

Pavāha, *m.* continuous flowing ; a stream. —**haka,** *a.* carrying away.

Pavāheti (pa + vah + e), to make to flow ; to cause to be carried away ; to remove. *aor.* —**esi.** *pp.* —**hita.** *abs.* —**hetvā.**

Pavāḷa, *m. nt.* coral ; a sprout.

Pavijjhati (pa + vidh + ya), to throw forth ; to shoot. *aor.* —**jhi.** *pp.* **paviddha.** *abs.* —**jhitvā.**

Paviṭṭha (*pp.* of **pavisati**) entered ; gone into.

Pavivitta, *a.* separated ; secluded.

Paviveka, *m.* solitude, seclusion ; retirement.

Pavisati (pa + vis + a), to go in ; to enter. *aor.* **pavisi.** *pr. p.* —**santa.** *abs.* —**sitvā.** *inf.* —**situŋ.**

Pavīṇa, *a.* clever ; skilful.

Pavuccati (pa + vac + ya), to be called, said, or pronounced. *pp.* **pavutta.**

Pavuttha, *pp.* of **pavasati.**

Paveṇī, *f.* tradition ; succession ; lineage ; breed ; a braid of hair.

Pavedana, *nt.* announcement.

Pavedeti (pa + vid + e), to declare ; to make known. *aor.* —**esi.** *pp.* —**dita.** *abs.* —**detvā.** *pr. p.* —**denta.**

Pavedhati (pa + vedh + a), to tremble ; to be agitated. *aor.* —**dhi.** *pp.* —**dhita.** *abs.* —**dhitvā.** *pr. p.* —**dhamāna.**

Pavesa, *m.* —**sana,** *nt.* entering ; entrance ; entry. —**saka,** *a.* one who makes enter.

Paveseti (pa + vis + e), to make enter ; to introduce ; to usher in. *aor.* —**esi.** *pp.* —**sita.** *abs.* —**setvā.** *pr. p.* —**senta.** *inf.* —**setuŋ.**

Pavesetu, *m.* an usher ; one who allows to enter.

Pasaŋsaka, 3. one who praises or flatters.

Pasaŋsati (pa + saŋs + a), to praise ; to commend. *aor.* **pasaŋsi.** *pp.* —**sita, pasattha.** *pr. p.* —**santa.** *pt. p.* —**sitabba,**—**siya.** *abs.*—**sitvā.** *inf.* —**situŋ.**

Pasaŋsana, *nt.* —**saŋsā,** *f.* praise ; commendation.

Pasaṅga, *m.* inclination ; attachment ; event ; occasion.

Pasata, *m.* a handful; ¼th of a seer.

Pasattha (*pp.* of **pasaŋsati**), extolled; commended.

Pasada, *m.* a kind of deer.

Pasanna (*pp.* of **pasīdati**) clear; bright; pleased; believing. **—citta, —mānasa,** *a.* having a gladdened or devoted mind.

Pasayha, *abs.* forcibly; by force.

Pasava, *m.* outflow; bringing forth; offspring.

Pasavati (pa + su + a), to bring forth; to give birth to; to flow; to accumulate. *aor.* **pasavi.** *pp.* **—vita.** *pr. p.* **—vanta.** *abs.* **—vitvā.**

Pasahati (pa + sah + a), to use force; to subdue; to oppress. *aor.* **pasahi.** *abs.* **—hitvā, pasayha.**

Pasahana, *nt.* overcoming; mastering.

Pasākha, *nt.* the body where it branches from the trunk.

Pasākhā, *f.* a small branch or twig.

Pasāda, *m.* clearness; brightness; joy; faith; the faculty of senses. **—daka,** *a.* making bright or clear; pleasing; making happy.

Pasādaniya, *a.* inspiring confidence.

Pasādeti (pa + sad + e), to gladden; to purify; to make faithful; to convert. *aor.* **—esi.** *pp.* **—dita.** *pr. p.* **—denta.** *abs.* **—detvā.** *pt. p.* **—detabba.**

Pasādhana, *nt.* an ornament; decoration.

Pasādheti (pa + sādh + e), to adorn; to decorate; to array. *aor.* **—esi.** *pp.* **—dhita.** *abs.* **—dhetvā, —dhiya.**

Pasāraṇa, *nt.* stretching out; spreading.

Pasāreti (pa + sar + e), to stretch out; to spread; to hold out; to offer for sale. *aor.* **—esi.** *pp.* **—rita.** *abs.* **—retvā.**

Pasāsati (pa + sās + a), to instruct; to rule; to govern. *aor.* **pasāsi.** *pp.* **—sita.**

Pasibbaka, *m.* a purse; sack; bag.

Pasīdati (pa + sad + a), to become bright; to be pleased or purified; to be clear or devoted. *aor.* **pasīdi.** *pp.* **pasanna.** *abs.* **—ditvā.** *pt p.* **—ditabba.**

Pasīdana, *nt.* **—nā,** *f.* devotion; clearness; gratification.

Pasu, *m.* a beast; quadruped. **—pati,** *m.* the god Isvara.

Pasuta, *a.* engaged in; attached to; doing.

Pasūta (*pp.* of **pasavati**), produced; delivered; born.

Pasūti, *f.* bringing forth; birth. **—kā,** *f.* a woman who has delivered a child. **—ghara,** *nt.* lying-in-home.

Passa, *m. nt.* side; flank.

Passati (dis + a; **dis** is changed to **pas.**), to see; to find; to understand. *aor.* **passi,** *pp.* **diṭṭha.** *pr. p.* **—santa, passamāna,** *abs.* **passitvā, disvā.**

Passaddha, *pp.* of **passambhati.**

Passaddhi, *f.* calmness; tranquillity; serenity.

Passambhati (pa + sambh + a), to calm down; to be quiet. *aor.* **—mbhi.** *abs.* **—bhitvā.**

Passambhanā, *f.* allayment; calmness.

Passambheti (pa + sambh + e), to make calm or allayed. *aor.* **—esi.** *pp.* **—bhita.** *abs.* **—bhetvā.** *pr. p.* **—bhenta.**

Passasati (pa + sas + a), to breathe out. *aor.* **passasi.** *pp.* **—sita.** *abs.* **—sitvā.** *pr. p.* **—santa.**

Passāva, *m.* urine.

Passāsa, *m.* exhalation. **—sī,** *m.* one who exhales.

Passituŋ, *inf.* to see.

Passitabba, *pt. p.* fit to be seen.

Pahata, *pp.* of **paharati.**

Pahaṭṭha (*pp.* of **pahaŋsati**), delighted ; very cheerful.

Paharaṇa, *nt.* beating ; a weapon to strike with. **—ṇaka,** *a.* hitting ; striking.

Paharati (pa + har + a), to beat ; to hit ; to strike. *aor.* **pahari.** *pr. p.* **—ranta.** *abs.* **—ritvā.** *inf.* **—rituŋ.**

Pahāna, *nt.* removal ; giving up ; abandoning ; avoidance.

Pahāya, *abs.* (of **pajahati**), having left or given up.

Pahāyī, 3. one who gives up or abandons.

Pahāra, *m.* a blow ; a stroke ; **—dāna,** *nt.* giving a blow ; assailing. **Ekappahārena** = all at once.

Pahāsa, *m.* great joy ; mirth.

Pahāseti (pa + has + e), to make one laugh ; to gladden. *aor.* **—esi.** *pp.* **pahāsita.**

Pahiṇana, *nt.* sending ; despatch.

Pahiṇagamana, *nt.* going as a messenger.

Pahiṇāti (pa + hi + ṇā), to send. *aor.* **pahiṇi.** *pr. p.* **—ṇanta.** *abs.* **pahiṇitvā.**

Pahita, *pp.* of the above.

Pahīna (*pp.* of **pajahati**), eliminated ; abandoned ; destroyed.

Pahīyati (pa + hā + ī + ya), to vanish ; to pass away ; to be abandoned. *aor.* **pahīyi.** *pp.* **pahīna.** *pr. p.* **—yamāna.** *abs.* **—yitvā.**

Pahū, *a.* able.

Pahūta, *a.* abundant ; much ; broad. **—jivha,** *a.* having a broad tongue. **—bhakkha,** *a.* having much to eat or eating much.

Paheṇaka, *nt.* a present fit to be sent to someone.

Pahoti (pa + hū + a), to be able, adequate, or sufficient.

Pahonaka, *a.* sufficient ; enough.

Paḷiguṇṭheti (pari + guṇṭh + e), to entangle ; to envelop. *aor.* **—esi.** *pp.* **—ṭhita.**

Paligha, *m.* a cross-bar ; an obstacle.

Paḷibujjhati (pari + budh + ya), to be delayed or spoiled ; to be obstructed. *aor.* **—jjhi.** *pp.* **paḷibuddha.** *abs.* **—jhitvā**

Paḷibujjhana, *nt.* becoming dirty.

Paḷibodha, *m.* obstruction ; hindrance ; impediment.

Paḷiveṭhana, *nt.* wrapping ; encircling.

Paḷiveṭheti (pari + veṭh + e), to wrap up ; to entwine ; to encircle. *aor.* **—esi.** *pp.* **—ṭhita.**

Paŋsu, *m.* soil ; dust. **—kūla,** *nt.* a dust heap. **—kūlacīvara,** *nt.* a robe made of rags taken from dust-bins. **—kūlika,** 3. one who wears such robes.

Pāka, *m.* cooking ; that which is cooked ; ripening. **—vaṭṭa,** *nt.* continuous supply of food.

Pākāra, *m.* encircling wall ; a rampart. **—parikkhitta,** *a.* surrounded by a wall.

Pāgabbhiya, *nt.* boldness ; impudence ; forwardness.

Pāguññatā, *f.* experience ; cleverness.

Pācaka, *a.* cooking; maturing; digesting; one who cooks.

Pācana, *nt.* a goad. See **Pājana.**

Pācariya, *m.* teacher's teacher.

Pācāpeti (pac + āpe), to cause to cook. *aor.* **—esi.** *pp.* **—pita.** *abs.* **—petvā.**

Pācikā, *f.* a female cook.

Pācīna, *a.* eastern. **—disā,** *f.* the east. **—mukha,** *a.* facing the east.

Pāceti, see **Pācāpeti.**

Pājana, *nt.* driving; a goad.

Pājeti (pa + aj + e), to drive; to lead. *aor.* **pājesi.** *pp.* **pājita.** *pr. p.* **pājenta.** *abs.* **pājetvā.** *caus.* **pājāpeti.**

Pāṭala, *a.* pale-red; pink.

Pāṭaliputta, *nt.* name of a city in Magadha, (present Patna).

Pāṭalī, *m.* the trumpet-flower tree.

Pāṭava, *m. nt.* skill.

Pāṭikaṅkha, *a.* to be desired or expected. **—khī,** 3. one who desires or expects.

Pāṭikā, *f.* half-moon stone at the entrance of a building or at the base of a flight of steps.

Pāṭikūlya, *nt.* loathsomeness.

Pāṭipada, *m.* the first day of a lunar fortnight.

Pāṭibhoga, *m.* a sponsor; a surety; bail; security.

Pāṭiyekka, *a.* separate; single. **—kaṇ,** *ad.* separately; individually.

Paṭihāra, Pāṭihīra, Pāṭihera, Pāṭihāriya, *nt.* a miracle; an extraordinary event. **—riya-pakkha,** *m.* an extra holiday.

Pāṭekka, see **Pāṭiyekka.**

Pāṭha, *m.* a passage; text-reading. **—ka,** *a.* reciter; one who reads.

Pāṭhīna, *m.* a kind of fish; a shad.

Pāṇa, *m.* life; breath; a living being. **—ghāta,** *m.* killing; slaying life. **—ghātī,** 3. one who destroys life. **—da,** *a.* one who preserves life. **—bhūta,** *m.* a living being. **—vadha,** *m.* destruction of life. **—sama,** *a.* dear as life. **—hara,** *a.* taking away life.

Pāṇaka, *m.* an insect.

Pāṇana, *nt.* breathing.

Pāṇi, *m.* the hand; the palm. **—tala,** *nt.* the palm of the hand. **—ggaha,** *m.* marriage.

Pāṇikā, *f.* a hand-like thing; a trowel.

Pāṇī, *m.* a living being.

Pāta, *m.* a fall; a throw.

Pātana, *nt.* bringing to fall; throwing down; killing.

Pātabba, *pt. p.* (of **pivati**), fit to be drunk.

Pātarāsa, *m.* morning meal.

Pātāla, *m.* an abyss; proclivity; the other side of the earth.

Pāti, *f.* a bowl; a dish.

Pāti (pā + a), to watch; to protect.

Pātika, *nt.* a small dish.

Pātita, *pp.* of **Pāteti.**

Pātimokkha, *m.* a collection of precepts contained in the Vinaya.

Pātī, *a.* (in cpds.) one who throws or shoots.

Pātu, *in.* in front; visible; manifest. **—kamma, —karaṇa,** *nt.* manifestation; making visible. **—bhāva,** *m.* appearance; coming into manifestation. **—bhūta,** *pp.* appeared.

Pātukamyatā, *f.* desire to drink.

Pātukaroti (pātu + kar + o), to manifest. *aor.* **—kari.** *pp.* **—kata.** *abs.* **—karitvā, —katvā.**

Pātukāma, *a.* desirous of drinking.

Pātubhavati (pātu + bhū + a), to become manifest; to appear. *aor.* —**bhavi.** *pp.* —**bhūta.** *abs.* —**bhavitvā.**

Pāturahosi, *aor.* of **pātubhavati.**

Pātuŋ, *inf.* to drink.

Pāteti (pat + e), to fell; to throw off; to kill. *aor.* **pātesi.** *pp.* **pātita.** *abs.* **pātetvā.**

Pāto, *in.* in the morning. —**va**, *in.* right early.

Pātheyya, *nt.* provision for a journey.

Pāda, *m. nt.* the foot; leg; a base; one-fourth of any measure or of a stanza. —**ka**, *a.* having feet or a basis; *nt.* a foundation or basis. —**kajjhāna**, *nt.* meditation forming a basis. —**kaṭhalikā**, *f.* a wooden block to wash feet on. —**ṅguṭṭha**, *nt.* the great toe. —**ṅguli**, *f.* a toe. —**ṭṭhika**, *nt.* bone of the leg. —**tala**, *nt.* the sole of the foot. —**paricārikā**, *f.* a wife. —**pīṭha**, *nt.* a foot-stool. —**puñchana**, *nt.* a matting for wiping feet. —**mūle**, at the feet. —**mūlika**, *m.* a servant; one who sits at one's feet. —**lola**, *a.* desirous of wandering about. —**sambāhana**, *nt.* massaging of feet.

Pādapa, *m.* a tree.

Pādāsi (*aor.* of **padāti**), he gave.

Pādukā, *f.* a slipper or shoe.

Pādūdara, *m.* a snake.

Pādodaka, *m.* water for washing feet.

Pāna, *nt.* drinking; a drink; a syrup. —**ka**, *nt.* a drink. —**maṇḍala**, —**āgāra**, *nt.* a drinking booth or tavern.

Pānīya, *nt.* water; a drink; beverage. —**ghaṭa**, *m.* water-pot. —**cāṭi**, *f.* drinking vessel. —**thālikā**, *f.* drinking cup —**bhājana**, *nt.* drinking vessel. —**māḷaka**, *nt.* —**sālā**, *f.* a hall where drinking water is kept.

Pāpa, *nt.* sin; evil; wrong action. *adj.* bad; sinful; wicked. —**kamma**, *nt.* crime; evil action. —**kammanta**,—**kammī**, *a.* evil-doer; a villain. —**kara**, —**kārī**, *a.* sinful; wicked. —**karaṇa**, *nt.* evil doing; committing sin. —**dhamma**, *a.* of evil character or habits. —**mitta**, *m.* bad companion; *adj.* having evil association. —**mittatā**, *f.* association with wicked people. —**saṅkappa**, *m.* evil thought. —**supina**, *nt.* an evil dream.

Pāpaka, *a.* wicked; sinful; (in cpds.): leading to.

Pāpaṇika, *m.* a shopkeeper.

Pāpikā, feminine of **pāpaka.**

Pāpita, *pp.* of **pāpeti.**

Pāpimantu, *a.* a sinner; the Wicked One.

Pāpiya, *a.* sinful.

Pāpuṇana, *nt.* attainment; arrival.

Pāpuṇāti (pa + ap + uṇā), to reach; to attain; to arrive at. *aor.* **pāpuṇi**, *pr. p.* —**ṇanta.** *abs.* —**ṇitvā**, **patvā.** *inf.* —**ṇituŋ**, **pattuŋ.**

Pāpuraṇa, *nt.* a cover; cloak; blanket.

Pāpurati (pa + ā + pur + a), to cover; to wrap with. (mostly used as **Pārupati**).

Pāpeti (pa + ap + e), to let go to; to cause to reach or attain. *aor.* **pāpesi.** *pp.* **pāpita.** *pr. p.* —**penta.** *abs.* —**petvā.**

Pābhata, *nt.* a present.

Pāmaṅga, *nt.* a waist-band.

Pāmokkha, *a.* chief ; first ; eminent. *m.* a leader.

Pāmojja, pāmujja, *nt.* delight ; joy ; happiness.

Pāya, *a.* (in cpds.) abounding with. **pāyena**, *ad.* for the most part ; mostly.

Pāyaka, 3. one who makes suck or drink.

Pāyāti (pa + ā + yā + a), to set out ; to start ; to go forth. *aor.* **pāyāsi.**

Pāyī, *a.* one who drinks.

Pāyeti (pā + e), to make suck or drink. *aor.* **pāyesi.** *pp.* **pāyita.** *pr. p.* **pāyenta, pāyamāna.** *abs.* **pāyetvā.**

Pāra, *nt.* the opposite shore ; the other side. **—gata**, *a.* one who has gone to the end or the other shore. **—gavesī**, *a.* looking for the final end or the other shore. **—gāmī**, 3. going to the other shore. **—gū, —ṅgata, —ppatta**, *a.* gone beyond ; passed ; crossed. **—lokika**, *a.* connected with the other world or future birth.

Pārada, *m.* quick-silver.

Pāradārika, *m.* adulterer.

Pāramitā, Pāramī, *f.* completeness ; perfection.

Pāramapariya, *nt.* tradition.

Pāraŋ, *ad.* beyond ; across ; over.

Pārājika, *a.* one who has committed the gravest transgression of the rules for bhikkhus.

Pārāp(v)ata, *m.* a pigeon.

Pārāyana, *nt.* final aim ; chief object.

Pāricariyā, *f.* service ; waiting on.

Pāricchattaka, *m.* the coral tree.

Pāripanthika, *a.* threatening ; dangerous ; a highwayman.

Pāripūri, *f.* fulfilment ; completion.

Pārima, *a.* yonder ; farther.

Pāribhogika, *a.* fit for use ; used.

Pārivaṭṭaka, *a.* exchanged ; bartered.

Pārisajja, *a.* belonging to an assembly ; member of a council.

Pārisuddhi, *f.* purity. **—sīla**, *nt.* purity of livelihood.

Pāruta, *pp.* of the following.

Pārupati (pa + ā + rup + a), to wrap in ; to veil ; to put on a robe. *aor.* **pārupi.** *abs.* **—pitvā.** *pr. p.* **—panta.**

Pārupana, *nt.* a cloak ; a robe.

Pārevata, *m.* pigeon.

Pāroha, *m.* fork of a tree ; a root descending from a branch (like that of a banyan tree).

Pāla, Pālaka, Pāletu, 3. a guard ; keeper ; protector.

Pālana, *nt.* **—nā**, *f.* protection ; preservation ; government.

Pāli, Pāḷi, *f.* a line ; range ; the canon of the Buddhist writings or the language in which it is written.

Pālicca, *nt.* greyness of hair.

Pālita, *pp.* of the following.

Pāleti (pāl + e), to protect ; to guard ; to preserve. *aor.* **—esi.** *pr. p.* **pālenta.** *pt. p.* **pāletabba.** *abs.* **pāletvā.** *inf.* **pāletuŋ.**

Pāvaka, *m.* fire.

Pāvacana, *nt.* the Scriptures.

Pāvassi, *aor.* of **pavassati.**

Pāvāra, *m.* a cloak ; mantle. **—rika**, a cloak-seller.

Pāvāḷa, *m.* the buttocks.

Pāvusa, *m.* rainy season ; a kind of fish.

Pāvussaka, *a.* belonging to the rainy season.

Pāsa, *m.* **Pāsaka**, *nt.* a sling; a snare; a button hole.

Pāsaka, *m.* a die; a throw.

Pāsaṇḍa, *nt.* heresy. **—ḍaka, —ḍika**, *m.* a heretic; sectarian.

Pāsāṇa, *m.* a stone; rock. **—gula**, *m.* a ball of stone. **—cetiya**, *nt.* a shrine made of stone. **—piṭṭhi**, *f.* the surface of a rock. **—phalaka**, *m.* a stone-slab. **—lekhā**, *f.* rock inscription.

Pāsāda, *m.* a mansion; palace; castle. **—tala**, *nt.* an upper storey or floor (of a mansion).

Pāsādika, *a.* pleasing; lovely; amiable.

Pāhuṇa, *m.* a guest. *nt.* meal for a guest; a present. **—ṇeyya**, *a.* worthy of hospitality.

Pāheti (pā + hi + e), to cause to send. *aor.* **pāhesi**.

Pi, *in.* (the enclitic form of **api**.) also; and also; even so; but; however; probably; perhaps.

Pika, *m.* a cuckoo.

Piṅgala, *a.* brown; tawny. **—netta**, *a.* having red eyes. **—makkhikā**, *f.* gadfly.

Picu, *nt.* cotton. **—paṭala**, *nt.* a film of cotton.

Piccha, *nt.* tail-feather; (any kind of) gum. **—chila**, *a.* slippery.

Piñja, *nt.* tail-feather; tail of a bird.

Piñjara, *a.* of a reddish colour.

Piññāka, *nt.* flour of oilseeds; poonac.

Piṭaka, *nt.* a basket; a container; one of the three main divisions of the Pāli Canon. **—ttaya**, *nt.* the three Piṭakas, *viz.* Vinaya, Sutta, and Abhidhamma. **—dhara**, *a.* one who knows the Piṭakas by heart.

Piṭṭha, *nt.* the back; hind part; surface; flour (of grain, etc.) **—khādaniya**, *nt.* sweets made of flour. **—dhītalikā**, *f.* a doll made of flour. **—piṇḍī**, *f.* a lump of flour.

Piṭṭhi, *f.* the back; upper side; top. **—kaṇṭaka**, *nt.* the back-bone. **—gata**, *a.* riding on an animal or on someone's back. **—passa**, *nt.* the hind part. *loc.* behind; at the back of. **—pāsāṇa**, *m.* a flat rock. **—maṃsika**, *a.* backbiting; one who blames someone in his absence. **—vaṃsa**, *m.* a back varandah.

Piṭhara, *m.* a big jar.

Piṇḍa, **—ḍaka**, *m.* a lump; a lump of food. **—cārika**, *a.* one who goes to collect alms. **—dāyaka**, 3. giver of alms. **—pāta**, *m.* a collection of alms. **—pātika**, 3. one who collects alms or eats only such food. **—ḍācāra**, *m.* going for collecting alms.

Piṇḍāya (*dat. sin.* of **piṇḍa**), for alms.

Piṇḍikamaṃsa, *nt.* the buttocks.

Piṇḍī, *f.* a cluster; bunch.

Piṇḍita, *pp.* of the following.

Piṇḍeti (piṇḍ + e), to ball together; to mix; to contract. *aor.* **—esi**. *abs.* **piṇḍetvā**.

Piṇḍolya, *nt.* going for collecting alms.

Pitāmaha, *m.* grandfather.

Pitika, *a.* (in cpds.) having a father; belonging to or come from a father.

Pitipakkha, *m.* father's side.

Pitu, *m.* father. **—kicca**, *nt.* duty of a father. **—ghāta**, *m.* parricide. **—santaka**, *a.* father's possession; belonging to a father.

Pitucchā, *f.* father's sister. **—putta**, *m.* aunt's son.

Pitta, *nt.* the bile. **—ādhika**, *a.* bilious.

Pithīyati (api + dhā + ī + ya ; *pass.* of **pidahati**), to be closed, shut, or obscured. *aor.* **—thīyi.**

Pidahati (api + dhā + a), to shut ; to close ; to cover. *aor.* **pidahi.** *pp.* **pidahita, pihita.** *abs.* **pidahitvā, pidhāya.**

Pidahana, *nt.* shutting ; closing.

Pidhāna, *nt.* a lid ; a cover.

Pināsa, *m.* catarrh.

Pipāsā, *f.* thirst.

Pipāsita (*pp.* of **pivāsati**) thirsty.

Pipillikā, pipīlikā, *f.* an ant.

Pipphala, —laka, *nt.* scissors.

Pipphalī, *f.* long pepper.

Piya, *a.* dear ; amiable ; beloved. *m.* the husband. *nt.* a dear thing. **—kamyatā**, *f.* desire for dear things or to become dear. **—tara**, *a.* more dear. **—tama**, *a.* most dear. **—dassana**, *a.* good-looking. **—bhāṇī, —vādī**, *a.* speaking pleasantly. **—rūpa**, *nt.* an enticing object of sight. **—vacana**, *nt.* a term of endearment. *adj.* speaking pleasant words. **—vippayoga**, *m.* separation from the beloved.

Piyaṅgu, *m.* a medicinal plant.

Piyatā, *f.* belovedness.

Piyā, *f.* the wife.

Piyāpāya, *a.* separation from what is beloved.

Piyāyati (*Deno.* from **piya**), to be fond of ; to hold dear ; to be devoted. *aor.* **piyāyi.** *pp.* **—yita.** *pr. p.* **—yanta, —yamāna,** *abs.* **—yitvā.**

Piyāyanā, *f.* love ; fondness.

Pilakkha, *m.* wave-leaved fig tree.

Pilandhati (api + nah + a), to adorn ; to put on ; to bedeck. *aor.* **—ndhi.** *pp.* **—dhita.** *abs.* **—dhiya, —dhitvā.**

Pilandhana, *nt.* an ornament ; putting on ; adorning.

Pilavati, Plavati (plav + a), to float ; to move quickly ; to swim. *aor.* **plavi.** *pp.* **plavita.** *abs.* **plavitvā.**

Pilotikā, *f.* a rag ; an old clothe.

Pillaka, *m.* a young of an animal.

Pivati, Pibati (pā + a ; **pā** is changed to **piba**), to drink. *aor.* **pivi.** *pp.* **pīta.** *pr. p.* **pivanta, —māna,** *abs.* **pivitvā,** *inf.* **pātuŋ, pivituŋ.**

Pivana, *nt.* drinking.

Pisati (pis + a), **Piŋsati** (pis + ŋ-a), to grind ; to crush. *aor.* **piŋsi.** *pp.* **piŋsita.** *abs.* **piŋsetvā.**

Pisana, Piŋsana, *nt.* grinding ; powdering.

Pisāca, —ka, *m.* a goblin or sprite.

Pisita, *nt.* flesh.

Pisuṇa, *nt.* slander ; malicious speech. **—ṇāvācā**, *f.* malicious speech.

Pihaka, *nt.* the spleen.

Pihayati (pih + ya), to desire ; to long for ; to endeavour. *aor.* **pihayi.** *pp.* **pihāyita.**

Pihāyanā, *f.* desire ; endearment.

Pihālu, *a.* covetous.

Pihita, *pp.* of **pidahati.**

Piḷakā, *f.* a boil ; a blister.

Piŋsati, see **pisati.**

Pīṭha, *nt.* chair ; a seat. **—ka**, *nt.* **—ṭhikā**, *f.* a small chair or bench.

Pīṭhasappī, *m.* a cripple.

Pīṇana, *nt.* gladdening; satisfaction.

Pīṇeti (pīṇ + e), to gladden; to please; to satisfy; to invigorate. *aor.* **pīṇesi.** *pp.* **pīṇita.** *abs.* **pīṇetvā.** *pr. p.* **pīṇenta.**

Pīta, *pp.* of **pivati.**

Pīta, **—ka,** *a.* yellow; golden coloured. *m.* yellow colour.

Pīti, *f.* joy; delight; emotion. **—pāmojja,** *nt.* joy and gladness. **—bhakkha,** *a.* feeding on joy. **—mana,** *a.* glad of heart; exhilarated. **—rasa,** *m.* taste or emotion of joy. **—sambojjhaṅga,** *m.* the joy-constituent of enlightenment. **—sahagata,** *a.* accompanied by joy.

Pīṇa, *a.* fat; swollen.

Pīḷaka, *a.* oppressing.

Pīḷana, *nt.* **pīḷā,** *f.* oppression; injury; damage.

Pīḷeti (pīḷ + e), to oppress; to crush; to molest; to subjugate. *aor.* **pīḷesi.** *pp.* **pīḷita.** *abs.* **pīḷetvā.**

Pukkusa, *m.* one who removes refuse.

Puggala, *m.* an individual; a person. **—paññatti,** *f.* classification of individuals. **—lika,** *a.* personal; individual.

Puṅgava, *m.* a bull; a noble person.

Puṅkha, *nt.* the feathered part of an arrow.

Pucimanda, *m.* the margosa tree.

Puccaṇḍa (pūti + aṇḍa), *nt.* a rotten egg.

Puccha, *nt.* tail.

Pucchaka, 3. one who asks questions.

Pucchati (pucch + a), to ask; to question. *aor.* **pucchi.** *pp.* **puṭṭha,** or **pucchita.** *pr. p.* **—chanta.** *abs.* **—chitvā.** *pt. p.* **—chitabba.** *inf.* **—chituŋ.**

Pucchā, *f.* a question.

Pujja, *a.* honourable; respectful.

Puñchati (puñch + a), to wipe off: to clean. *aor.* **puñchi.** *pp.* **puñchita.** *abs.* **—chitvā.** *pr. p.* **—chanta.** **—chamāna.**

Puñchana, *nt.* **—nī,** *f.* a cloth for wiping; a towel.

Puñja, *m.* a heap; pile; mass. **—kata,** *a.* piled; heaped.

Puñña, *nt.* merit; righteousness. **—kamma,** *nt.* meritorious action. **—kāma,** *a.* desirous of merit. **—kiriyā,** *f.* good action. **—kkhandha,** *m.* a mass of merit. **—kkhaya,** *m.* exhaustion of merit. **—tthika,** *a.* desirous of merit. **—pekkha,** *a.* hoping for merit. **—phala,** *nt.* the result of meritorious actions. **—bhāga,** *m.* a share of merit. **—bhāgī,** *a.* having a share in merit. **—vantu,** *a.* possessing merit; virtuous. **—ānubhāva,** *m.* the power of merit. **—ābhisanda,** *m.* accumulation of merit.

Puṭa, Puṭaka, *m. nt.* a container, (usually made of leaves); a pocket; a basket. **—baddha,** *a.* bound as a parcel. **—bhatta,** *nt.* a parcel of boiled rice. **—bhedana,** *nt.* opening of packages. **—ŋsa,** *a.* having a knapsack on one's shoulder.

Puṭṭha, (*pp.* of **poseti** :) fed; nourished; brought up. (*pp.* of **pucchati** :) asked or questioned by.

Puṇḍarīka, *nt.* white lotus.

Puṇṇa, (*pp.* of **pūrati**), full; complete. **—ghaṭa,** *m.* a full pitcher. **—canda,** *m.* full moon. **—patta,** *nt.* a gift or present. **—māsī,** **—mī,** *f.* full-moon day.

Puṇṇatā, *f.* **puṇṇatta,** *nt.* fulness.

Putta, *m.* a son ; a child. **—ka,** *m.* a little son. **—dāra,** children and wife.

Puttima, puttiya, *a.* having children.

Puthu, *in.* separated ; individual; far and wide ; separately. **—jjana,** *m.* a common worldling : uneducated person. **—bhūta,** *a.* widely spread. **—loma,** *m.* a fish.

Puthuka, *nt.* flatted corn. *m.* young of an animal.

Puthula, *a.* broad ; large.

Puthuvī, *f.* the earth

Puthuso, *ad.* diversely ; at variance.

Puna, *in.* again. **—divasa,** *m.* the following day. **—ppunaŋ,** *in.* again and again. **—bbhava,** *m.* birth in a new existence. **—vacana,** *nt.* **—rutti,** *f.* repitition. **—āgamana,** *nt.* coming again.

Puṇāti (pu + ṇā), to clean ; to sift. *aor.* **puṇi.** *abs.* **puṇitvā.**

Puṇeti (puna + eti), to come again.

Punnāga, *m.* the Alexandrian laurel tree.

Puppha, *nt.* flower ; the menstrual flux. **—gaccha,** *m.* a flowering plant or bush. **—gandha,** *m.* odour of flowers. **—cumbaṭaka,** *nt.* a chaplet of flowers. **—chaḍḍaka,** *m.* remover of withered flowers or rubbish ; a privy-cleaner. **—dāma,** *m.* a garland of flowers. **—dhara,** *a.* bearing flowers. **—paṭa,** *m. nt.* a cloth embroidered with flowers. **—muṭṭhi,** *m.* a handful of flowers. **—rāsi,** *m.* a heap of flowers. **—vatī,** *f.* a woman during her menstruation.

Pupphati (pupph + a), to flower ; to be blown. *aor.* **pupphi.** *pp.* **—phita.** *abs.* **—phitvā.**

Pubba, *m.* pus ; matter.

Pubba, *a.* former ; earlier ; eastern. *In cpds.* having been before, e.g. **gatapubba** = gone before. **—kamma,** *nt.* a deed done in a former existence. **—kicca,** *nt.* preliminary function. **—ṅgama,** *a.* going at the head ; preceding. **—carita,** *nt.* former life-story. **—aṇha,** *m.* forenoon. **—deva,** *m.* the ancient gods, i.e. Asuras. **—nimitta,** *nt.* a prognostic ; a portent. **—anta,** *m.* the Past ; the former end. **—purisa,** *m.* the ancestor. **—peta,** *m.* a deceased spirit. **—bhāga,** *m.* former part. *adj.* previous. **—yoga,** *m.* a former connection. **—videha,** *m.* name of the eastern continent.

Pubbanna, *nt.* a name given to 7 kinds of cereals such as rice, wheat.

Pubbā, *f.* the east.

Pubbācariya, *m.* the first teacher.

Pubbāpara, *a.* what proceeds and what follows ; former and latter.

Pubbuṭṭhāyī, *a.* getting up before (someone else).

Pubbe (*loc.*), formerly ; in the past. **—kata,** *a.* formerly done. **—nivāsa,** *m.* one's former state of existence. **—nivāsañāṇa,** *nt.* **—sānussati,** *f.* remembrance of one's former state of existence.

Puma, *m.* a male ; a man.

Pura, *nt.* a town or city.

Purakkhata, *pp.* put in front ; honoured ; esteemed.

Purakkharoti (purā + kar + o), to put in front ; to honour. *aor.* **—khari.** *pp.* **—khata.** *abs.* **—khatvā.**

Purato, *in.* in front of ; before.

Puratthā, *in.* the east. **—bhimukha,** *a.* looking eastward.

Puratthima, *a.* eastern.

Purā, *in.* formerly ; in the past.

Purāṇa, *a.* ancient ; old ; worn out ; used ; former. **—dutiyikā,** *f.* former wife. **—sālohita,** 3. former blood-relation.

Purātana, *a.* see **purāṇa.**

Purindada, *m.* an epithet of the king of Devas.

Purima, *a.* former ; earlier. **—jāti,** *f.* **—ttabhāva,** *m.* previous birth. **—taraŋ,** very early ; earlier than.

Purisa, *m.* a male ; a man. **—kāra,** *m.* manliness. **—thāma,** *m.* manly strength. **—damma,** *m.* a person to be trained or converted. **—dammasārathī,** *m.* guide of men who are to be restrained. **—parakkama,** *m.* manly effort. **—medha,** *m.* human sacrifice. **—liṅga, —vyañjana,** *nt.* the male organ. **—ājañña,** *m.* a remarkable man. **—ādaka,** *m.* a cannibal. **—ādhama,** *m.* a wicked man. **—sindriya,** *nt.* male faculty ; masculinity. **—suttama,** *m.* the highest of men.

Pure, *ad.* before ; formerly ; earlier. **—taraŋ,** *ad.* before any one else ; most early. **—cārika,** *a.* going before ; leading. **—java,** *a.* running in front. **—bhatta,** *nt.* forenoon.

Purekkhāra, *m.* putting in front; honour ; devotion.

Purohita, *m.* a king's religious adviser.

Pulava, —ka, *m.* a worm.

Pulina, *nt.* sand ; a sandy bank.

Pūga, *m.* a guild ; corporation. *nt.* a heap ; arecanut. **—rukkha,** *m.* the arecanut palm.

Pūjanā, Pūjā, *f.* veneration ; homage ; devotional offering.

Pūjaneyya, —nīya, pūjāraha, *a.* entitled to homage ; venerable.

Pūjiya, *a.* worthy to be honoured. *nt.* an object of veneration. **—māna,** *a.* being honoured.

Pūjita, *pp.* of the following.

Pūjeti (pūj + e), to honour ; to respect ; to offer something with devotion. *aor.* **—esi.** *pr. p.* **pūjenta, pūjayamāna.** *abs.* **pūjetvā.** *inf.* **pūjetuŋ.**

Pūti, Pūtika, *a.* rotten ; putrid ; stinking. **—kāya,** *m.* the body which contains foul things. **—gandha,** *m.* smell of a stinking thing. **—maccha,** *m.* stinking fish. **—mukha,** *a.* having a putrid mouth. **—mutta,** *nt.* cattle-urine. **—latā,** *f.* the creeper *Coccolus Cordifolius.* රසකිඳ.

Pūpa, *m. nt.* cake.

Pūpiya, *m.* cake-seller.

Pūya, *m.* pus.

Pūra, *a.* full ; full of.

Puraka, 3. one who fills, fulfils, or completes.

Pūrāpeti (*caus.* of the following), to make fill. *aor.* **—esi.** *pp.* **—pita.** *abs.* **—petvā.**

Pūreti (pūr + e), to fill ; to fulfil ; to complete. *aor.* **pūresi.** *pp.* **pūrita.** *pr. p.* **pūrenta.** *abs.* **pūretvā.** *inf.* **pūretuŋ.**

Pūva, *m. nt.* cake . bread.

Pūvika, *m.* dealer in cakes.

Pekkhaka, 3. one who is looking at.

Pekkhaṇa, *nt.* seeing ; sight.

Pekkhati (pa + ikkh + a), to see; to look at. *aor.* **pekkhi.** *pp.* **—khita.** *abs.* **—khitvā.** *pr. p.* **pekkhamāna.**

Pekhuṇa, *nt.* a peacock's tail-feather.

Pecca, *in.* after death.

Peta, *a.* dead; departed. *m.* a ghost. **—kicca,** *nt.* death-rites. **—yoni,** *f.* state of ghosts. **—loka,** *m.* the realm of goblins. **—vatthu,** *nt.* story about a ghost.

Pettika, *a.* paternal.

Pettivisaya, *m.* the world of manes.

Petteyya, *a.* respecting one's own father. **—tā,** *f.* filial piety.

Pema, *nt.* love; affection. **—nīya,** *a.* affectionate; amiable.

Peyya, *a.* drinkable, *nt.* a drink.

Peyyavajja, *nt.* kind speech.

Peyyāla, *nt.* an indication to show that a passage has been omitted.

Pelaka, *m.* a hare.

Pesaka, 3. sender; one who attends.

Pesakāra, *m.* a weaver.

Pesana, *nt.* sending out; a message; service. **—kāraka,** *m.* a servant. **—kārikā,** *f.* a maid servant.

Pesala, *a.* well behaved.

Pesi, Pesikā, *f.* a slice; the foetus in the third stage.

Pesita, *pp.* of **peseti.**

Pesīyati (*pass.* of **peseti**), to be sent. *pr. p.* **pesiyamāna.**

Pesuṇa, *nt.* slandering. **—kāraka,** *a.* one who slanders.

Pesuñña, *nt.* slander; calumny; backbiting.

Peseti (pes + e), to send out or forth; to employ; to send for. *aor.* **—esi.** *pp.* **pesita.** *pr. p.* **pesenta.** *abs.* **pesetvā.** *pt. p.* **pesetabba.**

Pessa, Pessiya, Pessika, *m.* a servant; a messenger.

Peḷā, *f.* a box or chest; a container.

Pokkhara, *nt.* a lotus; lotus plant; the tip of an elephant's trunk; the trunk of a lute. **—tā,** *f.* beauty. **—patta,** *nt.* lotus leaf. **—madhu,** *nt.* the honey sap of a lotus. **—vassa,** *nt.* a rain of flowers; a snow-storm.

Pokkharaṇī, *f.* a pond; an artificial pool.

Poṅkha, see **Puṅkha.**

Poṭṭhapāda, *m.* name of a month, September-October.

Poṭhana, *nt.* beating; striking.

Poṭheti, Potheti (poth + e), to beat; to strike; to snap (one's fingers). *aor.* **—esi.** *pp.* **poṭhita.** *abs.* **—etvā.** *pass.* **poṭhīyati.**

Poṇa, *a.* sloping down; prone; converging or leading to.

Pota, *m.* the young of an animal; a sprout or offshoot; a ship's boat; **—ka,** *m.* the young of an animal. **—potikā,** *fem.* of **potaka.** **—vāha,** *m.* a sailor.

Potthaka, *m. nt.* a book; a canvas for painting on.

Potthalikā, *f.* a modelled figure; a doll made of canvas.

Pothujjanika, *a.* belonging to ordinary man.

Ponobhavika, *a.* leading to rebirth.

Porāṇa, —ṇaka, *a.* ancient; old; former.

Porisa, *nt.* manliness; the height of a man (with upstretched hands).

Porisāda, *a.* a man-eater.

Porī, *f.* urbane ; polite.

Porohicca, *nt.* the office of a Purohita.

Posa, *m.* man.

Posaka, *a.* feeding ; nourishing ; one who brings up.

Posikā, *f.* a nurse ; a step-mother.

Posatha, see **uposatha**. —**thika**, *m.* one who observes fasting.

Posana, *nt.* bringing up ; nourishing ; feeding.

Posāvanika, *nt.* fee for bringing somebody up ; allowance ; sustenance.

Poseti (pus + e), to nourish ; to bring up ; to take care of ; to feed. *aor.* **posesi**. *pp.* **posita**. *pr. p.* **posenta**. *pt. p.* **posetabba**. *abs.* **posetvā**. *inf.* **posetuŋ**.

Plava, *m.* floating ; a raft. —**na**, *nt.* jumping ; floating.

Plavaṅgama, *m.* a monkey.

Ph.

Phaggu, *m.* a period of fasting.

Phagguṇa, *m.* name of a month, February-March. —**guṇī**, name of a constellation.

Phaṇa, *m.* the hood of a snake. —**ṇaka**, *nt.* an instrument shaped like a snake's hood, used for smoothing hair, etc.

Phaṇī, *m.* a cobra.

Phandati (phad + ŋ - a), to tremble ; to throb ; to stir. *aor.* **phandi**. *pp.* —**dita**. *pr. p.* —**damāna**, *abs.* —**ditvā**.

Phandana, *nt.* —**nā**, *f.* throbbing ; motion ; agitation.

Pharaṇa, *nt.* pervading ; suffusion ; thrill. —**ṇaka**, *a.* suffusing ; filling with.

Pharati (phar + a), to pervade ; to suffuse ; to fill. *aor.* **phari**. *pp.* **pharita**. *abs.* **pharitvā**. *pr. p.* **pharanta**.

Pharusa, *a.* rough ; harsh ; unkind. —**vacana**, *nt.* —**sā vācā**, *f.* rough speech.

Phala, *nt.* fruit ; nut ; result ; consequence ; fruition ; the blade of a weapon. —**citta**, *nt.* the fruition of the Path. —**ṭṭha**, *a.* stationed in the enjoyment of the Path. —**tthika**, *a.* looking for fruit. —**dāyī**, *a.* fruitful ; advantageous ; producing fruit. —**ruha**, *a.* grown from a seed. —**vantu**, *a.* bearing or having fruit. —**lāphala**, *nt.* various kinds of fruit. —**lāsava**, *m.* extract of fruit.

Phalaka, *m. nt.* a board ; plank ; a shield.

Phalati (phal + a), to bear fruit ; to burst open ; to split. *aor.* **phali**. *pp.* **phalita**. *abs.* **phalitvā**. *pr. p.* **phalanta**.

Phalī, *m.* (a tree) with fruit ; bearing fruit.

Phalu, *nt.* a joint or knot (of reed, etc.) —**bīja**, *nt.* a joint which produces a plant.

Phassa, *m.* touch ; contact.

Phasseti (phas + e), to touch ; to attain. *aor.* —**esi**. *pp.* —**sita**. *abs.* —**sitvā**.

Phāṇita, *nt.* treacle ; molasses. —**puṭa**, *m.* leaf-container of treacle.

Phātikamma, *nt.* restoration ; increase.

Phārusaka, *nt.* sweet lovi-lovi.

Phāla, *m.* a ploughshare ; an instrument to split wood ; one half or a slice of salted fish, etc.

Phālaka, 3. one who splits or breaks.

Phālana, *nt.* splitting.

Phāleti (phāl + e), to break; to split; to cut asunder. *aor.* **—esi.** *pp.* **phālita.** *pr. p.* **—lenta.** *abs.* **—letvā.** *inf.* **—etuṇ.**

Phāsu, *m.* ease; comfort. *adj.* comfortable; easy. **—ka,** *a.* pleasant, convenient.

Phāsukā, Phāsulikā, *f.* a rib; the flank.

Phiya, *nt.* an oar.

Phīta, *a.* opulent; prosperous; rich.

Phuṭa (*pp.* of **pharati**), pervaded; permeated; spread with.

Phuṭṭha, *pp.* of **Phusati.**

Phulla, Phullita, *pp.* fully opened or expanded; full of blossoms.

Phusati (phus + a), to touch; to reach; to attain. *aor.* **phusi.** *pr. p.* **phusanta, —māna.** *pp.* **phusita, phuṭṭha.** *abs.* **phusitvā.**

Phusana, *nt.* **—nā,** *f.* touch.

Phusita, —taka, *nt.* a drop; a touch.

Phusīyati (*pass.* of **phusati**), to be touched.

Phussa, *m.* name of a month, December-January; name of a constellation. *adj.* gaily coloured; auspicious. **—ratha,** *m.* a state carriage (running of its own accord in order to find an heir to a throne). **—rāga,** *m.* a topaz.

Pheggu, *nt.* wood surrounding the pith of a tree; a worthless thing.

Pheṇa, *nt.* foam; scum; froth. **—piṇḍa,** *m.* a lump of foam. **—ṇuddehaka,** *a.* throwing up foam.

Pheṇila, *m.* the soap-berry plant.

Phoṭa, *m.* **—ṭaka,** *nt.* a boil; blister.

Phoṭṭhabba, *nt.* touch; contact.

Phosita, *pp.* sprinkled.

B.

Baka, *m.* a crane; heron.

Bajjhati (*pass.* of **bandhati**), to be bound or captivated; to be caught (in a trap, etc.).

Battiṇsati, *f.* thirty-two.

Badara, *nt.* jujube fruit. **—missa,** *a.* mixed with jujube. **Badarī,** *f.* the jujube tree.

Badālatā, *f.* a creeper of sweet taste.

Baddha (*pp.* of **bandhati**), bound; trapped; fastened; made firm; put together. **—ñjalika,** *a.* keeping the hands reverently extended. **—rāva,** *m.* the cry of the trapped or caught. **—vera,** *nt.* contracted enmity. *adj.* having such enmity.

Badhira, *a.* deaf; a person who is deaf.

Bandha, *m.* **—dhana,** *nt.* bond; fetter; attachment; imprisonment.

Bandhati (bandh + a), to bind; to combine; to unite; to tie on; to imprison; to capture; to compose. *aor.* **bandhi.** *pp.* **baddha.** *pr. p.* **bandhanta.** *abs.* **—dhitvā, —dhiya.** *inf.* **—dhituṇ.** *pt. p.* **—dhitabba, —dhanīya.**

Bandhana, *nt.* binding; bondage; something to bind with. **—nāgāra,** *nt.* a prison. **—nāgārika,** *m.* a prisoner; prison-keeper.

Bandhava, *m.* kinsman; relative; relation.

Bandhāpeti (*caus.* of **bandhati**), to cause to be bound or fettered. *aor.* **—esi.** *pp.* **—pita.**

Bandhu, see **bandhava.** **—jīvaka,** *m.* the China-rose plant. **—mantu,** *a.* having relatives ; rich in kinsmen.

Babbaja, *nt.* the fragrant root of the *Andropogon Muricatus.* සැවැන්න..

Babbu, **—ka,** *m.* a cat.

Bala, *nt.* strength ; power ; force ; an army ; military force. **—kāya,** *m.* an army. **—koṭṭhaka,** *nt.* a stronghold ; fortress. **—kkāra,** *m.* violence ; application of force. **—da,** *a.* strength-giving ; bestowing power. **—dāna,** *nt.* bestowal of power. **—ppatta,** *a.* come into power ; grown strong. **—vantu,** *a.* powerful. **—vāhana,** *nt.* the soldiers and vehicles.

Balaṭṭha, Balattha, *m.* a soldier ; member of an army.

Balākā, *f.* a brown crane.

Bali, *m.* religious offering ; revenue ; tax. **—kamma,** an oblation. **—paṭiggāhaka,** *a.* receiving oblations or revenues. **—puṭṭha,** *m.* a crow. **—haraṇa,** *nt.* collecting of taxes.

Balivadda, *m.* an ox.

Balī, *a.* powerful ; strong.

Bavhābādha, *a.* full of sickness.

Bahala, *a.* thick ; dense. **—latta,** thickness.

Bahi, *in.* outer ; external ; outside. **—nagara,** *nt.* the outer city or outside the city. **—nikkhamana,** *nt.* going out ; **—gata,** *a.* gone outside.

Bahiddhā, *in.* outside ; outer.

Bahu, *a.* much ; many ; plenty ; abundant. *pl.* many persons. **—ka,** *a.* many. **—karaṇīya,** **—kicca,** *a.* having much to do ; busy. **—kāra,** *a.* of great service ; very useful. **—kkhattuŋ,** *ad.* many times. **—jana,** *m.* a mass of people. **—jāgara,** *a.* very wakeful. **—dhana,** *a.* with many riches. **—ppada,** *a.* many-footed ; giving much. **—bbīhi,** the Relative Compound. **—bhaṇḍa,** *a.* having an abundance of goods. **—bhāṇī,** *a.* garrulous ; talking much. **—bhāva,** *m.* abundance. **—mata,** *a.* much esteemed ; accepted by many. **—māna,** *m.* **—mānana,** *nt.* respect ; esteem ; veneration. **—mānita,** *a.* much esteemed. **—vacana,** *nt.* the plural number. **—vidha,** *a.* manifold ; multiform. **—ssuta,** *a.* very learned.

Bahutta, *nt.* manifoldness ; multiplicity.

Bahudhā, *ad.* in many ways.

Bahula, *a.* abundant ; frequent. **—tā,** *f.* **—tta,** *nt.* abundance. **—laŋ,** *ad.* mostly ; frequently. **—līkata,** *a.* practised frequently. **—līkaraṇa,** **—līkamma,** *nt.* **—līkāra,** *m.* continuous practice ; zealous exercise.

Bahulīkaroti (bahula + ī + kar + o), to take up seriously ; to increase. *aor.* **—kari,** *pp.* **—kata.**

Bahuso, *ad.* mostly ; frequently ; repeatedly.

Bāṇa, *m.* an arrow. **—dhi,** *m.* a quiver.

Bādhaka, *a.* preventing ; harassing ; obstructing. **—tta,** *nt.* the fact of being obstructive.

Bādhati (bādh + a), to hinder ; to obstruct ; to afflict ; to ensnare. *aor.* **bādhi.** *pp.* **bādhita.** *abs.* **bādhitvā.**

Bādhana, *nt.* hindrance ; affliction ; snaring ; catching.

Bādhā, *f.* hindrance ; prevention.

Bādhita, *pp.* of the following.

Bādheti (bādh + e), to oppress; to afflict; to harass; to ensnare; to prevent. *aor.* —**esi.** *pr. p.* **bādhenta.** *abs.* **bādhetvā.**

Bārasa, 3. twelve.

Bārāṇasī, *f.* the city of Benares. —**ṇaseyyaka,** *a.* made in or coming from Benares.

Bāla, *a.* young in years; ignorant; foolish. *m.* a child; a fool. —**ka,** *m.* a child.

Bālā, Bālikā, *f.* a girl.

Bālisika, *m.* a fisherman.

Bālya, *nt.* childhood; folly.

Bāvīsati, *f.* twenty-two.

Bāhā, *f.* the arm; a post; a handle. —**bala,** *nt.* power of the arm, i.e. manual labour.

Bāhita, *pp.* of **bāheti.**

Bāhira, *a.* external; outer; foreign. *nt.* outside. —**ka,** *a.* of another faith; outsider. —**kapabbajjā,** *f.* the ascetic life other than that of Buddhist monks.

Bāhiratta, *nt.* externality.

Bāhu, *m.* the arm.

Bāhujañña, *a.* belonging to the public.

Bāhulika, *a.* living in abundance.

Bāhulla, —**lya,** *nt.* abundance; luxurious living.

Bāhusacca, *nt.* great learning.

Bāheti (vah + e), to keep away; to ward off; to remove. *aor.* **bāhesi.** *pp.* **bāhita.** *abs.* **bāhetvā.**

Bāḷha, *a.* strong; much; excessive. —**haŋ,** *ad.* strongly; excessively; very much.

Bidala, *nt.* a split pea or bamboo; a lath.

Bindu, *nt.* a drop; a dot; a trifle. —**matta,** *a.* as much as a drop. —**mattaŋ,** *ad.* only a drop.

Bimba, *nt.* an image; figure; the disk (of the sun or moon);

Bimbā, *f.* name of the Prince Siddhartha's wife.

Bimbikā, Bimbī, *f.* the creeper *Brayonia Grandis,* which produces red oval fruits.

Bila, *nt.* a den; a hole; a portion.

Bilaṅga, *m.* vinegar. —**thālikā,** *f.* a kind of torture.

Bilaso, *ad.* in portions or heaps.

Billa, *m.* the marmelos tree.

Biḷāra, *m.* a cat. —**bhastā,** *f.* the bellows.

Biḷālī, *f.* a she cat; a kind of bulbuous plant.

Bīja, *nt.* seed; germ; generating element. —**kosa,** *m.* the capsule or seed vessel of flowers; the scrotum. —**gāma,** *m.* seed-kingdom. —**jāta,** *nt.* species of seed. —**bīja,** *nt.* plants propagated by seeds.

Bībhacca, *a.* awful; horrible.

Bīraṇa, *nt.* the grass **andropogon muricatus,** which produces fragrant roots. —**tthambha,** *m.* a bush of the abovesaid grass.

Bujjhati (budh + ya), to know to understand; to perceive; to be awake. *aor.* **bujjhi.** *pp.* **buddha.** *pr. p.* —**jhanta.** *abs.* —**jhitvā.**

Bujjhana, *nt.* awakening; attaining knowledge. —**naka,** *a.* intelligent; prudent.

Bujjhitu, *m.* one who awakes or becomes enlightened

Buḍḍha, *a.* aged; old. —**tara,** *a* older

Buddha, *m.* one who has attained enlightenment; the Enlightened One. —**kāraka-dhamma,** *m.* the practices bringing about Buddhahood. —**kāla,** *m.* the time when a Buddha appears. —**kolāhala,** *m.* the announcement about coming of a Buddha. —**kkhetta,** *nt.* the sphere where a Buddha's power exists. —**guṇa,** *m.* virtues of a Buddha. —**ṅkura,** *m.* one who is destined to be a Buddha. —**cakkhu,** *nt.* the faculty of complete intuition. —**ñāṇa,** *nt.* the boundless knowledge. —**antara,** *nt.* the interval between the appearance of one Buddha and the next. —**putta,** *m.* a disciple of a Buddha. —**bala,** *nt.* the force of a Buddha. —**bhāva,** *m.* the Buddhahood —**bhūmi,** *f.* the ground of Buddhahood. —**māmaka,** *a.* devoted or attached to the Buddha. —**rasmi,** —**raŋsi,** *f.* rays from the person of the B. —**līḷhā,** *f.* grace of a B. —**vacana,** *nt.* the teaching of the B. —**visaya,** *m.* the scope of a B. —**veneyya,** *a.* to be converted by a B. —**sāsana,** *nt.* the teaching of the B. —**ānubhāva,** *m.* the majestic power of the B. —**ānussati,** *f.* mindfulness upon the Buddha's virtues. —**ārammaṇa,** —**ālambana,** *a.* having its foundation in the B. —**upaṭṭhāka,** *a.* attending the B. —**uppāda,** *m.* the age in which a B. is born.

Buddhatta, *nt.* the state of a Buddha.

Buddhi, *f.* wisdom ; intelligence. —**mantu,** —**sampanna,** *a.* wise ; intelligent.

Budha, *m.* a wise man ; the planet Mercury. —**vāra,** *m.* Wednesday.

Bubbula, —**laka,** *nt.* a bubble.

Bubhukkhati (bhuj + kha ; **bhu** is doubled, the first **bh** is changed to **b** and **j** to **k**), to wish to eat. *aor.* —**khi.** *pp.* —**khita.**

Beluva, *m.* the tree *Aegle Marmelos.* —**pakka,** *nt.* a ripe fruit of marmelos. —**laṭṭhi,** *f.* a young marmelos tree. —**salāṭuka,** *nt.* unripe fruit of marmelos.

Bojjhaṅga, *nt.* a factor of knowledge or wisdom.

Bodha, *m.* **Bodhana,** *nt.* enlightenment ; knowledge. —**nīya,** —**neyya,** *a.* capable of being enlightened.

Bodhi, *f.* supreme knowledge ; the tree of wisdom. —**aṅgaṇa,** *nt.* the courtyard in which a Bo-tree stands. —**pakkhika,** —**pakkhiya,** *a.* belonging to enlightenment. —**pādapa,** —**rukkha,** *m.* the Bo-tree ; the *Ficus Religiosia.* —**pūjā,** *f.* —**maha,** *m.* offerings to a Bo-tree. —**maṇḍa,** *m.* the ground under the Bo-tree, where the Buddha sat at the time of His enlightenment. —**mūla,** *nt.* the foot of the Bo-tree.

Bodheti (budh + e), to awaken ; to enlighten. *aor.* —**esi.** *pp.* **bodhita.** *pr. p.* —**dhenta.** *abs.* —**etvā.**

Bodhetu, *m.* one who awakens or enlightens.

Bondi, *m.* the body.

Byaggha, *m.* a tiger.

Byañjana, *nt.* a syllable ; a consonant ; a sign or mark ; curry.

Byāpāda, *m.* malevolence.

Byāma, *m.* a fathom. —**ppabhā,** *f.* the halo extending around the Buddha.

Byūha, *m.* an array of troops ; a mass or collection.

Brahanta, *a.* vast ; lofty ; gigantic ; immense. (In cpds. it takes the form **brahā,** just like **mahā** from **mahanta**).

Brahma, *m.* the Brahma; the Creator. **—kāyika**, *a.* belonging to the company of Brahmas. **—ghosa**, *a.* having a sound similar to that of Brahma. **—cariyā**, *f.* religious life; complete chastity. **—cārī**, leading a chaste life. **—jacca**, *a.* belonging to the Brahman caste. **—ñña**, *nt.* **—ññatā**, *f.* brahmanhood; pure life. **—daṇḍa**, *m.* a (kind of) punishment by stopping all conversation and communication with one. **—deyya**, *nt.* a royal gift. **—ppatta**, *a.* arrived at the highest state. **—bandhu**, *m.* a relative of the Brahma, i.e. a Brahman. **—bhūta**, *a.* most excellent. **—loka**, *m.* the Brahma world. **—vimāna**, *nt.* mansion of a Brahma god. **—vihāra**, *m.* divine state of mind; a name collectively given to **mettā**, **karuṇā**, **muditā**, and **upekkhā**.

Brāhmaṇa, *m.* a man of the Brahman caste. **—kaññā**, *f.* a Brahman maiden. **—vācanaka**, *nt.* recitation of Vedas by Brahmans.

Brūti (brū + a), to say; to speak. *aor.* **abravi**. *pr. p.* **bruvanta**. *abs.* **bruvitvā**.

Brūhana, *nt.* development; increment.

Brūheti (brūh + e), to increase; to develop. *aor.* **—esi**. *pp.* **brūhita**. *pr. p.* **—henta**. *abs.* **—hetvā**.

Brūhetu, *m.* one who increases.

Bh.

Bhakkha, *a.* fit to be eaten; eatable. *nt.* food; prey. *In cpds.:* feeding on.

Bhakkhati (bhakkh + a), to eat; to feed upon. *aor.* **—kkhi**. *pp.* **—khita**. *in f.***—khituŋ**.

Bhakkhana, *nt.* eating.

Bhakkheti (bhakkh + e), see **Bhakkhati**.

Bhaga, *nt.* luck; fortune; the female organ. **—ndalā** *f.* the fistula. **—vantu**, *a.* fortunate. *m.* the Buddha.

Bhaginī, *f.* sister.

Bhagga (*pp.* of **bhañjati**), broken.

Bhaṅga, *m.* breaking up; dissolution. *nt.* the hempen cloth. **—kkhaṇa**, *m.* the moment of dissolution. **—gānupassanā**, *f.* insight into disruption.

Bhacca, *m.* a servant; a dependant. *adj.* to be nourished or brought up.

Bhajati (bhaj + a), to associate with; to keep company. *aor.* **bhaji**. *pp.* **bhajita**. *pr. p.* **bhajamāna**, *abs.* **bhajitvā**. *pt. p.* **—jitabba**.

Bhajjati (bhaj + a), to roast; to toast. *aor.* **bhajji**. *pp.* **bhajjita**. *pr. p.* **—jamāna**. *abs.* **—jitvā**. *pass.* **bhajjīyati**.

Bhañjaka, 3. one who breaks or spoils.

Bhañjati (bhañj + a), to break to destroy. *aor.* **bhañji**. *pp.* **bhagga**, **bhañjita**. *pr. p.* **—janta**, **—jamāna**. *abs.* **—jitvā**.

Bhañjana, *nt.* breakage; destruction. **—naka**, *a.* breaking; destroying.

Bhaṭa, *m.* a soldier; a constable; a hireling. **—senā**, an infantry.

Bhaṭṭha (*pp.* of **bhajjati**), roasted; fallen down; dropped.

Bhaṇati (bhaṇ + a), to speak; to tell; to preach. *aor.* **bhaṇi.** *pp.* **bhaṇita.** *pr. p.* **—ṇanta.** *pt. p.* **—ṇitabba.** *abs.* **bhaṇitvā.** *inf.* **bhaṇituŋ.**

Bhaṇe, *in.* a term often used for addressing inferiors.

Bhaṇḍa, **—ḍaka,** *nt.* goods; wares; implements; articles. **—ḍāgāra,** *nt.* a storehouse or treasury. **—ḍāgārika,** *m.* a store keeper or treasurer.

Bhaṇḍati (bhaḍ + a), **bhaṇḍeti** (bhaḍ + e), to quarrel. *aor.* **bhaṇḍi, —esi.** *abs.* **—ḍetvā.**

Bhaṇḍana, *nt.* a quarrel; a dispute.

Bhaṇḍikā, *f.* a bundle or parcel.

Bhaṇḍu, *m.* a person who is shaven. **—kamma,** *nt.* shaving.

Bhata (*pp.* of **bharati**), brought up; maintained; reared. *m.* a servant.

Bhataka, *m.* a hired servant.

Bhati, *f.* wages; fee.

Bhatta, *nt.* boiled rice; food; meal. **—kicca,** *nt.* taking of meals. **—kāraka,** *m.* a cook. **—kilamatha, —sammada,** *m.* drowsiness after a meal. **—gāma,** *m.* a village giving tribute or service. **—gga,** *nt.* a refectory. **—puṭa,** *nt.* a parcel of food. **—vissagga,** *m.* serving a meal. **—vetana,** *nt.* food and fees. **—velā,** *f.* meal-time.

Bhatti, *f.* devotion; belief; attachment. **—ka, —mantu,** *a.* devoted; believing in.

Bhattu, *m.* a husband; one who supports or brings up.

Bhadanta, bhaddanta, *a.* venerable; reverend. *m.* a venerable person.

Bhadda, *a.* august; auspicious; lucky; good. **—ka,** *nt.* a lucky or good thing. *adj.* of good quality; lucky. **—kaccānā,** *f.* another name for Rāhula's mother, Yasodharā. **—kumbha,** *m.* a full pitcher, (accepted as auspicious). **—ghaṭa,** *m.* a vessel used in drawing lots in a lottery. **—dāru,** *m.* a sort of pine, the deodar tree. **—padā,** *f.* name of a constellation. **—pīṭha,** *nt.* a rattan chair. **—mukha,** *a.* having a handsome face; a complementary address. **—yuga,** *nt.* the best pair.

Bhadra, same as **Bhadda.**

Bhaddā, **—ddikā,** *f.* a well-behaved woman.

Bhanta (*pp.* of **bhamati**), swaying; swerving. **—tatta,** *nt.* confusion; turmoil.

Bhante (*voc.* of **bhadanta**), Reverend Sir; O Lord.

Bhabba, *a.* able; capable; fit for. **—tā,** *f.* ability; fitness.

Bhama, *m.* a revolving thing; a whirlpool; swerving. **—kāra,** *m.* a turner.

Bhamati (bham + a), to revolve; to whirl about; to roam. *aor.* **bhami.** *pp.* **bhanta.** *pr. p.* **bhamanta.** *abs.* **—mitvā.**

Bhamara, *m.* a wasp.

Bhamarikā, *f.* a humming top.

Bhamu, —mukā, *f.* the eyebrow.

Bhaya, *nt.* fear; fright. **—ṅkara,** *a.* dreadful; horrible. **—dassāvī, —dassī,** *a.* realising the danger.

Bhayānaka, —yāvaha, *a.* frightful; horrible.

Bhara, *a.* (in cpds.) supporting. **Mātāpettibhara** = one who supports his parents.

Bharaṇa, *nt.* maintenance; bearing.

Bharati (bhar + a), to bear; to support; to maintain. *aor.* **bhari.** *pp.* **bhata.** *abs.* **bharitvā.**

Bharita, *pp.* filled with; full of; maintained.

Bhariyā, *f.* the wife.

Bhallātaka, *m.* the marking-nut tree. ඞදේල.

Bhava, *m.* the state of existence. **—gga,** *m.* the highest point of existence or of the universe. **—ṅga,** *nt.* the sub-consciousness. **—cakka,** *nt.* the wheel of rebirth. **—taṇhā, —netti,** *f.* craving for rebirth. **—ntaga, —ntagū,** *a.* gone to the end of existence. **—ntara,** *nt.* another existence. **—saŋyojana,** *nt.* fetter of rebirth. **—vābhava,** *m.* this or that life. **—vesanā,** *f.* longing for rebirth. **—vogha,** *m.* the flood of rebirth.

Bhavati (bhū + a), to become; to be; to exist. *aor.* **bhavi, abhavi.** *pp.* **bhūta.** *pr. p.* **bhavanta, bhavamāna.** *pt. p.* **bhavitabba.** *abs.* **bhavitvā, bhūtvā.** *inf.* **bhavituŋ.**

Bhavana, *nt.* becoming; a dwelling place.

Bhavanta, *a.* prosperous; a polite word often used in the place of "you."

Bhastā, *f.* the bellows; a leather bag.

Bhasma, *nt.* ashes. **—cchanna,** *a.* covered with ashes.

Bhassa, *nt.* useless talk. **—sārāmatā,** *f.* attachment to useless talk.

Bhassati (bhas + ya), to fall down; to drop; to descend. *aor.* **bhassi.** *pp.* **bhaṭṭha.** *pr. p.* **—santa, —samāna.** *abs.* **—sitvā.**

Bhassara, *a.* bright; shining; resplendent.

Bhā, *f.* the light; splendour.

Bhākuṭika, *a.* knitting the brows; frowning.

Bhāga, *m.* a portion; part; share; faction. **—vantu, bhāgī,** *a.* sharing in; partaking of.

Bhāgadheyya, —dheya, *nt.* fortune; fate.

Bhāgaso, *ad.* in parts; by portions.

Bhāgineyya, *m.* sister's son; nephew. **—yyā,** *f.* sister's daughter; niece.

Bhāgiya, *a.* (in cpds.) connected with; condusive to.

Bhāgīrathī, *f.* the Ganges.

Bhāgya, *nt.* good luck; fortune.

Bhājaka, bhājetu, *m.* one who divides or distributes.

Bhājana, *ger.* dividing; distribution.

Bhājana, *nt.* a bowl; dish; vessel; a container. **—vikati,** *f.* various kinds of dishes or vessels.

Bhājeti (bhāj + e), to divide; to distribute. *aor.* **—esi.** *pp.* **—jita.** *pr. p.* **—jenta.** *abs.* **—jetvā.** *pt. p.* **—jetabba.** *pass.* **bhājīyati.**

Bhāṇaka, 3. a reciter of the Scriptures. *m.* a big jar.

Bhāṇavāra, *m.* a section of the Scriptures, containing 8,000 letters.

Bhāṇī, *a.* speaking; reciting.

Bhāti (bhā + a), to shine. *aor.* **bhāsi.**

Bhātika, bhātu, *m.* a brother.

Bhānu, *m.* light; the sun. **—mantu,** *a.* luminous; *m.* the sun.

Bhāyati (bhī + a), to be afraid; to fear. *aor.* **bhāyi.** *pr. p.* **bhāyanta.** *pt. p.* **bhāyitabba.** *abs.* **bhāyitvā.**

Bhāyāpeti (*caus.* of **bhāyati**), to frighten. *aor.* **—esi.** *pp.* **—pita.** *abs.* **—petvā.**

Bhāra, *m.* a weight; load; burden; charge; task; an affair. **—nikkhepana,** *nt.* the laying down of a burden or charge. **—mocana,** *nt.* deliverance of a burden. **—vāhī,** 3. bearing the burden; one who carries an office. **—hāra,** 3. burden-bearer; load-carrier.

Bhārika, *a.* loaded; heavy; full of.

Bhāriya, *a.* weighty; grave; serious.

Bhāva, *m.* condition; nature; becoming.

Bhāvanā, *f.* increase; development by means of thought; meditation. **—nānuyoga,** *m.* application to meditation. **—maya,** *a.* accomplished by meditation. **—vidhāna,** *nt.* arrangement or process of meditation.

Bhāvanīya, *a.* to be cultivated; to be respected.

Bhāvita (*pp.* of **bhāveti**), developed. **—tatta,** *a.* well-trained; self-composed.

Bhāvī, *a.* going to be; inevitable.

Bhāveti (bhū + e), to increase; to cultivate; to develop. *aor.* **—esi.** *pp.* **bhāvita.** *pr. p.* **—venta, —vayamāna.** *pt. p.* **—vetabba.** *abs.* **—vetvā.** *inf.* **—vetuŋ.**

Bhāsati (bhās + a), to say; to speak; to shine. *aor.* **bhāsi.** *pp.* **bhāsita.** *pr. p.* **—santa.** *abs.* **—sitvā.** *pt. p.* **—sitabba.**

Bhāsana, *nt.* speech; saying; talk.

Bhāsā, *f.* language; dialect.

Bhāsitu, bhāsī, *m.* one who says or speaks.

Bhāsura, *a.* bright; shining.

Bhikkhaka, *m.* a beggar; mendicant.

Bhikkhati (bhikkh + a), to beg alms; to ask for. *aor.* **—kkhi.** *pr. p.* **—khanta, —khamāna.** *abs.* **—khitvā.**

Bhikkhana, *nt.* begging.

Bhikkhā, *f.* alms; food. **—cariyā,** *f.* **—cāra,** *m.* going about for alms. **—hāra,** *m.* food received by a mendicant.

Bhikkhu, *m.* a Buddhist monk. **—ṇī,** *f.* a Buddhist nun. **—bhāva,** *m.* monkhood.

Bhiṅka, *m.* a young elephant.

Bhiṅkāra, *m.* a water-jug.

Bhijjati (bhid + ya), to be broken or destroyed. *aor.* **—jji.** *pp.* **bhinna.** *pr. p.* **—jamāna.** *abs.* **—jitvā.**

Bhijjana, *nt.* breaking up. **—dhamma,** *a.* brittle; falling into ruin.

Bhitti, *f.* a wall. **—pāda,** *m.* the foot or foundation of a wall.

Bhindati (bhid + ŋ - a), to break; to split; to sever. *aor.* **bhindi.** *pp.* **bhindita, bhinna.** *pr. p.* **—danta.** *abs.* **—ditvā.** *inf.* **—dituŋ.**

Bhinna. *pp.* of the above. **—tta,** *nt.* **—bhāva,** *m.* state of being broken; diversity. **—nāva,** *a.* shipwrecked. **—paṭa.** *nt.* a torn clothe. **—mariyāda,** *a.* gone beyond the limits. **—sīla,** *a.* one who has broken some precepts.

Bhiyyo, —yoso, *in.* exceedingly; more; in a higher degree; repeatedly. **—yoso mattāya,** exceedingly; more than one's ability.

Bhisa, *nt.* the root of lotus plant. —**puppha**, *nt.* lotus flower. —**muḷāla**, *nt.* lotus bulb and roots.

Bhisakka, *m.* a physician.

Bhisi, *f.* a cushion; a pad; a bolster.

Bhiŋsana, —**naka**, *a.* horrible; dreadful; awe-inspiring.

Bhīta (*pp.* of **bhāyati**), frightened.

Bhīti, *f.* fear.

Bhīma, **bhīsana**, *a.* dreadful; horrible.

Bhīru, —**ruka**, *a.* timid; fearful; cowardly. —**ruttāna**, *nt.* refuge for the fearful.

Bhukkaraṇa, *nt.* **bhuṅkāra**, **bhukkāra**, *m.* barking (of a dog).

Bhuṅkaroti (bhuŋ + kar + o), to bark. *aor.* —**kari.** *pp.* —**kata.** *pr. p.* —**karonta.** *abs.* —**katvā**, —**karitvā.**

Bhuja, *m.* the hand. *adj.* crooked; bending. —**patta**, *m.* the Bhurja tree, a kind of willow.

Bhujaga, —**jaṅga**, —**jaṅgama**, *m.* a snake.

Bhujissa, *m.* a freeman.

Bhuñjaka, **bhuñjitu**, 3. one who eats or enjoys.

Bhuñjati (bhuj + ŋ - a), to eat; to enjoy. *aor.* **bhuñji.** *pp.* **bhutta.** *pr. p.* —**janta**, —**jamāna.** *pt. p.* —**jitabba.** *abs.* —**jitvā**, **bhuñjiya**, **bhutvā.** *inf.* —**jituŋ**, **bhottuŋ.**

Bhuñjana, *nt.* eating. —**kāla**, *m.* meal-time.

Bhuttāvī, *a.* one who has eaten.

Bhumma, *a.* terrestrial. (in cpds.) having stages or stories. —**ṭṭha**, *a.* situated on the earth. —**ttharaṇa**, *nt.* a ground covering; carpet. —**ntara**, *nt.* different stages or planes.

Bhusa, *nt.* chaff; husks (of corn). *adj.* much; abundant. —**saŋ**, *ad.* exceedingly; frequently.

Bhussati (bhus + ya), to bark. *aor.* **bhussi.** *pr. p.* —**santa**, —**samāna.** *abs.* —**sitvā.**

Bhū, *f.* the earth.

Bhūta (*pp.* of **bhavati**), become; born; produced. *nt.* an element; a ghost; living being; truth; that which is; what has happened. —**kāya**, *m.* the body, which is produced by elements. —**gāma**, *m.* vegetation. —**gāha**, *m.* possession by a demon. —**vādī**, *a.* truthful. —**vejja**, *m.* an exorcist.

Bhūtatta, *nt.* the fact of having become.

Bhūtika, *a.* composed of elements.

Bhūma, —**maka**, *a.* (in cpds.) having floors or stories.

Bhūmi, *f.* ground; earth; region; stage; plane. —**kampā**, *f.* an earthquake. —**gata**, *a.* situated on the ground or stored away in the ground. —**tala**, *nt.* ground surface. —**ppadesa**, —**bhāga**, *m.* a piece of land.

Bhūri, *f.* wisdom. *adj.* extensive; abundant. —**pañña**, —**medha**, *a.* of extensive wisdom.

Bhūsana, *nt.* **bhūsā**, *f.* an ornament; decoration.

Bhūsāpeti (*caus.* of the following), to cause to adorn or decorate. *aor.* —**esi.** *pp.* —**pita.** *abs.* —**petvā.**

Bhūseti (bhūs + e), to adorn; to decorate; to beautify. *aor.* —**esi.** *pp.* **bhūsita.** *pr. p.* **bhūsenta.** *abs.* —**setvā.**

Bheka, *m.* a frog.

Bhejja, *a.* brittle; breakable. *nt.* breaking or cutting off.

Bheṇḍivāla, *m.* a kind of missile.

Bheṇḍu, —ḍuka, *m.* a ball for playing ; a ball-shaped top or cupola.

Bhettu, *m.* one who breaks.

Bheda, *m.* breach ; disunion ; dissension. **—daka,** 3. one who breaks or causes disunion. **—kara,** *a.* bringing division or disunion.

Bhedana, *nt.* breach ; division ; disunion. **—naka,** *a.* fit to be broken. **—dhamma,** *a.* perishable.

Bhedita, *pp.* of the following.

Bhedeti (bhid + e), to cause to break, divide or disunite. *aor.* **—esi.** *pp.* **—dita.** *abs.* **—detvā.**

Bheraṇḍa, *m.* a jackal. **—ḍaka,** *nt.* the cry of a jackal.

Bherava, *a.* frightful.

Bheri, *f.* a drum. **—cāraṇa,** *nt.* proclamation through sounding a drum. **—tala,** *nt.* the surface of a drum. **—vādaka,** *m.* a drummer. **—vādana,** *nt.* sounding of a drum. **—sadda,** *m.* sound of a drum.

Bhesajja, *nt.* medicine. **—kapāla,** *nt.* medicine bowl.

Bho, *in.* (a familiar term of address), my dear ; friend.

Bhoga, *m.* possession ; wealth ; enjoyment ; the coil of a snake. **—kkhandha,** *m.* a mass of wealth. **—gāma,** *m.* a tributary village. **—mada,** *m.* pride of wealth. **—vantu,** *a.* wealthy.

Bhogī, *m.* snake ; a wealthy man. *adj.* (in cpds.) enjoying ; partaking in.

Bhogga, *a.* fit to be enjoyed or possessed.

Bhojaka, 3. one who feeds ; a collector of revenues. **Gāmabhojaka** = a village headman.

Bhojana, *nt.* food ; meal.

Bhojaniya, *a.* fit to be eaten. *nt.* soft food.

Bhojāpeti (bhuj + āpe), to feed or serve at meals. *aor.* **—esi.** *pp.* **—pita.** *abs.* **—petvā.**

Bhojī, *a.* feeding on.

Bhojeti (bhuj + e), to feed. *aor.* **—esi.** *pp.* **bhojita.** *abs.* **—jetvā.** *pr. p.* **—jenta, —jayamāna.** *inf.* **—jetuŋ.**

Bhojja, *nt.* an edible thing. *adj.* fit to be eaten.

Bhoti (*voc. sin.*) Dear Madam.

Bhottabba, see **Bhojja.**

Bhottuŋ, *inf.* to eat.

Bhovādī, *m.* a Brahman.

M.

Makaci, *m.* the bow-string hemp. **—vāka,** *nt.* the fibre of the above-said plant. **—vattha,** *nt.* a canvas.

Makara, *m.* a sea-monster ; a sword-fish. **—dantaka,** *nt.* a design in the shape of the teeth of a sword-fish.

Makaranda, *m.* the nectar of a flower.

Makasa, *m.* a mosquito. **—vāraṇa,** *nt.* mosquito net.

Makuṭa, *m. nt.* crest ; crown ; a coronet.

Makula, *nt.* bud ; a knob.

Makkaṭa, *m.* a monkey. **—ṭaka,** *m.* a spider. **—sutta,** *nt.* spider's thread.

Makkaṭī, *f.* a female monkey.

Makkha, *m.* depreciation of another's worth.

Makkhaṇa, *nt.* smearing ; anointing with.

Makkhikā, *f.* a fly.

Makkhita, *pp.* of **makkheti.**

Makkhī, *m.* one who depreciates another's worth.

Makkheti (makkh + e), to smear; to anoint; to rub off. *aor.* —**esi.** *pp.* —**khita.** *abs.* —**khetvā.**

Maga, *m.* a quadruped. —**sira**, name of a constellation

Magadha, *m.* the country of Magadha, which includes present Bihar and Orissa.

Magga, *m.* path; road; way. —**kilanta**, *a.* wearied by walking. —**kusala**, *a.* one who knows the road well. —**kkhāyī**, *a.* one who shows the right path. —**ṅga**, *nt.* the constituents of the Path, *viz.* right view, right aspiration, right speech, right conduct, right livelihood, right effort, right mindfulness, and right rapture. —**ñāṇa**, *nt.* knowledge of the Path. —**ññū**, —**vidū**, *a.* one who knows the path. —**ṭṭha**, *a.* one who is on the road or who has attained the Path. —**dūsī**, *m.* a highway robber. —**desaka**, *a.* one who points out the way. —**paṭipanna**, *a.* a traveller; one who has entered the Path. —**bhāvanā**, *f.* cultivation of the Path. —**mūḷha**, *a.* one who has lost the way. —**sacca**, *nt.* the truth concerning the Path.

Maggati (mag + a), to seek; to track; to trace out. *aor.* **maggi.** *pp.* —**gita.** *abs.* —**gitvā.**

Maggana, *nt.* —**nā**, *f.* search; tracing out.

Maggika, 3. a wayfarer.

Maggita, *pp.* of **maggati.**

Maggeti (mag + e), see **maggati.**

Maghavantu, *m.* an epithet of Sakka.

Maṅku, *a.* confused; downcast; in low spirits. —**bhāva**, *m.* moral weakness; downcastness. —**bhūta**, *a.* silent; downcast.

Maṅgala, *a.* auspicious; royal; lucky; festive. *nt.* festivity; good omen; ceremony; prosperity. —**kicca**, *nt.* festivity. —**kolāhala**, *m.* dispute about auspicious things or acts. —**divasa**, *m.* a festive day; the day of marriage. —**assa**, —**sindhava**, *m.* state horse. —**pokkharaṇī**, *f.* royal bathing pond.—**silāpaṭṭa**, *nt.* a slab used by a king to sit on. —**supina**, *nt.* a lucky dream. —**hatthī**, *m.* state elephant.

Maṅgura, *m.* a kind of river fish. *adj.* of dark yellow colour.

Maccu, *m.* death; the Death. —**tara**, *a.* one who overcomes death. —**dheyya**, *nt.* the sphere of Death. —**parāyaṇa**, —**pareta**, *a.* subject to death. —**pāsa**, *m.* the snare of Death. —**mukha**, *nt.* the mouth of —Death. —**rāja**, *m.* the king of death. —**vasa**, *m.* the power of death. —**hāyī**, *a.* victorious over death.

Maccha, *m.* a fish. —**ṇḍa**, *nt.* fish-egg. —**ṇḍī**, *f.* a kind of sugar having the appearance of fish-eggs. —**maṇsa**, *nt.* fish and flesh. —**bandha**, *m.* a fisherman.

Macchara, —**chariya**, *nt.* avarice; niggardliness. —**charī**, *m.* a miser.

Maccharāyati (*Deno.* from **macchariya**), to be selfish, greedy or miserly.

Macchī, *f.* a she-fish.

Macchera, see **Macchariya.**

Majja, *nt.* an intoxicant. —**na**, *nt.* intoxication; negligence. —**pa**, 3. one who drinks strong drink. —**pāna**, *nt.* drinking of liquors; an intoxicating drink. —**pāyī**, see **majjapa**. —**vikkayī**, *m.* seller of spirits.

Majjati (mad + ya), to be intoxicated. (maj + a), to polish; to wipe; to clean. *aor.* **majji**. *pp.* 1. **matta**. 2. **maṭṭha** or **majjita**. *pr. p.* **majjanta**. *abs.* **majjitvā**.

Majjanā, *f.* polishing; wiping; stroking.

Majjāra, *m.* a cat. —**jārī**, *f.* a she-cat.

Majjha, *m.* the middle; the waist. *adj.* middle. —**ṭṭha**, —**tta**, *a.* neutral; impartial; indifferent. —**ṇha**, *m.* the noon; midday. —**ttatā**, *f.* impartiality; equanimity. —**desa**, *m.* the middle country. —**ntika**, —**ntikasamaya**, *m.* the midday.

Majjhima, *a.* middle; medium; moderate; central. —**desa**, *m.* the middle country including the Ganges basin. —**purisa**, *m.* a man of moderate height; the 2nd person in grammar. —**yāma**, *m.* the middle portion of the night. —**vaya**, *m.* the middle age.

Mañca, *m.* a bed. —**ka**, *m.* a small bed. —**parāyaṇa**, *a.* confined to bed. —**pīṭha**, *nt.* beds and chairs; furniture. —**vāna**, *nt.* the netting of a bed.

Mañjarī, *f.* a bunch or cluster.

Mañjiṭṭha, —**jeṭṭha**, *a.* crimson. —**jiṭṭhā**, *f.* the red sanders tree, seeds of which are used as a jeweller's weight. මදට.

Mañju, *a.* charming; lovely. —**bhāṇaka**, —**ssara**, *a.* sweet-voiced; speaking sweetly.

Mañjūsaka, *m.* a celestial tree.

Mañjūsā, *f.* a casket; box.

Mañjeṭṭhī, *f.* the Bengal madder.

Maññati (man + ya), to imagine; to be of opinion; to deem. *aor.* **maññi**. *pp.* **maññita**. *pr. p.* **maññamāna**, *abs.* **maññitvā**.

Maññanā, *f.* **maññita**, *nt.* imagination; illusion.

Maññe, *in.* methinks; I imagine.

Maṭṭa, **maṭṭha**, *a.* smoothed; polished. —**sāṭaka**, *nt.* a fine cloth

Maṇi, *m.* a gem; jewel. —**kāra**, *m.* gem-cutter. —**kuṇḍala**, *nt.* jewelled earring. —**kkhandha**, *m.* a tremendous jewel. —**pallaṅka**, *m.* a jewel seat. —**bandha**, *m.* the wrist. —**maya**, *a.* made of precious stones. —**ratana**, *nt.* a valuable gem. —**vaṇṇa**, *a.* of the colour of crystal. —**sappa**, *m.* a kind of green snake.

Maṇḍa, *m.* the best part (of milk, etc.). *adj.* very clear.

Maṇḍana, *nt.* adornment; decoration. —**jātika**, *a.* desirous of adornment.

Maṇḍapa, *m.* temporary shed or pavilion.

Maṇḍala, *nt.* a circle; disk; round platform; circus ring; a round flat surface. —**māla**, *m.* a circular pavilion. —**lika**, *a.* belonging to a circle or a small country. —**lissara**, *m.* a governor of a province. —**ḍalī**, *a.* having a disk; circular.

Maṇḍita, *pp.* of **maṇḍeti**.

Maṇḍuka, *m.* a frog.

Maṇḍeti (maṇḍ + e), to adorn; to decorate. *aor.* —**esi**. *pp.* —**ḍita**. *abs.* —**ḍetvā**.

Mata (*pp.* of **maññati**), known; understood. *nt.* a view.

Mata (*pp.* of **marati**), dead —**kicca**, *nt.* rites for the dead.

Mataka, 3. the deceased. **—bhatta,** *nt.* food offered for the dead. **—vattha,** *nt.* cloth offered for the dead.

Mati, *f.* wisdom; idea. **—mantu,** *a.* wise. **—vippahīna,** *a.* foolish.

Matta (*pp.* of **majjati**), intoxicated; full of joy; proud of; conceited. **—hatthī,** *m.* a rutted elephant.

Matta (**—ka**), (in cpds.) of the size of; as much as. **—ññū,** *a.* knowing the measure or limit; moderate. **—ññutā,** *f.* moderation.

Mattā, *f.* a measure; quantity; moderation; size. **—sukha,** *nt.* limited happiness.

Mattikā, *f.* clay; soil. **—piṇḍa,** *m.* a lump of clay. **—bhājana,** *nt.* earthenware (vessel).

Matteyya, *a.* respecting one's mother. **—tā,** *f.* filial love towards one's mother.

Matthaka, *m.* the head; top; summit. *loc.* upon; at the distance of.

Matthaluṅga, *nt.* the brain.

Matthu, *nt.* the water separated from the curd.

Mathati (math + a), to shake about; to churn; to disturb. *aor.* **mathi.** *pp.* **mathita.** *abs.* **mathitvā.**

Mathana, *nt.* churning; disturbance.

Mada, *m.* pride; intoxication; conceit; sexual excess. **—nīya,** *a.* intoxicating; causing attachment.

Madana, *m.* the God of love. *nt.* intoxication.

Madirā, *f.* liquor made from cereals.

Maddati (madd + a), to crush; to trample on; to subjugate. *aor.* **maddi.** *pp.* **—dita.** *pr. p.* **—danta,** *abs.* **—ditvā, maddiya.**

Maddana, *nt.* crushing; trampling; threshing.

Maddava, *nt.* softness; mildness; a soft thing. *adj.* mild; gentle; soft.

Madhu, *nt.* honey; wine made from the blossom of *Bassia Latifolia.* **—ka,** *m.* the tree *Bassia Latifolia.* **—kara,** *m.* a bee. **—gaṇḍa, —paṭala,** *m.* a honeycomb. **—pa,** *m.* a bee; sucker of honey. **—piṇḍikā,** *f.* a ball of flour mixed with honey. **—bbata,** *m.* a bee. **—makkhita,** *a.* smeared with honey. **—meha,** *m.* diabetes. **—laṭṭhikā,** *f.* liquorice. **—lāja,** *m.* fried corn mixed with honey. **—līha,** *m.* a bee. **—ssava,** *a.* dripping with honey.

Madhukā, *f.* liquorice

Madhura, *a.* sweet. *nt.* sweet thing. **—ratta,** *nt.* **—ratā,** *f.* sweetness. **—ssara,** *a.* having a sweet voice. *m.* a sweet voice.

Madhvāsava, *m.* wine from the flowers of Bassia.

Mana, *m. nt.* mind; consciousness. (in cpds. it takes the form **mano**). **—kkāra, manasikāra,** *m.* ideation; consideration.

Manatā, *f.* (in cpds.) mentality. **Attamanatā,** = joyful mentality.

Manana, *nt.* thinking.

Manasikaroti (manasi + kar + o), to keep in mind; to think over. *aor.* **—kari.** *pp.* **—kata.** *pr. p.* **—ronta.** *abs.* **—katvā, —karitvā.** *pt. p.* **—kātabba.**

Manaŋ, *in.* nearly; well-nigh; almost; somewhat.

Manāpa, —āpika, *a.* pleasing; charming.

Manuja, *m.* a human being. **—jādhipa**, **—jinda**, *m.* lord of men ; a king.

Manuñña, *a.* delightful; pleasant.

Manussa, *m.* a human being. **—satta**, *nt.* human existence. **—bhāva**, *m.* state of a human being. **—bhūta**, *a.* one who has become a man. **—loka**, *m.* human world.

Manesikā, *f.* thought-reading.

Mano (form taken by **mana** in cpds.) **—kamma**, *nt.* mental action. **—java**, *a.* swift as thought. **—duccarita**, *nt.* bad mentality. **—dvāra**, *nt.* the threshold of consciousness. **—dhātu**, *f.* the ideational faculty. **—padosa**, *m.* ill-will. **—pasāda**, *m.* devotional feeling.**—pubbaṅgama**, *a.* directed by mind. **—maya**, *a.* mind-made. **—ratha**, *m.* wish. **—rama**, *a.* delightful. **—viññāṇa**, *nt.* the mind cognition. **—viññeyya**, *a.* to be comprehended by the mind. **—vitakka**, *m.* a thought. **—hara**, *a.* charming ; captivating.

Manosilā, *f.* red arsenic.

Manta, *nt.* a charm ; spell ; incantation. **—jjhāyaka**, *a.* one who studies the Holy Incantations.

Mantana, *nt.* **—nā**, *f.* consultation ; discussion.

Mantī, *m.* a counsellor ; a minister. **—tinī**, *f.* a woman councillor.

Manteti (mant + e), to consult ; to take counsel ; to discuss. *aor.* **—esi.** *pp.* **—tita.** *pr. p.* **—tenta, mantayamāna.** *abs.* **—tetvā.** *inf.* **—tetuŋ.**

Mantha, *m.* churning stick ; parched corn-flour.

Manthara, *m.* a tortoise.

Manda, *a.* slow ; dull ; lazy ; foolish ; yielding a little. *nt.* a little. **—datā**, *f.* **—datta**, *nt.* reduced state ; slowness ; stupidity. **—daŋ, mandamandaŋ**, *ad.* slowly ; little by little.

Mandākinī, *f.* name of a great lake, and of a river.

Mandāmukhī, *f.* a coal-pan.

Mandāra, *m.* name of a mountain.

Mandiya, *nt.* stupidity ; slackness.

Mandira, *nt.* a mansion ; a palace.

Mamaṅkāra, *m.* **mamatta**, *nt.* **mamāyanā**, *f.* selfish attachment.

Mamāyati (*Deno.* from **mama**), to be attached to ; to cherish. *aor.* **mamāyi.** *pp.* **—yita.** *pr. p.* **—yanta.** *abs.* **mamāyitvā.**

Mamma, mammaṭṭhāna, *nt.* a vital spot of the body ; a nerve centre. **—cchedaka**, *a.* wounding a vital spot ; very harsh or fatal.

Mammana, 3. one who stammers.

Mayaŋ (*nom. pl.* of **amha**), we.

Mayūkha, *m.* a ray of light.

Mayūra, *m.* peacock.

Maraṇa, *nt.* death. **—kāla**, *m.* time of death. **—cetanā**, *f.* intention to kill. **—dhamma**, *a.* subject to death. **—nta**, **—pariyosāna**, *a.* having death as its end. **—bhaya**, *nt.* fear of death. **—mañcaka**, *m.* death-bed. **—mukha**, *nt.* the mouth of Death. **—sati**, *f.* meditation on death. **—samaya**, *m.* time of death.

Marati (mar + a). to die. *aor.* **mari.** *pp.* **mata.** *pr. p.* **maranta, maramāna.** *pt. p.* **maritabba.** *abs.* **maritvā.** *inf.* **marituŋ.**

Marica, *nt.* pepper ; chillies.

Mariyādā, *f.* boundary ; limit.

Marīci, *f.* a ray of light ; mirage. —**cikā**, *f.* mirage. —**dhamma**, *a.* equal to mirage; unsubstantial.

Maru, *f.* sand ; a sandy waste. *m.* a deity.

Marumbā, *f.* pebbles.

Mala, *nt.* impurity ; stain ; rust ; dirt ; dung. —**tara**, *a.* more dirty or impure.

Malina, —**naka**, *a.* dirty ; stained ; impure. *nt.* impurity.

Malla, *m.* a wrestler ; a man of the Malla clan. —**yuddha**, *nt.* wrestling contest.

Mallaka, *m.* a vessel ; a receiver.

Mallikā, *f.* the (Arabian) jasmine.

Masāragalla, *nt.* a kind of precious stone.

Masi, *m.* soot ; charcoal dust.

Massu, *nt.* the beard. —**kamma** —**karaṇa**, *nt.* beard-dressing.

Maha, *m.* a religious festival.

Mahaggata, *a.* become great ; lofty.

Mahaggha, *a.* very costly. —**tā**, *f.* costliness.

Mahagghasa, *a.* eating much ; glutonous.

Mahaṇṇava, *m.* the great ocean.

Mahati (mah + a), to honour ; to revere. *aor.* **mahi.** *pp.* **mahita.** *abs.* **mahitvā.**

Mahatta, *nt.* greatness.

Mahaddhana, *a.* having great riches.

Mahanīya, *a.* respectable.

Mahanta, *a.* great ; big ; extensive. (*f.* **mahantī, mahatī**). —**tara**, *a.* greater ; more extensive. —**tā**, *f.* —**bhāva**, *m.* greatness.

Mahapphala, *a.* rich in result.

Mahabbala, *a.* having a great power or strong force. *nt.* a great strength or army.

Mahabbhaya, *nt.* great fear.

Mahallaka, *a.* old. *m.* an old man. —**tara**, *a.* older. —**llikā**, *f.* old woman.

Mahā (**mahanta** becomes **mahā** in compounds ; the last vowel **a** is often shortened euphonically). —**upāsaka**, *m.* a great follower of the Buddha. —**upāsikā**, *f.* a great female devotee. —**karuṇā**, *f.* great compassion. —**kāya**, *a.* having a fat or big body. —**gaṇa**, *m.* a great community. —**gaṇī**, 3. having many followers. —**jana**, *m.* the public. —**taṇha**, *a.* very greedy. —**tala**, *nt.* a large flat roof on the top of a palace. —**dhana**, *nt.* immense wealth. —**naraka**, —**niraya**, *m.* the great hell. —**nasa**, *nt.* the kitchen. —**nubhāva**, *a.* of great majesty. —**pañña**, *a.* very wise. —**patha**, *m.* high road. —**pitu**, *m.* father's elder brother. —**purisa**, *m.* a great man. —**bhūta**, *nt.* the four great elements. —**bhoga**, *a.* having great wealth. —**mati**, *m.* a great wise man. —**matta**, —**macca**, *m.* a chief minister. —**muni**, *m.* the great sage. —**megha**, *m.* a shower. —**yañña**, —**yāga**, *m.* a great sacrifice. —**yasa**, *a.* of great fame. —**raha**, *a.* very precious. —**rāja**, *m.* a great king. —**latāpasādhana**, *nt.* a ladies' parure called "great creeper." —**satta**, *m.* the great being. —**samudda**, *m.* the ocean. —**sara**, *nt.* a great lake. —**sāra**, —**sāla**, *a.* having immense wealth. —**sāvaka**, *m.* a great disciple.

Mahikā, *f.* the frost.

Mahiccha, *a.* greedy. **—tā**, *f.* greediness.

Mahita, *pp.* of **mahati.**

Mahiddhika, *a.* of great magical power.

Mahinda, *m.* a personal name; the chief of gods.

Mahilā, *f.* a woman.

Mahisa, *m.* a buffalo. **—maṇḍala**, *nt.* name of a country, present Mysore.

Mahissara, *m.* a great lord; the God Īsvara.

Mahī, *f.* the earth; name of a river. **—tala**, *nt.* the surface of the earth. **—dhara**, *m.* a mountain. **—pati**, **—pāla**, *m.* a king **—ruha**, *m.* a tree.

Mahesakkha, *a.* influential; possessing great power.

Mahesi (mahā + isi), *m.* the great sage.

Mahesī, *f.* a queen.

Mahogha, *m.* great flood.

Mahodadhi, *m.* the ocean.

Mahodara, *a.* having a big belly.

Mahoraga, *m.* a king of Nāgas.

Maŋsa, *nt.* flesh. **—pesi**, *f.* a slice of flesh. **—puñja**, *m.* a heap of flesh.

Mā, (*a prohibitive particle*), do not.

Mā, *m.* the moon.

Māgadha, **—dhaka**, *a.* belonging to Magadha. **—dhī**, *f.* the language of Magadha.

Māgavika, *m.* a huntsman.

Māgasira, *m.* name of a month, December-January.

Māgha, *m.* name of a month, January-February.

Māghāta, *m.* non-killing order.

Māṇava, **—vaka**, *m.* a young man. **—vikā**, **—vī**, *f.* a maiden.

Mātaṅga, *m.* an elephant; a low-caste man.

Mātalī, *m.* name of Indra's charioteer.

Mātāpitu, *m.* parents; the mother and the father.

Mātāpettika, *a.* come from father and mother. **—pettibhara**, *a.* supporting one's parents.

Mātāmaha, *m.* mother's father. **—mahī**, *f.* mother's mother.

Mātika, *a.* connected with mother. **—kā**, *f.* a water course; a table of contents; the code of Pātimokkha.

Mātipakkha, *m.* mother's side.

Mātu, *f.* mother. **—kucchi**, *m.* mother's womb. **—gāma**, *m.* a woman. **—ghāta**, *m.* matricide. **—ghātaka**, 3. a matricide. **—paṭṭhāna**, *nt.* looking after one's mother. **—posaka**, 3. supporting one's mother.

Mātucchā, *f.* mother's sister.

Mātula, *m.* maternal uncle. **—lānī**, *f.* maternal uncle's wife.

Mātuluṅga, *m.* the citron.

Mādisa, *a.* one like me.

Māṇa, *nt.* measure; measurement. **—kūṭa**, *m.* a false measure.

Māna, *m.* pride; conceit. **—tthaddha**, *a.* stubborn in pride. **—da**, *a.* inspiring respect.

Mānana, *nt.* paying honour or respect.

Mānasa, *nt.* mind; intention. *adj.* (in cpds.) having the intention of.

Mānita, *pp.* of **māneti.**

Mānī, 3. one who is proud.

Mānusa, *a.* human. *m.* a man. **—saka**, *a.* human. **—sī**, *f.* a woman.

Māneti (mān + e), to honour; to revere; to think highly. *aor.* **mānesi.** *pr. p.* **mānenta.** *abs.* **mānetvā.**

Māpeti (mā + āpe), to build; to construct; to create; to cause to appear by super-natural power. *aor.* —**esi.** *pp.* **māpita.** *abs.* **māpetvā.**

Māmaka, *a.* devoted to; loving.

Māyā, *f.* fraud; deceit; magic; jugglery. —**kāra,** 3. a juggler. —**yāvī,** *a.* deceitful; hypocritical; a magician.

Māra, *m.* the Evil One; the Tempter; death personified. —**kāyika,** *a.* belonging to the group of Māra deities. —**dheyya,** *nt.* the realm of Māra. —**bandhana,** *nt.* the fetter of Death. —**senā,** *f.* the army of Māra.

Māraka, *a.* bringing death; one who kills.

Māraṇa, *nt.* killing.

Mārāpana, *nt.* causing to be killed.

Mārāpeti (*caus.* of **māreti**), to cause to be killed. *aor.* —**esi.** *pp.* **mārāpita.** *abs.* —**petvā.** *pr. p.* —**penta.**

Mārita, *pp.* of **māreti.**

Mārisa, *a.* (found only in *Voc.*) Sir, Sirs.

Māruta, *m.* the wind.

Māreti (mar + e), to kill *aor.* **māresi.** *pr. p.* **māre[illegible]a.** *abs.* **māretvā.** *inf.* **māretuṃ.**

Māretu. *m.* killer.

Māla, —**laka,** *m.* a circular enclosure; a round yard.

Mālatī, *f.* great-flowered jasmine.

Mālā, *f.* a garland; wreath; flowers; a string of. —**kamma,** *nt.* garland work; a mural drawing. —**kāra,** *m.* garland-maker; a florist. —**gaccha,** *m.* a flowering plant. —**guṇa,** *m.* a string of flowers. —**guḷa,** *nt.* a cluster of flowers. —**cumbaṭaka,** *m.* a chaplet of flowers. —**dhara,** *a.* wearing a garland of flowers. —**dhārī,** —**bhārī,** *a.* wearing a wreath. —**puṭa,** *m.* a container of flowers. —**vaccha,** *nt.* a flower garden or flowery bed.

Mālika, mālī, *a.* having garlands or flowers. —**linī,** *f.* a woman wearing garlands.

Māluta, *m.* the wind.

Māluvā, *f.* a parasite creeper which slowly destroys the tree on which it has grown.

Mālūra, *m.* the marmelos tree.

Mālya, *nt.* a garland.

Māsa, *m.* a month; a kind of bean, *Phaseolus Indica.* —**sika,** *a.* occurring monthly; once a month.

Māsaka, *m.* a small coin, (the value of which is about an anna).

Miga, *m.* a beast; a quadruped; a deer. —**chāpaka,** —**potaka,** *m.* the young of a deer. —**taṇhikā,** *f.* mirage. —**dāya,** *m.* deer-park. —**mada,** *m.* the musk. —**luddaka,** *m.* a deer-hunter.

Migava, *nt.* hunting.

Miginda, *m.* the king of beasts; a lion.

Migī, *f.* a hind.

Micchatta, *nt.* falsehood.

Micchā, *in.* untruth; falsehood; false; wrongly; wrong. —**kammanta,** *m.* wrong conduct or action. —**gahaṇa,** *nt.* wrong conception. —**cāra,** *m.* wrong behaviour. —**cārī,** *a.* one who behaves wrongly. —**diṭṭhi,** *f.* wrong view; heresy. —**vācā,** *f.* wrong speech. —**paṇihita,** *a.* wrongly directed. —**vāyāma,** *m.* wrong effort. —**saṅkappa,** *m.* wrong intention.

Miñja, *nt.* **miñjā,** *f.* kernel; marrow; pith.

Miṇana, *nt.* measurement.

Miṇāti (mi + ṇā), to measure; to weigh; to balance. *aor.* **miṇi,** *pp.* **mita.** *pr. p.* **miṇanta.** *abs.* **miṇitvā.** *inf.* **miṇituṃ.** *pass.* **miṇīyati.**

Mita. *pp.* of the above. **—bhāṇī,** 3. one who speaks moderately.

Mitta, *m. nt.* a friend. **—ddu, —dubbhi, —dūbhī,** *m.* one who betrays his friends; a treacherous person. **—patirūpaka,** *a.* a false friend. **—bheda,** *m.* breaking of friendship or alliance.

Mithu, *in.* alternate; alternately; secretly. **—bheda,** *m.* breaking of alliance.

Mithuna, *nt.* a pair of a male and a female.

Middha, *nt.* torpor; drowsiness. **—dhī,** *a.* torpid; drowsy.

Miyyati, mīyati (mar + ya; **mar** is changed to **miy** and **mī**), to die. *pr. p.* **mīyamāna.**

Milakkha, *m.* a barbarian. **—desa,** *m.* a country where barbarians live.

Milāta (*pp.* of **milāyati**), withered. **—tā,** *f.* fadedness.

Milāyati (milā + ya), to be faded; to wither. *aor.* **—lāyi.** *pr. p.* **milāyamāna.** *abs.* **—yitvā.**

Missa, —saka, *a.* mixed; combined.

Missita, *pp.* of the following.

Misseti (miss + e), to mix. *aor.* **—esi.** *pr. p.* **—senta.** *abs.* **—setvā.**

Mihita, *nt.* a smile.

Mīna, *m.* a fish.

Mīyati, see **Miyyati.**

Mīḷha, *nt.* excrement; dung.

Mukula, *nt.* a bud.

Mukha, *nt.* mouth; face; entrance; opening; front. *adj.* foremost. **—tuṇḍa,** *nt.* beak. **—dvāra,** *nt.* the mouth. **—dhovana,** *nt.* washing of the face; rinsing the mouth. **—puñchana,** *nt.* a towel for wiping the face. **—pūra,** *nt.* a mouthful. *adj.* filling the mouth. **—vaṭṭi,** *f.* brim; rim; edge. **—vaṇṇa,** *m.* the features. **—vikāra,** *m.* contortion of the face; showing faces. **—saṅkocana,** *nt.* distortion of the mouth (as a sign of displeasure). **—saññata,** *a.* controlling one's mouth.

Mukhara, *a.* garrulous; talkative. **—ratā,** *f.* talkativeness.

Mukhādhāna, *nt.* a bridle.

Mukhullokaka, *a.* looking into a person's face.

Mukhodaka, *nt.* water for washing the face.

Mukhya, *a.* chief; foremost; most important.

Mugga, *m.* green peas.

Muggara, *m.* a club; mallet.

Muṅgusa, *m.* a mungoose.

Mucalinda, *m.* the tree *Barringtonia Acutangula.*

Muccati (muc + ya), to become free; to be saved or released. *aor.* **mucci.** *pp.* **mutta, muccita.** *pr. p.* **muccamāna.** *abs.* **—citvā.**

Mucchati (mucch + a), to become unconscious or infatuated; to faint. *aor.* **mucchi.** *pp.* **—chita.** *pr. p.* **—chanta.** *abs.* **—chitvā, mucchiya.**

Mucchana, *nt.* **—nā, mucchā,** *f.* fainting; unconsciousness; infatuation.

Mucchita, see under **Mucchati.**

Muñcaka, *a.* one who releases; emitting.

Muñcati (muc + ŋ - a), to release; to loosen; to deliver; to send off; to emit; to give up. *aor.* **muñci.** *pp.* **mutta, muñcita.** *pr. p.* **—canta, —camāna.** *abs.* **—citvā, —ciya.**

Muñcana, *nt.* releasing; giving up. **—naka,** *a.* emitting.

Muñja, *nt.* a kind of grass used in making slippers, etc.

Muṭṭha (*pp.* of **mussati**), forgotten. **—sacca,** *nt.* forgetfulness. **—ssatī,** *a.* forgetful.

Muṭṭhi, *m.* the fist; a handle. **—ka, —malla,** *m.* a wrestler; boxer. **—yuddha,** *nt.* boxing.

Muṇḍa, *a.* shaven; void of vegetation; bare. **—ka,** 3. a shaveling; shaven-headed. **—cchadda,** *m.* a building with a flat roof. **—ḍatta, muṇḍiya,** *nt.* the fact of being shaven.

Muṇḍeti (muṇḍ + e), to shave. *aor.* **—esi.** *pp.* **—ḍita.** *abs.* **—ḍetvā.**

Muta, *nt.* sense perceptions through nose, tongue and touch.

Mutiṇga, mudiṇga, *m.* a small drum.

Mutimantu, *a.* sensible.

Mutta, *pp.* of **muñcati.**

Mutta, *nt.* the urine. **—karaṇa,** *nt.* the male or female organ. **—vatthi,** *f.* the bladder.

Muttā, *f.* a pearl. **—cāra,** *a.* of loose habits. **—vali,** *f.* **—hāra,** *m.* a string of pearls. **—jāla,** *nt.* a net of pearls.

Mutti, *f.* release; freedom.

Mudita, *a.* glad; satisfied. **—mana,** *a.* with gladdened heart.

Muditā, *f.* sympathy in others' welfare.

Mudu, muduka, *a.* soft; mild; tender. **—citta, —hadaya,** *a.* of a tender heart. **—jātika,** *a.* of tender nature. **—tā,** *f.* **—tta,** *nt.* softness; plasticity. **—bhūta,** *a.* supple; malleable.

Muddaṅkaṇa, *nt.* printing.

Muddā, *f.* a seal; a stamp; an impression; gesture; printing. **—paka,** *m.* a printer. **—pana,** *nt.* printing. **—yanta,** *nt.* a printing press.

Muddāpeti (*Deno.* from **muddā**), to print. *aor.* **—esi.** *pp.* **—pita.** *abs.* **—petvā.**

Muddikā, *f.* a seal ring; signet ring.

Muddíkā, *f.* grape-vine; grapes. **—āsava,** *m.* wine.

Muddha, *a.* foolish; bewildered. **—dhātuka,** *a.* foolish in nature. **—tā,** *f.* foolishness.

Muddhā, *m.* the head; top; summit. **—dhaja,** *a.* lingual. *m.* hair. **—dhipāta,** *m.* splitting of the head. **—vasitta,** *a.* properly anointed (king).

Mudhā, *in.* gratis; for nothing.

Munāti (mun + a), to know; to understand. *aor.* **muni.** *pp.* **muta.**

Munī, *m.* a monk. **—nda,** *m.* the great sage.

Muyhati (muh + ya), to forget; to become dull; to infatuate. *aor.* **muyhi.** *pp.* **mūḷha.** *pr. p.* **—hamāna.** *abs.* **—hitvā.**

Muraja, *m.* a tamborine.

Murumurāyati (*Onom.* from **muru-muru**), to bite up with a craking sound.

Musala, *m.* a pestle. **—salī,** 3. with a pestle in hand.

Musā, *in.* falsehood; lie. **—vāda,** *m.* lying.

Mussati (mus + ya), to forget; to pass into oblivion. *aor.* **mussi.** *pp.* **muṭṭha.** *abs.* **mussitvā.**

Muhutta, *m. nt.* a moment; a minute. **—ttena,** *ad.* in a moment. **—ttika,** *a.* existing only for a moment. *m.* an astrologer.

Muḷāla, *nt.* lotus root. **—puppha,** *nt.* lotus flower.

Mūga, *a.* dumb; a dumb person.

Mūla, *nt.* root; money; cash; foot; bottom; origin; cause; foundation; beginning. **—kanda,** *m.* a bulbous root. **—bīja,** *nt.* plant germinating from root.

Mūlaka, *m.* the radish. *adj.* (in cpds.) being conditioned by; originating in.

Mūlika, *a.* fundamental; elementary.

Mūlya, *nt.* payment; wages.

Mūsā, *f.* a crucible.

Mūsika, *m.* **—sikā,** *f.* a rat; mouse. **—cchinna,** *a.* gnawed by mice. **—vacca,** *nt.* mice-dung.

Mūḷha (*pp.* of **muyhati**), gone astray; confused; erring; foolish.

Me (*dat.* and *gen. sing.* of **amha**), to me; my; mine.

Mekhalā, *f.* a girdle for women.

Megha, *m.* rain; a cloud. **—nāda,** *m.* a thunder. **—vaṇṇa,** *a.* cloud-coloured, i.e. black.

Mecaka, *a.* black; dark blue.

Mejjha, *a.* pure.

Meṇḍa, —ka, *m.* a ram; sheep.

Mettacitta, *a.* having a benevolent heart.

Mettā, *f.* amity; benevolence. **—kammaṭṭhāna,** *nt.* **—bhāvanā,** *f.* cultivation of benevolence. **—yanā,** *f.* friendly feeling. **—vihārī,** 3. abiding in kindliness.

Mettāyati (*Deno.* from **mettā**), to feel friendly; to be benevolent. *aor.* **—tāyi.** *abs.* **—yitvā.** *pr. p.* **—yanta.**

Metti, see **Mettā.**

Metteyya-nātha, *m.* the coming Buddha, Metteyya.

Methuna, *nt.* sexual intercourse; coupling **—dhamma,** *m.* same as the above.

Meda, *m.* the fat. **—kathālikā,** *f.* a saucepan for frying fat. **—vaṇṇa,** *a.* of the colour of fat.

Medinī, *f.* the earth.

Medha, *m.* a religious sacrifice.

Medhaga, *m.* a quarrel.

Medhā, *f.* wisdom. **—vī,** 3. the wise. **—vinī,** *f.* a wise woman.

Meraya, *nt.* fermented liquor.

Meru, *m.* name of the highest mountain in the world.

Melana, *nt.* a gathering; meeting.

Mesa, *m.* a ram.

Meha, *m.* a urinary affliction.

Mehana, *nt.* the male or female organ.

Mokkha, *m.* release; freedom; deliverance; the final release. **—ka,** 3. one who releases. **—magga,** *m.* the path leading to salvation.

Mokkhati (mokkh + a), to be free or saved.

Mogha, *a.* empty; vain; useless. **—purisa,** *m.* a stupid or useless person.

Moca, *m.* the plantain tree.

Mocana, *nt.* setting free; discharging.

Mocāpana, *nt.* causation of one's freedom; deliverance.

Moceti (muc + e), to deliver; to set free; to release. *aor.* **—esi.** *pp.* **mocita.** *pr. p.* **mocenta.** *abs.* **mocetvā, mociya.** *inf.* **mocetuṃ.**

Modaka, *m.* a globular sweetmeat.

Modati (mud + a), to rejoice; to be happy. *aor.* **modi.** *pp.* **modita.** *pr. p.* **modamāna.** *abs.* **moditvā.**

Modana, *nt.* **—nā,** *f.* rejoicing; enjoyment.

Mona, *nt.* wisdom; self-possession; silence.

Moneyya, *nt.* moral perfection.

Momuha, *a.* dull; silly; bewildered.

Mora, *m.* a peacock. **—piñja,** *nt.* peacock's tail.

Mosa, *m.* **mosana,** *nt.* theft.

Mosavajja, *nt.* untruth.

Moha, *m.* stupidity; delusion. **—kkhaya,** *m.* destruction of ignorance. **—carita,** *a.* of foolish habits. **—tama,** *m.* the darkness of ignorance. **—nīya,** **—neyya,** *a.* leading to infatuation.

Mohana, *nt.* making dull; enticement; allurement. **—naka,** *a.* bewildering; leading astray.

Moheti (muh + e), to deceive; to befool; to delude. *aor.* **—esi.** *pp.* **mohita.** *abs.* **mohetvā.**

Y.

Ya, *relative pron.* which; what; whatever.

Yakana, *nt.* the liver.

Yakkha, *m.* a demon. **—gaṇa,** *m.* a multitude of demons. **—gāha,** *m.* possession by a demon. **—tta,** *nt.* condition of a demon. **—bhūta,** *a.* born as a demon. **—samāgama,** *m.* meeting of the yakkhas. **—ādhipa,** *m.* the king of demons.

Yakkhinī, yakkhī, *f.* a demoness.

Yagghe, *a.* hortative particle used in addressing a superior person.

Yajati (yaj + a), to sacrifice; to give away alms or gifts. *aor.* **yaji.** *pp.* **yiṭṭha, yajita.** *abs.* **yajitvā.** *pr. p.* **yajamāna.**

Yajana, *nt.* the act of sacrificing; distribution of alms.

Yañña, *m.* see **Yāga.** **—sāmī,** *m.* the owner of a sacrifice. **—āvāṭa,** *m.* the sacrificial pit. **—ūpanīta,** *a.* brought for the sacrifice.

Yaṭṭhi, *m. f.* a stick; staff; a pole; walking stick. **—koṭi,** *f.* the end of a staff. **—madhukā,** *f.* the liquorice.

Yata (*pp.* of **yameti**), checked; controlled; restrained.

Yatati (yat + a), to exert oneself; to strive. *aor.* **yati.**

Yatana, *nt.* endeavour.

Yati, *m.* a monk.

Yato, *in.* from where; whence; since; because; on account of which.

Yattaka, *a.* however much.

Yattha, yatra, *ad.* wherever; where.

Yathatta, *nt.* reality; true nature.

Yathariva (yathā + iva), *in.* just as.

Yathā, *ad.* as; like; in relation to; according to; in whatever way; just as. **—kammaŋ,** *ad.* according to one's actions. **—kāmaŋ,** *ad.* according to one's wish; at random. **—kāmakārī,** 3. one who acts according to his wishes. **—kārī,** *a.* as he does. **—kāla,** *m.* suitable time. **—kālaŋ,** *ad.* at the proper time. **—kkamaŋ,** *ad.* in order; in succession. **—ṭhita,** *a.* as it was; just as he stood. **—tatha,** *a.*

true; real. —**tathaŋ**, *ad.* according to truth. —**dhammaŋ**, *ad.* according to the Law. —**dhota**, *a.* as if it were washed. —**nusiṭṭhaŋ**, *ad.* in accordance with the advice. —**nubhāvaŋ** *ad.* according to one's ability. —**pasādaŋ**, *ad.* according to one's gratification. —**pūrita**, *a.* as full as could be. —**phāsuka**, *a.* comfortable. —**balaŋ**, *ad.* according to one's strength. —**bhataŋ**, *ad.* as it was carried. —**bhirantaŋ**, *a.* as long as one likes. —**bhucca**, —**bhūta**, *a.* real; evident; in conformity with the truth. —**bhūtaŋ**, *ad.* in truth; in reality; in its real essence. —**rahaŋ**, *ad.* as is fit or proper. —**ruciŋ**, *ad.* according to liking. —**vato**, *ad.* in its real essence. —**vidhiŋ**, *ad.* duly; fitly. —**vihita**, *a.* as arranged. —**vuḍḍhaŋ**, *ad.* according to seniority.—**vutta**, *a.* aforesaid. —**vuttaŋ**, *ad.* as stated before.—**saka**, *a.* according to one's ownership. —**sakaŋ**, *ad.* each his own. —**sattiŋ**, *ad.* according to one's power. —**saddhaŋ**, *ad.* according to one's devotion. —**sukhaŋ**, *ad.* comfortably.

Yathicchitaŋ, *ad.* as one liked.

Yadā, *ad.* whenever; when.

Yadi, *in.* if; however. —**idaŋ**, *in.* which is this; that is; namely.

Yanta, *nt.* a machine. —**nāḷi**, *f.* a mechanical pipe —**mutta**, *a.* thrown or shot through a machine. —**yutta**, *a.* connected with a machine.

Yantika, *m.* a mechanic.

Yama, *m.* the ruler of the kingdom of the dead. —**dūta**, *m.* Death's messenger. —**purisa**, *m.* torturers in the hell. —**rāja**, *m.* same as **yama**, —**loka**, *m.* the world of the dead.

Yamaka, *a.* double; twin. *nt.* a pair; couple. —**sāla**, *m.* twin Sal trees.

Yava, *m.* barley. —**sūka**, *m.* the beard of barley.

Yavasa, *m.* a kind of grass.

Yasa, *m. nt.* (mano-group), fame; glory; success; retinue. —**dāyaka**, *a.* giver of wealth or repute. —**mahatta**, *nt.* greatness of fame or wealth; a high position. —**lābha**, *m.* gain of fame or wealth.

Yasodhara, *a.* famous.

Yasoladdha, *a.* got through fame.

Yahaŋ, **yahiŋ**, *ad.* where; wherever.

Yaŋ (*nt. sin.* of **ya**), which; whatever thing. *ad.* because of.

Yā (*f. sin.* of **ya**), whatever woman.

Yāga, *m.* sacrifice; alms-giving.

Yāgu, *f.* rice-gruel.

Yācaka, *m.* a beggar; one who requests. *f.* **yācikā**.

Yācati (yāc + a), to beg; to ask; to entreat. *aor.* **yāci**. *pp.* **yācita**. *pr. p.* **yācanta**, —**māna**. *abs.* **yācitvā**. *inf.* **yācituŋ**.

Yācana, *nt.* begging; entreaty. —**naka**, *a.* begging.

Yācayoga *a.* accessible to begging; ready to comply with another's request.

Yacitaka, *nt.* a borrowed thing.

Yājaka, *m.* one who causes to sacrifice.

Yāta (*pp.* of **yāti**), gone; proceeded.

Yāti (yā + a), to go on; to proceed. *abs.* **yātvā**.

Yātrā, *f.* travel; voyage; support of life.

Yāthāva, *a.* exact ; definite. **—vato**, *ad.* exactly.

Yādisa, **—saka**, *a.* whichever ; whatever ; which like.

Yāna, *nt.* a carriage ; vehicle ; going. **—ka**, *nt.* a small carriage. **—gata**, *a.* got up in a carriage. **—bhūmi**, *f.* a road accessible to a carriage.

Yānī, 3. one who drives in a carriage. **—kata**, *a.* made a habit of ; mastered.

Yāpana, *nt.* sustenance ; nourishment ; keeping up of the body. **—panīya**, *a.* sufficient for supporting one's life.

Yāpeti (yā + āpe), to nourish ; to keep up ; to support one's life. *aor.* **yāpesi**. *pp.* **yāpita**. *pr. p.* **yāpenta**. *abs.* **yāpetvā**.

Yāma, *m.* a watch of the night ; $\frac{1}{3}$ of a night. **—kālika**, *a.* something allowed to be taken by a B. monk after noon and in the night.

Yāva, *in.* up to ; as far as ; so far that. **—kālika**, *a.* temporary. **—jīva**, *a.* life-long. **—jīvaŋ**, *ad.* for the length of one's life. **—jīvika**, *a.* existing as long as one's life lasts. **—taka**, *a.* as much as ; as many as ; as far as. **—tatiyaŋ**, *ad.* up to the third time.

Yāvatā, *in.* as far as ; in comparison with. **—yukaŋ**, *ad.* as long as life lasts. **—vatihaŋ**, *ad.* as many days as.

Yiṭṭha (*pp.* of **yajati**), bestowed ; sacrificed.

Yuga, *nt.* a yoke ; a pair ; a couple ; an age or generation. **—nta**, *m.* the end of an age or generation. **—ggāha**, *m.* imperiousness ; rivalry ; competition. **—ggāhī**, 3. a rival ; a competent. **—cchidda**, *nt.* the hole of a yoke. **—naddha**, **—nandha**, *a.* congruous ; harmonious ; connected to a yoke. **—matta**, *a.* the distance of a yoke.

Yugala, **—laka**, *nt.* a pair or couple.

Yujjhati (yudh + ya), to fight ; to make war. *aor.* **yujjhi**. *pp.* **yujjhita**. *pr. p.* **—jhanta**, **—jhamāna**, *abs.* **yujjhitvā**, **yujjhiya**, *inf.* **—jhituŋ**.

Yuñjati (yuj + ŋ - a), to join with ; to engage in ; to endeavour. *aor.* **yuñji**. *pp.* **yutta**. *pr. p.* **—janta**. **—jamāna**. *abs.* **—jitvā**. *pt. p.* **—jitabba**.

Yutta (*pp.* of the above), yoked ; harnessed ; connected with ; given to ; engaged in ; proper. **—ka**, *a.* proper ; fit. **—kārī**, *a.* acting properly or rightly.

Yutti, *f.* justice ; fitness. **—tito**, *ad.* in accordance with justice.

Yuddha, *nt.* fight ; war ; battle. **—bhūmi**, *f.* **—maṇḍala**, *nt.* battle-field.

Yuva, *m.* a youth. (*nom. sin.* **yuvā**).

Yuvatī, *f.* a young woman.

Yūtha, *m.* a flock or herd of animals. **—jeṭṭha**, **—pa**, *m.* leader of a herd.

Yūpa, *m.* a sacrificial post.

Yūsa, *m.* juice ; soup.

Yena, *ad.* because of.

Yebhuyya, *a.* numerous ; most ; abundant. **—yyena**, *ad.* almost all ; mostly.

Yeva, *in.* (*emphatic particle*), even ; just ; also.

Yo (*nom. sin.* of **ya**), any person ; whoever.

Yoga, *m.* connection ; bond ; endeavour ; conjunction ; attachment ; effort ; mixture. **—kkhema**, *m.* release from the attachments. **—yutta**, *a.* bound by attachments. **—āva-**

cara, *m.* one who practises spiritual exercise. —**ātiga,** *a.* one who has conquered the bond of rebirth.

Yogī, see **Yogāvacara.**

Yogga, *a.* suitable ; fit for. *nt.* a vehicle ; a contrivance.

Yojaka, 3. one who joints, connects or yokes ; a composer.

Yojana, *nt.* yoking ; application ; a measure of length, which is about 7 miles.

Yojanā, *f.* construction ; suggestion ; proposal ; an exegesis.

Yojanika, *a.* having a **yojana** in extent.

Yojāpeti, *caus.* of **yojeti.**

Yojeti (yuj + e), to yoke ; to harness ; to combine ; to unite ; to mix ; to apply ; to prepare; to urge. *aor.* **yojesi.** *pp.* **yojita.** *pr. p.* —**jenta.** *abs.* **yojetvā, yojiya.**

Yotta, *nt.* a string ; a twine.

Yodha, *m.* a soldier. —**ājīva,** a warrior.

Yodheti (yudh + e), to fight ; to make war. *aor.* —**esi.** *pp.* —**dhita.** *abs.* —**dhetvā.**

Yoni, *f.* origin ; realm of existence ; the female organ ; knowledge. —**so,** *ad.* wisely ; properly ; judiciously . —**somanasikāra,** *m.* proper consideration.

Yobbana, yobbañña, *nt.* youth. —**mada,** *m.* the pride of youth.

R.

Rakkhaka, 3. one who guards, observes or keeps ; a guard.

Rakkhati (rakkh + a), to protect ; to guard ; to observe ; to preserve. *aor.* **rakkhi.** *pp.* —**khita.** *pr. p.* —**khanta.** *abs.* —**khitvā.** *pt. p.* —**khitabba.**

Rakkhana, *nt.* protection ; observance. —**naka,** *a.* observing ; guarding.

Rakkhā, *f.* protection ; safety ; shelter.

Rakkhiya, *a.* to be protected.

Raṅga, *m.* 1. dye ; paint ; 2. a stage ; theatre ; a play. —**kāra,** *m.* a dyer ; an actor. —**jāta,** *nt.* various kinds of dye. —**ratta,** *a.* dyed with. —**ājīva,** *m.* a painter or dyer.

Racayati (rac + aya), to arrange ; to compose ; to prepare. *aor.* —**yi.** *pp.* **racita.** *abs.* **racitvā.**

Racanā, *f.* arrangement ; a treatise.

Racchā, *f.* a street.

Raja, *m. nt.* (mano-group), dust ; dirt ; pollen ; defilement ; impurity. —**kkha,** *a.* (in cpds.) having defilement. —**kkhandha,** *m.* a cloud of dust.

Rajaka, *m.* a washer man.

Rajata, *nt.* silver. —**paṭṭa,** a silver plate or sheet.

Rajati (raj + a), to dye. *aor.* **raji.** *abs.* **rajitvā.** *pt. p.* **rajitabba.**

Rajana, *nt.* colouring ; dye ; dyeing. —**kamma,** *nt.* dyeing.

Rajanī, *f.* night.

Rajanīya, *a.* enticing ; apt to rouse excitement.

Rajojalla, *nt.* muddy dirt.

Rajoharaṇa, *nt.* removal of dirt ; a duster.

Rajja, *nt.* kingdom ; kingship. —**siri,** *f.* sovereignty. —**sīmā,** *f.* the border of a kingdom.

Rajjati (raj + ya), to find pleasure in ; to be attached to. *aor.* **rajji.** *pp.* **ratta.** *pr. p.* **rajjanta.** *abs.* **rajjitvā.**

Rajjana, *nt.* defilement.

Rajju, *f.* a rope ; a cord. —**gāhaka**, *m.* a land-surveyer.

Rañjati (rañj + a), to find delight in. *aor.* **rañji.** *pp.* **rañjita** or **ratta.** *pr. p.* —**janta**, —**jamāna.** *abs.* —**jitvā.**

Rañjeti (rañj + e), to give pleasure ; to colour ; to dye. *aor.* —**esi.** *pp.* —**jita.** *pr.p.* —**jenta.** *abs.* —**jetvā.**

Raṭṭha, *nt.* a country. —**piṇḍa**, *m.* food obtained from the people. —**vāsī**, —**vāsika**, 3. an inhabitant of a country.

Raṭṭhika, *a.* belonging to a country ; an official.

Raṇa, *nt.* war ; battle ; sin ; fault. —**ñjaha**, *a.* avoiding the disturbance of passions.

Rata (*pp.* of **ramati**), delighting in ; devoted to.

Ratana, *nt.* a gem ; precious thing ; a cubit. —**ttaya**, *nt.* the three precious things, *viz.* the Buddha, His doctrine, and His community. —**vara**, *nt.* the best of gems.

Ratanika, *a.* (in cpds.) having so many cubits in length or breadth.

Rati, *f.* attachment ; love ; liking for. —**kīḷā**, *f.* sexual intercourse.

Ratta, *a.* red. *nt.* blood. *pp.* dyed ; coloured ; infatuated with lust. —**kkha**, *a.* with red eyes. —**candana**, *nt.* red sandal-wood. —**phalā**, *f.* a creeper having red oval fruits. —**paduma**, *nt.* red lotus. —**maṇi**, *m.* a ruby. —**ātisāra**, *m.* the bloody diarrhoea.

Rattaññū, *a.* of long standing.

Rattandhakāra, *m.* nightly darkness.

Ratti, *f.* night. —**kkhaya**, *m.* the vane of the night. —**khitta**, *a.* shot in the night. —**bhāga**, *m.* night-time. —**bhojana**, *nt.* the supper.

Rattūparata, *a.* abstaining from eating at night.

Ratha, *m.* a carriage ; chariot. —**kāra**, *m.* chariot-maker ; carpenter. —**ṅga**, *nt.* parts of a carriage. —**gutti**, *f.* fender of a carriage. —**cakka**, *nt.* chariot-wheel. —**pañjara**, *m.* the body of a chariot. —**yuga**, *nt.* the chariot pole. —**reṇu**, *m.* a mote of dust. —**ācariya**, *m.* a charioteer ; driver. —**āṇīka**, *nt.* a group of war chariots. —**āroha**, *m.* a warrior in a chariot.

Rathika, *m.* one who fights in a chariot.

Rathikā, *f.* street.

Randha, *nt.* an opening ; cleft ; a weak spot ; fault. —**gavesī**, *m.* one who finds fault or weak points.

Randhaka, *m.* a cook.

Randhana, *nt.* cooking ; boiling.

Randheti (randh + e), to boil or cook. *aor.* —**esi.** *pp.* —**dhita.** *abs.* —**dhetvā.**

Ramaṇī, *f.* a woman.

Ramaṇīya, *a.* delightful ; charming.

Ramati (ram + a), to delight in ; to enjoy oneself. *aor.* **rami.** *pp.* **rata.** *pr. p.* **ramanta.** —**māna.** *abs.* **ramitvā**, *inf.* **ramituṃ.**

Ramaṇa, *nt.* enjoyment.

Rambhā, *f.* plantain tree.

Ramma, *a.* charming ; enjoyable.

Rava, *m.* sound ; roar ; cry. —**na**, *nt.* roaring ; howling.

Ravati (ru + a), to make a noise; to cry. *aor.* **ravi.** *pr. p.* **ravanta, ravamāna,** *abs.* **ravitvā.** *pp.* **ravita, ruta.**

Ravi, *m.* the sun. **—haŋsa,** *m.* a kind of bird.

Rasa, *m.* taste ; juice ; flavour ; quick-silver. **—gga,** *nt.* the finest quality of taste. **—ñjana,** *nt.* a sort of collyrium. **—taṇhā,** *f.* the thirst for taste. **—vatī,** *f.* kitchen. **—haraṇī,** *f.* the taste conductor.

Rasaka, *m.* a cook.

Rasmi, *f.* a cord ; a rein ; ray of light.

Rassa, *a.* short ; dwarfish ; stunted. **—tta,** *nt.* shortness.

Rahada, *m.* a lake.

Rahassa, *nt.* a secret.

Rahābhāva, *m.* the state of not being secret.

Rahita, *a.* deprived of ; without.

Raho, *in.* secretly ; in secrecy ; a lonely place. **—gata,** *a.* gone to a lonely place.

Raŋsi, *f.* light ; a ray. **—mantu,** *m.* the sun. *adj.* radiant.

Rāga, *m.* colour ; hue ; dye ; lust ; attachment. **—kkhaya,** *m.* destruction of lust. **—ggi,** *m.* the fire of lust. **—carita,** *a.* of lustful behaviour. **—ratta,** *a.* infatuated with lust.

Rāgī, *a.* lustful.

Rāja, *m.* king. **—kakudhabhaṇḍa,** *nt.* ensign of royalty ; regalia. **—kathā,** *f.* talk about kings. **—kammika,** *m.* a government official. **—kumāra,** *m.* a prince. **—kumārī, —kaññā,** *f.* a princess. **—kula,** *nt.* royal family ; king's palace. **—geha, —bhavana, —mandira,** *nt.* king's palace. **—ṅgaṇa,** *nt.* the courtyard of a palace. **—daṇḍa,** *m.* punishment ordered by a king. **—dāya,** *m.* a royal gift. **—dūta,** *m.* a king's messenger or envoy. **—devī,** *f.* a consort of a king. **—dhamma,** *m.* duty of a king. **—dhāni,** *f.* the royal city. **—dhītu, —puttī,** *f.* a king's daughter. **—nivesana,** *nt.* king's abode. **—ntepura,** *nt.* royal harem ; palace grounds. **—parisā,** *f.* retinue of a king ; a royal assembly. **—putta,** *m.* a prince. **—purisa,** *m.* one who is in the king's service. **—porisa,** *nt.* the government service. **—bali,** *m.* a tax to be given to a king. **—bhaṭa,** *m.* a soldier. **—bhaya,** *nt.* fear coming from a king. **—bhogga,** *a.* fit to be used by a king. **—mahāmatta,** *m.* the prime minister. **—mahesī,** *f.* a queen. **—muddā,** *f.* the royal seal. **—ratha,** *m.* the state carriage. **—vara,** *m.* a noble king. **—vallabha,** *a.* familiar with a king ; a king's favourite. **—sampatti,** *f.* splendour of a king.

Rājañña, *m.* a man of the warrior caste.

Rājati (rāj + a), to shine. *aor.* **rāji.** *pp.* **rājita.** *pr. p.* **rājamāna.**

Rājatta, *nt.* kingship.

Rājahaŋsa, *m.* royal swan (whose beak and feet are red).

Rājāṇā, *f.* king's command.

Rājānubhāva, *m.* the pomp or majesty of a king.

Rājāmacca, *m.* a royal minister.

Rājāyatana, *m.* the tree *Buchanania Latifolia.*

Rāji, *f.* a row ; line ; range ; dissension.

Rājita, *pp.* resplendent ; shining.

Rājiddhi, *f.* royal power.

Rājinī, *f.* a queen.

Rājisi, *m.* a royal seer.

Rājupaṭṭhāna, *nt.* attendance on a king.

Rājuyyāna, *nt.* a royal garden.

Rājorodha, *m.* a king's harem ; a royal concubine.

Rāmaṇeyyaka, *a.* pleasant ; agreeable ; lovely.

Rāva, *m.* a cry ; howling ; noise.

Rāsi, *m.* a heap ; quantity. **—vaḍḍhaka,** *m.* the controller of revenues.

Rāhaseyyaka, *a.* secluded ; secret.

Rāhu, *m.* name of an Asura king ; an eclipse. **—mukha,** *nt.* the mouth of Rāhu ; a certain punishment.

Riñcati (ric + ŋ - a), to neglect ; to abandon ; to empty. *aor.* **riñci.** *pp.* **ritta.** *abs.* **riñcitvā.** *pr. p.* **riñcamāna.**

Ritta (*pp.* of the above), devoid ; empty ; rid of. **—muṭṭhi,** *m.* an empty fist. **—hattha,** *a.* empty-handed.

Rukkha, *m.* a tree. **—gahaṇa,** *nt.* a thicket of trees. **—devatā,** *f.* a tree-sprite. **—mūla,** *nt.* the foot of a tree. **—mūlika,** 3. one who lives at the foot of a tree. **—susira,** *nt.* a hollow in a tree.

Ruci, *f.* liking ; choice ; inclination. **—ka,** *a.* (in cpds.) having the inclination.

Rucira, *a.* pleasant ; agreeable ; beautiful.

Ruccati (ruc + ya), to find delight in ; to like. *aor.* **rucci.** *pp.* **ruccita.** *abs.* **ruccitvā.**

Ruccana, *nt.* liking ; choice. **—naka,** *a.* pleasing ; satisfying.

Rujati (ruj + a), to feel pain ; to ache. *aor.* **ruji.** *abs.* **rujitvā.**

Rujana, *nt.* **rujā,** *f.* pain ; affliction. **—naka,** *a.* aching.

Rujjhati (rudh + ya), to be obstructed or prevented. *aor.* **rujjhi.** *pp.* **ruddha.**

Ruṭṭha (*pp.* of **russati**), vexed ; enraged.

Ruṇṇa (*pp.* of **rudati**), crying ; weeping ; lamentation.

Ruta, *nt.* cry of an animal.

Rudati (rud + a), to cry ; to lament. *aor.* **rudi.** *pp.* **rudita, ruta.** *pr. p.* **rudanta, —māna,** *abs.* **ruditvā.**

Rudammukha, *a.* with tearful face.

Ruddha, see under **Rujjhati.**

Rudhira, *nt.* blood.

Rundhati (rudh + ŋ - a), to prevent ; to obstruct ; to besiege ; to imprison. *aor.* **—dhi.** *pp.* **rundhita, ruddha.** *abs.* **—dhitvā.**

Rundhana, *nt.* prevention ; imprisonment.

Ruppati (rup + ya), to be vexed or changed. *aor.* **ruppi.** *pr. p.* **ruppamāna.**

Ruru, *m.* a kind of deer.

Ruha, *a.* (in cpds.) growing ; rising up ; ascending.

Ruhira, *nt.* blood.

Rūpa, *nt.* form ; figure ; image ; object of the eye ; a material composition. **—ka,** *nt.* a small figure ; a simile. **—taṇhā,** *f.* craving after form. **—dassana,** *nt.* seeing of an object. **—bhava,** *m.* the Brahma world. **—rāga,** *m.* desire to be born in the world of form. **—vantu,** *a.* handsome. **—sampatti,** *f.* beauty. **—siri,** *f.* personal splendour. **—ārammaṇa,** *nt.* a visible thing. **—āvacara,** *a.* belonging to the world of form.

Rūpiya, *nt.* silver ; a silver coin. **—maya,** *a.* made of silver.

Rūpinī, *f.* a beautiful woman.

Rūpī, *a.* having material qualities.

Rūpūpajīvinī, *f.* a harlot.

Rūḷha, *pp.* of the following.

Rūhati (ruh + a), to grow ; to ascend ; to heal (a wound). *aor.* **rūhi.**

Rūhana, *nt.* growing ; ascending ; rising.

Recana, *nt.* emission.

Reṇu, *m. f.* dust ; pollen.

Roga, *m.* disease ; illness. —**niḍḍa,** —**nīḷa,** *a.* the seat of disease. —**hārī,** *m.* a physician. —**ātura,** *a.* a sick person.

Rogī, 3. a patient.

Rocati (ruc + a), to shine. *aor.* **roci.**

Rocana, *nt.* liking ; choice ; shining.

Roceti (ruc + e), to give one's consent ; to like. *aor.* —**esi.** *pp.* **rocita.** *abs.* **rocetvā.**

Rodati (rud + a), to cry ; to lament. *aor.* **rodi.** *pp.* **rodita.** *pr. p.* **rodanta,** —**māna.** *abs.* **roditvā.** *inf.* **roditu ŋ.**

Rodha, *m.* **rodhana,** *nt.* obstruction ; prevention.

Ropa, ropaka, 3. a planter ; cultivator.

Ropita, *pp.* of the following.

Ropeti (rup + e), to plant ; to cultivate. *aor.* —**esi.** *pr. p.* **ropenta, ropayamāna.** *abs.* **ropetvā, ropiya.**

Roma, *nt.* hair on the body. —**ñca,** *m.* horripilation or bristling of hair.

Romaka, *a.* Roman.

Romanthati (?), to chew the cud ; to munch. *aor.* —**nthi.** *abs.* —**nthayitvā.**

Romanthana, *nt.* ruminating ; munching.

Roruva, *m.* name of a hell.

Rosa, *m.* anger. —**ka,** *a.* making angry.

Rosanā, *f.* enragement.

Roseti (rus + e), to make angry ; to irritate. *aor.* **rosesi.** *pp.* **rosita.** *abs.* **rosetvā.**

Rohati, see **Ruhati.**

Rohita, *a.* red. *m.* a kind of deer ; a kind of fish. —**maccha,** *m.* a salmon.

L.

Lakāra, *m.* a sail.

Lakuṇṭaka, *a.* dwarf.

Lakkha, *nt.* a mark ; a target ; a stake at gambling ; a mark in casting up accounts ; a hundred thousand.

Lakkhaṇa, *nt.* a sign ; mark ; characteristic ; a prognosticative mark ; a quality. —**pāṭhaka,** 3. an expert in interpreting signs. —**sampatti,** *f.* excellency of marks. —**sampanna,** *a.* endowed with auspicious signs.

Lakkhika, *a.* fortunate.

Lakkhita, *pp.* of **lakkheti.**

Lakkhī, *f.* good luck ; prosperity ; the deity of wealth.

Lakkheti (lakkh + e), to mark ; to distinguish ; to characterize. *aor.* —**esi.** *pp.* —**khita.** *abs.* —**khetvā.**

Laguḷa, *m.* a cudgle.

Lagga, *a.* stuck ; attached to.

Laggati (lag + a), to stick ; to attach ; to adhere to ; to hang from. *aor.* **laggi,** *pp.* **laggita.**

Laggana, *nt.* sticking ; attachment ; hanging from.

Laggeti (lug + e), to hang on ; to stick to. *aor.* —**esi.** *pp.* **laggita.** *abs.* **laggetvā.**

Laṅgī, *f.* a bolt ; a bar.

Laṅgula, *nt.* tail.

Laṅghaka, 3. a jumper; an acrobat.

Laṅghati (lagh + ŋ - a), to jump over; to hop. *aor.* **laṅghi.** *abs.* —**ghitvā.**

Laṅghana, *nt.* jumping; hopping.

Laṅghāpeti, *caus.* of **laṅghati.**

Laṅghī, *m.* a jumper; a threshold.

Laṅgheti (lagh + e), to jump over; to discharge; to transgress. *aor.* —**esi.** *pp.* **laṅghita.** *abs.* —**ghetvā.**

Lajjati (lajj + a), to be ashamed or abashed. *aor.* **lajji.** *pp.* **lajjita.** *pr. p.* **lajjanta,** —**māna.** *abs.* **lajjitvā.**

Lajjā, *f.* shame; bashfulness.

Lajjāpana, *nt.* putting to shame.

Lajjāpeti (*caus.* of **lajjati**), to make ashamed. *aor.* —**esi.** *pp.* —**pita.**

Lajjitabbaka, *a.* fit to be ashamed.

Lajjī, *a.* feeling shame; modest; conscientious.

Lacchati = **labhissati,** *fut.* of **labhati.**

Lañca, *m.* bribe. —**khādaka,** *a.* receiving bribe. —**dāna,** *nt.* bribery.

Lañcha, *m.* —**chana,** *nt.* a mark; an imprint.

Lañchaka, 3. one who marks or stamps.

Lañchati (lanch + a), **lañcheti** (lanch + e), to mark; to stamp; to seal. *aor.* **lañchi.** —**chesi.** *pp.* **lañchita.** *abs.* —**chitvā,** —**chetvā.**

Laṭukikā, *f.* the Indian quail.

Laṭṭhi, —**ṭhikā,** *f.* a staff; a young tree.

Laṇḍa, *m.* **laṇḍikā,** *f.* dung of animals.

Latā, *f.* a creeper. —**kamma,** *nt.* creeper-work (in painting).

Laddha (*pp.* of **labhati**), obtained; received. —**ka,** *a.* charming; pleasant. —**bba,** *pt. p.* what should be received. —**bhāva,** *m.* the fact of receiving or attainment. —**ssāda,** *a.* being refreshed; recovered from a trouble.

Laddhā, laddhāna, *abs.* (from **labhati**), having got, received, or attained.

Laddhi, *f.* a view or theory. —**ka,** *a.* having a certain view.

Laddhuŋ (= **labhituŋ**), *inf.* to get; to receive.

Lapati (lap + a), to speak; to talk; to prattle. *aor.* **lapi.** *pp.* **lapita.** *abs.* **lapitvā.**

Lapana, *nt.* the mouth; speech. —**ja,** *m.* a tooth.

Lapanā, *f.* prattling; flattering.

Labuja, *m.* the breadfruit tree.

Labbhati (labh + ya), to be obtained or received. *pp.* **laddha.** *pr. p.* **labbhamāna.**

Labbhā, *in.* possible; allowable; may be obtained.

Labhati (labh + a), to get; to obtain; to attain. *aor.* **labhi.** *pp.* **laddha.** *pr. p.* **labhanta.** *abs.* **labhitvā, laddhā.** *inf.* **labhituŋ, laddhuŋ.**

Lamba, *a.* hanging from; pendulous. —**ka,** *nt.* that which is hanging down; a pendulum.

Lambati (lab + ŋ - a), to hang down; to suspend. *aor.* **lambi.** *pr. p.* —**banta,** —**bamāna.** *abs.* —**bitvā.**

Lambeti (*caus.* of the above), to cause to hang or suspend. *aor.* —**esi.** *pp.* **lambita.** *abs.* —**betvā.**

Laya, *m.* a brief measure of time.

Lalanā, *f.* a woman.

Lalita, *nt.* grace ; charm.
Lava, *m.* a drop.
Lavaṅga, *nt.* the cloves.
Lavaṇa, *nt.* salt.
Lavana, *nt.* mowing ; reaping.
Lasati (las + a), to shine ; to play. *aor.* **lasi.**
Lasikā, *f.* synovic fluid.
Lasī, *f.* brains.
Lasuṇa, *nt.* garlic.
Lahu, *a.* light ; quick. *nt.* a short vowel. —**ka,** *a.* light ; trifling ; buoyant. —**kaŋ,** *ad.* quickly. —**tā,** *f.* lightness ; buoyancy. —**parivatta,** *a.* quickly changing.
Lahuŋ, lahuso, *ad.* quickly.
Lākhā, *f.* lac ; sealing wax. —**rasa,** *m.* lac-colouring.
Lāja, *m.* parched corn. —**pañcamaka,** *a.* having parched corn as the fifth.
Lāpa, *m.* a sort of quail.
Lāpu, lābu, *f.* gourd. —**kaṭāha,** *m.* the outer crust of a gourd used as a vessel.
Lābha, *m.* gain ; acquisition. —**kamyatā,** *f.* desire for gain. —**gga,** *m.* the highest gain. —**macchariya,** *nt.* selfishness in gain. —**sakkāra,** *m.* gain and honour.
Lābhā, *in.* it is profitable ; it is a gain.
Lābhī, 3. one who gains much.
Lāmaka, *a.* inferior ; low ; sinful.
Lāyaka, 3. a reaper ; mower.
Lāyati (lā + ya), to reap ; to mow. *aor.* **lāyi.** *pp.* **lāyita.** *abs.* **lāyitvā.**
Lālana, *nt.* dalliance ; lulling.
Lāleti (lal + e), to lull ; to quell ; to sooth. *aor.* **lālesi.** *pp.* **lālita.** *abs.* **lāletvā.**
Lāsa, *m.* **lāsana,** *nt.* dancing ; sport.
Likkhā, *f.* an egg of a louse ; a measure named after it.
Likhati (likh + a), to write ; to inscribe ; to carve ; to scratch. *aor.* **likhi.** *pp.* **likhita.** *pr. p* **likhanta.** *abs.* **likhitvā.** *inf.* **likhituŋ.**
Likhana, *nt.* writing ; cutting into pieces.
Likhāpeti (*caus.* of **likhati**), to make one write. *aor.* —**esi.** *abs.* —**petvā.**
Likhitaka, *m.* one who has been prescribed ; an outlaw.
Liṅga, *nt.* sign ; mark ; attribute ; feature ; the generative organ ; the gender (in grammar). —**vipallāsa,** *m.* —**parivattana,** *nt.* change of the gender or sex
Litta, *pp.* of **limpati.**
Lipi, *f.* a writing ; a letter. —**kāra,** *m.* a writer ; scribe ; clerk.
Limpati (lip + ŋ - a), to smear ; to stain ; to anoint. *aor.* **limpi.** *pp.* **litta.** *abs.* **limpitvā.**
Limpana, *nt.* smearing with.
Limpeti (lip + e), to anoint ; to smear ; to plaster. *aor.* —**esi.** *pp.* **limpita.** *pr. p.* **limpenta.** *abs.* —**petvā.** *caus.* **limpāpeti.**
Lihati (lih + a), to lick. *aor.* **lihi.** *abs.* **lihitvā.** *pr. p.* **lihamāna.**
Līna (*pp.* of **līyati**), shrunk ; shy ; reserved. —**tā,** *f.* —**tta,** *nt.* sluggishness ; shyness.
Līyati (li + ya), to shrink ; to wither ; to cling to. *aor.* **līyi.** *pp.* **līna,** *pr. p.* **līyamāna.** *abs.* **līyitvā.**
Līyana, *nt.* shrinking ; withering.
Līlā, *f.* grace ; charm.
Lujjati (luj + ya), to break up ; to fall apart. *aor.* **lujji.** *pp.* **lugga.** *abs.* **lujjitvā.**

Lujjana, *nt.* crumbling; dissolution.

Luñcati (luñc + a), to pull out; to uproot. *aor.* **luñci.** *pp.* **luñcita.** *abs.* **—citvā.**

Lutta (*pp.* of **lopeti**), cut off; elided; plundered of.

Ludda, *a.* fierce; cruel. *m.* huntsman. **—ka,** *m.* a hunter.

Luddha (*pp.* of **lubbhati**), greedy; covetous.

Lunāti (lu + nā), to cut off; to mow; to reap. *aor.* **luni.**

Lubbhati (lubh + ya), to be greedy; to covet. *aor.* **lubbhi.** *pp.* **luddha.**

Lubbhana, *nt.* greediness.

Lumpati (lup + ŋ - a), to plunder; to eat. *aor.* **lumpi.** *pp.* **lumpita.** *abs.* **—pitvā.**

Lumpana, *nt.* plundering; eating.

Luḷita, *pp.* stirred; disturbed.

Lūkha, *a.* rough; coarse; miserable. **—cīvara,** *a.* wearing coarse robes. **—tā,** *f.* coarseness. **—ppasanna,** *a.* devoted to a person who is shabby. **—ājīvī,** *a.* leading a miserable life.

Lūṇa, lūna (*pp.* of **lunāti**), reaped; mowed.

Lekhaka, *m.* a scribe; clerk; writer. **—khikā,** *f.* a female clerk.

Lekhana, *nt.* **lekhā,** *f.* writing; a letter; an inscription.

Lekhanī, *f.* a pen. **—mukha,** *nt.* a nib.

Lekhā, *f.* a line; the art of writing.

Leḍḍu, *m.* a clod of earth. **—pāta,** *m.* a stone's throw.

Leṇa, *nt.* safety; a cave; a rock cell.

Lepa, *m.* coating; plastering; a plaster.

Lepana, *nt.* smearing; coating.

Lepeti (lip + e), to plaster; to coat with; to smear. *aor.* **—esi.** *pp.* **lepita, litta,** *pr. p.* **lepenta.** *abs.* **lepetvā.**

Leyya, *a.* fit to be licked or sipped. *nt.* mucilaginous food.

Lesa, *m.* a trifle; a pretext; trick.

Loka, *m.* the world; the population. **—gga,** 3. the chief of the world. **—nāyaka, —nātha,** *m.* the lord of the world. **—nta,** *m.* the end of the world. **—ntagū,** *a.* one who has reached the end of the things worldly. **—ntara,** *nt.* a different world; the space between the worlds. **—ntarika,** *a.* situated between the worlds. **—nirodha,** *m.* destruction of the existence. **—pāla,** *m.* a guardian of the world. **—vajja,** *nt.* a common sin. **—vivaraṇa,** *nt.* unveiling of the universe. **—vohāra,** *m.* ordinary way of speaking. **—ādhipacca,** *nt.* domination of the world. **—ānukampā,** *f.* sympathy with the world of men. **—āyatika,** *a.* one who holds the view of nature-lore; a nihilist.

Lokika, lokiya, *a.* worldly; mundane.

Lokuttara, *a.* super-mundane; transcendental.

Locaka, 3. one who pulls out or uproots.

Locana, *nt.* the eye.

Loṇa, *nt.* salt. *adj.* salty. **—kāra,** *m.* salt-maker. **—dhūpana,** *nt.* flavouring with salt. **—phala,** *nt.* **—sakkharā,** *f.* a crystal of salt.

Loṇika, *a.* alkaline.

Loṇī, *f.* a salt-pan; a lagoon.

Lopa, *m.* elision; cutting off.

Lobha, *m.* greed ; covetousness. **—nīya,** *a.* to be coveted ; desirable. **—mūlaka,** *a.* having greed as its root.

Loma, *nt.* the hair on the body. **—kūpa,** *m.* a pore of the skin. **—haṭṭha,** *a.* having hair standing on the end. **—haŋsa,** *m.* **—haŋsana,** *nt.* horripilation.

Lomasa, *a.* hairy ; covered with hair. **—pāṇaka,** *m.* a caterpillar.

Lola, *a.* greedy ; unsteady. **—tā,** *f.* eagerness ; greed.

Lolupa, *a.* covetous ; greedy.

Loluppa, *nt.* greed.

Loleti (lul + e), to stir ; to shake ; to agitate.

Loha, *nt.* metal ; copper. **—kaṭāha,** *m.* a copper receptacle. **—kāra,** *m.* a coppersmith ; metal worker. **—kumbhī,** *f.* a pot made of copper. **—guḷa, —piṇḍa,** *m.* a lump of metal. **—jāla,** *nt.* a brass netting. **—thālaka,** *m.* a brass plate or bowl. **—pāsāda,** *m.* name of the palacial chapter house in Anuradhapura, which was covered with copper tiles. **—bhaṇḍa,** *nt.* copper ware. **—maya,** *a.* made of copper. **—māsaka,** *m.* a copper coin. **—salākā,** *f.* a brass wire or pin.

Lohita, *nt.* blood. *adj.* red. **—taka,** *a.* red. **—kkha,** *a.* having red eyes. **—candana,** *nt.* red sandal-wood. **—pakkhandikā,** *f.* bloody diarrhoea. **—bhakkha,** *a.* feeding on blood. **—tuppādaka,** *m.* one who sheds the blood (of a Buddha).

Lohitaṅka, *m.* a ruby.

V.

Va, a shortened form of **iva** or **eva.**

Vaka, *m.* a wolf.

Vakula, *m.* the tree *Mimusops Elengi.* මුනමල්.

Vakka, *nt.* the kidny.

Vakkala, *nt.* a garment made of bark ; the strips taken for that purpose. **—lī,** 3. wearing a bark-garment.

Vakkhati (*fut.* of **vadati**), he will say.

Vagga, *m.* a group ; a party chapter of a book. *adj.* dissociated ; dissentious. **—bandhana,** *nt.* forming of a group ; a gang ; a guild.

Vaggiya, *a.* (in cpds.) belonging to a group.

Vaggu, *a.* lovely ; pleasant. **—vada,** *a.* of lovely speech.

Vagguli, *f.* a bat.

Vaṅka, *a.* bent ; crooked ; dishonest, *nt.* a hook ; a fish-hook. **—ghasta,** *a.* having swallowed the hook. **—tā,** *f.* crookedness.

Vaṅga, *m.* the country of Bengal.

Vaca, *m. nt.* (mano-group), word ; saying.

Vacana, *nt.* utterance ; word ; saying ; a term ; an expression. **—kara,** *a.* obedient. **—kkhama,** *a.* willing to do what others bid. **—ttha,** *m.* meaning of a word. **—nīya,** *a.* fit to be spoken to or admonished. **—patha,** *m.* the way of saying.

Vacā, *f.* the sweet-flag plant ; orris root.

Vacī, *f.* speech ; word. **—gutta,** *a.* controlled in speech. **—kamma,** *nt.* verbal action. **—duccarita,** *nt.* misbehaviour in words. —**parama**, *a.* one who excels in words but not in actions. —**bheda**, *m.* an utterance. —**viññatti**, *f.* intimation by language. —**saṅkhāra**, *m.* antecedent for speech. —**samācāra**, *m.* good conduct in speech. —**sucarita**, *nt.* good action in speech.

Vacca, *nt.* excrement; faeces; dung. —**kuṭi**, *f.* a privy; lavatory. —**kūpa**, *m.* a privy pit. —**magga**, *m.* the anus. —**sodhaka**, *m.* a privy-cleaner.

Vaccha, *m.* a calf; the young of an animal. —**ka**, *m.* a small calf. —**giddhinī**, *f.* a cow longing for her calf. —**tara**, *m.* a big calf.

Vacchara, *nt.* an year.

Vacchala, *a.* affectionate.

Vaja, *m.* a cow-pen; cattle-fold.

Vajati (vaj + a), to go; to proceed. *aor.* **vaji**. *pr. p.* **vajamāna**.

Vajira, *nt.* a diamond; a thunderbolt. —**pāṇi**, —**hattha**, *m.* having a diamond mace in his hand, i.e. Sakka.

Vajja, *nt.* fault; a musical instrument. *adj.* which should be avoided; what should be told. —**nīya**, *a.* fit to be avoided or shunned.

Vajjana, *nt.* avoidance; shunning.

Vajjita, *pp.* of **vajjeti**.

Vajjī, *m.* a man of the Vajji clan.

Vajjeti (vaj + e), to avoid; to abstain from; to renounce. *aor.* —**esi**. *pt. p.* **vajjetabba**. *abs.* **vajjetvā**. *inf.* **vajjetuŋ**.

Vajjha, *a.* fit to be killed or punished. —**ppatta**, *a.* condemned. —**bheri**, *f.* the execution drum.

Vañcakā, 3. a cheat; fraudulent. —**cana**, *nt.* —**canā**, *f.* cheating; fraud. —**canika**, *a.* deceiving.

Vañceti (vañc + e), to cheat; to deceive. *aor.* —**esi**. *pp.* —**cita**. *pr. p.* —**centa**. *abs.* —**cetvā**.

Vañjha, *a.* barren. —**jhā**, *f.* a barren woman.

Vaṭa (—**rukkha**), *m.* a banyan tree.

Vaṭaŋsaka, *m.* a wreath for the head.

Vaṭuma, *nt.* a road; path.

Vaṭṭa, *a.* circular; round. *nt.* a circle; the cycle of rebirth; an expenditure or provision for alms.

Vaṭṭakā, *f.* a quail.

Vaṭṭati (vaṭṭ + a), to behove; to be right, fit, or proper; to turn round.

Vaṭṭana, *nt.* turning round.

Vaṭṭi, —**kā**, *f.* a wick; a roll; a gush of water, etc.; the edge; rim, or brim.

Vaṭṭula, *a.* circular.

Vaṭṭeti (vaṭṭ + e), to turn; to cause to move; to make a wick or roll; to make circular. *aor.* —**esi**. *pp.* **vaṭṭita**. *abs.* **vaṭṭetvā**.

Vaṭṭha, *pp.* wet with rain.

Vaṭhara, *a.* bulky; fat.

Vaḍḍha, —**ka**, *a.* augmenting; increasing. —**na**, *nt.* growth; increase; enlargement. —**naka** *a.* increasing; serving in.

Vaḍḍhakī, *m.* a carpenter.

Vaḍḍhati (vaḍḍh + a), to grow; to prosper. *aor.* **vaḍḍhi**, *pp.* —**ḍhita**. *pr. p.* —**ḍhanta**, —**ḍhamāna**, *abs.* —**ḍhitvā**.

Vaḍḍhi, *f.* increase; growth; profit; welfare; interest on money.

Vaḍḍheti (vaḍḍh + e), to increase; to cultivate; to rear or bring up; to get ready (of food); to serve in; to set into motion. *aor.* —**esi.** *pp.* —**ḍhita.** *pr. p.* —**ḍhenta.** *abs.* —**ḍhetvā.**

Vaṇa, *nt.* a wound; a sore; —**colaka,** *nt.* a rag for dressing a wound. —**paṭikamma,** *nt.* curing of a wound. —**bandhana,** *nt.* bandage for a wound.

Vaṇijjā, *f.* trade; trading.

Vaṇita, *pp.* wounded.

Vaṇippatha, *m.* a country where trade is going on.

Vaṇibbaka, *m.* a pauper.

Vaṇṭa, —**ka,** *nt.* a stalk. —**ṭika,** *a.* having a stalk.

Vaṇṇa, *m.* colour; appearance; colour of the skin; sort; caste; a letter; quality. —**ka,** *nt.* a dye. —**kasiṇa,** *nt.* a colour circle for the practice of meditation. —**da,** —**dada,** *a.* giving colour or beauty. —**dhātu,** *f.* condition of appearance; colour. —**pokkharatā,** *f.* beauty of complexion. —**vantu,** *a.* colourful. —**vādī,** 3. saying about one's virtues. —**sampanna,** *a.* endowed with beauty or colour.

Vaṇṇadāsī, *f.* a courtezan.

Vaṇṇanā, *f.* explanation; a commentary; praising.

Vaṇṇanīya, *a.* fit to be commented or praised.

Vaṇṇita, *pp.* of **vaṇṇeti.**

Vaṇṇī, *a.* (in cpds.) having the appearance of.

Vaṇṇu, *f.* sand. —**patha,** *m.* a sandy waste.

Vaṇṇeti (vaṇṇ + e), to describe; to explain; to comment on; to praise; to extol. *aor.* —**esi.** *pp.* **vaṇṇita.** *pr. p.* —**ṇenta.** *pt. p.* —**ṇetabba.** *abs.* —**ṇetvā.**

Vata, *in.* surely; certainly; indeed; alas.

Vata, *nt.* a religious duty or observance. —**pada,** *nt.* an item of good practice. —**vantu,** *a.* observant of religious duties. —**samādāna,** *nt.* taking up of a religious vow.

Vati, vatikā, *f.* a fence.

Vatika, *a.* (in cpds). having the habit of; acting like.

Vatta, *nt.* duty; service; function. —**paṭivatta,** *nt.* all kinds of duties. —**sampanna,** *a.* dutiful.

Vattaka, vattetu, 3. exercising; keeping on.

Vattati (vat + a), to exist; to happen; to take place; to go on. *aor.* **vatti.** *abs.* **vattitvā.** *pr. p.* **vattanta,** —**tamāna.** *inf.* **vattituŋ.** *pt. p.* **vattitabba.**

Vattabba (=**vaditabba**), *pt. p.* fit to be told.

Vattamāna, *a.* existing. *m.* the present period. —**nā,** *f.* the Present Tense. —**mānaka,** *a* existing; going on.

Vattikā, *f.* a thong; a wick.

Vattitabba, *pt. p.* to be continued, practised, or observed.

Vattī, *a.* (in cpds.) one who keeps up, practises, or causes to go on.

Vattu, *m.* one who speaks or says; sayer.

Vattuŋ, *inf.* (of **vadati**) to say.

Vatteti (*caus.* of **vattati**), keeps on; to make go on. *aor.* **vattesi.** *pp.* **vattita.** *pr. p.* —**tenta.** *abs.* **vattetvā,** *pt. p.* —**tetabba.** *inf.* —**tetuŋ.**

Vattha, *nt.* a cloth; garment; raiment. —**guyha,** *nt.* that which is concealed by a clothe, *i.e.* pudendum. —**ntara,** *nt.* species of cloth. —**yuga,** *nt.* a pair of suit or clothes.

Vatthi, *f.* the bladder ; a clyster ; the sheath (enveloping the male organ). **—kamma,** *nt.* using of clyster.

Vatthu, *nt.* a site ; ground ; field ; plot ; object ; a thing ; a substance ; a story. **—ka,** *a.* (in cpds.) having its ground in ; founded on. **—kata,** *a.* made a basis of ; practised thoroughly. **—gāthā,** *f.* the introductory stanzas. **—devatā,** *f.* a deity haunting a certain place. **—vijjā,** *f.* the science of building-sites. **—visadakiriyā,** *f.* cleansing of the fundamentals.

Vatvā, *abs.* (of **vadati**), having told or said.

Vadaññū, *a.* liberal ; bountiful ; giving ear to suplications. **—utā,** *f.* liberality.

Vadati (vad + a), to speak ; to say ; to tell. *aor.* **vadi.** *pp.* **vutta.** *pr. p.* **vadanta, vadamāna,** *pt. p.* **vattabba.** *abs-* **vatvā, vaditvā.**

Vadana, *nt.* the face ; speech ; utterance.

Vadāpana, *nt.* causing to speak.

Vadāpeti (*caus.* of **vadati**), to make somebody speak or say. *aor.* **—esi.** *pp.* **—pita.** *abs.* **—petvā.**

Vadeti (vad + e), to say ; to speak.

Vaddalikā, *f.* heaping of rain clouds.

Vaḋdha, see **Vuddha.**

Vaddhana, see **Vaḍḍhana.**

Vaddhāpacāyana, *nt.* respect towards elders.

Vadha, *m.* punishment ; killing ; execution. **—ka,** *m.* an executioner ; one who inflicts punishment.

Vadhita, *pp.* of **vadheti.**

Vadhukā, *f.* a young wife ; a daughter-in-law.

Vadhū, *f.* a woman.

Vadheti (vadh + e), to kill ; to tease or hurt. *aor.* **—esi.** *pr. p.* **vadhenta.** *abs.* **vadhitvā.**

Vana, *nt.* a wood ; forest. **—kammika,** *m.* one who works in the woods. **—gahana,** *nt.* a jungle thicket. **—gumba,** *m.* a cluster of trees. **—cara, —caraka, —cārī,** *a.* a forester. **—devatā,** *f.* a forest deity. **—ppati, —spati,** *m.* a big tree which bears fruit without flowers. **—pattha,** *nt.* a place far away in the forest. **—vāsī,** *a.* dwelling in the forest. **—saṇḍa,** *m.* a jungle thicket.

Vanatha, *m.* craving ; desire.

Vanika, *a.* (in cpds.) belonging to a forest.

Vanta (*pp.* of **vamati**), vomited ; renounced. **—kasāva,** *a.* one who has left behind all fault. **—mala,** *a.* stainless

Vandaka, 3. one who bows down or venerates.

Vandati (vand + a), to salute ; to pay homage ; to honour ; to adore. *aor.* **vandi.** *pp.* **vandita** *pr. p.* **vandanta. —māna.** *pt. p.* **—ditabba.** *abs.* **vanditvā, vandiya.**

Vandana, *nt.***—nā,** *f.* salutation ; homage.

Vandāpana, *nt.* causing one to pay homage.

Vandāpeti, *caus.* of **vandati.** *aor.* **—esi.** *pp.* **—dāpita.** *abs.* **—petvā.**

Vapati (vap + a), to sow ; to shave. *aor.* **vapi.** *pp.* **vapita, vutta.** *pr. p.* **vapanta.** *abs.* **vapitvā.**

Vapana, *nt.* sowing.

Vapu, *nt.* the body.

Vappa, *m.* sowing; name of a month, October-November. **—kāla,** *m.* sowing time. **—maṅgala,** *nt.* ploughing festival.

Vamati (vam + a), to vomit; to eject; to discharge. *aor.* **vami.** *pp.* **vanta, vamita.** *abs.* **vamitvā.**

Vamathu, *m.* **vamana,** *nt.* vomiting; discharged food.

Vambhana, *nt.* **—nā,** *f.* contempt; despite.

Vambhī, 3. one who treats with contempt.

Vambheti (vambh + e), to despise; to treat with contempt. *aor.* **—esi.** *pp.* **—bhita.** *pr. p.* **—bhenta.** *abs.* **—bhetvā.**

Vamma, *nt.* an armour. **—mī,** 3. wearing armour.

Vammika, *m.* an ant-hill.

Vammita, *pp.* of the following.

Vammeti (vam + e), to put on armour. *aor.* **—esi.** *abs.* **vammetvā.**

Vaya, *m. nt.* (mano-group), age; loss; decay; expenditure. **—karaṇa,** *nt.* expenditure. **—kalyāṇa,** *nt.* charm of youth. **—ṭṭha,** *a.* come to maturity. **—ppatta,** *a.* come of age; fit to marry.

Vayassa, *m.* a friend.

Vayha, *nt.* a vehicle; a litter.

Vara, *a.* excellent; noble. *m.* a boon; a favour. **—ṅganā,** *f.* a noble lady. **—da,** *a.* giver of the best things. **—dāna,** *nt.* granting of a boon or privilege. **—pañña,** *a.* having an excellent knowledge. **—lakkhaṇa,** *nt.* an excellent sign (on the body).

Varaka, *m.* a kind of grain.

Varaṇa, *m.* the tree *Cartaeva Roxburghii.*

Varattā, *f.* a thong; a strap.

Varāka, *a.* wretched; a miserable person.

Varāha, *m.* a hog; a boar. **—hī,** *f.* a sow.

Valañja, *nt.* (in cpds.) a track; trace; use; that which is secreted. **—na,** *nt.* resorting; using; acting as; easing the body. **—naka,** *a.* fit to be used or spent.

Valañjiyamāna, *a.* being used.

Valañjeti (valaj + e), to track; to trace; to use; to spend; to resort to. *aor.* **—esi.** *pp.* **—jita.** *pr. p.* **—jenta.** *abs.* **—jetvā.** *pt. p.* **—jetabba.**

Valaya, *nt.* a bangle; a bracelet; a loop. **—ākāra,** *a.* circular.

Valāhaka, *m.* a rain cloud.

Vali, *f.* a fold; a wrinkle. **—ka,** *a.* having folds.

Valita, *pp.* wrinkled.

Valittaca, *a.* with wrinkled skin.

Valīmukha, *m.* a monkey; the wrinkled faced.

Vallakī, *f.* an Indian lute.

Vallabha, *a.* favourite. **—tta,** *nt.* state of being a favourite.

Vallarī, *f.* a bunch; a cluster.

Valli, *f.* a creeper. **—hāraka,** 3. a collecter of creepers.

Vallibha, *m.* the pumpkin.

Vallūra, *nt.* dried flesh.

Vavatthapeti (vi + ava + ṭhā + āpe), to settle; to define; to fix; to designate. *aor.* **—esi.** *pp.* **—thāpita.** *abs.* **—petvā.**

Vavatthāpana, *nt.* definition; determination.

Vavattheti (vi + ava + ṭhā + e), to analyse; to define. *aor.* **—esi.** *pp.* **vavatthita.** *abs.* **—thetvā.**

Vasa, *m.* control; influence; authority. **—ga, —ṅgata,** *a.* being in someone's power. **—vattaka, —vattī,** *a.* wielding power; dominating. **—vattana,** *nt.* control; authority. **—ānuga, —ānuvattī,** *a.* obedient.

Vasati (vas + a), to live; to abide; to dwell; to stay. *aor.* **vasi.** *pp.* **vuttha, vusita.** *pr. p.* **vasanta, vasamāna.** *abs.* **vasitvā.** *pt. p.* **vasitabba.**

Vasana, *nt.* dwelling; living; a clothe. **—naka,** *a.* living in. **—naṭṭhāna,** *nt.* residence; dwelling place.

Vasanta (**—kāla**), *m.* the spring.

Vasala, *m.* an outcast; a person of low birth.

Vasā, *f.* the fat; grease.

Vasāpeti (*caus.* of **vasati**), to make live; to cause to dwell; to detain. *aor.* **—esi.** *pp.* **—pita.** *abs.* **—petvā.**

Vasippatta, *a.* one who has mastered well.

Vasī, *a.* mastering; having power. **—kata,** *a.* subjected; brought under one's power. **—bhāva,** *m.* mastery. **—bhūta,** *a.* having become a master over.

Vasu, *nt.* wealth. **—dhā, —ndharā, —matī,** *f.* the earth.

Vassa, *m., nt.* the year; rain. **—kāla,** *m.* rainy season. **—gga,** *nt.* seniority of monks.

Vassati (vas + a), to rain; to utter a cry (by some animal). *aor.* **vassi.** *pp.* **vassita;** (in the case of rain:) **vuṭṭha.** *pr. p.* **vassanta.** *abs.* **vassitvā.**

Vassana, *nt.* raining; cry of an animal.

Vassāna, *m.* the rainy season.

Vassāpanaka, *a.* causing to rain.

Vassāpeti (*caus.* of **vassati**), to cause to rain. *aor.* **—esi.** *pp.* **—pita.** *abs.* **—petvā.**

Vassika, *a.* belonging to the rainy season. (in cpds.) so many years old. **—sāṭikā,** *f.* a kind of rain coat used by B. monks during the rainy season.

Vassikā, *f.* great-flowered jasmine.

Vassita (*pp.* of **vassati**), wet with; *nt.* cry of an animal.

Vahati (vah + a), to bear; to carry; to do one's work; to flow. *aor.* **vahi.** *pp.* **vahita.** *pr. p.* **vahanta.** *abs.* **vahitvā.** *pt. p.* **vahitabba.**

Vahana, *nt.* carrying; bearing; flowing.

Vahitu, *m.* bearer.

Vaḷabāmukha, *nt.* a submarine fire.

Vaḷavā, *f.* a mare.

Vaŋsa, *m.* a race; lineage; family; a bamboo tree; a bamboo flute. **—kaḷīra,** *m.* the sprout of a bamboo. **—ja,** *a.* born in a certain clan or race. **—vaṇṇa,** *m.* the lapislazuli. **—āgata,** *a.* come down from father to son. **—ānupālaka,** *a.* preserving the lineage.

Vaŋsika, *a.* belonging to a clan or race.

Vā (*particle of disjunction*), or; either-or.

Vāka, *nt.* strips of bark (used for making garments). **—cīra,** *nt.* a bark garment. **—maya,** *a.* made of bark-strips.

Vākarā, vāgurā, *f.* a net for catching deer.

Vākkaraṇa, *nt.* conversation.

Vākya, *nt.* a sentence; saying.

Vāgurika, 3. one who uses nets in catching animals.

Vācaka, 3. one who teaches or recites.

Vācanaka, *nt.* recitation.

Vacanāmagga, *m.* the way of recitation or tradition.

Vācasika, *a.* connected with speech.

Vācā, *f.* word; speech; saying. **—nurakkhī,** *a.* guarding one's speech.

Vācāla, *a.* garrulous; talkative.

Vācuggata, *a.* learned by heart.

Vāceti (vac + e), to read; to teach; to recite. *aor.* **—esi.** *pp.* **vācita.** *pr. p.* **—centa.** *pt. p.* **vācetabba.** *abs.* **vācetvā.**

Vācetu, *m.* one who reads or teaches.

Vāja, *m.* the feather of an arrow; a kind of drink. **—peyya,** *nt.* a kind of sacrifice.

Vājī, *m.* a horse.

Vāṭa, vāṭaka, *m.* an enclosure.

Vāṇija, —ka, *m.* a merchant; trader.

Vāṇijja, *nt.* trade.

Vāṇī, *f.* word; speech.

Vāta, *m.* the wind; air. **—ghātaka,** *m.* the tree *Cassia Fistula.* **—java,** *a.* as swift as the wind. **—pāna,** *nt.* a window. **—maṇḍalikā,** *f.* a whirlwind. **—roga.—ābādha,** *m.* an illness caused by the wind humour. **—vuṭṭhi,** *f.* wind and rain. **—vega,** *m.* force of the wind.

Vātātapa, *m.* wind and heat.

Vātābhihata, *a.* shaken by the wind.

Vātāyana, *nt.* a window.

Vātāhaṭa, *a.* brought by the wind.

Vāti (vā + a), to blow; to emit some smell.

Vātika, *a.* caused by the wind humour.

Vātiṅgaṇa, *m.* the brinjal.

Vāterita, *a.* moved by the wind.

Vāda, *m.* theory; saying; creed; controversy. **—kāma,** *a.* desirous of disputation. **—kkhitta,** *a.* upset in a disputation. **—patha,** *m.* ground for a disputation.

Vādaka, 3. player on a musical instrument.

Vādana, *nt.* sounding of a musical instrument.

Vādita, *nt.* music.

Vādī, 3. one who disputes or preaches some doctrine; speaking of. **—vara,** *m.* the noblest of the view-holders.

Vāna, *nt.* craving; netting of a bed.

Vānara, *m.* a monkey. **—rī,** *f.* female monkey. **—rinda,** *m.* monkey-king.

Vāpi, *f.* a tank; a reservoir for water.

Vāpita, *pp.* sown.

Vāma, *a.* left; agreeable. **—passa,** *nt.* the left side.

Vāmana, —naka, *m.* a dwarf. *adj.* dwarfish.

Vāya, *m. nt.* (mano-group), the wind; air. See **Vāyo.**

Vāyati (vā + ya), to blow; to emit an odour; to weave. *aor.* **vāyi.** *pr. p.* **vāyanta, vāyamāna.** *abs.* **vāyitvā.**

Vāyana, *nt.* blowing; spreading of a smell.

Vāyamati (vi + ā + yam + a), to strive; to endeavour. *aor.* **vāyami.** *pr. p.* **vāyamanta.** *abs.* **—mitvā.**

Vāyasa, *m.* a crow.

Vāyasāri, *m.* an owl.

Vāyāma, *m.* exertion; striving.

Vāyita (*pp.* of **vāyati**), woven; plaited; blown.

Vāyima, *a.* woven.

Vāyu, *nt.* wind; the mobile principle.

Vāyo, the form taken by **vāya** (in cpds.) —**kasiṇa**, *nt.* wind taken as an object of meditation. —**dhātu**, *f.* the mobile principle.

Vāra, *m.* a turn; occasion; opportunity.

Vāraka, *m.* a jar.

Vāraṇa, *m.* an elephant; a kind of eagle. *nt.* warding off; obstruction; resistance.

Vāri, *nt.* water. —**gocara**, *a.* living in water. —**ja**, *a.* water-born. *m.* a fish. *nt.* a lotus. —**da**, —**dhara**, —**vāha**, *m.* a rain cloud. —**magga**, *m.* a drain; a conduit.

Vārita, *pp.* of **vāreti**.

Vāritta, *nt.* avoidance; an act that should not be done.

Vāriyamāna, *a.* being hindered, obstructed, or prevented.

Vāruṇī, *f.* spirituous liquor.

Vāreti (var + e), to prevent; to obstruct; to hinder. *aor.* **vāresi**. *pr. p.* **vārenta**, **vārayamāna**. *pt. p.* **vāretabba**. *abs.* **vāretvā**.

Vāla, *m.* hair of the tail. *adj.* fierce; malicious. —**kambala**, *nt.* a blanket made of horse-hair. —**gga**, *nt.* the tip of a hair. —**ṇḍupaka**, *m. nt.* a brush made of horse tail. —**vījanī**, *f.* a fan made of yak's tail. —**miga**, *m.* a beast of prey. —**vedhī**, *m.* an archer who can hit a hair.

Vāladhi, *m.* tail.

Vālikā, **vālukā**, *f.* sand. —**puñja**, *m.* a heap of sand. —**pulina**, *nt.* a sand bed. —**kantāra**, *m.* a sandy waste.

Vāsa, *m.* living; sojourn; habitation; a clothe; perfume. —**cuṇṇa**, *nt.* perfumed powder. —**ṭṭhāna**, *nt.* dwelling place.

Vāsana, *nt.* perfuming; making to inhabit.

Vāsanā, *f.* former impression; recollection of the past.

Vāsara, *m.* a day.

Vasava, *m.* the king of the gods.

Vāsi, *f.* an adze; a hatchet; a sharp knife. —**phala**, *nt.* the blade of a knife or axe. —**jaṭa**, *nt.* the handle of an axe.

Vāsika, **vāsī**, 3. (in cpds.) living in; dwelling in. *f.* **vāsinī**.

Vāsitaka, *nt.* perfumed powder; *adj.* scented.

Vāsudeva, *m.* the God Vishnu.

Vāseti (vas + e), to establish; to make dwell; to perfume. *aor.* **vāsesi**. *pp.* **vāsita**. *abs.* **vāsetvā**.

Vāha, *a.* carrying; leading. *m.* a leader; a cart; a cartload, *i.e.* 380 doṇas; a beast of burden; a torrent. —**ka**, 3. one who bears or carries away; leading to; a current.

Vāhasā, *in.* owing to; by dint of; on account of.

Vāhinī, *f.* an army; a river.

Vāhī, *a.* carrying; conveying; bearing.

Vāheti (vah + e), to convey; to lead to.

Vikaca, *a.* blown; blossoming.

Vikaṭa, *a.* changed; altered. *nt.* filth; dirt.

Vikati, *f.* a sort or kind; made of a shape. —**ka**, *a.* (in cpds.) of many sorts or shapes.

Vikatthati (vi + kath + a), to boast; to show off. *aor.* —**thi**. *pp.* —**thita**. *abs.* —**thitvā**.

Vikatthana, *nt.* boasting.

Vikatthaka, —**tthī**, 3. one who boasts.

Vikantati (vi + kant + a), to cut open. *aor.* —**nti**. *pp.* —**ntita**. *abs.* —**ntitvā**.

Vikantana, *nt.* cutting off; a knife to cut with.

Vikappa, *m.* thought; consideration; indecision; alternative. **—na,** *nt.* indefiniteness; assignment; apportioning.

Vikappeti (vi + kapp + e), to design; to intend; to assign; to arrange; to alter; to shape. *aor.* **—esi.** *pp.* **—ppita.** *pr. p.* **—penta.** *abs.* **—petvā.**

Vikampati (vi + kamp + a), to tremble; to be unsettled. *aor.* **—mpi.** *pp.* **—pita.** *abs.* **—pitvā.** *pr. p.* **—pamāna.**

Vikampana, *nt.* trembling.

Vikaroti (vi + kar + o), to undo; to alter. *aor.* **vikari.** *pp.* **vikata.**

Vikala, *a.* defective; in want of; being without. **—ka,** *a.* being short of.

Vikasati (vi + kas + a), to open out; to expand; to be blown. *aor.* **vikasi.** *pp.* **—sita.** *abs.* **—sitvā.**

Vikāra, *m.* change; alteration; reversion; disturbance; deformity; quality.

Vikāla, *m.* the wrong time; afternoon and the night. **—bhojana,** *nt.* taking food in the afternoon and night.

Vikāsa, *m.* expansion; opening.

Vikāseti (vi + kas + e), to illuminate; to make expand or open wide. *aor.* **—esi.** *pp.* **—sita.** *abs.* **—setvā.**

Vikiṇṇa (*pp.* of **vikirati**), scattered about; strewn all over. **—kesa,** *a.* with dishevelled hair.

Vikiraṇa, *nt.* scattering; dispersion.

Vikirati (vi + kir + a), to scatter; to spread; to sprinkle. *aor.* **vikiri.** *pr. p.* **—ranta, vikiramāna,** *abs.* **—ritvā.** *pass.* **vikirīyati.**

Vikuṇita, *pp.* distorted; deformed.

Vikubbati (vi + kar + o; **karo** is changed to **kubba**), to transform; to perform miracles. *aor.* **vikubbi.** *pp.* **—bita.**

Vikubbana, *nt.* miraculous transformation.

Vikūjati (vi + kūj + a), to chirp; to warble; to coo; to sing. *aor.* **vikūji.** *pp.* **—jita.**

Vikūjana, *nt.* cooing of a bird.

Vikūla, *a.* sloping down.

Vikopana, *nt.* upsetting; injuring.

Vikopeti (vi + kup + e), to upset; to injure; to destroy. *aor.* **—esi.** *pp.* **—pita.** *abs.* **—petvā.** *pr. p.* **—penta.**

Vikkanta, *nt.* heroism.

Vikkama, *m.* strength; heroism; stepping.

Vikkamati (vi + kam + a), to exert oneself; to step forward. *aor.* **vikkami.**

Vikkamana, *nt.* exertion; stepping.

Vikkaya, *m.* sale.

Vikkayika, vikketu, 3. a seller; salesman.

Vikkāyika, *a.* to be sold. **—bhaṇḍa,** *nt.* merchandise.

Vikkiṇāti (vi + ki + ṇā), to sell. *aor.* **vikkiṇi.** *pp.* **—kiṇita, —kīta.** *pr. p.* **—ṇanta.** *abs.* **—ṇitvā.** *inf.* **—ṇituŋ.**

Vikkhambha, *m.* diameter.

Vikkhambhana, *nt.* arrest; elimination; discarding; suppression.

Vikkhambheti (vi + khambh + e), to suppress; to discard; to extripate. *aor.* **—esi.** *pp.* **—bhita.** *pr. p.* **—bh nta.** *abs.* **—bhetvā.**

Vikkhāleti (vi + khāl + e), to wash off; to rinse one's mouth. *aor.* **—esi.** *pp.* **—lita.** *abs.* **—letvā.**

Vikkhitta (*pp.* of **vikkhipati**), upset; perplexed. **—citta,** *a.* of confused or upset mind.

Vikkhittaka, *a.* scattered all over. *nt.* such a corpse.

Vikkhipati (vi + khip + a), to disturb; to confuse. *aor.* **—khipi.** *pr. p.* **—panta.** *abs.* **—pitvā.**

Vikkhipana, *nt.* **vikkhepa,** *m.* disturbance; confusion; derangement.

Vikkhepaka, *a.* one who disturbs.

Vikkhobhana, *nt.* a great disturbance.

Vikkhobheti (vi + khubh + e), to shake or disturb thoroughly. *aor.* **—esi.** *pp.* **—bhita.** *abs.* **—bhetvā.**

Vigacchati (vi + gam + a), to depart; to disappear; to go away. *aor.* **—cchi.** *pr. p.* **—chanta, —chamāna.**

Vigata (*pp.* of the above), gone away; ceased; deprived of; being without. **—khila,** *a.* free from callosity. **—raja,** *a.* free from defilement. **—āsa,** *a.* free from desire. **—āsava,** *a.* free from depravity; a saint.

Vigama, *m.* **—mana,** *nt.* departure; disappearance; going away.

Vigayha (*abs.* from **vigāhati**), having entered or plunged into.

Vigarahati (vi + garah + a), to scold intensely; to abuse. *aor.* **—rahi.** *abs.* **—rahitvā.**

Vigalita (*pp.* of **vigalati**), displaced; dropped down.

Vigāhati (vi + gāh + a), to enter; to plunge into. *aor.* **vigāhi.** *pp.* **vigāḷha.** *pr. p.* **vigāhamāna.** *abs.* **vigāhitvā, —hetvā.** *inf.* **—hituṇ.**

Viggayha (*abs.* from **viggaṇhāti**), having quarrelled or analysed.

Viggaha, *m.* a dispute; quarrel; the body; resolution of words into their elements.

Viggāhikakathā, *f.* quarrelsome speech.

Vighaṭṭana, *nt.* knocking against.

Vighāṭana, *nt.* opening; unfastening.

Vighāṭeti (vi + ghaṭ + e), to unfasten; to break up; to open. *aor.* **—esi.** *pp.* **—ṭita.** *pr. p.* **—ṭenta.** *abs.* **—ṭetvā.**

Vighāta, *m.* destruction; distress; vexation; annoyance.

Vighāteti (vi + han + e), to kill; to destroy. *aor.* **—esi.** *pp.* **—tita.** *abs.* **—tetvā.**

Vighāsa, *m.* remains of food; scraps. **—sāda,** *m.* one who eats the remains of food.

Vicakkhaṇa, *a.* skilful; wise. *m.* a wise man.

Vicaya, *m.* investigation.

Vicaraṇa, *nt.* walking; going about.

Vicarati (vi + car + a), to go about; to wander. *aor.* **vicari.** *pp.* **vicarita.** *pr.p.* **vicaranta, —ramāna.** *abs.* **vicaritvā.** *inf.* **—rituṇ.**

Vicāra, *m.* **—raṇa,** *nt.* **—raṇā,** *f.* investigation; management; planning.

Vicāraka, 3. one who investigates or manages; a manager.

Vicāreti (vi + car + e), to think over; to manage; to plan; to administer. *aor.* **—esi.** *pp.* **—rita.** *pr. p.* **—renta.** *abs.* **—retvā.**

Vicikicchati (vi + kit + cha ; **ki** is doubled and the first **ki** is changed to **ci**), to doubt ; to hesitate ; to be distracted. *aor.* **—cchi.** *pp.* **—chita.**

Vicikicchā, *f.* doubt ; uncertainty.

Viciṇṇa, *pp.* of **vicināti.**

Vicita, *pp.* of **vicināti.**

Vicitta, *a.* variegated ; ornamented ; decorated.

Vicinana, *nt.* discrimination ; selection.

Vicināti (vi + ci + nā), to consider ; to discriminate ; to select ; to collect. *aor.* **vicini.** *pp.* **vicita.** *pr. p.* **vicinanta.** *abs.* **—nitvā.**

Vicinteti (vi + cit + e), to think over ; to consider. *aor.* **—esi.** *pp.* **—tita.** *pr. p.* **—tenta.** *abs.* **—tetvā.**

Vicuṇṇa, *a.* crushed up ; powdered ; broken into pieces.

Vicuṇṇeti (vi + cuṇṇ + e), to crush ; to powder ; to break into pieces. *aor.* **—esi.** *pp.* **—ṇita.** *abs.* **—ṇetvā.**

Vicchikā, *f.* a scorpion.

Vicchiddaka, *a.* full of holes ; perforated all over.

Vicchindati (vi + chid + ŋ - a), to cut off ; to interrupt ; to prevent. *aor.* **—ndi.** *pp.* **—chinna.** *pr. p.* **—danta, —damāna.** *abs.* **—nditvā.**

Viccheda, *m.* interruption ; cutting off.

Vijaṭana, *nt.* disentangling.

Vijaṭeti (vi + jaṭ + e), to unravel ; to comb out ; to disentangle. *aor.* **—esi.** *pp.* **—ṭita.** *abs.* **—ṭetvā.**

Vijana, *a.* deserted of people. **—vāta,** *a.* having an atmosphere of loneliness.

Vijambhati (vi + jambh + a), to rouse oneself ; to display activity ; to yawn. *aor.* **—mbhi.** *abs.* **—bhitvā.**

Vijambhanā, *f.* arousing ; activity.

Vijambhikā, *f.* yawning ; drowsiness.

Vijaya, *m.* victory ; triumph.

Vijayati (vi + ji + a), to conquer ; to triumph over. *aor.* **vijayi.**

Vijahati (vi + hā + a ; **hā** is doubled and the first **hā** is changed to **ja**), to abandon ; to forsake ; to leave ; to give up. *aor.* **vijahi.** *pp.* **—hita.** *pr. p.* **—hanta.** *abs.* **—hitvā, vihāya.** *pt. p.* **—hitabba.**

Vijāta, *pp.* of **vijāyati.**

Vijātā, *f.* a woman who has given birth to a child.

Vijātika, *a.* of a different nation ; an outsider ; foreigner.

Vijānana, *nt.* knowledge ; recognition.

Vijānāti (vi + ñā + nā ; **ñā** is changed to **jā**), to know ; to understand ; to perceive ; to recognize. *aor.* **vijāni.** *pp.* **viññāta,** *pr. p.* **—nanta.** *pt. p.* **—nitabba.** *abs.* **—nitvā, vijāniya.** *inf.* **—nituŋ.**

Vijāyati (vi + jan + ya), to bring forth ; to give birth. *aor.* **vijāyi.** *abs.* **vijāyitvā.**

Vijāyana, *nt.* bringing forth ; giving birth.

Vijāyantī, —yamānā, *f.* a woman bringing forth a child.

Vijāyinī, *f.* able to bear a child.

Vijita (*pp.* of **vijināti**), conquered ; subdued. *nt.* a kingdom. **—saṅgāma,** *a.* victorious ; by whom the battle has been won.

Vijināti. see **Jināti.**

Vijitāvī, 3. victorious.

Vijjati (vid + ya), to exist ; to be found. *pr. p.* **vijjanta, vijjamāna.**

Vijjantarikā, *f.* an interval of lightning.

Vijjā, *f.* higher knowledge ; science. **—caraṇa,** *nt.* special wisdom and virtue. **—ṭṭhāna,** *nt.* a subject of study ; arts and sciences. **—dhara,** *a.* a knower of charms ; a sorcerer. **—vimutti,** *f.* emancipation through wisdom.

Vijju, vijjutā, vijjullatā, *f.* a lightning.

Vijjotati (vi + jut + a), to shine. *aor.* **vijjoti.** *pp.* **—jotita.** *pr. p.* **—tamāna.**

Vijjhati (vidh + ya), to shoot ; to pierce ; to perforate. *aor.* **vijjhi.** *pp.* **viddha.** *pr. p.* **—jhanta, —jhamāna.** *abs.* **—jhitvā, vijjhiya.**

Vijjhana, *nt.* shooting ; piercing.

Vijjhāyati (vi + jhe + a), to be extinguished. *aor.* **—āyi.**

Viññatta=**viññāpita,** informed ; instructed.

Viññatti, *f.* intimation ; information.

Viññāṇa, *nt.* animation ; consciousness. **—ṇaka,** *a.* endowed with vitality. **—kkhandha,** *m.* the aggregate of life-force. **—ṭṭhiti,** *f.* stages of sentient beings. **—dhātu,** *f.* mind-element.

Viññāta (*pp.* of **vijānāti**), understood ; perceived ; known.

Viññātabba (*pt. p.* of **vijānāti**), what should be understood.

Viññātu, *m.* a perceiver ; one who knows.

Viññāpaka, 3. clever in instruction.

Viññāpana, *nt.* information ; introduction.

Viññāpaya, *a.* accessible to instruction.

Viññāpeti (vi + ñā + āpe), to inform ; to teach ; to intimate. *aor.* **—esi.** *pp.* **—pita.** *abs.* **—petvā.** *pr. p.* **—penta.**

Viññāpetu, *m.* an instructor ; one who intimates.

Viññāya (*abs.* from **vijānāti**), having known or learnt.

Viññāyati (*pass.* of **vijānāti**), to be known. *aor.* **—ñāyi.**

Viññū, *a.* wise ; *m.* a wise man. **—ñutā,** *f.* discretion ; puberty. **—uppasattha,** *a.* extolled by the wise.

Viññeyya, *a.* to be perceived.

Viṭaṅka, *m. nt.* a dovecot ; the line of projecting ends of beams.

Viṭapa, *m.* a branch ; fork of a tree ; the roots descending from branches.

Viṭapī, *m.* a tree.

Vitakka, *m.* reflexion ; thought. **—kana,** *nt.* contemplation.

Vitakketi (vi + tak + e), to reflect ; to consider. *aor.* **—esi.** *pp.* **—kita.** *pr. p.* **—kenta.** *abs.* **—ketvā.**

Vitacchikā, *f.* scabies.

Vitaccheti (vi + tacch + e), to peel ; to smooth. *aor.* **—esi.** *pp.* **—chita.**

Vitaṇḍavāda, *m.* sophistry. **—vādī,** *m.* a sophist.

Vitata (*pp.* of **vitanoti**), stretched ; extended ; diffused.

Vitatha, *a.* false ; untrue. *nt.* untruth.

Vitanoti (vi + tan + o), to stretch or spread out. *aor.* **vitani.**

Vitaraṇa, *nt.* distribution ; overcoming ; getting through.

Vitarati (vi + tar + a), to go through ; to distribute ; to remove. *aor.* **vitari.** *pp.* **vitarita, vitiṇṇa.**

Vitāna, *nt.* a canopy.

Vitiṇṇa, see under **Vitarati.**

Vitudati (vi + tud + a), to nudge; to prick. *aor.* **vitudi.** *abs.* **—ditvā.**

Vitudana, *nt.* pricking.

Vitunna, *pp.* of **vitudati.**

Vitta, *nt.* wealth; property.

Vitti, *f.* joy; happiness.

Vittha, *nt.* a bowl for drinking spirits.

Vitthata (*pp.* of **vittharati**), extended; wide; spread out.

Vitthambhana, *nt.* expansion; puffing; suffusion.

Vitthambheti (vi + thambh + e), to expand; to puff; to inflate. *aor.* **—esi.** *pp.* **—bhita.** *abs.* **—bhetvā.**

Vitthāra, *m.* explanation; detail; the breadth. **—kathā,** *f.* commentary. **—rato,** *ad.* in detail. **—rika,** *a.* wide-spread

Vitthāreti (vi + thar + e), to spread out; to explain; to expand. *aor.* **—esi.** *pp.* **—rita.** *pr. p.* **—renta.** *abs.* **—retvā.** *pass.* **vitthārīyati.**

Vitthinna, see **Vitthata.**

Vidatthi, *f.* a span.

Vidahati (vi + dhā + a), to arrange; to manage; to command. *aor.* **vidahi.** *pp.* **vihita, vidahita.** *abs.* **—hitvā.**

Vidāraṇa, *nt.* rending; splitting.

Vidāreti (vi + dar + e), to split; to rend. *aor.* **—esi.** *pp.* **—rita.** *pr. p.* **—renta.** *abs.* **—retvā.**

Vidālana, *nt.* splitting; bursting.

Vidāleti, see **Vidāreti.**

Vidita (*pp.* from the root **vid**), known; found out. **—tatta,** *nt.* the fact of having known.

Vidisā, *f.* an intermediate point of compass.

Vidugga, *nt.* a difficult passage; a fortress difficult to access.

Vidū, *a.* wise; skilled in. *m.* a wise man.

Vidūra, *a.* remote; distant.

Vidūsita (*pp.* of **vidūseti**), corrupted; depraved.

Videsa, *m.* a foreign country. **—sika, —sī,** *a.* foreign; a foreigner.

Viddasu, *m.* a wise man.

Viddesa, *m.* enmity.

Viddha (*pp.* of **vijjhati**), pierced; shot; struck.

Viddhaŋsaka, *a.* one who destroys; bringing destruction. **—sana,** *nt.* demolition; destruction.

Viddhaŋseti (vi + dhaŋs + e), to demolish; to destroy. *aor.* **—esi.** *pp.* **—sita, viddhasta.** *abs.* **—setvā.** *pr. p.* **—senta.**

Vidha, *a.* (in cpds.) of a kind; consisting of. —fold. **nānāvidha** = manifold.

Vidhamaka, *a.* one who destroys; destroying.

Vidhamati (vi + dham + e), to destroy; to ruin; to scatter. *aor.* **vidhami.** *pp.* **—mita.** *abs.* **—mitvā.**

Vidhameti (vi + dham + e), same as the above.

Vidhavā, *f.* a widow.

Vidhā, *f.* conceit; pride.

Vidhātu, *m.* the Creator.

Vidhāna, *nt.* arrangement; command; performance; process.

Vidhāyaka, *a.* one who arranges, manages or performs.

Vidhāvati (vi + dhāv + a), to run about; to roam. *aor.* **vidhāvi.** *abs.* **—vitvā.**

Vidhāvana, *nt.* running about.

Vidhi, *m.* method; way; luck; destiny; form. **—dhinā,** *ad.* in due method.

Vidhunāti (vi + dhu + nā), to shake off; to remove. *aor.* **vidhuni.** *pp.* **vidhūta, vidhunita.** *abs.* **—nitvā.**

Vidhūta, *pp.* of the above.

Vidhūpana, *nt.* a fan; fanning; flavouring; fumigation.

Vidhūpeti (vi + dhūp + e), to flavour; to fan; to fumigate; to scatter. *aor.* **—pesi.** *pp.* **—pita.** *pr. p.* **—payanta.** *abs.* **—petvā.**

Vidhūma, *a.* smokeless; passionless.

Vidheyya, *a.* obedient.

Vinaṭṭha (*pp.* of **vinassati**), destroyed; ruined; lost.

Vinata (*pp.* of **vinamati**), bent.

Vinatā, *f.* the mother of the Garuḍa race.

Vinaddha, *pp.* of the following.

Vinandhati (vi + nandh + a), to encircle; to twist round; to intertwine. *aor.* **—ndhi.** *abs.* **—dhitvā.**

Vinaya, *m.* discipline; the code of monastic discipline; removal. **—na,** *nt.* removal; taming; instruction. **—dhara,** *a.* an expert in Vinaya-code. **—piṭaka,** *nt.* the code of discipline for the B. monks. **—vādī,** *m.* one who speaks in accordance with the rules of conduct.

Vinaḷīkata, *pp.* destroyed; rendered useless.

Vinassati (vi + nas + ya), to be lost; to perish; to be destroyed. *aor.* **vinassi.** *pp.* **vinaṭṭha.** *pr. p.* **—santa, —samāna.** *abs.* **—sitvā.**

Vinassana, *nt.* perishing.

Vinā, *in.* without. **—bhāva,** *m.* separation.

Vināti (vi + nā), to weave. *aor.* **vini.** *pp.* **vīta.**

Vināma, *m.* **—mana,** *nt.* bending the body or limbs.

Vināmeti (vi + nam + e), to bend. *aor.* **—esi.** *pp.* **—mita.** *abs.* **—metvā.**

Vināyaka, *m.* a great leader; the Buddha.

Vināsa, *m.* destruction; ruin; loss. **—saka,** *a.* destroying; causing ruin. **—sana.** *nt.* destroying.

Vināseti (vi + nas + e), to cause ruin; to destroy; to spoil. *aor.* **—esi.** *pp.* **vināsita.** *pr. p.* **—senta.** *abs.* **—setvā.**

Viniggata (*pp.* of **viniggacchati**), come out from.

Vinicchaya, *m.* decision; judgement; trial; discrimination. **—kathā,** *f.* analytical discussion. **—ṭṭhāna,** *nt.* law-courts. **—sālā,** *f.* the hall of judgement.

Vinicchita, *pp.* of **vinicchet**i. decided; judged; discerned.

Vinicchināti (vi + ni + chi + nā), to investigate; to try; to decide. *aor.* **—chini.** *pp.* **—chita.** *abs.* **—chinitvā.**

Viniccheti (vi + ni + chi + e) to investigate; to judge. *aor.* **—esi.** *pp.* **—chita.** *abs.* **—chetvā.** *pr. p.* **—chenta.**

Vinidhāya, *abs.* (from **vinidahati**), having misplaced; asserting wrongly.

Vinipāta, *m.* a place of suffering; a bad falling. **—pātika,** *a.* destined to suffer in purgatory.

Vinipāteti (vi + ni + pat + e), to bring to ruin; to waste.

Vinibaddha (*pp.* of **vinibandhati**), bound to; connected with.

Vinibandha, *m.* bondage; attachment.

Vinibbhujati (vi + ni + bhuj + a), to separate; to discriminate. *aor.* **—bhuji.** *abs.* **—jitvā.**

Vinibbhoga, *m.* separation ; discrimination.

Vinimaya, *m.* reciprocity ; exchange.

Vinimoceti (vi + ni + muc + e), to free oneself ; to get rid of. *aor.* **—esi.** *pp.* **—cita.** *abs.* **—cetvā.**

Vinimmutta (*pp.* of **vinimuccati**), free from ; released.

Vinivaṭṭeti (vi + ni + vat + e), to turn or roll over ; to glide off. *aor.* **—esi.** *pp.* **—ṭita.** *abs.* **—ṭetvā.**

Vinivijjha, *abs.* of the following.

Vinivijjhati (vi + ni + vidh + ya), to pierce through. *aor.* **—jhi.** *pp.* **—viddha.** *abs.* **—jhitvā.**

Vinividdha, *pp.* of the above.

Viniveṭheti (vi + ni + veṭh + e), to disentangle ; to unwrap ; to free oneself from. *aor.* **—esi.** *pp.* **—ṭhita.** *abs.* **—ṭhetvā.**

Vinīta (*pp.* of **vineti**), trained ; educated.

Vinīvaraṇa, *a.* free from the obstructions to the progress of mind.

Vineti (vi + ni + e), to lead ; to train ; to instruct ; to remove. *aor.* **vinesi.** *pr. p.* **vinenta.** *pt. p.* **vinetabba.** *abs.* **vinetvā.**

Vinetu, *m.* trainer ; instructor ; remover.

Vineyya (*abs.* of **vineti**), having removed. *adj.* fit to be trained.

Vinoda, *m.* joy ; pleasure.

Vinodana, *nt.* removal ; dispelling.

Vinodeti (vi + nud + e), to dispel ; to remove ; to drive out. *aor.* **—esi.** *pp.* **—dita.** *abs.* **—detvā.**

Vinodetu, *m.* dispeller.

Vindaka, 3. one who enjoys or suffers.

Vindati (vid + ŋ - a), to enjoy ; to undergo ; to know ; to gain. *aor.* **vindi.** *pp.* **vindita.** *pr. p.* **—danta, —damāna.** *abs.* **vinditvā.** *pt. p.* **—ditabba.**

Vindiyamāna, *pr. p.* being endured or suffered.

Vipakkha, *a.* hostile. **—sevaka,** *a.* siding with the enemy.

Vipaccati (vi + pac + ya), to ripen ; to bear fruit. *aor.* **vipacci.** *pp.* **vipakka.** *pr. p.* **vipaccamāna.**

Vipajjati (vi + pad + ya), to fail ; to go wrong ; to perish. *aor.* **vipajji.** *pp.* **vipanna.**

Vipajjana, *nt.* failing ; perishing.

Vipatti, *f.* failure ; misfortune ; distress ; going wrong.

Vipatha, *m.* wrong path.

Vipanna, *pp.* of **vipajjati.** **—diṭṭhī,** *a.* one who has wrong views. **—sīla,** *a.* gone wrong in morals.

Vipariṇata (*pp.* of **vipariṇamati**), perverted ; lustful.

Vipariṇāma, *m.* change.

Vipariṇāmeti (vi + pari + nam + e), to change ; to alter. *aor.* **—esi.** *pp.* **—ṇāmita.**

Vipariyāya, vipariyesa, *m.* contrariness ; wrong state ; reversal.

Viparivattati (vi + pari + vat + a), to turn round ; to upset. *aor.* **—vatti.** *pp.* **—vattita.**

Viparivattana, *nt.* change ; reverse.

Viparīta, *a.* reversed ; changed ; wrong. **—tā,** *f.* contradistinction.

Vipallattha, *a.* deranged ; perverted ; upset.

Vipallāsa, *m.* derangement ; corruption ; perversion.

Vipassaka, *a.* gifted with introspection.

Vipassati (vi + dis + a), to see clearly; to have intuition. *aor.* **vipassi.** *abs.* **—sitvā.**

Vipassanā, *f.* insight. **—ñāṇa.** *nt.* ability of attaining insight. **—dhura,** *nt.* obligation of introspection.

Vipassī, 3. gifted with insight.

Vipāka, *m.* result; fruition; consequence of one's actions.

Vipina, *nt.* a forest.

Vipula, *a.* extensive; great; large. **—latā,** *f.* **—latta,** *nt.* abundance; excess; broadness.

Vippa, *m.* a brahman. **—kula.** *nt.* the brahman caste.

Vippakata, *a.* left unfinished.

Vippakāra, *m.* change; alteration.

Vippakiṇṇa, *pp.* of the following.

Vippakirati (vi + pa + kir + a), to strew all over; to confound; to destroy. *aor.* **—kiri.** *abs.* **—kiritvā.**

Vippajahati (vi + pa + hā + a), to give up; to abandon. *aor.* **—jahi.**

Vippaṭipajjati (vi + paṭi + pad + ya), to err; to fail; to commit sin. *aor.* **—pajji.**

Vippaṭipatti, *f.* wrong action; transgression of rules.

Vippaṭipanna (*pp.* of **vippaṭipajjati**), acting wrongly; gone wrong.

Vippaṭisāra, *m.* remorse; repentance. **—sārī,** *a.* remorseful; repentant.

Vippamutta, *pp.* released; set free; saved.

Vippayutta, *pp.* separated.

Vippayoga, *m.* separation.

Vippalapati (vi + pa + lap + a), to wail; to lament. *aor.* **—lapi.**

Vippalāpa, *m.* confused talk; wailing.

Vippavasati (vi + pa + vas + a), to be absent; to be away from home. *aor.* **—vasi.**

Vippavāsa, *m.* absence; living abroad.

Vippavuttha (*pp.* of **vippavasati**), absent; being away from home.

Vippasanna (*pp.* of the following), very clear; pure; bright.

Vippasīdati (vi + pa + sad + a), to become clear or bright; to be joyful. *aor.* **—sīdi.**

Vippahīna, *a.* abandoned; removed of.

Vipphandati (vi + phand + a), to struggle; to writhe. *aor.* **—ndi.** *pp.* **—dita.** *abs.* **—ditvā.**

Vipphandana, *nt.* writhing struggle.

Vipphāra, *m.* diffusion; pervasion. **—rika,** *a.* spreading out. **—rita,** *pp.* expanded; spread out.

Vipphuraṇa, *nt.* pervasion.

Vipphurati (vi + phur + a), to vibrate; to tremble; to diffuse. *aor.* **—uri.** *pp.* **—rita.** *pr. p.* **—ranta.**

Vipphuliṅga, *nt.* a spark.

Viphala, *a.* fruitless; useless.

Vibandha, *m.* a fetter.

Vibādhaka, *a.* preventing; doing harm.

Vibādhati (vi + badh + a), to hinder; to oppress; to obstruct.

Vibādhana, *nt.* obstruction; prevention.

Vibbhanta (*pp.* of **vibbhamati**), **—ka,** *a.* apostate; one who has forsaken the Order.

Vibbhamati (vi + bham + a), to go astray; to forsake the Order. *aor.* **—mi.** *abs.* **—mitvā.**

Vibhaṅga, *m.* distribution; division; classification.

Vibhajati (vi + bhaj + a), to divide ; to dissect ; to classify. *aor.* **vibhaji.** *pp.* **vibhatta, vibhajita.** *pr. p.* **—janta.** *abs.* **—jitvā.**

Vibhajja (*abs.* of the above), having divided or analysed. **—vāda,** *m.* the religion of reason. **—vādī,** *m.* one who accepts the Theravāda doctrine.

Vibhatta, *pp.* of **vibhajati.**

Vibhatti, *f.* division ; classification ; inflection of nouns and verbs ; a case in grammar. **—tika,** *a.* having divisions.

Vibhava, *m.* wealth ; prosperity.

Vibhāga, *m.* **vibhajana,** *nt.* distribution ; division ; classification.

Vibhāta, *pp.* of the following.

Vibhāti (vi + bhā + a), to become bright ; to shine forth.

Vibhāvana, *nt.* explanation ; making clear.

Vibhāvī, *a.* intelligent ; *m.* a wise man.

Vibhāveti (vi + bhū + a), to make clear ; to explain. *aor.* **—esi.** *pp.* **—vita.** *pr. p.* **—venta.** *abs.* **—vetvā.**

Vibhinna, *pp.* divided ; at variance.

Vibhītaka, *m.* **—takī,** *f.* *Beleric Myrobalan.* ඵුළු.

Vibhūta, *pp.* clear ; distinct.

Vibhūti, *f.* splendour ; glory.

Vibhūsana, *nt.* **vibhūsā,** *f.* an ornament ; decoration.

Vibhūseti (vi + bhūs + e), to adorn ; to embellish ; to beautify *aor.* **—esi.** *pp.* **—sita.** *abs.* **—setvā.**

Vimati, *f.* doubt ; perplexity. **—cchedaka,** *a.* removing perplexity.

Vimana, *a.* displeased ; distracted.

Vimala, *a.* clean ; spotless ; unstained.

Vimāna, *nt.* a mansion ; heavenly palace. **—peta,** *m.* a kind of spiritual beings liable to semi-punishment and semi-enjoyment. **—vatthu,** *nt.* a book containing stories about **vimānas.**

Vimāneti (vi + man + e), to disrespect ; to treat with contempt. *aor.* **—esi.** *pp.* **—nita.** *abs.* **—netvā.**

Vimukha, *a.* turning away from ; neglectful.

Vimuccati (vi + muc + ya), to be released ; to be emancipated. *aor.* **—cci.** *pp.* **vimutta.** *abs.* **—citvā.**

Vimuccana, *nt.* release.

Vimuñcati (vi + muc + ŋ - a), to release ; to be free. *aor.* **—ñci.** *pp.* **—ñcita.** *pr. p.* **—canta.** *abs.* **—citvā.**

Vimutta (*pp.* of **vimuccati**), freed ; released ; emancipated.

Vimutti, *f.* release ; deliverance ; emancipation. **—rasa,** *m.* the essence of emancipation. **—sukha,** *nt.* happiness of emancipation.

Vimokkha, *m.* deliverance ; release ; emancipation.

Vimocaka, 3. one who releases.

Vimocana, *nt.* release from ; discharging ; letting loose.

Vimoceti (vi + muc + e), to release ; to make free. *aor.* **—esi.** *pp.* **—cita.** *pr. p.* **—centa.** *abs.* **—cetvā.**

Vimoheti (vi + muh + e), to delude ; to bewilder ; to beguile. *aor.* **—esi.** *pp.* **—hita.** *abs.* **—hetvā.**

Vimhaya, *m.* astonishment ; surprise.

Vimhāpaka, 3. one who amazes or surprises. **—pana**. *nt.* surprising.

Vimhāpeti (vi + mhi + āpe), to astonish; to surprise. *aor.* **—esi**. *pp.* **vimhāpita**. *abs.* **—petvā**.

Vimhita, *pp.* astonished.

Viya (*a particle of comparison*), like; as.

Viyatta, *a.* learned; accomplished.

Viyūhati (vi + ūh + a), to remove; to scatter. *aor.* **viyūhi**. *pp.* **viyūḷha, viyūhita**. *abs.* **—hitvā**.

Viyūhana, *nt.* scattering; removal.

Viyūḷha, vyūḷha, *pp.* of **viyūhati**.

Viyoga, *m.* separation.

Viracita, *pp.* of the following.

Viracayati (vi + rac + ya), to compose; to put together. *aor.* **viraci, viracayi**.

Viraja, *a.* stainless; free from defilement.

Virajjati (vi + rad + ya), to detach oneself: to show lack of interest in. *aor.* **—jji**. *pp.* **viratta**. *abs.* **—jjitvā**. *pr. p.* **—jamāna**.

Virajjana, *nt.* discarding; to dismiss from enjoyment.

Virajjhati (vi + rādh + ya), to fail; to miss; to lose. *aor.* **—jjhi**. *pp.* **viraddha**. *abs.* **—jhitvā**.

Virata (*pp.* of **viramati**), abstaining from.

Virati, *f.* abstinence.

Viratta (*pp.* of **virajjati**), dispassioned; unattached to.

Viraddha (*pp.* of **virajjhati**), failed; missed.

Viramana, *nt.* abstinence; abstaining from.

Viramati (vi + ram + a), to abstain; to refrain; to desist; to cease. *aor.* **virami**. *pr. p.* **viramanta**. *abs.* **viramitvā**.

Virala, *a.* sparse; rare; thin.

Virava, virāva, *m.* cry; roar; shouting.

Viravati (vi + rav + a), to cry aloud; to shout; to utter a cry. *aor.* **viravi**. *pr. p.* **—vanta**. *abs.* **—vitvā**.

Viravana, *nt.* see **Virava**.

Viraha, *m.* separation; emptiness.

Virahita, *a.* empty; rid of; exempt from; without.

Virāga, *m.* dispassionateness; absence of desire. **—gatā**, *f.* absence of lust. **—gī**, *a.* passionless; emancipated.

Virājati (vi + raj + a), to shine; to be bright. *aor.* **virāji**. *pp.* **—jita**. *pr. p.* **—jamāna**.

Virājeti (vi + rāj + e), to discard; to remove; to destroy. *aor.* **—esi**. *abs.* **—jetvā**.

Virādhanā, *f.* failure.

Virādheti (vi + radh + e), to miss; to omit; to fail. *aor.* **—esi**. *pp.* **—dhita**. *abs.* **—dhetvā**.

Viriccati (*pass.* of **vireceti**), to get purged.

Viriccamāna (*pr. p.* of the above), being purged.

Viritta (*pp.* of the above), purged.

Viriya, *nt.* vigour; energy; effort; strength. **—bala**, *nt.* the power of energy. **—vantu**, *a.* energetic. **—samatā**, *f.* moderation of energy. **—ārambha**, *m.* application of exertion. **—yindriya**, *nt.* the faculty of energy.

Virujjhati (vi + rudh + ya), to oppose; to be hostile. *aor.* **—jjhi**. *pp.* **viruddha**. *pr. p.* **—jjhanta**. *abs.* **—jhitvā**.

Viruddha (*pp.* of the above), opposed; opposite; hostile. **—tā,** *f.* hostility; opposition.

Virūpa, *a.* deformed; ugly. **—tā,** *f.* ugliness.

Virūpakkha, *m.* name of the overlord of Nāgas.

Virūḷha (*pp.* of **virūhati**), grown; increased.

Virūḷhi, *f.* growth.

Virūhati (vi + ruh + a), to grow; to sprout; to increase. *aor.* **virūhi.** *pr. p.* **—hanta.** *abs.* **—hitvā.**

Virūhana, *nt.* **—nā,** *f.* growing; growth.

Vireka, *m.* **virecana,** *nt.* purging; a purgative.

Vireceti (vi + rec + e), to purge. *aor.* **—esi.** *pp.* **virecita.** *abs.* **—cetvā.**

Virocati (vi + ruc + a), to shine; to be brilliant. *aor.* **viroci.** *pr. p.* **—camāna.** *abs.* **—citvā.**

Virocana, *nt.* shining.

Viroceti (*caus.* of **virocati**), to illumine. *aor.* **—esi.** *pp.* **—cita.** *abs.* **—cetvā.**

Virodha, *m.* **—dhana,** *nt.* opposition; contradiction; obstruction.

Virodheti (vi + rudh + e), to render hostile; to cause obstruction. *aor.* **—esi.** *pp.* **—dhita.** *abs.* **—dhetvā.**

Vilagga, *pp.* stuck; attached. *m.* the waist.

Vilapati (vi + lap + a), to lament; to wail; to talk nonsense. *aor.* **vilapi.** *pr. p.* **—panta, —pamāna.** *abs.* **—pitvā.**

Vilambati (vi + lamb + a), to loiter; to tarry; to hang about. *aor.* **vilambi.** *pp.* **—bita.** *abs.* **—bitvā.**

Vilambana, *nt.* loitering; a cause for shame.

Vilaya, *m.* dissolution.

Vilasati (vi + las + a), to shine forth; to dally; to sport. *aor.* **vilasi.**

Vilasita (*pp.* of the above), gay; shining; splendid.

Vilāpa, *m.* wailing; idle talk.

Vilāsa, *m.* charm; grace; beauty; appearance; coquetry. **—sitā,** *f.* coquetry.

Vilāsinī, *f.* a woman.

Vilāsī, *a.* possessing charm or grace.

Vilitta (*pp.* of **vilimpeti**), anointed with.

Vilimpati (vi + lip + ŋ - a), to smear; to anoint.

Vilimpeti (vi + limp + e), to smear; to anoint. *aor.* **—esi.** *pr. p.* **—penta.** *abs.* **—petvā.**

Vilīna (*pp.* of the following), dissolved.

Vilīyati (vi + lī + ya), to melt; to be dissolved; to perish. *aor.* **vilīyi.** *pr. p.* **—yamāna.**

Vilīyana, *nt.* melting; dissolution.

Vilīva, *nt.* a slip of bamboo or reed. **—kāra,** *m.* a basket maker.

Vilugga (*pp.* of **vilujjati**), broken; crumbling to pieces.

Vilutta (*pp.* of **vilumpati**), plundered; robbed of.

Vilūna, *pp.* cut or torn off.

Vilekha, *m.* perplexity; scratching.

Vilepana, *nt.* ointment; cosmetic; toilet perfume.

Vilepita, *pp.* of the following.

Vilepeti (vi + lip + e), to anoint with. *aor.* **—esi.** *abs.* **—petvā.**

Vilokana, *nt.* looking at; investigation.

Viloketi (vi + lok + e), to look at ; to inspect. *aor.* **—esi.** *pp.* **—kita.** *pr. p.* **—kenta. —kayamāna.** *abs.* **—ketvā.**

Vilocana, *nt.* the eye.

Vilopa, *m.* **—pana,** *nt.* pillage ; plunder. **—paka,** 3. one who plunders or destroys.

Viloma, *a.* opposing ; disagreeing. **—matā,** *f.* disagreement ; discrepancy.

Vilometi (*Deno.* from **viloma**), to disagree with ; to dispute. *aor.* **—esi.** *abs.* **— metvā.**

Viloḷana, *nt.* stirring.

Viloḷeti (vi + luḷ + e), to stir ; to shake about.

Vivajjana, *nt.* abandoning ; abstaining from.

Vivajjeti (vi + vajj + e), to avoid ; to abandon ; to forsake. *aor.* **—esi.** *pp.* **—jita.** *pr. p.* **—jenta.** *abs.* **—jetvā, vivajjiya.**

Vivaṭa (*pp.* of **vivarati**), open ; laid bare ; unveiled.

Vivaṭṭa, *nt.* devolution of rebirth. **—kappa,** *m.* an ascending aeon.

Vivaṭṭati (vi + vaṭṭ + a), to move back ; to revolve ; to begin again. *aor.* **vivaṭṭi.** *pp.* **—ṭita.** *abs.* **—ṭṭitvā.**

Vivaṭṭana, *nt.* moving back ; turning away.

Vivaṭṭeti (vi + vaṭṭ + e), to turn back ; to divert ; to destroy. *aor.* **—esi.** *pp.* **—ṭita.** *abs.* **—ṭetvā.**

Vivaṇṇeti (vi + vaṇṇ + e), to dispraise ; to defame. *aor.* **—esi.** *pp.* **—ṇita.** *abs.* **—ṇetvā.**

Vivadati (vi + vad + a), to dispute ; to quarrel. *aor.* **vivadi.** *pr. p.* **—danta, —damāna.** *abs.* **—ditvā.**

Vivadana, *nt.* disputation.

Vivara, *nt.* an opening ; cleft ; fissure ; flaw.

Vivaraṇa, *nt.* opening ; unveiling ; revelation.

Vivarati (vi + var + a), to open ; to uncover ; to make clear ; to analyse. *aor.* **vivari.** *pp.* **vivaṭa.** *pr. p.* **—ranta, —ramāna.** *abs.* **—ritvā.** *inf.* **—rituṃ.**

Vivāda, *m.* dispute ; contention ; quarrel ; controversy. **—dī. —ka,** 3. one who disputes.

Vivāha, *m.* marriage. **—maṅgala,** *nt.* marriage ceremony.

Vivicca, *in.* aloof from ; separating oneself from.

Vivitta, *a.* secluded ; lonely ; solitary. **—tā,** *f.* seclusion.

Vividha, *a.* divers ; manifold.

Viveka, *m.* detachment ; seclusion.

Vivecana, *nt.* discrimination ; criticism.

Viveceti (vi + vic + e), to separate ; to discriminate ; to criticize. *aor.* **—esi.** *pp.* **—cita.** *abs.* **—cetvā.**

Visa, *nt.* poison ; venom. **—kaṇṭaka,** *nt.* a poisoned thorn ; a kind of sugar. **—pīta,** *a.* dipped into poison. **—rukkha,** *m.* a poisonous tree. **—vejja,** *m.* a physician who cures poison. **—salla,** *nt.* a poisoned dart.

Visañña, —ññī, *a.* unconscious.

Visaṭa, visata (*pp.* of **visarati**), spread ; diffused.

Visati (vis + a), see **Pavisati.**

Visattikā, *f.* attachment ; craving.

Visada, *a.* clean ; pure ; manifest. **—kiriyā,** *f.* making clear. **—tā,** *f.* **—bhāva,** *m.* clearness ; purity.

Visabhāga, *a.* different; contrary; uncommon.

Visama, *a.* uneven; unequal; disharmonious.

Visaya, *m.* locality; region; sphere; object; scope; sensual pleasure; footing.

Visayha, *a.* bearable; possible.

Visalla, *a.* free from grief; removed of the dart.

Visahati (vi + sah + a), to be able; to dare; to venture. *aor.* **visahi.** *pr. p.* **—hamāna.**

Visaŋyutta, *pp.* unyoked; detached from.

Visaŋyoga, *m.* disconnection; separation from.

Visaŋvāda, *m.* deceiving; a lie. **—daka,** *a.* untrustworthy. **—dana,** *nt.* lying.

Visaŋvādeti (vi + saŋ + vad + e), to deceive; to lie; to break one's word. *aor.* **—esi.** *pp.* **—vādita.** *pr. p.* **—denta.** *abs.* **—detvā.**

Visaŋsaṭṭha, *a.* separated; disconnected.

Visaṅkita, *a.* suspicious.

Visaṅkhāra, *m.* divestment of all material things.

Visākhā, *f.* name of a lunar mansion, and that of a female devotee of the Buddha.

Visāṇa, *nt.* a horn. **—maya,** *a.* made of horn.

Visāda, *m.* dejection; depression.

Visārada, *a.* self-possessed; confident; skilled.

Visāla, *a.* large; broad; extensive; bulky. **—kkhī,** *f.* (a woman) having large eyes. **—tā,** *f.* **—tta,** *nt.* largeness; immensity.

Visikhā, *f.* a street.

Visiṭṭha, *a.* distinguished; eminent; extraordinary. **—tara,** *a.* more prominent.

Visibbeti (vi + siv + e), to unsew; to warm oneself. *aor.* **—esi.** *abs.* **—betvā.**

Visīdati (vi + sad + a), to sink down; to be dejected. *aor.* **visīdi.**

Visīdana, *nt.* sinking; dejection.

Visīvana, *nt.* warming oneself.

Visīveti (vi + siv + e), to warm oneself. *aor.* **—esi.** *pr. p.* **—venta.** *abs.* **—vetvā.**

Visujjhati (vi + sudh + ya), to become clean or pure. *aor.* **—jjhi.** *pp.* **visuddha.** *pr. p.* **—jhamāna.** *abs.* **—jhitvā.**

Visuddha (*pp.* of the above), clean; pure; bright; stainless; sanctified. **—tā,** *f.* **—tta,** *nt.* purity; cleanliness.

Visuddhi, *f.* purity; holiness; splendour; excellency. **—deva,** *m.* a holy person. **—magga,** *m.* the path to obtain holiness.

Visuŋ, *ad.* separately; individually; apart. **—karaṇa,** *nt.* separation. **—katvā,** *abs.* having separated.

Visūka, *nt.* wriggling; a show. **—dassana,** *nt.* visiting shows.

Visūcikā, *f.* cholera.

Visesa, *m.* distinction; difference; attainment. **—ka,** *m.* a distinguishing mark. **—gāmī,** *a.* reaching distinction. **—bhāgiya,** *a.* leading to distinction or progress. **—sādhigama,** *m.* specific attainment.

Visesato, *ad.* distinctively; altogether.

Visesana, *nt.* distinction; attribute; an adjective.

Visesiya, **—sitabba,** *a.* to be qualified or defined.

Visesī, *a.* possessing distinction; one who qualifies.

Viseseti (vi + sis + e), to qualify; to define; to distinguish. *aor.* **—esi.** *pp.* **—sita.** *abs.* **—setvā.**

Visoka, *a.* free from grief.

Visodhana, *nt.* cleansing; purifying.

Visodheti (vi + sudh + e), to clean; to purify. *aor.* **—esi.** *pp.* **—dhita.** *pr. p.* **—dhenta.** *abs.* **—dhetvā, —dhiya.**

Visoseti (vi + sus + e), to cause to dry up; to make wither. *aor.* **—esi.** *pp.* **—sita.** *pr. p.* **—senta.** *abs.* **—setvā.**

Vissagandha, *m.* a smell like that of raw flesh.

Vissagga, *m.* donation; distribution.

Vissajjaka, *a.* giving out; distributing; one who answers a question.

Vissajjana, *nt.* bestowing; sending off; discharging; an answer; expenditure. **—naka,** *a.* answering; bestowing; expending.

Vissajjanīya,—jjitabba,—jjiya, *a.* to be distributed or answered.

Vissajjeti (vi + sajj + e), to answer; to distribute; to send off; to spend; to get rid of; to emit; to let loose. *aor.* **—esi.** *pp.* **—jita, vissaṭṭha,** *abs.* **—jetvā,** *pr. p.* **—jenta.**

Vissaṭṭhi, *f.* emission; discharge.

Vissattha (*pp.* of **vissasati**), confident; intimate; friendly.

Vissanda, *m.* **—dana,** *nt.* overflow; oozing.

Vissandati (vi + sand + a), to flow out; to overflow. *aor.* **—ndi.** *pp.* **—dita.** *pr. p.* **—damāna.** *abs.* **—ditvā.**

Vissamati (vi + sam + a), to rest; to repose; to recover from fatigue. *aor.* **—sami.** *pp.* **vissanta.** *pr. p.* **—samanta.** *abs.* **—mitvā.**

Vissara, *a.* a cry of distress.

Vissarati (vi + sar + a), to forget. *aor.* **vissari.** *pp.* **—sarita.** *abs.* **—ritvā.**

Vissasati (vi + sas + a), to confide in; to be friendly with. *aor.* **—sasi.** *pp.* **vissattha.** *pr. p.* **—santa.** *abs.* **—sitvā.**

Vissāsa, *m.* confidence; trust; intimacy. **—saka, —sika, —sāsī,** *a.* intimate; confidential; trustworthy.

Vissāsanīya, *a.* fit to be trusted; confidential.

Vissuta, *a.* famous; renowned.

Vihaga, vihaṅgama, *m.* a bird.

Vihaññati (vi + han + ya), to be vexed or grieved; to suffer hardship. *aor.* **—ññi.** *pr. p.* **—ñamāna.**

Vihata, *pp.* of the following.

Vihanati (vi + han + a), to kill; to put an end to; to remove. *aor.* **vihani.** *abs.* **vihantvā, vihanitvā.**

Viharati (vi + har + a), to live; to abide; to dwell; to sojourn. *aor.* **vihari.** *pr. p.* **viharanta, —ramāna.** *abs.* **viharitvā.**

Vihāya, *abs.* (from **vijahati**), having left or given up.

Vihāra, *m.* an abode; a dwelling place; mode of life; passing the time.

Vihārika, vihārī, *a.* (in cpds.) staying or sojourning; being in such and such a condition.

Vihiŋsati (vi + hiŋs + a), to hurt; to injure; to annoy. *aor.* **—hiŋsi.** *pr. p.* **—santa.** *abs.* **—sitvā.**

Vihiŋsanā, vihiŋsā, *f.* cruelty; injury; injuring. **—sāvitakka,** *m.* malign thought.

Vihita (*pp.* of **vidahati**), arranged; furnished; engaged upon.

Vihīna (*pp.* of **vihāyati**), left; lost; decreased.

Viheṭhaka, *a.* harassing; oppressing; annoying. **—jātika,** *a.* having the habit of harassing.

Viheṭhana, *nt.* oppression. **—naka,** *a.* doing harm.

Viheṭhiyamāna, *pr. p.p.* being oppressed or harassed.

Viheṭheti (vi + heṭh + e), to vex; to bring into difficulties. *aor.* **—esi.** *pp.* **—ṭhita.** *pr. p.* **—ṭhenta.** *abs.* **—ṭhetvā.**

Vihesaka, *a.* vexing; troubling.

Vihesā, *f.* vexation; annoyance; injury.

Vihesiyamāna, see **Viheṭhiyamāna.**

Viheseti (vi + his + e), see **Viheṭheti.**

Vīci, *f.* a wave; an interval.

Vījati (vīj + a), to fan. *aor.* **vīji.** *pp.* **vījita.** *abs.* **vījetvā.** *pr. p.* **vījayamāna.**

Vījana, *nt.* fanning.

Vījanī, *f.* a fan.

Vījiyamāna, *pr. p.p.* being fanned.

Vījeti (vīj + e), to fan. *aor.* **—esi.** *pr. p.* **vījenta.** *abs.* **vījetvā.**

Viṇā, *f.* a lute. **—daṇḍaka,** *m.* the neck of a lute. **—doṇi,** *f.* the sounding board of a lute. **—vāyana,** *nt.* playing of a lute.

Vīta (= **vigata**), *pp.* free from; being without; (= **vāyita**), woven. **—ccika,** *a.* flameless; glowing. **—gedha, —taṇha,** *a.* without greed or craving. **—mala,** *a.* stainless. **—moha,** *a.* without ignorance. **—rāga,** *a.* passionless. *m.* a saint.

Vītikkama, *m.* transgression; going beyond.

Vītikkamati (vi + ati + kam + a), to transgress; to go beyond. *aor.* **—kami.** *pp.* **vītikkanta.** *pr. p.* **—kamanta.** *abs.* **—kamitvā.**

Vītināmeti (vi + ati + nam + e), to spend time; to wait. *aor.* **—esi.** *pp.* **—nāmtia.** *abs.* **—metvā.**

Vītivatta (*pp.* of **vītivattati**), having passed, spent, or overcome.

Vītivatteti (vi + ati + vat + e), to overcome; to spend time. *aor.* **—esi.** *pp.* **—vattita.** *abs.* **—tetvā.**

Vītiharaṇa, *nt.* **vītihāra,** *m.* exchange of steps; a stride; carrying in between.

Vītiharati (vi + ati + har + a), to walk; to stride. *aor.* **—hari.** *abs.* **—ritvā.**

Vīthi, *f.* a street; a track. **—citta,** *nt.* process of cognition.

Vīmaŋsaka, *a.* one who investigates or tests.

Vīmaŋsana, *nt.* **vīmaŋsā,** *f.* experiment; investigation.

Vīmaŋsati (mān + sa; **mā** is doubled and the first **mā** is changed to **vī**; the second **mā** is shortened), to investigate; to test; to consider. *aor.* **vīmaŋsi.** *pp.* **—sita.** *pr. p.* **—santa.** *abs.* **—sitvā, vīmaŋsiya.**

Vīmaŋsī, 3. investigator.

Vīra, *a.* brave; heroic. *m.* a hero.

Vīyati (vā + ī + ya), to be woven.

Vīsati, *f.* twenty. **—ma,** *a.* twentieth. (in cpds. **vīsati** sometimes takes the form **vīsaŋ,** *e. g.* **vīsaŋvassasatikā**).

Vīhi, *m.* paddy.

Vuccati (vac + ya), to be said or called. *pr. p.* **vuccamāna.**

Vuṭṭha (*pp.* of **vassati**), wet with rain.

Vuṭṭhahati, vuṭṭhāti (u + ṭhā + a), to rise ; to arise ; to emerge from ; to be produced. *aor.* **vuṭṭhahi, vuṭṭhāsi**. *pp.* **vuṭṭhita**. *pr. p.* **—hanta**. *abs.* **vuṭṭhahitvā, vuṭṭhāya**

Vuṭṭhāpeti (*caus.* of the above) ; to rouse ; to turn away from ; to ordain. *aor.* **—esi**. *pp.* **—pita**. *abs.* **—petvā**.

Vuṭṭhi, *f.* rain. **—ka**, *a.* having rain.

Vuḍḍha, *a.* old ; venerable. **—tara**, *a.* elder ; older.

Vuḍḍhi, *f.* increase ; growth ; prosperity.

Vutta (*pp.* of **vadati**), said ; (from **vapati** :) sown ; shaven. *nt.* the thing sown or said. **—ppakāra**, *a.* having above-said qualities. **—ppakārena**, *ad.* in the way above explained. **—vādī**, 3. one who speaks what is said. **—sira**, *a.* with a shaven head.

Vutti, *f.* conduct ; habit ; practice ; usage ; livelihood. **—ka, vuttī**, *a.* having the habit or practice of. **—tā**, *f.* condition.

Vuttha (*pp.* of **vasati**), having dwelt or spent time. **—vassa**, *a.* having spent the rainy season.

Vuddha, see **Vuḍḍha**.

Vuddhi, see **Vuḍḍhi**. **—ppatta**, *a.* come of age ; fit to be married ; grown up.

Vuyhati (vah + ya), to be carried away or floated. *aor.* **vuyhi**. *pp.* **vūḷha**. *pr. p.* **—hamāna**.

Vusita (*pp.* of **vasati**), dwelt ; fulfilled ; come to perfection. **—tta**, *nt.* **—bhāva**, *m.* the fact of being dwelt.

Vussati, *pass.* of **vasati**.

Vupakaṭṭha, *a.* secluded.

Vūpasanta (*pp.* of **vūpasammati**), allayed ; calmed.

Vūpasama, *m.* **—mana**, *nt.* relief ; calmness ; cessation.

Vūpasameti (vi + upa + sam + e), to appease ; to allay ; to relieve. *aor.* **—esi**. *pp.* **—samita**. *pr. p.* **—samenta**. *abs.* **—metvā**.

Vūpasammati (vi + upa + sam + ya), to be assuaged or quieted ; to be extinguished.

Vūḷha, *pp.* of **vuyhati**.

Ve, *a particle of affirmation*, indeed ; truly ; surely.

Vekalla, *nt.* **—latā**, *f.* deformity ; deficiency.

Vega, *m.* force ; speed ; velocity ; impulse.

Vejayanta, *m.* name of Indra's palace.

Vejja, *m.* a physician ; doctor. **—kamma**, *nt.* medical treatment.

Veṭhaka, *a.* enveloping ; wrapping.

Veṭhana, *nt.* a wrapper ; a turban or head-dress.

Veṭhiyamāna, *pr. p. p.* being wrapped or twisted.

Veṭheti (veṭh + e), to wrap ; to twist round ; to envelope. *aor.* **veṭhesi**. *pp.* **veṭhita**. *pr. p.* **—ṭhenta**. *abs.* **—ṭhetvā**.

Veṇika, *m.* a player on a lute.

Veṇī, *f.* a braid of hair. **—kata**, *a.* plaited ; bound together as in a sheaf. **—karaṇa**, *nt.* making sheafs.

Veṇu, *m.* a bamboo. **—gumba**, *m.* a bush of bamboo. **—bali**, *m.* a tax to be paid in bamboo. **—vana**, *nt.* a bamboo grove.

Vetana, *nt.* wages ; hire ; payment ; fee.

Vetanika, 3. one who works for wages; a hireling.

Vetaraṇī, *f.* name of a river.

Vetasa, *m.* the rattan reed.

Vetālika, *m.* a court musician.

Veti (vi + i + a), to wane; to disappear.

Vetta, *nt.* a cane; a twig. **—gga**, *nt.* the sprout of a cane. **—latā**, *f.* cane creeper.

Veda, *m.* religious feeling; knowledge; the brahmanic canon of authorized religious teaching. **—gū**, *m.* one who has attained the highest knowledge. **—ntagū**, **—pāragū**, *m.* one who excells in the knowledge of the Vedas. **—jāta**, *a.* filled with joy.

Vedaka, 3. one who feels or suffers.

Vedanaṭṭa, *a.* afflicted with pain.

Vedanā, *f.* pain; sensation. **—kkhandha**, *m.* the aggregate of sensation.

Vedayita, *nt.* feeling; experience.

Vedi, *aor.* of **vidati** = to know.

Vedikā, **vedī**, *f.* a platform; a railing.

Vedita, *pp.* of **vedeti**.

Vediyati (vid + i + ya), to be felt or experienced. *pr. p.* **—yamāna**.

Vedeti (vid + e), to feel; to sense; to know. *aor.* **vedesi**. *pr. p.* **vedenta**. *abs.* **vedetvā**.

Vedeha, *a.* belonging to the Videha country.

Vedehīputta, *m.* son of a princess from Videha.

Vedha, *m.* **vedhana**, *nt.* piercing; shooting; pricking.

Vedhati (vidh + a), to tremble; to quake. *aor.* **vedhi**. *pp.* **vedhita**.

Vedhī, 3. one who shoots or hits.

Venayika, *m.* a nihilist; an expert in Vinaya.

Veneyya, *a.* accessible to instruction; tractable.

Vepulla, *nt.* **—latā**, *f.* full development; abundance.

Vebhaṅgiya, *a.* fit to be distributed.

Vema, *m.* a shuttle.

Vemajjha, *nt.* the middle; centre.

Vematika, *a.* doubtful.

Vematta, *nt.* **—ttatā**, *f.* difference; distinction.

Vemātika, *a.* having a different mother and the same father.

Vemānika, *a.* having a fairy palace. **—peta**, see **Vimānapeta**.

Veyyattiya, *nt.* lucidity; accomplishment.

Veyyākaraṇa, *nt.* explanation. 3. one who knows grammar or how to explain.

Veyyābādhika, *a.* causing injury or oppression.

Veyyāvacca, *nt.* duty; service; commission. **—kara**, 3. **—yāvatika**, 3. an attendant; servant; one who waits on.

Vera, *nt.* enmity; hatred.

Verajjaka, *a.* belonging to various countries.

Veramaṇī, *f.* abstinence.

Verambhavāta, *m.* a wind blowing in high altitudes.

Verika, **verī**, *a.* inimical; revengeful. *m.* an enemy.

Verocana, *m.* the sun.

Velā, *f.* time; shore; limit; boundary. **—tikkama**, *m.* going out of limits.

Vellita, *a.* crooked ; curly. —**gga**, *a.* having curly tips.

Vevacana, an epithet ; a synonym.

Vevaṇṇiya, *nt.* disfiguration ; discolouring.

Vesa, *m.* appearance ; dress.

Vesamma, *nt.* unequality ; disharmony.

Vesākha, *m.* name of a month, April-May.

Vesārajja, *nt.* self-confidence.

Vesiyā, vesī, *f.* a harlot ; a prostitute.

Vesma, *nt.* a dwelling place.

Vessa, *m.* a member of the third social grade.

Veḷu, see **Veṇu**. —**riya**, *nt.* a lapis lazuli.

Vehāsa, *m.* the sky. —**kuṭi**, *f.* an airy room upstairs. —**gamana**, *nt.* going through the air. —**ṭṭha**, *a.* situated in the sky.

Vo (*enclitic* from **tumha**), to you ; of you ; by you.

Vokiṇṇa, *pp.* covered with ; full of ; mixed up.

Vokkanta, see **Okkanta**.

Vokkanti, see **Okkanti**.

Vokkamati (vi + u + kam + a), to turn aside ; to deviate from. *aor.* **vokkami**. *pp.* **vokkanta**. *abs.* **vokkamma**, —**mitvā**.

Vocchijjati (vi + u + chid + ya), to be cut off or stopped. *aor.* —**jji**. *pp.* —**chinna**. *abs.* —**jjitvā**.

Vodaka, *a.* free from water.

Vodapana, *nt.* —**nā**, *f.* cleansing ; purification.

Vodapeti (vi + u + dā + āpe), to cleanse ; to purify. *aor.* —**esi**.

Vodāna, *nt.* purity ; sanctification.

Vomissaka, *a.* miscellaneous ; mixed.

Voropana, *nt.* depriving of.

Voropeti (vi + ava + rup + e), to deprive of ; to take away. *aor.* —**esi**. *pp.* **voropita**. *pr. p.* —**penta**. *abs.* —**petvā**.

Voloketi (vi + ava + lok + e), to examine ; to scrutinize.

Vosita, *a.* accomplished ; perfected.

Vossagga, *m.* —**sajana**, *nt.* donation ; relinquishing ; giving up.

Vossajati (vi + ava + saj + a), to give up ; to hand over ; to relinquish. *aor.* —**saji**. *pp.* **vossaṭṭha**. *abs.* —**jitvā, vossajja**.

Voharati (vi + ava + har + a), to use ; to express ; to call ; to trade ; to administrate. *aor.* **vohari**. *pp.* **voharita**. *pr. p.* —**ranta**. *abs.* —**haritvā**.

Vohariyamāna, *pr. p. p.* being called.

Vohāra, *m.* calling ; expression ; use ; trade ; jurisprudence ; current appellation.

Vohārika, *m.* a trader ; a judge. —**kāmacca**, *m.* the Chief Justice.

Vyaggha, *m.* a tiger.

Vyañjana, *nt.* a curry ; a distinctive mark ; a consonant ; a letter.

Vyañjayati (vi + añj + a), to indicate ; to characterise ; to denote. *aor.* —**jayi**. *pp.* —**jita**.

Vyatta, *a.* learned ; accomplished ; evident ; manifest. —**tara**, *a.* more learned or skilful. —**tā**, *f.* cleverness ; learning.

Vyathati (vyath + a), to oppress; to subdue. *aor.* **vyathi.** *pp.* **—thita.**

Vyantīkaroti (vi + anta + ī + kar + o), to abolish; to remove; to get rid of. *aor.* **—kari.** *pp.* **—kata.** *abs.* **—karitvā, —katvā.**

Vyantībhavati (vi + anta + ī + bhū + a), to cease; to stop; to come to an end. *aor.* **—bhavi.** *pp.* **—bhūta.**

Vyantībhāva, *m.* annihilation; destruction.

Vyamha, *nt.* a divine mansion.

Vyaya, see **Vaya.**

Vyasana, *nt.* misfortune; ruin; destruction.

Vyākata, *pp.* of **vyākaroti.**

Vyākaraṇa, *nt.* grammar; explanation; answer; declaration.

Vyākariyamāna, *pr. p. p.* being explained or declared.

Vyākaroti (vi + ā + kar + o), to explain; to declare; to answer. *aor.* **—kari.** *pp.* **—kata.** *abs.* **—karitvā.**

Vyākhyāti (vi + ā + khyā + a), to announce; to explain. *aor.* **—khyāsi.** *pp.* **—āta.**

Vyākula, *a.* perplexed; confused; entangled.

Vyādha, *m.* a huntsman.

Vyādhi, *m.* sickness; disease. **—ta,** *a.* affected with illness.

Vyāpaka, *a.* filling with; spreading; suffusing.

Vyāpajjati (vi + ā + pad + ya), to fail; to be troubled; to be vexed. *aor.* **—pajji.**

Vyāpajjanā, *f.* failing; ill will; anger.

Vyāpanna (*pp.* of **vyāpajjati**), gone wrong; malevolent; vexed.

Vyāpāda, *m.* ill will; malevolence.

Vyāpādeti (vi + ā + pad + e), to spoil; to vex.

Vyāpāra, *m.* occupation; work; business.

Vyāpārita (*pp.* of **vyāpāreti**), instigated; urged by.

Vyāpita, *pp.* of the following.

Vyāpeti (vi + ap + e), to pervade; to make full; to diffuse. *aor.* **—esi.** *pr. p.* **—penta.** *abs.* **—petvā.**

Vyābādheti (vi + ā + bādh + e), to do harm; to obstruct. *aor.* **—esi.** *pp.* **—dhita.** *abs.* **—etvā.**

Vyābhaṅgī, *f.* a carrying pole.

Vyāma, *m.* a fathom.

Vyāvaṭa, *a.* busy; active; engaged in; intent on.

Vyāsatta, *a.* attached to.

Vyāharati (vi + ā + har + a), to utter; to talk; to speak. *aor.* **—hari.** *pp.* **vyāhaṭa.** *abs.* **—ritvā.**

Vyūha, *m.* an array; grouping of troops.

S.

Sa, 1. (= **sva** in Sk.) *a.* one's own. (**Sehi kammehi** = through one's own actions. 2. a shortened form of **saha,** in compounds such as **sadevaka.**

Sa (= **so**), *Nom. sing.* of **ta** in *mas.* is often seen in this form, e.g. **Sa ve kāsāvam arahati.**

Saupādāna, *a.* showing attachment.

Saupādisesa, *a.* having the substratum of life remaining.

Saka, *a.* one's own. *m.* a relation. *nt.* one's own property. —**mana,** *a.* joyful.

Sakaṅkha, *a.* doubtful.

Sakaṭa, *m. nt.* a cart; wagon. —**bhāra,** —**vāha,** *m.* a cart-load. —**vyūha,** *m.* an array of wagons.

Sakaṇṭaka, *a.* thorny.

Sakadāgāmī, 3. one who has attained the second stage of the Path and to be reborn on the earth only once.

Sakabala, *a.* (saka + bala:) one's own strength; (sa + kabala:) with food in the mouth.

Sakamma, *nt.* one's own duty. —**ka,** *a.* transitive (*verb*).

Sakaraṇīya, *a.* one who still has something to do.

Sakala, *a.* whole; entire.

Sakalikā, *f.* a splinter.

Sakāsa, *m.* neighbourhood; presence.

Sakicca, *nt.* one's own business.

Sakiñcana, *a.* having worldly attachment.

Sakiŋ, *ad.* once.

Sakīya, *a.* one's own.

Sakuṇa, *m.* a bird. —**gghī,** *m.* a hawk. —**ṇī,** *f.* a she-bird.

Sakka, *a.* able; possible.

Sakka, *m.* a man of the Sākya race; the king of devas.

Sakkacca, *abs.* having well prepared, honoured, or respected. —**kārī,** 3. one who acts carefully. —**caŋ,** *ad.* carefully; thoroughly.

Sakkata (*pp.* of **sakkaroti**), honoured; duly attended.

Sakkatta, *nt.* the position as the ruler of devas.

Sakkatvā, *abs.* from **sakkaroti.**

Sakkarīyati (*pass.* of **sakkaroti**), to be honoured or respected. *pr. p.* —**riyamāna.**

Sakkaroti (saŋ + kar + o), to honour; to treat with respect; to receive hospitably. *aor.* **sakkari.** *pp.* **sakkata.** *pr. p.* —**karonta.** *pt. p.* —**ritabba, sakkātabba.** *abs.* **sakkatvā,** —**karitvā.** *inf.* —**karituŋ, sakkātuŋ.**

Sakkāya, *m.* the existing body. —**diṭṭhi.** *f.* heresy of individuality.

Sakkāra, *m.* honour; hospitality.

Sakkuṇāti (sak + uṇā), to be able. *aor.* —**kuṇi.** *pr. p.* —**ṇanta.** *abs.* —**ṇitvā.**

Sakkuṇeyyatta, *nt,* possibility; ability.

Sakkoti (sak + o), to be able. *aor.* **asakkhi.** *pr. p.* **sakkonta.**

Sakkharā, *f.* a crystal; gravel; juggery.

Sakkhali, —**likā,** *f.* the orifice (of the ear); a slice; the scale of fish.

Sakkhi, *in.* face to face; before one's eyes. —**ka,** —**khī,** *a.* an eyewitness; a witness. —**diṭṭha,** *a.* seen face to face. —**puṭṭha,** being asked as a witness.

Sakya, *a.* belonging to the Sākya race. —**muni,** *m.* the noble sage of the Sākyans.

Sakha, sakhi, *m.* a friend. **sakhitā,** *f.* friendship.

Sakhila, *a.* kindly in speech.

Sakhya, *nt.* friendship.

Sagabbha, *a.* pregnant.

Sagāha, *a.* full of ferocious animals.

Sagāmeyya, *a.* hailing from the same village.

Sagārava, *a.* respectful; **—vaŋ**, *ad.* respectfully. **—vatā**, *f.* respect.

Sagotta, *a.* of the same lineage; a kinsman.

Sagga, *m.* a place of happiness; heaven. **—kāya**, *m.* the heavenly assembly. **—magga**, *m.* the way to heaven. **—loka**, *m.* the heavenly region. **—saŋvattanika**, *a.* leading to heaven.

Sagguṇa, *m.* good quality.

Saṅkaḍḍhati (saŋ + kaḍḍh + a), to collect; to drag. *aor.* **—ḍḍhi.** *abs.* **—ḍhitvā.**

Saṅkati (sak + ŋ - a), to doubt; to hesitate; to be uncertain. *aor.* **saṅki.** *pp.* **saṅkita.** *pr. p.* **—kamāna.** *abs.* **saṅkitvā.**

Saṅkanta, *pp.* of **saṅkamati.**

Saṅkantati (saŋ + kant + a), to cut all round. *aor.* **—nti.** *pp.* **—tita.** *abs.* **—titvā.**

Saṅkantika, *a.* moving from one place to another. **—roga**, *m.* an epidemic.

Saṅkappa, *m.* intention; purpose.

Saṅkappeti (saŋ + kapp + e), to think about; to imagine. *aor.* **—esi.** *pp.* **—pita.** *abs.* **—petvā.**

Saṅkamati (saŋ + kam + a), to pass over to; to shift; to transmigrate. *aor.* **—kami.** *pp.* **saṅkanta.** *abs.* **—mitvā, saṅkamma.**

Saṅkamana, *nt.* a passage; a bridge; going over; to move from place to place.

Saṅkampati (saŋ + kamp + a), to tremble; to shake. *aor.* **—kampi.** *pp.* **—pita.** *abs.* **—pitvā.**

Saṅkara, *a.* blissful. *m.* blending; mixing.

Saṅkalana, *nt.* addition; collection.

Saṅkā, *f.* doubt; uncertainty.

Saṅkāyati (*Deno.* from **saṅkā**), to be doubtful or uncertain about. *aor.* **—kāyi.** *pp.* **—yita.**

Saṅkāra, *m.* rubbish. **—kūṭa**, *m.* rubbish heap. **—coḷa**, *nt.* a rag picked up from a rubbish heap. **—ṭṭhāna**, *nt.* a dust-bin; rubbish heap.

Saṅkiṇṇa (*pp.* of **saṅkirati**), full of; mixed; impure.

Saṅkita, *pp.* of **saṅkati.**

Saṅkittana, *nt.* making known; proclamation.

Saṅkiliṭṭha, *pp.* of the following.

Saṅkilissati (saŋ + kilis + ya), to become soiled or impure. *aor.* **—lissi.** *abs.* **—ssitvā.**

Saṅkilissana, *nt.* **—kilesa**, *m.* impurity; defilement.

Saṅkilesika, *a.* baneful; corrupting.

Saṅkī, *a.* doubtful.

Saṅkīyati (*pass.* of **saṅkati**), to be suspected.

Saṅku, *m.* a stake, a spike. **—patha**, *m.* a path to be gone with the help of stakes.

Saṅkucati (saŋ + kuc + a), to become contracted; to shrink; to clench. *aor.* **—kuci.** *pp.* **—kucita.** *abs.* **—kucitvā.**

Saṅkucana, *nt.* shrinkage.

Saṅkupita (*pp.* of **saṅkuppati**), enraged.

Saṅkula, *a.* full of; crowded.

Saṅketa, *m. nt.* a mark; appointed place; rendezvous. **—kamma**, *nt.* engagement.

Saṅkoca, *m.* contraction; grimace; distortion.

Saṅkoceti (saŋ + kuc + e), to contract or distort. *aor.* —**esi.** *pp.* —**cita.**

Saṅkopa, *m.* disturbance; agitation.

Saṅkha, *m.* a chank; a conch shell. —**kuṭṭhī,** *m.* one who is suffering with white scab. —**thāla,** *m.* a vessel made of conch shell. —**dhama,** 3. one who blows a conch shell. —**muṇḍika,** *nt.* a kind of torture; the shell-tonsure.

Saṅkhata (*pp.* of **saṅkharoti**), conditioned; repaired; produced by a cause.

Saṅkhaya, *m.* consumption; loss; destruction.

Saṅkharaṇa, *nt.* restoration; preparation.

Saṅkharoti (saŋ + kar + o), to restore; to prepare; to put together. *aor.* —**khari.** *pp.* —**khata.** *pr. p.* —**kharonta.** *abs.* —**ritvā.**

Saṅkhā, saṅkhyā, *f.* enumeration; calculation; a number; definition.

Saṅkhāta, *pp.* agreed on; reckoned. (in cpds.) so-called; named.

Saṅkhādati (saŋ + khād + a), to masticate. *aor.* —**khādi.** *pp.* —**dita.** *abs.* —**ditvā.**

Saṅkhāna, *nt.* calculation; counting.

Saṅkhāya (*abs.* from **saṅkhāti**), having considered or discriminated.

Saṅkhāra, *m.* essential condition; a thing conditioned, mental coefficients. —**kkhandha,** *m.* the aggregate of mental coefficients. —**dukkha,** *nt.* the evil of material life. —**loka,** *m.* the whole creation.

Saṅkhitta, *pp.* of the following.

Saṅkhipati (saŋ + khip + a), to contract; to abridge; to shorten; to fold. *aor.* —**khipi.** *pr. p.* —**panta,** —**pamāna.** *pt. p.* —**pitabba.** *abs.* —**pitvā.** *inf.* —**pituŋ.**

Saṅkhubhati (saŋ + khubh + a), to be agitated; to stir. *aor.* —**bhi.** *pp.* —**bhita.** *abs.* —**bhitvā.**

Saṅkhubhana, *nt.* stirring; agitation.

Saṅkhepa, *m.* abridgement; *nt.* abstract; condensed account; amassing.

Saṅkheyya, *a.* calculable.

Saṅkhobha, *m.* commotion; disturbance.

Saṅkhobheti (saŋ + khubh + e), to disturb; to stir; to upset. *aor.* —**esi.** *pp.* —**bhita.** *pr. p.* —**bhenta.** *abs.* —**bhetvā.**

Saṅga, *m.* attachment: clinging.

Saṅgacchati (saŋ + gam + a), to meet with; to come together, *aor.* —**cchi.** *pp.* **saṅgata.** *abs.* **saṅgantvā.**

Saṅgaṇikā, *f.* society. —**rāma,** —**rata,** *a.* fond of or delighting in society. —**rāmatā,** *f.* delight in company.

Saṅgaṇhāti (saŋ + gah + ṇhā), to treat kindly; to compile; to collect. *aor.* —**gaṇhi.** *pr. p.* —**gaṇhanta.** *pp.* —**gahita.** *abs.* —**gahetvā,** —**gaṇhitvā,** **saṅgayha.**

Saṅgāma, *m.* fight; battle. —**māvacara,** *a.* frequenting in the battle-field.

Saṅgāmeti (*Deno.* from **saṅgāma**), to fight; to come into conflict; to fight a battle. *aor.* **—esi.** *pp.* **—mita.** *abs.* **—metvā.**

Saṅgāyati (saŋ + gā + ya), to chant; to reherse. *aor.* **—gāyi.** *pp.* **saṅgīta.** *abs.* **—gāyitvā.**

Saṅgāha, *m.* a collection. **—ka,** 3. one who collects, compiles, treats kindly, or holds together. *m.* a charioteer.

Saṅgīta (*pp.* of **saṅgāyati**), chanted; uttered; sung.

Saṅgīti, *f.* rehersal; a convocation of the Buddhist clergy in order to settle questions of doctrine. **—kāraka,** *m.* the Elders who held the convocations.

Saṅgha, *m.* a multitude; an assemblage; the Buddhist clergy. **—kamma,** *nt.* an act performed by a chapter of Buddhist monks. **—gata,** *a.* gone into or given to the community. **—tthera,** *m.* the senior monk of a congregation. **—bhatta,** *nt.* food given to the community. **—bheda,** *m.* dissension among the Order. **—bhedaka,** 3. one who causes dissension in the community of monks. **—māmaka,** *a.* devoted to the community.

Saṅghaṭeti (saŋ + ghaṭ + e), to join together. *aor.* **—esi.** *pp.* **—ṭita.** *abs.* **—ṭetvā.**

Saṅghaṭṭana, *nt.* close contact; knocking against.

Saṅghaṭṭeti (saŋ + ghaṭṭ + e), to knock against; to provoke by scoffing. *aor.* **—esi.** *pp.* **—ṭṭita.** *abs.* **—ṭetvā.**

Saṅghāṭa, *m.* junction; union; a raft.

Saṅghāṭi, *f.* the upper robe of a Buddhist monk.

Saṅghāta, *m.* knocking together; snapping (of fingers); accumulation.

Saṅghika, *a.* belonging to the Order.

Saṅghī, 3. having a crowd of followers.

Saṅghuṭṭha (*pp.* of **saṅghoseti**), resounding with; proclaimed.

Sacitta, *nt.* one's own mind. **—ka,** *a.* endowed with mind.

Sace, *in.* if.

Sacetana, *a.* animate; conscious.

Sacca, *nt.* truth. *adj.* true; real. **—kiriyā,** *f.* a declaration on oath. **—paṭivedha, —ābhisamaya,** *m.* comprehension of the reality. **—vācā,** *f.* a truthful word. **—vādī,** 3. one who speaks the truth. **—sandha,** *a.* reliable.

Saccakāra, *m.* a pledge; ratification; payment in advance.

Saccāpeti (*Deno.* from **sacca**), to bind with an oath; to conjure. *aor.* **—esi.** *pp.* **—pita.**

Sacchikaraṇa, *nt.* realization; experiencing. **—raṇīya,** *a.* fit to be realized.

Sacchikaroti (sacchi + kar + o), to realize; to experience for oneself. *aor.* **—kari.** *pp.* **—kata.** *pr. p.* **—karonta.** *pt. p.* **—kātabba.** *abs.* **—katvā, —karitvā.** *inf.* **—kātuŋ, —karituŋ.**

Sacchikiriyā, *f.* see **Sacchikaraṇa.**

Sajati (saj + a), to embrace. *aor.* **saji.** *pr. p.* **sajamāna.** *abs.* **sajitvā.**

Sajana, *nt.* see **Parissajana.**

Sa-jana, *m.* a kinsman; one's own men.

Sajātika, *a.* of the same race or nation.

Sajīva, *a.* endowed with life.

Sajotibhūta, *a.* ablaze; aglow.

Sajjati (saj + ya), to cling to; to be attached. *aor.* **sajji.** *pp.* **saṭṭha.** *pr. p.* **sajjamāna.** *abs.* **sajjitvā.**

Sajjana, *nt.* attachment; decoration; preparation.

Saj-jana, *m.* a virtuous man.

Sajjita, *pp.* of **sajjeti.**

Sajju, *in.* instantly; speedily; at the same moment. **—kaŋ**, *ad.* quickly.

Sajjulasa, *m.* resin.

Sajjeti (saj + e), to prepare; to fit up; to decorate. *aor.* **—esi.** *pr. p.* **—jenta.** *abs.* **—jetvā, sajjiya.**

Sajjhāya, *m.* study; rehersal.

Sajjhāyati (saŋ + jhā + ya), to reherse; to recite; to study. *aor.* **—āyi.** *pp.* **—yita.** *abs.* **—yitvā.** *pr. p.* **—yamāna.**

Sajjhāyanā, *f.* recitation; study.

Sajjhu, *nt.* silver. **—maya**, *a.* made of silver.

Sañcaya, *m.* accumulation; quantity.

Sañcaraṇa, *nt.* wandering about.

Sañcarati (saŋ + car + a), to go about; to wander; to move; to frequent. *aor.* **—cari.** *pp.* **—carita.** *pr. p.* **—caranta.** *abs.* **—ritvā.**

Sañcāra, *m.* passage; movement; wandering.

Sañcāraṇa, *nt.* causing to move or act.

Sañcāreti (*caus.* of **sañcarati**), to cause to move about. *aor.* **—esi.** *pp.* **—rita.** *abs.* **—retvā.**

Sañcalati (saŋ + cal + a), to be unsteady or agitated. *aor.* **—cali.** *pp.* **—calita.**

Sañcalana, *nt.* agitation.

Sañcicca, *in.* with intention; purposely; discriminately.

Sañcita, *pp.* of **sañcināti.**

Sañcinana, *nt.* accumulation.

Sañcināti (saŋ + ci + nā), to accumulate. *aor.* **—cini.** *pr. p.* **—nanta.** *abs.* **—nitvā.**

Sañcuṇṇeti (saŋ + cuṇṇ + e), to crush; to powder. *aor.* **—esi.** *pp.* **—ṇita.** *abs.* **—ṇetvā.**

Sañcetanā, *f.* cognition; intention. **—tanika**, *a.* intentional.

Sañceteti (saŋ + cit + e), to think; to devise means. *aor.* **—esi.** *abs.* **—tetvā.**

Sañcodita (*pp.* of **sañcodeti**), instigated; excited.

Sañchanna (*pp.* of the following), covered with; full of.

Sañchādeti (saŋ + chad + e), to cover; to thatch. *aor.* **—esi.** *pp.* **—dita.** *abs.*— **detvā.**

Sañchindati (saŋ + chid + ŋ-a), to cut; to destroy. *aor.* **—ndi.** *pp.* **—chinna.** *abs.* **—nditvā.**

Sañjagghati (saŋ + jaggh + a), to laugh; to joke. *aor.* **—ghi.** *abs.* **—ghitvā.** *ger.* **—ghana**, *nt.*

Sañjanana, *nt.* production. *adj.* producing; generating.

Sañjaneti (saŋ + jan + e), to produce; to generate; to bring forth. *aor.* **—esi.** *pp.* **—janita.** *abs.* **—netvā.**

Sañjāta (*pp.* of sañjāyati), born; arisen.

Sañjāti, *f.* birth; outcome; origin.

Sañjānana, *nt.* recognition; perception.

Sañjānāti (saŋ + ñā + nā), to recognize; to be aware of; to know. *aor.* **—jāni.** *abs.* **—jānitvā.** *pr. p.* **—jānanta.**

Sañjāyati (saŋ + jan + ya), to be born or produced. *aor.* **—jāyi.** *pp.* **sañjāta.** *pr. p.* **—yamāna.** *abs.* **—yitvā.**

Sañjīvana, *a.* reviving.

Sañjhā, *f.* the evening. **—ghaṇa,** *m.* evening cloud. **—tapa,** *m.* evening sun.

Saññatta (= **saññāpita**), *pp.* induced; talked over; convinced.

Saññatti, *f.* information; pacification.

Saññā, *f.* sense; perception; mark; name; recognition; gesture. **—kkhandha,** *m.* the aggregate of perception. **—paka,** 3. one who makes understand. **—pana,** *nt.* convincing; making known.

Saññāṇa, *nt.* a mark or sign.

Saññāpeti (saŋ + ñā + āpe), to make known; to convince. *aor.* **—esi.** *pp.* **—pita.** *abs.* **—petvā.**

Saññita, *a.* so-called; named.

Saññī, *a.* conscious; having perception; being aware.

Saṭṭhi, *f.* sixty. **—hāyana,** *a.* sixty years old.

Saṭṭhuŋ, *inf.* to give up; to dismiss.

Saṭha, *a.* crafty; fraudulent. *m.* a cheat. **—tā,** *f.* craft.

Saṇati (saṇ + e), to make a noise.

Saṇṭhapana, *nt.* adjustment; establishing.

Saṇṭhapeti (saŋ + ṭhā + āpe), to settle; to adjust; to establish. *aor.* **—esi.** *abs.* **—petvā.**

Saṇṭhahana, *nt.* re-creation; coming into existence.

Saṇṭhāti (saŋ + ṭhā + a), to remain; to stand still; to be established. *aor.* **—ṭhāsi.** *abs.* **—ṭhahitvā.** *pr. p.* **—ṭhahanta.**

Saṇṭhāna, *nt.* shape; form; position.

Saṇṭhita, (*pp.* of **saṇṭhāti**), settled; established in.

Saṇṭhiti, *f.* stability; firmness; settling.

Saṇḍa, *m.* a grove; cluster; multitude.

Saṇḍāsa, *m.* pincers; tweezers.

Saṇha, *a.* smooth; soft; delicate; exquisite. **—karaṇī,** *f.* grinding stone; an instrument for smoothing.

Saṇheti (saṇh + e), to grind; to powder; to smooth; to brush down. *aor.* **—esi.** *pp.* **saṇhita.** *abs.* **—hetvā.**

Sata, *a.* mindful; conscious.

Sata, *nt.* a hundred. **—ka,** *nt.* group of a hundred. **—kkaku,** *a.* having a hundred projections. **—kkhattuŋ,** *ad.* a hundred times. **—dhā,** *ad.* in a hundred ways. **—pāka,** *nt.* (an oil) medicated for a hundred times. **—puññalakkhaṇa,** *a.* having the signs of innumerable merits. **—porisa,** *a.* of the height of a hundred men. **—sahassa,** *nt.* a hundred thousand.

Satata, *a.* constant; continual. **—taŋ,** *ad.* constantly; continually; always.

Satapatta, *nt.* a lotus. *m.* a woodpecker.

Satapadī, *m.* a centipede.

Satamūlī, *f.* the plant *Asparagus.*

Sataraŋsī, *m.* the sun.

Sati, *f.* memory; mindfulness. **—ndriya,** *nt.* the faculty of mindfulness. **—paṭṭhāna,** *nt.* application of mindfulness. **—mantu,** *a.* thoughtful; careful. **—sampajañña,** *nt.* memory and wisdom. **—sambojjhaṅga,** *m.* self-possession as a constituent of enlightenment. **—sammosa, —sammoha,** *m.* loss of memory; forgetfulness.

Satī, *f.* a chaste woman.

Satekiccha, *a.* curable; pardonable.

Satta, *m.* a creature; living being.

Satta, *a.* (the number) seven. **—ka,** *nt.* a group of seven. **—kkhattuŋ,** *ad.* seven times. **—guṇa,** *a.* sevenfold. **—tanti,** *a.* having seven strings. **—tālamatta,** *a.* about the height of seven palm trees. **—tiŋsā,** *f.* thirty-seven. **—paṇṇī,** *m.* the tree *Alstonia Scholaris.* **—bhūmaka,** *a.* consisting of seven stories. **—ratta,** *nt.* a week. **—rasa, —dasa,** 3. seventeen. **—vassika,** *a.* seven years old. **—vīsati,** *f.* twenty-seven. **—saṭṭhi,** *f.* sixty-seven. **—sattati,** *f.* seventy-seven.

Sattati, *f.* seventy.

Sattama, *a.* seventh. **—mī,** *f.* the seventh day; the locative case; the Conditional Mood.

Sattāha, *nt.* a week.

Satti, *f.* ability; power; strength; a spear; a dagger. **—sūla,** *nt.* the stake of a spear.

Sattu, *m.* an enemy; parched flour. **—bhastā,** *f.* a leather bag full of parched flour.

Sattha, *nt.* a science; an art; a lore; a knife; a lance. *m.* a caravan. **—ka,** *nt.* a pen-knife. **—kamma,** *nt.* surgical operation. **—kavāta,** *m.* a cutting pain. **—gamanīya,** *a.* (a path) to be passed with a caravan. **—vāha,** *m.* a caravan leader.

Satthi, *f.* the thigh.

Satthu, *m.* teacher; master, the Buddha.

Sadattha, *m.* one's own welfare.

Sadana, *nt.* a house.

Sadara, *a.* troublesome

Sadasa, *a.* with a fringe.

Sadassa, *m.* a good horse.

Sadā, *ad.* ever; always. **—tana,** *a.* eternal.

Sadāra, *m.* one's own wife.

Sadisa, *a.* equal; similar; like. **—tta,** *nt.* equality; similarity.

Sadevaka, *a.* including the devas.

Sadda, *m.* sound; noise; a word. **—ttha,** *m.* meaning of a word. **—vidū,** one who knows the meaning of various sounds. **—vedhī,** *m.* one who shoots by sound. **—sattha,** *nt.* grammar; science of words.

Saddala, *m.* a place covered with new grass.

Saddahati (saŋ + dhā + a), to believe; to have faith. *aor.* **—dahi.** *pp.* **—dahita.** *pr. p.* **—hanta, —hāna.** *abs.* **—hitvā.** *pt. p.* **—hitabba.**

Saddahana, *nt.* **—nā,** *f.* believing; trusting.

Saddāyati (*Deno.* from **sadda**), to make a noise; to shout. *aor.* **—dāyi.** *abs.* **—dāyitvā.** *pr. p.* **—yamāna.**

Saddūla, *m.* a leopard.

Saddha, *a.* believing ; faithful ; devoted.

Saddhamma, *m.* the true doctrine.

Saddhā, *f.* faith ; devotion. **—tabba,** *pt. p.* fit to be believed. **—deyya,** *a.* a gift in faith. **—dhana,** *nt.* the wealth of devotion. **—yika,** *a.* trustworthy. **—lū,** *a.* much devoted.

Saddhivihārika, —vihārī, 3. a co-resident ; an attending monk.

Saddhiŋ, *in.* with ; together. **—cara,** *a.* a companion ; a follower.

Sadhana, *a.* rich ; wealthy.

Sanantana, *a.* primeval ; old ; eternal.

Sanābhika, *a.* having a nave.

Santa (*pp.* of **sammati :**) calmed ; peaceful ; tired ; wearied. *adj.* existing. *m.* a virtuous man. **—kāya,** *a.* having a calmed body. **—tara,** *a.* more calmed. **—mānasa,** *a.* of tranquil mind. **—bhāva,** *m.* calmness.

Santaka, *a.* one's own ; *nt.* property. (sa + antaka :) limited.

Santajjeti (saŋ + tajj + e), to frighten ; to menace. *aor.* **—esi.** *pp.* **—jita.** *pr. p.* **—jenta, —jayamāna.** *abs.* **—jetvā.**

Santataŋ, *ad.* see **Satataŋ.**

Santati, *f.* continuity ; duration ; lineage.

Santatta, *pp.* of the following.

Santappati (saŋ + tap + ya), to be heated ; to grieve ; to sorrow. *aor.* **—ppi.** *pr. p.* **—pamāna.**

Santappita, *pp.* of the following.

Santappeti (saŋ + tapp + e), to satisfy ; to please. *aor.* **—esi.** *pr. p.* **—penta.** *abs.* **—petvā, santappiya.**

Santara-bāhira, *a.* with the inner and the outer. **—raŋ.** *ad.* within and without.

Santarati (saŋ + tar + a), to be in haste ; to go quickly. *aor.* **—tari.** *pr. p.* **—ramāna.**

Santasati (saŋ + tas + a), to fear ; to be terrified or disturbed. *aor.* **—tasi.** *pp.* **—tasita.** *pr. p.* **—tasanta.** *abs.* **—sitvā.**

Santāna, *nt.* continuity ; succession ; offspring ; a cobweb.

Santāpa, *m.* heat ; torment ; grief.

Santāpeti (saŋ + tap + e), to heat ; to burn ; to torment. *aor.* **—esi.** *pp.* **—pita.** *ab* **—petvā.**

Santāsa, *m.* fear ; trembling ; shock. **—sī,** *a.* trembling ; fearing.

Santi, *f.* peace, calmness; tranquillity. **—kamma,** *nt.* pacification ; an act of appeasing. **—pada,** *nt.* the tranquil state.

Santika, *a.* near. *nt.* vicinity ; presence. **santikā,** from. **—kāvacara,** *a.* keeping near ; intimate.

Santiṭṭhati (saŋ + ṭhā + a), to stand still ; to remain ; to be fixed or settled.

Santīraṇa, *nt.* investigation.

Santuṭṭha (*pp.* of **santussati**), pleased ; happy. **—tā,** *f.* state of contentment.

Santuṭṭhi, *f.* satisfaction ; contentment ; joy.

Santusita, see **Santuṭṭha.**

Santussaka, *a.* content; glad. **—sana,** *nt.* contentment; joy.

Santussati (saŋ + tus + ya), to be contented, pleased, or happy. *aor.* **—ssi.** *pr. p.* **—samāna.**

Santosa, *m.* joy; pleasure.

Santhata (*pp.* of **santharati**), covered with; spread. *nt.* a rug or mat.

Santhambheti (saŋ + thambh + e), to make stiff or rigid. to numb. *aor.* **—esi.** *pp.* **—bhita.** *abs.* **—bhetvā.**

Santhambhanā, *f.* stiffening; rigidity.

Santhara, *m.* a mat; a covering; a bed-sheet. **—ṇa,** *nt.* spreading; covering with.

Santharati (saŋ + thar + a), to spread; to strew; to cover with. *aor.* **—thari.** *abs.* **—tharitvā.** *caus.* **santharāpeti.**

Santhava, *m.* intimacy; acquaintance; sexual intercourse.

Santhāgāra, *m. nt.* a council hall; a mote hall.

Santhāra, *m.* covering; flooring.

Santhuta (*pp.* of **santhaveti**), acquainted; familiar.

Sanda, *a.* thick; dense. *m.* a flow. **—cchāya,** *a.* giving dense shade.

Sandati (sand + a), to flow. *aor.* **sandi.** *pp.* **sandita.** *abs.* **—ditvā.** *pr. p.* **—damāna.**

Sandassaka, 3. one who shows or instructs. **—sana,** *nt.* instruction; show; pointing out. **—ssiyamāna,** *a.* being instructed or pointed out.

Saŋdasseti (saŋ + dis + e), to point out; to explain. *aor.* **—esi.** *pp.* **—sita.** *abs.* **—setvā.**

Sandahati (saŋ + dhā + a), to connect; to unite; to fit. *aor.* **—dahi.** *pp.* **—hita.** *abs.* **—hitvā.**

Sandahana, *nt.* fitting; putting together.

Sandāna, *nt.* a chain; a tether.

Sandāleti (saŋ + dāl + e), to break; to shatter. *aor.* **—esi.** *pp.* **—lita.** *abs.* **—letvā.**

Sandiṭṭha (*pp.* of **sandissati**), seen together. *m.* a friend.

Sandiṭṭhika, *a.* visible; belonging to this life.

Sandita (*pp.* of **sandati**), flowed; chained.

Sandiddha, *pp.* smeared with poison.

Sandissati (saŋ + dis + ya), to be seen; to appear; to agree with. *pr. p.* **—samāna.**

Sandīpana, *nt.* **—nā,** *f.* kindling; making clear.

Sandīpeti (saŋ + dīp + e), to kindle; to make clear. *aor.* **—esi.** *pp.* **—pita.** *abs.* **—petvā.**

Sandesa, *m.* a message; a letter; a written document. **—hara,** *m.* a messenger. **—sāgāra,** *nt.* a post office.

Sandeha, *m.* doubt; one's own body.

Sandoha, *m.* a heap; a multitude.

Sandhana, *nt.* one's own property.

Sandhamati (saŋ + dham + a), to blow; to fan. *aor.* **—dhami.** *abs.* **—mitvā.**

Sandhātu, *m.* one who conciliates.

Sandhāna, *nt.* uniting; conciliation.

Sandhāya (*abs.* of **sandahati**), having united. *in.* with reference to; concerning.

Sandhāraka, *a.* bearing; restraining. **—raṇa,** *nt.* checking; bearing.

Sandhāreti (saŋ + dhar + e), to bear; to check; to hold up; to curb; to support. *aor.* **—esi.** *pp.* **—rita.** *abs.* **—retvā.** *pr. p.* **—renta.**

Sandhāvati (saŋ + dhāv + a), to run through; to transmigrate. *aor.* **—āvi.** *pp.* **—vita.** *abs.* **—vitvā.** *pr. p.* **—vanta, —vamāna.**

Sandhi, *f.* union; junction; joint; connection; agreement; euphonic combination. **—cchedaka,** *a.* one who can cut a brake into a house. **—mukha,** *nt.* opening of a break into a house.

Sandhīyati (*pass.* of **sandhāti**), to be connected, joined, or put together. *aor.* **—dhīyi.**

Sandhūpāyati (saŋ + dhūp + āya), to emit smoke. *aor.* **—pāyi.** *abs.* **—yitvā.**

Sandhūpeti (saŋ + dhūp + e), to fumigate. *aor.* **—esi.** *pp.* **—pita.** *abs.* **—petvā.**

Sandhovati, see **Dhovati.**

Sannaddha, *pp.* of the following.

Sannayhati (saŋ + nah + ya), to fasten; to arm oneself; to array. *aor.* **—yhi.** *abs.* **—ḥitvā, —nayha.**

Sannāha, *m.* armour; fastening together.

Sannikaṭṭha, *nt.* neighbourhood; vicinity.

Sannikāsa, *a.* resembling; looking like.

Sannicaya, *m.* accumulation; hoarding.

Sannicita, *pp.* accumulated; hoarded.

Sanniṭṭhāna, *nt.* conclusion; ascertainment.

Sannidhāna, *nt.* proximity; vicinity; storing.

Sannidhi, *m.* storing up; hoarding. **—kāraka,** 3. one who lays up in stocks. **—kata,** *a.* hoarded.

Sannipatati (saŋ + ni + pat + a), to assemble; to come together. *aor.* **—pati.** *pp.* **—patita.** *abs.* **—titvā.** *pr. p.* **—patanta.**

Sannipāta, *m.* assemblage; congregation; union of the humours of the body. **—pātika,** *a.* resulting from the union of the humours. **—pātana,** *nt.* calling together; convoking.

Sannipāteti (saŋ + ni + pat + e), to convoke; to call a meeting. *aor.* **—esi.** *pp.* **—pātita.** *abs.* **—tetvā.**

Sannibha, *a.* resembling.

Sannirumbhana, *nt.* restraining checking; suppression.

Sannirumbheti (saŋ + ni + rumbh + e), to restrain; to block; to impede. *aor.* **—esi.** *pp.* **—bhita.** *abs.* **—bhetvā.**

Sannivasati (saŋ + ni + vas + a) to live together. *aor.* **— vasi.**

Sannivāreti (saŋ + ni + var + e), to check; to prevent. *aor.* **—esi.** *abs.* **—retvā.**

Sannivāsa, *m.* association; living together.

Sannivesa, *m.* encampment; settlement.

Sannisinna, *pp.* of the following.

Sannisīdati (saŋ + ni + sad + a), to settle; to subside; to become quiet. *aor.* **—sīdi.** *abs.* **—ditvā.**

Sannissita, *a.* connected with; based on.

Sannihita, *pp.* put down; placed; arranged well.

Sanneti, (saŋ + ni + e), to mix; to knead. *aor.* **—esi.** *pp.* **sannita.** *abs.* **sannetvā.**

Sapajāpatika, *a.* with one's wife.

Sapati (sap + a), to swear; to curse. *aor.* **sapi.** *pp.* **sapita.** *abs.* **sapitvā.**

Sapatta, *m.* a rival; a foe. *adj.* hostile.

Sapattabhāra, *a.* having one's wings as one's whole burden.

Sapattī, *f.* a co-wife.

Sapatha, *m.* an oath.

Sapadāna, *a.* successive. **—naŋ,** *ad.* without interruption. **—cārikā,** *f.* to go on alms-begging not leaving a single house in his course.

Sapadi, *in.* instantly.

Sapāka, sopāka, *m.* an outcast; a dog-eater.

Sappa, *m.* a snake. **—potaka,** *m.* a young serpent.

Sappaccaya, *a.* having a cause; conditioned.

Sappañña, *a.* wise.

Sappaṭibhaya, *a.* dangerous; harmful.

Sappati (sapp + a), to crawl; to creep. *aor.* **sappi.**

Sappana, *nt.* crawling.

Sappāṇaka, *a.* containing animate beings.

Sappāya, *a.* beneficial; wholesome; suitable. **—tā,** *f.* wholesomeness.

Sappi, *nt.* ghee; clarified butter.

Sappītika, *a.* accompanied by joy.

Sapharī, *f.* a sheet fish.

Saphala, *a.* having its reward; bearing fruit.

Sabala, *a.* strong; spotted; variegated.

Sabba, *a.* all; every; whole; entire. **—kaniṭṭha,** *a.* the youngest of all. **—kammika,** *a.* (a minister) doing all work. **—ññū, —vidū,** *a.* all-knowing; *m.* the Omniscient One. **—ññutā,** *f.* omniscience. **—ṭṭhaka,** *a.* consisting eight of each kind. **—tthaka,** *a.* concerned with every thing; a do-all. **—paṭhama,** *a.* foremost. **—paṭhamaŋ,** *ad.* before all; very early. **—sata,** *a.* consisting a hundred of each. **—sovaṇṇa,** *a.* entirely made of gold. **—ssa,** *nt.* the whole of one's property. **—ssaharaṇa,** *nt.* confiscation of one's whole property.

Sabbato, *in.* from every side; in every respect.

Sabbattha, sabbatra, *ad.* everywhere.

Sabbathā, *ad.* in everyway.

Sabbadā, *ad* always; everyday.

Sabbadhi, *ad.* everywhere.

Sabbaso, *ad.* altogether; in every respect.

Sabbhi (= Sk. **sadbhih,** with the wise. But in Pali it is sometimes used as an *adj.*) the virtuous.

Sabrahmaka, *a.* including the Brahma world.

Sabrahmacārī, *m.* a fellow monk.

Sabhaggata, *a.* come to an assembly.

Sabhā, *f.* an assembly; a hall for meeting.

Sabhāga, *a.* common ; being of the same division. **—ṭṭhāna,** *nt.* a convenient place. **—vuttī,** *a.* living in mutual courtesy.

Sabhāva, *m.* nature ; condition ; disposition ; reality. **—dhamma,** *m.* principle of nature.

Sabhojana, *a.* (sa + bhojana :), with food ; (sa + ubho + jana :) where there is a couple, a wife and a husband. (The 2nd reading is found in the Vinaya).

Sama, *a.* even ; equal ; level ; similar. *m.* clamness ; tranquility. **—ka,** *a.* equal ; like ; same. **—maŋ,** *ad.* evenly ; equally. **—mena,** *ad.* impartially.

Samagga, *a.* being in unity. **—karaṇa,** *nt.* peace-making. **—tta,** *nt.* agreement ; state of being united. **—rata, —ārāma,** *a.* rejoicing in peace.

Samaṅgitā, *f.* the fact of being endowed.

Samaṅgī, —gībhūta, *a.* endowed with ; possessing.

Samacariyā, *f.* living in spiritual calm.

Samacitta, *a.* possessed of equanimity. **—tā,** *f.* equality in mind.

Samajātika, *a.* of the same caste.

Samajja, *nt.* a festive gathering ; a theatrical display. **—ṭṭhāna,** *nt.* an arena. **—ābhicaraṇa,** *nt.* visiting fairs or festivals.

Samaññā, *f.* designation. **—ñāta,** *a.* designated.

Samaṇa, *m.* a recluse. **—kuttika,** *m.* a bogus monk. **—ṇī,** *f.* a nun. **—ṇuddesa,** *m.* a novice.

Samatā, *f.* equality ; eveness ; normal state.

Samatikkanta, *pp.* of **—tikkamati.**

Samatikkama, *m.* **—mana,** *nt.* passing beyond ; overcoming.

Samatikkamati (saŋ + ati + kam + a), to pass over ; to transcend ; to remove. *aor.* **—kami.** *abs.* **—kamitvā.**

Samatittika, *a.* brimful.

Samativattati (saŋ + ati + vat + a), to overcome ; to transcend. *aor.* **—vatti.** *pp.* **—vatta, —vattita.**

Samatta, *a.* complete ; entire.

Samatta, *nt.* see **Samatā.**

Samattha, *a.* able ; skilful. **—tā,** *f.* ability ; proficiency.

Samatha, *m.* calm ; quietude of heart ; settlement of legal questions. **—bhāvanā,** *f.* the way of concentrating the mind.

Samadhigacchati (saŋ + adhi + gam + a), to attain ; to understand clearly. *aor.* **—cchi,** *pp.* **—gata.** *abs.* **—gantvā.**

Samanantara, *a.* immediate ; nearest. **—tarā,** *ad.* just after.

Samanugāhati (saŋ + anu + gah + a), to ask for reasons. *aor.* **—gāhi.** *abs.* **—gāhitvā.**

Samanuñña, *a.* approving. **—ññā,** *f.* approval. **—ñāta,** *a.* approved ; allowed.

Samanupassati (saŋ + anu + dis + a), to see ; to perceive. *aor.* **—passi.** *pr. p.* **—samāna.** *abs.* **—sitvā.**

Samanubhāsati (saŋ + anu + bhās + a), to converse together. *aor.* **—bhāsi.**

Samanubhāsanā, *f.* conversation ; rehearsal.

Samanuyuñjati (saŋ + anu + yuj + ŋ - a), to cross question. *aor.* **—ñji.** *abs.* **—jitvā.**

Samanussarati (saŋ + anu + sar + a), to recollect; to call to mind. *aor.* **—sari.** *pr. p.* **—ranta.** *abs.* **—saritvā.**

Samanta, *a.* all; entire. **—cakkhu,** *a.* all-seeing; the Omniscient One. **—pāsādika,** *a.* all-pleasing. **—bhaddaka,** *a.* completely auspicious.

Samantā, —ntato, *ad.* all around; everywhere.

Samannāgata, *a.* endowed with; possessed of.

Samannāharati (saŋ + anu + ā + har + a), to collect together. *aor.* **—hari.** *pp.* **—haṭa,** *abs.* **—haritvā.**

Samappeti (saŋ + ap + e), to hand over; to consign; to apply. *aor.* **—esi.** *pp.* **—ppita.** *abs.* **—etvā, —ppiya.**

Samaya, *m.* time; congregation; season; occation; religion. **—ntara,** *nt.* different religions.

Samara, *nt.* battle.

Samala, *a.* impure; contaminated.

Samalaṅkata, *pp.* of the following.

Samalaṅkaroti (saŋ + alaŋ + kar + o), to decorate; to adorn. *aor.* **—kari.** *abs.* **—karitvā.**

Samavāya, *m.* combination; coming together.

Samavekkhati (saŋ + ava + ikkh + a), to consider; to examine. *aor.* **—kkhi.**

Samavepākinī, *f.* promoting good digestion.

Samassāsa, *m.* relief; refreshment.

Samassāseti (saŋ + ā + sas + e), to relieve; to refresh. *aor.* **—esi.** *abs.* **—setvā.**

Samā, *f.* an year.

Samākaḍḍhati (saŋ + ā + kaḍḍh + a), to pull along. *aor.* **—ḍḍhi.** *abs.* **—ḍhitvā.**

Samākaḍḍhana, *nt.* pulling; dragging.

Samākiṇṇa, samākula, *a.* filled or covered with; crowded together.

Samāgacchati (saŋ + ā + gam + a), to meet together; to assemble. *aor.* **—cchi.** *pp.* **samāgata.** *abs.* **—gantvā, —gamma.**

Samāgama, *m.* meeting with; an assembly.

Samācarati (saŋ + ā + car + a), to behave; to act; to practise. *aor.* **—cari.** *pr. p.* **—caranta.** *abs.* **—caritvā.**

Samācaraṇa, *nt.* **samācāra,** *m.* conduct; behaviour.

Samādapaka, —dapetu, *m.* instigator. **—pana,** *nt.* instigation.

Samādapeti (saŋ + ā + dā + āpe), to instigate. *aor.* **—esi.** *pp.* **—pita.** *abs.* **—petvā.**

Samādahati (saŋ + ā + dhā + a), to put together; to concentrate; to kindle (fire). *aor.* **—dahi.** *pr. p.* **—hanta.** *abs.* **—hitvā.**

Samādāti (saŋ + ā + dā + a), to take; to accept. *abs.* **samādāya.**

Samādāna, *nt.* taking; observance; acceptance.

Samādiyati (*pass.* of **samādāti**), to take upon oneself. *aor.* **—diyi.** *pp.* **samādinna.** *abs.* **—diyitvā.** *pr. p.* **—diyanta.**

Samādisati (saŋ + ā + dis + a), to indicate; to command. *aor.* **—disi.** *pp.* **samādiṭṭha.** *abs.* **—disitvā.**

Samādhāna, *nt.* putting together; concentration.

Samādhi, *m.* meditation; one-pointedness of the mind. **—ja,** *a.* produced by concentration. **—bala,** *nt.* the power of concentration. **—bhāvanā,** *f.* cultivation of concentration. **—saŋvattanika,** *a.* conducive to concentration. **—sambojjhaṅga,** *m.* concentration as a constituent of enlightenment.

Samādhiyati (saŋ + ā + dhā + i + ya), to be calmed or concentrated. *aor.* **—dhiyi.**

Samāna, *a.* equal; same; similar. **—gatika,** *a.* identical. **—tta,** *nt.* **—tā,** *f.* **—bhāva,** *m.* identity; equality. **—ttatā,** *f.* impartiality; sociability. **—vassika,** *a.* equal in seniority; of the same age. **—saŋvāsaka,** *a.* belonging to the same communion.

Samānīta, *pp.* of the following.

Samāneti (saŋ + ā + nī + a), to bring together; to compare; to calculate. *aor.* **—esi.** *abs.* **—netvā.**

Samāpajjati (saŋ + ā + pad + ya), to enter upon; to engage in. *aor.* **—pajji.** *pr. p.* **—janta, —jamāna,** *abs.* **—jitvā, —pajja.**

Samāpajjana, *nt.* entering upon; passing through.

Samāpatti, *f.* attainment; an enjoying stage of meditation.

Samāpanna, *pp.* of **samāpajjati.**

Samāpeti (saŋ + ap + e), to conclude; to finish; to complete. *aor.* **—esi.** *pp.* **—pita.** *abs.* **—petvā.**

Samāyāti (saŋ + ā + yā + a), to come together; to be united. *pp.* **samāyāta.**

Samāyuta, *a.* combined; possessed with.

Samāyoga, *m.* combination; conjunction.

Samāraka, *a.* including Māra devas.

Samāraddha (*pp.* of **samārabhati**), begun.

Samārabhati (saŋ + ā + rabh + a), to begin; to undertake; to kill. *aor.* **—rabhi.** *abs.* **—bhitvā.**

Samārambha, *m.* undertaking; activity; injury; slaughter.

Samāruhati (saŋ + ā + ruh + a), to climb up; to ascend. *aor.* **—ruhi.** *pp.* **—rūḷha.** *abs.* **—hitvā, samāruyha.**

Samāruhana, *nt.* climbing; ascending.

Samārūḷha, *pp.* of the above.

Samāropana, *nt.* raising up; putting on.

Samāropeti (saŋ + ā + rup + e), to make ascend; to put on; to entrust. *aor.* **—esi.** *pp.* **—pita.** *abs.* **—petvā.**

Samāvahati (saŋ + ā + vah + a), to bring about. *aor.*—**vahi.** *pr. p.*—**vahanta.**

Samāsa, *m.* compound; an abridgement.

Samāseti (saŋ + ās + e), to associate; to combine; to abridge. *aor.* **—esi.** *pp.* **—sita.** *abs.* **—setvā.**

Samāhata (*pp.* of **samāhanati**), struck; hit.

Samāhita, *pp.* settled; composed; collected of mind.

Samijjhati (saŋ + idh + ya), to succeed ; to prosper ; to take effect. *aor.* —**jjhi.** *pp.* **samiddha.** *abs.* —**jhitvā.**

Samita (*pp.* of **sameti**), calmed ; appeased. —**tta,** *nt.* state of being calmed. —**tāvī,** *m.* one who has quieted himself.

Samitaŋ, *ad.* always ; continuously.

Samiti, *f.* an assembly ; a society.

Samiddha (*pp.* of **samijjhati**), successful ; rich.

Samiddhi, *f.* success ; prosperity.

Samīpa, *a.* near ; close. —**ga,** *a.* got near. —**cārī,** *a.* being near. —**ṭṭha,** *a.* standing near ; not far. —**ṭṭhāna,** *nt.* a place near by.

Samīraṇa, *m.* the wind.

Samīrati (saŋ + īr + a), to blow ; to move. *pp.* **samīrita.**

Samīreti (saŋ + īr + e), to utter ; to speak. *aor.* —**esi.** *pp.* —**rita.** *abs.* —**retvā.**

Samukkaŋseti (saŋ + u + kas + e), to extol ; to praise. *aor.* —**esi.** *pp.* —**sita.** *abs.* —**setvā.**

Samugga, *m.* a casket.

Samuggacchati (saŋ + u + gam + a), to arise ; to come to existence. *aor.* —**chi.** *abs.* —**ggantvā.**

Samuggata, *pp.* of the above.

Samuggaṇhāti (saŋ + u + gah + ṇhā), to learn well. *aor.* —**gaṇhi.** *pp.* —**gahita.** *abs.* —**hetvā.**

Samuggama, *m.* rise ; origin.

Samuggirati (saŋ + u + gir + a), to utter ; to throw out ; to emit. *aor.* —**giri.**

Samuggiraṇa, utterance.

Samugghāta, *m.* jostling ; knocking against ; uprooting ; removal. —**taka,** *a.* abolishing ; removing.

Samugghāteti (saŋ + u + ghāt + e), to abolish ; to uproot ; to remove. *aor.* —**esi.** *pp.* —**tita.** *abs.* —**tetvā.**

Samucita, *pp.* accumulated.

Samuccaya, *m.* collection ; accumulation.

Samucchindati (saŋ + u + chid + ŋ - a), to extirpate ; to abolish ; to destroy. *aor.* —**ndi.** *abs.* —**ndiya,** —**nditvā.**

Samucchinna, *pp.* of the above.

Samucchindana, *nt.* —**ccheda,** *m.* extirpation ; destruction.

Samujjala, *a.* resplendent ; shining.

Samuṭṭhahati, **samuṭṭhāti,** (saŋ + u + ṭhā + a), to rise up ; to originate. *aor.* —**ṭhahi.** *pp.* —**ṭhita.** *abs.* —**hitvā.**

Samuṭṭhāna, *nt.* origination ; cause. —**nika,** *a.* originating.

Samuṭṭhāpaka, *a.* occasioning ; producing.

Samuṭṭhāpeti (saŋ + u + ṭhā + āpe), to raise ; to produce ; to originate. *aor.* —**esi.** *pp.* —**pita.** *abs.* —**petvā.**

Samuṭṭhita, *pp.* of **samuṭṭhāti.**

Samuttarati (saŋ + u + tar + a), to pass over. *aor.* —**tari.** *pp.* **samuttiṇṇa.** *abs.* —**taritvā.** *ger.* —**taraṇa.**

Samuttejaka, *a.* instigating ; inciting. —**jana,** *nt.* instigation.

Samuttejeti (saŋ + u + tij + e), to sharpen ; to instigate. *aor.* —**esi.** *pp.* —**jita.** *abs.* —**jetvā.**

Samudaya, *m.* rise ; origin ; produce. —**sacca,** *nt.* the truth of origination.

Samudāgata, *pp.* arisen; resulted. **—gama,** *m.* rising; produce.

Samudācarati (saŋ + u + ā + car + a), to behave towards; to occur to; to frequent. *aor.* **—cari.** *pp.* **—carita.** *abs.* **—caritvā.**

Samudācaraṇa, *nt.* **—cāra,** *m.* behaviour; habit; practice; familiarity.

Samudāciṇṇa (*pp.* of **samudācarati**), practised; indulged in.

Samudāya, *m.* a multitude.

Samudāharati (saŋ + u + ā + har + a), to speak; to utter. *aor.* **—hari.** *pp.* **—haṭa.** *abs.* **—haritvā.**

Samudāharaṇa, *nt.* **—hāra,** *m.* conversation; utterance.

Samudita, *pp.* of **samudeti.**

Samudīraṇa, *nt.* utterance; movement.

Samudīreti (saŋ + u + īr + e), to utter; to move. *aor.* **—esi.** *pp.* **—dīrita.** *abs.* **—retvā.**

Samudeti (saŋ + u + i + a), to arise. *aor.* **—esi.**

Samudda, *m.* the sea. **—ṭṭhaka,** *a.* situated in the ocean.

Samuddhaṭa, *pp.* of **samuddharati.**

Samuddharaṇa, *nt.* pulling out; salvation.

Samuddharati (saŋ + u + har + a), to lift up; to take out; to save from. *aor.* **—dhari.** *abs.* **—dharitvā.**

Samupagacchati (saŋ + upa + gam + a), to approach. *aor.* **—cchi.** *pp.* **—pagata.** *abs.* **—gantvā, —gamma.**

Samupagamana, *nt.* approach.

Samupasobhita, *a.* adorned; endowed with.

Samupeta, *pp.* endowed with.

Samuppajjati (saŋ + u + pad + ya), to arise; to be produced. *aor.* **—jji.** *abs.* **—jitvā.**

Samuppanna, *pp.* of the above.

Samubbahati (saŋ + u + vah + a), to bear; to carry. *aor.* **—bahi.** *pr. p.* **—bahanta.** *abs.* **—bahitvā.** *ger.* **—bahana.**

Samubbhavati (saŋ + u + bhū + a), to arise; to be produced. *aor.* **—bhavi.** *pp.* **—bhūta.** *abs.* **—bhavitvā.**

Samullapati (saŋ + u + lap + a), to converse friendly. *aor.* **—lapi.** *pp.* **—lapita.** *abs.* **—pitvā.**

Samullapana, *nt.* **—lāpa,** *m.* conversation.

Samussaya, *m.* the body; accumulation.

Samussāpeti (saŋ + us + āpe), to raise; to hoist. *aor.* **—esi.** *pp.* **—pita.** *abs.* **—petvā.**

Samussāheti (saŋ + u + sah + e), to instigate. *aor.* **—esi.** *pp.* **—hita.** *abs.* **—hetvā.**

Samussita, *pp.* elevated; lifted; raised; arrogant.

Samūlaka, *a.* including the root.

Samūha, *m.* multitude; a mass; aggregation.

Samūhata, *pp.* of the following.

Samūhanati (saŋ + u + han + a), to uproot; to abolish; to remove.

Samekkhati (saŋ + ikkh + a), to look for; to consider. *aor.* **—kkhi.** *pp.* **—khita.** *abs.* **—khitvā, —khiya.**

Sameta (*pp.* of the following), endowed or connected with; combined.

Sameti (saŋ + i + a), to come together; to meet; to agree with; to compare; to make even; to appease. *aor.* **samesi.** *abs.* **sametvā.**

Samerita, *pp.* moved; set in motion.

Samokiṇṇa, *pp.* of the following.

Samokirati (saŋ + ava + kir + a), to sprinkle; to strew. *aor.* **—kiri.** *abs.* **—kiritvā.**

Samokiraṇa, *nt.* sprinkling; strewing.

Samotata, *pp.* strewn all over; spread.

Samotarati (saŋ + ava + tar + a), to descend (into water). *aor.* **—tari.** *pp.* **—tiṇṇa.** *abs.* **—taritvā.**

Samodahati (saŋ + ava + dah + a), to put together; to keep in. *aor.* **—dahi.** *pp.* **—dahita.** *abs.* **—dahitvā.**

Samodahana, *nt.* keeping or putting in.

Samodhāna, *nt.* collocation; combination; to be contained in.

Samodhāneti (*Deno.* from **samodhāna**), to connect; to fit together. *aor.* **—esi.** *abs.* **—netvā.**

Samosaraṇa, *nt.* coming together; meeting.

Samosarati (saŋ + ava + sar + a), to come together; to assemble. *aor.* **—sari.** *pp.* **—saṭa.** *abs.* **—saritvā.**

Samoha, *a.* infatuated.

Samohita (*pp.* of **samodahati**), included; covered with; put together.

Sampakampati (saŋ + pa + kamp + a), to tremble; to be shaken. *aor.* **—mpi.** *pp.* **—pita.**

Sampajañña, *nt.* discrimination; comprehension.

Sampajāna, *a.* thoughtful.

Sampajjati (saŋ + pad + ya), to succeed; to prosper; to happen; to become. *aor.* **—pajji.** *pp.* **—panna.** *pr. p.* **—jjamāna.** *abs.* **—jitvā.**

Sampajjana, *nt.* success; prosperity; becoming.

Sampajjalita (*pp.* of **—jalati**), in flames; ablaze.

Sampaṭicchati (saŋ + pati + is + a), to receive; to accept. *aor.* **—cchi.** *pp.* **—chita.** *abs.* **—chitvā.**

Sampaṭicchana, *nt.* acceptance; agreement.

Sampati, *in.* just now.

Sampatita (*pp.* of **sampatati**), fallen; happened.

Sampatta (*pp.* of **sampāpuṇāti**), reached; arrived; come to.

Sampatti, sampadā, *f.* fortune; happiness; success; attainment.

Sampadāna, *nt.* handing on; giving over; the dative case.

Sampadālana, *nt.* tearing; splitting.

Sampadāḷeti (saŋ + pa + daḷ + e), to tear; to split; to burst open. *aor.* **—esi.** *pp.* **—lita.** *abs.* **—letvā.**

Sampadussati (saŋ + pa + dus + ya), to be corrupted. *aor.* **—dussi.** *pp.* **—paduṭṭha.** *abs.* **—sitvā.**

Sampadussana, *nt.* corruption.

Sampadosa, *m.* wickedness.

Sampanna (*pp.* of **sampajjati**), successful; complete; abounding in; endowed with.

Sampayāta, *pp.* gone forth; proceeded.

Sampayutta, *a.* associated; connected.

Sampayoga, *m.* union; association; connection.

Sampayojeti (saŋ + pa + yuj + e), to join; to associate with; to litigate. *aor.* **—esi.** *pp.* **—jita.** *abs.* **—jetvā.**

Samparāya, *m.* future state; the next world. **—yika,** *a.* belonging to the next world.

Samparivajjeti (saŋ + pari + vaj + e), to avoid; to shun. *aor.* **—esi.** *pp.* **—jita** *abs.* **—jetvā.**

Samparivattati (saŋ + pari + vat + a), to turn; to roll about. *aor.* **—vatti.** *abs.* **—vattitvā.** *caus.* **samparivatteti.**

Samparivāreti (saŋ + pari + var + e), to surround; to wait upon; to attend on. *aor.* **—esi.** *pp.* **—vārita.** *abs.* **—retvā.**

Sampavatteti (saŋ + pa + vat + e), to set going. *aor.* **—esi.** *pp.* **—ttita.**

Sampavedhati (saŋ + pa + vidh + a), to be shaken violently; to be highly affected. *aor.* **—vedhi.** *pp.* **—dhita.** *caus.* **sampavedheti.**

Sampasāda, *m.* pleasure; serenity. **—daniya,** *a.* leading to serenity; inspiring faith.

Sampasādeti (saŋ + pa + sad + e), to gladden; to purify. *aor.* **—esi.** *pp.* **—dita.** *abs.* **—detvā.**

Sampasāreti (saŋ + pa + sar + e), to spread; to stretch out. *aor.* **—esi.** *pp.* **—rita.** *abs.* **—retvā.**

Sampasīdati (saŋ + pa + sad + a), to be pleased; to become clear; to be tranquillized. *aor.* **—sīdi.** *abs.* **—ditvā.**

Sampasīdana, *nt.* joy; happiness; becoming clear.

Sampassati (saŋ + dis + a), to see; to behold; to consider. *aor.* **—ssi.** *pr. p.* **—santa, —samāna.** *abs.* **—sitvā.**

Sampahaṭṭha (*pp.* of **sampahaŋsati**), gladdened; joyful; beaten; refined; wrought.

Sampahaŋsaka, *a.* gladdening. **—sana,** *nt.* being glad; pleasure.

Sampahaŋsati (saŋ + pa + has + a), to be glad. *aor.* **—ŋsi.** *caus.* **sampahaŋseti.** *aor.* **—esi.** *pp.* **—sita.** *abs.* **—setvā.**

Sampahāra, *m.* strife, battle; striking.

Sampāta, *m.* falling together. concurrence; collision.

Sampādaka, *a.* one who prepares or supplies. **—dana,** *nt.* supplying; making ready.

Sampādiyati (*pass.* of **sampādeti**), to be supplied.

Sampādeti (saŋ + pad + e), to try to accomplish; to supply; to prepare. *aor.* **—esi.** *pp.* **—dita.** *abs.* **—detvā.**

Sampāpaka, *a.* leading to; bringing. **—pana,** *nt.* leading; getting to.

Sampāpuṇāti (saŋ + pa + ap + uṇā), to reach; to attain; to meet with. *aor.* **—puṇi.** *pp.* **sampatta.** *pr. p.* **—ṇanta.** *abs.* **—puṇitvā.**

Sampiṇḍana, *nt.* combination; connection; addition.

Sampiṇḍeti (saŋ + piṇḍ + e), to unite ; to combine ; to ball together ; to abridge. *aor.* **—esi.** *pp.* **—ḍita.** *abs.* **—ḍetvā.**

Sampiyāyati (*Deno.* from **sampiya**), to treat kindly ; to be attached or devoted to ; to be fond of. *aor.* **—yāyi.** *pp.* **—yita.** *pr. p.* **—yanta, —yamāna.** *abs.* **—yitvā.**

Sampīṇeti (saŋ + pī + ṇā + e), to satisfy ; to gladden ; to please. *aor.* **—esi.** *pp.* **—ṇita.** *abs.* **—ṇetvā.**

Sampīḷeti (saŋ + pīḷ + e), to oppress ; to worry ; to crush. *aor.* **—esi.** *pp.* **—ḷita.** *abs.* **—ḷetvā.**

Sampucchati (saŋ + pucch + a), to ask ; to take permission. *aor.* **—cchi.** *pp.* **—puṭṭha.**

Sampuṇṇa (*pp.* of **sampūrati**), full ; complete ; filled.

Sampupphita, *pp.* in full bloom.

Sampūjeti (saŋ + pūj + e), to honour ; to respect. *aor.* **—esi.** *pp.* **—jita.** *pr. p.* **—jenta.** *abs.* **—jetvā.**

Sampūreti (saŋ + pūr + e), to fill ; to accomplish. *aor.* **—esi.** *pp.* **—rita.** *abs.* **—retvā.**

Sampha, *nt.* frivolity ; useless talk. **—ppalāpa,** *m.* talking nonsense.

Samphassa, *m.* touch ; contact.

Samphuṭṭha, *pp.* of **samphusati.**

Samphulla, *a.* full-blown.

Samphusati (saŋ + phus + a), to touch ; to come in contact with. *aor.* **—phusi.** *abs.* **—sitvā.**

Samphusanā, *f.* touch ; contact.

Samphusita, *pp.* touched ; well fitted.

Sambaddha, *pp.* of **sambandhati.**

Sambandha, *m.* connection.

Sambandhati (saŋ + bandh + a), to bind together ; to unite. *aor.* **—ndhi.** *abs.* **—ndhitvā.**

Sambandhana, *nt.* binding together ; connection.

Sambala, *nt.* provision.

Sambahula, *a.* many.

Sambādha, *m.* pressure ; crowding ; inconvenience. **—dhana,** *nt.* obstruction.

Sambādheti (saŋ + bādh + e), to be crowded ; to obstruct. *aor.* **—esi.** *abs.* **—dhetvā.**

Sambāhati (saŋ + bāh + a), to massage ; to rub ; to shampoo. *aor.* **—bāhi.** *abs.* **—hitvā.**

Sambāhana, *nt.* rubbing ; massaging.

Sambuka, *m.* an oyster ; a shell.

Sambujjhati (saŋ + budh + ya), to understand clearly ; to know perfectly. *aor.* **—jjhi.** *pp.* **—buddha.** *abs.* **—jhitvā.**

Sambuddha, *m.* the Omniscient One.

Sambojjhaṅga, *m.* constituent of enlightenment.

Sambodhana, *nt.* arousing ; the vocative case.

Sambodhi, *f.* enlightenment ; the highest wisdom.

Sambodheti (saŋ + budh + e), to teach ; to make understand. *aor.* **—esi.**

Sambhagga, *pp.* of the following.

Sambhañjati (saŋ + bhañj + a), to break ; to split. *aor.* **—ñji.** *abs.* **—ñjitvā.**

Sambhata, *pp.* brought together; stored up.

Sambhatta, *a.* a friend; a devoted person.

Sambhama, *m.* excitement; confusion.

Sambhamati (saŋ + bham + a), to revolve. *aor.* **—bhami.** *abs.* **—mitvā.**

Sambhava, *m.* origin; birth; production; semen virile.

Sambhavati (saŋ + bhū + a), to arise; to be produced or present; to exist; to be together with. *aor.* **—bhavi.** *pp.* **—bhūta.**

Sambhavana, *nt.* coming into existence.

Sambhavesī, 3. one who is seeking birth.

Sambhāra, *m.* materials; requisite ingredients; accumulation; a heap.

Sambhāvanā, *f.* honour; reverence; esteem. **—vanīya,** *a.* venerable.

Sambhāveti (saŋ + bhū + e), to esteem; to honour; to mix with. *aor.* **—esi.** *pp.* **—vita.** *abs.* **—vetvā.**

Sambhīta, *pp.* terrified.

Sambhuñjati (saŋ + bhuj + ŋ - a), to eat together. *aor.* **—ñji.** *abs.* **—jitvā.**

Sambhūta (*pp.* of **sambhavati**), arisen from.

Sambheda, *m.* mixing up; confusion.

Sambhoga, *m.* eating or living together with.

Sambhoti, see **Sambhavati.**

Samma (a term of familiar address; seen only in *voc.*) my dear.

Samma, *nt.* a cymbal.

Sammakkhana, *nt.* smearing.

Sammakkheti (saŋ + makkh + e), to smear. *aor.* **—esi.** *pp.* **—khita.** *abs.* **—khetvā.**

Sammaggata, *a.* who has come to the right path.

Sammajjati (saŋ + majj + a), to sweep; to polish. *aor.* **—jji.** *pp.* **—jjita, sammaṭṭha.** *pr. p.* **—janta.** *abs.* **—jitvā.** *pt. p.* **—jitabba.**

Sammajjanī, *f.* a broom.

Sammata, *pp.* agreed upon; authorized; honoured; appointed for.

Sammatāla, *m.* a cymbal.

Sammati (sam + a), to be appeased or calmed; to cease; to rest; to dwell; to be weary.

Sammatta (saŋ + matta), *pp.* intoxicated; much delighted. (*Abstr.* from **sammā**:) correctness; righteousness.

Sammada, *m.* drowsiness after a meal.

Sammadakkhāta, *a.* well preached.

Sammadaññā, —ñāya, *abs.* having understood perfectly.

Sammad'eva, *in.* properly; in completeness.

Sammadda, *m.* crowding.

Sammaddati (saŋ + madd + a), to trample down; to crush. *aor.* **—maddi.** *pp.* **—dita.** *abs.* **—ditvā.**

Sammaddana, *nt.* trampling; crushing.

Sammaddasa, *a.* having right views; seeing rightly.

Sammanteti (saŋ + mant + e), to consult together. *aor.* **—esi.** *pp.* **—tita.** *abs.* **—tetvā.**

Sammannati (saŋ + man + a), to authorize; to agree to; to assent; to select. *aor.* **—nni.** *pp.* **—nita, sammata.** *abs.* **—nitvā.**

Sammappaññā, *f.* right knowledge.

Sammappadhāna, *nt.* right exertion.

Sammasati (saŋ + mas + a), to grasp; to touch; to know thoroughly; to meditate on. *aor.* **—masi.** *pp.* **—masita.** *abs.* **—sitvā.**

Sammā, *in.* properly; rightly; thoroughly. **—ājīva,** *m.* right means of livelihood. **—kammanta,** *m.* right conduct. **—diṭṭhi,** *f.* right belief. **—diṭṭhika,** *a.* having right views. **—paṭipatti,** *f.* right mental disposition. **—paṭipanna,** rightly disposed. **—vattanā,** *f.* proper conduct. **—vācā,** *f.* right speech. **—vāyāma,** *m.* right effort. **—vimutti,** *f.* right emencipation. **—saṅkappa,** *m.* right intention. **—sati,** *f.* right memory. **—samādhi,** *m.* right concentration. **—sambuddha,** *m.* the perfectly Enlightened One. **—sambodhi,** *f.* perfect enlightenment.

Sammāna, *m.* **—nanā,** *f.* honour; respect.

Sammiñjati (saŋ + inj + a), to bend back; to double up. *aor.* **—ñji.** *pp.* **—jita.** *pr. p.* **—janta.** *abs.* **—jitvā.**

Sammissa, *a.* mixed. **—tā,** *f.* the state of being mixed.

Sammisseti (saŋ + mis + e), to mix; to confuse. *aor.* **—esi.** *pp.* **—sita.** *abs.* **—setvā.**

Sammukha, *a.* face to face with. *loc.* in the presence. **—khā,** *in.* in front; face to face.

Sammucchati (sam + mus + ya), to infatuate. *aor.* **—chi.** *pp.* **—chita.** *abs.* **—chitvā.**

Sammuti, *f.* general opinion; consent; selection; permission.

Sammudita, *a.* delighting in.

Sammuyhati (saŋ + muh + ya), to forget; to be bewildered or infatuated. *aor.* **—yhi.** *pp.* **—mūḷha.** *abs.* **—yhitvā, —muyha.**

Sammuyhana, *nt.* forgetting; bewilderment.

Sammussati (saŋ + mus + ya), to forget. *aor.* **—ssi.** *pp.* **sammuṭṭha.** *abs.* **—sitvā.**

Sammūḷha (*pp.* of **sammuyhati**), forgotten; infatuated.

Sammodaka, 3. one who speaks friendly.

Sammodati (saŋ + mud + a), to rejoice; to delight; to exchange friendly greetings. *aor.* **—modi.** *abs.* **—ditvā.**

Sammodanā, *f.* rejoicing; compliment; mixing. **—danīya,** *a.* to be rejoiced; pleasant.

Sammosa, —moha, *m.* confusion; delusion.

Sayañjāta, *a.* born from oneself; sprung up spontaniously.

Sayati (si + a), to sleep; to lie down. *aor.* **sayi.** *pr. p.* **sayanta, sayamāna.** *abs.* **sayitvā.**

Sayana, *nt.* a bed; sleeping. **—nighara,** *nt.* a sleeping room.

Sayambhū, *m.* the Creator.

Sayaŋ, *in.* self; by oneself. **—kata,** *a.* done by oneself; made by itself. **—vara,** *m.* self-choice.

Sayāna, *a.* sleeping; lying down.

Sayāpeti (*caus.* of **sayati**), to make sleep or lie down.

Sayha, *a.* bearable; able to endure.

Sara, *m.* an arrow; a sound; a vowel; a lake; a kind of reed. **—tuṇḍa,** *nt.* the point of an arrow. **—tīra,** *nt.* the bank of a lake. **—bhaṅga,** *m.* arrow-breaking. **—bhañña,** *nt.* intoning; a particular mode of recitation. **—bhāṇaka,** 3. one who recites the sacred texts.

Saraka, *m.* a drinking vessel.

Saraja, *a.* dusty; impure.

Saraṇa, *nt.* protection; help; refuge; a shelter. **—ṇāgamana,** *nt.* taking refuge.

Saraṇīya, *a.* fit to be remembered.

Sarati (sar + a), to remember; to move along. *aor.* **sari.** *abs.* **saritvā.** *pr. p.* **saranta.**

Sarada, *m.* the autumn; a year. **—samaya,** *m.* the season following on the rains.

Saritabba, *pt. p.* fit to be remembered.

Saritā, *f.* a river.

Saritu, *m.* one who remembers.

Sarīra, *nt.* the body. **—kicca,** *nt.* easing of the body; bodily function; obsequies. **—ṭṭha,** *a.* deposited in the body. **—dhātu,** *f.* a body relic of the Buddha. **—nissanda,** *m.* excretion of the body. **—ppabhā,** *f.* lustre of the body. **—maŋsa,** *nt.* the flesh of the body. **—vaṇṇa,** *m.* the appearance of the body. **—valañja,** *m.* discharge from the body. **—valañjaṭṭhāna,** *nt.* a place where the people ease their bodies. **—saṇṭhāna,** *nt.* bodily form; features.

Sarūpa, *a.* of the same form; having a form. **—tā,** *f.* similarity.

Saroja, saroruha, *nt.* a lotus.

Salakkhaṇa, *a.* together with the characteristics. *nt.* one's own characteristic.

Salabha, *m.* a moth; a grasshopper.

Salākā, *f.* a blade of grass; ribs of a parasol; a surgical instrument; tickets consisting of slips of wood; a lot. **—vutta,** *a.* subsisting by means of food tickets. **—kagga,** *nt.* a room for distributing tickets. **—gāha,** *m.* taking of tickets or votes. **—gāhāpaka,** 3. distributor of voting tickets. **—bhatta,** *nt.* food to be distributed by tickets.

Salāṭu, —ka, *a.* unripe.

Salābha, *m.* one's own advantage or gain.

Salila, *nt.* water. **—dhārā,** *f.* a shower of water.

Salla, *m.* a dart; spike; stake; quill of a porcupine; surgical instrument. **—ka,** *m.* a porcupine. **—viddha,** *a.* pierced by a dart.

Sallakatta, *m.* a surgeon. **—kattiya,** *nt.* surgery.

Sallakkhaṇa, *nt.* **—ṇā,** *f.* discernment; consideration.

Sallakkheti (saŋ + lakkh + e), to observe; to consider. *aor.* **—esi.** *pp.* **—khita.** *abs.* **—khetvā.** *pr. p.* **—khenta.**

Sallapati (saŋ + lap + a), to converse; to talk with. *aor.* **—lapi.** *pr. p.* **—panta.** *abs.* **—pitvā.**

Sallapana, *nt.* talking.

Sallahuka, *a.* light; frugal.

Sallāpa, *m.* friendly talk.

Sallikhati (saṇ + likh + a), to cut into slices. *aor.* —**khi.** *pp.* —**khita.** *abs.* —**khitvā.**

Sallīna, *pp.* of the following.

Sallīyati (saṇ + lī + ya), to become secluded. *aor.* —**līyi.** *abs.* —**yitvā.**

Sallīyanā, *f.* stolidity ; seclusion.

Sallekha, *m.* austere penance.

Savaṅka, *a.* having bendings.

Savaṇa, *nt.* hearing ; the ear.

Savaṇīya, *a.* pleasant to hear.

Savana, *nt.* flowing.

Savati (su + a), to flow. *aor.* **savi.** *pr. p.* **savanta.** *abs.* **savitvā.**

Savantī, *f.* a river.

Savighāta, *a.* bringing vexation.

Saviññāṇaka, *a.* animate ; conscious.

Savitakka, *a.* accompanied by reasoning.

Savera, *a.* connected with enmity.

Savyañjana, *a.* together with condiments or well sounding letters.

Sasa, *m.* a hare. —**lakkhaṇa,** —**lañchana,** *nt.* the sign of hare in the moon. —**visāṇa,** *nt.* a hare's horn, (an impossibility).

Sasakkaṇ, *ad.* surely ; certainly.

Sasaṅka, *m.* the moon.

Sasattha, *a.* bearing weapons.

Sasambhāra, *a.* with the ingredients or constituents.

Sasī, *m.* the moon.

Sasīsaṇ, *ad.* together with the head ; up to the head.

aSsura, *m.* father-in-law.

Sasena, *n.* accompanied by an army.

Sassa, *nt.* corn ; crop. —**kamma,** *nt.* agriculture. —**kāla,** harvest time.

Sassata, *a.* eternal. —**diṭṭhi,** *f.* —**vāda,** *m.* eternalism. —**vādī,** *m.* eternalist.

Sassati, *f.* eternity. —**tika,** *a.* eternalist.

Sassamaṇa-brāhmaṇa, *a.* including religious teachers and brahmans.

Sassāmika, *a.* having a husband or an owner.

Sassirīka, *a.* glorious ; resplendent.

Sassu, *f.* mother-in-law.

Saha (*conjunctive particle*), with ; together ; accompanied by. —**gata,** *a.* connected or endowed with. —**ja,** —**jāta,** *a.* born at the same time or together. —**jīvī,** *a.* living together with. —**nandī,** *a.* rejoicing together. —**dhammika,** *a.* co-religionist. —**bhū,** *a.* arising together with. —**yoga,** *m.* connection ; co-operation ; application of **saha.** —**vāsa,** *m.* living together. —**seyyā,** *f.* sharing the same bedroom. —**sokī,** *a.* sharing another's sorrow.

Saha, *a.* enduring.

Sahakāra, *m.* a sort of fragrant mango.

Sahati (sah + a), to bear ; to endure ; to be able ; to overcome. *aor.* **sahi.** *pr. p.* **sahanta, sahamāna.** *abs.* **sahitvā.**

Sahattha, *m.* one's own hand.

Sahana, *nt.* endurance.

Sahavya, *nt.* —**vyatā,** *f.* companionship.

Sahasā, *ad.* suddenly ; forcibly.

Sahassa, *nt.* a thousand. **—kkha,** *m.* the thousand-eyed Sakka. **—kkhattuŋ,** *ad.* a thousand times. **—gghanaka,** *a.* worth a thousand. **—tthavikā,** *f.* **—bhaṇḍikā,** *f.* a bag containing a thousand pieces of gold coins. **—dhā,** *ad.* in a thousand ways. **—netta,** see **—kkha. —raŋsī,** *m.* the sun. **—āra,** *a.* having a thousand spokes.

Sahassika, *a.* consisting of a thousand. **—sīlokadhātu,** *f.* a thousand-fold world.

Sahāya, —yaka, *m.* a friend ; an ally. **—tā,** *f.* friendship.

Sahita, *a.* accompanied with ; united ; keeping together ; consistent. *nt.* literature ; scriptures ; a piece of wood to generate fire by rubbing on.

Sahitabba (*pt. p.* of **sahati**), to be endured.

Sahitu, *m.* one who endures.

Sahetuka, *a.* having a cause.

Sahoḍha, *a.* together with the stolen goods.

Saḷāyatana, *nt.* the six organs of sense. *viz :* eye, ear, nose, tongue, body, and mind.

Saŋyata, *a.* restrained ; self-controlled. **—tta,** *a.* having one's mind restrained. **—cārī,** *a.* living in self-control.

Saŋyama, *m.* **—mana,** *nt.* restraint ; self-control ; abstinence. **—mī,** *m.* a recluse ; one who restrains his senses.

Saŋyameti (saŋ + yam + e), to restrain ; to practise self-control. *aor.* **—esi.** *pp.* **—mita.** *pr. p.* **—menta.** *abs.* **—metvā.**

Saŋyuta, saŋyutta (*pp.* of **saŋyuñjati**), connected ; combined ; bound together.

Saŋyūhati (saŋ + ūh + a), to form into a mass. *aor.* **—hi.** *pp.* **saŋyūḷha.**

Saŋyoga, *m.* a bond ; union ; association ; fetter ; an euphonic combination.

Saŋyojana, *nt.* connection ; fettering. **—niya,** *a.* favourable to the **saŋyojanas.**

Saŋyojeti (saŋ + yuj + e), to join ; to combine ; to bind. *aor.* **—esi.** *pp.* **—jita.** *pr. p.* **—jenta.** *abs.* **—jetvā.**

Saŋrakkhati (saŋ + rakkh + a), to guard ; to ward off. *aor.* **—kkhi.** *pp.* **—khita.** *abs.* **—khitvā.**

Saŋrakkhanā, *f.* guarding ; protection.

Saŋvacchara, *nt.* a year.

Saŋvaṭṭati (saŋ + vat + a), to be dissolved. *aor.* **—ṭṭi.**

Saŋvaṭṭana, *nt.* rolling ; dissolution.

Saŋvaḍḍha (*pp.* of the following), grown up ; brought up.

Saŋvaḍḍhati (saŋ + vaḍḍh + a), to grow ; to increase. *aor.* **—ḍḍhi.** *pr. p.* **—ḍhamāna.** *abs.* **—ḍhitvā.**

Saŋvaḍḍheti (*caus.* of the above), to rear ; to nourish ; to bring up. *aor.* **—esi.** *pp.* **—ḍhita.** *abs.* **—ḍhetvā.**

Saŋvannanā, *f.* exposition ; explanation ; praise.

Saŋvaṇṇeti (saŋ + vaṇṇ + e), to explain ; to comment ; to praise. *aor.* **—esi.** *pp.* **—ṇita.** *pt. p.* **—ṇetabba.** *abs.* **—ṇetvā.**

Saŋvattati (saŋ + vat + a), to exsist ; to lead to. *aor.* **—vatti.** *pp.* **—vattita.**

Saŋvattanika, *a.* conducive to; involving.

Saŋvatteti (*caus.* of **saŋvattati**), to make go on or continue, *aor.* **—esi**. *pp.* **—vattita**. *abs.* **—tetvā**.

Saŋvaddha, see **Saŋvaḍḍha**. **—na,** *nt.* growth ; bringing up ; growing.

Saŋvara, *m.* restraint. **—ṇa,** *nt.* restriction ; obstruction ; shutting.

Saŋvarati (saŋ + var + a), to restrain ; to shut ; to cover. *aor.* **—vari**. *pp.* **saŋvuta**. *abs.* **—varitvā**.

Saŋvarī, *f.* the night.

Saŋvasati (saŋ + vas + a), to associate ; to live together ; to cohabitate. *aor.* **—vasi**. *pp.* **—vasita**. *abs.* **—vasitvā**.

Saŋvāsa, *m.* co-residence ; intimacy ; sexual intercourse.

Saŋvigga (*pp.* of the following), agitated ; moved by fear.

Saŋvijjati (saŋ + vid + ya), to be found ; to exist ; to be agitated or moved. *aor.*—**jji**. *pr. p.* **—jamāna**.

Saŋvidahati (saŋ + vi + dhā + a), to arrange ; to give orders ; to prepare. *aor.* **—dahi**. *pp.* **—vihita**. *abs.* **—dahitvā**. *pr. p.* **—dahamāna**. *pt. p.* **—hitabba**.

Saŋvidahana, *nt.* arrangement ; giving orders.

Saŋvidhāna, *nt.* see the above.

Saŋvidhāya (*abs.* from **saŋvidahati**), having arranged. **—yaka,** 3. one who arranges or manages.

Saŋvidhātuŋ (*inf.* from **saŋvidahati**), to arrange ; to issue commands.

Saŋvibhajati (saŋ + vi + bhaj + a), to divide ; to share. *aor.* **—bhaji**. *pp.* **—jita**. **—vibhatta**. *abs.* **—vibhajja, —jitvā**.

Saŋvibhajana, *nt.* **—vibhāga,** *m.* dividing ; sharing.

Saŋvibhāgī, 3. generous ; openhanded.

Saŋvihita, *pp.* of **saŋvidahati**.

Saŋvuta, *pp.* of **saŋvarati**. **—tindriya,** *a.* having the senses under control.

Saŋvega, *m.* anxiety ; agitation ; religious emotion.

Saŋvejaniya, *a.* apt to cause emotion or anxiety.

Saŋvejeti (saŋ + vij + e), to cause emotion or agitation. *aor.* **—esi**. *pp.* **—jita**. *abs.* **—jetvā**.

Saŋsagga, *m.* contact ; association.

Saŋsaṭṭha, *pp.* mixed with ; joined ; associating with.

Saŋsatta, *pp.* adhering ; clinging.

Saŋsandati (saŋ + sand + a), to fit ; to agree ; to run together. *aor.* **—sandi**. *pp.* **—dita**. *abs.* **—ditvā**.

Saŋsandeti (*caus.* of the above), to make fit ; to compare. *aor.* **—esi**. *abs.* **—detvā**.

Saŋsappati (saŋ + sap + a), to creep along ; to crawl ; to move slowly. *aor.* **—ppi**. *abs.* **—pitvā**.

Saŋsappana, *nt.* writhing ; struggling.

Saŋsaya, *m.* doubt.

Saŋsarati (saŋ + sar + a), to move about continuously ; to transmigrate. *aor.* **—sari**. *pp.* **—sarita**. *abs.* **—ritvā**.

Saŋsaraṇa, *nt.* moving about ; wandering.

Saŋsāra, *m.* faring on ; transmigration. **—cakka,** *nt.* the wheel of rebirth. **—dukkha,** *nt.* the ill of transmigration. **—sāgara,** *m.* the ocean of rebirth.

Saŋsijjhati (saŋ + siddh + ya), to be fulfilled; to succeed. *aor.* **—jjhi.** *pp.* **—siddha.**

Saŋsiddhi, *f.* success.

Saŋsibbita (*pp.* of **saŋsibbati**), sewn; entwined.

Saŋsīdati (saŋ + sad + a), to sink down; to lose heart; to fail in. *aor.* **saŋsīdi.** *pr. p.* **—damāna.** *abs.* **—sīditvā.**

Saŋsīdana, *nt.* sinking down.

Saŋsīna, *pp.* fallen off.

Saŋsuddha, *pp.* pure. **—gahaṇika,** *a.* of pure descent.

Saŋsuddhi, *f.* purity.

Saŋsūcaka, *a.* indicating.

Saŋsedaja, *a.* born from moisture.

Saŋseva, *m.* **—vanā,** *f.* associating.

Saŋsevati (saŋ + sev + a), to associate; to attend. *aor.* **—sevi.** *pp.* **—vita.** *pr. p.* **—vamāna.** *abs.* **– vitvā.**

Saŋsevī, *a.* one who associates.

Saŋhata, *a.* firm; compact.

Saŋharaṇa, *nt.* gathering; folding.

Saŋharati (saŋ + har + a), to collect; to draw together; to fold up. *aor.* **—hari.** *pp.* **saŋhaṭa,** **—harita.** *pr. p.* **—ranta.** *abs.* **—ritvā.**

Saŋhāra, *m.* abridgement; compilation. **—ka,** *a.* drawing together.

Saŋhārima, *a.* movable.

Saŋhita, *a.* equipped with; possessed of. **—tā,** *f.* connection; euphonic agreement.

Sā, *m.* a dog.

Sā, *f.* (*Nom.* from ta,) she.

Sāka, *m. nt.* vegetable; pot herb. **—paṇṇa,** *nt.* vegetable leaf.

Sākacchā, *f.* conversation; discussion.

Sākaṭika, *m.* a carter.

Sākalya, *nt.* totality.

Sākiya, 3. belonging to the Sākya race. **—yānī,** *f.* a woman of the Sākya race.

Sākuṇika, sākuntika, *m.* a fowler; a bird-catcher.

Sākhā, *f.* a branch. **—nagara,** *nt.* a suburb. **—palāsa,** *nt.* branches and leaves. **—bhaṅga,** *m.* a broken branch. **—miga,** *m.* a monkey.

Sākhī, *m.* a tree.

Sāgataŋ, *in.* hail; welcome.

Sāgara, *m.* the sea; ocean.

Sāgāra, *a.* living in a house.

Sācariyaka, *a.* together with one's teacher.

Sāṭaka, *m.* **sāṭikā,** *f.* a clothe; a cloak.

Sāṭheyya, *nt.* craft; treachery.

Sāṇa, *nt.* hemp; hempen cloth.

Sāṇi, *f.* a screen; a curtain. **—pasibbaka,** *m.* a sack. **—pākāra,** *m.* a screen wall, (made with hempen cloth).

Sāta, *nt.* pleasure; comfort. *adj.* pleasant; agreeable.

Sātakumbha, *nt.* gold.

Sātacca, *nt.* continuation; perseverance. **—kārī,** 3. acting continuously. **—kiriyā,** *f.* perseverance.

Sātatika, *a.* acting continuously.

Sātireka, *a.* having something in excess.

Sāttha, —thaka, *a.* useful; advantageous; with the meaning.

Sādara, *a.* affectionate; showing regard. **—raŋ,** *ad.* affectionately.

Sādiyati (sad + i + ya), to accept; to enjoy; to agree to; to permit. *aor.* **—diyi.** *pp.* **sādita.** *pr. p.* **—yanta, —yamāna.** *abs.* **—yitvā.**

Sadiyana, *nt.* **—yanā,** *f.* acceptance; appropriation.

Sādisa, *a.* like; similar.

Sādu, *a.* sweet; pleasant. **—tara,** *a.* more sweet or pleasant. **—rasa,** *a.* having a pleasant taste.

Sādhaka, *a.* effecting; accomplishing. *nt.* a proof.

Sādhana, *nt.* proving; settling; effecting; clearing a debt.

Sādhāraṇa, *a.* common; general.

Sādhika, *a.* having something in excess.

Sādhita (*pp.* of **sādheti**).

Sādhiya, *a.* that which can be accomplished.

Sādhu, *a.* good; virtuous; profitable. *ad.* well; thoroughly. **—kaŋ,** *ad.* well; thoroughly. **—kamyatā,** *f.* desire for proficiency. **—kāra,** *m.* cheering; applause; approval; saying "well."**—kīḷana,** *nt.* a sacred festivity. **—rūpa,** *a.* of good dispositions. **—sammata,** *a.* highly honoured; accepted by the virtuous.

Sādhu, *in.* yes; alright.

Sādheti (sādh + e), to accomplish; to effect; to prepare; to perform; to clear a debt. *aor.* **—esi.** *pp.* **sādhita.** *abs.* **sādhetvā.** *pr. p.* **—dhenta.**

Sānu, *f. nt.* a table land.

Sānucara, *a.* together with followers.

Sānuvajja, *a.* blamable.

Sāpa, *m.* a curse.

Sāpateyya, *nt.* property, wealth.

Sāpattika, *a.* one who has transgressed a Vinaya rule.

Sāpadesa, *a.* with reasons.

Sāpekkha, sāpekha, *a.* hopeful; expecting; longing for.

Sāma, *a.* black; dark. *m.* peace; name of a portion of Veda.

Sāmaŋ, *in.* oneself; by oneself.

Sāmaggi, *f.* **—giya,** *nt.* concord; unity.

Sāmacca, *a.* together with the ministers or friends.

Sāmañña, *nt.* conformity; generality; the state of a monk. **—tā,** *f.* congruity; respect for the religious mendicants. **—phala,** *nt.* fruit of the life of a recluse.

Sāmaṇaka, *a.* worthy or needful for a monk.

Samaṇera, *m.* a novice of a monk. **—ṇerī,** *f.* a female apprentice of a nun.

Sāmatthiya, *nt.* ability.

Sāmanta, *nt.* neighbourhood; vicinity. *adj.* bordering; neighbouring.

Sāmayika, *a.* religious; temporary.

Sāmā, *f.* a kind of medical plant; a woman of dark complexion.

Sāmājika, *m.* a member (of an assembly).

Sāmika, *m.* the husband; the owner.

Sāminī, *f.* mistress ; a female owner.

Sāmivacana, *nt.* the genitive case.

Sāmisa, *a.* fleshy ; carnal ; smeared with food.

Sāmī, *m.* owner ; lord ; master ; husband.

Sāmīci, *f.* proper course ; friendly treatment. **—kamma**, *nt.* proper act ; homage. **—paṭipanna**, *a.* entered into the proper course.

Sāmuddika, *a.* seafaring ; marine.

Sāyaka, *a.* one who tastes.

Sāyaṇha, *m.* evening ; **—samaya**, **—kāla**, *m.* the latter part of the afternoon.

Sāyati (sā + ya), to taste. *aor.* **sāyi**. *pp.* **sāyita**. *pr. p.* **sāyanta**. *abs.* **sāyitvā**.

Sāra, *m.* essence ; the pith of a tree ; the choicest part. *adj.* essential ; excellent ; strong.**—gandha**, *m.* odour of the heart of a tree. **—gavesī**, *a.* one who seeks the essence. **—maya**, *a.* made of hard wood. **—sūci**, *f.* a needle made of hard wood. **—vantu**, *a.* valuable ; having kernel or pith.

Sārakkha, *a.* guarded.

Sārajjati (saŋ + raj + ya), to be attached to. *aor.* **—jji**. *pp.* **sāratta**. *abs.* **—jitvā**.

Sārajjanā, *f.* attachment.

Sāratta (*pp.* of **sārajjati**), impassioned ; enamoured.

Sārathi, **—thī**, *m.* a charioteer; a coachman ; a driver.

Sārada, **—dika**, *a.* autumnal.

Sāraddha, *a.* passionate ; warm.

Sārameya, *m.* a dog.

Sārambha, *m.* impetuosity ; anger ; involving danger to living beings.

Sārasa, *m.* a water bird.

Sāraṇīya, *a.* what should be reminded.

Sāribā, *f.* the *Sarsaparilla* plant.

Sārī, *a.* (in cpds.) wandering ; following.

Sārīrika, *a.* connected with the body.

Sāruppa, *a.* fit ; suitable ; proper.

Sāreti (sar + e), to remind ; to lead ; to make move along. *aor.* **sāresi**. *pp.* **sārita**. *pt. p.* **sāretabba**. *abs.* **sāretvā**.

Sāla, *m.* brother-in-law ; a Sal tree. **—rukkha**, *m.* the tree *Shorea Robusta* **—vana**, *nt.* a Sal grove. **—laṭṭhi**. *f.* a young Sal tree.

Sālaya, *a.* having attachment.

Sālā, *f.* a hall ; a shed.

Sālākiya, *nt.* opthalmology.

Sāli, *m.* a good kind of rice. **—kkhetta**, *nt.* a rice-field. **—gabbha**, *m.* ripening young rice. **—bhatta**, *nt.* boiled rice of Sāli.

Sālikā, *f.* a myna-bird.

Sālittaka-sippa, *nt.* the art of slinging stones.

Sāluka, *nt.* the root of water-lily.

Sāvaka, *m.* a hearer ; a disciple. **—tta**, *nt.* the state of a disciple. **—saṅgha**, *m.* the congregation of disciples. **—vikā** *f.* a female disciple.

Sāvajja, *a.* blamable ; faulty ; *nt.* what is censurable. **—tā**, *f.* guilt ; blamability.

Sāvaṭṭa, *a.* containing whirlpools.

Sāvaṇa, *nt.* announcement: proclamation. *m.* name of a month, July-August.

Sāvatthī, *f.* name of the metropolis of the Kingdom of Kosala.

Sāvasesa, *a.* incomplete; with a remainder.

Sāveti (su + e), to make hear; to announce; to declare. *aor.* **—esi.** *pp.* **sāvita.** *pr. p.* **sāventa, sāvayamāna.** *pt. p.* **—vetabba.** *abs.* **sāvetvā.**

Sāvetu, *m.* one who announces.

Sāsaṅka, *a.* suspicious.

Sāsati (sās + a), to teach; to instruct; to rule. *aor.* **sāsi.** *pp.* **sāsita.**

Sāsana, *nt.* teaching; order; message; doctrine; a letter. **—kara, —kārī, —kāraka,** *a.* complying with one's order or teaching. **—ntaradhāna,** *nt.* disappearance of the teaching of the Buddha. **—hara,** *m.* a messenger. **—āvacara,** *a.* observing the religious rules.

Sāsanika, *a.* connected with Buddhism.

Sāsapa, *m.* a mustard seed.

Sāsava, *a.* connected with the depravities.

Sāhatthika, *a.* done with one's own hand.

Sāhasa, *nt.* violence; arbitrary action. **—sika,** *a.* violent; savage.

Sāhu, *in.* good; well.

Sāḷava, *m.* a salad.

Sikatā, *f.* sand.

Sikkhati (sikkh + a), to learn; to train oneself; to practise. *aor.* **sikkhi.** *pp.* **sikkhita.** *pr. p.* **—khanta, —khamāna.** *abs.* **—khitvā.** *pt. p.* **—khitabba.**

Sikkhana, *nt.* learning; training.

Sikkhamānā, *f.* a female novice undergoing a probationary course.

Sikkhā, *f.* study; discipline. **—kāma,** *a.* anxious to observe religious rules. **—paka, —panaka,** 3. a teacher; trainer. **—pada,** *nt.* a precept; a religious rule. **—pana,** *nt.* teaching; instruction. **—samādāna,** *nt.* taking the precepts upon oneself.

Sikkhita, *pp.* of **sikkhati.**

Sikhaṇḍa, *m.* the crest of a peacock. **—ṇḍī,** *m.* a peacock.

Sikhara, *nt.* the top: summit; peak of a mountain. **—rī,** *m.* a mountain.

Sikhā, *f.* crest; top-knot; a flame.

Sikhī, *m.* fire; peacock.

Sigāla, *m.* a jackal. **—laka,** *nt.* a jackal's howl.

Siggu, *m.* the horse radish tree. මුරුංගා.

Siṅga, *nt.* a horn.

Siṅgāra, *m.* erotic sentiment.

Siṅgivera, *nt.* ginger.

Siṅgī, *a.* possessing horns. *nt.* gold. **—nada, —vaṇṇa,** *nt.* gold.

Siṅghati (siṅgh + a), to sniff; to smell. *aor.* **—ghi.** *abs.* **—ghitvā.**

Siṅghāṭaka, *m. nt.* anything of the shape of a cross; a place where four roads meet

Siṅghānikā, *f.* mucus of the nose ; snot.

Sijjhati (sidh + ya), to happen ; to succeed ; to avail. *aor.* **sijjhi**. *pp.* **siddha**.

Sijjhana, *nt.* happening ; success.

Siñcaka, *a.* one who waters or sprinkles.—**cana**, *nt.* sprinkling.

Siñcati (sic + ŋ + a), to pour ; to sprinkle. *aor.* **siñci**. *pp.* **sitta, siñcita**. *pr. p.* —**camāna**. *abs.* **siñcitvā**. *caus.* **siñcāpeti**.

Sita, *a.* white ; depending on ; attached. *nt.* a smile.

Sitta, *pp.* of **siñcati**.

Sittha, *nt.* wax ; a grain of boiled rice. —**āvakārakaŋ**, *ad.* scattering boiled rice all over.

Sitthaka, *nt.* bees-wax.

Sithila, *a.* loose ; lax ; yielding. —**tta**, *nt.* looseness.

Siddha (*pp.* of **sijjhati**), ended ; accomplished ; happened. —**ttha**, *a.* one who has accomplished his task. *m.* the mustard.

Siddha, *a.* a semi-divine being ; a magician.

Siddhatthaka, *nt.* mustard seed.

Siddhi, *f.* accomplishment ; success.

Sinâna, *nt.* bathing ; bath.

Siniddha, *a.* smooth ; glossy ; pliable ; soft ; loving.

Sineha, sneha, *m.* affection ; love ; oil ; fat. —**hana**, *nt.* oiling. —**bindu**, *nt.* a drop of oil.

Sineheti (*Deno.* from **sineha**), to love ; to smear with oil.

Sindī, *f.* the date palm.

Sindūra, *m.* red arsenic.

Sindhava, *a.* belonging to Sindh ; *m.* rock salt ; a Sindh horse.

Sindhu, *m.* ocean ; a river. —**raṭṭha**, *nt.* the country of Sindh. —**saṅgama**, *m.* the mouth or confluence of a river.

Sipāṭikā, *f.* the pericap ; a small case.

Sippa, *nt.* art ; craft. —**ṭṭhāna**, —**āyatana**, *nt.* a branch of knowledge ; a craft. —**sālā**, *f.* a school (for arts).

Sippika, sippī, *m.* an artist ; a craftsman.

Sippikā, *f.* an oyster.

Sibbati (siv + ya), to stitch ; to sew. *aor.* **sibbi**. *pp.* **sibbita**. *abs.* **sibbitvā**.

Sibbana, *nt.* sewing.

Sibbanī, *f.* seamstress ; craving. —**magga**, *m.* the suture.

Sibbeti (siv + e), to sew. *aor.* —**esi**. *pp.* **sibbita**. *abs.* —**betvā**. *pr. p.* —**benta**.

Simbalī, *m.* the silk-cotton tree.

Sira, *m. nt.* (mano-group) the head.

Sirā, *f.* a tendon ; vein.

Siri, sirī, *f.* luck ; glory ; wealth; splendour ; the goddess of luck. —**gabbha**, *m.* the bedroom of a noble person ; the royal bed chamber. —**mantu**, *a.* glorious. —**vilāsa**, *m.* the pomp and splendour —**sayana**, *nt.* the royal bed ; state couch. —**ndhara**, *a.* glorious.

Sirivāsa, *m.* turpentine.

Sirīsa, *m.* the tree *Acacia Sirissa.*

Siro (is the form taken by **sira** in cpds.), —**jāla**, *a.* veil for the head. —**ruha**, *m. nt.* hair. —**maṇi**, *m.* a diadem ; a jewelled crest. —**veṭhana**, *nt.* a turban.

Silā, *f.* a stone. **—guḷa**, *m.* a ball of stone. **—tthambha**, *m.* a stone pillar. **—paṭṭa**, *nt.* a slab of stone. **—pākāra**, *m.* a stone wall. **—maya**, *a.* made of stone.

Silāghati (silāgh + a), to extol ; to boast. *aor.* **—ghi.**

Silāghā, *f.* praise.

Siliṭṭha, *a.* smooth. **—tā**, *f.* smoothness.

Siluccaya, *m.* a rock.

Silutta, *m.* rat-snake.

Silesa, *m.* a riddle ; a rhetoric figure ; an adhesive substance.

Silesuma, *m.* the phlegm.

Siloka, *m.* fame ; a verse.

Siva, *a.* sheltering ; safe. *m.* the God Siva. *nt.* a safe place ; the Nirvāna.

Sivikā, *f.* a palanquin ; a litter.

Sisira, *m.* the winter ; cold season. *adj.* cool.

Sissa, *m.* a pupil ; a student.

Sīgha, *a.* quick ; rapid, swift. **—gāmī**, *a.* going or moving quickly. **—taraŋ**, *ad.* very soon ; more quickly. **—sīghaŋ**, *ad.* very quickly ; hastily. **—sota.** *a.* having a running stream. **— ghaŋ**, *ad.* quickly ; swiftly.

Sīta, *a.* cool ; cold. *nt.* coolness ; cold. **—bhīruka**, *a.* susceptible of cold.

Sītala, *a.* cool ; cold. *nt.* coolness.

Sītā, *f.* a furrow.

Sītibhāva, *m.* coolness ; calm.

Sītibhūta, *pp.* calmed ; tranquillized.

Sītodaka, *nt.* cool water.

Sīdati (sad + a), to sink ; to subside ; to yield. *aor.* **sīdi.** *pp.* **sīna.** *abs.* **sīditvā.** *pr. p.* **sīdamāna.**

Sīdana, *nt.* sinking.

Sīna, *pp.* of **sīdati.**

Sīpada, *nt.* elephantiasis (of the leg).

Sīmaṭṭha, *a.* situated within or on the boundary.

Sīmantinī, *f.* a woman.

Sīmā, *f.* a boundary ; a limit ; a chapter house for Buddhist monks. **—kata**, *a.* limited. **—tiga**, *a.* gone over the limits. **—samugghāta**, *m.* abolishing of a former boundary. **—sammuti**, *f.* fixing of a new boundary ; convention of a chapter house.

Sīla, *nt.* nature ; habit ; moral practice ; code of morality. **—kathā**, *f.* exposition of the duties of morality. **—kkhandha**, *m.* all that belongs to moral practices. **—gandha**, *m.* the fragrance (= fame) of the good works. **—bbata, —vata**, *nt.* ceremonial observances. **—bheda**, *m.* breach of morality. **—maya**, *a.* connected with morality. **—vantu**, *a.* virtuous; observing the moral practices. **—vipatti**, *f.* moral transgression. **—vipanna**, *a.* one who has trespassed the moral precepts. **—sampatti**, *f.* accomplishment of morals. **—sampanna**, *a.* observing the moral precepts.

Sīlana, *nt.* practising ; restraining.

Sīlika, **sīlī**, *a.* (in cpds.) having the nature of.

Sīvathikā, *f.* a place where the dead bodies are thrown to rot away.

Sīsa, *nt.* the head; the highest point; an ear of corn; heading of an article; the lead. —**kapāla**, —**kaṭāha**, *m.* the skull. —**cchavi**, *f.* the skin of the head. —**cchejja**, *a.* resulting in decapitation. —**cchedana**, *nt.* decapitation. —**ppacālana**, *nt.* swaying of the head. —**paramparā**, *f.* changing from one's head to another's in carrying a burden. —**veṭhana**, *nt.* a turban; a head-wrap. —**ābādha**, *m.* disease of the head.

Sīha, *m.* a lion. —**camma**, *nt.* lion's hide. —**nāda**, *m.* lion's roar; a brave speech. —**nādika**, *a.* one who utters a lion's roar. —**pañjara**, *m.* a lion's cage; a kind of window. —**potaka**, *m.* a young lion. —**vikkīḷita**, *nt.* lion's play. —**seyyā**, *f.* lying on the right side. —**ssara**, *a.* having a voice like a lion. —**hanu**, *a.* having a jaw like that of a lion.

Sīhaḷa, *a.* belonging to Ceylon; *m.* a Sinhalese —**dīpa**, *m.* the island of Ceylon. —**bhāsā**, *f.* the Sinhalese language.

Su, a *prep.* expressing the notion of: well, happily and thorough.

Suka, *m.* a parrot.

Sukaṭa, **sukata**, *a.* well done. *nt.* meritorious act.

Sukara, *a.* easy; easily done.

Sukumāra, *a.* delicate. —**tā**, *f.* delicateness.

Sukusala, *a.* very skilful.

Sukka, *a.* white; pure; good; bright. *nt.* virtue. —**pakkha**, *m.* the bright half of a month.

Sukkha, *a.* dry.

Sukkhati (sukkh + a), to be dried up. *aor.* **sukkhi**, *pr. p.* —**khamāna**. *abs.* **sukkhitvā**.

Sukkhana, *nt.* drying up.

Sukkhāpana, *nt.* making dry.

Sukkhāpeti (*caus.* of **sukkhati**), to make dry. *aor.* —**esi**. *pp.* —**khita**. *abs.* —**khetvā**.

Sukha, *nt.* happiness; comfort. —**kāma**, *a.* longing for happiness. —**tthika**, —**tthī**, *a.* longing for happiness. —**da**, *a.* producing happiness. —**nisinna**, *a.* comfortably seated. —**paṭisaŋvedī**, *a.* experiencing happiness. —**ppatta**, *a.* happy. —**bhāgiya**, *a.* participating in happiness. —**yānaka**, *nt.* an easy-going cart. —**vipāka**, *a.* resulting in happiness. —**viharaṇa**, *nt.* comfortable living. —**saŋvāsa**, *m.* pleasant to associate with. —**samphassa**, *a.* pleasant to touch. —**sammata**, *a.* deemed a pleasure.

Sukhaŋ, *ad.* easily; comfortably.

Sukhāyati (*Deno.* from **sukha**), to be comfortable or happy.

Sukhāvaha, *a.* bringing happiness.

Sukhita (*pp.* of **sukheti**), happy; blest; glad.

Sukhī, 3. see the above.

Sukhuma, *a.* subtle; minute; fine; exquisite. —**tara**, *a.* very fine or subtle. —**tta**, *nt.* —**tā**, *f.* fineness; delicacy.

Sukhumāla, *a.* tender; delicate; refined. —**tā**, *f.* delicate constitution.

Sukheti (su + khan + e), to make happy. *aor.* —**esi**. *pp.* **sukhita**.

Sukhedhita, *a.* delicately nurtured.

Sukhesī, 3. looking for pleasure.

Sugata, *a.* faring well ; happy. *m.* the Buddha. —**tālaya,** *m.* dwelling place of the Buddha ; imitation of the Buddha.

Sugati, *f.* a happy state.

Sug(k)atī, *a.* righteous.

Sugandha, *m.* fragrance ; pleasant odour. *adj.* fragrant. —**ndhī,** —**dhika,** *a.* fragrant.

Sugahana, *nt.* a good grip.

Sugutta, sugopita, *pp.* well guarded or protected.

Suggahita, *a.* grasped tightly ; well learnt ; attentive.

Suṅka, *m.* toll ; tax. —**ghāta,** *m.* evasion of customs duties. —**ṭṭhāna,** *nt.* taxing place ; customs house.

Suṅkika, *m.* a collector of taxes.

Sucarita, *nt.* right conduct.

Suci, *a* pure ; clean. *nt.* goodness ; a pure thing. —**kamma,** *a.* whose actions are pure. —**gandha,** *a.* having a sweet smell. —**jātika,** *a.* liking cleanliness.—**vasana,** *a.* having a clean dress.

Sucitta, sucittita, *a.* much variegated ; well painted.

Succhanna, *a.* well covered or thatched.

Sujana, *m.* a virtuous man.

Sujā, *f.* the sacrificial ladle ; name of Sakka's wife.

Sujāta, *pp.* well born ; of good birth.

Sujjhati (sudh + ya), to become clean or pure. *aor.* **sujjhi.** *pr. p.* —**jhamāna.** *pp.* **suddha.** *abs.* —**jhitvā.**

Suñña, *a.* empty ; void.—**gāma,** *m.* a deserted village. —**tā,** *f.* emptiness. —**āgāra,** *nt.* an empty place.

Suṭṭhu, *in.* well. —**tā,** *f.* excellence.

Suṇa, *m.* a dog.

Suṇāti (su + ṇā), to hear. *aor.* **suṇi.** *pp.* **suta.** *pr. p.* **suṇanta, suṇamāna.** *pt. p.* **sotabba, suṇitabba.** *abs.* **sutvā, suṇitvā.** *inf.* **sotuŋ, suṇituŋ.**

Suṇisā, suṇha, *f.* a daughter-in-law.

Suta, *m.* a son.

Suta (*pp.* of **suṇāti**), heard. *nt.* the sacred lore ; learning ; that which is heard —**dhara,** remembering what has been learnt or heard. —**vantu,** *a.* learned.

Sutatta, *pp.* much heated.

Sutanu, *a.* having a handsome body or a slender waist.

Sutappaya, *a.* easily satisfied.

Suti, *f.* hearing ; tradition ; rumour ; the Vedas. —**hīna,** *a.* deaf.

Sutta (*pp.* of **supati**), slept ; dorment ; asleep.

Sutta, *nt.* a thread ; a string ; a discourse ; an aphorism. —**kantana,** *nt.* spinning. —**kāra,** *m.* a composer of grammatical aphorisms. —**guḷa,** *nt.* a ball of string. —**piṭaka,** *nt.* the portion of the Buddhist Scriptures containing discourses. —**maya,** *a.* made of threads.

Suttanta, *m. nt.* a discourse. —**ntika,** *a.* one who has learnt a portion or the whole of the Suttapiṭaka.

Sutti, *f.* a pearl oyster.

Sudanta, *a.* well tamed.

Sudassa, *a.* easily seen. —**sana,** *a.* having a good appearance.

Sudaŋ, a pleonestic particle.

Sudiṭṭha, *a.* well seen.

Sudinna, *a.* well given.

Suduttara, *a.* very difficult to escape from.

Sudukkara, *a.* very difficult to do.

Sududdasa, *a.* very difficult to see.

Sudubbala, *a.* very weak.

Sudullabha, *a.* very difficult to obtain.

Sudesita, *a.* well preached.

Sudda, *m.* a person of the Sūdra caste.

Suddha, *a.* clean; pure; unmixed; simple. **—tā,** *f.* **—tta,** *nt.* purity. **—ājīva,** *a.* living a pure life; *m.* clean livelihood. **—āvāsa,** *m.* the pure abode (in Brahma heaven). **—āvāsika,** *a.* living in the Pure Abode.

Suddhi, *f.* purity; purification. **—magga,** *m.* the path of purification.

Sudhanta, *pp.* well blown or purified.

Sudhammatā, *f.* good nature.

Sudhā, *f.* the embrosia; lime; chunnam. **—kamma,** *nt.* white-washing; coating with cement or plaster. **—kara,** *m.* the moon.

Sudhī, *m.* a wise man.

Sudhota, *pp.* well washed; thoroughly clean.

Sunakha, *m.* a dog. **—khī,** *f.* a bitch.

Sunahāta, *pp.* well bathed.

Sunisita, *pp.* well whetted or sharpened.

Sundara, *a.* good; nice; beautiful. **—tara,** *a.* better; more beautiful.

Supakka, *a.* thoroughly ripe.

Supaṭipanna, *a.* entered upon the right path.

Supaṇṇa, *m.* a kind of fairy bird.

Supati (sup + a), to sleep. *aor.* **supi.** *pp.* **sutta.** *pr. p.* **supanta.** *abs.* **supitvā.**

Suparikammakata, *a.* well prepared or polished.

Suparihīna, *a.* thoroughly bereft; much emaciated.

Supina, —naka, —nanta, *nt.* a dream. **—pāṭhaka,** *m.* a dream-teller.

Supupphita, *a.* covered with flowers; fully blown.

Supoṭhita, —thita, *pp.* thoroughly beaten.

Suppa, *m. nt.* a winnoing basket.

Suppaṭividdha, *pp.* thoroughly understood.

Suppatiṭṭhita, *pp.* firmly established.

Suppatīta, *a.* well pleased.

Suppadhaŋsiya, *a.* easily assaulted or overwhelmed.

Suppabhāta, *nt.* a good daybreak; good morning.

Suppavedita, *a.* well preached.

Suppasanna, *a.* very clear; very pleased; full of faith.

Suphassita, *a.* well fitted.

Subahu, *a.* very many.

Subbaca, *a.* obedient; meek; compliant.

Subbata, *a.* of good conduct.

Subbuṭṭhi, *f.* abundant rainfall.

Subha, *a.* lucky; auspicious; pleasant. *nt.* welfare; beauty. **—kiṇṇa,** *m.* the lustrous devas. **—nimitta,** *nt.* an auspicious sign; a beautiful object.

Subhaga, *a.* lucky ; fortunate.

Subhara, *a.* easily supported or satisfied.

Subhikkha, *a.* having plenty of food.

Sumati, *m.* a wise man.

Sumana, *a.* glad. **—puppha**, *nt.* jasmine flower. **—makula**, *nt.* a jasmine bud. **—mālā**, *f.* a garland of jasmine.

Sumanā, *f.* jasmine ; a glad woman.

Sumanohara, *a.* very charming.

Sumānasa, *a.* joyful.

Sumāpita, *pp.* well built.

Sumutta, *pp.* well released.

Sumedha, **—dhasa**, *a.* wise.

Suyiṭṭha, *a.* well sacrificed.

Suyutta, *a.* well arranged or suited.

Sura, *m.* a god ; deity. **—nadī**, *f.* the celestial river. **—nātha**, *m.* the king of devas. **—patha**, *m.* the sky. **—ripu**, *m.* the enemy of gods, i.e. an **Asura**.

Surata, *a.* well-loving ; devoted ; attached.

Suratta, *a.* well dyed ; very red.

Surabhi, *a.* fragrant. **—gandha**, *m.* fragrance.

Surā, *f.* intoxicating liquor. **—ghaṭa**, *m.* a pitcher of liquor. **—chaṇa**, *m.* a drinking festival. **—dhutta**, *m.* a drunkard. **—pāna**, *nt.* drinking of strong liquor ; a strong drink. **—pāyikā**, *f.* a drunkard woman. **—pīta**, *a.* one who has drunk. **—mada**, *m.* tipsiness. **—meraya**, *nt.* rum and spirits. **—soṇḍa**, **—ḍaka**, *a.* addicted to strong drinks. *m.* a drunkard.

Suriya, *m.* the sun. **—ggāha**, *m.* eclipse of the sun. **—maṇḍala**, *nt.* the orb of the sun. **—tthaṅgama**, *m.* the sun-set. **—raŋsi**, **—rasmi**, *f.* rays of the sun. **—uggamana**, *nt.* the sun-rise.

Surusurukārakaŋ, *ad.* making a hissing sound while eating.

Suruṅgā, *f.* a prison.

Surūpa, **—pī**, *a.* handsome. *f.* **—pinī**.

Suladdha, *a.* well gained.

Sulabha, *a.* easy to be obtained.

Suva, *m.* a parrot.

Suvaca, see **Subbaca**.

Suvaṇṇa, *nt.* gold. *adj.* of good colour ; beautiful. **—kāra**, *m.* a goldsmith. **—gabbha**, *m.* a safe room for gold. **—guhā**, *f.* a golden cave. **—tā**, *f.* beauty of complexion. **—paṭṭa**, *nt.* a sheat of gold. **—pīṭhaka**, *nt.* a golden chair. **—maya**, *a.* made of gold. **—bhiṅkāra**, *m.* a golden pitcher. **—vaṇṇa**, *a.* gold-coloured. **—haŋsa**, *m.* golden swan.

Suvatthi (su + atthi), hail !

Suvammita, *pp.* well harnessed or armoured.

Suvavatthāpita, *a.* well defined or ascertained.

Suvāṇa, *m.* a dog. **—doṇi**, *f.* a dogs' trough.

Suvijāna, *a.* easily understood.

Suviññāpaya, *a.* easy to instruct.

Suvibhatta, *pp.* well divided or arranged.

Suvilitta, *pp.* well perfumed.

Suvimhita, *pp.* much astonished.

Suvisada, *a.* very clear.

Suvuṭṭhika, *a.* having abundant rain.

Suve, *ad.* tomorrow.

Susaṅkhata, *pp.* well prepared.

Susaññata, *a.* thoroughly restrained.

Susaṇṭhāna, *a.* having a good design ; well featured.

Susamāraddha, *pp.* thoroughly undertaken.

Susamāhita, *pp.* well grounded; well restrained.

Susamucchinna, *pp.* thoroughly eradicated.

Susāna, *nt.* cemetery. **—gopaka,** *m.* a cemetery-keeper.

Susikkhita, *pp.* well-trained ; thoroughly learnt.

Susira, *nt.* a hollow. *adj.* perforated ; having a hole.

Susīla, *a.* virtuous.

Susu, *m.* a young one ; a boy. *adj.* young.

Susukā, *f.* an alligator.

Susukka, *a.* very white.

Susuddha, *a.* very clean.

Sussati (sus + ya), to wither ; to be dried. *aor.* **sussi.** *pp.* **sukkha.** *pr. p.* **sussamāna.** *abs.* **sussitvā.**

Sussaratā, *f.* the fact of having a sweet voice.

Sussūsati (su + sa ; **su** is doubled and the second **u** is lengthened), to listen. *aor.* **—sūsi.**

Sussūsā, *f.* wish to hear ; obedience.

Suhajja, *nt.* amity ; friendship.

Suhada, *m.* a friend.

Suhita, *a.* satisfied.

Sūka, *m.* awn of barley, etc.

Sūkara, *m.* a pig ; a hog. **—potaka,** *m.* the young of a pig. **—maṃsa,** *nt.* pork.

Sūkarika, *m.* a dealer in swine ; pork-butcher.

Sūcaka, *a.* indicating ; one who indicates or informs.

Sūcana, *nt.* indication.

Sūci, *f.* a needle ; a hairpin ; a small door-bolt. **—kā,** *f.* a bolt ; a table of contents. **—kāra,** *m.* a needle-maker. **—ghaṭikā,** *f.* a bolt-holder. **—ghara,** *nt.* a needle case. **—mukha,** *m.* a mosquito. **—loma,** *a.* having hair like needles. **—vijjhana,** *nt.* an awl.

Sūju, *a.* upright.

Sūnā, *f.* a butcher's block. **—ghara,** *nt.* slaughter house.

Sūta, *m.* charioteer.

Sūtighara, *nt.* lying-in-chamber

Sūda, sūdaka, *m.* a cook.

Sūna, *a.* swollen.

Sūnu, *m.* a son.

Sūpa, *m.* curry.

Sūpatittha (su + upa + tittha), with beautiful fords.

Sūpadhārita, *pp.* well considered.

Sūpika, *m.* a cook.

Sūpeyya, *a.* suitable for curry. **—paṇṇa,** *nt.* curry leaf.

Sūyati (*pass.* of **suṇāti**), to be heard. *pr. p.* **sūyamāna.**

Sūra, *a.* valiant ; courageous. *m.* a hero. **—tā,** *f.* **bhāva,** *m.* valour.

Sūra, sūriya, *m.* the sun.

Seka, *m.* sprinkling.

Sekha, sekkha, *m.* a learner ; one who is in the course of perfection.

Sekhara, *nt.* a garland for the crest.

Sekhiya, *a.* connected with training.

Secana, *nt.* see **Seka.**

Seṭṭha, *a.* foremost; excellent. **—tara**, *a.* more excellent. **—sammata**, *a.* considered the best.

Seṭṭhi, **—ṭhī**, *m.* a millionaire. **—ṭṭhāna**, *nt.* the position of a **seṭṭhi.** **—jāyā**, **—bhariyā**, *f.* a millionaire's wife.

Seṇi, *f.* a guild. **Seṇiya**, *m.* a guild-master.

Seta, *a.* white; pure. *m.* the white colour. **—kuṭṭha**, *nt.* white leprosy. **—cchatta**, *nt.* a white parasol, which is an emblem of royalty. **—pacchāda**, *a.* with white covering.

Setaṭṭhikā, *f.* the mildew.

Seti (si + a), to sleep. *pr. p.* **senta, semāna.**

Setu, *m.* a bridge.

Seda, *m.* sweat; perspiration. **—ka**, *a.* sweating; transpiring. **—na**, *nt.* boiling by steam. **—āvakkhitta**, *a.* sweat-covered

Sedeti (sid + e), to cause to transpire; to steam. *aor.* **—esi.** *pp.* **sedita.** *abs.* **sedetvā.**

Sena, **senaka**, *m.* a hawk.

Senā, *f.* an army. **—nāyaka**, **—pati**, **—nī**, *m.* a general. **—pacca**, *nt.* the office of a general. **— byūha**, *m.* an array of troops.

Senāsana, *nt.* lodging; sleeping place. **—gāhāpaka**, *m.* one who allots lodging places. **—cārikā**, *f.* wandering from lodging to lodging. **—paññāpaka**, *m.* regulater of lodging places.

Sephālikā, *f.* a plant producing fragrant flowers.

Semānaka, *a.* lying down.

Semha, *nt.* phlegm. **—hika**, *a.* a man of phlegmatic humour.

Seyya, *a.* better; excellent.

Seyyathā pi, *in.* just as. **—thī'daŋ**, *in.* as follows.

Seyyā, *f.* a bed; bedding; sleep.

Seyyo, *in.* it is better.

Sericārī, *a.* acting according to one's liking.

Seritā, *f.* independence; freedom.

Serivihārī, *a.* living at one's own choice.

Sela, *m.* a rock; stone. **—maya**, *a.* made of stone.

Seleyya, *nt.* gum benjamin.

Sevaka, *m.* a servant; an attendant. *adj.* serving; associating.

Sevati (sev + a), to serve; to associate with; to make use of; to practise. *aor.* **sevi.** *pp.* **sevita.** *pr. p.* **sevanta, sevamāna.** *abs.* **sevitvā.** *pt.p* **sevitabba.**

Sevā, *f.* service.

Sevāla, *m.* moss; slime; the aquatic plant *Vallisnaria Octandra.*

Sevī, 3. one who associates or practises.

Sesa, *a.* remaining; left.

Seseti (sis + e), to leave over. *aor.* **—esi.** *pp.* **sesita.** *abs.* **sesetvā.**

So (*Nom. sing.* of **ta**), *m.* he.

Soka, *m.* grief; sorrow. **—ggi**, *m.* the fire of sorrow. **—pareta**, *a.* overcome with grief. **—vinodana**, *nt.* dispelling grief. **—salla**, *nt.* the dart of sorrow.

Sokī, *a.* sorrowful.

Sokhya, *nt.* health ; happiness.

Sokhumma, *nt.* fineness.

Sogandhika, *nt.* the white water-lily.

Socati (suc + a), to mourn ; to grieve. *aor.* **soci.** *pp.* **socita.** *pr. p.* **socanta, socamāna.** *pt. p.* **socitabba.** *abs.* **socitvā.** *inf.* **socituŋ.**

Soceyya, *nt.* purity.

Soṇa, *m.* a dog. **Soṇī,** *f.* a bitch.

Soṇita, *nt.* blood.

Soṇī, *f.* the waist.

Soṇḍa, —ka, *a.* addicted to.

Soṇḍā, *f.* an elephant's trunk ; a woman addicted to drink, etc.

Soṇḍika, *m.* a seller of spirits.

Soṇḍikā, soṇḍī, *f.* a natural tank in a rock.

Soṇṇa, *nt.* gold. **—maya,** *a.* made of gold.

Sota, *nt.* the ear. *m.* a stream ; torrent ; flood. **—dvāra,** *nt.* the auditory sensation. **—bila,** *nt.* the orifice of the ear. **—vantu,** *a.* one who has ears. **—viññāṇa,** *nt.* auditory cognition. **—viññeyya,** *a.* cognizable by hearing. **—āyatana,** *nt.* the sense of hearing.

Sotabba, *pt. p.* fit to be heard.

Sotāpatti, *f.* entering upon the Noble Path.

Sotāpanna, *a.* one who has entered the stream of Path.

Sotindriya, *nt.* the faculty of hearing.

Sotu, *m.* hearer. **—kāma,** *a.* willing to hear.

Sotuŋ, *inf.* to hear.

Sotthi, *f.* well-being ; safety ; blessing. **—kamma,** *nt.* blessing. **—bhāva,** *m.* safety. **—sālā,** *f.* a hospital ; a senatorium.

Sodaka, *a.* wet ; dripping.

Sodariya, *a.* born of the same mother.

Sodhaka, *a.* one who cleanses, corrects, or purifies.

Sodhana, *nt.* cleansing ; correcting.

Sodhāpeti (*caus.* of **sodheti**), to cause to clean or correct. *aor.* **—esi.** *pp.* **—pita.** *abs.* **—petvā.**

Sodheti (sudh + e), to make clean ; to purify ; to correct ; to clear a debt. *aor.* **—esi.** *pp.* **—dhita.** *pr. p.* **—dhenta, sodhayamāna.** *pt. p.* **—dhetabba.** *abs.* **sodhetvā.**

Sopāka, *m.* a low-caste man.

Sopāna, *m. nt.* stairs ; a ladder. **—panti,** *f.* a flight of steps. **—pāda,** *m.* the foot of the steps. **—phalaka,** *nt.* a step of a staircase. **—sīsa,** *nt.* the top of a staircase.

Soppa, *nt.* sleep.

Sobbha, *nt.* a pit ; a pool of water.

Sobhagga, *nt.* splendour ; beauty. **—ppatta,** *a.* endowed with beauty or splendour.

Sobhaṇa, —na, *a.* shining ; beautiful.

Sobhati (subh + a), to shine ; to be splendid ; to look beautiful. *aor.* **sobhi.** *pp.* **sobhita.** *pr. p.* **sobhanta, sobhamāna.** *abs.* **sobhitvā.**

Sobhā, *f.* splendour ; beauty.

Sobheti (*caus.* of **sobhati**), to make resplendent ; to adorn. *aor.* **—esi.** *pp.* **sobhita.** *pr.p* **sobhenta.** *abs.* **sobhetvā.**

Soma, *m.* the moon.

Somanassa, *nt.* joy ; delight; happiness

Somma, *a.* gentle ; agreeable ; pleasing.

Soracca, *nt.* gentleness ; meekness.

Sovaggika, *a.* leading to heaven.

Sovacassatā, *f.* suavity ; obedience.

Sovaṇṇa, *nt.* gold. **—ya, —maya,** *a.* golden.

Sovatthika, *nt.* a svastika ; a mark like S on the hood of a cobra.

Sovīraka, *m.* sour gruel ; vinegar.

Sosa, *m.* drying up ; consumption.

Sosana, *nt.* causing to dry.

Sosānika, *a.* one who lives in a cemetery.

Soseti (sus + e), to cause to dry or wither. *aor.* **—esi.** *pp.* **sosita.** *pr. p.* **sosenta.** *abs.* **sosetvā.**

Sohajja, *nt.* friendship.

Sneha, *m.* love ; oil.

Svākāra, *a.* being of good disposition.

Svākkhāta, *a.* well preached.

Svāgata, *a.* welcome ; learnt by heart.

Svātana, *a.* relating to the morrow. **—nāya,** *dat.* for the morrow.

Sve, *ad.* tomorrow.

H.

Haññati (han + ya), to be killed or destroyed. *aor.* **haññi.** *pr. p.* **haññamāna.**

Haññana, *nt.* torture ; distress ; killing.

Haṭa, *pp.* of **harati.**

Haṭṭha (*pp.* of **haṃsati**), joyful ; happy ; bristling. **—tuṭṭha,** *a.* full of mirth. **—loma,** *a.* with bristling hairs.

Haṭha, *m.* violence.

Hata (*pp.* of **hanati**), killed ; injured ; destroyed. **—bhāva,** *m.* the fact of being destroyed. **—ntarāya,** *a.* one who has removed obstacles. **—āvakāsa,** *a.* one who has cut off every occasion of good and evil.

Hattha, *m.* the hand ; a handle ; a cubit. **—ka,** *m.* a hand-like thing. *adj.* having hands. **—kamma,** *nt.* manual labour. **—gata,** *a.* come into the possession. **—gahaṇa,** *nt.* **—gāha,** *m.* seizing by the hand. **—cchinna,** *a.* whose hand is cut off. **—ccheda,** *m* **—chedana,** *nt.* cutting off the hand. **—tala,** *nt.* the palm of the hand. **—pasāraṇa,** *nt.* stretching out one's hand. **—pāsa,** *m.* a hand's length. **—vaṭṭaka,** *m.* a hand-cart. **—vikāra,** *m.* motion of the hand. **—sāra,** *m.* the most valuable thing. **—āpalekhana,** *a.* licking the hands after taking meals. **—ābharaṇa,** *nt.* a bracelet.

Hatthatthara, *m.* elephant rug

Hatthācariya, *m.* elephant trainer.

Hatthāroha, *m.* an elephant driver.

Hatthi, the shortened form of **Hatthī** (= an elephant). **—kantavīṇā,** *f.* a lute enticing elephants. **—kalabha,** the young of an elephant. **—kumbha,** *m.* the frontal globe of an elephant. **—kula,** *nt.* elephant species. **—kkhandha,** *m.* the back of an elephant. **—gopaka,** *m.* an elephant keeper. —**danta**, *m. nt.* ivory. —**damaka**, *m.* elephant tamer. —**damma**, *m.* an elephant in training. —**pada**, *nt.* an elephant's foot or step. —**pākāra**, *m.* a wall with figures of elephants in relief. —**ppabhinna**, *a.* a furious elephant. —**bandha**, —**meṇḍa**, *m.* an elephant keeper. —**matta**, *a.* as big as an elephant. —**māraka**, *a.* elephant hunter. —**yāna**, *nt.* an elephant carriage or a riding elephant. —**yuddha**, *nt.* combat of elephants. —**rūpaka**, *nt.* figure of an elephant. —**laṇḍa**, *m.* elephant dung. —**liṅgasakuṇa**, *m.* a vulture with a bill like an elephant's trunk. —**sālā**, *f.* elephant stable. — **sippa**, *nt.* the knowledge of elephant training. —**soṇḍā**, *f.* the trunk of an elephant.

Hatthinī, *f.* a she-elephant.

Hatthī, *m.* an elephant.

Hadaya, *nt.* the heart. —**ṅgama**, *a.* pleasant ; charming ; agreeable. —**maŋsa**, *nt.* the flesh of the heart. —**vatthu**, *nt.* the substance of the heart. —**santāpa**, *m.* grief. —**ssita**, —**nissita**, *a.* connected with the heart.

Hanati, hanti (han + a), to kill ; to strike ; to injure. *aor.* **hani.** *pp.* **hata.** *pr. p.* **hananta, hanamāna.** *abs.* **hantvā, hanitvā.** *inf.* **hantuŋ, hanituŋ,** *pt. p.* **hantabba, hanitabba.**

Hanana, *nt.* killing ; striking.

Hanu, hanukā, *f.* the jaw.

Hantu, *m.* one who kills or strikes.

Handa (*an exhortative emphatic particle*), well then ; now ; come along.

Hambho, a particle used in addressing equals.

Hammiya, *nt.* a long, storied building.

Haya, *m.* a horse. —**vāhī**, *a.* drawn by horses.

Hayānīka, *nt.* a cavalry.

Hara, *m.* the God Ísvara.

Haraṇa, *nt.* carrying. —**ka**, *a.* carrying ; movable.

Harati (har + a), to carry ; to take away ; to plunder ; to steal. *aor.* **hari.** *pp.* **haṭa,** *pr. p.* **haranta, haramāna.** *abs.* **haritvā.** *inf.* **harituŋ.**

Harāyati (*Deno.* from **hiri**), to be ashamed, depressed or vexed; to worry. *aor.* **harāyi.** *abs.* **harāyitvā.**

Harāpeti (*caus.* of **harati**), to make carry or take away. *aor.* —**esi.** *pp.* —**pita.** *abs.* —**petvā.**

Hari, *m.* the God Vishnu.

Hariṇa, *m.* a deer.

Harita, *a.* green ; tawny ; fresh. *nt.* vegetables ; greens. —**tta**, *nt.* greenness ; freshness.

Haritabba, *pt. p.* (of **harati**), to be carried or removed.

Haritāla, *nt.* yellow orpiment.

Haritu, *m.* one who carries away.

Harittaca, *a.* gold-coloured.

Harissavaṇṇa, *a.* having a golden hue.

Harītaka, *nt.* —**takī**, *f.* yellow myrobalan.

Hare, a particle used in addressing inferiors.

Hala, *nt.* a plough.

Halaŋ, *in.* enough ; why should.

Halāhala, *nt.* a deadly poison.

Haliddā, *f.* turmeric.

Haliddī, *f.* same as the above.

Have, *in.* surely ; indeed.

Havya, *nt.* an oblation.

Hasati (has + a), to smile ; to laugh. *aor.* **hasi.** *pp.* **hasita.** *pr. p.* **hasanta, hasamāna.** *pt. p.* **hasitabba.** *abs.* **hasitvā.**

Hasana, hasita, *nt.* laughter.

Hasituppāda, *m.* aesthetic faculty.

Hassa, *nt.* laughter ; joke ; jest.

Haŋsa, *m.* a swan. —**potaka,** *m.* a young swan.

Haŋsati (haŋs + a), to bristle ; to stand on the end (said of hair) ; to be glad. *aor.* **haŋsi.**

Haŋsana, *nt.* bristling.

Haŋsī, *f.* of **haŋsa.**

Haŋseti, *caus.* of **haŋsati.**

Hā, *in.* alas !

Hāṭaka, *nt.* a kind of gold.

Hātabba (*pt. p.* of **hāyati**), fit to be avoided or given up.

Hātuŋ (*inf.* of **hāyati**), to remove; to give up.

Hānabhāgiya, *a.* conducive to relinquishment.

Hāni, *f.* decrease ; loss ; falling off.

Hāpaka, *a.* causing decrease or loss ; reducing.

Hāpana, *nt.* lessening ; reduction.

Hāpeti (hā + āpe), to omit ; to neglect ; to reduce ; to delay. *aor.* **hāpesi.** *pp.* **hāpita.** *pr. p.* **hāpenta.** *abs.* **hāpetvā.**

Hāyati (hā + ya), to diminish ; to dwindle ; to waste away. *aor.* **hāyi.** *pp.* **hīna,** *pr. p.* **hāyanta, hāyamāna.** *abs.* **hāyitvā.**

Hāyana, *nt.* diminution ; decay ; decrease ; a year.

Hāyī, *a.* one who gives up or leaves behind.

Hāra, *m.* a string (of pearls, etc.); a necklace. —**ka,** *a.* carrying ; removing.

Hāriya, *a.* portable ; capable of being carried.

Hāsa, *m.* laughter ; mirth. —**kara,** *a.* giving pleasure.

Hāseti (has + e), to make laugh ; to gladden. *aor.* **hāsesi.** *pp.* **hāsita.** *pr. p.* **hāsenta, hāsayamāna.** *abs.* **hāsetvā.**

Hi, *in.* because ; indeed.

Hikkā, *f.* hiccup.

Hiṅgu, *nt.* the exudation of asafoetida plant.

Hiṅgulaka, *nt.* **hiṅguli,** *f.* vermilion.

Hita, *nt.* benefit ; blessing ; good ; welfare. *adj.* useful ; beneficial. *m.* a friend. —**kara,** *a.* doing what is beneficial. —**āvaha,** *a.* beneficial.

Hitesī, 3. benefactor ; desiring another's welfare.

Hintāla, *m.* the marshy date palm.

Hima, *nt.* snow ; ice. —**vantu,** *a.* having snow or ice ; the Himalaya mountains.

Hiyyo, *ad.* yesterday.

Hirañña, *nt.* unwrought gold.

Hiri, *f.* shyness ; sense of shame. —**kopīna,** *nt.* that which arouses shyness, i.e. the male or female organ. —**mantu,** *a.* modest ; bashful.

Hirīyati (*Deno.* from **hiri**), to blush ; to be shy or ashamed.

Hirīyanā, *f.* see **Hiri.**

Hirottappa, *nt.* shame and fear for sin.

Hiŋsati (hiŋs + a), to hurt; to injure; to tease. *aor.* **hiŋsi.** *pp.* **hiŋsita.** *pr. p.* **—santa, —samāna.** *abs.* **hiŋsitvā.**

Hiŋsana, *nt.* **—nā,** *f.* **hiŋsā,** *f.* teasing; injury; hurting.

Hiŋsāpeti (*caus.* of **hiŋsati**), to cause to hurt or injure. *aor.* **—esi.** *pp.* **—pita.** *abs.* **—petvā.**

Hīna, *a.* low; inferior; base; despicable. **—jacca,** *a.* having a low birth. **—viriya,** *a.* lacking in energy. **—ādhimuttika,** *a.* having low inclinations.

Hīyati (*pass.* of **hāyati**), to be decreased or dwindled; to decay; to be left or given up. *aor.* **hīyi.** *pr. p.* **hīyamāna.**

Hīyo, see **Hiyyo.**

Hīra, —ka, *nt.* a splinter; a stripe.

Hīlana, *nt.* **—nā,** *f.* disdain; contempt.

Hīḷeti (hīḷ + e), to scorn; to disdain; to despise. *aor.* **—esi.** *pp.* **hīḷita.** *abs.* **hīḷetvā.** *pr. p.* **hīḷayamāna.**

Huta, *nt.* the thing sacrificed; an oblation.

Hutāsana, *nt.* fire.

Hutta, *nt.* sacrifice.

Hutvā, *abs.* (of **hoti**), having been.

Huraŋ, *a.* in the other world; in another existence.

Huṅkāra, *m.* the sound "huŋ."

He, *a vocative particle.* hey; eh; ere; my dear.

Heṭṭhato, *ad.* from below.

Heṭṭhā, *ad.* below; down; underneath. **—bhāga,** *m.* the lower portion. **—mañce,** *ad.* under the bed.

Heṭṭhima, *a.* lower.

Heṭhaka, 3. one who harasses or troubles.

Heṭhanā, *f.* harassing.

Heṭheti (heṭh + e), to harass; to worry; to injure. *aor.* **—esi.** *pp.* **heṭhita.** *pr. p.* **heṭhenta, heṭhayamāna.** *abs.* **heṭhetvā.**

Hetu, *m.* cause; reason; condition. **—ka,** *a.* connected with a cause. **—ppabhava,** *a.* arising from a cause. **—vāda,** *m.* the theory of cause.

Hema, *nt.* gold. **—jāla,** *nt.* a golden netting.

Hemanta, *m.* the winter. **—ntika,** *a.* belonging to the winter; icy cold.

Hemavaṇṇa, *a.* golden coloured.

Hemavataka, *a.* living in the Himalayas.

Herañññika, *m.* a goldsmith; a money-changer.

Hesā, *f.* **hesārava,** *m.* the neighing of a horse.

Hoti (hū + a), to be; to exist. *aor.* **ahosi.** *pr. p.* **honta.** *pt. p.* **hotabba.** *inf.* **hotuŋ.**

Homa, *nt.* oblation.

Horā, *f.* hour. **—pāṭhaka,** *m.* an astrologer. **—yanta,** *nt.* any device showing the time; a clock.

Horālocana, *nt.* a watch; a clock.